Houghton Mifflin

Mathematics

HOUGHTON MIFFLIN

BOSTON • MORRIS PLAINS, NJ

California • Colorado • Georgia • Illinois • New Jersey • Texas

ISBN 0-618-08179-8

5 6 7 8 9 DW 06 05 04 03 02

Authors

Senior Authors

Dr. Carole Greenes
Professor of Mathematics Education
Boston University
Boston, MA

Dr. Miriam A. Leiva
Distinguished Professor of Mathematics, Emerita
University of North Carolina
Charlotte, NC

Dr. Bruce R. Vogeli
Clifford Brewster Upton Professor of Mathematics
Teachers College, Columbia University
New York, NY

Program Authors

Dr. Matt Larson
Curriculum Specialist for Mathematics
Lincoln Public Schools
Lincoln, NE

Dr. Jean M. Shaw
Professor of Elementary Education
University of Mississippi
Oxford, MS

Dr. Lee Stiff
Professor of Mathematics Education
North Carolina State University
Raleigh, NC

Content Reviewers

Lawrence Braden (Grades 5–6)
Mathematics Teacher
St. Paul's School
Concord, NH

Dr. Don Chakerian (Grades 3–4)
Emeritus Professor of Mathematics
University of California
Davis, CA

Dr. Kurt Kreith (Grades 3–4)
Emeritus Professor of Mathematics
University of California
Davis, CA

Dr. Liping Ma (Grades K–2)
Visiting Scholar
Carnegie Foundation for the Advancement of Teaching
Menlo Park, CA

Dr. David Wright (Grades 5–6)
Professor of Mathematics
Brigham Young University
Provo, UT

Reviewers

California Math Teacher Advisory Board

Grade K

Lee Arsenian
Hoover Street Elementary School
Los Angeles, CA

Kathy Dyer
Alice Birney Elementary School
Fresno, CA

Paula Ferrett
Hyatt Elementary School
Riverside, CA

Linda Hill
Crestline Elementary School
Barstow, CA

Rene Jimenez
Ralph J. Bunche Elementary School
Compton, CA

Christina Kruse-Pennes
Cesar Chavez Elementary School
Richmond, CA

Mary L. Paredes
Cahuenga Elementary School
Los Angeles, CA

Grade 1

Michelle Enriquez
Crestline Elementary School
Barstow, CA

Terri Ortiz
Sunny Brae Ave. Elementary School
Winnetka, CA

Shelia Patterson
Cypress School
Tulare, CA

Maria Tarabotto
Hazeltine Elementary School
Van Nuys, CA

Grade 2

Nancy Burgei
Blossom Hill School
Los Gatos, CA

Tracy Green
Figarden School
Fresno, CA

Barbara Page
Elihu Beard Elementary School
Modesto, CA

Barbara Park
Sunny Brae Ave. Elementary School
Winnetka, CA

Kim Seto
Sierra Madre School
Sierra Madre, CA

Judy Trette
Gregory Gardens Elementary School
Pleasant Hill, CA

Grade 3

Rita Bennett
Santa Susana Elementary School
Simi Valley, CA

Karen Choi
Pasadena Unified Education Center
Pasadena, CA

Karen Ciraulo
Kingswood Elementary School
Citrus Heights, CA

Cheryl Dultz
Kingswood Elementary School
Citrus Heights, CA

Doug Hedin
Park Oaks Elementary School
Thousand Oaks, CA

Vicky Holman
Mount Pleasant Elementary School
San Jose, CA

Sylvia Kyle
Chester Nimitz Elementary School
Cupertino, CA

Jennifer Rader
Desert Trails Elementary School
Adelanto, CA

Fran Range-Long
Alice Birney Elementary School
Fresno, CA

Karlene Seitz
Citrus Glen Elementary School
Ventura, CA

Grade 4

Marilyn Higbie
Jane Addams Elementary School
Long Beach, CA

Beth Holguin
Graystone Elementary School
San Jose, CA

Tarie Lewis
Melrose Elementary School
Oakland, CA

Sandra Jo McIntee
Haynes Street School
West Hills, CA

Mike Tokmakoff
Hoover Street Elementary School
Los Angeles, CA

Nancy Yee
Valhalla Elementary School
Pleasant Hill, CA

Grade 5

Patty Jernigan
Santa Susana
Simi Valley, CA

Joe Koski
Nu-View Elementary School
Nuevo, CA

Bill Laraway
Silver Oak Elementary
San Jose, CA

Steve Monson
Castro Elementary School
El Cerrito, CA

Sherri Qualls
Weibel Elementary School.
Fremont, CA

Arlene Sackman
Earlimart Middle School
Earlimart, CA

Robyn Suskin
Sierra Madre School
Sierra Madre, CA

Grade 6

Herb Brown
Lake Gregory Elementary School
Crestline, CA

German Palabyab
Harding Elementary School
El Cerrito, CA

Carole Patty
West Riverside Elementary School
Riverside,CA

Maureen Smith
Patterson Elementary School
Fremont, CA

Jeff Varn
Sierra Madre Elementary School
Sierra Madre, CA

Family Letter

Dear Family,

Every parent hopes his or her child will be confident and successful in school. *Houghton Mifflin Mathematics* is designed to provide children with a solid foundation in mathematics that will help lead to such success.

This program is based on the Mathematics Content Standards for California. The goals of this program are

- Providing a curriculum that balances skills, conceptual understanding, and problem solving
- Providing instruction and practice to help children become proficient in computational skills
- Helping children become good mathematical problem solvers
- Enabling children to use correct mathematical terms to communicate their understanding of math concepts

Look for the standards box in each lesson.

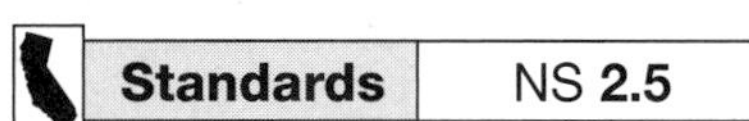

The notation in this box represents the following standard.

Number Sense 2.5 **Compute and perform simple multiplication and division of fractions and apply these procedures to solving problems.**

On pages vi–ix you will find a full listing of all the Mathematics Content Standards for California for Grade 5.

As you work with your child throughout the year, the listing of these standards will help you understand what he or she is learning in each lesson.

We trust your child will have a successful year!

Sincerely,
Houghton Mifflin Company

California
MATH STANDARDS

By the end of grade five, students increase their facility with the four basic arithmetic operations applied to fractions, decimals, and positive and negative numbers. They know and use common measuring units to determine length and area and know and use formulas to determine the volume of simple geometric figures. Students know the concept of angle measurement and use a protractor and compass to solve problems. They use grids, tables, graphs, and charts to record and analyze data.

Number Sense (NS)

1.0 Students compute with very large and very small numbers, positive integers, decimals, and fractions and understand the relationship between decimals, fractions, and percents. They understand the relative magnitudes of numbers:

- **1.1** Estimate, round, and manipulate very large (e.g., millions) and very small (e.g., thousandths) numbers.
- **1.2** Interpret percents as a part of a hundred; find decimal and percent equivalents for common fractions and explain why they represent the same value; compute a given percent of a whole number.
- **1.3** Understand and compute positive integer powers of nonnegative integers; compute examples as repeated multiplication.
- **1.4** Determine the prime factors of all numbers through 50 and write the numbers as the product of their prime factors by using exponents to show multiples of a factor (e.g., $24 = 2 \times 2 \times 2 \times 3 = 2^3 \times 3$).
- **1.5** Identify and represent on a number line decimals, fractions, mixed numbers, and positive and negative integers.

2.0 Students perform calculations and solve problems involving addition, subtraction, and simple multiplication and division of fractions and decimals:

- **2.1** Add, subtract, multiply, and divide with decimals; add with negative integers; subtract positive integers from negative integers; and verify the reasonableness of the results.

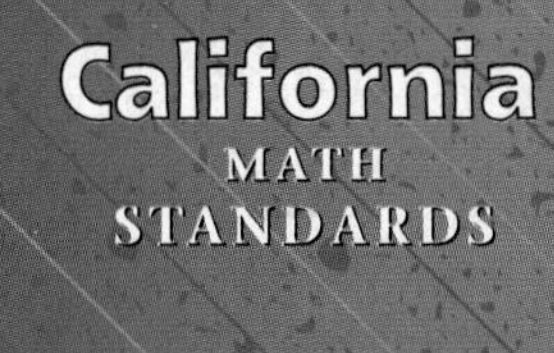

2.2 Demonstrate proficiency with division, including division with positive decimals and long division with multidigit divisors.

2.3 Solve simple problems, including ones arising in concrete situations, involving the addition and subtraction of fractions and mixed numbers (like and unlike denominators of 20 or less), and express answers in the simplest form.

2.4 Understand the concept of multiplication and division of fractions.

2.5 Compute and perform simple multiplication and division of fractions and apply these procedures to solving problems.

Algebra and Functions (AF)

1.0 Students use variables in simple expressions, compute the value of the expression for specific values of the variable, and plot and interpret the results:

1.1 Use information taken from a graph or equation to answer questions about a problem situation.

1.2 Use a letter to represent an unknown number; write and evaluate simple algebraic expressions in one variable by substitution.

1.3 Know and use the distributive property in equations and expressions with variables.

1.4 Identify and graph ordered pairs in the four quadrants of the coordinate plane.

1.5 Solve problems involving linear functions with integer values; write the equation; and graph the resulting ordered pairs of integers on a grid.

Measurement and Geometry (MG)

1.0 Students understand and compute the volumes and areas of simple objects:

1.1 Derive and use the formula for the area of a triangle and of a parallelogram by comparing it with the formula for the area of a rectangle (i.e., two of the same triangles make a parallelogram with twice the area; a parallelogram is compared with a rectangle of the same area by cutting and pasting a right triangle on the parallelogram).

1.2 Construct a cube and rectangular box from two-dimensional patterns and use these patterns to compute the surface area for these objects.

1.3 Understand the concept of volume and use the appropriate units in common measuring systems (i.e., cubic centimeter

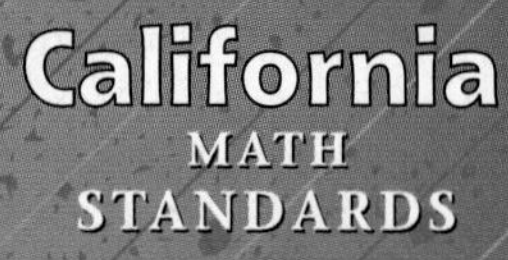

[cm^3], cubic meter [m^3], cubic inch [in^3], cubic yard [yd^3]), to compute the volume of rectangular solids.

1.4 Differentiate between, and use appropriate units of measure for, two- and three-dimensional objects (i.e., find the perimeter, area, volume).

2.0 Students identify, describe, and classify the properties of, and the relationships between, plane and solid geometric figures:

2.1 Measure, identify, and draw angles, perpendicular and parallel lines, rectangles, and triangles by using appropriate tools (e.g., straightedge, ruler, compass, protractor, drawing software).

2.2 Know that the sum of the angles of any triangle is 180° and the sum of the angles of any quadrilateral is 360° and use this information to solve problems.

2.3 Visualize and draw two-dimensional views of three-dimensional objects made from rectangular solids.

Statistics, Data Analysis, and Probability (SDP)

1.0 Students display, analyze, compare, and interpret different data sets, including data sets of different sizes:

1.1 Know the concepts of mean, median, and mode; compute and compare simple examples to show that they may differ.

1.2 Organize and display single-variable data in appropriate graphs and representations (e.g., histograms, circle graphs) and explain which types of graphs are appropriate for various data sets.

1.3 Use fractions and percentages to compare data sets of different sizes.

1.4 Identify ordered pairs of data from a graph and interpret the meaning of the data in terms of the situation depicted by the graph.

1.5 Know how to write ordered pairs correctly; for example, (x, y).

Mathematical Reasoning (MR)

1.0 Students make decisions about how to approach problems:

1.1 Analyze problems by identifying relationships, distinguishing relevant from irrelevant information, sequencing and prioritizing information, and observing patterns.

1.2 Determine when and how to break a problem into simpler parts.

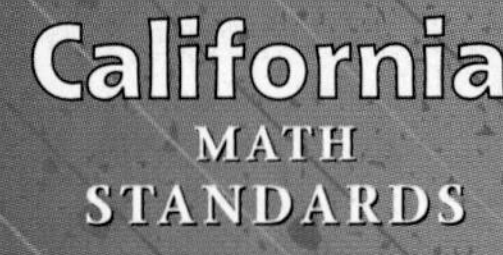

2.0 Students use strategies, skills, and concepts in finding solutions:

2.1 Use estimation to verify the reasonableness of calculated results.

2.2 Apply strategies and results from simpler problems to more complex problems.

2.3 Use a variety of methods, such as words, numbers, symbols, charts, graphs, tables, diagrams, and models, to explain mathematical reasoning.

2.4 Express the solution clearly and logically by using the appropriate mathematical notation and terms and clear language; support solutions with evidence in both verbal and symbolic work.

2.5 Indicate the relative advantages of exact and approximate solutions to problems and give answers to a specified degree of accuracy.

2.6 Make precise calculations and check the validity of the results from the context of the problem.

3.0 Students move beyond a particular problem by generalizing to other situations:

3.1 Evaluate the reasonableness of the solution in the context of the original situation.

3.2 Note the method of deriving the solution and demonstrate a conceptual understanding of the derivation by solving similar problems.

3.3 Develop generalizations of the results obtained and apply them in other circumstances.

Contents

Remembering Your Facts

CHAPTER 1 Whole Numbers, Decimals, and Integers

Addition, Subtraction, and Equations

Multiplication

Division and Equations

CHAPTER 5 Measurement and Integers

Data, Statistics, and Probability

Number Theory and Addition and Subtraction of Fractions

Multiplication and Division of Fractions

Multiplication and Division of Decimals

Geometry and Measurement

Ratio and Percent

Integers and the Coordinate Plane

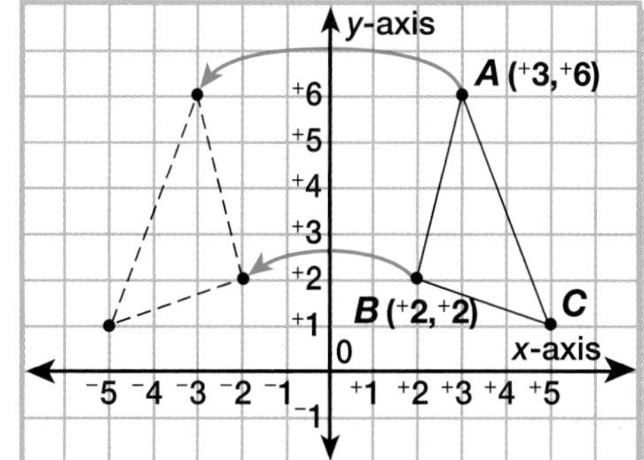

Book Resources

Addition Facts

Add.

1. 4 + 6	**2.** 3 + 6	**3.** 9 + 9	**4.** 5 + 8	**5.** 3 + 3
6. 6 + 6	**7.** 3 + 9	**8.** 2 + 2	**9.** 3 + 7	**10.** 5 + 5
11. 7 + 7	**12.** 6 + 9	**13.** 5 + 6	**14.** 4 + 5	**15.** 2 + 3
16. 5 + 7	**17.** 2 + 9	**18.** 7 + 9	**19.** 6 + 8	**20.** 2 + 7
21. 4 + 4	**22.** 3 + 5	**23.** 9 + 5	**24.** 9 + 8	**25.** 7 + 8
26. 2 + 5	**27.** 2 + 6	**28.** 8 + 8	**29.** 6 + 7	**30.** 3 + 8
31. 2 + 4	**32.** 4 + 7	**33.** 4 + 8	**34.** 9 + 7	**35.** 9 + 6
36. 4 + 8	**37.** 5 + 9	**38.** 3 + 4	**39.** 2 + 8	**40.** 8 + 9

Subtraction Facts

Subtract.

1. 10 − 5	**2.** 15 − 9	**3.** 12 − 5	**4.** 11 − 3	**5.** 6 − 2
6. 4 − 2	**7.** 14 − 7	**8.** 17 − 9	**9.** 16 − 8	**10.** 17 − 8
11. 9 − 3	**12.** 5 − 2	**13.** 16 − 7	**14.** 16 − 9	**15.** 14 − 6
16. 11 − 4	**17.** 13 − 6	**18.** 15 − 7	**19.** 15 − 6	**20.** 14 − 5
21. 13 − 4	**22.** 8 − 4	**23.** 10 − 3	**24.** 7 − 3	**25.** 8 − 3
26. 12 − 4	**27.** 11 − 5	**28.** 11 − 2	**29.** 9 − 4	**30.** 10 − 4
31. 7 − 2	**32.** 9 − 2	**33.** 14 − 9	**34.** 8 − 2	**35.** 10 − 2
36. 12 − 6	**37.** 18 − 9	**38.** 13 − 5	**39.** 12 − 3	**40.** 6 − 3

Multiplication Facts

Multiply.

1. 3×3	**2.** 8×6	**3.** 8×4	**4.** 9×3	**5.** 7×9
6. 8×5	**7.** 9×7	**8.** 4×2	**9.** 6×6	**10.** 6×9
11. 9×9	**12.** 9×2	**13.** 7×4	**14.** 3×2	**15.** 8×3
16. 6×3	**17.** 7×5	**18.** 9×8	**19.** 5×4	**20.** 7×6
21. 6×4	**22.** 8×7	**23.** 8×2	**24.** 6×5	**25.** 8×8
26. 5×5	**27.** 8×9	**28.** 4×3	**29.** 9×6	**30.** 6×2
31. 9×5	**32.** 5×9	**33.** 7×3	**34.** 7×7	**35.** 5×2
36. 2×2	**37.** 5×3	**38.** 9×4	**39.** 7×2	**40.** 4×4

Division Facts

Divide.

1. 18 ÷ 3	**2.** 6 ÷ 2	**3.** 63 ÷ 7	**4.** 63 ÷ 9	**5.** 48 ÷ 6
6. 36 ÷ 4	**7.** 16 ÷ 4	**8.** 21 ÷ 3	**9.** 12 ÷ 3	**10.** 10 ÷ 2
11. 72 ÷ 8	**12.** 64 ÷ 8	**13.** 72 ÷ 9	**14.** 49 ÷ 7	**15.** 4 ÷ 2
16. 25 ÷ 5	**17.** 54 ÷ 9	**18.** 35 ÷ 5	**19.** 24 ÷ 3	**20.** 8 ÷ 2
21. 45 ÷ 5	**22.** 54 ÷ 6	**23.** 56 ÷ 7	**24.** 42 ÷ 6	**25.** 28 ÷ 4
26. 36 ÷ 6	**27.** 81 ÷ 9	**28.** 40 ÷ 5	**29.** 27 ÷ 3	**30.** 9 ÷ 3
31. 15 ÷ 3	**32.** 14 ÷ 2	**33.** 45 ÷ 9	**34.** 12 ÷ 2	**35.** 16 ÷ 2
36. 32 ÷ 4	**37.** 30 ÷ 5	**38.** 18 ÷ 2	**39.** 20 ÷ 4	**40.** 24 ÷ 4

Whole Numbers, Decimals, and Integers

Why Learn About Whole Numbers, Decimals, and Integers?

For solving different kinds of problems, people need different kinds of numbers—whole numbers, decimals, positive numbers, and negative numbers.

Very large numbers are needed to describe some distances, such as the earth's distance from the sun. Negative numbers are used to describe temperatures below zero.

You can easily count the number of people who came to see the waterfalls, but you cannot count the number of gallons of water going over the falls.

NO SMOKING
HURRICANE DECK

Reviewing Vocabulary

Understanding math language helps you become a successful problem solver. Here are some math vocabulary words you should know.

place value the position of a digit in a number that determines the value of the digit

expanded form a way to write a number as a sum of the values of the digits

standard form a way to write a number using only numerals with commas and decimal points

Reading Words and Symbols

When you read mathematics, sometimes you read only words, sometimes you read words and symbols, and sometimes you read only symbols.

All of these statements represent the same number.

- one thousand, two hundred thirty-four
- $(1 \times 1000) + (2 \times 100) + (3 \times 10) + (4 \times 1)$
- 1,234

Try These

1. Write the place value of the 7 in each number.
   - **a.** 7,412
   - **b.** 40,763
   - **c.** 38,527
   - **d.** 716,413
   - **e.** 2,671
   - **f.** 574,621

2. Write each number in standard and expanded forms.
   - **a.** three hundred sixty-five
   - **b.** four thousand, one hundred eleven
   - **c.** sixty-seven thousand, five hundred
   - **d.** seven hundred eighty-nine thousand, four hundred fifty-two

3. Fill in the blanks with the correct numbers.
   - **a.** In expanded form, 657 is (■ × 100) + (■ × 10) + (■ × 1).
   - **b.** Eight thousand, five hundred twelve is ■,■■■ in standard form.

Upcoming Vocabulary

Write About It **Here are some other vocabulary words** you will learn in this chapter. Watch for these words. Write their definitions in your journal.

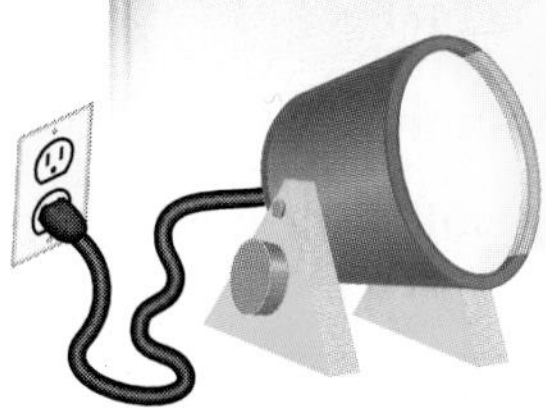

base

exponent

power of ten

negative numbers

opposite

integers

Place Value to Hundred Thousands

You will learn how to read and write numbers through hundred thousands in standard and expanded form.

Review Vocabulary
period
standard form
expanded form
place value

Learn About It

The United States has 383,611 square miles of protected land.

In a number, each group of 3 digits separated by a comma is called a **period**.

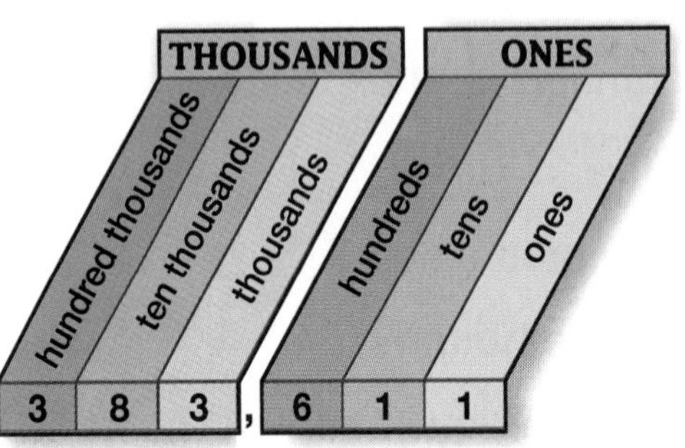

Different Ways to Read and Write Numbers

You can use standard form.

383,611

You can use expanded form.

$300{,}000 + 80{,}000 + 3{,}000 + 600 + 10 + 1$
$= (3 \times 100{,}000) + (8 \times 10{,}000) + (3 \times 1{,}000) + (6 \times 100) + (1 \times 10) + (1 \times 1)$

You can use word form.

three hundred eighty-three thousand, six hundred eleven

You can use short word form.

383 thousand, 611

Explain Your Thinking

► What happens to each **place value** as you move from right to left in a number?

Guided Practice

Write each number in word form and in expanded form.

1. 25,078 **2.** 693,412 **3.** 151,940

Ask Yourself

- What is the greatest place value in the number?
- What is the value for each place?

Standards NS 1.0 MR 2.0, 2.3

Independent Practice

Write the value of each underlined digit in short word form.

4. 2,346 **5.** 34,501 **6.** 257,824 **7.** 649,192

Read each number. Then write it in short word form.

8. 6,780 **9.** 48,309 **10.** 586,147 **11.** 870,148

Write each number in standard form.

12. 8 thousand, 752 **13.** 240 thousand, 357 **14.** 872 thousand,12

15. one hundred forty thousand, four

16. eight hundred thirty thousand, three hundred four

17. 300,000 + 5,000 + 30 + 1 **18.** 900,000 + 10,000 + 4,000 + 60

19. 60,000 + 5 **20.** 800,000 + 800 + 8

Problem Solving • Reasoning

Use Data **Use the facts to answer Problems 21–22.**

21. Which California park is the largest?

22. Which California park is the smallest?

23. **Analyze** Brazil has 552,191 square miles of protected land. What is the value of each 5 in 552,191? What is the value of each 1 in 552,191?

24. Greenland has three hundred seventy-nine thousand, three hundred forty-five square miles of protected land. Write this number in standard form.

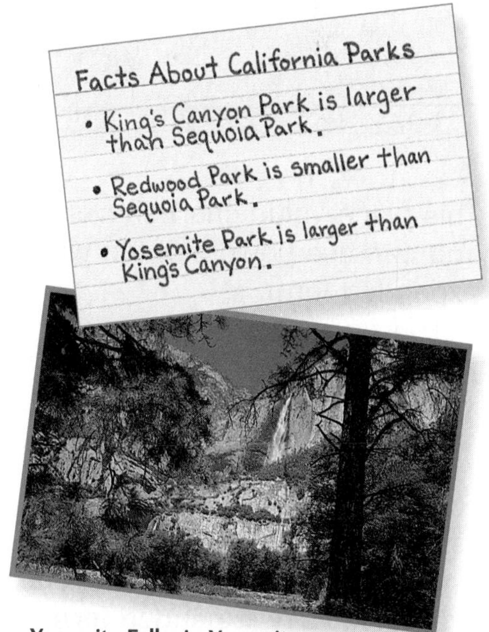

Yosemite Falls, in Yosemite National Park.

Mixed Review • Test Prep

Solve.

25. 5,000 − 4,691 **26.** 832 + 428 **27.** 6,290 − 95

28. 2 × 47 **29.** 7 × 60 **30.** 9 × 23

31 A number has three digits. The hundreds digit is half the ones digit. The three digits add up to 11. The tens digit is greater than the sum of the other two digits. What is the number?

A 182 **B** 256 **C** 281 **D** 652

Extra Practice See Set A on page 38.

Exponents

You will learn how to read and write numbers through hundred thousands with exponents.

New Vocabulary
base
exponent
power of ten

Learn About It

A short way to write the product $10 \times 10 \times 10 \times 10 \times 10$ is 10^5. To read 10^5, say "ten to the fifth power." The 10 is the base. The small raised 5 is the exponent. The **base** is the factor that is repeated in the product. The **exponent** shows the number of times the base is used as a factor.

THOUSANDS			ONES		
hundred thousands	ten thousands	thousands	hundreds	tens	ones
100,000	10,000	1,000	100	10	1
$10 \times 10 \times 10 \times 10 \times 10$	$10 \times 10 \times 10 \times 10$	$10 \times 10 \times 10$	10×10	10	1
10^5	10^4	10^3	10^2	10^1	10^0

Think:
Note the pattern.
$1{,}000 = 10^3$
$100 = 10^2$
$10 = 10^1$
$1 = 10^0$

This place-value chart shows each place as a **power of ten.** You can use powers of ten when you write numbers in expanded form.

Different Ways to Write 562,412

You can use expanded form.

$(5 \times 100{,}000) + (6 \times 10{,}000) + (2 \times 1{,}000) + (4 \times 100) + (1 \times 10) + (2 \times 1)$

You can use expanded form with exponents.

$(5 \times 10^5) + (6 \times 10^4) + (2 \times 10^3) + (4 \times 10^2) + (1 \times 10^1) + (2 \times 10^0)$

Another Example

2 as the Base

$2 \times 2 \times 2 \times 2 = 2^4$

Read: "two to the fourth"

The base is 2. The exponent is 4.

Explain Your Thinking

- ▶ What happens to the powers of ten as you move from left to right?
- ▶ Why does it make sense that 10^0 is equal to 1?

Standards NS **1.3** AF **1.0, 1.2** MR **2.3**

Guided Practice

Write each number in expanded form with exponents.

1. 47,052 **2.** 712,943 **3.** 823,930

> **Ask Yourself**
> - What power of ten represents the greatest place value?

Independent Practice

Write each number in standard form.

4. 6×10^5 **5.** 4×10^2 **6.** 2×10^4 **7.** 3×10^1 **8.** 9×10^3

9. $(7 \times 10^4) + (5 \times 10^3) + (3 \times 10^2) + (2 \times 10^1) + (8 \times 10^0)$

10. $(6 \times 10^5) + (4 \times 10^4) + (3 \times 10^3) + (5 \times 10^1) + (7 \times 10^0)$

11. The base is five, and the exponent is two.

Complete each pattern.

12.
$2^5 = 32$
$2^4 = 16$
$2^3 = 8$
$2^2 = 4$
$2^1 = $ ■
$2^0 = $ ■

13.
$64 \div 2 = 32$
$32 \div 2 = 16$
$16 \div 2 = 8$
$8 \div 2 = 4$
$4 \div 2 = $ ■
■ $\div 2 = $ ■

14.
$3^5 = 243$
$3^4 = 81$
$3^3 = 27$
$3^2 = $ ■
$3^1 = $ ■
$3^0 = $ ■

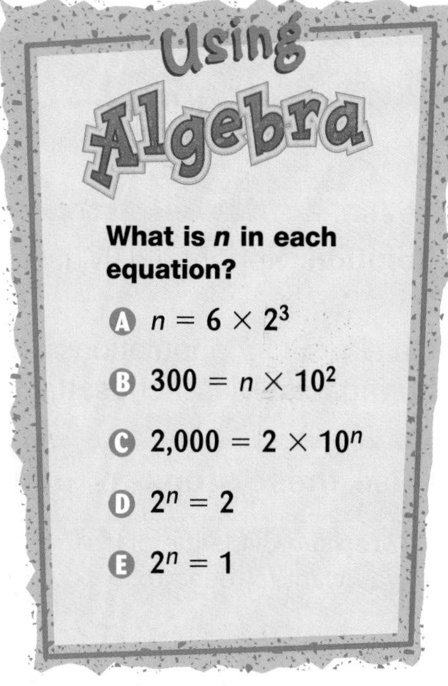

What is *n* in each equation?

A $n = 6 \times 2^3$

B $300 = n \times 10^2$

C $2{,}000 = 2 \times 10^n$

D $2^n = 2$

E $2^n = 1$

Problem Solving • Reasoning

15. A googol is a very large number. It is 1 followed by 100 zeros. Write a googol as a power of ten.

16. What is the sum of 3^3 and 2^4?

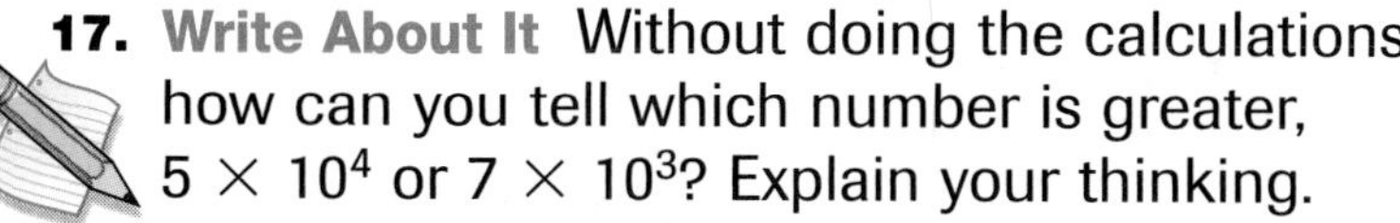

17. **Write About It** Without doing the calculations, how can you tell which number is greater, 5×10^4 or 7×10^3? Explain your thinking.

Mixed Review • Test Prep

Solve.

18. $6{,}437 + 1{,}595$ **19.** $8{,}079 - 5{,}412$ **20.** $6{,}532 + 2{,}097$ **21.** $7{,}790 - 1{,}785$ **22.** $3{,}409 + 4{,}868$

23 What is the remainder when 358 is divided by 9?

A 40 **C** 8

B 39 **D** 7

Extra Practice See Set B on page 38.

Lesson 3 Compare, Order, and Round Whole Numbers

You will learn how to compare, order, and round numbers through hundred thousands.

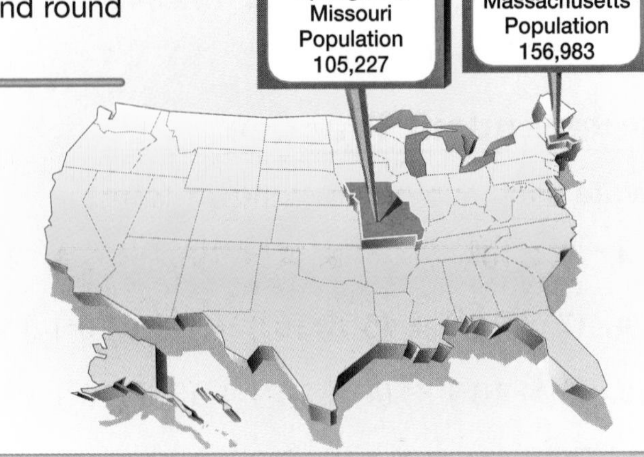

Learn About It

A city named Springfield can be found in many states. Missouri and Massachusetts have cities named Springfield. Which Springfield has the greater population?

Compare 156,983 and 105,227.

Step 1 Line up the numbers by place value.

156,983
105,227

Step 2 Start from the left. Compare the digits until they are different.

156,983
105,227

The ten thousands digits are different. 5 is greater than 0, so 156,983 > 105,227.

Solution: Springfield, Massachusetts, has the greater population.

On signs, city populations are often rounded. What is the population of Springfield, Massachusetts, to the nearest ten thousand?

Use these steps to round.

Step 1 Circle the place you want to round to.

1⑤6,983
↑
rounding place

Step 2 Look at the digit to its right.

1⑤6,983
↑
digit to the right

Step 3 If that digit is 5 or greater, increase the rounding place digit by 1. If that digit is less than 5, do not change the rounding place digit. Then replace all digits to the right with zeros.

1⑤6,983
↓
160,000

6 > 5
Change 5 to 6.
Write zeros to the right.

Solution: The population of Springfield, Massachusetts, is 160,000 to the nearest ten thousand.

 Standards NS 1.1

Other Examples

A. Order 3 Numbers

Order 143,416, 143,687, and 142,825 from least to greatest.

- Line up the digits.
- Compare from the left.
- Continue comparing.

```
1 4 3, 4 1 6
1 4 3, 6 8 7  ←— greatest number
1 4 2, 8 2 5  ←— least number
```

$142{,}825 < 143{,}416 < 143{,}687$

B. Round a 9

Round 389,762 to the nearest thousand.

38⑨,762
↑
$7 > 5$

So, the number rounds to 390,000.

Explain Your Thinking

▶ Why do you start at the left to compare numbers?

▶ Why is the digit 5 used to decide how to round the digit to the left?

Guided Practice

Compare. Write >, <, or = for each ●.

1. 25,431 ● 25,661
2. 725,042 ● 724,742

Order each set of numbers from greatest to least.

3. 43,055 422,007 42,007
4. 812,661 814,475 813,677

Round to the place of the underlined digit.

5. <u>5</u>45
6. <u>2</u>8,621
7. 5<u>7</u>,421
8. <u>2</u>75,813

Ask Yourself

- Are the numbers lined up by place value?
- Where are the digits different?
- What is the digit to the right of the place I am rounding to?

Independent Practice

Compare. Write >, <, or = for each ●.

9. 12,198 ● 1,219
10. 5,555 ● 5,557
11. 46,117 ● 46,117
12. 245,672 ● 45,802
13. 138,042 ● 138,024
14. 782,450 ● 827,405

Order each set of numbers from least to greatest.

15. 1,374; 1,536; 1,437
16. 8,714; 8,764; 8,734
17. 44,991; 44,278; 44,717
18. 21,672; 21,872; 2,924
19. 541,536; 511,394; 601,345
20. 316,725; 316,728; 316,825

Round to the place of the underlined digit.

21. $5\underline{8}1$ **22.** $\underline{7}22$ **23.** $5,\underline{2}61$ **24.** $\underline{6},652$

25. $4,1\underline{2}7$ **26.** $1\underline{9},014$ **27.** $\underline{3}5,722$ **28.** $7\underline{4},127$

29. $6\underline{4}5,024$ **30.** $\underline{7}52,814$ **31.** $8\underline{6}4,120$ **32.** $\underline{5}92,107$

Round each number.

33. 28,652 to the nearest thousand.

34. 85,197 to the nearest ten thousand.

35. 259,802 to the nearest thousand.

36. 624,314 to the nearest hundred thousand.

Problem Solving • Reasoning

Use the table for Problems 37–40.

37. Arrange the cities in order from the least to the greatest population.

38. Analyze Round each city's population to the nearest hundred thousand. Order the rounded populations from least to greatest. What do you notice?

39. Which two cities have populations that round to the same number when they are rounded to the nearest hundred thousand?

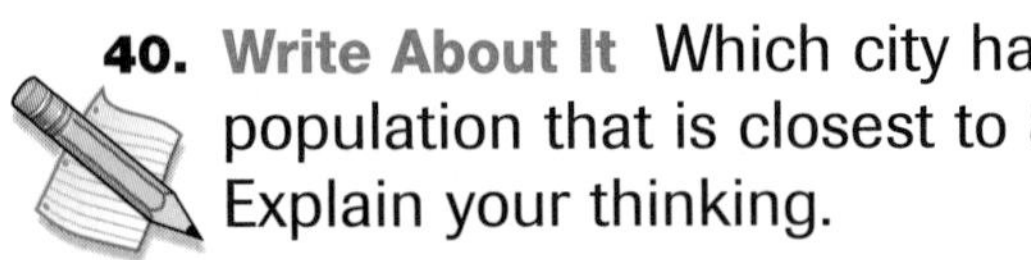

40. Write About It Which city has a population that is closest to 800,000? Explain your thinking.

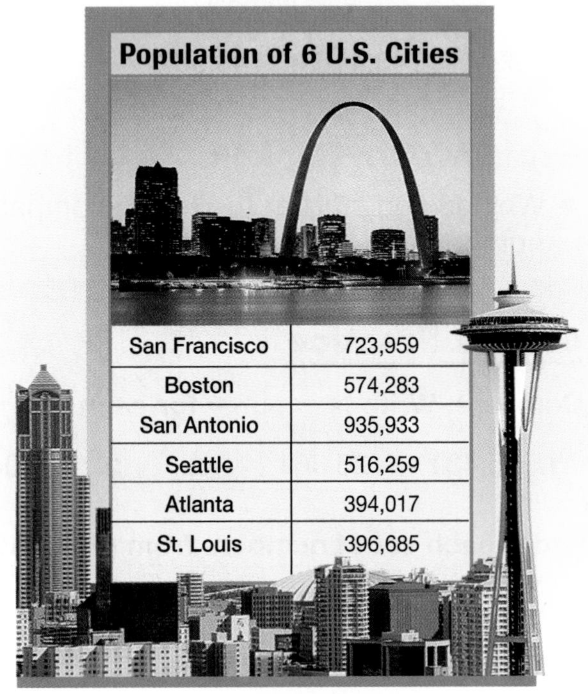

Population of 6 U.S. Cities

City	Population
San Francisco	723,959
Boston	574,283
San Antonio	935,933
Seattle	516,259
Atlanta	394,017
St. Louis	396,685

Mixed Review • Test Prep

Multiply or divide.

41. $17\overline{)51}$ **42.** 22×8 **43.** $19\overline{)95}$ **44.** $7,632 \times 5$

45. 15×7 **46.** $12\overline{)144}$ **47.** $14\overline{)98}$ **48.** 39×9

49 The difference between some number and 17 is 43. What is the number?

A 26 **C** 36

B 34 **D** 60

Extra Practice See Set C on page 38.

Practice Game

Digit Challenge

Practice place value by playing this game with a partner or several friends. Two to six can play. Try to be the first person to score 10 points.

Players 2–6

What You'll Need

- *4 sets of number cards, numbered 0–9*
- *a game board for each player with 6 rectangles, side by side*

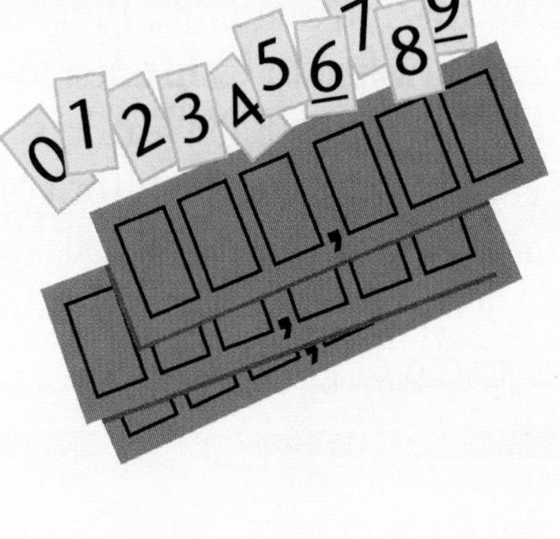

Here's What to Do

1. Shuffle the cards and place them in a stack.
2. Each player draws a card and places it on his or her game board. Once placed, the card cannot be moved.
3. Repeat Step 2 until each player has drawn and placed 6 cards.
4. The player who makes the greatest number scores a point.
5. Return all the cards to the deck and reshuffle.

Repeat Steps 2–5.

The first player to score a total of 10 points is the winner.

Share Your Thinking How would your strategy change if you played this game to make the smallest possible number?

Problem-Solving Skill: Estimated or Exact Amounts

You will learn how to recognize whether amounts are estimates or are exact.

Numbers can be used to represent exact amounts or estimated amounts. Read this report about the California Gold Rush.

San Francisco, California Dec. 23, 1852

Gold was discovered near Sacramento on January 24, 1848. Walking over land for 4 to 8 months, thousands of people rushed to California to seek their fortunes. In 1849, at least 32,000 people arrived to search for gold in the California hills. In 1850, about 44,000 people rushed into California in search of gold.

The port of San Francisco was a busy place during these years. In addition to the people who came by land from other states, nearly 40,000 more people came to California by sea during 1849 and 1850. The California Gold Rush peaked in 1852 when more than $80 million worth of gold was found.

Sometimes the amounts we use are exact.

We use an exact amount when an amount can be counted or measured.

Sometimes the amounts we use are estimates.

We use an estimate for an amount that cannot be measured easily. Any amount that is not exact is an estimate.

Some words in the report can help you identify that an amount is an estimate.

thousands	at least	4 to 8
about	nearly	more than

Look Back Is the number of travelers who came by sea exact? How can you decide whether an amount is exact or estimated?

 Standards MR 1.0, 2.0, 3.0

Left: When gold was discovered in 1848, only 800 people lived in San Francisco. *Right:* By the early 1850s the population had exploded to about 250,000.

Guided Practice

Decide if an amount is estimated or exact.

1. By 1853, nearly 250,000 people had rushed to California. Is the number of people who had rushed to California an exact amount or an estimated amount? Explain.

   Think: What word will tell you whether the amount is estimated?

2. Many gold seekers earned from $12 to $15 a day. One gold seeker was reported to have earned $128 in one day. Which amount is exact? Which amount is an estimate?

   Think: Which amount has been counted accurately?

Choose a Strategy

Solve. Use these or other strategies.

Problem-Solving Strategies

- **Write an Equation**
- **Draw a Diagram**
- **Make a Table**
- **Guess and Check**

Use the Gold Rush information on pages 12 and 13 to answer Problems 3–6.

3. About how many people altogether traveled over land to California in 1849 and 1850?

4. To the nearest thousand, by how much did San Francisco's population grow from 1848 to 1853?

5. How many gold seekers altogether arrived in 1849 and 1850? Is your answer exact or an estimate?

6. Could you say that about 300,000 people had rushed to California by 1853? Explain why or why not.

7. Juan has 4 more Gold Rush souvenirs than Carla. They have 32 souvenirs altogether. How many souvenirs does Juan have? How many souvenirs does Carla have?

8. Suppose an ounce of gold is worth about $300.00. Mei Lin has saved $40 a week for 2 months. Does she have enough to buy an ounce of gold? Explain your thinking.

9. At a Gold Rush gift shop, souvenir hats are $7.95 each and gold pans are $11.50 each. Is $30 enough money to buy 2 hats and 1 gold pan? Explain.

10. A newspaper article about the Gold Rush has 1,582 words. If the article fills 4 columns, about how many words are in each column?

Extra Practice See 1–4 on page 41.

Millions and Billions

You will learn how to read, write, compare, and order numbers in the millions and billions.

Learn About It

In 1999, the population of China reached 1,246,871,951. The population of the United States reached 272,639,608 and the population of India reached 1,000,848,550.

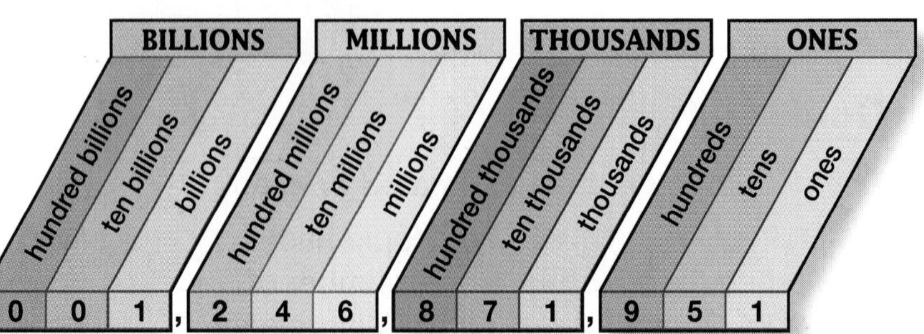

How could you order the populations from least to greatest?

Different Ways to Read and Write Numbers

You can use standard form.	1,246,871,951
You can use expanded form.	$(1 \times 1{,}000{,}000{,}000) + (2 \times 100{,}000{,}000) + (4 \times 10{,}000{,}000)$ $+ (6 \times 1{,}000{,}000) + (8 \times 100{,}000) + (7 \times 10{,}000)$ $+ (1 \times 1{,}000) + (9 \times 100) + (5 \times 10) + (1 \times 1)$
You can use expanded form with exponents.	$(1 \times 10^9) + (2 \times 10^8) + (4 \times 10^7) + (6 \times 10^6) + (8 \times 10^5)$ $+ (7 \times 10^4) + (1 \times 10^3) + (9 \times 10^2) + (5 \times 10^1) + (1 \times 10^0)$
You can use short word form.	1 billion, 246 million, 871 thousand, 951
You can use word form.	one billion, two hundred forty-six million, eight hundred seventy-one thousand, nine hundred fifty-one

Compare and order large numbers in the same way as small numbers.

- Line up the place values.
- Compare the digits in the places until they are different.

```
  272,639,608  ←  the least number
1,246,871,951  ←  the greatest number
1,000,848,550
  ↑
2 > 0
```

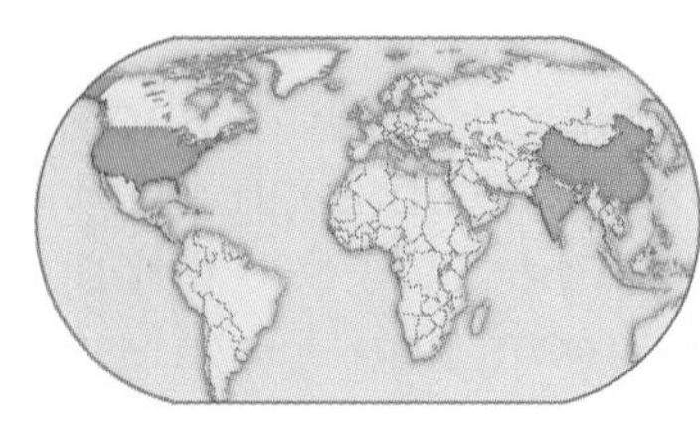

Solution: From least to greatest, the populations are 272,639,608; 1,000,848,550; 1,246,871,951.

 Standards NS **1.0, 1.1** MR **1.0, 1.1, 2.4, 2.3**

Explain Your Thinking

- ▶ Explain why a thousand million is the same as a billion.
- ▶ Why is 2.5 million the same as 2,500,000?

Guided Practice

Write the numbers in short word form, expanded form, and expanded form using exponents.

1. 213,456,075 **2.** 45,678,092,143

Order each set of numbers from greatest to least.

3. 345,678,219 34,578,219 134,786,234

4. 45,342,123 245,673,451 6,789,342,501

Ask Yourself

- What place comes before each comma?
- What power of ten is in the greatest place value?
- Where are the digits different?

Independent Practice

Write the value of the underlined digit in short word form.

5. $\underline{8}$76,541 **6.** 2,$\underline{3}$46,780,102 **7.** 4$\underline{5}$6,073,969,208

Read the number. Then write it in short word form.

8. 796,806 **9.** 234,158,672 **10.** 7,542,908,685

Write in standard form.

11. 8 million, 345 thousand, 752

12. 92 billion, 34 million, 25

13. one hundred nine million, three hundred forty-two

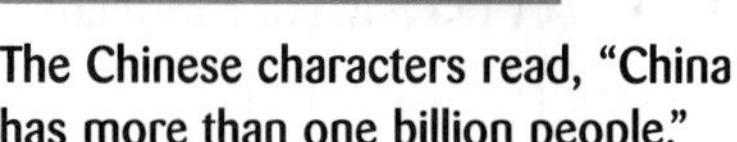

The Chinese characters read, "China has more than one billion people."

14. three billion, fourteen million, five hundred eighty-five

15. $(8 \times 10^{10}) + (5 \times 10^9) + (3 \times 10^8) + (2 \times 10^7) + (4 \times 10^6) + (6 \times 10^5) + (1 \times 10^4) + (7 \times 10^3) + (9 \times 10^2) + (5 \times 10^1) + (4 \times 10^0)$

16. $(9 \times 10^9) + (2 \times 10^7) + (8 \times 10^6) + (7 \times 10^3) + (3 \times 10^2) + (7 \times 10^0)$

Write in expanded form using exponents.

17. 78,056,432,941 **18.** 245,087,705 **19.** 19,650,120

Order each set of numbers from least to greatest.

20. 67,564,321
67,823,430
67,478,043

21. 345,652,189,234
345,658,145,037
345,658,123,078

22. 23,456,701
2,356,701
24,356,701

Algebra • Equations **Substitute the correct value for *n*.**

23. $n - 1 = 999{,}999$

24. $n + 1 = 1{,}000{,}000{,}000$

25. $n - 1{,}000 = 9{,}999{,}000$

Problem Solving • Reasoning

Use Data **Use the diagram for Problems 26 and 27.**

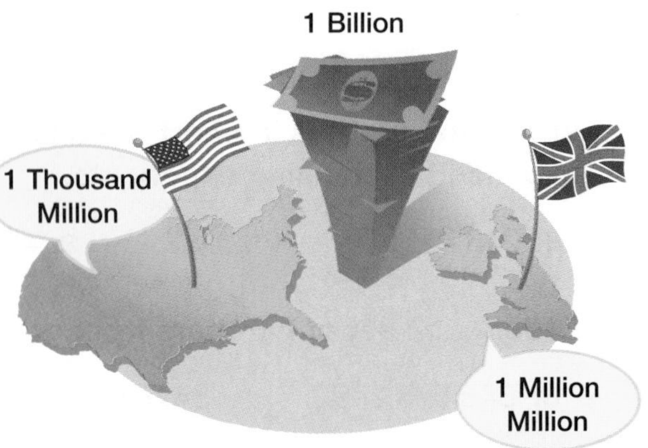

In England, the word *billion* has a different meaning. There, it means one million million.

26. **Compare** Use exponents to write an American billion and an English billion. Is the exponent the same for both numbers?

27. **Analyze** Would you rather have a billion dollars in England or in the United States? Explain.

28. Order the numbers 6×10^6, 7×10^5, and 4×10^2 from greatest to least.

29. **Write About It** Write the number in standard form that represents one million tens. Explain your thinking.

Mixed Review • Test Prep

Solve.

30. 47×22

31. $63 + 34$

32. 19×40

33. 21×6

34. $38 + 55$

Write the letter of the correct answer.

35. Which sum is closest to 6,000?

A 4,172 + 523 **B** 3,999 + 2,003 **C** 2,453 + 3,544 **D** 4,128 + 2,500

36. Which difference is closest to 6,000?

F 7,502 − 502 **G** 8,000 − 1,593 **H** 9,000 − 3,980 **J** 10,000 − 3,980

Logical Thinking

Numbers

Use all of these digits exactly once to write the number described in standard form.

1. the greatest possible number
2. the smallest possible number if the first digit is greater than 0

Extra Practice See Set D on page 39.

Relative Magnitude

Sometimes the same number can seem very large, very small, or about right.

When does 1,000,000 seem very large?

Few people in the world are able to spend $1,000,000 on a work of art. So it is big news when it happens.

One million dollars is a large amount of money to spend on a single painting.

Millions Spent on Modern Art

Picassos accounted for more than $164 million of the auction total, and were eight of the ten most expensive works. His cubist "Woman Sitting in an Armchair," sold for $24.7 million.

When does 1,000,000 seem to be small?

Major Hollywood movies cost tens of millions of dollars to make, even as much as $100,000,000.

One million dollars seems a small amount of money to make a movie.

Low Budget Film Big Hit!

Made with a budget of only $1,000,000, the film has nevertheless done well in screenings abroad because of its presentation and grand scale. The screenwriter said the film has a certain unmatched authenticity.

When does 1,000,000 seem about right?

There are many cities in the world with populations of 1,000,000 or more.

One million seems about right for the population of a major city.

Urban Populations (rounded)

Münich, Germany	1,179,000
Philadelphia, U.S.	1,435,000
Lagos, Nigeria	1,704,000
Hangzhou, China	1,477,000

Explain Your Thinking

- Think of other examples in which 1,000,000 seems large, small, or about right.
- When does 1,000 seem large? small? about right?

Round Large Numbers

You will learn how to round numbers to the nearest million and billion.

Learn About It

A newspaper reporter is doing a story on the number of books in The Library of Congress. The library has 14,941,834 books. The reporter wants to round this number to the nearest million.

Round **14,941,834** to the nearest million.

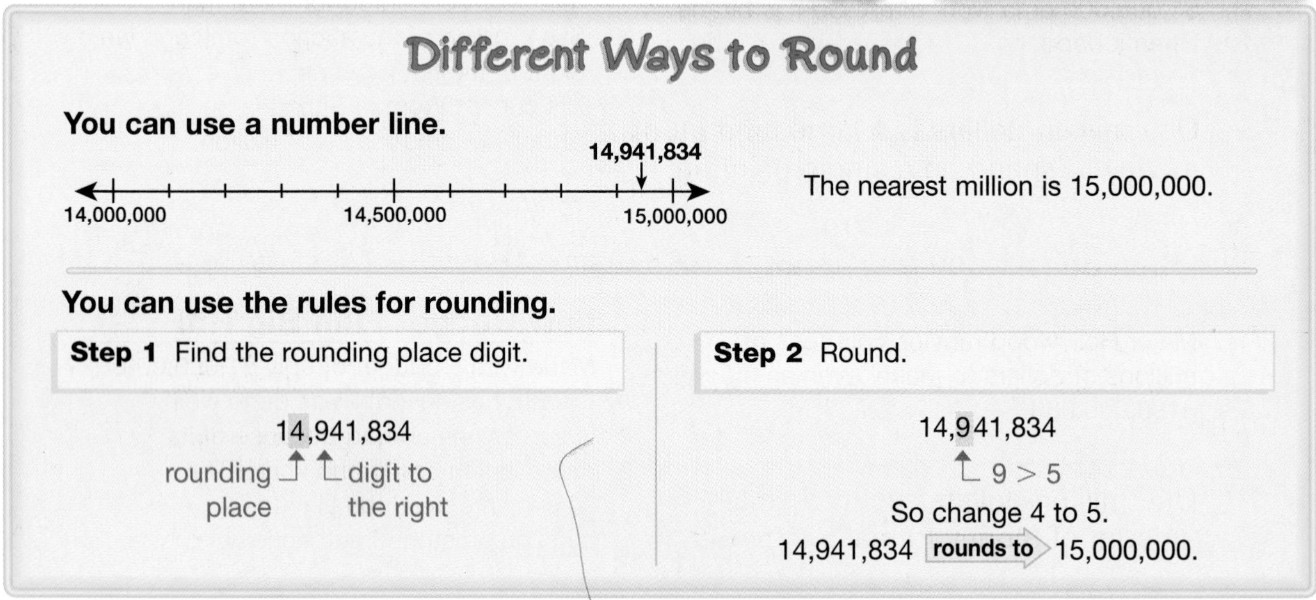

Different Ways to Round

You can use a number line.

The nearest million is 15,000,000.

You can use the rules for rounding.

Step 1 Find the rounding place digit.

14,941,834

rounding place — digit to the right

Step 2 Round.

14,941,834

$9 > 5$

So change 4 to 5.

14,941,834 **rounds to** 15,000,000.

Solution: 14,941,834 rounded to the nearest million is 15,000,000.

Another Example

Round to the nearest billion.

25,632,127,689

rounding place — $6 > 5$

25,632,127,689 **rounds to** 26,000,000,000.

Explain Your Thinking

► How are rounding to the nearest million and to the nearest billion similar? How are they different?

Guided Practice

Round each number to the nearest million.

1. 6,123,478 **2.** 473,892,315

Round each number to the nearest billion.

3. 17,894,321,560 **4.** 236,289,562,012

Ask Yourself

- What is the digit to the right of the place to which I am rounding?

Standards NS **1.0, 1.1**

Independent Practice

Round to the nearest million. Write the answers in short word form.

5. 2,478,923 **6.** 4,723,561 **7.** 8,923,452 **8.** 25,178,029

9. 57,690,345 **10.** 73,328,159 **11.** 168,034,526 **12.** 367,236,854

Round to the nearest billion. Write the answers in short word form.

13. 5,678,433,210 **14.** 6,493,451,723 **15.** 8,765,430,921

16. 24,375,689,321 **17.** 36,563,782,901 **18.** 67,834,526,019

19. 124,784,361,093 **20.** 458,294,567,210 **21.** 845,321,687,988

Round to the place of the underlined digit.

22. 8$\underline{9}$9 **23.** 3,$\underline{8}$27 **24.** $\underline{5}$4,328 **25.** $\underline{3}$5,642

26. $\underline{3}$72,589 **27.** 5$\underline{6}$4,378 **28.** 2$\underline{9}$,567,452 **29.** 1$\underline{0}$2,436,745

Problem Solving • Reasoning

30. An encyclopedia contains 21,873,526 words. How many words is that to the nearest million? to the nearest ten million?

31. **Estimate** Another encyclopedia contains 6,315 articles. If the average article is 2,000 words long, how many words are there in the encyclopedia, to the nearest million words?

32. **Analyze** If ten-digit codes are used to catalog books, how many different codes are possible? Every code must have ten digits, but zeros can be used for any digit. For example, 0000000000 is the first acceptable code.

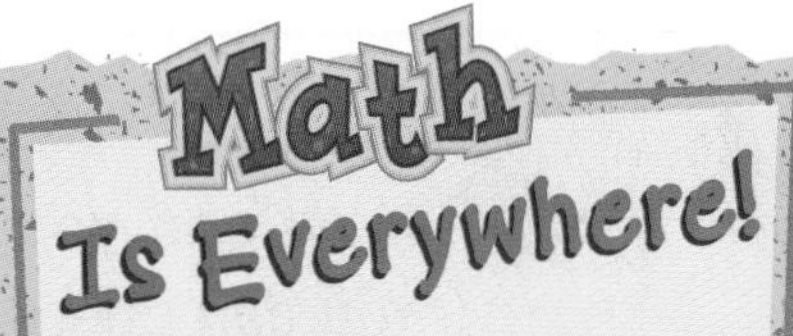

ENGLISH A magazine article is often written to a specific number of words. To estimate word count, multiply the number of words in one line by the number of lines. Which article has about 1,500 words?

	Lines	Words in a line
A	186	8
B	168	9
C	136	11

Mixed Review • Test Prep

Add or subtract.

33. 6,487 − 5,593 **34.** 7,218 + 4,568 **35.** 5,201 − 3,874

36. 7,790 + 1,785 **37.** 4,576 − 4,571 **38.** 5,102 + 909

39 What is the product of 70 and 22?

A 92 **B** 144 **C** 154 **D** 1,540

Extra Practice See Set E on page 39.

Problem-Solving Strategy: Guess and Check

You will learn how to solve a problem by guessing and checking.

Sometimes the quickest way to solve a problem is to try a few numbers and check the results.

Problem The quiz show host said, "A whole number can be divided by 5 and 2 with a remainder of 0. The number is greater than 30 and less than 50. What is the number?"

Understand

What is the question?

What is the number?

What do you know?

- It is a whole number that can be divided by 5 and 2.
- It is greater than 30, and it is less than 50.

Plan

How can you find the answer?

You can guess and check to help solve the problem. Make a guess. Check to see whether your guess is correct. If not, use the result to improve your guess.

Solve

Guess	Check		
Try 35.	$5\overline{)35}$ = 7	$2\overline{)35}$ = 17 R1	The number 35 can be divided by 5 but not by 2. The answer is not 35.
Try 40. It is an even number and it is between 30 and 50.	$5\overline{)40}$ = 8	$2\overline{)40}$ = 20	The number 40 can be divided by 5 and by 2. A possible answer is 40.

Solution: The number is 40.

Look Back

Look back at the problem.

Check to make sure that 40 is the only possible answer.

Standards | MR 1.0, 1.1, 1.2, 2.0, 3.0, 3.1

Remember:
- Understand
- Plan
- Solve
- Look Back

Guided Practice

Solve each problem, using the Guess and Check strategy.

1. Marla has 18 tickets. Each ticket is either red or blue. There are twice as many blue tickets as red tickets. How many blue tickets are there? How many red tickets?

   Think: What information should you start with?

2. The fifth grade made $25.00 on a talent show. They received only $5 bills and $1 bills and collected a total of 9 bills in the cash box. What combination of bills did they have?

   Think: Which types of bills are in the cash box?

Choose a Strategy

Solve. Use these or other strategies.

Problem-Solving Strategies

- **Draw a Diagram**
- **Find a Pattern**
- **Guess and Check**
- **Make a Model**

3. The sixth-grade students made $25.00 on their show. They have $10, $5, and $1 bills and 8 bills in all. How many of each bill did they have?

4. Carlo has 6 more trading cards than Ashley. Together they have 54 cards. How many cards does Carlo have? How many cards does Ashley have?

5. There are cats, dogs, and birds at the fifth-grade pet show. If there are 9 pets in all, and they have 30 legs altogether, how many birds are there in the show?

6. Alex, Sue, and Jo sold tickets for a show. Alex sold 52 tickets. Sue sold 10 more tickets than Alex. Jo sold 10 more tickets than Sue. How many tickets did Alex, Sue, and Jo sell in all?

7. In 1906, the famous escape artist, Houdini, jumped into San Francisco Bay with a metal ball chained to his feet. This time, he escaped safely. If Houdini and the ball weighed 225 pounds altogether, and Houdini weighed twice as much as the ball, how much did the ball weigh?

8. Use the numbers 1 to 8 to complete this magic square. Put a different digit in each square so that the numbers in each row, column, and diagonal have a sum of up to 15.

		9

Extra Practice See 5–7 on page 41.

Quick Check

Check Your Understanding of Lessons 1–7

Write each in word form and expanded form.

1. 15,806 **2.** 205,019 **3.** 650,250,055

Write each in standard form.

4. 5×10^4 **5.** $(8 \times 10^3) + (2 \times 10^2)$

6. $(5 \times 10^5) + (3 \times 10^4) + (2 \times 10^3) + (6 \times 10^2) + (4 \times 10^1)$

Compare. Write >, <, or = for each ⬬.

7. 23,456 ⬬ 32,645 **8.** 541,621 ⬬ 541,612 **9.** 999,989 ⬬ 999,899

Round each to the underlined place.

10. $\underline{3}2{,}650{,}112$ **11.** $21\underline{9}{,}760{,}224$ **12.** $1{,}9\underline{9}9{,}999{,}999$

Solve.

13. A rectangle has a perimeter of 20 cm. Two of the sides are 2 cm longer than the other two sides. How long is each side?

14. Ms. Chu bought 3 T-shirts for $19.95 each and a pair of socks for $5.85. About how much money did she spend? Do you need to find an estimated or an exact amount? Explain.

How did you do?

If you had difficulty with any items in the Quick Check, you can use the following pages for review and extra practice.

California Standards	Items	Review These Pages	Do These Extra Practice Items
Number Sense: **1.0**	1–3	pages 4–5, 14–16	Set A, page 38 Set D, page 39
Number Sense: **1.3**	4–6	pages 6–7	Set B, page 38
Number Sense: **1.1**	7–12	pages 8–10, 18–19	Set C, page 38 Set E, page 39
Math Reasoning: **2.5**	13–14	pages 12–13, 20–21	1–7, page 41

Test Prep • Cumulative Review

Maintaining the Standards

Choose the letter of the correct answer. If a correct answer is not here, choose NH.

1 What is the value of 10^4?

A 40
B 1,000
C 4,000
D 10,000

2 Which of these is *not* rounded correctly?

F 5,513,111 to 6,000,000
G 7,682,099 to 8,000,000
H 12,600,343 to 12,000,000
J 39,199,999 to 39,000,000

3 In which of the following situations would it *not* be a good idea to round the numbers?

A a teacher counting her students
B a musician counting the number of people in the audience
C a person describing the distance between two places
D a runner in a marathon counting the other runners

4 A used car is advertised in the newspaper for $12,850. Round this figure to the nearest thousand dollars.

F $13,900 **H** $12,900
G $13,000 **J** $12,000

5 What is the sum of 10^2 and 10^3?

A 1,100 **C** NH
B 100,000 **D** 20^5

6 Ten years ago a mother was three times as old as her son was. The sum of their ages today is 60. How old is the mother today?

F 60 years old
G 50 years old
H 40 years old
J 30 years old

7 If the following mountains were ordered from lowest to highest elevation, which mountain would be second on the list?

Mountain	Elevation (feet)
Mt. Rainier	14,410
Mt. McKinley	20,320
Mt. Whitney	14,494
Mt. Elbert	14,433
Mt. Hood	11,239

A Mt. Rainier **C** Mt. McKinley
B Mt. Whitney **D** Mt. Elbert

8 Josh says, "I am thinking of a whole number that is greater than 54 and less than 72. The number can be divided by 2 and 3, but not 5." What number is Josh thinking of?

Explain How could you find the number?

Internet Test Prep
Visit **www.eduplace.com/kids/mhm** for more *Test Prep Practice.*

Place Value and Decimals

You will learn how to read and write decimals as small as one thousandth.

Review Vocabulary
decimal
decimal point
standard form

Learn About It

In basketball, a field goal average is the number of successful shots divided by the number of attempts. It is often shown as a **decimal**. In one season, Jim's field goal average was 0.584. What does 0.584 mean?

Use the place-value chart to understand decimals.

The value of numbers to the right of the **decimal point** is less than 1.

WHOLE NUMBERS				DECIMALS		
hundreds	tens	ones		tenths	hundredths	thousandths
		0	.	5	8	4

decimal point

Standard form: 0.584
Word form: five hundred eighty-four thousandths

Solution: Jim's average was 584 thousandths or $\frac{584}{1,000}$.

Another Example

Decimals Greater Than 1

Write 2.035 in word form.

two and thirty-five thousandths

Explain Your Thinking

▶ Why does the value of the last digit help you read a decimal?

Guided Practice

Write each decimal in words.

1. 2.7 **2.** 0.15 **3.** 0.094

4. 3.826 **5.** 45.073 **6.** 2,430.75

7. 1.005 **8.** 10.67 **9.** 103.06

Ask Yourself

- What word did I write in for the decimal point?

Independent Practice

In words, what is the value of the underlined digit?

10. 5.7<u>7</u> **11.** 6.<u>2</u>45 **12.** 7.8<u>8</u>

13. 8.37<u>4</u> **14.** 8.10<u>9</u> **15.** 4.<u>7</u>3

16. <u>3</u>.990 **17.** 0.0<u>3</u>2 **18.** 0.2<u>0</u>4

Make a place-value chart. Write each decimal in the chart and in words.

19. 0.019 **20.** 0.5 **21.** 0.34 **22.** 25.4

23. 0.789 **24.** 4.306 **25.** 0.082 **26.** 3.1

Write in standard form.

27. five tenths

28. twenty-four hundredths

29. one hundred thirty-eight thousandths

30. nine hundredths

31. twenty-five thousandths

32. eleven and seven tenths

33. five and twenty-three hundredths

34. twelve and four thousandths

Problem Solving • Reasoning

Use Data **Use the graph for Problems 35–37.**

35. What was Jim's best season?

36. What was his worst season?

37. **Analyze** Rounded to the nearest tenth, what was Jim's overall average?

38. Write a decimal to the thousandths place that is equivalent to one.

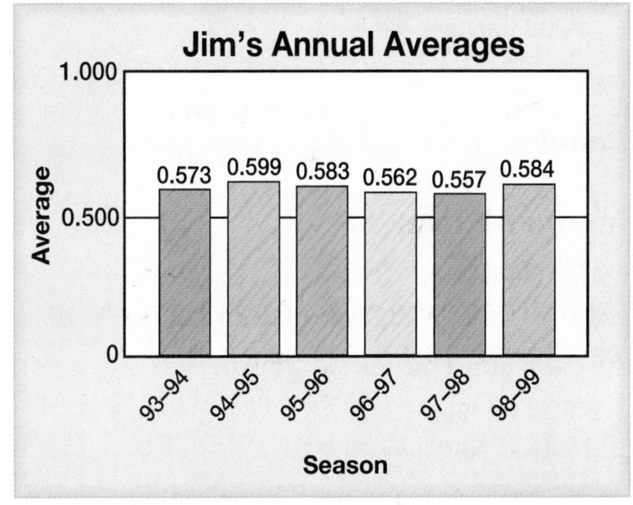

Mixed Review • Test Prep

Round to the nearest ten. *(pages 8–10)*

39. 44 **40.** 167 **41.** 2,355 **42.** 60,981

Write the letter of the correct anwer. *(pages 8–10)*

43 Which number could have been rounded to the nearest hundred?

A 800 **B** 801 **C** 810 **D** 850

44 Which number could have been rounded to the nearest ten?

F 800 **G** 801 **H** 811 **J** 8,011

Extra Practice See Set F on page 39.

LESSON 9

Compare and Order Decimals Less Than One

You will learn how to compare and order decimals as small as one thousandth.

Learn About It

Which number is greater?

Compare **0.5** and **0.25**.

Different Ways to Compare Decimals

You can use a number line.

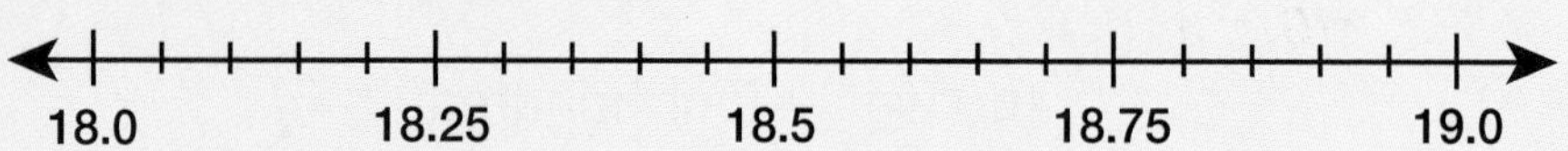

0.5 is to the right of 0.25, so 0.5 > 0.25.

You can compare digits.

- Align the decimal points.
- Compare digits from left to right until they are different.

0.50
0.25

Since 5 > 2, 0.5 > 0.25.

Solution: 0.5 is greater than 0.25.

Another Example

Order Decimals

Order 0.506, 0.534, and 0.525 from least to greatest.

0.506 ← least
0.534 ← greatest
0.525

0.506 < 0.525 < 0.534

Explain Your Thinking

▶ Why is it important to align the decimal points when comparing decimals?

Guided Practice

Compare the decimals. Write >, <, or = for each ●.

1. 0.45 ● 0.88 **2.** 0.6 ● 0.06 **3.** 0.153 ● 0.2

Order each set of numbers from least to greatest.

4. 0.3 0.520 0.08 **5.** 0.825 0.07 0.25

Ask Yourself

- Did I line up the decimal points?
- Did I find the first place where the digits are different?

Standards NS 1.0, 1.1, 1.5

Independent Practice

Compare. Write >, <, or = for each ●.

6. 0.09 ● 0.11 **7.** 0.945 ● 0.941 **8.** 0.30 ● 0.300 **9.** 0.26 ● 0.3

10. 0.9 ● 0.5 **11.** 0.321 ● 0.27 **12.** 0.013 ● 0.13 **13.** 0.9 ● 0.900

Order each set of decimals from greatest to least.

14. 0.35 0.53 0.05 **15.** 0.15 0.009 0.8 **16.** 0.42 0.12 0.25

17. 0.35 0.5 0.432 **18.** 0.25 0.7 0.825 **19.** 0.78 0.713 0.33

20. 0.7 0.13 0.76 **21.** 0.9 0.003 0.59 0.662 **22.** 0.3 0.081 0.2 0.02

n **Algebra • Properties** **Compare. Write >, <, or = for each ●, given $a = 0.895$, $b = 0.75$, $c = 0.075$, and $d = 0$.**

23. b ● c **24.** c ● b **25.** a ● d **26.** c ● d

Problem Solving • Reasoning

27. **Analyze** What digits could you put in the ■ to make the statement 0.23 ■ > 0.234 true? Explain.

28. **Compare** Do 0.3, 0.30, and 0.300 represent the same value? Explain your thinking.

29. Many libraries use a system of decimals to classify books and order them on the shelves. Three books are numbered 0.971, 0.978, and 0.97. Which book should be first on the shelf?

30. **Write Your Own** Write a problem that can be solved by comparing four decimals. Have a partner check your work.

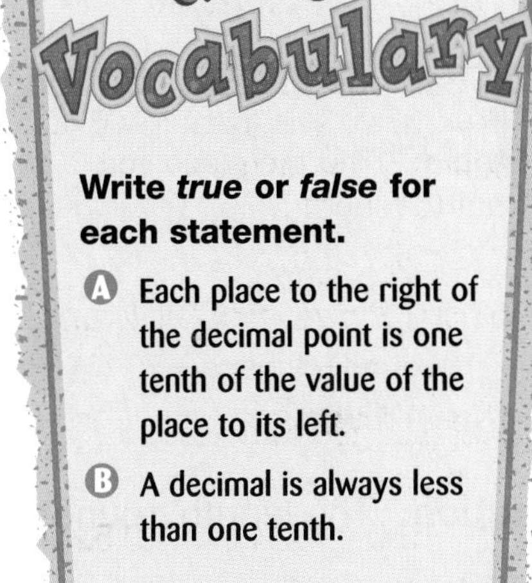

Mixed Review • Test Prep

What is the place value of the underlined digit? *(pages 4–5, 24–25)*

31. $36\underline{2},011$ **32.** $98.7\underline{6}5$ **33.** $3,67\underline{9}.23$

Write the letter of the correct answer. *(pages 14–16)*

34 Which number has a one in the ones, ten thousands, hundred thousands, and millions places?

A 1,010,001 **C** 1,110,001

B 1,101,001 **D** 1,110,010

Extra Practice See Set G on page 40.

Round Decimals

You will learn how to round decimals to the nearest tenth and hundredth.

Learn About It

An engineer's plan shows that the Verrazano Narrows Bridge in New York City is 0.807 mile long. How long is it to the nearest hundredth of a mile?

Round 0.807 to the nearest hundredth.

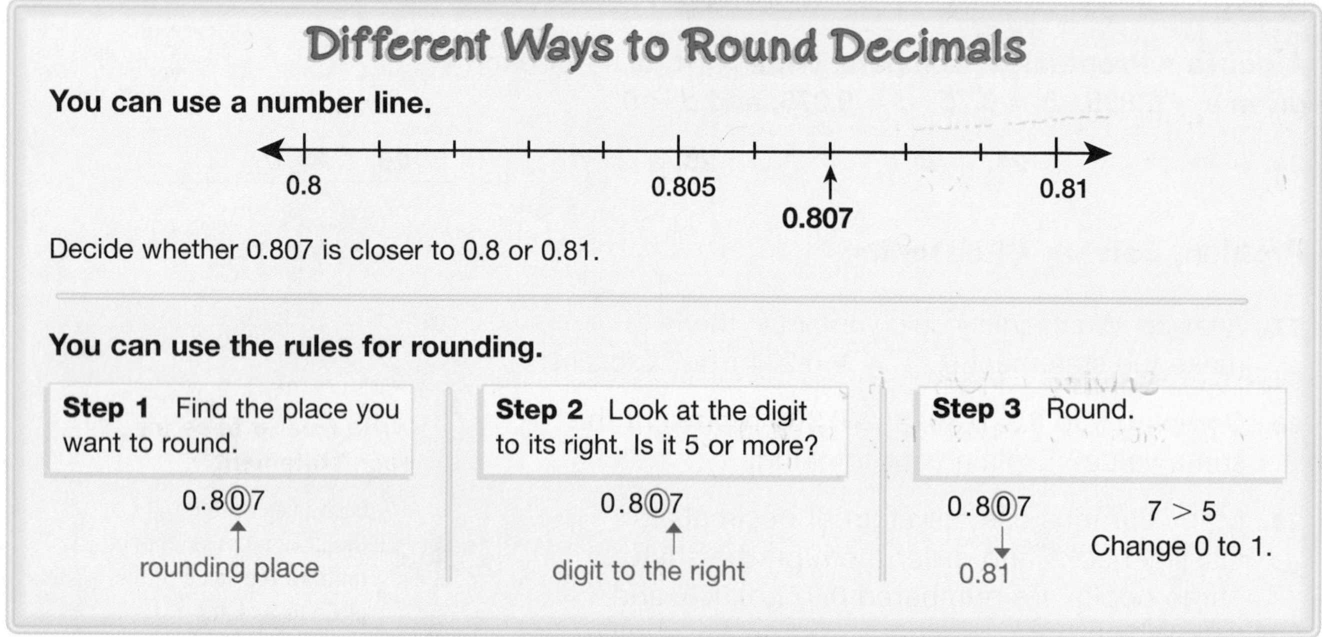

Different Ways to Round Decimals

You can use a number line.

Decide whether 0.807 is closer to 0.8 or 0.81.

You can use the rules for rounding.

Step 1 Find the place you want to round.

0.8⓪7
↑
rounding place

Step 2 Look at the digit to its right. Is it 5 or more?

0.8⓪7
↑
digit to the right

Step 3 Round.

0.8⓪7
↓
0.81

$7 > 5$
Change 0 to 1.

Solution: The length, rounded to the nearest hundredth, is 0.81 mile.

Other Examples

A. Round to the Nearest Tenth

0.④18

↑ $1 < 5$ 0.418 **rounds to** 0.4

B. Round to the Nearest Whole Number

②.798

↑ 7 is equal to or greater than 5 2.798 **rounds to** 3

Explain Your Thinking

▶ How is rounding a decimal like rounding whole numbers?

Guided Practice

Use a number line to round to the place value of the underlined digit.

1. $0.0\underline{8}5$ **2.** $0.5\underline{7}2$ **3.** $0.1\underline{4}5$ **4.** $\underline{3}.957$

Ask Yourself

- Do I change the rounding place digit?

Standards NS **1.0, 1.1, 1.5** MR **1.0**

Independent Practice

Round to the nearest tenth.

5. 0.457	**6.** 0.81	**7.** 0.672	**8.** 0.93
9. 2.79	**10.** 3.456	**11.** 4.321	**12.** 12.57
13. 0.124	**14.** 0.317	**15.** 0.543	**16.** 0.781

Round to the nearest hundredth.

17. 0.234	**18.** 0.568	**19.** 0.695	**20.** 0.852
21. 2.147	**22.** 3.672	**23.** 16.176	**24.** 27.452
25. 3.156	**26.** 6.782	**27.** 7.346	**28.** 33.31

Round to the nearest whole number.

29. 1.4	**30.** 2.8	**31.** 3.45	**32.** 4.67
33. 8.34	**34.** 9.91	**35.** 7.123	**36.** 8.672

Problem Solving • Reasoning

37. The Mackinac Straits Bridge in Michigan is 0.72 mile long. What is its length to the nearest tenth of a mile?

38. The Golden Gate Bridge is 0.795 mile long. Round its length to the nearest hundredth of a mile.

39. **Compare** Which bridge is closest to one mile in length, the Verrazano Bridge, the Mackinac Straits Bridge, or the Golden Gate Bridge?

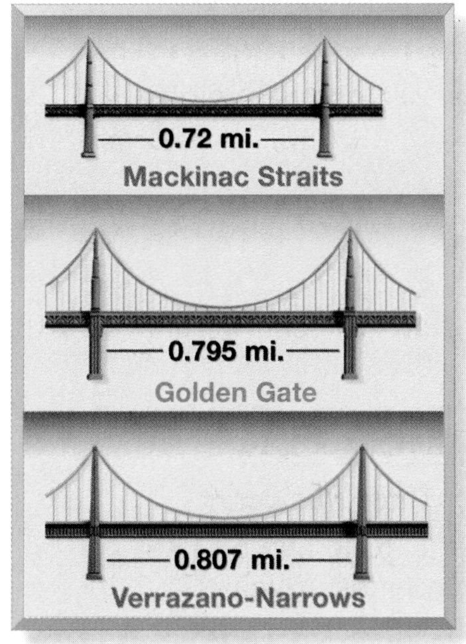

Mixed Review • Test Prep

Write >, <, or = for each ⬬. *(pages 26–27)*

40. 0.678 ⬬ 0.7 **41.** 0.167 ⬬ 0.166 **42.** 0.682 ⬬ 0.683

43 The dividend is forty-four, the divisor is seven, the quotient is six, and the remainder is two. Select the correct equation.

A 44 ÷ 6 = 7 R2 **C** 44 ÷ 7 = 2 R6

B 44 ÷ 2 = 7 R6 **D** 44 ÷ 7 = 6 R2

Extra Practice See Set H on page 40.

Compare and Order Decimals and Whole Numbers

You will learn how to compare and order decimals and whole numbers.

Rene Girard, Special Olympics Speed Skater

Learn About It

In 1988, one participant in a Special Olympics speed-skating event finished in 18.75 seconds. Another participant finished in 18.34 seconds. Which time was shorter?

Compare **18.75** and **18.34**.

Different Ways to Compare Decimals

You can use a number line.

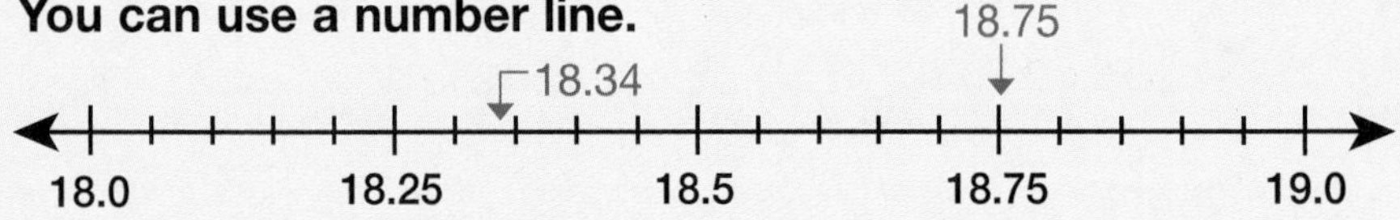

Since 18.75 is to the right of 18.34 on the number line, 18.75 > 18.34.

You can compare digits.

Align the decimal points. Compare digits until they are different.

```
1 8 . 7 5
1 8 . 3 4
↑ ↑     └ Since 7 > 3, then 18.75 > 18.34.
same same
```

Solution: The shorter time was 18.34 seconds.

Another Example

Order Three Numbers

Order 5, 5.43, and 5.419 from greatest to least.

5. 0 0 0 5. 4 3 0 5. 4 1 9	Write zeros if necessary. Looking at the tenths place, the least number is 5.000.
5. 4 3 0 5. 4 1 9	Looking at the hundredths place, the next greatest number is 5.43.

Ordered from greatest to least, the numbers are 5.43, 5.419, 5.

Explain Your Thinking

▶ Writing a zero to the right of a whole number multiplies its value by 10. Why can you write zeros at the end of a decimal number without changing the value of the number?

 Standards NS **1.0, 1.1, 1.5**

Guided Practice

Compare. Write >, <, or = for each ●.

1. 0.017 ● 1.016 **2.** 0.546 ● 5.2 **3.** 1.017 ● 2

Order each set of numbers from least to greatest.

4. 1.432 1,432 14.32 **5.** 1.78 0.613 1

Ask Yourself

- What is the first place from the left in which the digits are different?
- How do the digits in that place compare?

Independent Practice

Compare. Write >, <, or = for each ●.

6. 8 ● 9.123 **7.** 4.1 ● 0.875 **8.** 3 ● 3.000 **9.** 4.567 ● 5

10. 17 ● 16.882 **11.** 25.2 ● 252 **12.** 1.523 ● 1,523 **13.** 9.9 ● 9.900

Order each set of numbers from greatest to least.

14. 4 0.425 4.25 **15.** 0.6 0.68 68 **16.** 2,543 2.543 25.43

17. 0.34 0.4 3 **18.** 3.4 5 4.35 **19.** 0.72 7.2 7

Problem Solving • Reasoning

Use Data **Use the table for Problems 22 and 23.**

20. The quotient of two whole numbers is 15. The product is 240. What are the numbers?

21. **Analyze** If $n > 7.047$, what whole number could n stand for? Give an example to support your thinking.

22. **Compare** Order the figure skating singles silver points from least to greatest.

23. **Write About It** Do the gold points or the silver points have a greater range? Explain your answer.

Special Olympics Results Figure-Skating Singles

Gold Points	Silver Points
222.36	205.03
250.99	208.74
245.22	158.59
248.84	177.26
215.35	162.40

Erin Rynberk, Special Olympics Figure Skater

Mixed Review • Test Prep

Solve.

24. $295 + 10$ **25.** 100×6 **26.** 224×3 **27.** $305 - 16$ **28.** 546×24

29 What is the sum of 721,500 and four thousand, twelve?

A 725,512 **B** 725,620 **C** 761,512 **D** 1,121,512

Extra Practice See Set I on page 40.

Negative Numbers and the Number Line

You will learn how to compare integers and decimals.

New Vocabulary
negative numbers
opposite
integers

Learn About It

The whole numbers 0, 1, 2, 3, 4, 5, ... , can be shown on a number line. You can extend the number line to the left of 0 and label it with numbers that are less than 0. Numbers less than zero are called **negative numbers**.

Negative 7, or $^{-}7$, is the **opposite** of positive 7, or $^{+}7$. $^{+}7$ is another way to write the counting number 7.

This number line shows the set of integers from $^{-}7$ to $^{+}7$.

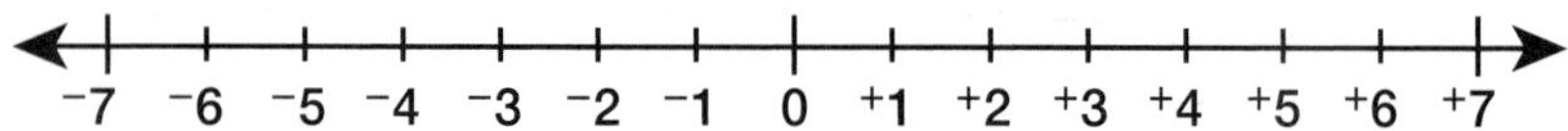

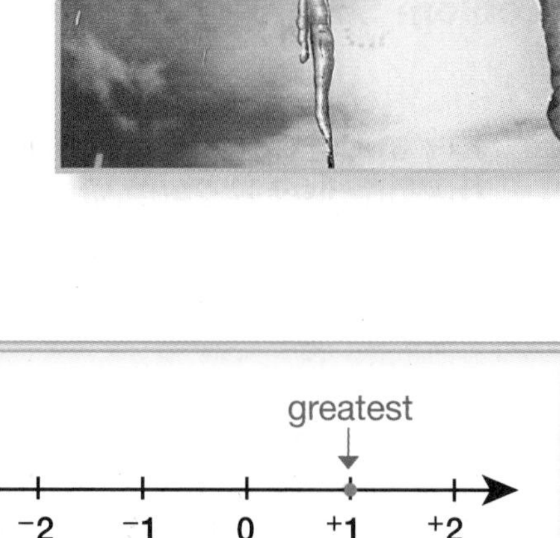

The **integers** include zero, the positive whole numbers and their opposites.

Water freezes at 0°C. When the temperature changes from $^{-}3$°C to $^{+}1$°C, ice will start to melt.

You can use a number line to compare integers just as you compare other numbers.

Use a number line to compare $^{-}3$ and $^{+}1$.

- Locate each integer on the number line.
- Compare. The integer farthest to the left is least and the integer farthest to the right is greatest.

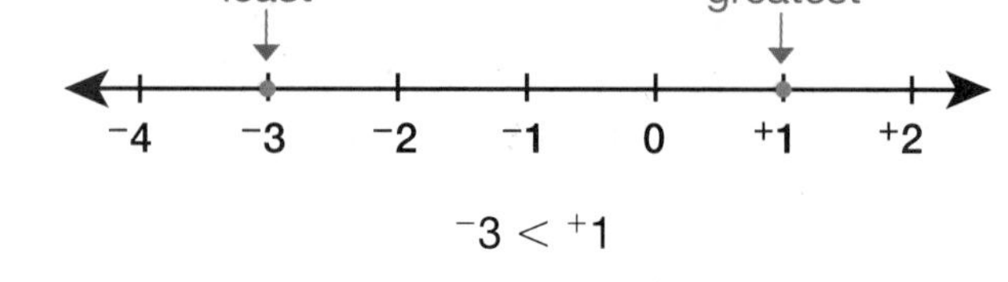

$^{-}3 < {}^{+}1$

Another Example

Compare Decimals

You can label a number line with positive and negative decimals.

Compare $^{-}1.5$ and 0.

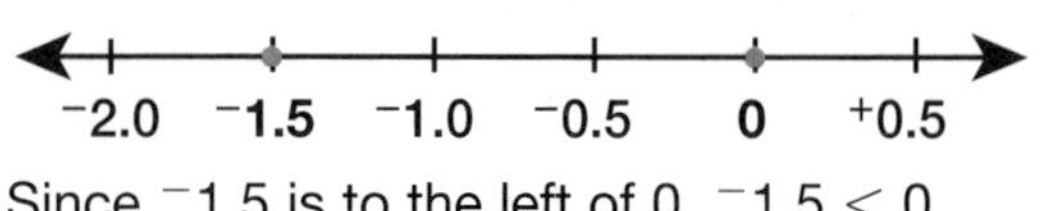

Since $^{-}1.5$ is to the left of 0, $^{-}1.5 < 0$.

Explain Your Thinking

▶ What are the opposites of the integers from $^{+}1$ to $^{+}9$?

▶ How are positive integers and negative integers alike?

Standards NS **1.5**

Guided Practice

Compare. Draw a number line from $^{-}3.5$ to $^{+}3.5$ and label each 0.5 unit. Write >, <, or = for each ●.

1. $^{+}1.5$ ● $^{+}2.5$ **2.** $^{+}1$ ● $^{-}1$ **3.** $^{-}2.5$ ● 0

4. $^{-}3$ ● $^{-}1$ **5.** $^{+}0.5$ ● $^{+}2.5$ **6.** $^{+}3$ ● $^{+}2$

Ask Yourself

- Did I check that the number to the left is less than the number to the right on my number line?

Independent Practice

Compare. Draw a number line from $^{-}3.5$ to $^{+}3.5$ and label each 0.5 unit. Write >, <, or = for each ●.

7. $^{+}2$ ● $^{-}1$ **8.** $^{-}2.5$ ● $^{-}2$ **9.** $^{+}0.5$ ● $^{-}3$ **10.** $^{+}1.5$ ● 0

11. $^{-}1.5$ ● $^{+}3$ **12.** $^{+}2.5$ ● $^{-}1.5$ **13.** $^{-}1$ ● $^{+}1$ **14.** $^{+}2$ ● 0

15. $^{-}0.5$ ● $^{-}2.5$ **16.** 0 ● $^{-}1$ **17.** $^{-}2.5$ ● $^{-}2.5$ **18.** $^{+}1.5$ ● $^{-}2$

Problem Solving • Reasoning

Solve. Choose a method.

Computation Methods

- **Mental Math**
- **Estimation**
- **Pencil and Paper**

19. On a cold day, a thermometer showed $^{-}10$°F in the morning, $^{+}4$°F at noon, and $^{-}5$°F in the evening. Order the temperatures from lowest to highest.

20. The low temperatures for five days in Barrow, AK, were 6°F, 8°F, 4°F, 2°F, and 5°F. What was the average, or mean, low temperature?

21. **Analyze** The temperature was 2°F at 6 A.M. By noon, it had increased by 10°. By 6 P.M., it had fallen by 5°. What was the temperature at 6 P.M.?

22. **Write About It** On Dec. 28, La Crosse, WI, reported temperatures from $^{-}8$°F to $^{-}1$°F. What was the high temperature of the day? Explain.

Mixed Review • Test Prep

Round each number to its greatest place value. *(pages 18–19)*

23. 1,277 **24.** 10,700 **25.** 274,919 **26.** 6,922,080

Write the letter of the correct answer. *(pages 4–5, 28–29)*

27 Which number could have been rounded to the nearest thousand?

A 1,010 **C** 20,500
B 8,007 **D** 607,000

28 Which number could have been rounded to the nearest tenth?

F 1 **H** 1.25
G 1.03 **J** 1.3

Extra Practice See Set J on page 40.

Problem-Solving Application: Use a Table

You will learn how to solve a problem by using a table.

You can use a table to solve a problem.

Problem Tyler is making a Thai wrap sandwich with ginger chicken, rice, and peanut sauce. He wants to use 2 of these 4 fillings: carrots, peppers, cabbage, and cucumber. How many different combinations of 2 fillings are there?

What is the question?

How many different combinations of 2 fillings are there?

What do you know?

- There are 4 kinds of fillings.
- Each combination must have two kinds of fillings.

Start with what you know.

Make a table to organize the information. Use the fillings as labels for the columns.

Wrap Fillings

carrots	peppers	cabbage	cucumbers

Use ✓ to show which fillings to use for each combination.

There are 6 possible combinations.

Wrap Fillings

carrots	peppers	cabbage	cucumbers
✓	✓		
✓		✓	
✓			✓
	✓	✓	
	✓		✓
		✓	✓

Look Back

Look back at the problem.

For what kinds of problems does it help to use a table?

Standards | MR 1.0, 1.1, 2.0, 2.1, 2.3, 3.0, 3.1, 3.3

Left: Asian cuisine has become popular in many parts of the world.
Right: Traditional beef tamales are made by cooking dough and meat filling inside corn husks.

Guided Practice

Make and use a table to solve each problem.

1. Jose can choose 3 toppings for his taco. There are 4 toppings that he likes: cheese, tomato, onions, and peppers. How many ways can he order a taco with 3 different toppings?

   Think: How many combinations of 3 toppings are there?

2. Pizza Palace's large pizzas are $12 and medium pizzas are $9. Leigh ordered some pizzas of both sizes. She paid $45.00 for her order. How many of each size did she buy?

   Think: What is a reasonable number of pizzas to buy for $45?

Choose a Strategy

Solve. Use these or other strategies.

Problem-Solving Strategies

- **Guess and Check**
- **Make a Table**
- **Draw a Diagram**
- **Use Logical Thinking**

3. A recipe for Southwest taco pie uses one 16-oz can of refried beans. The recipe serves 6 people. How many ounces of beans are needed to make 30 servings?

4. A restaurant has square tables where one person can sit on each side. How can the tables be arranged to exactly fit a party of 10? How many tables are needed?

5. Erin has $3 more than Tamara. Together they have $23 to pay for dinner. How much money does each girl have?

6. Michael paid for some nachos with 6 coins worth $1.05. He had only quarters and dimes. How many of each coin did he have?

7. A circular pie is cut into 8 pieces. What is the least number of cuts that can be made?

8. How many times does the numeral 5 appear when you write the numbers from 1 to 100?

9. Which costs more, five large pizzas for $12 each, or seven medium pizzas for $9 each?

10. Bob's lunch cost $4.20. He paid with a $5 bill and got 5 coins in change. What coins was he given?

Extra Practice See 8–11 on page 41.

Quick Check

Check Your Understanding of Lessons 8–13

Write in standard form.

1. thirty-seven hundredths

2. two and five thousandths

Compare. Use >, <, or = for each ●.

3. 0.61 ● 0.16 **4.** 0.5 ● 0.05 **5.** 0.812 ● 0.9 **6.** 0.27 ● 0.270

Round to the nearest hundredth.

7. 0.923 **8.** 0.087 **9.** 5.609 **10.** 2.395

Order each set of numbers from least to greatest.

11. 0.52 5.2 0.5 0.025 5

12. 2.8 8.2 2 8 0.28 0.82

Compare. Use >, <, or = for each ●.

13. $^{-}8$ ● $^{-}10$ **14.** $^{-}0.5$ ● $^{-}1.5$ **15.** $^{-}12$ ● $^{-}11.5$ **16.** $^{-}4.5$ ● $^{-}4.50$

Make a table to solve this problem.

17. Rita wants two different toppings on her sandwich. She can choose from 5 toppings: cheese, lettuce, tomato, pickles and onion. How many ways can Rita choose 2 toppings?

How did you do?

If you had difficulty with any items in the Quick Check, you can use the following pages for review and extra practice.

California Standards	Items	Review These Pages	Do These Extra Practice Items
Number Sense: **1.1**	1–2	pages 24–25	Set F, page 39
Number Sense: **1.1, 1.5**	3–6	pages 26–27	Set G, page 40
Number Sense: **1.1**	7–10	pages 28–29	Set H, page 40
Number Sense: **1.1**	11–12	pages 30–31	Set I, page 40
Number Sense: **1.5**	13–16	pages 32–33	Set J, page 40
Math Reasoning: **1.0, 1.1, 2.3**	17	pages 34–35	8–11, page 41

Test Prep • Cumulative Review

Maintaining the Standards

Choose the letter of the correct answer.

1. In words, what is the value of the digit 8 in 24,600,158?
   - **A** eight ones
   - **B** eight tenths
   - **C** eight hundredths
   - **D** eight thousandths

2. Between which two numbers does 0.005 fall on this number line?

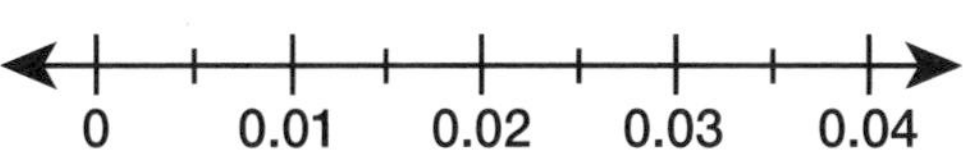

   - **F** 0 and 0.01
   - **G** 0.01 and 0.02
   - **H** 0.02 and 0.03
   - **J** 0.03 and 0.04

3. Which number is the greatest?
   - **A** 23.008
   - **B** 23.07
   - **C** 23.1
   - **D** 23.099

4. Devin has a quarter, a nickel, a dime, and a penny. He plans to give two of the coins to his sister. Find all the possible combinations of two coins he could give her. How many combinations are there?
   - **F** 2 combinations
   - **G** 4 combinations
   - **H** 6 combinations
   - **J** 8 combinations

5. Which number could be at point *R* on this number line?

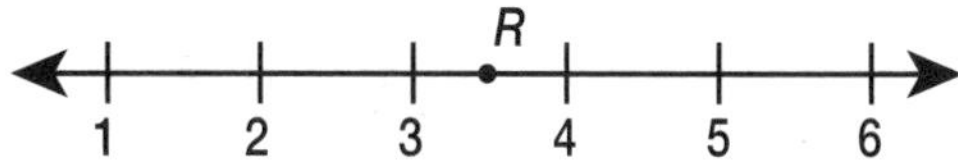

   - **A** 2.34
   - **B** 2.6
   - **C** 3.462
   - **D** 4.01

6. When rounding 234.82 to a certain place, Bryan wrote 230. When rounding 368.19 to the same place, he wrote 370. What will Bryan write when he rounds 514.99 to the same place?
   - **F** 520
   - **G** 515
   - **H** 514
   - **J** 510

7. Round 57.017 to the nearest tenth.
   - **A** 60
   - **B** 58
   - **C** 57.02
   - **D** 57.0

8. Bethany said, "$^{-}5 > {}^{-}1$." Jessie said, "$^{-}5 < {}^{-}1$." Who is right?

   Explain How could you settle their disagreement?

Internet Test Prep
Visit **www.eduplace.com/kids/mhm** for more *Test Prep Practice.*

Extra Practice

Set A *(Lesson 1, pages 4–5)*

Write each number in word form and in expanded form.

1. 73,412 **2.** 14,608 **3.** 9,812 **4.** 23,987

5. 42,654 **6.** 4,860 **7.** 57,749 **8.** 32,541

9. 681,299 **10.** 376,300 **11.** 150,002 **12.** 762,431

13. 167,907 **14.** 493,544 **15.** 721,012 **16.** 254,069

Set B *(Lesson 2, pages 6–7)*

Write each number in expanded form with exponents.

1. 32,667 **2.** 45,908 **3.** 9,812 **4.** 72,306

5. 64,753 **6.** 80,776 **7.** 22,325 **8.** 41,913

9. 237,009 **10.** 156,098 **11.** 834,517 **12.** 489,310

13. 575,132 **14.** 664,583 **15.** 169,347 **16.** 235,962

Set C *(Lesson 3, pages 8–10)*

Compare. Write >, <, or = for each ⬬.

1. 17,645 ⬬ 9,891 **2.** 5,468 ⬬ 552,468

3. 23,917 ⬬ 23,871 **4.** 64,728 ⬬ 46,728

5. 9,701 ⬬ 9,710 **6.** 5,499 ⬬ 15,944

7. 345,876 ⬬ 345,876 **8.** 456,890 ⬬ 465,812

9. 125,000 ⬬ 124,776 **10.** 988,334 ⬬ 988,443

11. 554,309 ⬬ 554,000 **12.** 312,745 ⬬ 899,604

Extra Practice

Set D *(Lesson 5, pages 14–16)*

Write each in short word form.

1. 25,600,357

2. 67,312,875

3. 3,070,653

4. 66,954,332

5. 34,669,213

6. 76,000,952

7. 22,766,450,002

8. 765,923,549,855

9. 231,677,908,200

10. 345,806,321,765

11. 712,600,952,341

12. 487,933,003,762

Set E *(Lesson 6, pages 18–19)*

Round to the underlined place.

1. 2$\underline{7}$2

2. $\underline{5}$,812

3. 7,$\underline{6}$43

4. 4$\underline{6}$,829

5. $\underline{2}$4,999

6. 1,0$\underline{4}$5,001

7. 36,$\underline{7}$25,450

8. 28,63$\underline{5}$,914

9. 3$\underline{9}$8,762,431

10. 1$\underline{2}$,643,776,803

11. 214,$\underline{8}$86,575,003

12. $\underline{9}$05,436,957,800

Set F *(Lesson 8, pages 24–25)*

In words, what is the value of the underlined digit?

1. 2.$\underline{6}$

2. 6.2$\underline{7}$

3. $\underline{9}$.4

4. 3.$\underline{0}$1

5. $\underline{7}$.31

6. 3.0$\underline{5}$

7. 4.$\underline{5}$4

8. $\underline{5}$.27

9. 0.$\underline{0}$96

10. 8.00$\underline{2}$

11. 6.$\underline{4}$72

12. 8.46$\underline{0}$

13. 1.1$\underline{1}$

14. 0.$\underline{4}$06

15. 3.8$\underline{9}$6

16. 2.$\underline{5}$49

Extra Practice

Set G (Lesson 9, pages 26–27)

Compare. Write >, <, or = for each ●.

1. 0.65 ● 0.56
2. 0.09 ● 0.19
3. 0.13 ● 0.130
4. 0.971 ● 0.917
5. 0.3 ● 0.31
6. 0.079 ● 0.790
7. 0.645 ● 0.465
8. 0.47 ● 0.50
9. 0.8 ● 0.78
10. 0.2 ● 0.200
11. 0.095 ● 0.950
12. 0.389 ● 0.839

Set H (Lesson 10, pages 28–29)

Round to the nearest tenth.

1. 0.79
2. 0.28
3. 0.05
4. 0.92
5. 0.671
6. 0.312
7. 0.458
8. 0.061
9. 8.954
10. 7.238
11. 3.356
12. 5.512
13. 9.025
14. 5.052
15. 9.323
16. 8.771

Set I (Lesson 11, pages 30–31)

Compare. Write >, <, or = for each ●.

1. 7.6 ● 7.60
2. 3.1 ● 3.01
3. 7 ● 7.008
4. 13.466 ● 13.644
5. 82.3 ● 8.230
6. 12.7 ● 12.735
7. 0.801 ● 8.01
8. 43.45 ● 4.345
9. 3 ● 3.000
10. 9.02 ● 2.09
11. 1.825 ● 1.852
12. 4.997 ● 5.003

Set J (Lesson 12, pages 32–33)

Compare. Write >, <, or = for each ●.

1. $^{+}7$ ● $^{-}8$
2. $^{-}2$ ● $^{-}3$
3. $^{-}7$ ● $^{+}6$
4. $^{+}1$ ● $^{-}0.5$
5. $^{-}1.5$ ● $^{-}2.5$
6. $^{-}15$ ● $^{-}1.5$
7. $^{-}10$ ● $^{-}11$
8. $^{+}4$ ● $^{-}4.5$
9. $^{-}3$ ● $^{-}3.0$
10. $^{-}9.0$ ● $^{-}8.5$
11. $^{-}1$ ● 0
12. $^{-}4$ ● $^{-}5$

Extra Practice • Problem Solving

Tell whether each problem requires an estimated or exact answer. Then solve. *(Lesson 4, pages 12–13)*

1. A school show costs $2,000 to produce. The school theater has 400 seats. If tickets sell for $8 each, how many tickets would have to be sold to pay for the cost of the show?
2. Mount Everest is 866 feet taller than another mountain in Nepal called Kangchenjunga. If Kangchenjunga is 28,169 feet tall, about how tall is Mount Everest?
3. How many 2-in. by 2-in. squares will fit inside a 3-in. by 5-in. rectangle without overlapping?
4. Which costs more: 5 small lemons for 33¢ each or 3 large ones for 49¢ each?

Solve each problem, using the Guess and Check strategy. *(Lesson 7, pages 20–21)*

5. What is the greatest 3-digit number you can write whose digits have a sum of 20?
6. Arrange the numbers 2, 4, 6, 8, and 10 in the circles below so the sum in both directions is the same.
7. Marla has 16 nickels and pennies. She has 3 times as many pennies as nickels. What is the total value of the coins?

Make and use a table to solve each problem. *(Lesson 13, pages 34–35)*

8. A bag contains a red, a yellow, a green, and a blue marble. If you choose two marbles from the bag, how many different color combinations are possible?
9. Suppose you added one more marble of each color to the bag in Problem 8. Now how many different color combinations will be possible?
10. How many different three-digit numbers can you make from the digits 1, 2, and 3 if each digit is used only once?
11. How many different four-digit numbers can you make from the digits 1, 2, 3, and 4 if each digit is used only once?

Chapter Review

Reviewing Vocabulary

Write *always, sometimes,* or *never* for each question. Give an example to support your answer.

1. A number with 6 in the millions place is greater than a number with 5 in the millions place.
2. If you are rounding a number to the nearest hundredth, and the thousandths digit is less than 5, the hundredths digit will stay the same.
3. If you round a number to any place, the final digit will be 0.
4. If a number has six digits and no decimal point, the expanded form will begin with a number times 10^6.

Find and correct any errors in each form if the standard form is 562,415,081.

5. expanded form	$(5 \times 100{,}000{,}000) + (6 \times 10{,}000{,}000) + (2 \times 1{,}000{,}000) + (4 \times 100{,}000) + (10 \times 10{,}000) + (5 \times 1{,}000) + (8 \times 10) + (1 \times 1)$
6. expanded form with exponents	$(5 \times 10^9) + (6 \times 10^8) + (2 \times 10^7) + (4 \times 10^6) + (1 \times 10^5) + (5 \times 10^4) + (8 \times 10^2) + (1 \times 10^1)$
7. word form	five hundred sixty-two billion, four hundred fifteen thousand, eighty-one
8. short word form	562 million, 41 thousand, 581

Reviewing Concepts and Skills

Write each number in short word form and expanded form with exponents. *(pages 4–7, 14–16)*

9. 14,245 **10.** 63,422 **11.** 58,003 **12.** 174,689

13. 256,987 **14.** 302,405 **15.** 42,998,998 **16.** 840,146,825

Write each decimal in words. *(pages 24–25)*

17. 0.765 **18.** 1.4 **19.** 6.57 **20.** 4.706

Compare. Write >, <, or = for each ●. *(pages 8–10, 14–15, 32–33)*

21. 9,654 ● 9,564

22. 23,550 ● 23,005

23. 2,086,754 ● 286,754

24. 62,145,799 ● 62,345,799

25. 462,950,003 ● 472,943,219

26. 0.432 ● 0.342

27. 0.725 ● 0.7

28. 5.08 ● 5.080

29. $^{-}3$ ● $^{+}3$

30. $^{-}4.5$ ● $^{-}5.5$

Round to the underlined digit. *(pages 8–10, 18–19, 28–29)*

31. 6,$\underline{5}$22

32. $\underline{4}$5,230

33. $\underline{1}$9,891

34. $\underline{1}$56,873

35. 49$\underline{9}$,999

36. 3,4$\underline{6}$7,810

37. $\underline{2}$5,671,988

38. 7,82$\underline{6}$,466,812

39. 0.$\underline{7}$5

40. 0.$\underline{0}$89

41. 8.7$\underline{9}$9

42. 5.$\underline{7}$09

Solve. *(pages 12–13, 20–21, 34–35)*

43. A bag contained one counter in each of these colors: red, yellow, blue, black, and green. If Alex reached into the bag and took out two counters at random, what color combinations could he get?

44. Gabriela correctly rounded one of these numbers to 2,000,000. Which number was it?

1,456,821 22,450,989 1,562,419 250,618

45. Dana has 5 coins worth 42¢. What coins does she have?

Brain Teasers Math Reasoning

Product Power

How many different ways can you find to write 500,000 as a product of two whole numbers where one of the numbers is a power of ten?

Round and Round

If you round a whole number to the nearest million, the result is 6,000,000. How many numbers would fit this description?

Internet Brain Teasers
Visit **www.eduplace.com/kids/mhm** for more *Brain Teasers.*

Chapter Test

Write each number in short word form and in expanded form with exponents.

1. 23,812 **2.** 78,654 **3.** 37,005

4. 237,945 **5.** 181,978 **6.** 412,600

7. 45,780,321 **8.** 212,988,753 **9.** 5,089,765,434

Write each number in word form.

10. 0.6 **11.** 0.79 **12.** 0.832

13. 2.8 **14.** 3.65 **15.** 7.913

Compare. Write >, <, or = for each ●.

16. 8,745 ● 8,745 **17.** 42,090 ● 42,900

18. 78,634 ● 78,364 **19.** 3,112,856 ● 312,856

20. 54,677,809 ● 54,767,809 **21.** 867,428,302 ● 876,482,302

22. 0.445 ● 0.643 **23.** 0.832 ● 0.8 **24.** 0.560 ● 0.56

25. 3.743 ● 7.343 **26.** 6 ● 5.999 **27.** 3.05 ● 3.005

28. $^-7$ ● $^+6$ **29.** $^-3.5$ ● $^-0.5$ **30.** $^-10.5$ ● $^-11$

Round to the underlined digit.

31. 4,$\underline{8}$33 **32.** $\underline{6}$3,412 **33.** 4$\underline{7}$,659

34. $\underline{3}$78,942 **35.** 1$\underline{5}$8,055 **36.** 28$\underline{8}$,002

37. 2,43$\underline{6}$,957 **38.** $\underline{9}$7,655,044 **39.** 3,778,$\underline{9}$12,553

40. 0.$\underline{4}$3 **41.** 0.$\underline{0}$98 **42.** 0.1$\underline{4}$4

43. 3.$\underline{8}$72 **44.** 6.2$\underline{3}$6 **45.** 2.$\underline{3}$01

Solve.

46. What is the greatest number Jeannette can make using these digit cards?

4 7

47. Tony says that it's possible for a number with 2 digits to be less than a number with 1 digit. Give an example of two numbers he might be thinking of.

48. Kevin's apartment number is 4 less than Jenn's. The sum of the two numbers is 88. What are the numbers?

49. When you round a six-digit number to the nearest hundred thousand, the result is 500,000. What are the least and greatest whole numbers that fit this description?

50. A photography studio has six backdrops that show a forest, a blue sky with clouds, mountains, stars, a garden, and a fireplace. Customers can order a special package that includes pictures taken against two different backdrops. How many backdrop combinations are possible for the special package?

Write About It

Solve each problem. Use correct math vocabulary to explain your thinking.

1. Imagine that you could tape 12 meter sticks together to form a cube.

- **a.** How many centimeter cubes would it take to cover the floor of your meter cube? Explain how you know.
- **b.** How many layers like this could you make inside the cube? Explain how you know.
- **c.** How many centimeter cubes would it take to fill your meter cube? Explain how you know.
- **d.** How many meter cubes would you need to hold 1 billion centimeter cubes?

2. Explain the steps you use to round a number to the nearest tenth. Tell what to do if the number in the tenths place is a 9 and the number in the hundredths place is 5 or greater.

3. Explain.

- **a.** If one whole number has six digits and another whole number has seven digits, which is greater? Why?
- **b.** Can you compare two decimal numbers by counting the digits? Explain why or why not.

Another Look

Use numbers from the article to solve each problem.

Amazing Facts About Insects

There may be as many as 3,000,000 different species of insects, although scientists have studied only about 750,000 of them.

For such tiny creatures, insects have amazing abilities. For example:

- Termites may be only 0.28 inches long, but they can lay up to 3,000 eggs in a day, or 1,095,000 in a year.
- An ant is only about 0.125 inches long, but it is estimated that there are one quadrillion (one million billion) ants living on Earth.
- A mosquito has a mass of only 1.1 milligrams, but it can take in 1.5 times its own mass in blood.

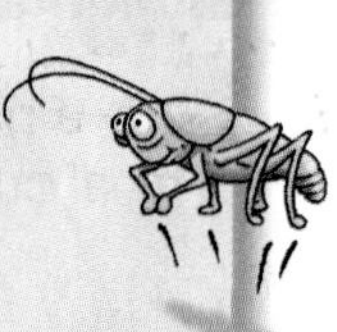

- A cockroach can run 1.635 yards in only 1 second.
- A tiny flea can jump a distance of 13.3 inches or up to 7.75 inches high.

Solve.

1. Pick three whole numbers from the article. Write the numbers in short word form and in expanded form using exponents. Then write the numbers you picked in order from least to greatest.
2. **Compare** What insects are smaller, termites or ants? Explain.
3. Rounded to the nearest inch, how high can a flea jump?
4. Write the least number from the article in a place-value chart.

5. **Write About It** Do you think the numbers in this article are estimated or exact amounts? Explain your thinking.

Standards NS **1.0, 1.1, 1.3** MR **1.0, 1.1, 2.0, 2.5**

Enrichment

Scientific Notation

Using scientific notation is a way of writing numbers with many places.

4.3×10^5 2.65×10^3 7.2×10^8

New Vocabulary
scientific notation

In **scientific notation**, a number is expressed as the product of a number between 1 and 10 and a power of 10.

Write 820,000 using scientific notation.

Step 1 Place a decimal point so the digits form a number between 1 and 10.

8.20000, or 8.2, is between 1 and 10

Step 2 Multiply the number you found in Step 1 by a power of 10 to make it equal to the original number.

$820{,}000 = 8.2 \times 10 \times 10 \times 10 \times 10 \times 10$
$= 8.2 \times 10^5$

Write 6.3×10^4 using standard notation.

Step 1 Look at the power of 10 to find how many times you need to multiply the first factor by 10.

$10^4 = 10 \times 10 \times 10 \times 10$

Step 2 Multiply.

$6.3 \times 10^4 = 6.3 \times 10 \times 10 \times 10 \times 10$
$= 63{,}000$

Write each number using scientific notation.

1. 4,200
2. 42,000
3. 52,000
4. 120,000
5. 670,000
6. 425,000
7. 3,450,000
8. 652,000,000
9. Which of the numbers you wrote using scientific notation is the greatest? the least?
10. Write each number shown at the top of this page in standard notation.

Explain Your Thinking

- When you are writing a number using scientific notation, how can you tell where to place the decimal point to create the first factor?
- How can you tell which power of ten to use as the second factor?

Standards NS **1.1, 1.3**

CHAPTER 2

Addition, Subtraction, and Equations

Why Learn About Addition, Subtraction, and Equations?

Knowing how to add and subtract helps you to solve many kinds of problems. You will learn to use algebra to represent a problem and express the relationships between quantities.

You add when you know two driving distances and want to find the total number of miles. You can use an equation to express a relationship between distance and time.

These students are solving an equation. The quantities on each side of the equals sign must have the same value. Can you find the value of *d*?

5 + d = 17
d = 17 - 5
d

Reviewing Vocabulary

Understanding math language helps you become a successful problem solver. Here are some math vocabulary words you should know.

addend	a number to be added in an addition expression
sum	the answer in addition
difference	the answer in subtraction
parentheses	symbols used to show which operations in an expression should be done first

Reading Words and Symbols

When you read mathematics, sometimes you read only words, sometimes you read words and symbols, and sometimes you read only symbols.

There are different ways to read and write addition.

$$\begin{array}{r} 4{,}385 \\ +\ 1{,}729 \\ \hline 6{,}114 \end{array}$$

$4{,}385 + 1{,}729 = 6{,}114$

4,385 ↑ addend; 1,729 ↑ addend; 6,114 ↑ sum

- ▶ 4,385 plus 1,729 equals 6,114.
- ▶ The sum of 4,385 and 1,729 is 6,114.

There are different ways to read and write subtraction.

$$\begin{array}{r} 6{,}025 \\ -\ 574 \\ \hline 5{,}451 \end{array}$$

$6{,}025 - 574 = 5{,}451$

5,451 ↑ difference

- ▶ 6,025 minus 574 equals 5,451.
- ▶ The difference between 6,025 and 574 is 5,451.

Try These

1. Write whether ■ represents an addend, a sum, or a difference. Then find the missing value.

   a. 2,350 + 822 = ■ b. 1,865 − 744 = ■

   c. 5,488 + ■ = 7,025 d. ■ + 866 = 2,442

2. Write *true* or *false* for each statement.

   a. When you add two counting numbers, the sum is always greater than either addend.

   b. When you add or subtract numbers, it's important to write them so that digits with the same place value align.

   c. Writing zeros after a number does not change the value of the number.

   d. If you know that 600 + ■ = 2,000, then you also know that 2,000 − 600 = ■.

   e. When you add or subtract amounts with dollars and cents, you are actually adding or subtracting decimal numbers.

3. Fill in the blanks with numbers that work.

   If ■ is an addend and ■ is the sum, then the other addend must be ■.

Upcoming Vocabulary

Write About It **Here are some other vocabulary words** you will learn in this chapter. Watch for these words. Write their definitions in your journal.

variable

algebraic expression

simplify

equation

evaluate

inverse operations

function

function table

LESSON 1

Add Whole Numbers

You will learn how to estimate sums and add whole numbers with up to five digits.

Review Vocabulary
sum

Learn About It

Ronan checked his Web site and found that he had received 6,395 hits. Two weeks later he had received 2,768 more. How many hits was this in all?

Add. **6,395 + 2,768 = *n***

Find 6,395 + 2,768.

Step 1 Add the ones.

Regroup 10 ones as 1 ten whenever possible.

13 ones = 1 ten 3 ones

$$\begin{array}{r} \scriptstyle 1 \\ 6,395 \\ +\ 2,768 \\ \hline 3 \end{array}$$

Step 2 Add the tens.

Regroup 10 tens as 1 hundred whenever possible.

16 tens = 1 hundred 6 tens

$$\begin{array}{r} \scriptstyle 1\ 1 \\ 6,395 \\ +\ 2,768 \\ \hline 63 \end{array}$$

Step 3 Add the hundreds.

Regroup 10 hundreds as 1 thousand whenever possible.

11 hundreds = 1 thousand 1 hundred

$$\begin{array}{r} \scriptstyle 1\ 1\ 1 \\ 6,395 \\ +\ 2,768 \\ \hline 163 \end{array}$$

Step 4 Add the thousands.

If necessary, also write the ten thousands digit in the **sum**.

$$\begin{array}{r} \scriptstyle 1\ 1\ 1 \\ 6,395 \\ +\ 2,768 \\ \hline 9,163 \end{array}$$

Solution: Ronan's Web site received 9,163 hits in all.

Estimate to check.

6,395 rounds to 6,000

2,768 rounds to 3,000

6,000 + 3,000 = 9,000

The answer is close to 9,000.

Explain Your Thinking

▶ When is it necessary to regroup in adding whole numbers?

Guided Practice

Add. Estimate to check that your answer is reasonable.

1. $\begin{array}{r} 457 \\ +\ 285 \\ \hline \end{array}$

2. $\begin{array}{r} 6,701 \\ +\ 3,495 \\ \hline \end{array}$

3. $\begin{array}{r} 54,187 \\ 3,456 \\ +\ 12,579 \\ \hline \end{array}$

4. 7,814 + 543

5. 34,516 + 478 + 2,347

Ask Yourself

- Do I need to regroup?
- Where should I write the regrouped numbers?

Standards NS 1.0, 1.1 MR 1.0, 1.1, 2.0, 2.1

Independent Practice

Add. Estimate to check.

6. 746 + 459
7. 952 + 374
8. 843 + 199
9. 587 + 96
10. 2,874 + 1,568
11. 3,985 + 439
12. 4,782 + 561
13. 5,768 + 3,492
14. 16,083 + 24,569
15. 17,985 + 26,832
16. 24,781 + 1,245 + 37,844
17. 46,839 + 980 + 9,402
18. 67,019 + 5,672 + 467
19. 89,516 + 462 + 6,709
20. 72,459 + 1,456 + 12,347

21. 564 + 328
22. 722 + 588
23. 1,235 + 8,299
24. 6,784 + 5,896
25. 4,569 + 367
26. 7,658 + 376 + 3,258
27. 45,056 + 12,345
28. 79,546 + 58,918
29. 67,942 + 578 + 4,672

Algebra • Patterns **Find each sum when $n = 1{,}000{,}000$.**

30. $n + 9$
31. $n + 9{,}000$
32. $n + 9{,}000{,}000$

Problem Solving • Reasoning

Use Data **Use the data to solve Problems 33–36.**

33. **Estimate** The table shows the weekly hits on Ronan's Web site for the month of November. Estimate the number of hits in November.

34. Compute the total number of hits in November.

35. **Analyze** At 12:00 A.M. on November 1, Ronan's Web site showed 64,572 hits. How many hits were shown at the end of November?

36. **Write About It** Why were there so few hits in Week 4? Explain your thinking.

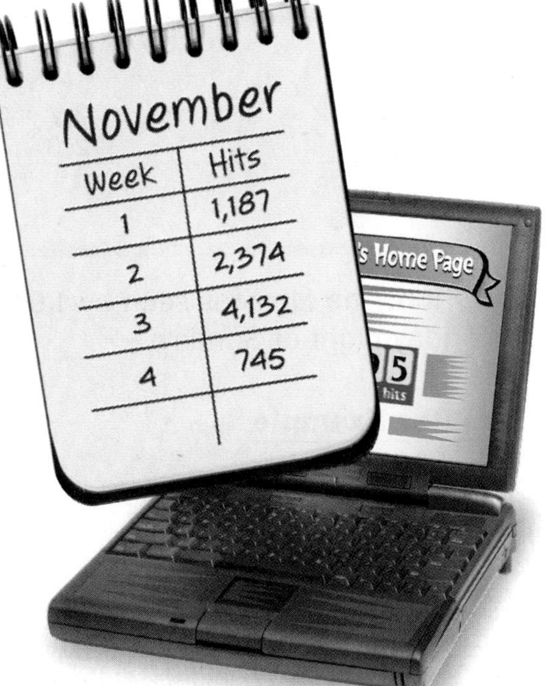

Mixed Review • Test Prep

Write the value of each underlined digit in short word form. *(pages 4–5, 14–15)*

37. 293
38. 1,094
39. 52,584
40. 29,747,916

41. When you round 68,341,002 to the nearest million, what is the result? *(pages 18–19)*

A 8,000,000 **B** 60,000,000 **C** 68,000,000 **D** 70,000,000

Extra Practice See Set A on page 82.

Subtract Whole Numbers

You will learn how to subtract whole numbers with up to five digits.

Learn About It

A new feature film was seen by 3,452 people during the first weekend it was open. If 2,374 people saw the film on Saturday, how many saw the film on Friday night or Sunday?

Subtract. **3,452 − 2,374 = *n***

Find 3,452 − 2,374.

Step 1 Subtract the ones. Since 4 > 2, you must regroup 1 ten as 10 ones.	**Step 2** Subtract the tens. Since 7 > 4, regroup 1 hundred as 10 tens.	**Step 3** Subtract the hundreds.	**Step 4** Subtract the thousands.
$\begin{array}{r} {}^{4\ 12} \\ 3{,}4\not{5}\not{2} \\ -\ 2{,}374 \\ \hline 8 \end{array}$	$\begin{array}{r} {}^{3\ 14\ 12} \\ 3{,}\not{4}\not{5}\not{2} \\ -\ 2{,}374 \\ \hline 78 \end{array}$	$\begin{array}{r} {}^{3\ 14\ 12} \\ 3{,}\not{4}\not{5}\not{2} \\ -\ 2{,}374 \\ \hline 078 \end{array}$	$\begin{array}{r} {}^{3\ 14\ 12} \\ 3{,}\not{4}\not{5}\not{2} \\ -\ 2{,}374 \\ \hline 1{,}078 \end{array}$

Solution: The film was seen by 1,078 people on Friday night or Sunday.

Check.

$$\begin{array}{r} {}^{1\ 1} \\ 1{,}078 \\ +\ 2{,}374 \\ \hline 3{,}452 \end{array}$$

Subtraction and addition are inverse operations. So you can check subtraction by adding.

Another Example

Zeros in Subtraction

30,062 − 17,874 = *n*

$$\begin{array}{r} {}^{2\ 9\ \ 9\ 15\ 12} \\ \not{3}\not{0}{,}\not{0}\not{6}\not{2} \\ -\ 17{,}874 \\ \hline 12{,}188 \end{array}$$

← When you subtract tens, you can't subtract 7 tens from 5 tens, but there are no hundreds or thousands to regroup.

Regroup 1 ten thousand as 9 thousands, 9 hundreds, and 10 tens.

Explain Your Thinking

- ▶ When is it necessary to regroup when you are subtracting whole numbers?
- ▶ How do you regroup tens when there is a zero in the hundreds place?

Standards NS 1.0, 1.1 MR 2.0, 2.1

Guided Practice

Subtract. Add to check your answer.

1. 829 − 287

2. 3,402 − 1,689

3. 42,317 − 19,675

4. 6,015 − 4,987 **5.** 68,615 − 3,786 **6.** 867 − 328

> **Ask Yourself**
> - Do I need to regroup?
> - Where should I write the regrouped numbers?

Independent Practice

Subtract. Add to check your answer.

7. 746 − 199 **8.** 752 − 97 **9.** 500 − 354 **10.** 674 − 286 **11.** 3,958 − 498

12. 34,440 − 5,485 **13.** 56,583 − 9,407 **14.** 67,109 − 15,479 **15.** 75,406 − 16,789 **16.** 80,412 − 667

17. 6,896 − 5,908 **18.** 4567 − 369 **19.** 7,685 − 3,858

20. 45,650 − 18,728 **21.** 74,846 − 57,908 **22.** 88,429 − 4,689

Problem Solving • Reasoning

Solve.

23. The first full-length animated feature was released in 1937. In 1995 the first completely computer-generated full-length film was released. How many years apart were the two films released?

24. **Compare** There are 23,662 movie theaters in the United States and 14,960 in Ukraine. How many more are there in the United States?

25. **Estimate** The Rivoli Theater sold 12,217 tickets and the Capital sold 2,250. About how many more tickets did the Rivoli sell?

> **Using Vocabulary**
>
> **Write a subtraction sentence that fits each description.**
>
> **A** The difference between two whole numbers is 168.
>
> **B** When a three-digit whole number is subtracted from a four-digit whole number, the difference is close to 1,000.

Mixed Review • Test Prep

Round to the underlined place. *(pages 8–9, 18–19)*

26. 3$\underline{3}$5 **27.** 17,$\underline{3}$16 **28.** 6$\underline{6}$,818 **29.** $\underline{4}$63,524

30 What is 6×10^4? *(pages 6–7)*

A 6,000 **C** 60,000 **B** 10,000 **D** 600,000

Extra Practice See Set B on page 82.

LESSON 3

Problem-Solving Skill: Too Much or Too Little Information

You will learn how to find the information needed to solve a problem.

When a problem has too much information, you must decide which information is important. When a problem does not give enough information, you must decide what is missing.

At the county fair, 9,576 tickets were sold on Saturday and 10,598 were sold on Sunday. Saturday's ticket sales included 3,085 child tickets, 4,112 adult tickets and some senior tickets. The fair collected $15,412.32 on Saturday and $12,672.51 on Sunday.

Sometimes you have too much information.

How many tickets for seniors were sold on Saturday?

What facts do I need?

- the total number of tickets sold on Saturday (9,576)
- the number of child tickets (3,085) and adult tickets (4,112) sold on Saturday

There is additional information provided, but I don't need it.

How can I solve the problem?

- Find the number of non-senior tickets sold on Saturday
  3,085 + 4,112 = 7,197
- Subtract this total from the total ticket sales for Saturday.
  9,576 − 7,197 = 2,379

On Saturday, 2,379 senior tickets were sold.

Sometimes you have too little information.

How much money did the fair collect in a week?

What facts do I need?

- the amount of money collected each day for one week

Information for ticket sales during the week is not given. There is not enough information to solve the problem.

Look Back Provide more information for the problem and solve it.

Standards MR 1.0, 1.1, 2.0, 3.0, 3.2

LEFT: Prize-winning cow at a county fair.
RIGHT: Prize winning apple pie at a county fair.

Guided Practice

Solve each if you can. If a problem is incomplete, tell what information you would need to solve it.

1. At the county fair, Parking Lot 1 was full at 1:00 P.M. It can hold 775 cars. Lot 2 was full by 2:00 P.M. It can hold 850 cars. How many cars were parked in both parking lots?

   Think: Which numbers in the problem tell how many cars there were?

2. On Saturday the county fair opened at 9:00 A.M. and stayed open until midnight. On Sunday it opened at 10:00 A.M. For how many hours was the fair open on the weekend?

   Think: Is there too much or too little information in this problem?

Choose a Strategy

Solve each if you can. Choose these or other strategies. If a problem is incomplete, tell what information you would need to solve it.

Problem-Solving Strategies

- **Draw a Diagram**
- **Guess and Check**
- **Make a Table**
- **Work Backward**

3. Mr. and Mrs. Gregorio took their five children to the fair. Each child in the family got $4 less than the next older brother or sister to spend at the fair. If the oldest child received $20, how much did the youngest receive?

4. A booth at the county fair sells 24-inch long sandwiches. Zita plans to share a sandwich with some friends. If she wants to cut the sandwich into equal-sized pieces, how many cuts will she need to make?

5. Hanna won many prizes playing games at the county fair. If she gives 11 to her friend Carla, she will have 47 left and Carla will have 18 in all. How many prizes does Hanna have?

6. Four rides are located side by side. The Flying Saucer is between the Zipper and the Octopus. The Zipper is next to the Bobsled. Which rides are at the ends of the row?

7. Steve has 12 more ride tickets than Adam. Together they have 36 ride tickets. How many tickets does each boy have?

8. Hanna waited in line for a ride 10 min less than Steve. Steve waited 10 min less than Zita. If Zita waited 30 min, how long did Hanna wait?

Extra Practice See 1–4 on page 85.

LESSON 4

Add Decimals

You will learn how to add decimals.

Learn About It

Sharee took a pedometer with her on a charity walk so she could measure the distance she traveled. When she reached Checkpoint 2, she had walked 7.38 miles. She then walked 3.91 miles to the finish line. How many miles did she walk in all?

Add. **7.38 + 3.91 = *n***

Find 7.38 + 3.91.

Step 1 Write the addends so that digits with the same place value align (line up).

$$\begin{array}{r} 7.38 \\ +\ 3.91 \\ \hline 9 \end{array}$$

Use the decimal point as a guide. Then add the hundredths.

Step 2 Add the tenths. Regroup 12 tenths as 1 one and 2 tenths.

$$\begin{array}{r} \scriptstyle 1 \\ 7.38 \\ +\ 3.91 \\ \hline 29 \end{array}$$

Step 3 Add the ones.

$$\begin{array}{r} \scriptstyle 1 \\ 7.38 \\ +\ 3.91 \\ \hline 11.29 \end{array}$$

Put a decimal point in the sum so it lines up with the decimal points in the addends.

Solution: Sharee walked 11.29 miles in all.

Explain Your Thinking

- ▶ When is it necessary to regroup when adding decimals?
- ▶ Why is it important to align the decimal points in the addends?

Guided Practice

Find each sum. Estimate to check that your answer is reasonable.

1. $\begin{array}{r} 4.517 \\ +\ 2.824 \\ \hline \end{array}$

2. $\begin{array}{r} \$57.99 \\ +\ 4.23 \\ \hline \end{array}$

3. $\begin{array}{r} 54.1 \\ 8.376 \\ +\ 12 \\ \hline \end{array}$

4. 78.94 + 5.57

5. 19.07 + 1.23

6. 82.59 + 19.6

7. 8 + 4.794 + 2.3

Ask Yourself

- Did I write the addends so digits with the same place value align?
- Did I remember to write the decimal point in the answer?

Standards NS 1.0, 2.0, 2.1 MR 2.3

Independent Practice

Add. Estimate to check that your answer is reasonable.

8. $8.49 + 4.59

9. 9.527 + 3.75

10. 178.03 + 8.4

11. 1.699 + 90.5

12. $10.00 + 8.05

13. $51.70 + 83.62

14. 78.427 + 27.309

15. 85.076 + 7.925

16. 5.76 + 28.569

17. 41.75 + 9.863

18. 31.85 5.8 + 53.85

19. $8.03 9.80 + 24.57

20. 7.9 5.662 + 14.038

21. 4.887 46.2 + 7.09

22. 8.7 4.47 4.46 + 6.592

23. 28.5 + 85.7

24. 2.06 + 46.99

25. 0.007 + 0.925

26. 7.48 + 0.351

27. 11.2 + 16.801

28. 20.49 + 17.5 + 0.001

29. 5.05 + 1.3

30. 2.089 + 5 + 4.8

31. 6.792 + 5.78 + 4.6

Problem Solving • Reasoning

Use Data **Sharee used her pedometer to keep track of how far she walked every week in July. Use the table she made to solve Problems 32–34.**

Walking Distances in Miles	
Week 1	6.94
Week 2	12.73
Week 3	9.3
Week 4	10.25

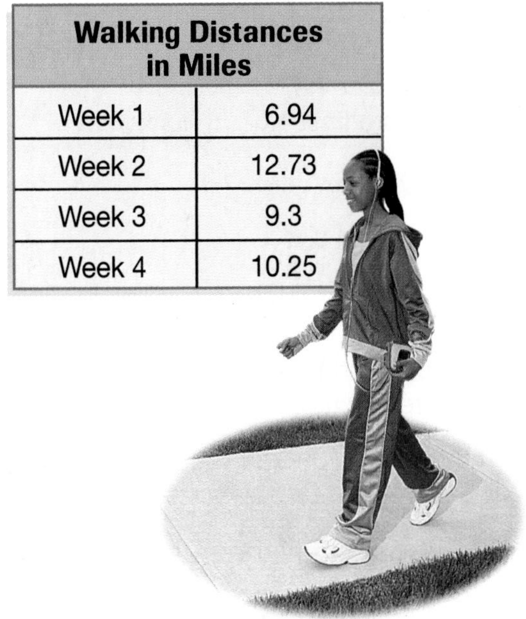

32. **Analyze** During which two weeks did Sharee's distance total about 17 miles?

33. **Estimate** Estimate how far Sharee walked in July.

34. Sharee walked 20.7 miles during the month of August. How many miles did she walk during July and August combined?

35. **Analyze** Write the missing digits.

6 ■ ■ . 5
\+ 1 7 . ■
■ 3 2 . 1

Mixed Review • Test Prep

Write each number in standard form. *(pages 24–25)*

36. six tenths

37. five and sixty-seven thousandths

38. twenty-three and four hundredths

39. seven hundred twenty-one thousandths

40 Find 46,072 written in expanded form. *(pages 6–7)*

A $(4 \times 10^3) + (6 \times 10^2) + (7 \times 10^1) + (2 \times 10^0)$

B $(4 \times 10^4) + (6 \times 10^3) + (7 \times 10^1) + (2 \times 10^0)$

C $(4 \times 10^4) + (6 \times 10^3) + (7 \times 10^2) + (2 \times 10^1)$

D $(4 \times 10^5) + (6 \times 10^4) + (7 \times 10^3) + (2 \times 10^2)$

Extra Practice See Set C on page 83.

LESSON 5

Subtract Decimals

You will learn how to subtract decimals.

Learn About It

The average annual rainfall in Los Angeles is 14.85 inches. In Savannah, Georgia, the average annual rainfall is 48.61 inches. On average, how many more inches of rain does Savannah receive each year than Los Angeles?

Savannah, Georgia

Los Angeles, California

Subtract. **48.61 − 14.85 = *n***

Find 48.61 − 14.85.

Step 1 Align decimal points. Subtract the hundredths.

$$\begin{array}{r} \overset{5\ 11}{48.\not{6}\not{1}} \\ -\ 14.85 \\ \hline 6 \end{array}$$

You need to regroup 6 tenths as 5 tenths and 10 hundredths.

Step 2 Subtract the tenths.

$$\begin{array}{r} \overset{7\ 15\ 11}{4\not{8}.\not{6}\not{1}} \\ -\ 14.85 \\ \hline 76 \end{array}$$

You need to regroup 8 ones as 7 ones and 10 tenths.

Step 3 Subtract the ones. Write the decimal point in the answer.

$$\begin{array}{r} \overset{7\ 15\ 11}{4\not{8}.\not{6}\not{1}} \\ -\ 14.85 \\ \hline 3.76 \end{array}$$

Step 4 Subtract the tens.

$$\begin{array}{r} \overset{7\ 15\ 11}{4\not{8}.\not{6}\not{1}} \\ -\ 14.85 \\ \hline 33.76 \end{array}$$

Solution: Savannah receives 33.76 inches more rain each year.

Another Example

Zeros as Placeholders

Find 27.5 − 2.71.

$$\begin{array}{r} \overset{6\ 14\ 10}{2\not{7}.\not{5}\not{0}} \\ -\ 2.71 \\ \hline 24.79 \end{array}$$

Explain Your Thinking

- Why does the value of a number stay the same when you write a zero after the final digit to the right of the decimal point?
- Why is it helpful to write zeros when you are lining up digits in a subtraction problem?
- How is subtraction with decimals like subtraction with whole numbers? How is it different?

Standards NS 2.0 MR 2.3

Guided Practice

Subtract. Add to check your answer.

1. 4.5 − 3.7

2. 7.0 − 3.47

3. $4.18 − 2.99

4. 7.514 − 5.439

5. 84.016 − 47.869

> **Ask Yourself**
>
> - Have I aligned the digits correctly?
> - Have I included zeros where I need them to subtract?

Independent Practice

Subtract. Add to check your answer.

6. 5.6 − 4.9

7. 9.2 − 3.7

8. 12.5 − 9.8

9. 8.4 − 3.6

10. 13.0 − 8.4

11. $3.45 − 0.79

12. 47.32 − 5.61

13. 57.68 − 24.92

14. $28.09 − 17.99

15. $43.72 − 27.65

16. 6.74 − 5.89

17. 4.56 − 3.67

18. 65.23 − 37.68

19. 4.056 − 2.345

20. 29.547 − 18.918

21. 0.623 − 0.097

Problem Solving • Reasoning

Use Data **Use the table at the right to answer Problems 22 and 23.**

Wettest Inhabited Places	Average Annual Rainfall (in.)
Buenaventura, Colombia	265.47
Monrovia, Liberia	202.01
Pago Pago, American Samoa	196.46

22. **Compare** What is the difference in annual rainfall between Monrovia and Pago Pago?

23. **Estimate** Which two cities have a difference in annual rainfall of about 63 inches?

24. **Analyze** The sum of two numbers is 16.4. Their difference is 0.8. What are the two numbers?

Mixed Review • Test Prep

Compare the decimals. Write >, <, or =. *(pages 26–27)*

25. 0.08 ● 0.10

26. 0.40 ● 0.400

27. 0.75 ● 0.075

28. 0.015 ● 0.15

29 Which decimal has been rounded to the nearest tenth? *(pages 28–29)*

A 0.544 **B** 0.54 **C** 5.4 **D** 54.40

Extra Practice See Set D on page 83.

Problem-Solving Strategy: Work Backward

You will learn how to solve a problem by working backward.

Sometimes you can start with what you know in a problem and work backward.

Problem At a track-and-field meet, the winner of the pole-vault event cleared a height of 3.20 m. This was 0.10 m more than the height cleared by the second-place vaulter. The second-place height was 0.05 m more than the third-place height. What height did the third-place vaulter clear?

Understand

What is the question?
What height did the third-place vaulter clear?

What do you know?
The winner cleared a height of 3.20 m. This was 0.10 m more than the second-place height. The second-place height was 0.05 m more than the third-place height.

How can you find the answer?
Start with what you know and work backward.

Decide what operation to use for each step.

Start with the 3.20 m cleared by the winner.

First Place	Second Place	Third Place
3.20 m	3.20 m − 0.10 m 3.10 m	3.10 m − 0.05 m 3.05 m
This height was 0.10 m more than the second-place height.	The second-place height was 0.05 m more than the third-place height.	The third-place height was 3.05 m.

Look Back

Look back at your problem.
Is your answer reasonable?

Standards MR 1.0, 1.2, 2.0, 2.6, 3.0, 3.1

Remember:
- ► Understand
- ► Plan
- ► Solve
- ► Look Back

Guided Practice

Solve each problem using the Work Backward strategy.

1. During practice, Maggie ran 3 more laps than Tasha. Sonia ran 5 more laps than Tasha. Carmen ran 2 fewer laps than Sonia. Sonia ran 6 laps. How many laps did each girl run?

   Think: Which girl should you use first? Why?

2. A store has 15 large jackets. There are 2 fewer medium jackets than large ones. There are 3 fewer small jackets than medium ones. How many small jackets are there?

   Think: What information will you start with?

Choose a Strategy

Solve. Use these or other strategies.

Problem-Solving Strategies

- Find a Pattern
- Draw a Diagram
- Guess and Check
- Work Backward

3. An Olympic track-and-field team has 121 athletes and 16 coaches and trainers. If 57 of the athletes are women, how many are men?

4. Leo watched a sports event on TV for twice as long as Ella. Together, they watched for 2 hours. For how long did each person watch the event?

5. Ella trained for 4 hours on Friday, which was one hour more than she trained on Thursday and one hour less than on Saturday. How many hours did she train over the three days?

6. Tyler notices a pattern in his long-jump distances. So far they have been 3.2 m, 3.325 m, 3.45 m, 3.575 m, and 3.7 m. Find a pattern. What is the next distance in your pattern?

7. How many more rolls of pole-vault tape would be needed to extend the arrangement to form a triangle?

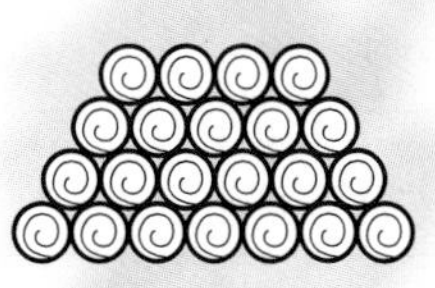

8. In the 400-m hurdle event, the distance from the starting line to the first hurdle is 45 m. The distance between the hurdles is 35 m. The distance from the last hurdle to the finish line is 40 m. How many hurdles do the runners jump?

Extra Practice See 5–8 on page 85.

Quick Check

Check Your Understanding of Lessons 1–6

Add. Estimate to check that your answer is reasonable.

1. $351 + 728$
2. $493 + 362$
3. $4{,}721 + 4{,}419$
4. $23{,}014 + 30{,}629$
5. $2.4 + 3.6$
6. $6.57 + 32.35$
7. $62.35 + 7.9$
8. $\$8.32 + 27.91$

Subtract. Estimate to check that your answer is reasonable.

9. $2{,}465 - 234$
10. $4{,}893 - 527$
11. $6{,}021 - 2{,}429$
12. $32{,}609 - 29{,}759$
13. $5.75 - 0.69$
14. $35.62 - 9.86$
15. $67.4 - 23.07$
16. $\$19.95 - 11.99$

Solve.

17. The high temperature on Wednesday was 75.3°F. Monday's high temperature was 4.9°F greater than Tuesday's. Wednesday's high temperature was 2.7°F greater than Tuesday's. Friday's high temperature was 76°F. How warm was it on Monday and Tuesday?

How did you do?

If you had difficulty with any items in the Quick Check, you can use the following pages for review and extra practice.

California Standards	Items	Review These Pages	Do These Extra Practice Items
Number Sense: **1.0, 1.1** Math Reasoning: **2.1**	1–4	pages 52–53	Set A, page 82
Number Sense: **1.0, 1.1** Math Reasoning: **2.1**	9–12	pages 54–55	Set B, page 82
Number Sense: **1.0, 2.0**	5–8	pages 58–59	Set C, page 83
Number Sense: **1.0, 2.0**	13–16	pages 60–61	Set D, page 83
Math Reasoning: **1.1, 1.2**	17	pages 56–57, 62–63	1–8, page 85

Test Prep • Cumulative Review

Maintaining the Standards

Choose the letter of the correct answer.

1. Frank added these numbers and then estimated to check the sum. Which number is likely to be his estimate?

$$\begin{array}{r} 13{,}078 \\ +\ 59{,}512 \\ \hline \end{array}$$

A 50,000 **C** 70,000
B 60,000 **D** 80,000

2. What is the value of 10^6?

F 60
G 100,000
H 1,000,000
J 6,000,000

3. In words, what is the value of the digit 6 in 324.672?

A six tens
B six tenths
C six hundredths
D six thousandths

4. On June 1, Miguel put $18.75 into his checking account. On June 4, he took out $23.89. On June 15, he put in $135.52. On June 23, he took out $83.06. At the end of the month, he had $525.73 in his account. How much was in the account at the beginning of June?

F $47.32
G $154.27
H $478.41
J $573.05

5. Starting at her house, Hannah walked north for a certain distance and then 0.5 blocks west. Then she walked 1 block north where she met a friend. Together they walked 1.5 blocks east, 1.5 blocks south, and 0.5 blocks west. In all, Hannah walked 7.5 blocks. How far did Hannah walk by herself?

A 4 blocks **C** 2 blocks
B 2.5 blocks **D** 1.5 blocks

6. Which of these is *not* rounded correctly?

F 2,155,684 to 2,200,000
G 3,545,210 to 3,500,000
H 4,350,008 to 4,300,000
J 5,092,546 to 5,100,000

7. Which number is the greatest?

A 9.786
B 9.867
C 9.876
D 8.976

8. An inchworm was in a jar that was 9 cm tall. It climbed 3 cm up the side of the jar and then slid back 2 cm, climbed 3 cm up and then slid 2 cm back, and so on. On which climb was the inchworm finally able to go over the top of the jar?

Explain How did you find your answer?

Internet Test Prep
Visit **www.eduplace.com/kids/mhm** for more *Test Prep Practice.*

LESSON 7 Expressions and Equations

You will learn how to simplify expressions and write equations.

New Vocabulary
expression
simplify
equation

Learn About It

The school math club is having a bake sale. Ms. Ahto, the club's advisor, offered a giant blueberry muffin to the first student who could show whether or not these two expressions are equal.

An **expression** is a combination of numbers, operation signs, and grouping symbols. The parentheses show which operation should be done first.

When you **simplify** an expression, you do all the operations and write the result. Always complete the operations inside the parentheses first.

Simplify 48 − (17 + 1) − 12.

Step 1 Add the numbers inside the parentheses first.

$48 - (17 + 1) - 12$
$48 - 18 - 12$

Step 2 Add or subtract from left to right.

$48 - 18 - 12$
$30 - 12$
18

Simplify (6 + 8) + (9 − 4) − 1.

Step 1 Add or subtract the numbers inside each pair of parentheses.

$(6 + 8) + (9 - 4) - 1$
$14 + 5 - 1$

Step 2 Add or subtract the resulting numbers.

$14 + 5 - 1$
$19 - 1$
18

Solution: Both expressions simplify to 18, so the expressions are equal.

An **equation** is a statement which shows that two mathematical expressions are equal. Since the two expressions above are equal, you can use them to write this equation.

$$48 - (17 + 1) - 12 = (6 + 8) + (9 - 4) - 1$$

Standards Reviews Grade 4 Standards

Another Example

Three Sets of Parentheses

(12 + 4) + (4 + 5) − (8 − 4)
= 16 + 9 − 4
= 25 − 4
= 21

The expression simplifies to 21.

Explain Your Thinking

▶ What would happen if you did not use parentheses to show which operations belong together?

Guided Practice

Simplify.

1. 5 + (8 − 6)

2. (14 + 2) − 5

3. 25 + (4 + 20) − 6

4. (12 + 13) − (8 + 4)

5. 0.3 + (5.2 − 4.1) + 7.3

6. (4.2 + 3.33) − 0.03

Ask Yourself

- Which operation should I start with?
- Have I simplified the expression completely?

Independent Practice

Simplify.

7. (12 + 6) − 3

8. 9 + (18 − 9) + 6

9. (8 + 2) + (3 + 4)

10. (21 − 3) − (4 + 2) + (3 + 5)

11. (27 − 2) − (20 − 5)

12. 0.5 + (12.4 − 0.2) + 3.2

13. 12.95 − (4. 9 − 2.25) + 1.4

Write >, <, or = for each ●.

14. 11 + (32 − 7) ● (11 + 32) − 7

15. 26 − (19 + 6) ● (26 − 19) + 6

16. 1.38 + (4.5 + 2.46) ● (1.38 + 4.5) + 2.46

17. 18.22 − (15.3 − 2.01) ● (18.22 − 15.3) − 2.01

If $n = 2$, write *true* or *false* for each expression.

Ⓐ $n = (20 - 16) - 2$

Ⓑ $n = 8 - (4 - 2)$

Ⓒ $n = 1.5 + (1 - 0.5)$

Ⓓ $n = (6.5 + 2.5) - 7$

Use mental math to calculate.

18. (7 + 2) − 9 + 8

19. (4 + 2) + (3 + 3) + (7 − 1)

20. (5 + 5) + 2 + (2 + 2)

21. (4 + 4) + 4 − (2 + 2)

Problem Solving • Reasoning

Solve. Choose a method.

Computation Methods

- Mental Math
- Estimation
- Paper and Pencil

22. **Analyze** Treats at the club bake sale were arranged on two rectangular tables. One table was 2 ft wide and 3 ft long. The other was 2 ft wide and 5 ft long. If the 2-ft sides were side by side, what was the perimeter of the two tables?

23. **Estimate** The money from the bake sale will help fund a club trip. The club raised $50.65 from the bake sale and has an additional $125.00 in the club treasury. If the cost of the trip is $167.50, does the club have enough money to pay for it?

24. Tasha brought $2.50 to spend at the bake sale. She spent $0.55 on a brownie and $0.85 on a slice of cake. How much money did she have left?

25. Alex bought a cookie for $0.15 and a slice of cake for $0.85. Gabe bought two brownies for $0.55 each. How much money did they pay in all?

26. **Logical Thinking** If 6 coins have a total value of 51¢, what could the coins be?

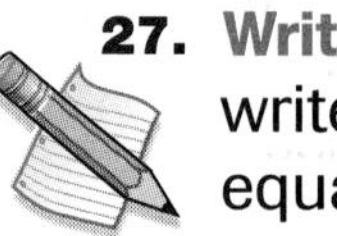

27. **Write About It** Use parentheses to write two different expressions with equal values.

Mixed Review • Test Prep

Write two division sentences you could make with the numbers in each multiplication sentence.

28. $4 \times 7 = 28$ **29.** $9 \times 5 = 45$ **30.** $6 \times 8 = 48$ **31.** $12 \times 5 = 60$

32 Which number is divisible by both 2 and 4?

A 42 **B** 34 **C** 24 **D** 18

Digit Problem

The price, in cents, of a slice of pie at the bake sale is a two-digit number. The ones digit is 2 less than the tens digit. The sum of the digits is 12. How much does a slice of pie cost?

Extra Practice See Set E on page 83.

Moving Parentheses

You can use the operations in an algebraic expression to help you predict whether the value will change if you move the parentheses.

addition only

$(5 + 4) + 6$ ● $5 + (4 + 6)$

$9 + 6$ ● $5 + 10$

15 ● 15

$15 = 15$

If the expression contains only addition, then moving the parentheses will not change the value.

subtraction only

$12 - (4 - 3)$ ● $(12 - 4) - 3$

$12 - 1$ ● $8 - 3$

11 ● 5

$11 \neq 5$

If the expression contains only subtraction, then moving the parentheses changes the value.

addition followed by subtraction

$(7 + 6) - 5$ ● $7 + (6 - 5)$

$13 - 5$ ● $7 + 1$

8 ● 8

$8 = 8$

If the expression contains addition followed by subtraction, then moving the parentheses does not change the value.

subtraction followed by addition

$(10 - 2) + 3$ ● $10 - (2 + 3)$

$8 + 5$ ● $10 - 5$

11 ● 5

$11 \neq 5$

If the expression contains subtraction followed by addition, then moving the parentheses changes the value.

Explain Your Thinking

- ► If all the numbers in an expression are added together, why does the value stay the same if the parentheses are moved?
- ► If an expression contains a minus sign followed by parentheses, the value may change if the parentheses are moved. Why?

Write and Evaluate Expressions

You will learn how to write and evaluate addition and subtraction expressions containing variables.

New Vocabulary
variable
algebraic expression
evaluate

Learn About It

Matt went on 4 more rides than Jessica did at Kids' Kingdom amusement park.

Since you don't know how many rides Jessica went on, you can use a **variable**, such as x or n, to stand for Jessica's rides. You can compare Matt's number of rides with Jessica's by writing an algebraic expression.

Expressions that contain variables are called **algebraic expressions**.

Write an algebraic expression.

Suppose Jessica went on 1 ride.	Suppose Jessica went on 10 rides.	Suppose Jessica went on *n* rides.
Then $1 + 4$ is an expression that shows how many rides Matt went on.	Then $10 + 4$ is an expression that shows how many rides Matt went on.	Then $n + 4$ is an expression that shows how many rides Matt went on.

Algebraic expressions allow you to do the same calculations with different numbers.

To **evaluate** an expression, substitute a number for the variable.

Evaluate the algebraic expression.

If Jessica went on 3 rides, how many rides did Matt go on?

Write the expression.	Substitute 3 for *n*.	Simplify.
$n + 4$ ↑ variable	$3 + 4$ ↑ number	$3 + 4 = 7$

If Jessica went on 3 rides, then Matt went on 7 rides.

 Standards AF 1.0, 1.2

Another Example

Write an Algebraic Expression in Words
Translate the expression $n - 3$ into words.

- In the expression, the variable is *n*. Substitute the words *some number* for the variable.
- The expression becomes *some number* − 3.
- The symbols "− 3" mean *subtract three.*
- The expression becomes *subtract three from some number.*

Other Possible Answers

There is often more than one way to write an algebraic expression in words. Other possible ways include

- **three less than some number**
- **subtract three from some number**
- **take three away from a number**
- **a number minus three**

Explain Your Thinking

▶ Why is a variable used in an algebraic expression?

▶ Why might someone want to write an algebraic expression in words?

▶ Why are there more ways to describe a situation in words than in algebraic terms?

Guided Practice

Write an algebraic expression for each word phrase.

1. some number plus 6 **2.** 8 less than a number

Translate each algebraic expression into words.

3. $k + 9$ **4.** $11 - z$ **5.** $14 + t$ **6.** $b - 4$

Evaluate each expression when $t = 12$.

7. $t + 11$ **8.** $22 - t$ **9.** $t - 8$ **10.** $13 + t$

Ask Yourself

- Do the words describe an addition expression or a subtraction expression?
- What words did I use for the variables?

Independent Practice

Write an algebraic expression for each word phrase.
Use the variable *x* to represent the unknown number.

11. subtract 10 from a number **12.** 9 plus a number

13. 3 more than a number **14.** a number and 18 more

15. a number plus 1 **16.** subtract 7 from a number

17. add 5 to a number **18.** take 15 away from a number

19. a number plus 2 more **20.** 6 is reduced by a number

21. 4 is decreased by a number **22.** 21 is increased by a number

Write each algebraic expression in words.

23. $14 - d$ **24.** $35 - g$ **25.** $m + 7$ **26.** $p - 19$ **27.** $27 + w$

Match.

28. a number plus 3 **a.** $y - 6$

29. $n + 6$ **b.** $3 + x$

30. 6 less than a number **c.** $b + 3$

31. $y - 36$ **d.** 36 plus a number

32. 3 increased by a number **e.** a number increased by 6

33. $36 + x$ **f.** 36 less than a number

Evaluate each expression when $p = 18$ and $m = 20$.

34. $12 + p$ **35.** $p - 9$ **36.** $34 - p$ **37.** $32 + p - 14$

38. $(6 + 4) + m$ **39.** $m - (2 + 7)$ **40.** $(12 - 8) + m$ **41.** $m + (20 - 5)$

Problem Solving • Reasoning

Use a variable to write an expression in Problems 42–44.

42. There were 25 children riding on the Ferris wheel and some others riding on the merry-go-round. If n children are on the merry-go-round, write an algebraic expression that describes the number of children on both rides.

43. Chris runs the Ferris wheel and can earn $60 in regular wages in a day plus a bonus for working an extra hour. Write an algebraic expression that describes the total amount she can earn in a day.

44. **Analyze** Alex had $20. He spent some of his money on admission to the park, rides, and treats. Write an expression that describes the amount he has left.

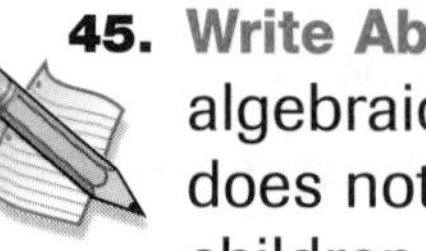

45. **Write About It** Explain whether the algebraic expression $25 - n$ does or does not describe the number of children on the merry-go-round in Problem 42.

Mixed Review • Test Prep

Write two subtraction sentences you could make with the numbers in each addition sentence.

46. $7 + 9 = 16$ **47.** $8 + 4 = 12$ **48.** $14 + 8 = 22$ **49.** $32 + 35 = 67$

50 When would the temperature be about 30°F?

A on the ski slopes **C** on a hot summer day

B on a cool night **D** inside an oven

Extra Practice See Set F on page 84.

Practice Game

Express Yourself

Play this game with a partner or small group to practice creating expressions that match given values.

What You'll Need

- *one set of 12 variable cards* (Teaching Tool 1)
- *one set of value cards* (Teaching Tool 2)
- *a timer*

Players
2

Here's What to Do

1. One player shuffles the cards in each set and places them facedown in two piles. Each player takes one variable card and one value card.
2. A player sets the timer for five minutes. The object of the game is to write addition and subtraction expressions that result in the number on the value card when the *n*-value is substituted for the variable.
3. The second player starts the timer. Players record their expressions and then check each one.
4. Points are awarded as follows.
   - 2 points for each correct expression
   - 1 extra point for using more than one operation in an expression
   - 2 points for using parentheses in an expression

   At the end of the game, players add their points to see who has won.

Share Your Thinking What thinking helps you create an expression with the correct value?

Write and Solve Equations

You will learn how to write addition and subtraction equations and how to use related number sentences and inverse operations to solve them.

New Vocabulary
inverse operations

Learn About It

Amanda is going to visit the Statue of Liberty. Using a coupon for \$2.00 off the price of her ferry ticket, Amanda only pays \$1.00. Write and solve an equation to show how much a ticket would cost without the coupon.

Step 1 Write an equation. Use the variable p to represent the regular price of a ticket. Use an equals sign to connect two equal mathematical expressions.	$p - 2 = 1$	When you subtract \$2 from the regular price, the reduced price is \$1.
Step 2 To find the value of p, think of the missing number.	$p - 2 = 1$	**Think:** What number minus 2 is equal to 1?
Step 3 Write the value you found for p.	$p = 3$	
Step 4 Check the result by substituting 3 for p in the original equation.	$p - 2 = 1$ $3 - 2 = 1$ $1 = 1$	The left side is equal to the right side, so $p = 3$ is correct.

Solution: The cost of a ferry ticket to the Statue of Liberty is \$3.00.

Another Example

Use Inverse Operations

Solve. $p + 4 = 11$

$p = 11 - 4$

$11 - 4 = 7$, so $p = 7$

Check: $p + 4 = 11$

$7 + 4 = 11$

$11 = 11$ ✔

Explain Your Thinking

- ► How was subtraction used to solve this addition equation?
- ► Addition and subtraction are called **inverse operations**. Explain why.
- ► How can you check the solution to an equation?

Standards AF **1.0, 1.1, 1.2**

Guided Practice

Solve and check.

1. $x + 6 = 14$ **2.** $23 - n = 19$ **3.** $5 + d = 17$

4. $y - 2 = 16$ **5.** $61 + w = 72$ **6.** $r - 14 = 35$

> **Ask Yourself**
> • What operation can I use to find the unknown number?

Independent Practice

Solve and check.

7. $4 + z = 10$ **8.** $5 + p = 12$ **9.** $6 + m = 9$ **10.** $12 + t = 19$

11. $t + 8 = 15$ **12.** $q + 6 = 15$ **13.** $n + 9 = 20$ **14.** $c + 2 = 19$

15. $14 - g = 8$ **16.** $16 - e = 11$ **17.** $18 - b = 15$ **18.** $11 - v = 0$

19. $n - 9 = 8$ **20.** $r - 12 = 9$ **21.** $y - 10 = 13$ **22.** $b - 14 = 2$

Problem Solving • Reasoning

Write an equation to solve each problem.

23. Ben used a coupon to pay for a purchase at the grocery store. The original price of his purchase was \$12.00. The coupon reduced the price to \$7.50. What was the value of the coupon?

24. **Analyze** Find the value of p when $p + 4$ is equal to each number.

a. 14 **b.** 21 **c.** 6 **d.** 30

25. Angelina had two coupons with a combined value of \$8.20. If one of the coupons was worth \$3.50, how much was the other one worth?

26. **Write Your Own** Write an equation that is true when the variable is equal to 7. Explain the thinking that helped you create your equation.

THE INTERNET Businesses circulate coupons on the Internet. A Web site offers a coupon worth \$3.00. If 10,500 people download and print the coupons, what is the total value of the coupons?

Mixed Review • Test Prep

Solve. *(pages 52–53)*

27. $24{,}865 + 5{,}914$ **28.** $72{,}460 + 1{,}250$ **29.** $43{,}910 + 79{,}048$ **30.** $91{,}033 + 8{,}152$

31 Which sum is the closest estimate for $35.012 + 7.9$? *(pages 58–59)*

A 35.79 **B** 42 **C** 43 **D** 114

Extra Practice See Set G on page 84.

LESSON 10

Variables and Functions

You will learn how to use a function table to solve addition and subtraction equations.

New Vocabulary
function
function table

Learn About It

A **function** is a rule that relates two variables, such as x and y. For each value of x, there is exactly one related value of y.

Ana made these designs with square pattern blocks. Find a pattern. How many blocks is she likely to need for Design 10?

1 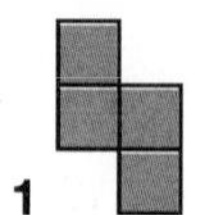 2 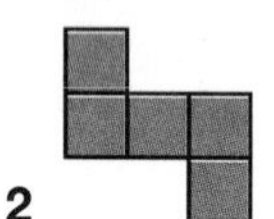 3 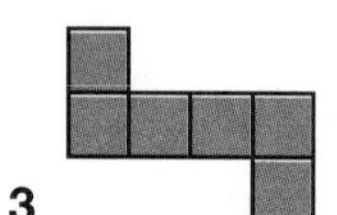 4 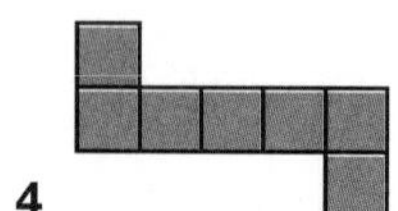

Solve.

Step 1 Organize the information from the problem in a table. Write the design number in the first column. Write the number of blocks in the second column.

Design Number	Number of Blocks
1	4
2	5
3	6
4	7

The table of values is called a **function table** because there is exactly one entry in the second column for each entry in the first.

Step 2 Write the equation that describes the relation between x and y.

The number of blocks is always equal to 3 more than the design number.

$$y = x + 3$$

number of blocks (y) design number (x)

Step 3 To find the number of blocks in design 10, substitute 10 for x and simplify.

$y = x + 3$
$y = 10 + 3$
$y = 13$

Solution: There will be 13 blocks in Design 10.

Another Example

Find the Value

The rule $y = x - 3$ describes a function. What is the value of y when $x = 6$?

Substitute 6 for x in the equation.

$y = 6 - 3$
$y = 3$

Explain Your Thinking

- How could you find out how many blocks would be in design 100?
- Why is it useful to write a function to describe a pattern?
- What are some other pairs of values that would fit in the function table for the second example?

Standards AF 1.0, 1.1, 1.5 MR 1.0, 1.1

Guided Practice

Copy and complete each function table.

1. $y = 5 + x$

x	y
4	■
3	■
2	■
1	■

2. $y = x - 0.5$

x	y
2.5	■
2.0	■
4.5	■
1.0	■

3. $y = x + 4$

x	y
12	■
■	14
8	■
■	10

Ask Yourself

- What value did I use for x?
- How did I get the value of y?
- Did a pattern help me find the missing values?

Independent Practice

Copy and complete each function table.

4. $y = 17 - x$

x	y
8	■
10	■
5	■
7	■

5. $y = 3 + x$

x	y
4	■
6	■
1	■
8	■

6. $y = x - 5$

x	y
15	■
20	■
25	■
30	■

7. $y = 1.5 + x$

x	y
2.5	■
1.5	■
1	■
0	■

Problem Solving • Reasoning

Use the designs for Problems 8–10.

8. Make a function table to show how the number of circles in the first three designs is related to the design number.

9. Make a function table to show how the number of triangles in the first three designs is related to the design number.

10. How many circles and triangles will be in Design 8?

11. **Analyze** Write an expression for the number of circles in the nth design. Write an expression for the number of triangles in the nth design.

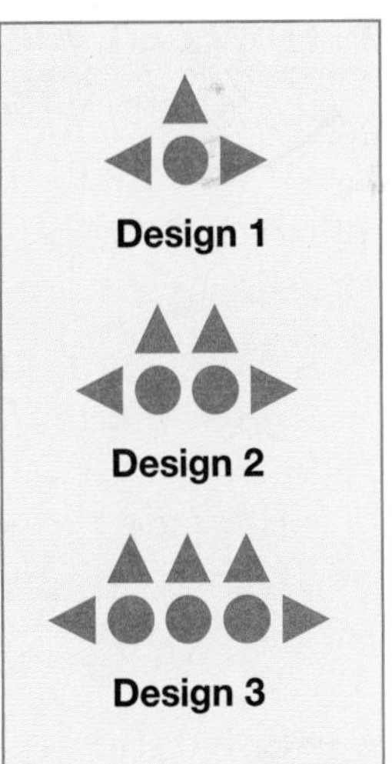

Mixed Review • Test Prep

Write each fraction in simplest form.

12. $\frac{6}{8}$ **13.** $\frac{6}{12}$ **14.** $\frac{3}{3}$ **15.** $\frac{10}{15}$

16 Which decimal means $\frac{45}{100}$? *(pages 24–25)*

A 0.045 **B** 0.405 **C** 0.45 **D** 4.5

Extra Practice See Set H on page 84.

Problem-Solving Application: Use an Equation

You will learn how to solve problems using equations.

In many problems, there is some information given and an amount you need to find. Often you can use an equation to help you find the unknown amount.

Problem Anita collects stuffed animals. She buys a lion and a leopard for a total of \$15.10. If the lion costs \$6.25, how much does the leopard cost?

Stuffed-Animal Prices

Animal	Price
Lion	\$6.25
Zebra	\$9.35
Toucan	\$8.99
Monkey	\$7.29
Leopard	???

Understand

What is the question?
How much does the leopard cost?

What do you know?
- The total cost for both animals is \$15.10.
- The lion costs \$6.25.

Plan

How can you find the answer?
If you know the sum and one addend, you can write an addition equation to find the other addend.

Solve

- Write the equation in words.
  cost of lion + cost of leopard = total cost
- Replace the words with the values you know.
  Use a variable to represent the cost of the leopard.

  $\$6.25 + c = \$15.10$
- Solve the equation.

  $c = \$15.10 - \$6.25$
  $c = \$8.85$

The cost of the leopard is \$8.85.

Look Back

Look back at the problem.
How can you estimate to check if your answer is reasonable?

Standards AF **1.0, 1.1, 1.2** MR **2.0, 2.1, 2.3**

The first Teddy Bear was made in honor of President Theodore Roosevelt.

Remember:
- ► Understand
- ► Plan
- ► Solve
- ► Look Back

Guided Practice

Use an equation to solve each money problem. Show all your work.

1. A stuffed elephant is on sale for $4.30 off its regular price. If the sale price is $9.95, what is the regular price?

   Think: Will the regular price of the toy be more or less than $9.95?

2. Mike buys a stuffed alligator and gives the clerk $15.00. If he gets $3.45 in change, what was the cost of the toy?

   Think: What will the variable in the equation represent?

Choose a Strategy

Solve. Use these or other strategies. Use the table on page 78 for Problems 3–8.

Problem-Solving Strategies

- **Write an Equation**
- **Guess and Check**
- **Draw a Diagram**

3. Barry bought two stuffed animals. He paid $18.34. Which two animals did Barry buy?

4. Sanjay buys a zebra, a toucan, and a monkey. Suppose he has $30. Can Sanjay also buy a lion? Explain.

5. Mr. Barros has $50 to spend on prizes for the math contest. Can he afford to buy one animal of each type listed in the table?

6. Carla wants to buy 3 lions that are on sale. The sale is $2.50 off the regular price of the toy. How much money will she spend?

7. Eli bought 3 lions and Cody bought 2 zebras. Who spent more money on stuffed animals?

8. What combination of stuffed animals could Sara buy that would give her the least change from a $20 bill?

9. Jenny wants to buy a large teddy bear. She has saved $22.55 towards the cost of the teddy bear. If the teddy bear costs $49.99, how much more money does Jenny need to save?

10. Jamila paid $7.75 for two stuffed animals. The price of one stuffed animal was 25¢ more than the price of the other stuffed animal. How much did each animal cost?

Extra Practice See 9–11 on page 85.

Quick Check

Check Your Understanding of Lessons 7–11

Simplify.

1. $(5 + 9) - 6$ **2.** $(6 - 2) + (11 - 4)$ **3.** $18.45 - (12.7 - 4.68)$

Write an algebraic expression using *n* to represent the unknown number. Then evaluate for $n = 12$.

4. a number plus 7

5. 5 less than a number

6. subtract 8 from a number

7. 10 more than a number

Solve and check.

8. $9 + m = 17$ **9.** $d - 16 = 10$ **10.** $b - 7 = 8$ **11.** $t + 12 = 20$

Copy and complete each function table.

12. $y = 6 + x$

x	*y*
5	■
10	■
3	■
8	■

13. $y = 10 - x$

x	*y*
8	■
1	■
5	■
9	■

14. $y = x - 3$

x	*y*
12	■
8	■
■	7
■	13

15. $y = 2.5 + x$

x	*y*
1.5	■
■	5
■	6
0	■

Solve.

16. A CD is on sale for $2.75 less than its regular price. If the sale price is $16.20, what is the regular price?

How did you do?

If you had difficulty with any items in the Quick Check, you can use the following pages for review and extra practice.

California Standards	Items	Review These Pages	Do These Extra Practice Items
Algebra and Functions: **1.0** Math Reasoning: **1.2, 2.4**	1–3	pages 66–68	Set E, page 83
Algebra and Functions: **1.2**	4–7	pages 70–72	Set F, page 84
Algebra and Functions: **1.1, 1.2**	8–11	pages 74–75	Set G, page 84
Algebra and Functions: **1.2, 1.5**	12–15	pages 76–77	Set H, page 84
Math Reasoning: **1.0, 2.1**	16	pages 78–79	9–11, page 85

Test Prep • Cumulative Review

Maintaining the Standards

Choose the letter of the correct answer. If a correct answer is not here, choose NH.

1 Evaluate $14 - t$ when $t = 6$.

A 8 **C** 20
B 9 **D** 22

2 Miranda spent $4.10 on lunch. Which two items did she buy?

Item	Cost
Chili	$2.95
Vegetable soup	$2.35
Grilled cheese	$2.85
Juice	$1.15
Lemonade	$0.95

F vegetable soup, juice
G chili, lemonade
H chili, juice
J grilled cheese, juice

3 Sonia has $8 more than Veronica. Veronica has $6 more than Pablo. Pablo has $3.85. How much money does Sonia have?

A $9.85 **C** $14.00
B $11.85 **D** $17.85

4 Write *two billion, six million, twelve* in standard form.

F 206,012
G 2,600,012
H 206,000,012
J 2,006,000,012

5 Which number does p represent in this number sentence?

$$7 + 0.5 + 0.09 + p = 7.596$$

A 6 **C** 0.06
B 0.6 **D** 0.006

6 Between which two numbers does 0.69 fall on this number line?

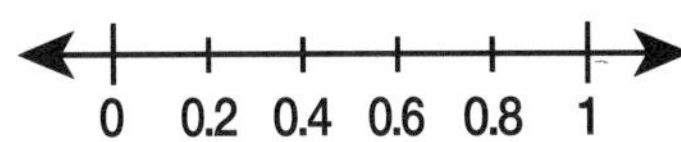

F 0 and 0.2
G 0.2 and 0.4
H 0.4 and 0.6
J 0.6 and 0.8

7 Jerry has $20 to spend at the amusement park. After paying $12.75 for admission and a ride pass, how much will Jerry have to spend on lunch?

A $32.75 **C** $7.75
B $8.25 **D** NH

8 Mrs. Mayer needs to buy two school uniforms for her daughter. A blouse costs $15.99. A skirt costs $23.59. Mrs. Mayer estimates she will need about $100 to pay for the uniforms.

Explain Is Mrs. Mayer's estimate reasonable?

Safe Site

Internet Test Prep
Visit **www.eduplace.com/kids/mhm** for more *Test Prep Practice.*

Extra Practice

Set A *(Lesson 1, pages 52–53)*

Add. Estimate to check that your answer is reasonable.

1. $76 + 412$
2. $686 + 231$
3. $706 + 97$
4. $5{,}610 + 5{,}485$
5. $278 + 1{,}864$
6. $8{,}603 + 587$
7. $9{,}706 + 3{,}048$
8. $42{,}103 + 34{,}572$
9. $545 + 36{,}789$
10. $28{,}589 + 23{,}721$
11. $46{,}418 + 2{,}509$
12. $13{,}659 + 27{,}821$
13. $72{,}314 + 27{,}921$
14. $42{,}617 + 19{,}373$
15. $478 + 356 + 273 + 151$
16. $2{,}705 + 1{,}592 + 3{,}007 + 9{,}108$
17. $18{,}472 + 30{,}903 + 3{,}684$
18. $26{,}783 + 5{,}206 + 483$
19. $55{,}408 + 765 + 207$
20. $42{,}557 + 31{,}006 + 23$

Set B *(Lesson 2, pages 54–55)*

Subtract. Estimate to check that your answer is reasonable.

1. $246 - 188$
2. $413 - 67$
3. $700 - 643$
4. $886 - 487$
5. $3{,}542 - 715$
6. $7{,}365 - 273$
7. $5{,}308 - 3{,}591$
8. $4{,}628 - 3{,}747$
9. $24{,}400 - 18{,}684$
10. $79{,}043 - 68{,}976$
11. $80{,}604 - 50{,}934$
12. $81{,}130 - 74{,}086$
13. $65{,}720 - 4{,}893$
14. $72{,}463 - 509$
15. $73{,}265 - 56$
16. $60{,}000 - 29{,}874$
17. $16{,}549 - 16{,}492$
18. $24{,}001 - 23{,}957$
19. $95{,}678 - 89{,}679$
20. $90{,}090 - 8{,}088$

Extra Practice

Set C *(Lesson 4, pages 58–59)*

Add. Estimate to check that your answer is reasonable.

1. $\begin{array}{r} 1.3 \\ +\ 4.7 \\ \hline \end{array}$ **2.** $\begin{array}{r} 7.42 \\ +\ 22.58 \\ \hline \end{array}$ **3.** $\begin{array}{r} 2.09 \\ +\ 56.43 \\ \hline \end{array}$ **4.** $\begin{array}{r} \$8.65 \\ +\ 40.25 \\ \hline \end{array}$

5. $\begin{array}{r} \$27.45 \\ +\ 53.75 \\ \hline \end{array}$ **6.** $\begin{array}{r} 23.6 \\ +\ 7.42 \\ \hline \end{array}$ **7.** $\begin{array}{l} \ \ 5 \\ +\ 3.821 \\ \hline \end{array}$ **8.** $\begin{array}{l} \ \ 7.3 \\ +\ 5.682 \\ \hline \end{array}$

9. 51 + 6 + 3.2 **10.** 0.005 + 15.712 **11.** 5.824 + 3.45 **12.** 17.06 + 5.6

13. $\begin{array}{r} 93.14 \\ 5.78 \\ +\ 235.309 \\ \hline \end{array}$ **14.** $\begin{array}{r} 15.735 \\ 3.284 \\ +\ 71.697 \\ \hline \end{array}$ **15.** $\begin{array}{r} \$2.86 \\ 6.99 \\ +\ 42.00 \\ \hline \end{array}$ **16.** $\begin{array}{r} 9.652 \\ 86.40 \\ +\ 71.308 \\ \hline \end{array}$

Set D *(Lesson 5, pages 60–61)*

Subtract. Estimate to check that your answer is reasonable.

1. $\begin{array}{r} 4.4 \\ -\ 3.5 \\ \hline \end{array}$ **2.** $\begin{array}{r} 7.4 \\ -\ 5.6 \\ \hline \end{array}$ **3.** $\begin{array}{r} 12.4 \\ -\ 8.9 \\ \hline \end{array}$ **4.** $\begin{array}{r} 50 \\ -\ 4.2 \\ \hline \end{array}$

5. $\begin{array}{r} 5.87 \\ -\ 1.09 \\ \hline \end{array}$ **6.** $\begin{array}{r} 42.24 \\ -\ 0.86 \\ \hline \end{array}$ **7.** $\begin{array}{r} \$47.75 \\ -\ 12.99 \\ \hline \end{array}$ **8.** $\begin{array}{r} 43.62 \\ -\ 10.80 \\ \hline \end{array}$

9. 5.038 - 1.429 **10.** 92.745 − 81.819 **11.** 78.493 − 57.565 **12.** 24.63 − 15.44

13. $\begin{array}{r} 5.650 \\ -\ 0.789 \\ \hline \end{array}$ **14.** $\begin{array}{r} 8.262 \\ -\ 7.464 \\ \hline \end{array}$ **15.** $\begin{array}{r} 66.978 \\ -\ 36.980 \\ \hline \end{array}$ **16.** $\begin{array}{r} 47.500 \\ -\ 46.071 \\ \hline \end{array}$

Set E *(Lesson 7, pages 66–68)*

Simplify.

1. 3 + (8 − 5) **2.** (5 + 7) − 6 **3.** 76 + (33 − 19)

4. 54 + (5 + 48) − 21 **5.** (22 + 33) − (10 + 15) **6.** 38 + (82 + 15) − 29

7. 23 + (8.5 − 6.9) **8.** (7.67 − 0.99) − 5.3 **9.** (0.4 + 3.5) + (3.6 − 0.8)

10. 5.4 + (4.2 − 2.1) **11.** (15 + 3.4) − 7 **12.** 43.7 + (5.6 + 4) − 6.6

13. (5.6 + 7.44) − 0.05 **14.** (15.1 − 3.72) + 4.93 **15.** (4 + 3.06) − (2.05 − 1.45)

Extra Practice

Set F (Lesson 8, pages 70–71)

Evaluate each expression when $n = 16$.

1. $15 + n$ **2.** $n - 9$ **3.** $n + (8 + 5)$

4. $56 + (n - 8)$ **5.** $34 + (6 + n)$ **6.** $n + (42 - 39)$

7. $37 - (n + 3)$ **8.** $(n + 29) - 45$ **9.** $(3 - 3) + n - (28 - 15)$

10. $n + (5 + 6) - (25 - 16)$ **11.** $17 + (n - 6) + 8$ **12.** $(47 + n) - 18$

13. $(17 - n) + (5 + 2)$ **14.** $(n + 7) - 9$ **15.** $(n - 16) + (n + 16)$

Set G (Lesson 9, pages 74–75)

Solve and check.

1. $3 + p = 21$ **2.** $27 - a = 0$ **3.** $d + 35 = 38$ **4.** $t + 15 = 61$

5. $r + 12 = 21$ **6.** $b + 4 = 16$ **7.** $c + 5 = 24$ **8.** $23 - h = 9$

9. $23 - f = 12$ **10.** $12 - c = 5$ **11.** $0 + t = 15$ **12.** $s + 6 = 15$

13. $x - 10 = 17$ **14.** $d - 15 = 3$ **15.** $17 + v = 19$ **16.** $v - 24 = 25$

Set H (Lesson 10, pages 76–77)

Complete each function table.

1. $y = 3 + x$

x	y
3	■
12	■
7	■
9	■

2. $y = 8 - x$

x	y
6	■
0	■
■	7
4	■

3. $y = x + 2$

x	y
12	■
■	5
7	■
■	13

4. $y = 1.5 + x$

x	y
2.5	■
■	3
6	■
0	■

5. $y = 6 + x$

x	y
■	10
10	■
7	■
■	7

6. $y = 10 - x$

x	y
8	■
1	■
5	■
6	■

7. $y = x - 2.5$

x	y
4	■
6	■
■	7
■	8

8. $y = 2.5 + x$

x	y
5	■
■	5
■	6
3	■

Extra Practice • Problem Solving

Solve. If a problem is incomplete, tell what information you would need to solve it. *(Lesson 3, pages 56–57)*

1. Anita sold 23 raffle tickets on Wednesday, 187 tickets on Saturday, and 63 tickets on Sunday. How many tickets did she sell on the weekend?

2. Carlos and Mike play soccer three times a week. Last week, Carlos scored 7 fewer goals than Mike. How many goals did each boy score?

3. Marta collects stamps and has over 4,000 stamps in her album. Most of her stamps are from the United States and the rest are from Europe. How many stamps are from the United States?

4. Two Grade 5 classes are going on a field trip. One class has 24 students and the other class has 26 students. There are 22 girls, 28 boys, and 2 teachers going on the field trip. How many are going in all?

Solve. Use the Work-Backward strategy or another strategy. *(Lesson 6, pages 62–63)*

5. Jennifer has been saving up for a CD that costs $16.75. If she saved $4 last week and $3 this week, how much money does she still have to save?

6. Tony got on the elevator and traveled up 6 floors and then down 5 floors. If he got off at the eighth floor, on what floor did he get on the elevator?

7. In a mystery number game, a number was added to 17. The result was 46. What was the mystery number?

8. Brenda gave 3 concert passes to her sister and 2 to her brother. If she has 5 passes left, how many passes did she start out with?

Solve. *(Lesson 11, pages 78–79)*

9. Lysha brought $20 to spend at the movies. After paying for her ticket and snacks, she had $8.35 left. How much did it cost Lysha to go to the movies?

10. Corinne planted beans in science class. In the first week, her bean plant grew 3.5 centimeters. In the second week, it grew another 4.1 centimeters. How tall was the bean plant after the first two weeks?

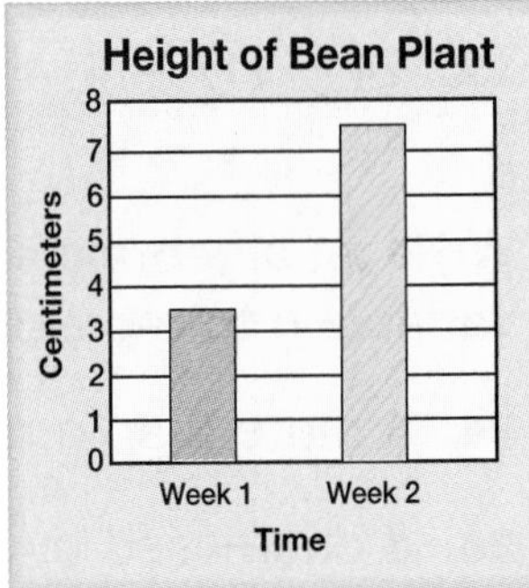

11. The Smithson Theater can hold 450 people. During a performance, an usher counted 17 empty seats. How many people were seated in the theater?

Chapter Review

Reviewing Vocabulary

Write *always, sometimes,* or *never* for each statement. Give an example to support your answer.

1. An addend is less than the sum when adding whole numbers.
2. The difference is greater than the first number when one whole number is subtracted from another.
3. All decimals need to be rounded to whole numbers when estimating sums.

Reviewing Concepts and Skills

Add. Check your answer by estimating. *(pages 52–53, 58–59)*

4. 57 + 346

5. 328 + 389

6. 4,015 + 679

7. 10.6 + 28.3

8. \$501.64 + 109.37

9. 45.67 + 3.80

10. 93.06 + 456.73 + 841.47

11. 36,845 + 52,214 + 7,543

Subtract. Check your answer by estimating. *(pages 54–55, 60–61)*

12. 2,574 − 346

13. 8,756 − 3,389

14. 56,946 − 23,679

15. 82.6 − 24.8

16. 5.342 − 4.554

17. \$202.76 − 35.99

18. 65,634 − 33,435

19. 50,820 − 34,752

Write $>$, $<$ or $=$ for each ●.

20. $12 + (24 - 6)$ ● $(12 + 24) - 6$

21. $4.25 + (3.2 + 6.51)$ ● $(4.25 + 3.2) + 6.51$

22. $24 - (17 + 4)$ ● $(24 - 17) + 4$

23. $(6.4 - 3.42)$ ● $(12.00 + 9.02)$

Write an algebraic expression for each word phrase. Use the variable *n* to represent the unknown number. *(pages 70–72)*

24. 4 more than a number

25. subtract 6 from a number

26. 8 decreased by a number

27. 42 is increased by a number

Find the value of q when $q + 5$ is equal to each number. *(pages 74–75)*

28. 21 **29.** 10 **30.** 26 **31.** 52

Complete each function table. *(pages 76–77)*

32. $y = 14 - x$

x	y
2	■
11	■
6	■
5	■

33. $y = 3 + x$

x	y
4	■
2	■
■	6
8	■

34. $y = x + 7$

x	y
2	■
■	10
7	■
■	11

Solve. *(pages 56–57, 62–63, 78–79)*

35. Shawna was given $40.00 for her birthday. She wants to buy shorts that cost $17.95 and a top that costs $9.95. Does she have enough money? Explain.

36. The amusement park had 4,612 visitors in the morning and another 1,486 in the afternoon. How many people visited the park altogether?

37. A parking lot holds 200 vehicles. Andrew counted 73 empty spaces in the parking lot. How many vehicles are parked in the parking lot?

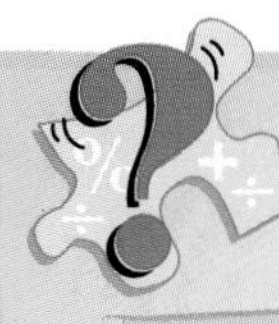

Brain Teasers Math Reasoning

Numbers in a Wheel

Put the digits 1, 2, 3, 4, and 5 in the circles so that the sums across and down both are 8.

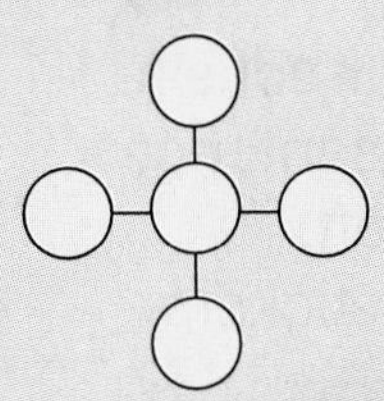

Dot to Dot

Copy the dots onto a sheet of paper.

• • •
• • •
• • •

Join all the dots by drawing 4 connected line segments without lifting your pencil.

Internet Brain Teasers

Visit **www.eduplace.com/kids/mhm** for more *Brain Teasers.*

Chapter Test

Add or subtract. Check your answer by estimating.

1. $\begin{array}{r} 2{,}437 \\ +\ 583 \\ \hline \end{array}$

2. $\begin{array}{r} 1{,}031 \\ -\ 462 \\ \hline \end{array}$

3. $\begin{array}{r} 24{,}672 \\ -\ 5{,}743 \\ \hline \end{array}$

4. $\begin{array}{r} 62{,}818 \\ +\ 15{,}483 \\ \hline \end{array}$

5. $\begin{array}{r} \$27.75 \\ -\ 6.99 \\ \hline \end{array}$

6. $\begin{array}{r} 25.73 \\ +\ 13.90 \\ \hline \end{array}$

7. $\begin{array}{r} 475.620 \\ +\ 126.753 \\ \hline \end{array}$

8. $\begin{array}{r} 5{,}927 \\ -\ 888 \\ \hline \end{array}$

9. $\begin{array}{r} 28{,}463 \\ +\ 60{,}578 \\ \hline \end{array}$

10. $\begin{array}{r} 117.75 \\ -\ 8.56 \\ \hline \end{array}$

11. $\begin{array}{r} 26{,}751 \\ +\ 7{,}039 \\ \hline \end{array}$

12. $\begin{array}{r} 45.030 \\ -\ 26.751 \\ \hline \end{array}$

13. Which expression has a value of 4?

a. $(72 + 36) - 32$ **b.** $72 - (36 - 32)$ **c.** $(72 - 36) - 32$

Simplify.

14. $(15 + 7) - 4$ **15.** $43 + (6 + 5) - 4$ **16.** $(8.25 - 0.33) - 5.2 + 3$

Solve and check.

17. $9 - w = 0$ **18.** $3 + q = 14$ **19.** $8 + s = 20$

20. $v - 7 = 40$ **21.** $p + 0 = 13$ **22.** $t - 9 = 19$

Solve.

23. You have 44 stickers. You give some to your cousin and now you have 38 left. Write a number sentence to represent how many stickers you have left. Use a variable to represent the number of stickers you gave your cousin.

24. It took Gloria 57.05 seconds to run a race. Jennifer's time in the same race was 0.65 seconds slower than Gloria's. What was Jennifer's time in the race?

25. Marcus made 48 cookies and 24 muffins for the class party. He kept 12 cookies and 6 muffins for his family. Which expression represents the number of cookies and muffins Marcus can take to the party?

a. $(48 - 24) + (12 - 6)$

b. $(48 - 12) + (24 + 6)$

c. $48 + 24 - (12 - 6)$

d. $48 + 24 - (12 + 6)$

Write About It

Solve each problem. Use correct math vocabulary to explain your thinking.

1. Explain.

a. How does estimating help determine whether a sum or difference is reasonable?

b. Why is it possible to check the solution to any equation?

2. Lucas completed this addition.

a. Explain what he did wrong.

b. Show how to find the correct sum.

```
   1 1 1
   15.75
+  6.359
   8.034
```

3. Explain the steps you would use to estimate the reasonableness of each answer.

a. 15,898 subtracted from 27,057

b. 18.5 minus 14.67

c. $n + 9 = 11$

Another Look

Use numbers from the box to solve the problems. Some numbers may be used more than once and others may not be used at all.

2.72	3,246	2.444	4,253
3,208	3.246	2.562	3,802
3,162	1,740	5.112	2.604

Find the number that makes each equation true.

1. $2{,}641 + x = 5{,}849$
2. $5{,}993 - n = 1{,}740$
3. $p + 1{,}831 = 4{,}993$
4. $c + 3.005 = 6.251$
5. $a + 3.063 = 5.783$
6. $6.06 - r = 3.456$
7. $6.583 - t = 4.021$
8. $3.456 + k = 6.018$
9. Choose two numbers from the box that make this equation true.

$$z - y = 2{,}513$$

10. **Estimate** Estimate to determine which is greater, 4,253 − 3,246 or 3,246 − 1,740. Explain your thinking.

11. **Write Your Own** Write an equation that can be solved using one of the numbers from the box.

Standards NS **1.0, 1.1, 2.0, 2.1**

Enrichment

Balancing a Checkbook

You can use a checkbook to keep a record of the money you put in and take out of a bank account.

A deposit is the amount of money added to an account.

A withdrawal is the amount of money subtracted from an account.

Date	Withdrawal	Deposit	Balance
4/2			$25.00
4/9		$10.00	$35.00
4/12	$5.00		$30.00

Recording a Deposit

Write the amount of the money in the deposit column.
Add the deposit to the previous balance to find the new balance.

Date	Withdrawal	Deposit	Balance
4/2			$25.00
4/9		**$10.00**	$35.00

$10.00 + $25.00 = $35.00

Recording a Withdrawal

Write the amount of the money in the withdrawal column.
Subtract the withdrawal from the previous balance to find the new balance.

Date	Withdrawal	Deposit	Balance
4/2			$25.00
4/9		$10.00	$35.00
4/12	**$5.00**		$30.00

$35.00 – $5.00 = $30.00

Copy and complete each checkbook.

1.

Date	Withdrawal	Deposit	Balance
6/22			$12.74
6/28			$6.52
7/11			$10.00

2.

Date	Withdrawal	Deposit	Balance
1/5			$21.00
1/6	$4.00		
1/9		$6.55	

Explain Your Thinking

- ▶ In which column would you write interest you receive from the bank?
- ▶ If you withdrew money from this account to pay a bill, in which column would you enter the amount of money?

Standards NS **2.0, 2.1** MR **3.0**

CHAPTER 3

Multiplication

Why Learn About Multiplication?

Knowing your basic facts helps you when you are multiplying large numbers.

When you buy several rolls of film each with 24 exposures and want to know how many pictures you can take, you can use multiplication.

Each of these people bought a ticket to take a trip on this ferryboat. The person in charge of the ferry can multiply to find what the total of the fares should be.

MIDTOWN
MAN.

Reading Mathematics

Reviewing Vocabulary

Understanding math language helps you become a successful problem solver. Here are some math vocabulary words you should know.

factors numbers that are multiplied to get a product

product the answer in a multiplication problem

regroup to exchange 10 smaller units for one larger one or one larger unit for 10 smaller ones

estimate a number close to an exact amount that tells about how much or about how many

multiple a number that is the product of the given number and a counting number

Reading Words and Symbols

When you read mathematics, sometimes you read only words, sometimes you read words and symbols, and sometimes you read only symbols.

All of these statements represent the same problem.

- three groups of six
- 3 times 6
- 3×6
- 6×3
- $\begin{array}{r} 6 \\ \times\ 3 \\ \hline \end{array}$

Try These

1. Write whether n represents a factor or a product. Then find the value of n.

   a. $8 \times n = 40$

   b. $\begin{array}{r} n \\ \times 7 \\ \hline 63 \end{array}$

   c. $n \times 6 = 42$

   d. $\begin{array}{r} 8 \\ \times n \\ \hline 56 \end{array}$

   e. $n = 8 \times 4$

   f. $n \times 9 = 81$

2. Write *true* or *false* for each statement.

   a. When you multiply two whole numbers, the product is always greater than either factor.

   b. When you multiply any whole number by 10, the ones digit in the product is 0.

   c. If you know a product and one factor that is greater than 0, you can divide to find the other factor.

   d. When you change the order of the factors in a multiplication, the product changes.

   e. The multiplication 8×9 gives the same result as $8 \times 3 \times 3$.

3. Fill in the blanks with numbers that work.

   If ____ is a **factor** and ____ is the **product**, then the other **factor** must be ____.

Upcoming Vocabulary

Write About It **Here are some other vocabulary words** you will learn in this chapter. Watch for these words. Write their definitions in your journal.

Distributive Property

partial products

Model the Distributive Property

You will learn how to use the Distributive Property to help you multiply.

New Vocabulary
Distributive Property
partial products

Learn About It

You can draw a rectangular array to show how to find a product.

A rectangle is 5 units wide and 16 units long. You can use simple multiplication facts to find the area of the rectangle.

Materials
grid paper
straightedge
colored pencils

Step 1 With a straightedge, draw a rectangle 5 units wide and 16 units long.

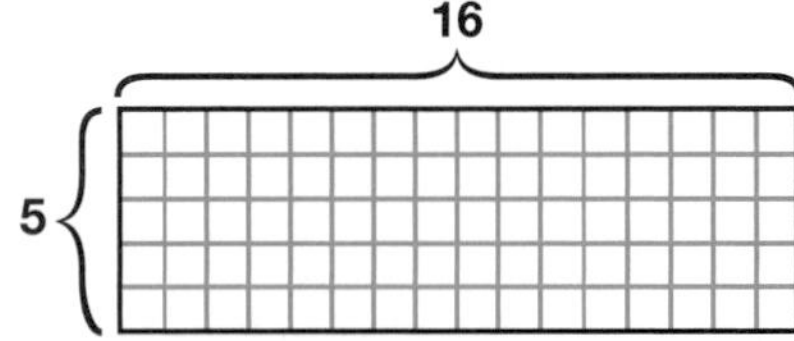

- What multiplication expression describes the area of the rectangle?
- Would it be easier to find the area of the rectangle if you divided it into two parts? Explain.

Step 2 The diagram shows one way to divide the rectangle. Divide your rectangle and shade each part.

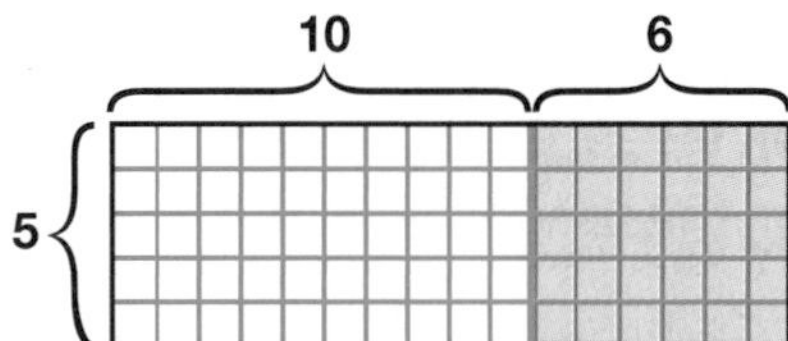

- How does the diagram show 5×16?
- How does it show $(5 \times 10) + (5 \times 6)$?
- How does it show $5 \times (10 + 6)$?

 Standards AF 1.3 MR 2.0, 2.3

Step 3 Find the area of the rectangle.
Use the **Distributive Property**.

$$\begin{aligned} \text{Area} &= 5 \times 16 \\ &= (5 \times 10) + (5 \times 6) \\ &= 50 + 30 \leftarrow \text{partial products} \\ &= 80 \end{aligned}$$

Distributive Property

When you multiply the sum of two or more addends by a factor, the product is the same as if you multiplied each addend by the factor and then added the partial products.

Try It Out

List the partial products for each and find their sums. Then write a multiplication sentence for each.

1.

2.

3.

4.

Draw and divide a rectangle to show each product. Use the Distributive Property to find the product.

5. 6×18
6. 7×25
7. 8×34
8. 9×42

Write about it! Talk about it!

Use what you have learned to answer these questions.

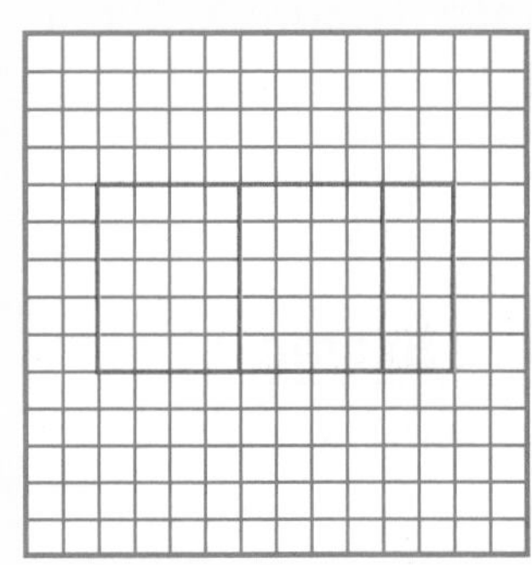

9. When you use the Distributive Property to find areas of rectangles, why does it make sense to divide the rectangles so you get groups of 10?
10. Would the Distributive Property work if you divided a rectangle into three parts? Explain.
11. Give an example of a mental math problem that can be solved easily by using the Distributive Property. Show how to solve it.

Extra Practice See Set A on page 120.

LESSON 2

Multiply by a One-Digit Number

You will learn how to multiply by one-digit numbers.

Learn About It

A mouse's heart can beat 637 times a minute. At this rate, how many times does a mouse's heart beat in 5 minutes?

Multiply. $5 \times 637 = n$

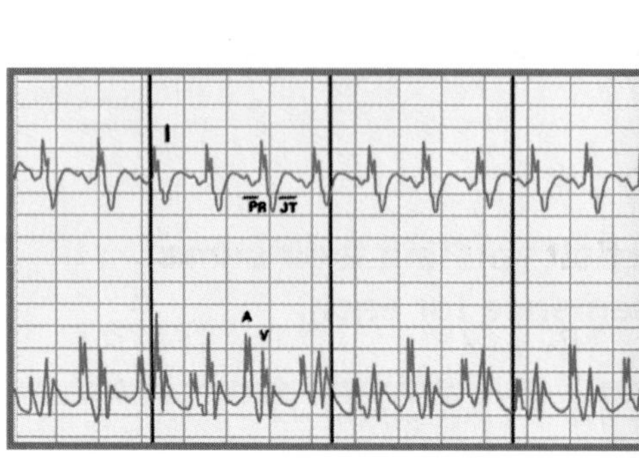

Find 5 × 637.

Step 1 Multiply the ones. Regroup if you can.

$$\begin{array}{r} {}^{3} \\ 637 \\ \times \quad 5 \\ \hline 5 \end{array}$$

5 × 7 ones = 35 ones
35 ones = 3 tens + 5 ones

Step 2 Multiply the tens. Add the regrouped tens. Regroup if you can.

$$\begin{array}{r} {}^{1\,3} \\ 637 \\ \times \quad 5 \\ \hline 85 \end{array}$$

5 × 3 tens = 15 tens
15 tens + 3 tens = 18 tens
18 tens = 1 hundred + 8 tens

Step 3 Multiply the hundreds. Add the regrouped hundreds.

$$\begin{array}{r} {}^{1\,3} \\ 637 \\ \times \quad 5 \\ \hline 3{,}185 \end{array}$$

5 × 6 hundreds = 30 hundreds
30 hundreds + 1 hundred = 31 hundreds

Estimate to check. When you round 637 to 600 and multiply by 5, you get 3,000, which is close to 3,185. So the answer is reasonable.

Solution: A mouse's heart beats 3,185 times in 5 minutes.

Another Example

Multiply With Money

6 × \$5.99

$$\begin{array}{r} {}^{5\,5} \\ \$5.99 \\ \times \quad 6 \\ \hline \$35.94 \end{array}$$

Explain Your Thinking

▶ The Distributive Property says that
5 × 637 = 5 × (600 + 30 + 7).
How is the Distributive Property used in the money example?

Standards NS 1.0, 2.0, 2.1 MR 2.0, 2.1

Guided Practice

Find the product. Estimate to check that your answer is reasonable.

> **Ask Yourself**
> - Do I need to regroup?
> - Did I remember to add regrouped numbers?

1. 51 × 6 **2.** 673 × 4 **3.** 4,187 × 4 **4.** $2.35 × 9

5. $0.89 × 7 **6.** 3,672 × 8 **7.** 5,125 × 5

Independent Practice

Multiply. Estimate to check that your answer is reasonable.

8. 51 × 5 **9.** 32 × 4 **10.** 74 × 3 **11.** $2.78 × 6 **12.** 753 × 2 **13.** 555 × 5

14. 741 × 3 **15.** $9.53 × 7 **16.** 826 × 8 **17.** 417 × 9

18. 754 × 6 **19.** 2,975 × 5 **20.** $84.62 × 6 **21.** 6,758 × 4

22. 9,183 × 3 **23.** 7,185 × 7 **24.** 77 × 6 **25.** 88 × 2

Problem Solving • Reasoning

26. A golden hamster's heart beats 276 times in 1 minute. How many times does the hamster's heart beat in 8 minutes?

27. **Estimate** A shrew's heart beats about 4 times faster than a golden hamster's. About how many times would the shrew's heart beat in 6 minutes?

28. **Logical Thinking** In the farm club pet show, 44 pets are entered. There are 3 times as many dogs as cats and half as many ferrets as dogs. How many of each are there?

29. **Write About It** How could you use the Distributive Property to calculate 4 × 259? Explain your thinking.

Write a multiplication sentence for each description.

Ⓐ The product is 5 times a five-digit whole number.

Ⓑ Three times an amount of money is $129.78.

Ⓒ The product of a six-digit number and a one-digit number is double the six-digit number.

Mixed Review • Test Prep

Write the value of each underlined digit in short word form. *(pages 4–5, 14–16)*

30. $8,\underline{4}67$ **31.** $\underline{3}2,994$ **32.** $\underline{4}56,789$ **33.** $1\underline{2}2,212,111$

34 What is 25,702,115 rounded to the nearest million? *(pages 18–19)*

A 26,000,000 **B** 25,702,000 **C** 25,000,000 **D** 6,000,000

Extra Practice See Set B on page 120.

LESSON 3

Multiply With Zeros

You will learn how to multiply numbers that contain zeros.

Learn About It

One train car can carry a maximum of 108 passengers. How many passengers could be on 6 completely filled cars?

Multiply. $\mathbf{6 \times 108 = n}$

Find 6 × 108.

Step 1 Multiply the ones. Regroup if you can.

$$\begin{array}{r} \scriptstyle 4 \\ 108 \\ \times \quad 6 \\ \hline 8 \end{array}$$

6 × 8 ones = 48 ones
48 ones = 4 tens + 8 ones

Step 2 Multiply the tens. 6 × 0 tens is 0, but there are 4 regrouped tens to be added.

$$\begin{array}{r} \scriptstyle 4 \\ 108 \\ \times \quad 6 \\ \hline 48 \end{array}$$

6 × 0 tens = 0 tens
0 tens + 4 tens = 4 tens

Step 3 Multiply the hundreds.

$$\begin{array}{r} \scriptstyle 4 \\ 108 \\ \times \quad 6 \\ \hline 648 \end{array}$$

6 × 1 hundred = 6 hundreds

Solution: There could be 648 passengers.

Estimate to check. When you round 108 to 100 and multiply by 6, you get 600, which is close to 648. So the answer is reasonable.

Another Example

Use the Distributive Property

$8 \times 20{,}102 = n$

$$\begin{aligned} 8 \times 20{,}102 &= 8 \times (20{,}000 + 100 + 2) \\ &= (8 \times 20{,}000) + (8 \times 100) + (8 \times 2) \\ &= 160{,}000 + 800 + 16 \\ &= 160{,}816 \end{aligned}$$

Explain Your Thinking

▶ If there are zeros in a factor, can you always assume that there will be zeros in the product? Explain.

Standards NS **1.0** AF **1.3** MR **2.0, 2.1**

Guided Practice

Find the product. Estimate to check.

1. 706 × 7

2. 3,009 × 4

3. 6,102 × 5

4. 41,101 × 5

> **Ask Yourself**
> - Did I use the Distributive Property to multiply?

Independent Practice

Multiply. Check your answer by estimating.

5. 602 × 6

6. 805 × 2

7. 202 × 3

8. $4.05 × 4

9. $8.09 × 5

10. $9.03 × 9

11. 3,056 × 4

12. $14.08 × 6

13. 8,706 × 3

14. $10.05 × 8

15. 4,002 × 8

16. 5,080 × 7

17. 32,405 × 7

18. 29,078 × 9

19. 47,009 × 8

Problem Solving • Reasoning

20. Cleveland, Ohio, is 2,550 miles from Los Angeles, California. If a train makes four roundtrips from Cleveland to Los Angeles, how far does it travel?

21. **Logical Thinking** In the future, airplanes may carry up to 700 passengers. A train car can carry up to 208 passengers. How many airplanes would be needed to carry as many people as 9 train cars?

22. **Analyze** Find digits that make the multiplication true. Can you find two different answers?

■■,8■4
× 6
■4,■24

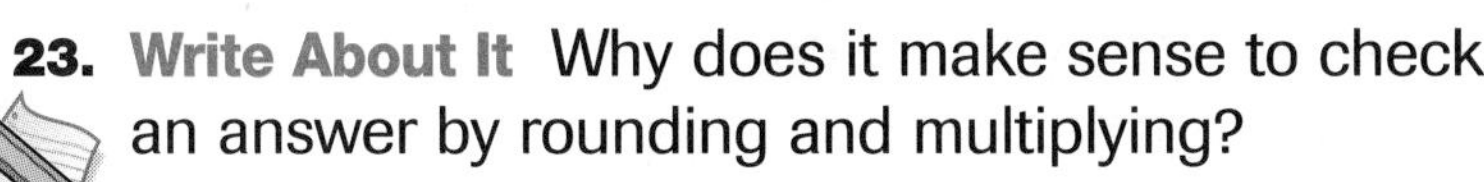

23. **Write About It** Why does it make sense to check an answer by rounding and multiplying?

TRANSPORTATION

Double-decker airplanes are being developed because the number of air travelers is expected to triple over the next 20 years.

In 1997, Los Angeles International Airport was the fourth busiest in the world, with 60,143,000 passengers. If the number of travelers triples as expected, about how many passengers will use that airport in 2017?

Mixed Review • Test Prep

Solve. *(pages 52–55)*

24. 5,242 + 8,617

25. 62,175 − 33,052

26. 42,094 − 9,527

27 What is the sum of 58,891 and 22,002? *(pages 52–53)*

A 65,893 **B** 72,893 **C** 80,893 **D** 115,893

Extra Practice See Set C on page 121.

Problem-Solving Skill: Estimated or Exact Answers

You will learn when you can solve a problem by estimating and when you should calculate the exact answer.

When you solve a problem, you can sometimes use an estimate. An estimate is quick and easy to do. Sometimes you need an exact answer. An exact answer gives you precise information.

Look at the situations below.

Sometimes an estimate is all you need.

Danita and Rani are selling houseplants at the school sale. Danita counts her money. She has about $72. Rani has not counted her money, but she has sold 17 plants.

Does Rani have more or less money than Danita?

The cost of one plant, $3.95, is less than $4.

$$
\begin{aligned}
17 \times \$4 &= (10 \times \$4) + (7 \times \$4) \\
&= \$40 + \$28 \\
&= \$68
\end{aligned}
$$

Seventeen plants cost less than $68, so Rani must have less money than Danita.

Sometimes you need an exact answer.

Jeff sold 9 houseplants and has exactly $35.45. Since 9 × $4 is $36, this amount is about right. Still, Jeff wants to be sure he hasn't lost any coins.

$$
\begin{array}{r}
{}^{8\,4} \\
\$3.95 \\
\times \quad 9 \\
\hline
\$35.55
\end{array}
$$

The total should be $35.55, so Jeff has lost a dime. He replaces it before he hands in the money at school.

Look Back Why is it a good idea to decide whether you need an estimated answer or an exact one before you start to solve a problem?

 Standards NS **1.0** MR **1.0, 2.0, 2.5, 3.0**

Guided Practice

Answer by estimating or calculating.

1. The school hopes to sell $3,000 worth of plants. If 284 students have average sales of $12 each, will the school meet its fundraising goal?

   Think: How can you be sure that an estimate will not be greater than the actual product?

2. The school plans to use some of the money raised by the sale to buy 5 new printers. Each printer costs $468. What will be the total cost?

   Think: Should you use an estimate or calculate the exact amount to find the total cost?

Choose a Strategy

Solve. Use these or other strategies.

Problem-Solving Strategies

- **Make a Model**
- **Solve a Simpler Problem**
- **Find a Pattern**
- **Draw a Diagram**

3. Jeff sold 9 houseplants for $35.55. How much less would he have collected if the price of a plant were $3.25 instead of $3.95?

4. A rectangular seed package has a perimeter of 32 in. What lengths and widths are possible? Use whole numbers to answer.

5. About 1 out of every 5 people Jeff spoke to agreed to buy a houseplant. He sold 9 plants. About how many people did Jeff speak to?

6. For each plant sold, the school keeps $2. The remaining $1.95 goes to the nursery. If the school kept $2,268, how many plants were sold?

7. Jodie is buying 4 packages of seeds. She can choose tomatoes, cucumbers, lettuce, beans, peas, or zucchini. How many possible choices of 4 different packages of seeds are there?

8. A morning-glory vine can grow 15 cm in 1 week. How much could a morning glory grow in 9 weeks? How many weeks will it take the vine to grow more than 1 meter?

9. Mrs. Tran planted beans, peppers, zucchini, and tomatoes in her garden. Use the clues to determine which type of plant is in each section.

   - The zucchini section borders only one other section.
   - The tomatoes are between the beans and the peppers.
   - Section 4 does not contain beans or peppers.
   - The beans are not in Section 1.

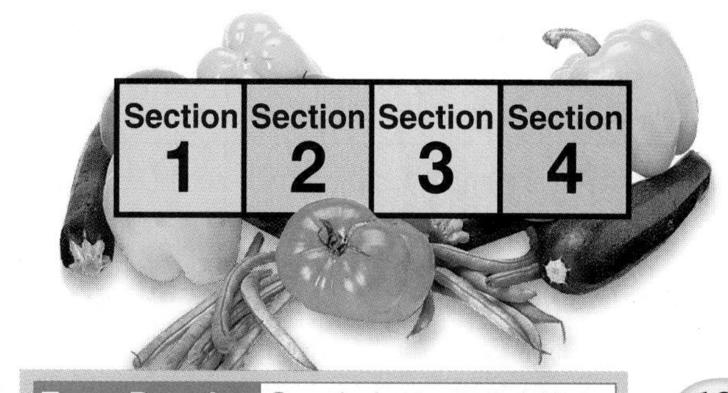

Extra Practice See 1–4 on page 123.

Quick Check

Check Your Understanding of Lessons 1–4

Multiply. Estimate to check that your answer is reasonable.

1. 359×4
2. $\$8.27 \times 7$
3. 199×5
4. 722×9
5. $4{,}327 \times 3$
6. $\$72.49 \times 6$
7. $5{,}445 \times 8$
8. $9{,}226 \times 7$

Multiply. Check your answer by estimating.

9. 602×6
10. 805×2
11. 202×3
12. $\$4.05 \times 4$
13. $8{,}402 \times 4$
14. $\$30.98 \times 5$
15. $26{,}500 \times 4$
16. $52{,}009 \times 8$

Answer by estimating or by calculating.

17. Jenna is buying 8 packages of writing paper that cost $4.27 for each package. Will her purchase cost more or less than $33? Explain.

How did you do?

If you had difficulty with any items in the Quick Check, you can use the following pages for review and extra practice.

California Standards	Items	Review These Pages	Do These Extra Practice Items
Number Sense: **1.0, 2.0** Math Reasoning: **2.1**	1–8	pages 98–99	Set B, page 120
Number Sense: **1.0, 2.0** Math Reasoning: **2.1**	9–16	pages 100–101	Set C, page 121
Math Reasoning: **2.1, 2.5**	17	pages 102–103	1–4, page 123

Test Prep • Cumulative Review

Maintaining the Standards

Choose the letter of the correct answer.

1. Elaine multiplied these factors and then estimated to check the product. Which number is likely to be her estimate?

$$\begin{array}{r} 19{,}783 \\ \times \quad 8 \\ \hline \end{array}$$

A 16,000 **C** 158,264
B 80,000 **D** 160,000

2. Which expression has the greatest value when $x = 9$?

F $x - 5$ **H** $5 - x$
G $x + 5$ **J** $(x - 2) + 6$

3. A video game is on sale for $3.35 less than its regular price. If the sale price is $15.48, which is the *best* description of the regular price?

A a little more than $3
B a little less than $15
C a little more than $15
D a little more than $18

4. Mr. Kim needs 12,000 pencils for a convention. A large box contains 13,000 pencils. A small box contains 2,050 pencils. Mr. Kim decides to order 6 small boxes instead of 1 large one. Which number sentence shows that he will have enough pencils?

F $13{,}000 - 12{,}000 = 1{,}000$
G $13{,}000 - 2{,}000 = 11{,}000$
H $2{,}000 \times 6 = 12{,}000$
J $3{,}000 \times 6 = 18{,}000$

5. Which equation describes the number of ● in the array below?

A $19 \times 4 = (10 \times 4) + (9 \times 4)$
B $19 \times 4 = (10 \times 4) - (9 \times 4)$
C $19 \times 4 = (10 + 4) \times (9 + 4)$
D $19 \times 4 = (10 \times 4) \times (9 \times 4)$

6. Which is the standard form of this number?

eight million, eight hundred seven thousand, four hundred forty-two

F 800,742 **H** 8,804,742
G 8,007,442 **J** 8,807,442

7. Which is the greatest number?

A 8×10^9 **C** 8×10^8
B 9×10^8 **D** 9×10^9

8. Look at the computations below.

$$\begin{array}{r} 14.53 \\ +\ 26.085 \\ \hline 40.615 \end{array} \qquad \begin{array}{r} 40.615 \\ -\ 14.53 \\ \hline \end{array}$$

Explain How can you use the first answer to find the second?

Safe Site

Internet Test Prep
Visit **www.eduplace.com/kids/mhm** for more *Test Prep Practice.*

Mental Math: Multiply Multiples of 10, 100, and 1,000

You will learn how to multiply a number by a multiple of 10, 100, or 1,000 mentally.

Learn About It

Around the world, about 40,000 thunderstorms occur each day. About how many thunderstorms occur every week?

There are 7 days in a week.

Multiply. $7 \times 40{,}000 = n$

Different Ways to Multiply Multiples of 10

You can use patterns.

$7 \times 4 = 28$
$7 \times 40 = 280$
$7 \times 400 = 2{,}800$
$7 \times 4{,}000 = 28{,}000$
$7 \times 40{,}000 = 280{,}000$

You can use mental math.

$7 \times 40{,}000 = 7 \times 4 \times 10{,}000$
$= 28 \times 10{,}000$
$= 280{,}000$

Solution: About 280,000 thunderstorms occur every week.

Other Examples

A. First Product Ends in Zero

Find $6 \times 5{,}000$.

$6 \times 5 = 30$
$6 \times 50 = 300$
$6 \times 500 = 3{,}000$
$6 \times 5{,}000 = 30{,}000$

B. Both Factors Are Multiples of 10

Find $8{,}000 \times 4{,}000$.

$8{,}000 \times 4{,}000 = 8 \times 1{,}000 \times 4 \times 1{,}000$
$= 8 \times 4 \times 1{,}000 \times 1{,}000$
$= 32{,}000{,}000$

Explain Your Thinking

- ▶ Does the number of zeros in the product always equal the number of zeros in the factors? Explain.
- ▶ How can you tell that $80 \times 40 = 8 \times 400$ without doing the multiplication?

Standards	NS 1.0	AF 1.0	MR 1.1, 2.3, 3.0

Guided Practice

Use a pattern or mental math to find each product.

1. 4 × 90 **2.** 7 × 500 **3.** 5 × 700

4. 800 × 50 **5.** 40 × 6,000 **6.** 60 × 4,000

> **Ask Yourself**
>
> - Did I check the number of zeros in the product?

Independent Practice

Use mental math to find each product.

7. 80 × 4 **8.** 50 × 9 **9.** 400 × 7 **10.** 700 × 7

11. 600 × 8 **12.** 3,000 × 4 **13.** 4,000 × 6 **14.** 2,000 × 8

15. 5,000 × 5 **16.** 9,000 × 7 **17.** 50 × 40 **18.** 80 × 90

19. 700 × 70 **20.** 4,000 × 30 **21.** 7,000 × 40 **22.** 5,000 × 50

23. 30 × 90 **24.** 40 × 500 **25.** 50 × 1,000 **26.** 700 × 70

27. 40 × 400 **28.** 30 × 300 **29.** 20 × 90 **30.** 6,000 × 30

31. 80 × 800 **32.** 7,000 × 30 **33.** 70 × 8,000 **34.** 60 × 60

35. 30 × 8,000 **36.** 9,000 × 50 **37.** 20 × 500 **38.** 20 × 5,000

Choose the greater product without multiplying first. Write $>$ or $<$ for each ●.

39. 90 × 50 ● 7 × 600 **40.** 900 × 3 ● 400 × 8

41. 60 × 3,000 ● 600 × 30 **42.** 50 × 3,000 ● 5 × 3 × 1,000

43. 20 × 4,000 ● 30 × 3,000 **44.** 70 × 4,000 ● 80 × 2,000

n **Algebra • Expressions** **What value of *n* makes each expression equal to 10,000?**

45. 100 × n **46.** 10 × n **47.** 5 × n **48.** 10^n **49.** n^2

Write *true* or *false*. Give an example for each.

50. When you multiply any whole number by a multiple of 10, the ones digit of the product will be zero.

51. When you multiply a multiple of 1,000 by a multiple of 10, the product will always have four zeros.

Problem Solving • Reasoning

Use Data **Use the table to answer Problems 52 and 53.**

52. Olympia, Washington, is a rainy city. What has been the average total yearly rainfall?

53. Compare The average rainfall data are based on observations over a 50-year period. In all, how much rain fell during the 50 winters? during the 50 springs? How much more rain fell in the winters?

Olympia, Washington Average Rainfall (over 50 years)	
Season	**Average Annual Rainfall**
Winter	22 in.
Spring	10 in.
Summer	4 in.
Fall	15 in.

54. Estimate Sound travels about 1,100 feet in 1 second. Light travels many times faster than sound. If you see a flash of lightning but hear the thunder 5 seconds later, about how far away did the lightning strike?

55. Write About It Tornadoes can travel up to 60 miles in 1 hour. At this speed, how far could a tornado travel in 3 hours?

Mixed Review • Test Prep

Add or subtract. Then estimate to check. *(pages 58–61)*

56. $43.72 + 61.03$

57. $943.02 - 88.91$

58. $3.9678 - 2.0341$

59. $552.300 - 34.126$

60 What is the difference between 467.01 and 162.9? *(pages 60–61)*

A 436.2 **B** 304.11 **C** 275.1 **D** 67.01

Products

Write *true* or *false* for each. Give examples to support your answers.

1. The product of two 2-digit numbers is always a 4-digit number.
2. The product of two 3-digit numbers is always less than 1,000,000.
3. The product of two multiples of 10 is always a multiple of 100.

Extra Practice See Set D on page 121.

Practice Game

How Many Factors?

Play this game with a partner to practice working with multiples of 10, 100, and 1,000.

What You'll Need

- *4 sets of number cards, numbered 1–10*
- *number cube with sides marked 10, 10, 100, 100, 1,000, 1,000*
- *minute timer*

Players
2

Here's What To Do

1. Each player takes two cards and rolls the number cube.
2. The player multiplies the numbers on the two cards and then multiplies by the number rolled on the cube to get a product.
3. Players have one minute to write as many different multiplication sentences as they can for their product. The *factors* in each multiplication sentence must be different, not just in a different order.
4. Players exchange and check lists. Players score one point for each correct sentence and lose one point for each incorrect sentence. The player with the most points wins the round.

Play as many rounds as you like. Make a table to keep track of the scores.

8 X 3 X 100 = 2,400
8 X 30 X 10 = 2,400
80 X 30 = 2,400
800 X 3 = 2,400
8 X 300 = 2,400
600 X 4 = 2,400
6 X 400 = 2,400
60 X 40 = 2,400
12 X 200 = 2,400

Share Your Thinking How can you find many different multiplication sentences that have the same product?

Multiply by Multiples of 10

You will learn how to multiply any whole number by a multiple of 10.

Learn About It

The Benz Spider, a motor car built in 1902, could go 35 miles in one hour. If a car traveled today at this speed without stopping, it could go from Portland, Maine, to Orlando, Florida, in 40 hours. How far is it from Portland to Orlando?

Multiply. $\mathbf{40 \times 35 = n}$

Different Ways to Multiply by Multiples of 10

You can change the order of the factors.

Think: $40 \times 35 = 4 \times 10 \times 35$
$= 10 \times 4 \times 35$
$= 4 \times 35 \times 10$

Find 4×35.

$$\begin{array}{r} 35 \\ \times\ 4 \\ \hline 140 \end{array}$$

Multiply the result by 10.

$140 \times 10 = 1{,}400$

You can multiply by multiples of 10.

Since 40 is a multiple of 10, the ones digit in the product must be 0.

Write 0 in the ones place.
Then multiply 35 by 4.

$$\begin{array}{r} 35 \\ \times\ 40 \\ \hline 1{,}400 \end{array}$$

Solution: It is 1,400 miles from Portland to Orlando.

Explain Your Thinking

- In a product of two whole numbers, if one of the factors is a multiple of 10, why is the ones digit always 0?

Guided Practice

Use a pattern to find each product.

1. 389×7 **2.** 389×70 **3.** 389×700

> **Ask Yourself**
> - How many places in the product will contain zeros?

Independent Practice

Multiply.

4. 59 × 10 **5.** 32 × 40 **6.** 74 × 30 **7.** 88 × 60

8. 265 × 30 **9.** 376 × 20 **10.** 402 × 60 **11.** 675 × 70

12. 3,970 × 80 **13.** 4,784 × 90 **14.** 56 × 10 **15.** 66 × 60

16. 534 × 70 **17.** 784 × 50 **18.** 2,975 × 20 **19.** 8,462 × 80

Problem Solving • Reasoning

Solve. Choose a method.

Computation Methods

- Mental Math
- Estimation
- Paper and Pencil

Use Data **Use the table for Problems 20 and 21.**

From \ To	New Orleans	New York	Phoenix
Boston	1,541 mi	213 mi	2,664 mi
San Jose	2,225 mi	2,992 mi	756 mi
Seattle	2,606 mi	2,900 mi	1,482 mi

20. **Logical Thinking** Siena and Rosa drove from one city to another. They drove 12 hours a day for 5 days. Their average speed was about 50 miles an hour. What were the two cities?

21. **Analyze** Brian is driving from Boston to New Orleans. He wants to drive 8 hours a day for 4 days. He plans to drive 55 miles an hour. Why is his plan reasonable?

22. **Write About It** Use patterns to find the products. Explain what you did.

83 × 6 83 × 60 83 × 600
830 × 6 8,300 × 6

Mixed Review • Test Prep

Write an algebraic expression for each phrase. Use the variable *n*. *(pages 70–72)*

23. a number decreased by five **24.** the sum of a number and twelve

25. a number increased by two **26.** seven less than a number

27 If $n = 2$, what is the value of $20 - (n + 8)$? *(pages 70–72)*

A 30 **B** 26 **C** 20 **D** 10

Extra Practice See Set E on page 122.

Problem-Solving Strategy: Write an Equation

You will learn how to use an equation to represent a word problem.

Sometimes you can write an equation to solve a problem. This strategy works well with problems that involve number patterns.

Problem Melina asks a friend to roll three number cubes labeled from 1 to 6 and to find the sum of the numbers on the tops and bottoms of all three cubes. Then Melina holds up a card with 21 on it.

To keep her friends from catching on, Melina uses a different number of cubes each time. What number should be on the card when she uses 5 cubes? 8 cubes? 11 cubes?

Understand

What is the question?

What number should be on the card when Melina uses 5 cubes? 8 cubes? 11 cubes?

What do you know?

- No matter how a cube rolls, the sum of the top and bottom numbers is always 7.

How can you find the answer?

Write an equation to represent the sum for n cubes.

Solve

Write an equation.

The sum equals the number of cubes times 7.

$s = n \times 7$	for $n = 5$	for $n = 8$	for $n = 11$
$s \rightarrow$ sum	$s = 5 \times 7$	$s = 8 \times 7$	$s = 11 \times 7$
$n \rightarrow$ number of cubes	$s = 35$	$s = 56$	$s = 77$

Look Back

Look back at the problem.

For what kinds of problems is writing an equation a good strategy?

Standards AF **1.1** MR **1.0, 2.0, 2.3, 2.4, 3.0**

Guided Practice

Write an equation for each problem.

1. Travis circles the date of his birthday on the calendar, doubles it, and then adds 10. The result is 38. What equation could you use to find his birthday?

   Think: How can you find his result before he added 10?

2. A rectangle is 24 inches long and has a perimeter of 84 inches. Mindy found the width of the rectangle without measuring. What equation did she use?

   Think: How many widths and lengths are counted in the perimeter?

Choose a Strategy

Solve. Use these or other strategies.

Problem-Solving Strategies

- **Guess and Check**
- **Make a Table**
- **Work Backward**
- **Write an Equation**

3. The sides of a standard number cube are labeled from 1 to 6. What is the sum of the numbers on all the sides of 8 standard number cubes?

4. Wei drew 8 shapes—rectangles and triangles—that have a total of 28 sides. How many shapes of each type did Wei draw?

5. There are 10 coins on a table. The total value of the coins is 93¢. What are the coins?

6. When you multiply a mystery number by 6 and then subtract 54, the result is 1,500. What is the number?

7. Why does this number trick work?
   - Choose any number.
   - Add 8.
   - Subtract 10.
   - Add 2.
   - The answer is the number you started with.

8. Find a rule that changes each number in the top row to the number below it. Then use the rule to fill in the missing numbers.

Starting Number	1	2	3	4	5	6
Result	3	6		12		

Extra Practice See 5–9 on page 123.

Multiply by Two-Digit Numbers

You will learn how to multiply by a two-digit number.

Review Vocabulary
Distributive Property

Learn About It

The 111th annual Rose Parade in Pasadena, California, had 56 floats decorated entirely with flowers, seeds, vegetables, and even seaweed. After the parade the floats were lined up for exhibition. If the space needed for each float was 185 feet, how far did people walk to see all the floats?

Multiply. **56 × 185 = *n***

Find 56 × 185.

Step 1 Multiply by the ones digit.

```
  53
  185
×  56
 1110  ← 6 × 185
```

Step 2 Multiply by the tens digit.

```
  42
  53
  185
×  56
 1110
 9250  ← 50 × 185
```

Step 3. Add the partial products.

```
   42
   53
   185
 ×  56
  1110
+ 9250
10,360
```

Check by estimating.

56 rounds to 60

185 rounds to 200

60 × 200 = 12,000

Both numbers were rounded to greater numbers, so 12,000 is a reasonable estimate for 10,360.

Solution: People walked about 10,360 feet to see all the floats.

Another Example

Multiplying Money

Find $29.99 × 12.

```
  11 1
 $29.99
×    12
  59 98
+ 299 90
$359.88  ←
```

Insert the decimal point and $ in the final product to show dollars and cents.

Explain Your Thinking

- How could you use the **Distributive Property** to multiply 2 two-digit numbers?
- When you multiply by the tens digit, why do you write a zero in the ones column?

Standards NS **1.0** AF **1.0, 1.3** MR **2.0, 2.1**

Guided Practice

Find each product. Estimate to check.

1. 57×26 **2.** 71×34 **3.** 406×25 **4.** $\$14.88 \times 25$

Ask Yourself

- Did I align the digits correctly to add the partial products?

Independent Practice

Multiply. Estimate to check.

5. 59×15 **6.** 36×19 **7.** 74×24 **8.** $\$0.78 \times 33$ **9.** 53×46 **10.** $\$1.39 \times 5$

11. 605 × 52 **12.** \$4.62 × 63 **13.** 758 × 76 **14.** 918 × 87

15. 826 × 98 **16.** 66¢ × 59 **17.** 78 × 68 **18.** 35 × 77

19. 378 × 68 **20.** 495 × 54 **21.** 1,785 × 23 **22.** \$64.82 × 36

23. 22 × 109 **24.** 18 × \$1.03 **25.** 79 × 189 **26.** 24 × \$0.99

Problem Solving • Reasoning

27. A Web site sells videos of the Rose Bowl game for \$19.95. The videos are packed in boxes of 12. How much is each box of videos worth?

28. **Analyze** A player carries the ball an average of 141 yards in 12 games. Is his record closer to 4,000 or 2,000 yards for the 12 games? Explain.

29. **Logical Thinking** A company bought 573 tickets for a pre-game rally at the Rose Bowl. Each ticket cost \$35. How much did the company spend?

30. **Write About It** A crowd of 8,500 people attended the first Rose Bowl game in 1902. Today, the Rose Bowl holds 12 times as many people as attended the first game. About how many people does the Rose Bowl hold today? Explain.

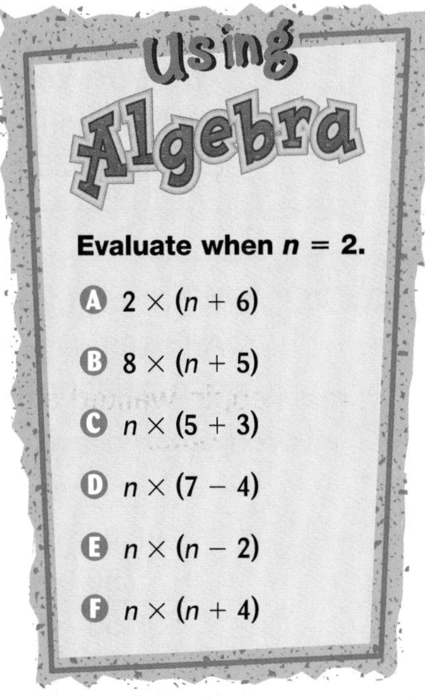

Evaluate when $n = 2$.

A $2 \times (n + 6)$

B $8 \times (n + 5)$

C $n \times (5 + 3)$

D $n \times (7 - 4)$

E $n \times (n - 2)$

F $n \times (n + 4)$

Mixed Review • Test Prep

Solve. *(pages 98–99)*

31. 423 × 7 **32.** 3,256 ÷ 4 **33.** 64,154 × 4 **34.** 99,999 ÷ 3

35 What is the correct product for 8 × 31,002? *(pages 98–99)*

A 24,816 **C** 248,160

B 248,016 **D** 320,016

Extra Practice See Set F on page 122.

Problem-Solving Application: Use Operations

You will learn how to choose an operation to solve a problem.

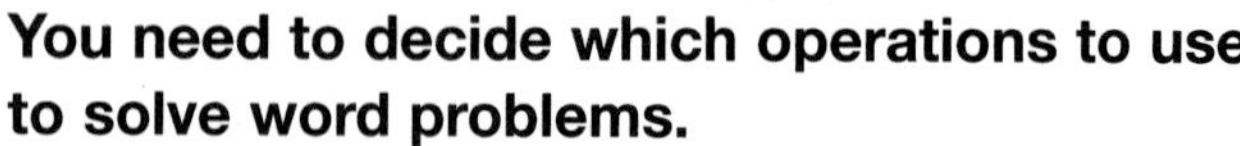

You need to decide which operations to use to solve word problems.

Six friends plan to go scuba diving with Under-the-Sea Tours. If everyone on the trip dives for a full day and needs one air tank refill, what will be the total cost?

What is the question?

How much will it cost for the six people to go scuba diving?

What do you know?

Each person will pay $88 for the day plus $7.50 for an air tank refill.

What can you do to find the answer?

Add $88 + $7.50 to find the total cost for one person. Then multiply by 6.

$$\begin{array}{r} \$88.00 \\ +\ \ 7.50 \\ \hline \$95.50 \end{array}$$

The cost for one person is $95.50.

$$\begin{array}{r} \$95.50 \\ \times\ \ \ \ 6 \\ \hline \$573.00 \end{array}$$

The total cost for 6 people is $573.00.

Look back at the problem.

If you add 6 × $88 and 6 × $7.50, will your answer be the same? Tell why.

Standards NS 1.0, 2.0, 2.1 MR 1.0, 1.2, 2.0, 3.0

Dolphins are amazing divers! They can dive to depths of 1,000 feet and stay submerged for up to 15 minutes.

Remember:
- Understand
- Plan
- Solve
- Look Back

Guided Practice

Solve and check.

1. Seaview Tours charges $99 for scuba diving, 3 meals, and 2 snacks. Crystal Tours charges $75 for the scuba diving, plus $5 for each meal and $2.50 for each snack. Which company offers a better deal?

   Think: How can you find the total cost for Crystal Tours?

2. Under-the-Sea Tours has 8 boats. Each boat can carry up to 24 divers. If the company charges $99 per day for each diver, estimate the maximum amount of money the company could expect to receive one day.

   Think: Which number can you round to find 8×24 quickly?

Choose a Strategy

Solve. Use these or other strategies.

Problem-Solving Strategies

- **Guess and Check**
- **Find a Pattern**
- **Work Backward**
- **Write an Equation**

3. Divers on a tour are offered a souvenir sweatshirt for $18 or a T-shirt for $9. If the company sells 6 shirts for a total of $90, how many of each type of shirt did they sell?

4. The snack bar on the Crystal Tours boat sells sandwiches for $5.00 and drinks for $1.50. One day it sold $227 worth of food, including 48 drinks. How many sandwiches did it sell?

5. Jamal plans to take scuba-diving lessons before he goes diving. He has saved $380 to pay for everything. If lessons cost $250, how much will he have left for diving?

6. A company charges $38 to rent a diving suit and air tank for 1 day. For each additional day, they charge half price. How much would it cost to rent scuba gear for 4 days?

7. Under-the-Sea Tours rents underwater cameras for $45 for up to 1 day. If there are 15 customers on the half-day tour and 8 of them rent cameras, how much will the group pay in all?

8. Under-the-Sea Tours made $2,079 from a diving trip on which each customer paid $99 for a full day of diving. How many customers were on this trip?

Extra Practice See 10–13 on page 123.

Quick Check

Check Your Understanding of Lessons 5–9

Use mental math to find the product.

1. 30×7
2. 800×5
3. $3{,}000 \times 4$
4. 600×90
5. $3{,}000 \times 60$

Multiply.

6. 26×10
7. 54×30
8. 278×50
9. $6{,}359 \times 60$
10. $27{,}955 \times 40$

Solve.

11. Kelsey counted the total number of sides on some square pattern blocks. If there were 48 sides, how many blocks were there?

Multiply. Estimate to check that your answer is reasonable.

12. 37×12
13. 49×53
14. $\$2.95 \times 35$
15. 756×47
16. $8{,}168 \times 96$

Solve.

17. It costs $9.95 to go indoor rock climbing at a community center. The center also offers a group rate of $150 for up to 20 people. If 14 friends want to go rock climbing, is it cheaper or more expensive to pay the group rate? by how much?

How did you do?

If you had difficulty with any items in the Quick Check, you can use the following pages for review and extra practice.

California Standards	Items	Review These Pages	Do These Extra Practice Items
Number Sense: **1.0, 2.0** Math Reasoning: **2.1**	1–5	pages 106–108	Set D, page 121
Number Sense: **1.0, 2.0**	6–10	pages 110–111	Set E, page 122
Algebra and Functions: **1.1, 1.2** Math Reasoning: **2.3, 2.4, 3.2**	11	pages 112–113	5–9, page 123
Number Sense: **1.0, 2.0** Math Reasoning: **2.1**	12–16	pages 114–115	Set F, page 122
Math Reasoning: **1.1, 2.1, 2.4, 2.6, 3.1**	17	pages 116–117	10–13, page 123

Test Prep • Cumulative Review

Maintaining the Standards

Choose the letter of the correct answer.

1. Dustin is in charge of planning a luncheon. Of the 235 people expected to attend, 123 will be between the ages of 8 and 15. He plans to spend $12 for every person who attends. How much money does Dustin plan to spend?

   A $4,104 **C** $1,476
   B $2,820 **D** $1,344

2. Sue bought a teddy bear, a yo-yo, and a puzzle. She paid $26.42, including $1.26 tax. How much change should Sue receive if she gave the clerk $30?

   F $1.26 **H** $3.58
   G $2.32 **J** $4.84

3. Which is the greatest number?

   A 627,959 **C** 627,995
   B 967,995 **D** 2,267,599

4. Beth's dictionary has 1,586 pages. Bill's dictionary has 8 more pages than Beth's. Barry's dictionary has more pages than Bill's. Which question cannot be answered?

   F How many pages does Bill's dictionary have?
   G Who has the dictionary with the most pages?
   H How many pages does Barry's dictionary have?
   J Who has the dictionary with the fewest pages?

5. Tyler plays a question game. He will score 7 points for one correct answer, 8 points for two correct answers, 9 points for three correct answers, and so on. Which expression shows how many points Tyler will score for 10 correct answers?

   A $x \times 7$ **C** $x \times 6$
   B $x + 6$ **D** $x + 7$

6. Wesley made this table to show how the width of a rectangle compares to its length. Which equation could he write?

width (w)	length (l)
2	4
3	5
4	6

   F $4 + l = w$ **H** $w = l + 2$
   G $w = l + 4$ **J** $l = w + 2$

7. What is 839,679 rounded to the nearest million?

   A 800,000 **C** 1,000,000
   B 900,000 **D** 2,000,000

8. Tara used 5 whole rolls of film to take 144 photos at a family reunion. Some of the rolls had 36 exposures and some had 24 exposures. How many rolls of each kind did she use?

   Explain What strategy did you use to solve this problem?

Safe Site

Internet Test Prep
Visit **www.eduplace.com/kids/mhm** for more *Test Prep Practice.*

Extra Practice

Set A (Lesson 1, pages 96–97)

Draw and divide a rectangle to show each product. Use the Distributive Property to find the product.

1. 5×14 **2.** 8×23 **3.** 6×19 **4.** 7×15

5. 9×37 **6.** 4×46 **7.** 7×33 **8.** 8×27

Set B (Lesson 2, pages 98–99)

Multiply. Check your answer by estimating.

1. 35×7 **2.** 76×4 **3.** $\$69 \times 6$

4. 42×8 **5.** 632×7 **6.** $\$1.27 \times 6$

7. 858×4 **8.** 537×2 **9.** $4,216 \times 5$

10. $7,519 \times 4$ **11.** $3,468 \times 7$ **12.** $\$28.15 \times 3$

13. $2,153 \times 4$ **14.** $6,119 \times 3$ **15.** $9,273 \times 9$

16. 72×8 **17.** 647×3 **18.** $\$4.99 \times 6$

19. $2,949 \times 3$ **20.** $\$36.55 \times 9$ **21.** $2,564 \times 8$

Extra Practice

Set C (Lesson 3, pages 100–101)

Multiply. Check your answer by estimating.

1. 701×4
2. $\$6.06 \times 6$
3. 905×2
4. 402×9
5. $6{,}802 \times 5$
6. $4{,}073 \times 8$
7. $3{,}710 \times 3$
8. $9{,}067 \times 4$
9. $51{,}068 \times 7$
10. $67{,}209 \times 2$
11. $80{,}742 \times 5$
12. $55{,}360 \times 4$
13. 503×9
14. $5{,}003 \times 9$
15. $50{,}003 \times 9$

Set D (Lesson 5, pages 106–108)

Use mental math to find the product.

1. 60×8
2. 80×7
3. 40×9
4. 50×5
5. 200×4
6. 400×6
7. 700×3
8. 900×2
9. $8{,}000 \times 8$
10. $5{,}000 \times 9$
11. $6{,}000 \times 7$
12. $2{,}000 \times 5$
13. 300×20
14. 600×40
15. $2{,}000 \times 70$

Extra Practice

Set E (Lesson 6, pages 110–111)

Multiply.

1. 62×10
2. 47×30
3. 82×70
4. 61×50
5. 258×30
6. 567×60
7. $\$7.25 \times 40$
8. 308×60
9. $4{,}231 \times 70$
10. $\$62.50 \times 20$
11. $6{,}045 \times 30$
12. $3{,}287 \times 40$
13. 699×80
14. $\$3.98 \times 60$
15. $1{,}458 \times 50$

Set F (Lesson 8, pages 114–115)

Multiply. Check your answer by estimating.

1. 45×46
2. 37×82
3. 52×49
4. $\$75 \times 35$
5. 135×25
6. 427×68
7. $\$3.96 \times 73$
8. 514×98
9. $6{,}759 \times 81$
10. $3{,}812 \times 66$
11. $\$47.85 \times 32$
12. $6{,}697 \times 24$
13. 64×97
14. 289×71
15. $\$7.85 \times 42$

Extra Practice • Problem Solving

Solve by estimating or calculating. *(Lesson 4, pages 102–103)*

1. Carly saved $57 each month for six months. About how much money did she have at the end of the sixth month?

2. Four friends each ordered the daily lunch special at a restaurant. If the special cost $5.95, what was the total cost of the meal?

3. Mr. Suarez makes clay sculptures. At a craft fair, he sold 8 sculptures for $24.60 each. How much money did he earn from the sales?

4. The seats in a theater are sold out every night for five nights. If there are 2,050 seats in the theater, how many people will see the show?

Write an equation to solve each problem. *(Lesson 7, pages 112–113)*

5. When you multiply a mystery number by 7, the result is 490. What is the number?

6. Sixty identical tickets to a show cost a total of $540. How much does each ticket cost?

7. If you multiply Geena's age by 30, the result is 270. How old is Geena?

8. The rectangle at the right has an area of 240 square inches. How long is it?

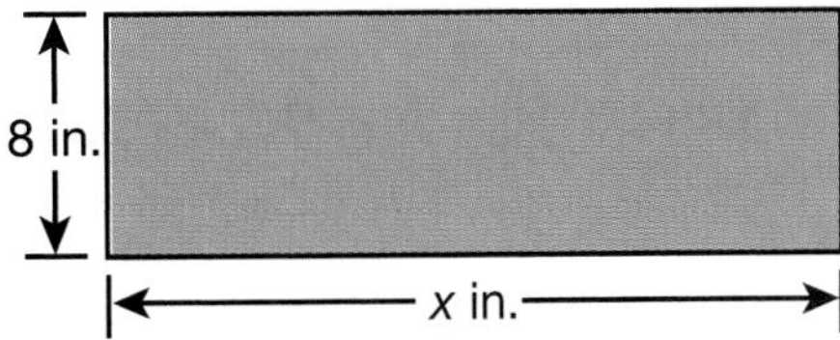

9. Billy bought 3 yards of rope that cost $2.59 a yard. How much change did Billy get from a $20 bill?

Solve. *(Lesson 9, pages 116–117)*

10. Vijay sells 4 CDs for $8.75 each and 5 CDs for $12.50 each. How much money does he receive from his customers?

11. Ride tickets sell for 75¢ apiece and it costs 3 tickets to ride the Ferris wheel. How much would it cost for 58 people to ride the Ferris wheel?

12. Mario's grandmother tells him that, as a graduation present, she will give him double any amount of money he manages to save during the month of June. He earns $45 in June, but he spends $18.50. How much will his grandmother give him?

13. The regular price of a room at a hotel is $85, but guests who stay three days can get a special rate of $210 for their whole stay. What is the difference in price between the special three-day rate and the cost if the regular price were paid for three days?

Chapter Review

Reviewing Vocabulary

Write *always, sometimes,* or *never* for each question. Give an example to support your answer.

1. When you change the order of the factors, the product will also change.
2. If the ones digit of one factor is zero, there will be a zero in the ones digit of the product.
3. When you multiply any whole number by a multiple of ten, the ones digit in the product is zero.
4. The product in multiplication will have more digits than either factor.

Write a definition.

5. Distributive Property
6. partial product
7. multiple of ten

Reviewing Concepts and Skills

Multiply. Check your answer by estimating. *(pages 98–101)*

8. 47×6
9. 32×3
10. $\$65 \times 9$
11. 383×4
12. $\$5.64 \times 7$
13. 455×8
14. $8{,}620 \times 5$
15. 503×2
16. $\$30.75 \times 6$
17. $\$93.06 \times 8$
18. $6{,}045 \times 7$
19. $9{,}704 \times 4$

Complete each multiplication pattern. *(pages 106–108)*

20. 7×6
21. 7×60
22. 7×600
23. $7 \times 6{,}000$
24. 50×8
25. 50×80
26. 50×800
27. $50 \times 8{,}000$

28. 62 × 7

29. 62 × 70

30. 62 × 700

31. 62 × 7,000

32. 457 × 9

33. 457 × 90

34. 457 × 900

35. 457 × 9,000

Multiply. Check your answer by estimating. *(pages 110–111, 114–115)*

36. 82 × 50

37. 425 × 30

38. 512 × 80

39. 372 × 20

40. 79 × 47

41. 695 × 76

42. 358 × 54

43. 742 × 66

44. 2,387 × 59

45. 7,921 × 32

46. 9,615 × 84

47. 1,386 × 28

Answer by estimating or calculating. *(pages 102–103, 112–113, 116–117)*

48. Each student in the class pays $27.50 for a field trip. If there are 31 students, how much will they pay in all?

49. Admission to an in-line skating rink is $3.25 per student. Will $150 be enough to pay the admission for 40 students?

50. A hotdog stand sells hotdogs for $2.25 and drinks for $1.00. If $204 worth of food was sold, including 78 drinks, how many hotdogs were sold?

Brain Teasers Math Reasoning

Find the Factors

The product of three consecutive numbers is about 24,000. What are the numbers?

One Thousand One

Multiply several two-digit numbers by 1,001. What pattern can you find? Why does the pattern work?

Internet Brain Teasers
Visit **www.eduplace.com/kids/mhm** for more *Brain Teasers.*

Chapter Test

Multiply. Check your answer by estimating.

1. 65×3

2. $\$42 \times 8$

3. 717×9

4. 32×4

5. 465×6

6. $5{,}685 \times 3$

7. $\$40.18 \times 4$

8. $7{,}952 \times 5$

9. $6{,}072 \times 8$

10. $2{,}907 \times 4$

11. $7{,}420 \times 2$

12. $8{,}012 \times 9$

13. 95×20

14. 83×40

15. 246×60

16. $1{,}985 \times 30$

17. 582×70

18. $2{,}831 \times 80$

19. 79×50

20. $4{,}482 \times 90$

Multiply. Check your answer by estimating.

21. 54×89

22. 72×13

23. 456×97

24. 235×15

25. $5{,}289 \times 43$

26. $9{,}439 \times 21$

27. $8{,}356 \times 78$

28. $4{,}326 \times 62$

29. 419×77

30. $5{,}309 \times 23$

31. $1{,}023 \times 64$

32. $3{,}997 \times 46$

33. $2{,}601 \times 85$

34. $\$15.95 \times 18$

35. $1{,}478 \times 66$

36. 51×307

37. $89 \times 1{,}042$

38. $27 \times \$17.95$

Solve.

39. Kelly makes fancy wreaths for people's front doors and sells them for $23.50 each. If she sells 47 wreaths, how much money will she receive from her customers?

40. The Green River in Kentucky is 360 miles long. The Arkansas River is about four times as long as the Green River. How long is the Arkansas River?

Write About It

Solve each problem. Use correct math vocabulary to explain your thinking.

1. Explain.

a. What is the Distributive Property?

b. How are you using the Distributive Property when you multiply one two-digit number by another?

2. Steve completed this multiplication.

a. Explain what he did wrong.

b. Show how to find the correct product.

$$\begin{array}{r} \scriptstyle 4 \\ 56 \\ \times\ 38 \\ \hline 448 \\ +\ 168 \\ \hline 616 \end{array}$$

3. Explain the steps you would use to find each product.

a. a three-digit number is multiplied by 1,000

b. a two-digit number is multiplied by 60

c. $52.36 is multiplied by 24

4. Describe three different situations where you would need to estimate the product of two numbers.

Another Look

Kira made this shopping list of supplies for her new pet-sitting business.

Shopping List

6 pet dishes	3 leashes
10 brushes	25 pet toys
6 water bottles	3 pairs of nail clippers
3 bags of pine shavings	2 rabbit cages

At the pet store, she found this list of prices.

Pet Dish	$2.75	Pine Shavings	$5.98
Leash	$6.25	Pet Toys	$5.98
Rabbit Cage	$79.99	Dog Food	$6.99
Water Bottle	$5.80	Cat Food	$0.59
Nail Clippers	$3.68	Rabbit Food	$4.69
Brush	$6.00	Bird Seed	$3.95

Solve.

1. What was the cost of all the supplies Kira bought?
2. During the first month her business was open, Kira used 4 bags of dog food, 36 cans of cat food, and 8 bags of rabbit food. What was the total cost of the food for the animals?
3. Find the total cost of all the items Kira bought for her business, including food.
4. In her first month, Kira looked after 6 dogs, 4 cats, and 10 rabbits for five days each. She charges $10 a day for each animal. Did Kira earn enough money to cover her expenses and give her some profit? If so, about how much was the profit?

Standards	NS **1.0, 2.0, 2.1** MR **1.0, 2.0, 2.1**

Enrichment

Multiply by 11

There's a shortcut you can use to multiply any number by 11.

Here's how to find 36,795 × 11.

Step 1 Multiply the number by 1.	**Step 2** Multiply the number by 10.	**Step 3** Add the results from Steps 1 and 2.
36,795 × 1 = 36,795	36,795 × 10 = 367,950	36,795 + 367,950 404,745

To multiply any number by 11, add the number to 10 times itself.

Use the shortcut to find each product.

1. 23 × 11 **2.** 654 × 11 **3.** 999 × 11 **4.** 7,280 × 11

5. 62,459 × 11 **6.** 83,530 × 11 **7.** 514,677 × 11 **8.** 558,999 × 11

9. How could you adapt this method to multiply any number by 111?

10. What shortcut could you use to multiply any number by 22?

11. What shortcut could you use to multiply any number by 444?

Use a shortcut to find each product.

12. 57 × 33 **13.** 29 × 77 **14.** 345 × 55 **15.** 2,475 × 88

16. 754 × 111 **17.** 459 × 333 **18.** 529 × 888 **19.** 620 × 999

Explain Your Thinking

► Explain how you can use a shortcut in any multiplication where all the digits in one of the factors are the same.

► What other shortcut could you use to multiply any number by 9? by 99?

Standards NS **1.0** MR **1.0, 1.1, 1.2**

Division and Equations

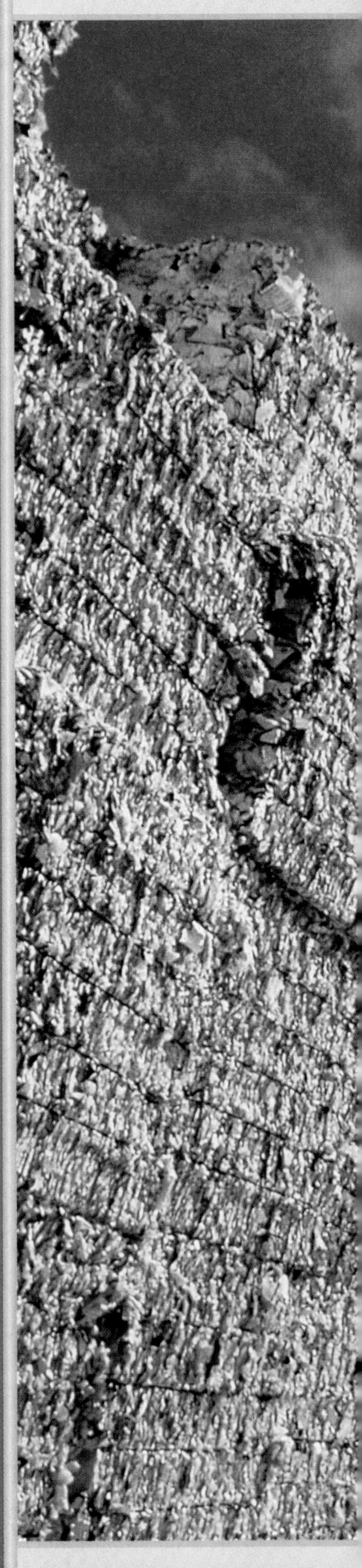

Why Learn About Division and Equations?

Division is used in many situations where it is important to have equal groups of things. Using equations can help you find answers to questions that involve patterns.

When you go on a hike, you can divide the distance you hike by the number of hours it takes to find your average hiking speed.

At this recycling plant, paper is bundled into equal-sized bales. The plant operators can find the number of bales they can make by dividing the total weight of the paper by the weight of one bale.

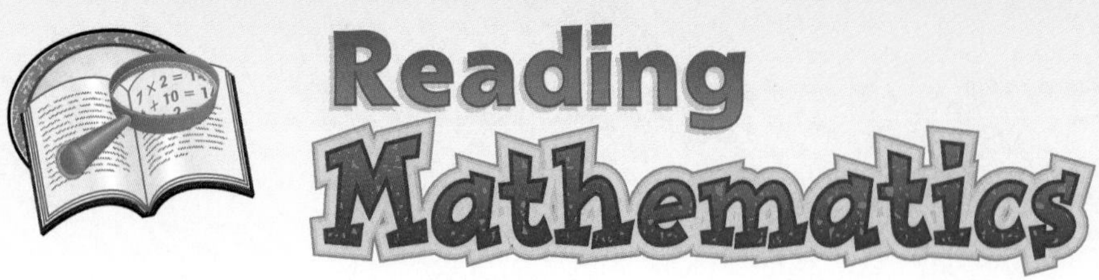

Reviewing Vocabulary

Understanding math language helps you become a successful problem solver. Here are some math vocabulary words you should know.

dividend the number that is divided in division

divisor the number by which a number is being divided

quotient the answer in division

remainder the number left over after one number is divided by another

mean the sum of a set of numbers divided by the number of addends

Distributive Property when you multiply two addends by a factor, the answer is the same as if you multiply each addend by the factor and then add the products

function a rule that shows how to use one or more operations with one number to get another number

function table a table that shows the numbers and the results for a function

Reading Words and Symbols

When you read mathematics, sometimes you read only words, sometimes you read words and symbols, and sometimes you read only symbols.

All of these statements represent the same problem.

- Twelve divided by four
- 12 divided by 4
- $12 \div 4$
- $4\overline{)12}$
- $4 \times ■ = 12$

Try These

1. Tell if ■ represents the divisor, the dividend, or the quotient. Then find the value of ■.

   a. $\begin{array}{r} \blacksquare \\ 4\overline{)36} \end{array}$ **b.** $\begin{array}{r} \blacksquare \\ 6\overline{)48} \end{array}$ **c.** $\begin{array}{r} 4 \\ 7\overline{)\blacksquare} \end{array}$

   d. $72 \div 8 = \blacksquare$ **e.** $35 \div \blacksquare = 5$ **f.** $\blacksquare \div 7 = 8$

2. Write *true* or *false* for each statement.

   a. When you divide counting numbers, the dividend is always less than the quotient.

   b. When you divide counting numbers, the divisor is never larger than the quotient.

   c. If you know the quotient and the divisor, you can always find the dividend.

   d. If there is no remainder, you can switch the divisor and the quotient and the resulting statement will still be true.

   e. The divisor in a division statement can never be zero.

   f. The quotient in a division statement can never be zero.

3. Fill in each ■ with numbers that work.

   a. If ■ is the **dividend** and ■ is the **divisor**, then the **quotient** is ■.

   b. If ■ is the **dividend** and 3 is the **divisor**, then ■ is the **quotient** and ■ is the remainder.

Upcoming Vocabulary

Write About It **Here are some other vocabulary words** you will learn in this chapter. Watch for these words. Write their definitions in your journal.

inverse operations

One-Digit Divisors

You will learn how thinking about place value helps you divide.

Review Vocabulary
quotient
remainder

Learn About It

Single servings of yogurt are sold in packages of 4. How many packages can be made from 378 single servings? How many servings are left over?

Divide. **378 ÷ 4** $\quad 4\overline{)378}$

Find 378 ÷ 4.

Step 1 Decide where to place the first digit of the **quotient.**

Think: $4\overline{)3\text{ hundreds}}$? hundreds

4 > 3 There are not enough hundreds to divide.

$4\overline{)378}$

37 > 4 Place the first digit in the tens place.

Step 2 Divide the tens.

Think: $4\overline{)37\text{ tens}}$? tens

$$\begin{array}{r} 9 \\ 4\overline{)378} \\ -\,36 \\ \hline 1 \end{array}$$

Multiply. 9 × 4
Subtract. 37 − 36
Compare. 1 < 4

Step 3 Bring down the ones. Divide the ones. Write the **remainder.**

Think: $4\overline{)18\text{ ones}}$? ones

$$\begin{array}{r} 94\text{ R2} \\ 4\overline{)378} \\ -\,36 \\ \hline 18 \\ -\,16 \\ \hline 2 \end{array}$$

The remainder is 2.
Bring down 8 ones.
Multiply. 4 × 4
Subtract. 18 − 16
Compare. 2 < 4

Check: Multiply. Then add.

(94 × 4) + 2 = 378
The sum equals the dividend, so the quotient and remainder are correct.

Solution: You can make 94 packages of yogurt from 378 single servings. There will be 2 servings left over.

Other Examples

A. Dividing Money

$$\begin{array}{r} \$\ 27.15 \\ 5\overline{)\$135.75} \\ -\,10 \\ \hline 35 \\ -\,35 \\ \hline 07 \\ -\,5 \\ \hline 25 \\ -\,25 \\ \hline 0 \end{array}$$

Check:

$$\begin{array}{r} \$\ 27.15 \\ \times\quad\ 5 \\ \hline \$135.75 \end{array}$$

B. Zeros in the Dividend

$$\begin{array}{r} 718\text{ R1} \\ 6\overline{)4{,}309} \\ -\,42 \\ \hline 10 \\ -\,6 \\ \hline 49 \\ -\,48 \\ \hline 1 \end{array}$$

Check:

$$\begin{array}{r} 718 \\ \times\quad 6 \\ \hline 4{,}308 \\ +\quad\ 1 \\ \hline 4{,}309 \end{array}$$

Explain Your Thinking

- ▶ Why must the remainder always be less than the divisor?
- ▶ How is the answer check in Example B different from Example A?

Guided Practice

Divide.

1. $6\overline{)582}$ **2.** $8\overline{)9{,}614}$ **3.** $5\overline{)4{,}217}$

4. $26.16 ÷ 4 **5.** 8,104 ÷ 7 **6.** 9,642 ÷ 9

Ask Yourself

- Can I divide the first digit in the dividend?
- Where should I write the first digit?

Independent Practice

Divide.

7. $6\overline{)550}$ **8.** $5\overline{)\$2.85}$ **9.** $3\overline{)702}$ **10.** $7\overline{)6{,}387}$

11. $4\overline{)\$58.20}$ **12.** $8\overline{)5{,}975}$ **13.** $9\overline{)36{,}217}$ **14.** $3\overline{)45{,}809}$

15. $9\overline{)\$582.39}$ **16.** $6\overline{)793{,}481}$ **17.** $9\overline{)867{,}042}$ **18.** $7\overline{)\$4{,}124.47}$

19. 894 ÷ 4 **20.** 763 ÷ 2 **21.** $48.72 ÷ 3 **22.** 8,067 ÷ 5

23. $567.12 ÷ 6 **24.** 62,384 ÷ 8 **25.** 715,482 ÷ 9 **26.** 860,174 ÷ 7

Problem Solving • Reasoning

27. On average, each American eats about 5 kg of chocolate a year. When Catherine read this, she said that the students in her class would eat about 165 kg a year. How many students are in her class?

28. **Estimate** A case of pudding packages sells for $31.68. If each package costs $1.98, how many packages are in a case?

29. **Analyze** The Grocery Stop is offering a special price for chocolate pudding–three packs (with four servings in each pack) for $5.80. At that price, what is the cost of each serving?

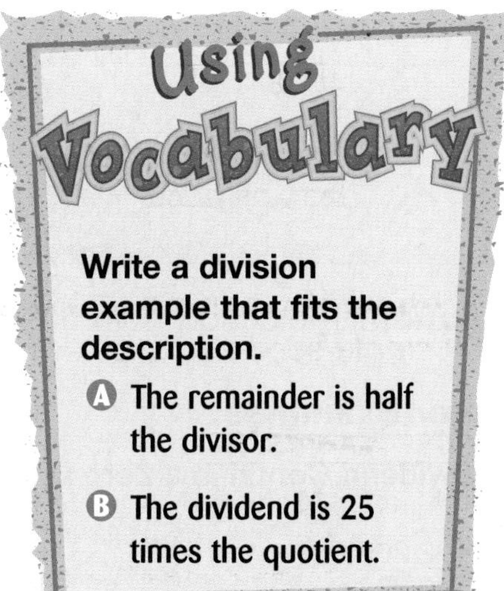

Mixed Review • Test Prep

Write the value of the underlined digit. *(pages 4–5, 14–15)*

30. 1,$\underline{8}$40 **31.** 4$\underline{2}$3,578 **32.** $\underline{6}$97,852,421 **33.** 1$\underline{2}$,890,124,562

34 What is the difference between 872 and 349? *(pages 54–55)*

A 523 **B** 533 **C** 537 **D** 1,221

Zeros in the Quotient

You will learn when to put zeros in the quotient.

Learn About It

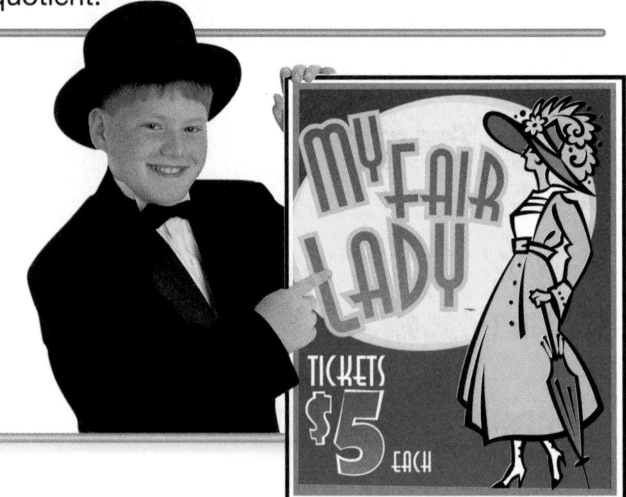

Tickets to a school production of *My Fair Lady* cost \$5. If the school took in a total of \$2,515, how many tickets were sold?

Divide. **2,515 ÷ 5 = *n*** **5)2,515**

Find 2,515 ÷ 5.

Step 1 Decide where to place the first digit of the quotient. Then divide.

Think: 5)2 thousands → ? thousands

There are not enough thousands to divide.

Think: 5)25 hundreds → ? hundreds

```
    5
 5)2,515
 - 25    Multiply. 5 × 5
    0    Subtract. 25 − 25
         Compare. 0 < 5
```

Step 2 Bring down the tens. Divide the tens.

Think: 5)1 ten → ? ten

There are not enough tens to divide.

```
    50
 5)2,515   Write 0 in the tens
 - 25↓     place to show that the
    01     quotient has 0 tens.
```

Step 3 Bring down the ones. Divide the ones.

Think: 5)15 ones → ? ones

```
    503
 5)2,515
 - 25 ↓
    015   Multiply. 3 × 5
   - 15   Subtract. 15 − 15
      0   There is no remainder.
```

Check: Multiply.

503 × 5 = 2,515

Solution: The school sold 503 tickets.

Other Examples

A. Dividend Contains a Zero Digit

```
   2,265 R3
 4)9,063
 - 8↓
   10   ← Bring down the zero from
  - 8     the hundreds place.
    26
  - 24
     23
   - 20
      3
```

B. Divide Into Zero

```
     700 R4
 7)4,904
  - 49↓
     00  ← The result is 0, but there are
    - 0    more places to divide. Write 0
     04    in the quotient, because
    - 0    0 tens ÷ 7 = 0 tens, and continue.
      4
```

Explain Your Thinking

- ▶ In Example A, what would happen if you did not bring down the zero?
- ▶ In Example B, why does the division continue after you get a result of zero?

Guided Practice

Ask Yourself

- Where do I write the first digit?
- How do I know when the division is done?

Divide.

1. $7\overline{)284}$ **2.** $4\overline{)3,602}$ **3.** $8\overline{)34,421}$

4. 301 ÷ 5 **5.** 2,881 ÷ 3 **6.** 240,120 ÷ 6

Independent Practice

Divide.

7. $7\overline{)568}$ **8.** $3\overline{)624}$ **9.** $2\overline{)801}$ **10.** $8\overline{)5,632}$

11. $4\overline{)3,603}$ **12.** $8\overline{)4,803}$ **13.** $7\overline{)28,210}$ **14.** $5\overline{)43,004}$

15. 70,200 ÷ 9 **16.** 63,564 ÷ 7 **17.** 627,153 ÷ 3 **18.** 457,287 ÷ 9

Problem Solving • Reasoning

19. **Analyze** A school production of *Oklahoma!* played for two nights. Tickets sold for $9. The play raised $3,213 the first night and $3,249 the second night. How many tickets were sold?

20. **Compare** The Star Theater sells tickets for $5 and can seat an audience of 1,152. The Bright Circle Theater sells tickets for $8 and earns $5,440 when every seat is sold. Which theater has more seats?

21. One of the longest running shows on Broadway was *Grease*, which was performed 3,388 times over 7 years. On average, about how many times was the show performed in each year?

22. The movie version of *My Fair Lady* was released in 1964. Kelsey has watched the movie 7 times, for a total of 1,190 min. How long is the movie?

Mixed Review • Test Prep

Solve. *(pages 52–53, 54–55, 98–99)*

23. 6,974 + 3,429 **24.** 8,342 − 6,987 **25.** 387 × 6 **26.** 2,284 × 5

27 What is the product of 315 and 4? *(pages 98–99)*

A 319 **B** 1,240 **C** 1,260 **D** 12,420

Extra Practice See Set B on page 178.

LESSON 3 Estimate Quotients

You will learn how to estimate quotients, using basic multiplication facts.

Learn About It

Marta is decorating a pair of jeans with colored beads. At the craft store, she buys 6 packages of beads in different colors. If there are 2,340 beads in all, about how many beads are in each package?

Estimate. $2{,}340 \div 6 = n$ $\quad 6\overline{)2{,}340}$

To estimate the quotient, you can use numbers that are easy to divide mentally.

Estimate 2,340 ÷ 6.

Step 1 Decide where to place the first digit of the quotient. Then use basic multiplication facts to find a multiple of the divisor that is close to the dividend.

$$\begin{array}{r} \text{? hundreds} \\ 6\overline{)2{,}340} \end{array}$$

Think: What value of n makes $6 \times n$ close to 23?

$6 \times 4 = 24$

24 is close to 23.

Step 2 Use basic facts and multiples of 10 to estimate.

$$\begin{array}{r} 400 \\ 6\overline{)2{,}400} \end{array}$$

2,400 is close to the dividend.

The estimated quotient is 400.

Solution: There are about 400 beads in each package.

Other Examples

A. Three-Digit Dividend

$$5\overline{)347} \longrightarrow \begin{array}{r} 70 \\ 5\overline{)350} \end{array}$$

$347 \div 5$ is about 70.

B. Five-Digit Dividend

$$4\overline{)21{,}654} \longrightarrow \begin{array}{r} 5{,}000 \\ 4\overline{)20{,}000} \end{array}$$

$21{,}654 \div 4$ is about 5,000.

Explain Your Thinking

- In each case, is the estimated quotient too large or too small?
- Without doing all of the division, how do you know how many digits there will be in a quotient?

Standards NS **1.0, 2.2** AF **1.0, 1.2** MR **2.0, 2.1**

Guided Practice

Estimate the quotient. Tell what numbers you used for the dividend and the divisor.

1. $8\overline{)658}$ **2.** $5\overline{)2,674}$ **3.** $4\overline{)17,000}$

4. 2,274 ÷ 3 **5.** 36,140 ÷ 7 **6.** 563,217 ÷ 9

> **Ask Yourself**
> - What multiplication fact will help me?
> - How many digits should be in the estimated quotient?

Independent Practice

Estimate the quotient.

7. $7\overline{)223}$ **8.** $8\overline{)334}$ **9.** $9\overline{)713}$ **10.** $5\overline{)4,400}$

11. $7\overline{)1,498}$ **12.** $8\overline{)4,109}$ **13.** $3\overline{)15,210}$ **14.** $9\overline{)42,825}$

15. $8\overline{)39,041}$ **16.** $6\overline{)162,400}$ **17.** $9\overline{)340,000}$ **18.** $4\overline{)294,020}$

19. 248 ÷ 5 **20.** 209 ÷ 3 **21.** 2,500 ÷ 6 **22.** 3,512 ÷ 4

23. 16,945 ÷ 7 **24.** 46,120 ÷ 8 **25.** 640,000 ÷ 9 **26.** 491,342 ÷ 8

Problem Solving • Reasoning

27. **Analyze** A package of beads costs 85¢. If you have $4.80, can you buy 6 packages? Explain how you can use estimation to decide.

28. A bead pattern has 8 rows. If there are 336 beads in the pattern, about how many beads are in each row?

29. **Estimate** A beaded gown costs $2,148. That gown is five times as expensive as a second beaded gown. About how much does the second gown cost?

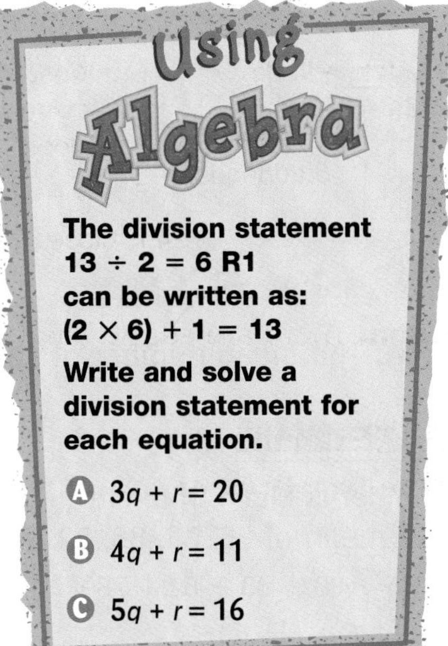

Mixed Review • Test Prep

Solve. *(pages 58–59, 60–61)*

30. 1.58 + 3.7 **31.** 6.784 − 2.49 **32.** 3.871 + 2.7 **33.** 6.4 + 4.72

Choose the letter of the correct answer. *(pages 98–99, 134–135)*

34 Solve for *n*. 129 × 6 = *n*

A 135 **C** 674
B 624 **D** 774

35 Solve for *m*. 1,107 ÷ 9 = *m*

F 23 **H** 223
G 123 **J** 323

Extra Practice See Set C on page 178.

Find the Mean

You will learn that the mean value is a single number that helps you represent a whole group of numbers.

Review Vocabulary
mean

Learn About It

What is the mean number of strikes for the top five bowlers on this team?

The **mean** tells you how many strikes each player would have if the total stayed the same and all the players had the same number of strikes.

To find the mean, first find the sum of the numbers. Then divide by the number of addends.

TOP FIVE BOWLERS

Name	Strikes
Pablo Gonzales	48
Erica Walker	46
Alfonso Montez	44
Maria Rivera	35
Allan Davidson	32

Find the mean of 48, 46, 44, 35, and 32.

Step 1 Add all the numbers.

$$\begin{array}{r} 48 \\ 46 \\ 44 \\ 35 \\ +\ 32 \\ \hline 205 \end{array}$$

There are 5 addends.

Step 2 Divide the sum by the number of addends.

$$5\overline{)205} = 41$$

Step 3 Check that your answer is reasonable.

The mean, 41, is between the smallest number, 32, and the largest, 48.

Solution: The mean number of strikes for these bowlers is 41.

Another Example

One Number Is Much Different

Find the mean of 85, 83, 86, 82, 78, and 12.

Add: $85 + 83 + 86 + 82 + 78 + 12 = 426$

Divide: $426 \div 6 = 71$

The mean is 71.

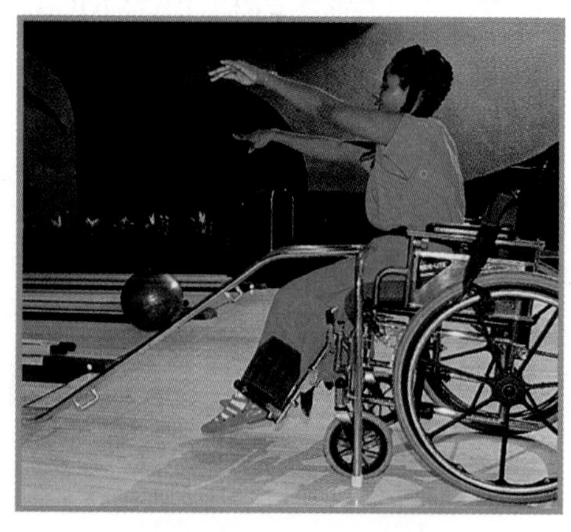

Explain Your Thinking

- Why is the mean for the set of numbers in Another Example less than most of the numbers?
- Is the mean a good representative for this set of numbers in Another Example? Why or why not?

Guided Practice

Find the mean.

1. 2, 3, 7, 8, 10

2. 4, 11, 4, 6, 3, 8

3. $85, $37, $94

4. 170, 187, 153, 170

Ask Yourself

- Did I divide by the correct number of addends?
- Is my answer reasonable?

Independent Practice

Find the mean. Compare with the set of numbers to make sure the answer is reasonable.

5. 3, 5, 7, 8, 12

6. 9, 9, 16, 16, 20, 20

7. 29, 10, 15, 18

8. $36, $56, $85

9. 82, 92, 70, 98, 84, 90

10. 28, 8, 30, 35, 66, 54, 45

11. 70, 50, 30, 20, 40, 20, 60, 30, 40

12. 72, 65, 36, 57, 87, 97, 57, 65

13. 110, 108, 98, 60, 139

14. 100, 200, 300, 300

15. 150, 255, 558

16. 152, 453, 202, 129

17. 503, 922, 512, 361, 837

18. 204, 205, 238, 98, 105, 128

Problem Solving • Reasoning

Use Data **Use the table for Problems 19 and 20.**

19. What is the mean bowling score?

20. **Analyze** A bowling game is the sum of the scores in 10 frames. What was Juan's mean score in a frame?

21. **Write About It** After playing one game, three people have a mean bowling score of 142. What could their individual scores be?

Bowling Scores	
Marty	148
Dana	162
Aileen	214
Juan	210
Geoff	234
Paul	166

Mixed Review • Test Prep

Solve. *(pages 162–164)*

22. $678 + (8 \times 4) = n$

23. $(81 \div 9) \times 3 = n$

24. $(49 \div 7) - 7 = n$

Choose the letter of the correct answer. *(4–5, 24–25)*

25 What is the value of the 6 in 1,316,894?

A 6 **C** 6,000

B 600 **D** 60,000

26 What is the value of the 6 in 23.561?

F 6 ones **H** 6 hundredths

G 6 tenths **J** 6 tens

Extra Practice See Set D on page 178.

Problem-Solving Skill: Interpret Remainders

You will learn how to solve problems involving remainders.

When you solve a problem that has a remainder, you need to decide how to interpret the remainder.

Look at the situations below.

Sometimes you increase the quotient.

One hundred three hikers sign up for a hike. Each group can have a maximum of 8 people. How many hiking groups will there be?

$$8\overline{)103} = 12 \text{ R}7$$

There will be 12 full groups of 8 people. Another group is needed for the last 7 hikers. In all, there will be 13 hiking groups.

Sometimes you drop the remainder.

After the hike, the participants feasted on 309 slices of pizza. If each whole pizza contains 6 slices, how many whole pizzas did they eat?

$$6\overline{)309} = 51 \text{ R}3$$

The hikers ate 51 whole pizzas.

Sometimes the remainder is the answer.

There are 57 life jackets available for white-water rafting. Each raft must have 8 life jackets. How many spare life jackets are there?

$$8\overline{)57} = 7 \text{ R}1$$

There is 1 spare life jacket.

Look Back Why does thinking about the questions in each situation help you decide what to do with the remainder?

Standards | NS **2.2** MR **1.0, 2.0, 2.6, 3.0, 3.1**

An amphitheater in Red Rocks Park west of Denver, Colorado.

Guided Practice

Solve.

1. The park rangers are cutting 7-foot lengths of rope. How many lengths of rope can they make from 85 feet of rope?

   Think: Can a length be made with less than 7 feet?

2. An outdoor amphitheater has 300 seats. The seats are in groups of 8 plus one smaller group. How many seats are in the smaller group?

   Think: Will the answer be less than 8 or more than 8?

Choose a Strategy

Solve. Use these or other strategies.

Problem-Solving Strategies

- **Guess and Check**
- **Work Backward**
- **Write an Equation**
- **Make a Table**

3. Rita took 71 photographs on her camping trip, and she wants to put them in an album. If each page holds 6 pictures, how many pages will she need for her photographs?

4. Together, Kamala and Fallon have handed out 64 camping brochures. Kamala handed out 6 more brochures than Fallon. How many brochures did each girl hand out?

5. Miguel made 40 sandwiches for his hiking group. He made half as many sandwiches with peanut butter as with strawberry jam. The rest are cheese sandwiches. He made 9 peanut butter sandwiches. How many cheese sandwiches did he make?

6. Anna Louise took 96 pictures of her camping trip. She used up twice as many rolls of 12 pictures as rolls of 24. How many of each size did she use? Jessica used the same number of the shorter rolls as Anna Louise. How many pictures did Jessica take?

7. Forty children are going on a hike, and each child will be given 2 energy bars. One box contains 6 bars. How many boxes of energy bars are needed for the hike?

8. Connor bought some shirts for his camping trip. The sweatshirts cost $16 and the T-shirts cost $10. If he spent $46, how many of each type of shirt did Connor buy?

Extra Practice See 1–4 on page 181.

Quick Check

Check Your Understanding of Lessons 1–5

Divide.

1. $9\overline{)585}$ **2.** $6\overline{)1,946}$ **3.** \$24.90 ÷ 6 **4.** $3\overline{)10,763}$

Divide.

5. $7\overline{)9,945}$ **6.** $6\overline{)3,016}$ **7.** \$40.20 ÷ 5 **8.** $7\overline{)22,052}$

Estimate the quotient.

9. $4\overline{)852}$ **10.** $7\overline{)36,512}$ **11.** $8\overline{)2,248}$ **12.** $6\overline{)47,994}$

Find the mean. Compare with the set of numbers to make sure the answer is reasonable.

13. 6, 12, 15, 15, 22 **14.** 645, 285, 314, 298, 580, 602

Solve.

15. Dara is ordering sticks of glitter glue for her craft store. Last month, the store sold 723 sticks. If the sticks come in packages of 8, how many packages will Dara need to order to replace what was sold?

How did you do?

If you had difficulty with any items in the Quick Check, you can use the following pages for review and extra practice.

California Standards	Items	Review These Pages	Do These Extra Practice Items
Number Sense: **1.0, 2.0, 2.1, 2.2**	1–4	pages 134–135	Set A, page 178
Number Sense: **1.0, 2.2**	5–8	pages 136–137	Set B, page 178
Number Sense: **1.0, 2.2** Math Reasoning: **2.5**	9–12	pages 138–139	Set C, page 178
Number Sense: **1.0, 2.2** Statistics, Data, Probability: **1.1**	13–14	pages 140–141	Set D, page 178
Math Reasoning: **1.1, 2.6, 3.1**	15	pages 142–143	1–4, page 181

Test Prep • Cumulative Review

Maintaining the Standards

Choose the letter of the correct answer.

1. Divide. $8.64 ÷ 4

   A $216 **C** $2.16

   B $21.60 **D** $2.11

2. If the following 1996 city populations were ordered from greatest to least, which would be the fourth population in the series?

City	Population
Mexico City	9,815,795
Jakarta, Indonesia	9,160,500
Bombay, India	9,925,891
Sao Paulo, Brazil	9,393,753
Shanghai, China	8,930,000

   F Bombay **H** Jakarta

   G Shanghai **J** Mexico City

3. In May, 42,872 people visited a Web site. In June, 18,305 people visited the same Web site. Estimate how many more visitors there were in May than in June.

   A 25,000 **C** 43,000

   B 30,000 **D** 60,000

4. Harrison is going to buy 3 shirts. Each shirt costs $18.79. How much should he expect to pay the clerk?

   F about $40.00

   G about $60.00

   H about $75.00

   J about $100.00

5. Sabrina's English grades are 85, 89, 90, 93, 94, and 71. Find her mean grade.

   A 94 **C** 87

   B 92 **D** 71

6. A shelf can hold a maximum of 30 pounds. Which 3 items can be put on the shelf at the same time?

Item	Weight in Pounds
1	14.95
2	14.89
3	7.008
4	8.056

   F items 1, 2, and 3

   G items 1, 2, and 4

   H items 2, 3, and 4

   J items 1, 3, and 4

7. Which value for *r* makes this statement true?

   $36 \times 7 = (30 \times 7) + (r \times 7)$

   A 36 **C** 7

   B 30 **D** 6

8. A shoe manufacturer can put, at most, 7 pairs of shoes into each shipping box. To fill an order for 307 pairs of shoes, Marla says they will need 43 shipping boxes. Jason says they need 44. Who is right?

   Explain How do you know?

Internet Test Prep
Visit **www.eduplace.com/kids/mhm** for more *Test Prep Practice.*

Divide by Multiples of 10, 100, and 1,000

You will learn how to use patterns and mental math to divide by multiples of 10, 100, and 1,000.

Learn About It

In 8 hours, the moon travels about 16,000 miles. How far does the moon travel in one hour?

Basic division facts and patterns will help you divide, using mental math.

Divide. **16,000 ÷ 8 = *n***

Find 16,000 ÷ 8.

16 ÷ 8 = 2
160 ÷ 8 = 20
1,600 ÷ 8 = 200
16,000 ÷ 8 = 2,000

Think: What do you notice about the pattern of zeros?

Solution: The moon travels about 2,000 miles in 1 hour.

Another Example

Dividend and Divisor Are Multiples of 10

Find 28,000 ÷ 7,000

28 ÷ 7 = 4
280 ÷ 70 = 4
2,800 ÷ 700 = 4
28,000 ÷ 7,000 = 4

Think: Is the pattern of zero's the same as above?

Explain Your Thinking

► In Another Example, the quotient is always 4. How do the dividend and divisor change?

Guided Practice

Divide. Use mental math.

1. 800 ÷ 4 **2.** 3,500 ÷ 5 **3.** 6,000 ÷ 20

4. $7\overline{)49{,}000}$ **5.** $30\overline{)9{,}000}$ **6.** $50\overline{)4{,}000}$

7. $800\overline{)6{,}400}$ **8.** $900\overline{)36{,}000}$ **9.** 200,000 ÷ 4,000

Ask Yourself

- Which basic division fact should I use?
- Did I write the correct number of zeros?

Independent Practice

Divide. Use mental math. Check by multiplying.

10. 280 ÷ 70 **11.** 540 ÷ 90 **12.** 18,000 ÷ 600

13. 4,800 ÷ 800 **14.** 24,000 ÷ 8,000 **15.** 32,000 ÷ 40

16. 10,000 ÷ 2,000 **17.** 2,700 ÷ 3 **18.** 630,000 ÷ 900

19. 2,500 ÷ 50 **20.** 42,000 ÷ 7,000 **21.** 3,000 ÷ 60

22. 480,000 ÷ 60 **23.** 81,000 ÷ 900 **24.** 490,000 ÷ 70

25. 180,000 ÷ 2,000 **26.** 56,000 ÷ 8,000 **27.** 36,000 ÷ 600

28. $80\overline{)64{,}000}$ **29.** $300\overline{)900{,}000}$ **30.** $1{,}000\overline{)700{,}000}$

31. $700\overline{)140{,}000}$ **32.** $50\overline{)25{,}000}$ **33.** $4{,}000\overline{)120{,}000}$

Problem Solving • Reasoning

34. The distance around Earth is about four times the distance around the Moon. If the distance around Earth is about 24,000 miles, what is the distance around the Moon?

35. The distance from Earth to the Moon is about 240,000 miles. The *Ulysses* spacecraft can travel about 30,000 miles in one hour. How long would it take *Ulysses* to travel 240,000 miles?

36. **Analyze** A deep crater on the Moon, called Bailly, is about 12,000 feet deep. The Mariana Trench—the deepest point in the Pacific Ocean—is about 36,000 feet below sea level. How many times deeper than the Bailly Crater is Mariana Trench?

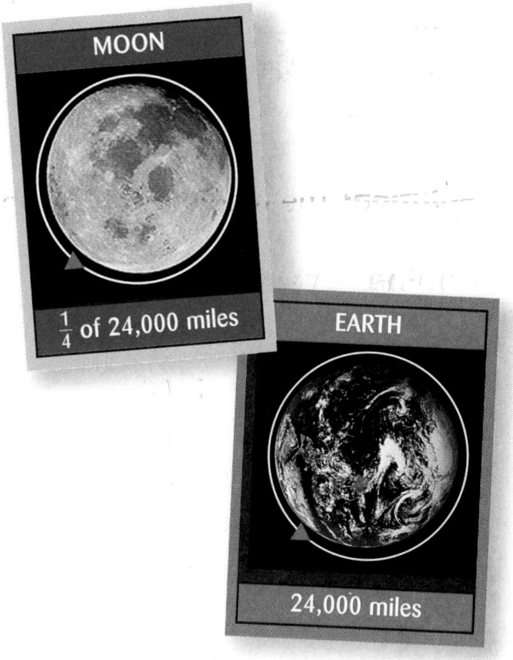

Mixed Review • Test Prep

Round the number to the underlined place. *(pages 8–9, 18–19)*

37. $7\underline{9}9$ **38.** $4{,}\underline{5}27$ **39.** $7\underline{4}{,}562$ **40.** $\underline{3}02{,}965$ **41.** $\underline{2}{,}895{,}743$

Write the letter of the correct answer. *(pages 54–55, 106–107)*

42 2,400 − 199 = n

A 2,200 **C** 2,201

B 2,199 **D** 2,599

43 3,000 × 50 = n

F 350 **H** 15,000

G 1,500 **J** 150,000

Extra Practice See Set E on page 179.

Divide by Two-Digit Numbers

You will learn how to divide by a two-digit number and how to estimate the first digit of the quotient.

Learn About It

A box of raisin cereal contains about 12 servings. If there are 279 raisins in the box, about how many raisins would you expect to get in one serving?

Divide. **279 ÷ 12** $\quad 12\overline{)279}$

Find 279 ÷ 12.

Step 1 Use an estimate to predict the first digit in the quotient. Test your prediction by dividing.

Think: 24 ÷ 12 = 2 $\quad 12\overline{)240}$ with quotient 20

```
    2
12)279    Multiply. 2 × 12
 - 24 ←   Subtract. 27 − 24
    3     Compare. 3 < 12
```

Step 2 Bring down the ones. Divide the ones and record the remainder.

Think: 36 ÷ 12 = 3 $\quad 12\overline{)39}$ with quotient 3

```
   23 R3
12)279
 - 24↓
    39    Multiply. 3 × 12
  - 36 ←  Subtract. 39 − 36
     3    Compare. 3 < 12
```

Check: Multiply the quotient by the divisor and add the remainder.

(23 × 12) + 3 = 279

The result equals the dividend, so the quotient is correct.

Solution: You would expect to get about 23 raisins in one serving.

Another Example

Zeros in the Quotient

Find 852 ÷ 42.

Think: $42\overline{)840}$ with quotient 20

```
   20 R12
42)852
 - 84
    12
   - 0
    12
```

Explain Your Thinking

- ▶ In the example at the left, how do you know that there must be two digits in the quotient?
- ▶ Why do you continue dividing even though you can't make any groups of 42 in the third line of the division example?

Guided Practice

Divide.

1. $11\overline{)89}$ **2.** $45\overline{)905}$ **3.** $19\overline{)798}$

4. 91 ÷ 27 **5.** 68 ÷ 31 **6.** 663 ÷ 82

Ask Yourself

- What basic fact can I use to estimate the first digit of the quotient?

Independent Practice

Divide.

7. $20\overline{)87}$ **8.** $26\overline{)84}$ **9.** $31\overline{)93}$ **10.** $27\overline{)56}$

11. $32\overline{)74}$ **12.** $43\overline{)86}$ **13.** $21\overline{)66}$ **14.** $32\overline{)98}$

15. $31\overline{)961}$ **16.** $15\overline{)724}$ **17.** $41\overline{)825}$ **18.** $41\overline{)945}$

19. $11\overline{)669}$ **20.** $61\overline{)860}$ **21.** $42\overline{)882}$ **22.** $81\overline{)415}$

23. 47 ÷ 22 **24.** 88 ÷ 44 **25.** 99 ÷ 32 **26.** 60 ÷ 29

27. 390 ÷ 75 **28.** 544 ÷ 32 **29.** 378 ÷ 62 **30.** 519 ÷ 51

Problem Solving • Reasoning

31. A recipe for one pan of cereal squares uses 50 mL of corn syrup. How many pans of squares could you make with 867 mL of corn syrup?

32. **Analyze** One serving of frosted wheat cereal is 35 grams. How many complete servings are there in a 475-gram package?

33. **Estimate** One 30-gram serving of toasted rice cereal contains 22 grams of starch. About how many grams of starch are in a 700-gram box of cereal? Show how you made your estimate.

Math Is Everywhere!

SCIENCE Information about the contents of packaged food is printed on the label. You might see this on a cereal package label.

Protein	**4 g**
Fat	**2 g**
Carbohydrate	**21 g**

About how many times as much carbohydrate is there as

Ⓐ protein? Ⓑ fat?

Ⓒ protein/fat combined?

Mixed Review • Test Prep

Solve. *(pages 58–59, 60–61, 110–111, 114–115)*

34. 3.415 + 2.79 **35.** 9.0 − 6.77

36. 6,704 × 40 **37.** $1.25 × 12

38 Write 3 and 5 thousandths in standard form. *(pages 24–25)*

A 3.5 **B** 3.05 **C** 3.005 **D** 3.0005

Extra Practice See Set F on page 179.

Estimated Quotient Is Too Large

You will learn what to do when an estimated digit in the quotient is too large.

Learn About It

At the World Weightlifting Championships in 1999, a woman in the 54-kilogram class set a world record by lifting 131 kg. If a 30-liter aquarium filled with water equals about 33 kg, how many aquariums would it take to equal the amount she lifted?

Divide. **131 ÷ 33** $33\overline{)131}$

Find 131 ÷ 33.

Step 1 Estimate to place the first digit in the quotient.

Think: $30\overline{)120}$ with quotient 4

$$\begin{array}{r} 4 \\ 33\overline{)131} \\ -\,132 \\ \hline \end{array}$$
← You can't subtract 132 from 131.

Step 2 Try a smaller number.

$$\begin{array}{r} 3\text{ R}32 \\ 33\overline{)131} \\ -\,99 \\ \hline 32 \end{array}$$

Multiply. 3 × 33
← Subtract. 131 − 99
Compare. 32 < 33

Solution: It would take almost 4 full aquariums to match the weight lifted by the world champion.

Explain Your Thinking

▶ How do you know when an estimated digit in the quotient is too large?

Guided Practice

Divide.

1. $64\overline{)316}$ **2.** $92\overline{)724}$ **3.** $24\overline{)620}$

4. 558 ÷ 64 **5.** 650 ÷ 24 **6.** 823 ÷ 23

Ask Yourself

- Did I estimate the first digit of the quotient?

Standards NS **2.2** AF **1.0, 1.2, 1.5**

Independent Practice

Divide.

7. $64\overline{)439}$ **8.** $52\overline{)464}$ **9.** $92\overline{)734}$ **10.** $33\overline{)275}$

11. $93\overline{)362}$ **12.** $92\overline{)549}$ **13.** $84\overline{)568}$ **14.** $72\overline{)632}$

15. $73\overline{)431}$ **16.** $43\overline{)808}$ **17.** $31\overline{)899}$ **18.** $32\overline{)612}$

19. 618 ÷ 32 **20.** 814 ÷ 21 **21.** 884 ÷ 34 **22.** 523 ÷ 53

23. 639 ÷ 22 **24.** 314 ÷ 63 **25.** 649 ÷ 13 **26.** 828 ÷ 42

n **Algebra • Functions** **Copy and complete each function table or write the rule.**

27. Rule: Divide by 12

Input	Output
24	■
48	■
144	■
192	■

28. Rule: Divide by 25

Input	Output
50	■
■	3
■	5
200	■

29. Rule: ■

Input	Output
200	10
240	12
360	18
480	24

Problem Solving • Reasoning

Use Data **Use the data for the Problems 30–31.**

30. **Estimate** The chimpanzee lifted 270 kg. About how many times its own mass was the chimpanzee able to lift?

31. If the child could lift as many times her own mass as the chimp can, could she lift a 200-kilogram object? Explain.

32. **Analyze** The Goliath beetle is the heaviest beetle in the world. It can weigh up to 100 grams. If there are 1,000 grams in a kilogram, about how many Goliath beetles would weigh a kilogram?

46 kg

6,000 kg

84 g

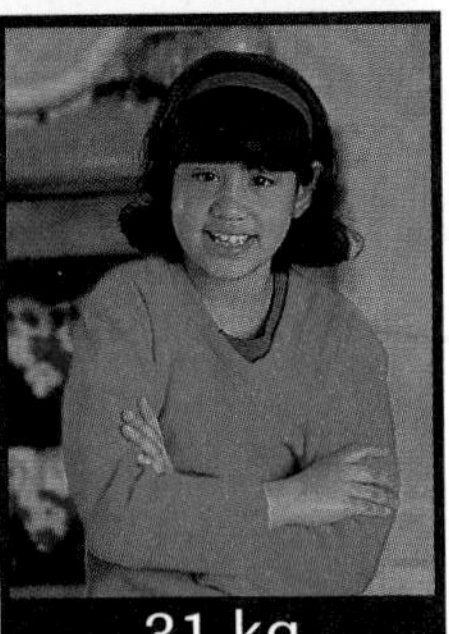

31 kg

Mixed Review • Test Prep

Write the value of the underlined digit. *(pages 4–5, 24–25)*

33. $2.\underline{3}$ **34** $7.0\underline{8}$ **35.** $3.00\underline{6}$ **36.** $1\underline{2}.874$

37 Solve. \$10.00 − \$4.99 = *n* *(pages 60–61)*

A \$14.99 **B** \$5.11 **C** \$6.01 **D** \$5.01

Extra Practice See Set G on page 179.

LESSON 9

Estimated Quotient Is Too Small

You will learn what to do when an estimated digit in the quotient is too small.

Learn About It

The average American eats about 65 quarts of popcorn a year. If you do eat this much popcorn, about how many years will it take you to consume 455 quarts?

Divide. $455 \div 65 = n$ $\quad 65\overline{)455}$

Find 455 ÷ 65.

Step 1 Estimate the first digit of the quotient.

Think: $70\overline{)420}$ → 6

$$\begin{array}{r} 6 \\ 65\overline{)455} \\ -\,390 \\ \hline 65 \end{array}$$

← You can make another group of 65 from this remainder. The estimated quotient is too small.

Step 2 Try a larger number.

$$\begin{array}{r} 7 \\ 65\overline{)455} \\ -\,455 \\ \hline 0 \end{array}$$

Multiply. 7 × 65
Subtract. 455 − 455
There is no remainder.

Solution: It will take you 7 years to eat 455 quarts of popcorn.

Explain Your Thinking

- ► How can you tell when an estimated digit in the quotient is too small?
- ► When are you likely to underestimate a quotient?

Guided Practice

Divide.

1. $46\overline{)420}$ **2.** $27\overline{)139}$ **3.** $38\overline{)234}$

4. 440 ÷ 5 **5.** 230 ÷ 45 **6.** 107 ÷ 15

7. 782 ÷ 16 **8.** 961 ÷ 31 **9.** 625 ÷ 24

Ask Yourself

- Did I use compatible numbers?
- Did I write the remainder?

Independent Practice

Divide.

10. $75\overline{)626}$ **11.** $18\overline{)176}$ **12.** $29\overline{)203}$ **13.** $86\overline{)430}$

14. $38\overline{)314}$ **15.** $67\overline{)408}$ **16.** $15\overline{)123}$ **17.** $26\overline{)209}$

18. $28\overline{)224}$ **19.** $16\overline{)120}$ **20.** $35\overline{)285}$ **21.** $46\overline{)444}$

22. $37\overline{)333}$ **23.** $76\overline{)593}$ **24.** $66\overline{)660}$ **25.** $65\overline{)520}$

26. $816 \div 27$ **27.** $629 \div 17$ **28.** $218 \div 23$ **29.** $329 \div 47$

30. $782 \div 26$ **31.** $702 \div 15$ **32.** $613 \div 67$ **33.** $600 \div 75$

n **Algebra • Equations** **Use what you know about multiplication and division to find the missing number.**

34. $n \div 4 = 208$ **35.** $n \div 8 = 60$ R4 **36.** $n \div 60 = 4$ **37.** $n \div 5 = 20$ R3

Problem Solving • Reasoning

38. **Analyze** The Popperific Popcorn Company sells 6 different popcorn flavors in large, decorated tubs. If Katie orders 25 matching tubs containing 150 gal of popcorn in all, how much popcorn is in each tub?

39. **Analyze** The staff at a theater snack counter have found that 35 oz of popcorn kernels makes enough popcorn to fill 40 small bags. How many small bags could they fill with 280 oz of kernels?

40. At a factory outlet, customers spend an average of $65 every hour on specialty popcorn. If the average daily sales are $585, how long is the store open each day?

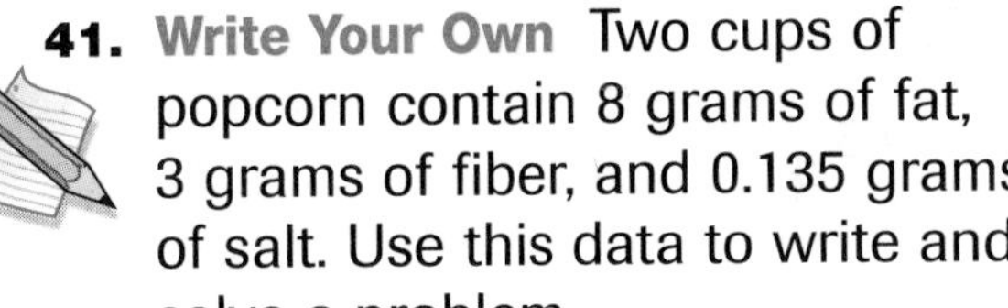

41. **Write Your Own** Two cups of popcorn contain 8 grams of fat, 3 grams of fiber, and 0.135 grams of salt. Use this data to write and solve a problem.

Mixed Review • Test Prep

Round the number to the underlined place. *(pages 28–29)*

42. $0.\underline{4}6$ **43.** $0.67\underline{8}9$ **44.** $1.4\underline{5}4$ **45.** $15.\underline{3}2$

Write the letter of the correct answer. *(pages 14–15)*

46 What is $(7 \times 10^4) + (3 \times 10^3) + (2 \times 10^2) + (5 \times 10^1)$ in standard form?

A 7,325 **B** 70,325 **C** 73,250 **D** 70,000,325

47 What is five million, sixty thousand, forty-three in standard form?

F 5,060,043 **G** 5,006,430 **H** 500,430 **J** 5,643

Extra Practice See Set H on page 179.

Four-and Five-Digit Dividends

You will learn how to divide a two-digit number into a dividend with up to five digits.

Learn About It

In 1997 a 12-year-old boy rode a lawn mower across the United States. He traveled a distance of 5,416 km to raise money to help a sick child. He followed a route suggested by the police and rode between two escort vehicles. The trip took 42 days. What was the mean number of kilometers he traveled each day?

Divide. **5,416 ÷ 42** **42)5,416**

12-Year-Old Rides Lawn Mower Cross-Country

…help raise money for a …hild, a twelve year old boy …is lawnmower across the country. Driving along …oulders of roads at a …of 10 miles per hour th… …l in Washingto… …2 days and ov… The boy rai… …ney to help… …ration nee… friend.

Find 5,416 ÷ 42.

Step 1 Estimate the first digit of the quotient. Then divide the hundreds.

Think: $40\overline{)4{,}000}$ = 100

Try 1 hundred.

```
     1
42)5,416   Multiply. 1 × 42
 - 4 2  ←  Subtract. 54 − 42
   1 2     Compare. 12 < 42
```

Step 2 Bring down the tens. Divide the tens.

Think: $40\overline{)1{,}200}$ = 30

Try 3 tens.

```
     13
42)5,416
 - 4 2↓
   1 2 1
 - 1 2 6  ← Estimate is
            too large.
            Try 2 tens.
```

```
     12
42)5,416
 - 4 2↓
   1 2 1    Multiply. 2 × 42
   - 84  ←  Subtract. 121 − 84
     37     Compare. 37 < 42
```

Step 3 Bring down the ones. Divide the ones.

Think: $40\overline{)360}$ = 9

Try 9 ones.

```
     129
42)5,416
 - 4 2↓
   121
  - 84↓
   376
 - 378  ← Estimate is too
          large. Try 8 ones.
```

```
     128 R40
42)5,416
 - 4 2↓
   121
  - 84↓
   376
 - 336
    40
```

Check: Multiply. Then add.

(42 × 128) + 40 = 5,416

The result equals the dividend, so the quotient is correct.

Solution: The mean distance traveled was between 128 km and 129 km each day.

 Standards NS **1.0, 2.2** AF **1.0, 1.2**

Another Example

Zeros in the Quotient

Find 72,096 ÷ 24.

Think: $25\overline{)75{,}000}$ = 3,000

$$\begin{array}{r} 3{,}004 \\ 24\overline{)72{,}096} \\ -72\phantom{{,}096} \\ \hline 00 \\ -0 \\ \hline 09 \\ -0 \\ \hline 96 \\ -96 \\ \hline 0 \end{array}$$

Explain Your Thinking

- ▶ Why is it helpful to estimate a quotient before you divide?
- ▶ How can you estimate a quotient when you are using very large numbers?
- ▶ When do you write a zero in the quotient?

Guided Practice

Ask Yourself

- Where should I write the first digit of the quotient?
- Is the estimated digit in the quotient too high or too low?

Divide.

1. $14\overline{)5{,}634}$
2. $38\overline{)6{,}375}$
3. $42\overline{)5{,}425}$
4. 17,860 ÷ 38
5. 19,857 ÷ 32
6. 40,952 ÷ 87
7. 29,622 ÷ 12
8. 85,215 ÷ 25
9. 91,233 ÷ 73

Independent Practice

Divide.

10. $17\overline{)5{,}185}$
11. $48\overline{)2{,}400}$
12. $73\overline{)7{,}408}$
13. $36\overline{)7{,}239}$
14. $32\overline{)1{,}684}$
15. $43\overline{)1{,}068}$
16. $64\overline{)2{,}240}$
17. $23\overline{)1{,}104}$
18. $54\overline{)11{,}144}$
19. $59\overline{)35{,}424}$
20. $91\overline{)27{,}636}$
21. $62\overline{)26{,}935}$
22. $73\overline{)36{,}898}$
23. $47\overline{)26{,}320}$
24. $93\overline{)43{,}815}$
25. $56\overline{)22{,}393}$
26. 9,427 ÷ 31
27. 9,454 ÷ 47
28. 7,664 ÷ 58
29. 4,800 ÷ 24
30. 16,819 ÷ 83
31. 35,190 ÷ 94
32. 42,398 ÷ 46
33. 10,542 ÷ 15
34. 93,438 ÷ 16
35. 82,675 ÷ 25
36. 75,223 ÷ 29
37. 20,702 ÷ 98

Algebra • Equations **If q is the quotient and r is the remainder, write and solve a division problem for each equation.**

38. $20q + r = 3{,}221$
39. $35q + r = 7{,}805$
40. $29q + r = 16{,}258$
41. $52q + r = 89{,}162$
42. $11q + r = 1{,}090$
43. $15q + r = 3{,}333$

Problem Solving • Reasoning

44. In 1992, four men drove their snowmobiles from Anchorage, Alaska, to Dartmouth, Nova Scotia. The trip covered 10,252 mi in 56 days. What was the mean distance they traveled each day?

45. **Analyze** In 1992, an athlete rode a unicycle from Newport, Oregon, to Washington, D.C. The trip took 44 days, covering an average of 74 mi each day. How far is it from Newport to Washington?

46. **Compare** In 1980, a man walked 3,008 mi on stilts from Los Angeles to Bowen, Kentucky. The trip took 158 days. In 1891, a stilt walker traveled from Paris, France, to Moscow, Russia, going 1,830 mi in about 54 days. Who traveled faster?

47. **Write Your Own** Use the information in Problems 44–46 to write your own problem. Give your problem to a partner to solve.

Mixed Review • Test Prep

Solve. *(pages 58–59, 60–61, 110–111, 114–115)*

48. 8.7 + 1.999

49. 7.3 − 4.067

50. 40 × 5,000

51. 5,239 × 25

Choose the letter of the correct answer. *(pages 8–9)*

52. What is 825 rounded to the nearest ten?

A 800 **C** 830

B 820 **D** 900

53. What is 6.075 rounded to the nearest tenth?

F 6 **H** 6.1

G 6.0 **J** 6.08

Logical Thinking

Properties

Write *true* or *false*.
Give examples to support your answer.

For any counting numbers, a, b, and c:

1. $(a + b) - c = a + (b - c)$

2. $a + b = b + a$

3. $a \div b = b \div a$

4. $(a \times b) \times 0 = 0$

Extra Practice See Set I on page 180.

Practice Game

Quotient Quest

Practice estimating quotients by playing this game in small groups. Try to be the first to get to 10 points!

Players 2

What You'll Need

- *four sets of number cards (Teaching Tool 3) or a deck of cards with the face cards and 10s removed*
- *division frames like the one shown*

Here's What to Do

1. Shuffle the cards and give five cards to each player.
2. Arrange your cards in a division frame like the one shown here. Use estimation to help you place the cards so the quotient will be as small as possible.
3. Divide to find your quotient and compare with the other player's quotient. The player with the smaller quotient gets 1 point. If both quotients are the same, the smaller remainder gets the point. If the remainders are the same, both players get 1 point.

Take turns dealing the cards, repeating steps 1 to 3. The first player to get a total of 10 points wins.

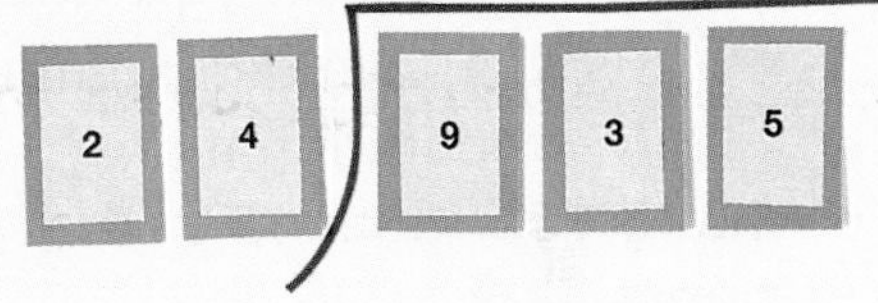

Share Your Thinking What strategy can you use to find the least possible quotient?

Standards NS 2.2 MR 2.1

Problem-Solving Strategy: Draw a Diagram

You will learn how a diagram can help you think about and solve a problem.

Sometimes you can solve a problem by drawing a diagram.

Problem Two companies leased all the space in an 18-story building. Company A has twice as many floors as Company B. How many floors does each company have?

Understand

What is the question?
How many floors does each of the two companies have?

What do you know?
Together the companies have 18 floors.

Plan

How can you find the answer?
You can use number strips to draw a picture that represents the information.

Solve

Draw two strips.
Make one strip twice the length of the other.

Company A

Company B

18 floors

Each small rectangle must represent 6 floors.

Company A must have 12 floors, while Company B has the other 6.

Look Back

Look back at the problem.
For what kind of problems would you use the Draw a Diagram strategy?

Standards MR 1.0, 1.1, 2.0, 2.3, 3.0

Remember:
- ▶ Understand
- ▶ Plan
- ▶ Solve
- ▶ Look Back

Guided Practice

Draw a diagram to solve each problem.

1. Two buildings have 60 floors altogether. Building A has 3 floors for every 2 floors of Building B. How many floors does each building have?

Think: How many floors does each rectangle represent?

2. An office has 245 men working in it. There are 37 more women than men. How many workers are there altogether?

Men | 245
Women | 37

Think: How can I find the number of women first?

Choose a Strategy

Solve. Use these or other strategies.

Problem-Solving Strategies

- **Draw a Diagram**
- **Make a Table**
- **Work Backward**
- **Write an Equation**

3. Sally bought 3 tickets to the observation deck at the top of a skyscraper. She paid with a five-dollar bill and got 50¢ change. What was the cost of each ticket?

4. The building superintendent planted 4 bushes in the first row of the garden. Each row has one more bush than the row before it. How many bushes are in the sixth row?

5. The Sears Tower and the John Hancock Center have 210 stories altogether. If the Sears Tower is 10 stories taller than the John Hancock Center, how many stories does the John Hancock Center have?

6. Sal and Theresa got on a hotel elevator on the 16th floor. The elevator went down eight floors, then went up six floors, down ten, and finally up three floors. What floor did the elevator finally stop on?

7. Find the mean height of the Sears Tower (1,454 ft), the John Hancock Center (1,127 ft), and the Empire State Building (1,250 ft).

8. The Imperial Building has 375 offices. If there are 25 floors of offices, what is the mean number of offices on each floor of the building?

Extra Practice See 5–7 on page 181.

Quick Check

Check Your Understanding of Lessons 6–11

Divide using mental math. Check by multiplying.

1. 640 ÷ 80

2. 32,000 ÷ 80

3. 72,000 ÷ 600

Divide.

4. $30\overline{)92}$

5. $72\overline{)436}$

6. $47\overline{)947}$

7. 630 ÷ 91

8. 729 ÷ 68

9. 589 ÷ 75

10. $48\overline{)338}$

11. $28\overline{)229}$

12. $85\overline{)595}$

13. 4,850 ÷ 91

14. 2,040 ÷ 34

15. 15,799 ÷ 63

Solve.

16. On Thursday at summer camp, the children could choose to go swimming or go on a hike. In all 91 children either went swimming or went on a hike. For every 3 children who chose hiking, 4 children chose swimming. How many children went swimming? How many children went on a hike?

How did you do?

If you had difficulty with any items in the Quick Check, you can use the following pages for review and extra practice.

California Standards	Items	Review These Pages	Do These Extra Practice Items
Number Sense: **1.0, 2.2**	1–3	pages 146–147	Set E, page 179
Number Sense: **1.0, 2.2**	4–6	pages 148–149	Set F, page 179
Number Sense: **1.0, 2.2** Math Reasoning: **3.3**	7–9	pages 150–151	Set G, page 179
Number Sense: **1.0, 2.2** Math Reasoning: **3.3**	10–12	pages 152–153	Set H, page 179
Number Sense: **1.0, 2.2**	13–15	pages 154–156	Set I, page 180
Math Reasoning: **1.1, 2.3**	16	pages 158–159	5–7, page 181

Test Prep • Cumulative Review

Maintaining the Standards

Choose the letter of the correct answer.
If a correct answer is not here, choose NH.

1. Divide. $800 \div 40$

   A 2
   B 4
   C 20
   D 200

2. Julia needs to put 315 straws into boxes. If she wants to put 63 straws in each box, how many boxes will she need?

   F 2
   G 3
   H 4
   J NH

3. Lee wrote the following equations:

   $2 \times 3{,}000 = 200 \times 30$

   $8 \times 4{,}000 = 800 \times 40$

   $5 \times 2{,}000 = 500 \times 20$

   How would Lee finish this equation?

   $9 \times 6{,}000 = \blacksquare$

   A 90×60
   B 900×60
   C 900×600
   D $9{,}000 \times 60$

4. Which is the greatest number?

   F $^{-}5$
   G $^{-}7$
   H $^{-}3$
   J $^{-}12$

5. Which is the greatest product?

   A $321{,}765 \times 2$
   B $456{,}132 \times 2$
   C $34{,}689 \times 8$
   D $178{,}634 \times 3$

6. Martin has 4.5 yards of cable for a project. He buys 5.75 yards more. How many yards of cable does he have now?

   F 10.25 yards
   G 9.575 yards
   H 9.25 yards
   J 6.2 yards

7. Which value for t makes this equation true?

   $4{,}009 \times 3 = (4{,}000 \times t) + (9 \times 3)$

   A 4,009
   B 4,000
   C 9
   D 3

8. Patrick has $500 to spend on bookshelves. Each bookshelf costs $89.59. He plans to buy 5.

   Explain Does Patrick need an exact answer or can he use an estimate to make sure he has enough money?

Safe Site

Internet Test Prep
Visit **www.eduplace.com/kids/mhm** for more *Test Prep Practice.*

Write and Evaluate Expressions

You will learn how to describe patterns using variables, numbers, and mathematical operations.

Learn About It

Elena has a part-time baby-sitting job where she earns $4 an hour. She also gets a weekly allowance of $5.

Write an algebraic expression you can use to find the total amount of money Elena will get in one week if she works for n hours. Then use the expression to see how much money she will get if she works for 10 hours.

Write an algebraic expression.

Step 1 Write an expression for the amount Elena earns at work.

If Elena works for 2 hours, she earns 2 × $4.

If Elena works for 3 hours, she earns 3 × $4.

If Elena works for n hours, she earns n × $4.

You can write $n \times 4$ in several different ways.

$n \times 4 \quad n \bullet 4$

$4 \times n \quad 4 \bullet n \quad 4n$

Step 2 Add the amount Elena gets for her allowance to the amount she earns at work.

$4n + 5$

or

$5 + (4n)$

Elena gets $4n$ dollars from work and 5 dollars for her allowance, so she earns $4n + 5$ dollars in a week where she works for n hours.

Step 3 Substitute 10 for n in the expression to see how much money Elena will get if she works for 10 hours.

$$\begin{aligned} 4n + 5 &= (4 \times 10) + 5 \\ &= 40 + 5 \\ &= 45 \end{aligned}$$

Commutative Property

The Commutative Property states that when you multiply or add numbers, you can change the order of the numbers without changing the result.

Solution: If Elena works for 10 hours in one week, she will get a total of $45.

Another Example

An Algebraic Expression in Words

Write $n \div 4$ in words.

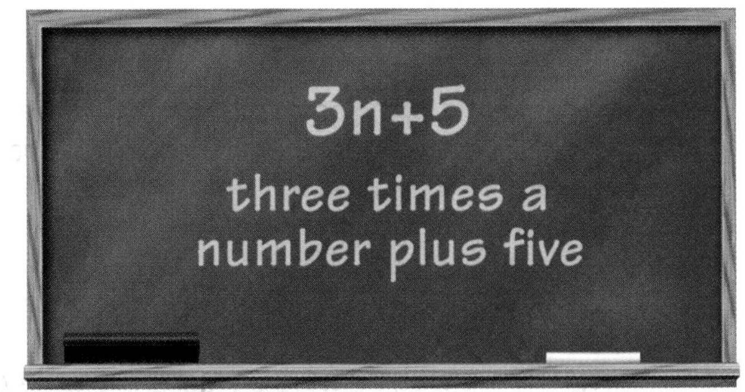

In the expression $n \div 4$, the variable is n. Substitute the words **a number** for the variable.

The expression becomes **a number ÷ 4**.

The symbols **÷ 4** mean divided by 4.

The expression becomes a *number divided by four.*

Explain Your Thinking

- ▶ Why can't you use the Commutative Property to rewrite $n \div 4$ as $4 \div n$?
- ▶ What everyday situations might be described by the expression $n \div 4$?

Guided Practice

Ask Yourself

- Did I use a variable for "a number"?
- Did I use symbols for the operation?

Write each word phrase as an algebraic expression.

1. 6 times a number **2.** 4 more than a number

3. 8 less than a number **4.** 7 less than (3 times a number)

Write each algebraic expression in words.

5. $d + 12$ **6.** $10p$ **7.** $4t + 5$ **8.** $(n \div 5) + 8$

Evaluate each expression.

9. $5s + 2$, if $s = 8$ **10.** $48 \div s$, if $s = 6$ **11.** $s \div 3$, if $s = 30$

Independent Practice

Write each word phrase as an algebraic expression.

12. a number plus 2 **13.** 9 times a number

14. a number divided by 3 **15.** a number multiplied by 4

16. 1 less than a number **17.** 3 times a number

18. 2 more than (7 times a number) **19.** 6 times a number is decreased by 6

20. (a number times 9) plus 3 more **21.** 1 more than (a number divided by 2)

Write and Solve Equations

You will learn how to write and solve multiplication and division equations.

New Vocabulary
inverse operations

Learn About It

Alex collects stamps. He can put 9 stamps on each page in his stamp album. How many pages does he need to display 45 stamps?

Write and solve an equation to solve the problem.

Let p represent the number of pages.

Equation: $9 \times p = 45$ ← total number of stamps

↑ 9: stamps on one page
↑ p: number of pages

Solve. $\mathbf{9p = 45}$

Different Ways to Solve an Equation

You can make a function table.

Use patterns and multiplication to complete the table.

Use the table to find the number of pages that would be needed to display 45 stamps.

$9p = 45$

Rule: $9p$ = total number of stamps

$p = 5$

Number of Pages (p)	Number of Stamps
1	9
2	18
3	27
4	36
5	**45**

You can use inverse operations.

Multiplication and division are inverse operations.

$9p = 45$ **Think:** I know that 9 times a number is equal to 45, so $45 \div 9$ must be equal to the number.

$45 \div 9 = 5$, so p must be equal to 5.

Solution: He needs 5 pages to display 45 stamps.

Check the result by substituting 5 for p in the original equation.

$9p = 45$
$9 \times 5 = 45$
$45 = 45$ ← The left side is equal to the right side, so $p = 5$ is correct.

Explain Your Thinking

▶ Describe two ways to solve $t \div 6 = 4$.

Standards AF 1.0, 1.1, 1.2, 1.5 MR 1.0, 2.3

Guided Practice

Solve.

1. $4d = 20$ **2.** $c \div 9 = 45$ **3.** $8s = 32$

Write an equation for each situation.

4. 8 times the number of stamps on each page equals 32 stamps in all.

5. A number of stamps shared over 5 pages equals 10 stamps on each page.

Ask Yourself

- What operation can I use to find the unknown number?
- Do I use a variable for the number of stamps?

Independent Practice

Solve by using any method.

6. $42 = 7k$ **7.** $55 = 11y$ **8.** $b \div 7 = 5$ **9.** $n \div 6 = 5$

10. $x \div 8 = 2$ **11.** $y \div 3 = 12$ **12.** $17z = 34$ **13.** $21 = 3q$

14. $6c = 18$ **15.** $5x = 45$ **16.** $12p = 48$ **17.** $3x = 33$

Write and solve an equation for each situation.

18. A number of stamps on 13 pages equals 5 stamps on each page.

19. 4 stamps on each page times a number of pages equals 72 stamps.

Problem Solving • Reasoning

20. Use Alex's equation to find out how many pages Alex would need for each number of stamps.

a. 45 **b.** 27 **c.** 72 **d.** 135

21. What does t represent, when $t \div 6$ equals each number? when $2t$ equals each number?

a. 5 **b.** 30 **c.** 8 **d.** 14

22. At an auction a collector bought a five-cent stamp for 10,000 times its original value. How much did that collector pay, in dollars, for that five-cent stamp?

23. First-class rates for letters and packages are determined by weight. The first ounce costs \$0.33 and each additional ounce costs \$0.22. What does it cost to mail an 8-oz package?

Mixed Review • Test Prep

Simplify. *(pages 98–99, 134–135, 162–164)*

24. $(9 \times 3) + (7 \times 3)$ **25.** \$6.45 $\times$ 8 **26.** $(2 \times 9) + (9 \times 4)$ **27.** \$9.35 $\div$ 5

28 What is the quotient if the dividend is 1,755 and the divisor is 39? *(pages 154–155)*

A 45 **B** 47 R 3 **C** 1,794 **D** 68,445

Extra Practice See Set K on page 180.

Model Equations

You will learn what happens when you perform the same operation on both sides of an equation.

Review Vocabulary
Distributive Property

Learn About It

You can use counters to model the equation $x + 4 = 8$.

The blue variable card represents the number of hidden counters.

$$x + 4 = 8$$

How many counters are hidden under the blue card?

The solution is $x = 4$.

Use counters to see what happens when you perform the same operation on both sides of an equation.

Add 2 to each side.

$x + 4 + 2 = 8 + 2$

$x + 6 = 10$

- Solve $x + 6 = 10$.

Subtract 2 from each side.

$x + 4 - 2 = 8 - 2$

$x + 2 = 6$

- Solve $x + 2 = 6$.

What do you notice about the solution of each new equation?

Multiply both sides by 3.

$3 \times (x + 4) = 3 \times 8$

$3(x + 4) = 24$

Simplify using the **Distributive Property.**

$(3 \times x) + (3 \times 4) = 24$

$3x + 12 = 24$

- What happens when you substitute the solution of $x + 4 = 8$ into the equation $3x + 12 = 24$?

Distributive Property

According to the **Distributive Property**, when you multiply two addends by a factor, the answer is the same as if you multiply each addend by the factor and then add the products.

$3 \times (4 + 5) = (3 \times 4) + (3 \times 5)$

or $3 \times 9 = 12 + 15$

$27 = 27$

The Distributive Property is also true for differences.

$3 \times (7 - 2) = (3 \times 7) - (3 \times 2)$

or $3 \times 5 = 21 - 6$

$15 = 15$

Standards AF **1.0, 1.1, 1.2, 1.3** MR **2.3**

Try It Out

Use the equation $x + 3 = 5$ for Problems 1–4.

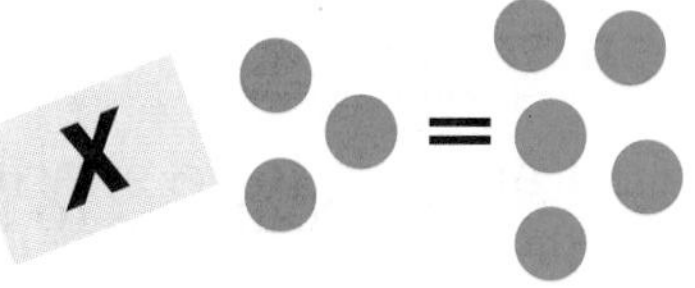

1. Solve the equation.
2. Add 2 to both sides. Solve the new equation.
3. Subtract 1 from both sides. Solve the new equation.
4. Multiply both sides by 3. Substitute the solution to the original equation in the new equation.

Use the equation $3x = 15$ for Problems 5–8.

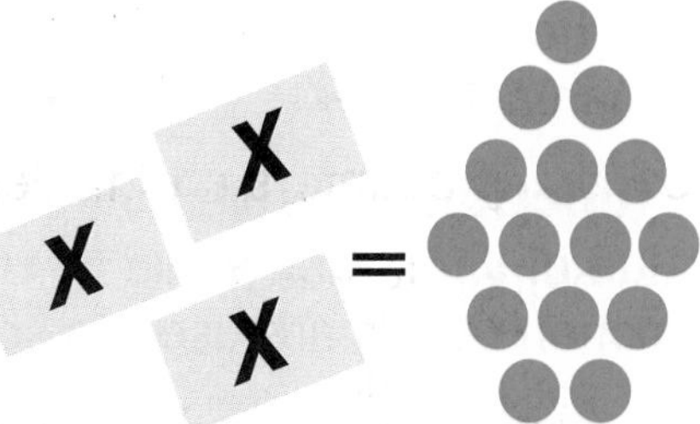

5. Solve the equation.
6. Multiply both sides by 10. Solve the new equation.
7. Add 5 to both sides. Substitute the solution to the original equation in the new equation.
8. Subtract 2 from both sides. Substitute the solution to the original equation in the new equation.

Use the equation $x = 6$ for Problems 9–10.

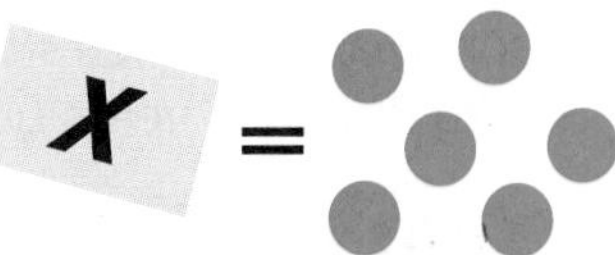

9. What operation could you perform on both sides to get the new equation $6x = 36$?
10. What operation could you perform on both sides to get the new equation $x - 3 = 3$?

Write about it! Talk about it!

Use what you have learned to answer these questions.

11. What happens to the value of the variable when you perform the same operation on both sides of an equation?
12. An equation shows that two mathematical expressions are equal. What happens to the relationship between the two expressions when you perform the same operation on both sides of an equation?
13. Tell how you could use what you have learned to find the solution to an equation such as $8x + 3 = 27$.

Functions and Variables

You will learn how to use a function table to solve equations involving multiplication and division.

Review Vocabulary
function table
function

Learn About It

Most animals have shorter life spans than people have. For example, one year in the life of a horse is about the same as 3 years of a human's life.

You can use a **function table** like the one at the right to show the ages of horses and equivalent human ages. For each age given for a horse, there is exactly one equivalent human age.

Age of Horse in Years	Equivalent Human Age
1	3
2	6
3	9
4	12

A **function** is a rule that gives exactly one value of y for each value of x. Functions and function tables are used to solve problems.

If the age of a horse is equivalent to 21 human years, what is its actual age?

Write an equation for a function.

Each year in a horse's life (x) is like 3 human years (y).

$y = 3 \times x$ or $y = 3x$

Use the equation to fill in the table.

The table shows that the horse age equivalent to 21 human years is 7 years.

If $x = 5$, then $y = 3 \times 5 = 15$. →
If $x = 6$, then $y = 3 \times 6 = 18$. →
If $x = 7$, then $y = 3 \times 7 = 21$. →
If $x = 8$, then $y = 3 \times 8 = 24$. →

x	y
5	15
6	18
7	21
8	24

Solution: The horse is actually 7 years old.

Another Example

Two Operations

This function combines multiplication and addition: $b = 2a + 1$

Find the value of a that makes $b = 13$.

For any value of a, the function tells you to multiply by 2 and then add 1. Complete a function table.

When $a = 6$, $b = 13$.

If $a = 1$, then $b = 2 \times 1 + 1 = 3$. →
If $a = 2$, then $b = 2 \times 2 + 1 = 5$. →
If $a = 3$, then $b = 2 \times 3 + 1 = 7$. →
If $a = 4$, then $b = 2 \times 4 + 1 = 9$. →
If $a = 5$, then $b = 2 \times 5 + 1 = 11$. →
If $a = 6$, then $b = 2 \times 6 + 1 = 13$. →

a	b
1	3
2	5
3	7
4	9
5	11
6	13

 Standards AF 1.0, 1.1, 1.2, 1.5 MR 1.0, 1.1, 2.0

Explain Your Thinking

- ► Why can any two variables, such as a and b in the second example, be used in a function rule?
- ► In the second example, why did you multiply by 2 before adding 1?

Guided Practice

Ask Yourself

- What value did I use for x?
- Did I do the operations in parentheses first?

Find the value of y when $x = 4$.

1. $y = 5x$

2. $y = 16 \div x$

3. $y = x \times 8$

4. $y = 5x + 3$

5. $y = 5x - 3$

6. $y = (16 \div x) + 3$

Independent Practice

Find the value of y when $x = 5$.

7. $y = 4x$

8. $y = 4x + 7$

9. $y = 4x - 7$

10. $y = 4x \div 10$

11. $y = 30 \div x$

12. $y = (30 \div x) + 3$

13. $y = (30 \div x) - 4$

14. $y = 7 \times (30 \div x)$

15. $y = 3 + 4x$

16. $y = 13 - 2x$

17. $y = 3x - 15$

18. $y = (x + 10) \div 3$

Write an equation for each function.

19. y is equal to the product of 4 and x.

20. y is equal to 1 less than x.

21. y is equal to 1 less than the product of 4 and x.

22. b is equal to 5 more than the product of 6 and a.

Describe each function in words.

23. $y = 12x$

24. $y = 6x - 5$

25. $y = 9 + 2x$

26. $f = 12 - 5g$

27. $t = s \div 6$

28. $q = (100 + r) \div 3$

Write a function to describe each situation.

29. A year in a deer's life is like 8 years of a person's life.

30. The real age of a bear is equivalent to its age in human years divided by 4.

31. Your age in months is a function of your age in years.

32. The number of days is a function of the number of weeks.

Problem-Solving Application: Use Equations

You will learn how to translate word problems into algebra problems.

When you solve a word problem, you have to decide which operations to use.

Problem Gilita deposits the same amount of money in her bank account every week. After 4 weeks her bank balance has increased by $12. How much does she deposit each week?

Understand

What is the question?

How much money does Gilita deposit each week?

What do you know?

- Gilita deposits the same amount each week.
- In 4 weeks she deposited $12.

Plan

What can you do to find the answer?

Write a multiplication equation to describe the situation.

Let d represent the amount Gilita deposits each week.

$4d = 12$ 4 weeks times d dollars per week equals $12.

Solve

Solve the equation.

$$4d = 12$$
$$d = 3$$

$4 \times 3 = 12$, so she must deposit $3 each week.

Gilita deposits $3 in her account each week.

Look Back

Look back at the question. Is your answer reasonable?

Do both sides of the equation have the same value when you substitute the solution value, 3, for d?

Standards AF **1.0, 1.1, 1.2** MR **1.0, 2.0, 3.0**

A printer at the Bureau of Printing and Engraving is checking one-dollar bills.

Remember:
- ▶ Understand
- ▶ Plan
- ▶ Solve
- ▶ Look Back

Guided Practice

Solve.

1. Marta has 3 times as much money in her bank account as Matt. If Marta has $47.25, how much money does Matt have in his account?

   Think: Do I multiply or divide to solve this problem?

2. Carla deposited money into her bank account twice as often this month as her sister Connie. If Carla made 4 deposits, how many did Connie make?

   Think: Has Connie deposited money more or less often than Carla?

Choose a Strategy

Solve. Use these or other strategies.

Problem-Solving Strategies

- **Guess and Check**
- **Use a Table**
- **Find a Pattern**
- **Write an Equation**

3. Marisol has a total of $27.50 in her left and right pockets. Her left pocket contains $3.50 more than her right pocket. How much money is in each of Marisol's two pockets?

4. John's sister has $4.95 in dimes and quarters in her piggy bank. There are 3 fewer dimes than quarters. How many quarters and dimes are in the piggy bank?

5. For every $10 Rita saves, her aunt gives her an extra $2. If Rita saves $40 on her own, how much will she have after her aunt gives her the extra money?

6. Look for a pattern in the list of amounts of money.
   $0.75, $0.50, $1.50, $1.25, $2.25, $2.00
   What is the next amount of money likely to be?

7. Greg has $6.25 in quarters, dimes, and nickels. If he has twice as many quarters as dimes and twice as many dimes as nickels, how many of each coin does he have?

8. Each week, Samantha deposits in the bank $7.25 from her newspaper route. Will she have enough in 4 weeks to buy a birthday gift for her mother that costs $27.75?

Extra Practice See Set 8–11 on page 181.

Quick Check

Check Your Understanding of Lessons 12–16

Evaluate each expression.

1. $3 \times r$, if $r = 8$

2. $14 \times n$, if $n = 1$

3. $4v + 6$, if $v = 7$

4. $(c \div 8) + 3$, if $c = 48$

5. $12 \times p$, if $p = 5$

6. $(8 \times 4) \times z$, if $z = 0$

Solve.

7. $9g = 36$

8. $24 = 2r$

9. $66 = 11p$

10. $49 = t \times 7$

11. $54 \div 6 = d$

12. $12x = 72$

Find the value of *y* when *x* = 6.

13. $y = 3x$

14. $y = 14 - 2x$

15. $y = (36 \div x) + 4$

16. $y = 2x - 10$

17. $y = 7(x - 4)$

18. $y = 3x - 18$

Solve.

19. The mean number of songs on a CD in Nicole's collection is about 12. If she has a total of 121 songs, how many CDs does she have?

How did you do?

If you had difficulty with any items in the Quick Check, you can use the following pages for review and extra practice.

California Standards	Items	Review These Pages	Do These Extra Practice Items
Algebra and Functions: **1.2**	1–6	pages 162–164	Set J, page 180
Algebra and Functions: **1.2**	7–12	pages 166–167	Set K, page 180
Algebra and Functions: **1.5**	13–18	pages 170–172	Set L, page 180
Algebra and Functions: **1.1, 1.2** Math Reasoning: **1.0, 1.2, 2.4, 2.6**	19	pages 174–175	8–11, page 181

Test Prep • Cumulative Review

Maintaining the Standards

Choose the letter of the correct answer.

1. Write an algebraic expression for this word sentence. Fifteen campers share *n* marshmallows.

   A $15 - n$

   B $15 + n$

   C $n \cdot 15$

   D $n \div 15$

2. Which number belongs in the box?

   $3 \times 10 \times 100 = 3{,}000$

   $30 \times 10 \times 100 = 30{,}000$

   $300 \times 10 \times 100 = 300{,}000$

   $3{,}000 \times 10 \times 100 = ■$

   F 5,000,000

   G 3,000,000

   H 333,000

   J 3,110

3. Eric weighed 112 ounces when he was born. Today he weighs 19 times that amount. How many ounces does Eric weigh today?

   A 218 oz

   B 1,120 oz

   C 2,128 oz

   D 202,128 oz

4. What is the value of $10^3 \times 10^2$?

   F 1,000

   G 10,000

   H 100,000

   J 1,000,000

5. What is the value of *y* when $x = 5$?

   $$y = 2x + 3$$

   A 5

   B 10

   C 13

   D 28

6. The world record height reached by an airplane is 123,523.58 ft. The record for a hot air balloon is 113,739.9 ft. How much higher did the airplane fly?

   F 9,783.68 ft

   G 10,783.68 ft

   H 114,386.48 ft

   J 118,256.42 ft

7. Which expression does *not* equal 4,500?

   A 9×500

   B 90×50

   C 900×50

   D 900×5

8. Multiply 4×36 mentally.

   Explain How could you use the Distributive Property to do this?

Safe Site

Internet Test Prep
Visit **www.eduplace.com/kids/mhm** for more *Test Prep Practice.*

Extra Practice

Set A (Lesson 1, pages 134–135)

Divide.

1. $3\overline{)393}$ **2.** $4\overline{)644}$ **3.** $2\overline{)\$1.46}$ **4.** $5\overline{)705}$

5. $6\overline{)5{,}473}$ **6.** $7\overline{)1{,}605}$ **7.** $9\overline{)6{,}641}$ **8.** $4\overline{)\$64.44}$

9. $8\overline{)25{,}412}$ **10.** $3\overline{)\$428.61}$ **11.** $70{,}655 \div 5$ **12.** $42{,}862 \div 6$

13. $576{,}999 \div 9$ **14.** $\$10{,}524 \div 2$ **15.** $490{,}826 \div 8$ **16.** $684{,}996 \div 7$

Set B (Lesson 2, pages 136–137)

Divide.

1. $7\overline{)496}$ **2.** $9\overline{)368}$ **3.** $4\overline{)832}$ **4.** $5\overline{)3{,}540}$

5. $3\overline{)7{,}206}$ **6.** $2\overline{)6{,}164}$ **7.** $4\overline{)42{,}003}$ **8.** $7\overline{)63{,}562}$

9. $7\overline{)63{,}427}$ **10.** $6\overline{)54{,}128}$ **11.** $9\overline{)18{,}024}$ **12.** $5\overline{)605{,}050}$

13. $605 \div 6$ **14.** $6{,}406 \div 8$ **15.** $14{,}210 \div 2$ **16.** $625{,}185 \div 3$

Set C (Lesson 3, pages 138–139)

Estimate the quotient.

1. $5\overline{)622}$ **2.** $6\overline{)204}$ **3.** $9\overline{)834}$ **4.** $6\overline{)3{,}966}$

5. $3\overline{)18{,}320}$ **6.** $4\overline{)1{,}734}$ **7.** $7\overline{)21{,}568}$ **8.** $2\overline{)49{,}626}$

9. $8\overline{)42{,}666}$ **10.** $9\overline{)290{,}000}$ **11.** $8\overline{)332{,}164}$ **12.** $4\overline{)375{,}166}$

13. $395 \div 9$ **14.** $2{,}906 \div 7$ **15.** $16{,}715 \div 5$ **16.** $295{,}612 \div 3$

Set D (Lesson 4, pages 140–141)

Find the mean.

1. 2, 6, 8, 9, 10

2. 4, 7, 8, 9, 12, 14

3. 16, 9, 14, 17

4. 14, 4, 20, 25, 46, 42, 59

5. $24, $47, $73

6. 90, 60, 40, 50, 60, 20, 60, 84

7. 416, 412, 400, 86, 141

8. 216, 432, 840

9. 173, 270, 573, 320

10. 607, 706, 816, 165, 861

Extra Practice

Set E (Lesson 6, pages 146–147)

Divide. Use mental math. Check by multiplying.

1. $240 \div 60$ **2.** $560 \div 80$ **3.** $6,000 \div 10$

4. $2,100 \div 300$ **5.** $1,800 \div 20$ **6.** $14,000 \div 70$

7. $3,600 \div 60$ **8.** $64,000 \div 8,000$ **9.** $720,000 \div 80$

10. $45,000 \div 5,000$ **11.** $49,000 \div 7,000$ **12.** $10,000 \div 200$

13. $90\overline{)27,000}$ **14.** $5,000\overline{)350,000}$ **15.** $3,000\overline{)810,000}$

Set F (Lesson 7, pages 148–149)

Divide.

1. $12\overline{)53}$ **2.** $16\overline{)98}$ **3.** $24\overline{)72}$ **4.** $19\overline{)59}$

5. $22\overline{)245}$ **6.** $33\overline{)646}$ **7.** $49\overline{)919}$ **8.** $65\overline{)702}$

9. $73\overline{)918}$ **10.** $60\overline{)856}$ **11.** $18\overline{)567}$ **12.** $43\overline{)879}$

13. $84 \div 42$ **14.** $5,466 \div 32$ **15.** $727 \div 46$ **16.** $486 \div 61$

Set G (Lesson 8, pages 150–151)

Divide.

1. $63\overline{)230}$ **2.** $64\overline{)294}$ **3.** $41\overline{)358}$ **4.** $84\overline{)636}$

5. $54\overline{)294}$ **6.** $83\overline{)228}$ **7.** $62\overline{)538}$ **8.** $33\overline{)707}$

9. $21\overline{)788}$ **10.** $42\overline{)342}$ **11.** $81\overline{)628}$ **12.** $91\overline{)448}$

13. $599 \div 12$ **14.** $536 \div 56$ **15.** $719 \div 31$ **16.** $726 \div 21$

Set H (Lesson 9, pages 152–153)

Divide.

1. $35\overline{)717}$ **2.** $19\overline{)184}$ **3.** $38\overline{)275}$ **4.** $66\overline{)360}$

5. $28\overline{)216}$ **6.** $47\overline{)209}$ **7.** $25\overline{)238}$ **8.** $16\overline{)108}$

9. $46\overline{)458}$ **10.** $16\overline{)136}$ **11.** $18\overline{)562}$ **12.** $45\overline{)410}$

13. $684 \div 16$ **14.** $408 \div 26$ **15.** $265 \div 37$ **16.** $200 \div 25$

Extra Practice

Set I (Lesson 10, pages 154–156)

Divide.

1. $24\overline{)7{,}252}$
2. $46\overline{)1{,}286}$
3. $62\overline{)1{,}406}$
4. $19\overline{)7{,}365}$
5. $13\overline{)1{,}065}$
6. $33\overline{)2{,}168}$
7. $47\overline{)4{,}562}$
8. $82\overline{)27{,}424}$
9. $63\overline{)25{,}864}$
10. $26\overline{)14{,}610}$
11. $82\overline{)46{,}613}$
12. $65\overline{)23{,}486}$
13. $8{,}316 \div 21$
14. $8{,}324 \div 56$
15. $25{,}169 \div 49$
16. $15{,}678 \div 23$

Set J (Lesson 12, pages 162–164)

Evaluate each expression.

1. $x + 5$, if $x = 3$
2. $10 - r$, if $r = 6$
3. $6p$, if $p = 2$
4. $z - 8$, if $z = 20$
5. $m \div 5$, if $m = 15$
6. $30 \div b$, if $b = 6$
7. $(s - 6) \div 2$, if $s = 8$
8. $(t + 7) \times 5$, if $t = 4$
9. $3n + 2$, if $n = 8$
10. $18 - (f \div 3)$, if $f = 12$
11. $(18 - f) \div 3$, if $f = 12$
12. $2c - 9$, if $c = 15$
13. $9 \times (g + 17)$, if $g = 13$
14. $(h \div 2) \times 6$, if $h = 40$
15. $84 - 3d$, if $d = 25$

Set K (Lesson 13, pages 166–167)

Solve. Use any method.

1. $5x = 25$
2. $2b = 14$
3. $10g = 110$
4. $4r = 24$
5. $64 = 8k$
6. $72 = 9p$
7. $c \div 8 = 48$
8. $w \div 3 = 9$
9. $v \div 6 = 6$
10. $42b = 84$
11. $35 = 7q$
12. $z \div 3 = 18$
13. $4x = 48$
14. $7z = 49$
15. $21 \div z = 7$
16. $72 \div a = 8$

Set L (Lesson 15, pages 170–172)

Find the value of *y* when *x* = 3.

1. $y = 3x$
2. $y = 14 + x$
3. $y = 9 \div x$
4. $y = 3x - 6$
5. $y = 2x + 4$
6. $y = 5x - 6$
7. $y = (4x) \div 2$
8. $y = 27 \div x$
9. $y = 5 + (33 \div x)$
10. $y = (21 \div x) + 6$
11. $y = 2 + (7x)$
12. $y = 12 - (4x)$
13. $y = 4x - 8$
14. $y = (x + 6) \div 3$
15. $y = (x + 3) + 4$

Extra Practice • Problem Solving

Solve. *(Lesson 5, pages 142–143)*

1. Lina is making costumes for the school play. If she needs 3 yd of fabric for each costume, how many can she make from 35 yd?

2. Laura has collected 82 stamps and is putting them in her album. If 9 stamps fit on one page, how many pages will she need?

3. Juan has 17 feet of rope. He cut the rope into as many 5-feet sections as possible. He gave away the rest. How much rope did he give away?

4. There are 53 people waiting in line for the flame ride at the amusement park. If each car holds 6 people, how many cars can be filled?

Solve. *(Lesson 11, pages 158–159)*

5. For the party, 105 red and blue balloons were inflated. There were 3 red balloons for every 2 blue balloons. How many blue balloons are there? How many red balloons?

6. Gavin is taller than Ralph, John, and Daniel. John is shorter than Ralph. Daniel is not the shortest. Glenn is taller than Gavin. Who is the shortest?

7. There are 35 girls in the fifth grade. There are 8 more boys than girls in that fifth grade. How many students are in that fifth grade?

Solve. *(Lesson 16, pages 174–175)*

8. Ella scored 3 times as many points as Gary in the basketball game. If Ella scored 21 points, how many did Gary score?

9. The Moniz family bought tickets to the zoo for $47.95. What was the cost for each person if all 5 people paid the same price?

10. Your brother is half as old as your sister. If your sister is 18, how old is your brother?

11. Dominic wrote the ages of his family members: 6, 11, 39, 41, and 63. What is the mean age?

Chapter Review

Reviewing Vocabulary

Write *always, sometimes,* or *never* for each question. Give an example to support your answer.

1. When you divide a number by 1, the result is the same number.
2. If there are zeros in the dividend, there will be zeros in the quotient.
3. When you are finding the mean of a group of numbers, first find the sum of the numbers and then divide the sum by the number of addends.
4. A function is a rule that gives two values of y for each value of x.

Write a definition.

5. Commutative Property
6. equation
7. inverse operations
8. mean

Reviewing Concepts and Skills

Divide. *(pages 134–135, 136–137)*

9. $4\overline{)848}$ **10.** $6\overline{)2{,}014}$ **11.** $9\overline{)672{,}461}$

12. $7\overline{)49{,}079}$ **13.** $12\overline{)18{,}024}$ **14.** $2\overline{)414}$

Estimate the quotient. *(pages 138–139)*

15. $6\overline{)315}$ **16.** $9\overline{)44{,}256}$ **17.** $5\overline{)16{,}205}$ **18.** $7\overline{)55{,}049}$

Find the mean. Compare with the set of numbers to make sure the answer is reasonable. *(pages 140–141)*

19. 18, 10, 15, 19, 23

20. 157, 231, 375, 240, 136, 97

21. 300, 900, 600

22. 75, 62, 85, 86, 73, 72, 71, 60

Divide. Use mental math. *(pages 146–147)*

23. $420 \div 60$ **24.** $32{,}000 \div 40$ **25.** $81{,}000 \div 90$ **26.** $60\overline{)540{,}000}$

Divide. *(pages 148–149, 150–151, 152–153, 154–156)*

27. $30\overline{)95}$ **28.** $41\overline{)83}$ **29.** $16\overline{)616}$ **30.** $32\overline{)514}$

31. $44\overline{)814}$ **32.** $33\overline{)668}$ **33.** $55\overline{)245}$ **34.** $22\overline{)204}$

35. $19\overline{)2,834}$ **36.** $76\overline{)8,462}$ **37.** $87\overline{)21,484}$ **38.** $15\overline{)30,655}$

Evaluate each expression. *(pages 162–164)*

39. $5 \times x$, if $x = 3$ **40.** $3n + 6$, if $n = 6$ **41.** $(25 \div s) + 4$, if $s = 5$

Solve. *(pages 166–167)*

42. $6x = 42$ **43.** $18r = 54$ **44.** $c \div 7 = 7$

Find the value of y when $x = 4$. *(pages 170–172)*

45. $y = 8x$ **46.** $y = 6x + 2$ **47.** $y = (x + 6) \div 2$

Solve. *(pages 142–143, 158–159, 174–175)*

48. There are 86 people waiting to go on a sightseeing trip. Each mini-bus can hold 9 people. How many mini-buses will be needed for the 86 people?

49. Darla earns the same amount for each hour she works. Her pay for working 6 hours was $48. How much does Darla earn each hour she works?

50. A rope is 75 inches long. It is cut into two parts, so that one part is twice as long as the other. How long is each part?

Brain Teasers Math Reasoning

Find the Number

The number can be divided by 50 and 20. It is greater than 300. It is less than 500. What is the number?

Number Puzzle

Replace the ■ each time with the same number. What do you notice? What numbers can you use to make this number sentence true?

(■ ÷ ■) − (■ ÷ ■) = 0

Internet Brain Teasers
Visit **www.eduplace.com/kids/mhm** for more *Brain Teasers.*

Chapter Test

Divide.

1. $5\overline{)655}$
2. $3\overline{)6,517}$
3. $6\overline{)18,709}$
4. $7\overline{)7,372}$
5. $8\overline{)32,406}$
6. $9\overline{)2,521}$

Estimate the quotient.

7. $3\overline{)598}$
8. $6\overline{)19,206}$
9. $8\overline{)70,789}$

Find the mean.

10. 6, 9, 8, 5, 12, 14, 7, 11
11. 968, 527, 635, 420, 585

Divide. Use mental math.

12. $350 \div 70$
13. $28,000 \div 40$
14. $60,000 \div 50$

Divide.

15. $21\overline{)442}$
16. $27\overline{)198}$
17. $81\overline{)476}$
18. $34\overline{)596}$
19. $32\overline{)928}$
20. $12\overline{)785}$
21. $63\overline{)989}$
22. $43\overline{)872}$
23. $779 \div 19$
24. $7,162 \div 26$
25. $55,055 \div 55$
26. $12,062 \div 34$

Evaluate each expression.

27. $x - 9$, if $x = 18$
28. $n \div 6$, if $n = 30$
29. $5t$, if $t = 12$

Solve.

30. $2g = 14$
31. $p + 4 = 51$
32. $w - 8 = 0$
33. $m \div 4 = 20$

Find the value of y when $x = 6$.

34. $y = 24 \div x$
35. $y = x + 19$
36. $y = 3x + 2$

Solve.

37. Brenda kept track of the high temperatures for one week. They were 62°F, 60°F, 71°F, 74°F, 70°F, 61°F, 64°F. What was the mean high temperature for that week?

38. Rocky has 78 baseball cards. He put all 78 baseball cards in plastic pages that hold 9 cards each. He filled as many plastic pages as possible. How many cards were on the page that was not full?

39. The library has 216 biographies. There are 5 biographies of men for every 4 biographies of women. How many biographies of women are there?

40. Michelle scored 4 times as many points as Tammy. If Michelle scored 28 points, how many points did Tammy score?

Write About It

Solve each problem. Use correct math vocabulary to explain your thinking.

1. Tina completed this division.

```
      2 013 R5
  49)88,652
    - 88
      0 65
      - 49
       162
     - 147
        15
```

a. Explain what she did wrong.

b. Show how to find the correct quotient and remainder.

2. Three students wrote the algebraic expression $4n + 2$ in words.
Cheryl wrote "4 more than two times a number."
Robert wrote "4 times the sum of a number and 2."
Clark wrote "2 more than 4 times a number."

a. Who wrote the correct phrase?

b. Explain why each of the other phrases is not correct.

c. Write each of the other two word phrases as algebraic expressions.

Another Look

Use the ticket information to solve each problem. Show your work using models, numbers, or words.

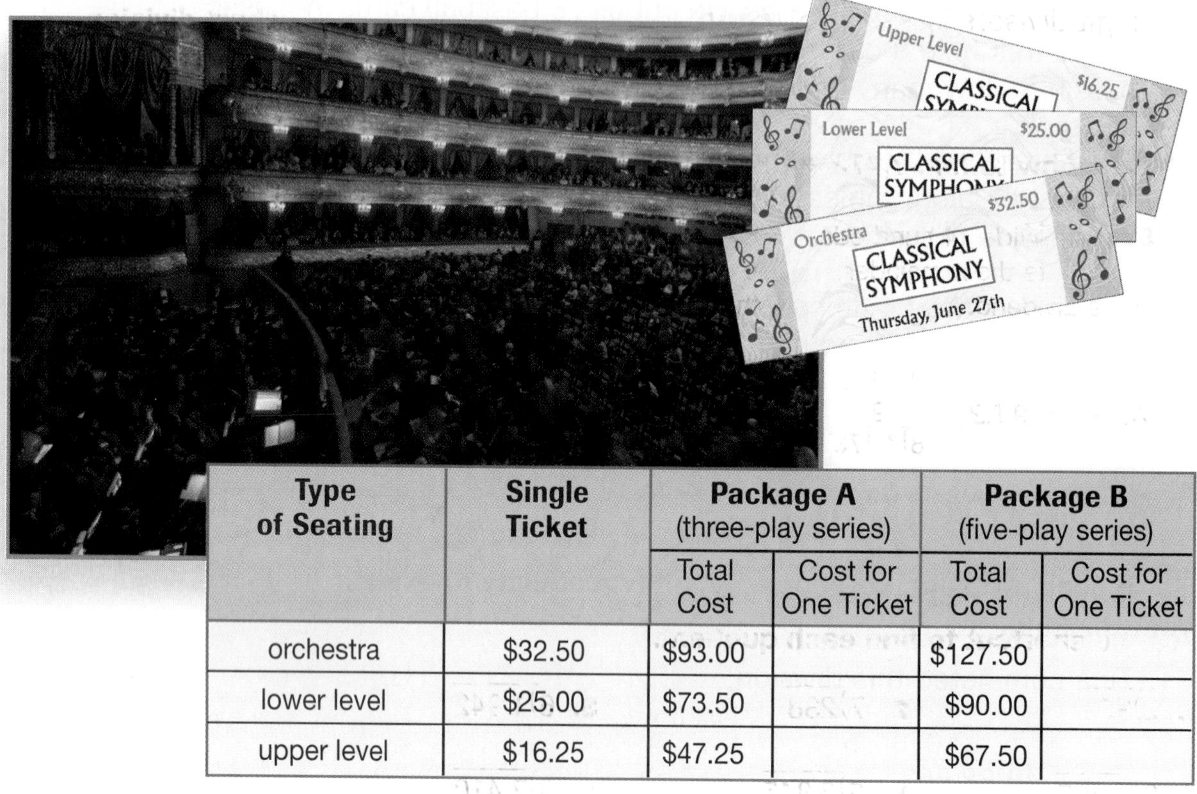

Type of Seating	Single Ticket	Package A (three-play series)		Package B (five-play series)	
		Total Cost	Cost for One Ticket	Total Cost	Cost for One Ticket
orchestra	$32.50	$93.00		$127.50	
lower level	$25.00	$73.50		$90.00	
upper level	$16.25	$47.25		$67.50	

1. How much is the cost for one ticket for each type of seating in packages A and B? Copy and complete the chart by finding the cost for one ticket for packages A and B.
2. Use your chart to compare ticket prices. For each type of seating, which is the best buy: a single ticket, a ticket from package A, or a ticket from package B?
3. **Look Back** Find the differences in price between a single ticket and a ticket from packages A and B. How much would you save with each package for each type of seating? Which package offers the greatest savings?
4. **Analyze** How does knowing the price for one ticket help when comparing ticket packages?

Standards NS 2.0 MR 2.0, 2.4, 2.6

Enrichment

Short Division

A shortcut you can use to divide with one-digit divisors is **short division**.

New Vocabulary
short division

Here's how to find 7,473 ÷ 8.

Step 1 Divide 74 hundreds by 8. Write the remainder in the dividend.	**Step 2** Divide 27 tens by 8. Write the remainder in the dividend.	**Step 3** Divide 33 by 8. Write the last remainder in the quotient.
Think: 74 ÷ 8 = 9 R2	**Think:** 27 ÷ 8 = 3 R3	**Think:** 33 ÷ 8 = 4 R1
Write: $8\overline{)74^{2}73}$ with quotient 9	**Write:** $8\overline{)74^{2}7^{3}3}$ with quotient 9 3	**Write:** $8\overline{)74^{2}7^{3}3}$ with quotient 9 3 4 R1

Use the shortcut to find each quotient.

1. $2\overline{)329}$ **2.** $7\overline{)238}$ **3.** $6\overline{)1{,}942}$

4. $8\overline{)4{,}265}$ **5.** $5\overline{)2{,}345}$ **6.** $3\overline{)7{,}410}$

7. $4\overline{)2{,}525}$ **8.** $9\overline{)8{,}035}$ **9.** $6\overline{)10{,}533}$

What do the circled numbers represent?

10. $4\overline{)7^{(3)}3^{(1)}6\,5}$ with quotient 1 8 41 R(1)

Explain Your Thinking

► When you are dividing a number using the shortcut method, how can you tell where to place the remainder in the dividend?

Standards NS 2.2

CHAPTER 5

Measurement and Integers

Why Learn About Measurement and Integers?

Measurement can help you find the distance down a hill and the weight of a sled. Integers can help you describe temperature.

When you read a train or a bus schedule, you use units of time to find how long a trip will take. When you add your score in a game of miniature golf, you add integers.

These boys just came down the hill on their sled. They used integers to read the thermometer before they went outside to play.

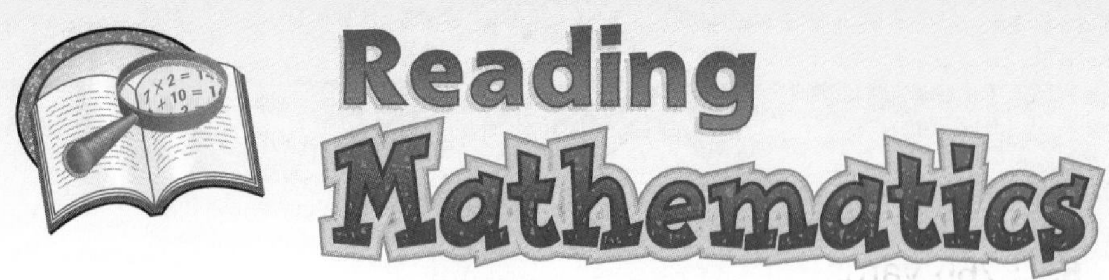

Reviewing Vocabulary

Understanding math language helps you become a successful problem solver. Here are some units of measure you should recognize.

Customary Units of Measure	Metric Units of Measure
Length	**Length**
1 foot (ft) = 12 inches (in.)	1 meter (m) = 100 centimeters (cm)
1 yard (yd) = 3 feet (ft)	1 kilometer (km) = 1,000 meters (m)
1 mile (mi) = 5,280 feet (ft)	
Capacity	**Capacity**
1 pint (pt) = 2 cups (c)	1 liter (L) = 1,000 milliliters (mL)
1 quart (qt) = 2 pints (pt)	
1 gallon (gal) = 4 quarts (qt)	
Weight	**Mass**
1 pound (lb) = 16 ounces (oz)	1 kilogram (kg) = 1,000 grams (g)
1 ton (T) = 2,000 pounds (lb)	

Reading Words and Symbols

When you read mathematics, sometimes you read only words, sometimes you read words and symbols, and sometimes you read only symbols.

Measurements are often written with symbols.

Larger and smaller metric units are created by adding prefixes to the names of basic units. These prefixes tell how large the unit is compared with the basic unit.

- The **meter** (m) is the basic unit of length
- 1 **kilo**meter = 1,000 m
- 1 **centi**meter = 0.01 m
- 1 **milli**meter = 0.001 m

Try These

1. Write each measurement using the symbol.

   a. 12 inches
   b. 1,760 yards
   c. 8 ounces
   d. 2 pints
   e. 1 kilometer
   f. 100 centimeters
   g. 1,000 grams
   h. 0.001 kilogram

2. Rewrite each amount from Exercise 1, using a different unit.

3. Write *true* or *false* for each statement.

   a. A pound is equal to 32 oz.
   b. A pencil weighs about 2 lb.
   c. Milk can come in quart containers.
   d. The length of a sheet of standard letter-size paper is 11 in.
   e. A kilometer is equal to 10 meters.
   f. There are 1,000 grams in 1 kilogram.

4. Write the customary unit you would use to measure each.

   a. the length of a nail
   b. the height of a room
   c. the amount of water in a fish tank
   d. the weight of a hummingbird

Upcoming Vocabulary

Write About It **Here are some other vocabulary words** you will learn in this chapter. Watch for these words. Write their definitions in your journal.

area	**unit square**	**decimeter (dm)**
unit length	**capacity**	**millimeter (mm)**
perimeter	**metric ton (t)**	**absolute value**
	milligram (mg)	

Customary Units of Length

You will learn how to measure lengths to the nearest fraction of an inch.

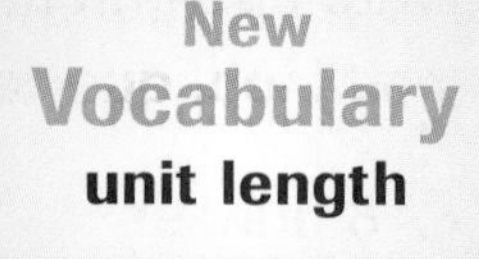

Learn About It

The system of measurement used in the United States is called the customary system of measurement. Some standard **unit lengths** in this system include mile (mi), yard (yd), foot (ft), and inch (in.). Inches are used to measure short lengths.

Materials

ruler marked in sixteenths of an inch

Measure the length of the purple line segment below, using a unit length of 1 inch.

Measuring With Customary Units of Length

Measure the length to the nearest inch.

- Where do you place the left end of a ruler when measuring length?
- Is the length of the above line segment closer to 3 in. or 4 in.? How can you tell?

Measure the length to the nearest half inch.

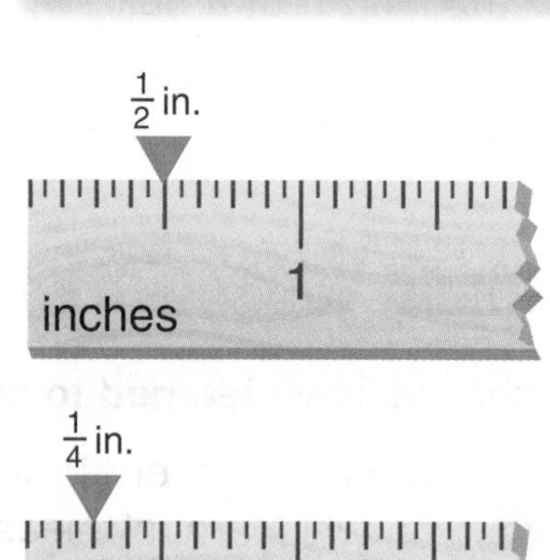

- The length of the segment lies between which two half-inch marks?
- What is the length to the nearest half inch?

Measure the length to the nearest quarter inch.

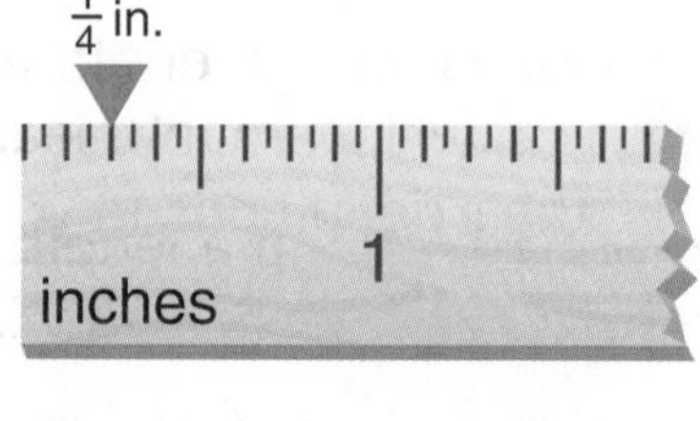

- The length of the segment lies between which two quarter-inch marks?
- What is the length to the nearest quarter inch?

Measure the length to the nearest eighth inch.

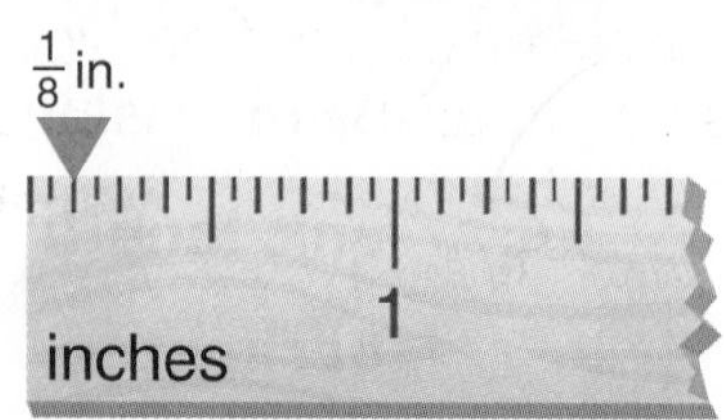

- What is the length to the nearest eighth inch? Explain how you know.

Try It Out

Use a ruler. Measure each line segment to the nearest inch, half inch, quarter inch, and eighth inch.

1.

2.

3.

4.

5.

6.

7.

8.

Write about it! Talk about it!

Use what you have learned to answer these questions.

9. Does measuring a length to the nearest customary unit produce an exact measurement? Explain.

10. How is measuring a length to the nearest unit like rounding a number? How is it different?

11. Choose an object from your classroom and measure its length to the nearest inch, half inch, quarter inch, and eighth inch. Which measure best describes its length? Tell why.

Perimeter and Area in Customary Units

You will learn how to find the perimeter and area of rectangular figures.

New Vocabulary
perimeter
unit square
area

Learn About It

Sophie is finding the perimeter and area of a rug that is 8 ft by 60 in.

You can measure **perimeter** (P) (the distance around a plane figure) by finding the sum of the lengths of its sides. A rectangle has two opposite sides of equal length (l) and two other sides of equal length (w). The perimeter of a rectangle is $P = 2l + 2w$.

A **unit square** is a square with sides one unit long. You can measure **area** (A) by finding the number of unit squares that cover a surface with no overlap. The area of a rectangle with length (l) and width (w) is $A = l \times w$.

To find the perimeter and area of the rug, you can change 60 inches into feet.

Changing Customary Units of Length

60 in. = ■ ft

- Use the table to find the relationship between inches and feet. 12 in = 1 ft
- Divide by 12 to find the number of feet. $60 \div 12 = 5$; 60 in = 5 ft

Customary Units of Length
12 inches (in.) = 1 foot (ft)
3 feet = 1 yard (yd)
36 inches = 1 yard
5,280 feet = 1 mile (mi)
1,760 yards = 1 mile

Find the perimeter and area of the rug.

Perimeter: $P = 2l + 2w$

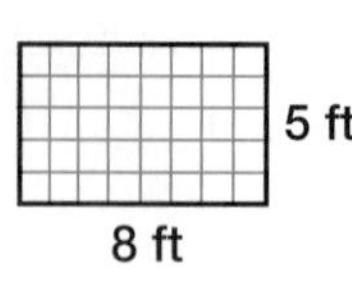

$P = 2(8) + 2(5)$
$= 16 + 10$
$= 26$ ft

Area: $A = l \times w$

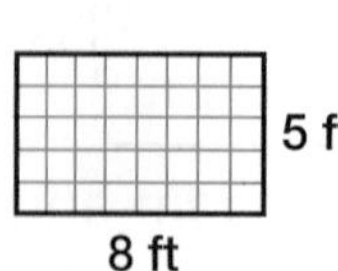

$A = 8 \times 5$
$= 40\ ft^2$

The symbol ft^2 tells you that the area unit being used is 1 square foot.
Write: 1 ft^2
Read: 1 square foot

Solution: The perimeter of the rug is 26 ft; its area is 40 ft^2.

 Standards NS **1.0, 2.2** MG **1.0, 1.4**

Other Examples

A. Change Inches to Feet and Inches

54 in. = ■ ft ■ in.

Since 12 in. = 1 ft, divide 54 by 12.
$54 \div 12 = 4$ R6

54 in. = 4 ft 6 in.

B. Change Yards and Feet to Feet

5 yd 2 ft = ■ ft

Since 1 yd = 3 ft., multiply 5 by 3.
$5 \times 3 = 15$; then add the 2 ft
$15 + 2 = 17$

5 yd 2 ft = 17 ft

Explain Your Thinking

- ▶ Do you multiply or divide to change a smaller unit to a larger unit? a larger unit to a smaller unit?
- ▶ Show that a rectangle that is 3 units by 4 units contains 12 unit squares.

Guided Practice

Ask Yourself

- Should I use $P = 2l + 2w$ or $A = l \times w$?
- Should I multiply or divide to change units?

Find the perimeter and area of each rectangle.

1. K L M N — 3 in., 4 in.

2. P S R Q — 5 ft, 5 ft

Complete.

3. 2 ft = ■ in.

4. 6 ft = ■ yd

5. 4 mi = ■ ft

6. 3,520 yd = ■ mi

7. 3 yd = ■ in.

8. 32 in. = ■ ft ■ in.

Independent Practice

Find the perimeter and area of each rectangle.

9. 2 ft, 3 ft

10. 10 yd, 16 yd

11. 5 in., 9 in.

12. 15 in., 25 in.

13.

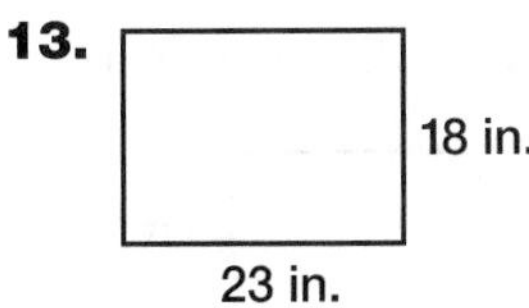

14.

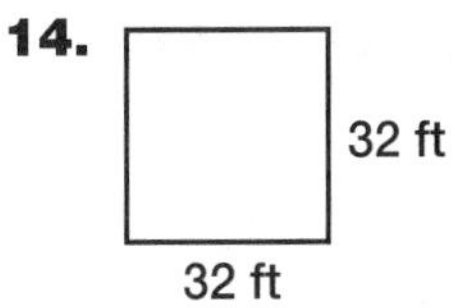

Complete.

15. 7 ft = ■ in.

16. ■ in. = 2 yd

17. ■ in. = 5 ft

18. 2 mi = ■ ft

19. 15 yd = ■ ft

20. ■ in. = 2 ft 6 in.

21. ■ ft = 3 yd 1 ft

22. 6,000 ft = ■ mi ■ ft

23. 125 in. = ■ ft ■ in.

The perimeter and the length of one side of each rectangle is given. Find the length of the missing side. Then find the area.

24. $P = 32$ yd; 6 yd

25. $P = 120$ in.; 30 in.

26. $P = 19$ mi; 2.5 mi

Problem Solving • Reasoning

Use the floor plan of a bedroom for Problems 27–30.

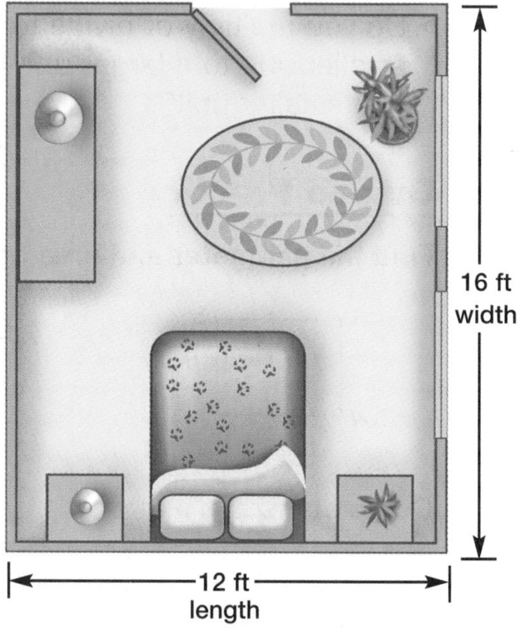

27. A wallpaper border will be applied to the walls. What is the maximum length of border that should be bought?

28. **Logical Thinking** If the length of this room was halved, and the width was doubled, what would be the new perimeter and the new area of the room?

29. **Analyze** New wall-to-wall carpeting is to be installed on the floor of the room. How many square feet of carpeting should be bought?

30. **Write About It** One quart of paint covers between 125 and 150 square feet. Will one quart of paint be enough to paint the ceiling? Explain.

Mixed Review • Test Prep

Compare. Write $>$, $<$, or $=$ for each ●. *(pages 30–31)*

31. 4.12 ● 4.21 **32.** 1.06 ● 0.99 **33.** 7.2 ● 7.20

34. 11.6 ● 1.16 **35.** 0.55 ● 0.505 **36.** 24.400 ● 24.4

37 For exercise, Lee walks $\frac{1}{2}$ mi every other day. How many miles does Lee walk in 2 weeks? *(pages 34–35)*

A 1 mi **B** $2\frac{1}{2}$ mi **C** $3\frac{1}{2}$ mi **D** 7 mi

Logical Thinking

Time

If a clock chimes once every $\frac{1}{4}$ hour, how many times does it chime in 6 hours?

Extra Practice See Set A on page 230.

Two-Dimensional Thinking

If you know the area of a figure in square feet, you can find the area in square yards or square inches.

1 square inch (in.^{2})

1 in.

1 in.

1 square foot (ft^2)

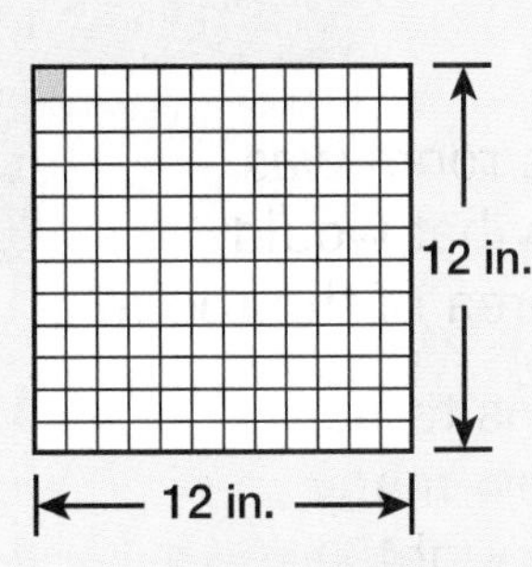

144 square inches

1 square yard (yd^2)

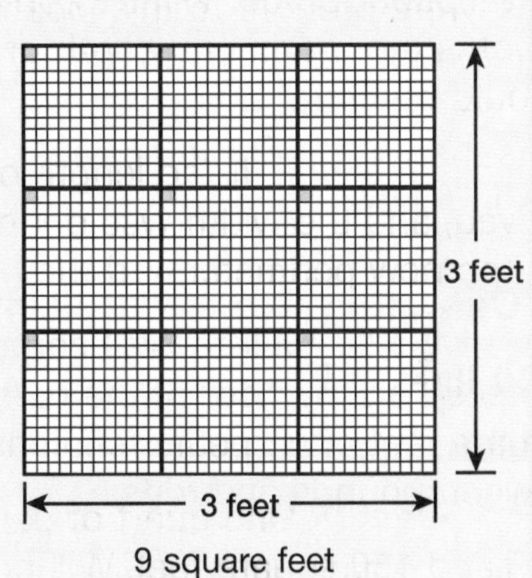

9 square feet

You can use division or multiplication to change from one unit to another.

288 in.^{2} = ■ ft^2

288 in.^{2} = 2 ft^2

Divide to change from smaller to larger units.
$288 \div 144 = 2$

5 yd^2 = ■ ft^2

5 yd^2 = 45 ft^2

Multiply to change from larger to smaller units.
$5 \times 9 = 45$

Try These

Complete each equivalent measure.

1. 576 in.^{2} = ■ ft^2 **2.** 2,880 in.^{2} = ■ ft^2 **3.** 14,400 in.^{2} = ■ ft^2

4. 2 yd^2 = ■ ft^2 **5.** 5 yd^2 = ■ ft^2 **6.** 10 yd^2 = ■ ft^2

7. 36 ft^2 = ■ yd^2 **8.** 225 ft^2 = ■ yd^2 **9.** 900 ft^2 = ■ yd^2

10. 4 ft^2 = ■ in.^{2} **11.** 3 ft^2 = ■ in.^{2} **12.** 10 ft^2 = ■ in.^{2}

Customary Units of Weight and Capacity

You will learn how to change one customary unit of weight or capacity to another.

New Vocabulary
capacity

Learn About It

Stonehenge, on Salisbury Plain, in England, is a favorite tourist attraction. The stones, some of them weighing as much as 90,000 pounds, were brought to this location and arranged about 4,000 years ago.

What is the weight of the heaviest stones in tons?

Changing Customary Units of Weight

90,000 lb = ■ T

- Use the table to find the relationship between pounds and tons. 2,000 lb = 1 T
- Divide by 2,000 to find the number of tons. 90,000 ÷ 2,000 = 45; 90,000 lb = 45 T

Customary Units of Weight		
16 ounces (oz)	=	1 pound (lb)
2,000 pounds	=	1 ton (T)

Solution: The heaviest stones at Stonehenge weigh about 45 tons.

Capacity is the amount that a container can hold.

How many quarts are in 20 gallons?

Changing Customary Units of Capacity

20 gal = ■ qt

- Use the table to find the relationship between gallons and quarts. 1 gal = 4 qt
- Multiply by 4 to find the number of quarts. 20 × 4 = 80; 20 gal = 80 qt

Customary Units of Capacity		
8 fluid ounces (fl oz)	=	1 cup (c)
2 cups	=	1 pint (pt)
16 fluid ounces	=	1 pint
2 pints	=	1 quart (qt)
4 quarts	=	1 gallon (gal)

Explain Your Thinking

▶ When changing from one unit to another, how do you know whether to multiply or divide?

 Standards AF 1.0, 1.2

Guided Practice

Complete.

1. 32 oz = ■ lb
2. ■ lb = 2 T
3. ■ c = 2 pt
4. 8 qt = ■ gal
5. 6 pt = ■ qt
6. ■ pt = 64 fl oz

Ask Yourself

- Do I multiply or divide to change smaller units to larger units? larger units to smaller units?

Independent Practice

Complete.

7. 5 T = ■ lb
8. ■ lb = 176 oz
9. 18,000 lb = ■ T
10. ■ oz = 7 lb
11. 4 T = ■ lb
12. ■ lb = 48 oz
13. 72 oz = ■ lb ■ oz
14. 15,500 lb = ■ T ■ lb
15. 12 c = ■ pt
16. ■ gal = 12 qt
17. 2 pt = ■ c
18. ■ pt = 10 qt
19. 7 qt = ■ pt
20. 26 qt = ■ gal ■ qt
21. 30 pt = ■ gal ■ qt

n **Algebra • Expressions Simplify each expression given a = 8 oz, b = 6 lb, and c = 12 lb 8 oz.**

22. $a + a$
23. $c - a$
24. $(c - b) + a$
25. $2c$

Problem Solving • Reasoning

26. **Compare** A British pint is 20 fluid ounces. How many customary pints equal 4 British pints? Express 2 British pints in customary quarts and fluid ounces.

27. There are 296 tourists, weighing an average of 150 lb each, on a plane. If the plane can carry a maximum of 84,400 lb, how many tons of additional weight can be carried?

28. **Analyze** About 26,400 soft drinks are sold at a cricket match. Each drink is 16 fluid ounces. How many gallons is this?

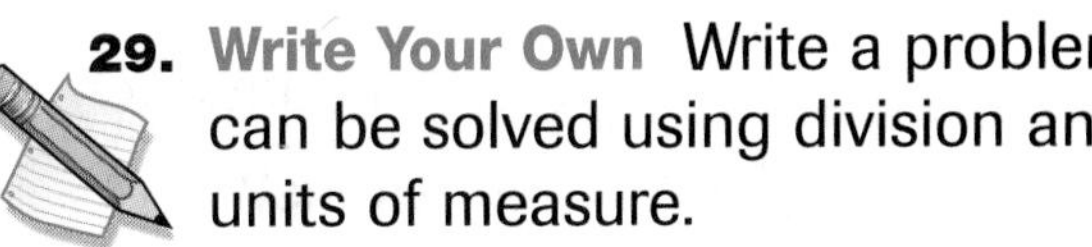

29. **Write Your Own** Write a problem that can be solved using division and units of measure.

Mixed Review • Test Prep

Order the numbers in each set from least to greatest. *(pages 26–27)*

30. 4.3 1.9 10.4 7.1 3.5
31. 0.5 0.65 1.5 0.25 0.09

32. What algebraic expression or equation represents the phrase fourteen less than a number? *(pages 70–71)*

A $14 - 14 = n$ **C** $14 - n$

B $14 - n = 14$ **D** $n - 14$

Extra Practice See Set B on page 230.

Problem-Solving Skill: Solve Multistep Problems

You will learn to solve problems that involve more than one step.

Sometimes it helps to break a problem into simpler steps.

Mr. and Mrs. Kole and their two children, ages 6 and 3, plan to visit the zoo. Will the tickets to the zoo cost less than $50.00?

Find the cost of tickets for the adults.

What is the cost of each adult ticket? → $18.00
How many adult tickets are needed? → × 2
How much will the adult tickets cost? → $36.00

Find the cost of tickets for the children.

What is the cost of each child ticket? → $8.00
How many child tickets are needed? → × 2
How much will the child tickets cost? → $16.00

Find the total cost of the tickets.

$$\begin{array}{r} \$36.00 \\ +\ 16.00 \\ \hline \$52.00 \end{array}$$

Solution: No, the tickets for the visit will cost $52.00 which is more than $50.00.

Look Back What information given in the problem did you need to answer the question that was asked?

 Standards NS **2.0, 2.1** MR **1.0, 1.2, 2.0, 3.0**

Guided Practice

Solve. Use the information from p. 200 and the signs at the right to help you.

1. How much more would it cost the Kole family to visit the wild animal park than the zoo?

   Think: How much more does it cost for each ticket?

2. How much would the Kole family save by buying zoo and park combo tickets instead of separate tickets?

   Think: What is the cost of separate tickets?

Choose a Strategy

Solve. Use these or other strategies.

Problem-Solving Strategies

- **Find a Pattern**
- **Make a Table**
- **Write an Equation**
- **Guess and Check**

3. Julia is saving to buy a child's ticket to the wild animal park. She has saved $7.53 so far. How much more money does she need to save to have enough money to buy the child's ticket?

4. Together Chen and Lou have visited the zoo a total of 12 times. Chen has visited the zoo 3 times as often as Lou. How many times has each boy visited the zoo?

5. Three hundred forty-six children from Greenview School will be visiting the zoo. What is the least number of buses that will be needed if each bus can carry 45 children?

6. On Sunday, Kari spent $24.00. On Monday, she spent $12.00. On Tuesday, she spent $6.00. If she continues this pattern of spending, how much will she spend on Thursday?

7. Mr. and Mrs. Wilson want to buy zoo and park combo tickets for themselves, 1 teenage child, and 2 children between the ages of 3 and 11. How much will the tickets cost?

8. Charlie bought 3 adult tickets to the wild animal park. Charlie gave the ticket seller one $20 bill, three $10 bills, and four $5 bills. How much change should he receive?

Extra Practice See 1–4 on page 233.

Metric Units of Length

You will learn how to measure lengths in metric units and how to change from one unit to another.

New Vocabulary
decimeter (dm)
millimeter (mm)

Learn About It

Use a ruler to measure to the nearest decimeter, centimeter, and millimeter.

The metric system is a system of measurement based on 10 and powers of 10 that is used in many countries. In the United States, scientists use the metric system for their measurements.

Materials
centimeter ruler

Measure the length of the line segment below using metric units.

Measuring With Metric Units of Length

Measure the length to the nearest decimeter.

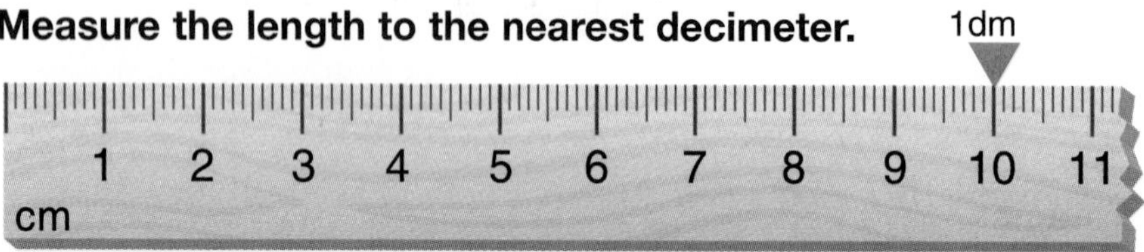

- 1 **decimeter** (1 dm) = 10 cm
- Between which two decimeter marks is the length of the line segment above?
- What is the length of the segment to the nearest decimeter?

Measure the length to the nearest centimeter.

- Is the length of the segment closer to 9 cm or 10 cm? How can you tell?
- What is the length of the segment to the nearest centimeter?

1cm
1 2 3
cm

Measure the length to the nearest millimeter.

- 1 **millimeter** (1 mm) = 0.1 cm
  How many millimeters are in 1 cm?
- What is the length of the line segment to the nearest millimeter?

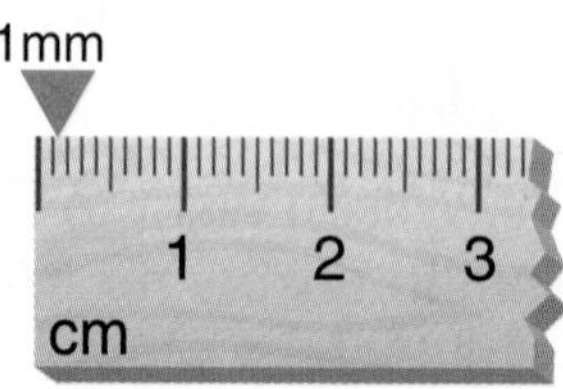

Standards MR **2.3, 2.5, 3.0, 3.3**

Changing Metric Units of Length

To change from one metric unit of length to another, multiply or divide by a power of 10. Powers of 10 include 10, 100, and 1,000.

Metric Units of Length
10 millimeters (mm) = 1 centimeter (cm)
10 centimeters = 1 decimeter (dm)
10 decimeters = 1 meter (m)
1,000 meters = 1 kilometer (km)

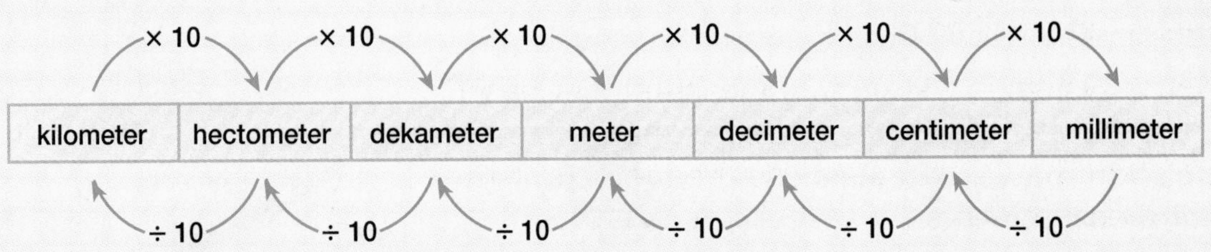

Multiply to change from a larger unit to a smaller unit.

2 cm = ■ mm

$2 \times 10 = 20$

2 cm = 20 mm

Divide to change from a smaller unit to a larger unit.

5,000 m = ■ km

$5{,}000 \div 1{,}000 = 5$

5,000 m = 5 km

Metric Prefixes
kilo–: 1,000
hecto–: 100
deka–: 10
deci–: 0.1
centi–: 0.01
milli–: 0.001

Notice that multiplying a number by 10 is the same as moving the decimal point in the number 1 place to the right. Dividing a number by 1,000 is the same as moving the decimal point in the number 3 places to the left.

- What happens to the decimal point when you multiply a number by 100? by 1,000? Give an example for each answer.
- What happens to the decimal point in a dividend when you divide by 10? by 100? Give an example for each answer.

Try It Out

Write the metric unit you would use to measure each.

1. length of your hair **2.** width of a parking lot

3. distance from Los Angeles to New York

Use a ruler. Measure each line segment to the nearest decimeter, centimeter, and millimeter.

4. ____

5. ____

6. ____

7. ____

8. ___________________________________

9. ____

Complete.

10. 3 m = ■ cm

11. ■ dm = 10m

12. 600 mm = ■ dm

13. 3,400 cm = ■ m

14. 500 cm = ■ dm

15. ■ mm = 25 cm

16. 2 km = ■ m

17. 750 dm = ■ cm

18. ■ mm = 8 m

19. 225 m = ■ cm

20. 8 m = ■ dm

21. 15,000 m = ■ km

Write about it! Talk about it!

Use what you have learned to answer each question.

22. Does measuring a length to the nearest metric unit produce an exact measurent? Explain.

23. Choose an object from your classroom and measure its length to the nearest millimeter, centimeter, and decimeter. Which measure best describes its length? Tell why.

24. How is changing from one metric unit to another like changing from one customary unit to another? How is it different?

Extra Practice See Set C on page 231.

Practice Game

Estimating Measures

Practice your skill by playing this estimation game in a small group. Try to make estimates that are as close as possible to the actual measurement.

What You'll Need

- *metric measurement tools (centimeter ruler, meter stick)*
- *a chart like the one shown (Teaching Tool 4)*

To Be Measured	Estimate	Measurement

Players
2

Here's What to Do

1. Pick one player to be the "chooser". This player thinks of a distance or object to be measured with the tools provided.
2. Each player records in a table like the one shown what will be measured. Then they estimate the measurement and record it. Players must include appropriate metric units with their estimates.
3. The "chooser" picks the appropriate tool and makes the measurement.
4. Players compare their estimates to the actual measurement. The player who has the estimate that is closest to the actual measurement is the "chooser" for the next round. Continue playing until everyone gets a chance to be the "chooser".

Share Your Thinking What helps you make good estimates?

Metric Units of Mass and Capacity

You will learn how to change from one metric unit of capacity or mass to another.

New Vocabulary
metric ton (t)
milligram (mg)

Learn About It

A great white shark can have a mass as great as 2,000 kg. What is the mass of a great white shark in **metric tons**?

Changing Metric Units of Mass

2,000 kg = ■ t

- Use the table to find the relationship between kilograms and metric tons. — 1,000 kg = 1 t
- Divide by 1,000 to find the number of metric tons. — 2,000 ÷ 1,000 = 2; 2,000 kg = 2 t

Metric Units of Mass		
1,000 milligrams (mg)	=	1 gram (g)
1,000 grams	=	1 kilogram (kg)
1,000 kilograms	=	1 metric ton (t)

Solution: A great white shark can have a mass of about 2 metric tons.

Changing Metric Units of Capacity

50 L = ■ mL

- Use the table to find the relationship between liters and milliliters. — 1 L = 1,000 mL
- Multiply by 1,000 to find the number of milliliters. — 1,000 × 50 = 50,000; 50 L = 50,000 mL

Metric Units of Capacity		
1,000 milliliters (mL)	=	1 liter (L)
10 deciliters (dL)	=	1 liter (L)

Solution: 50 L = 50,000 mL

Explain Your Thinking

▶ If you compared your mass with that of a great white shark, would you use kilograms or metric tons? Why?

▶ What power of 10 would you use to change liters to milliliters? Would you multiply or divide?

Standards | NS **1.1, 2.1** MR **1.1, 2.3**

Guided Practice

Complete.

1. 2 L = ■ mL
2. 3,000 mL = ■ L
3. 8,000 kg = ■ t
4. 6 g = ■ mg
5. 31,000 mg = ■ g
6. 5 t = ■ kg

Ask Yourself

- Which power of 10 do I use?
- Do I multiply or divide?

Independent Practice

Complete.

7. 4 kg = ■ g
8. 7 L = ■ mL
9. 7,000 g = ■ kg
10. 8 t = ■ kg
11. 2 L = ■ dL
12. 13 g = ■ mg
13. 5,000 kg = ■ t
14. 25,000 mg = ■ g
15. 2.5 kg = ■ g

Compare. Write >, <, or = for each ●.

16. 2 t ● 20,000 kg
17. 2,000 g ● 3 kg
18. 12 kg ● 10,000 g
19. 2,000 mL ● 20 L
20. 8 L ● 8,000 mL
21. 400 kg ● 4 t

Problem Solving • Reasoning

Choose the most reasonable measure for each.

22. a juice can
    a. 3.5 mL **b.** 35 mL **c.** 350 mL
23. a package of fish food
    a. 65 g **b.** 65 mg **c.** 6 kg
24. a whale
    a. 120 t **b.** 120 kg **c.** 1,200 g
25. an eyedropper
    a. 5 L **b.** 5 mL **c.** 5 g

Using Vocabulary

Which metric unit of length, mass, or capacity would you choose to measure each of these? Tell why.

- **A** the amount of water in a glass of water
- **B** the length of a pencil
- **C** the amount of medicine in a medicine dropper
- **D** the mass of a train

Mixed Review • Test Prep

Write each number in words. *(pages 24–25)*

26. 8.075
27. 710,044
28. 2,052,600

Choose the letter of the correct answer. *(pages 24–25)*

29. What number in standard form represents one hundred million?
    A 1,000 **B** 1,000,000 **C** 10,000,000 **D** 100,000,000

30. What number in standard form represents one thousandth?
    F 0.0001 **G** 0.001 **H** 0.01 **J** 0.1

Extra Practice See Set D on page 231.

Add and Subtract Units of Time

You will learn how to use addition and subtraction to solve problems involving time and schedules.

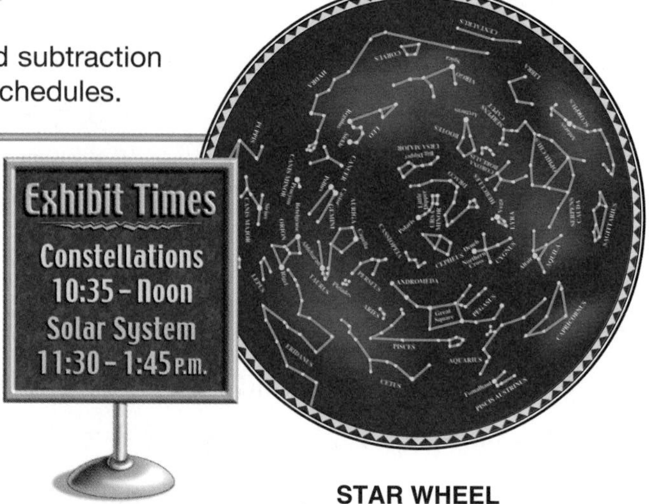

STAR WHEEL

Learn About It

The sign shows the starting and ending times of a video exhibit of the constellations at the planetarium. What is the length of the video in hours and minutes?

Subtract. **12:00 – 10:35**

Find 12:00 – 10:35.

Step 1 To subtract 35 min from 0 min, regroup 12 h as 11 h 60 min.

$$\begin{array}{r} \overset{11}{\cancel{12}}\text{ h }\overset{60}{\cancel{00}}\text{ min} \\ -10\text{ h }35\text{ min} \\ \hline \end{array}$$

Step 2 Subtract the minutes. Then subtract the hours.

$$\begin{array}{r} \overset{11}{\cancel{12}}\text{ h }\overset{60}{\cancel{00}}\text{ min} \\ -10\text{ h }35\text{ min} \\ \hline 1\text{ h }25\text{ min} \end{array}$$

Solution: The video is 1 hour 25 minutes long.

Another Example

Elapsed Time From A.M. to P.M.

How long is it from 11:30 A.M. until 1:45 P.M.?

$$\begin{array}{r} 30\text{ min} \\ +\ 1\text{ h }45\text{ min} \\ \hline 1\text{ h }75\text{ min} = 2\text{ h }15\text{ min} \end{array}$$

The time between 11:30 A.M. and noon is 30 min.

The time between noon and 1:45 P.M. is 1 h 45 min.

Add. If necessary, simplify your answer.

Explain Your Thinking

- ▶ How can you find the length of an event that starts before noon or midnight and lasts until after?
- ▶ When does an answer of hours and minutes need to be simplified? Give an example.

Guided Practice

How many hours and minutes are there between these times?

1. 7:05 A.M. to 11:30 A.M. **2.** 3:45 P.M. to 9:10 P.M.

3. 11:15 P.M. to 1:35 A.M. **4.** 5:05 A.M. to 4:55 P.M.

Ask Yourself

- Are the times from A.M. to P.M. or P.M. to A.M.?
- Do I need to regroup or simplify?

 Standards MR **1.1** AF **1.0, 1.2**

Independent Practice

How many hours and minutes are there between these times?

5. 1:10 P.M. to 7:10 P.M.
6. 7:40 A.M. to 9:50 A.M.
7. 6:05 P.M. to 10:15 P.M.

8. 2:25 A.M. to 8:15 A.M.
9. 4:30 P.M. to 5:05 P.M.
10. 9:35 A.M. to 10:50 A.M.

11. 8:00 A.M. to 2:30 P.M.
12. 9:20 P.M. to 1:15 A.M.
13. 4:30 A.M. to 9:30 P.M.

14. 8:17 P.M. to 3:02 A.M.
15. 2:44 A.M. to 12:07 P.M.
16. 11:48 P.M. to 10:06 A.M.

n **Algebra • Equations** **Find the time represented by *t*.**

17. 2:30 P.M. $- t =$ 1 h 15 min

18. $t -$ 3:45 A.M. $=$ 2 h 30 min

Problem Solving • Reasoning

Use Data **Use the sign to answer Problems 19–21.**

19. How long is the moon exhibit?

20. **Analyze** Which exhibit is the longest? Explain your answer.

21. **Write About It** Amy arrives at the planetarium at 4:25 P.M. How long does she have to wait until the moon exhibit begins? Explain your thinking.

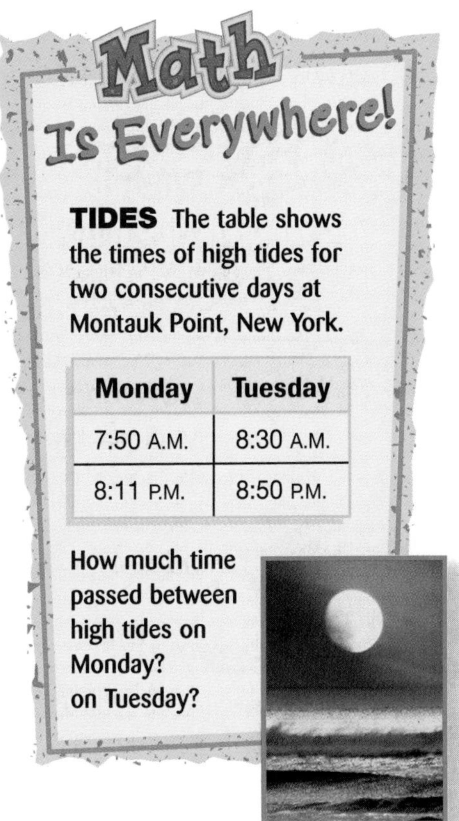

TIDES The table shows the times of high tides for two consecutive days at Montauk Point, New York.

Monday	Tuesday
7:50 A.M.	8:30 A.M.
8:11 P.M.	8:50 P.M.

How much time passed between high tides on Monday? on Tuesday?

Mixed Review • Test Prep

Evaluate each expression for $n = 12$. *(pages 70–71)*

22. $n + 8$
23. $n \div 6$
24. $100 \times n$
25. $144 \div n$

26 The largest butterfly in the world has a wingspan of 0.28 m. The smallest has a wingspan of 15 mm. What is the difference in length between these two wingspans? *(pages 54–55)*

A 13 mm
B 14.72 mm
C 265 mm
D 1.3 m

Problem-Solving Strategy: Make a Table

You will learn how making a table can help you to solve a problem.

Sometimes information in a problem can be organized in a table.

Problem Watermelon seeds should be planted in soil that has been at a temperature of 70°F or warmer for at least 3 consecutive days. If the soil temperature was 65°F on Monday and rose by 1.3 degrees each day for a week, on what day could you begin planting watermelon seeds?

What is the question?
Which day will be the third consecutive day on which the soil temperature will be 70°F or greater?

How can you find the answer?
Make a table to calculate and record the temperature each day.

Make a table. Begin with the given temperature on Monday.

Day	Temperature Calculation	Soil Temperature (°F)
Monday	65	65
Tuesday	65 + 1.3	66.3
Wednesday	66.3 + 1.3	67.6
Thursday	67.6 + 1.3	68.9
Friday	68.9 + 1.3	70.2
Saturday	70.2 + 1.3	71.5
Sunday	71.5 + 1.3	72.8

You can plant the seeds on Sunday, because it is the third consecutive day with a soil temperature of 70°F or more.

Look Back

Look back at the problem.
For what kinds of problems is it helpful to make a table?

Standards SDP **1.0** MR **1.0, 2.0, 2.3, 3.0, 3.2**

Remember:
- Understand
- Plan
- Solve
- Look Back

Guided Practice

Solve.

1. It takes Shira 4 minutes to plant 8 seedlings. At this rate, how long would it take her to plant 2 dozen seedlings? 4 dozen? 6 dozen?

   Think: How many seedlings are in a dozen?

2. On four consecutive days Marc planted 14 bulbs, 15 bulbs, 17 bulbs, and 20 bulbs. Find a pattern. What are the next 2 numbers in your pattern?

   Think: What pattern can you find in the differences?

Choose a Strategy

Solve. Use these or other strategies.

Problem-Solving Strategies

- **Make a Table**
- **Work Backward**
- **Guess and Check**
- **Write an Equation**

3. In the metric system, temperature is measured in degrees Celsius (°C). To change a temperature from degrees Fahrenheit to degrees Celsius, use the equation below.

   $$C = (F - 32) \times 5 \div 9$$

   Change each temperature in the table to Celsius.

Type of Plant	Best Soil Temperature for Planting (for 3 consecutive days)
tomatoes	60°F
sweet corn	65°F
squash	70°F
cantaloupe	75°F

4. A shelf holds 207 vegetable seed and flower seed packages. There are 25 more packages of vegetable seeds than flower seeds. How many packages are there of each type?

5. You used 11 coins to pay for a pair of gardening gloves. The total value of the coins is $2.25. If the coins were all quarters, dimes, and nickels, how many coins of each type did you use?

6. Each park needs 15 bags of grass seed. If there are 105 bags, how many parks can be seeded?

7. Find two whole numbers that have a sum of 23 and a product of 130.

Extra Practice See 5–8 on page 233.

Quick Check

Check Your Understanding of Lessons 1–8

Find the perimeter and area of rectangle *BCDE*.

1.

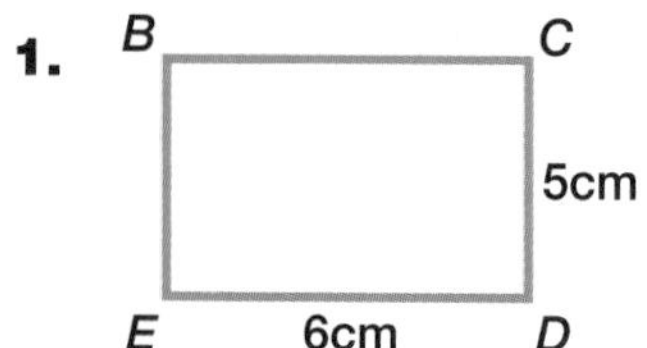

Complete.

2. 3 qt = ■ pt

3. ■ lb = 64 oz

4. 13,500 lb = ■ T ■ lb

5. 50 oz = ■ lb ■ oz

6. 15 m = ■ cm

7. 8,500 mm = ■ cm

8. 4,000 kg = ■ t

9. 6,000 mL = ■ L

10. 15 g = ■ mg

How many hours and minutes are between these times?

11. 4:20 P.M. to 6:15 P.M.

12. 2:00 A.M. to 2:00 P.M.

Solve.

13. Ron has 2 pounds of cream cheese. He uses 14 ounces to bake a cake. How many pounds and ounces of cream cheese does he have left?

14. If there are 8 commercials shown during a 30-minute TV show, how many commercials might be shown in 90 minutes? 120 minutes?

How did you do?

If you had difficulty with any items in the Quick Check, you can use the following pages for review and extra practice.

California Standards	Items	Review These Pages	Do These Extra Practice Items
Measurement and Geometry: **1.1, 1.4**	1	pages 194–196	Set A, page 230
Measurement and Geometry: **1.1, 1.4**	2–5	pages 198–199	Set B, page 230
Math Reasoning: **1.0, 2.0**	6-7	pages 202–204	Set C, page 231
Measurement and Geometry: **1.1, 1.4**	8–10	pages 206–207	Set D, page 231
Number Sense: **2.3**	11–12	pages 208–209	Set E, page 231
Math Reasoning: **1.0, 2.0**	13	pages 200–201	1–4, page 233
Math Reasoning: **1.0, 2.0**	14	pages 210–211	5–8, page 233

Test Prep • Cumulative Review

Maintaining the Standards

Choose the letter of the correct answer.

1. What is the perimeter of this rectangle?

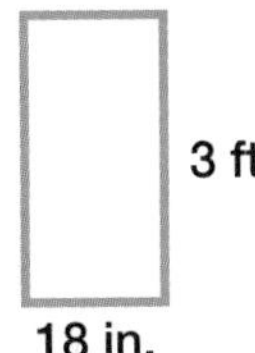

A 42 ft **C** 54 in.
B 108 in. **D** 42 in.

2. Kari subtracted these numbers and then estimated to check the difference. Which number is likely to be her estimate?

$$\begin{array}{r} 64.032 \\ -\ 19.895 \\ \hline \end{array}$$

F 30 **H** 55
G 44 **J** 84

3. Trains *A*, *B*, *C*, and *D* leave a station in order at intervals of 35 minutes. If Train *B* left at 8:15 A.M., what time was it when Train *A* left the station?

A 7:20 A.M. **C** 7:50 A.M.
B 7:40 A.M. **D** 8:50 A.M.

4. The equation $4t - 2 = r$ relates the temperature t at 6:00 A.M. and the temperature r at 11:00 A.M. The temperature at 6:00 A.M. was 2°F. What was the temperature at 11:00 A.M.?

F 1°F **H** 4°F
G 2°F **J** 6°F

5. If Megan divides her age by 2 and then adds 36, she will get her mother's age. Megan's mother is 40 years old. How old is Megan?

A 72 **C** 8
B 24 **D** 4

6. Measure this line segment to the nearest $\frac{1}{2}$ inch.

F $3\frac{1}{2}$ in. **H** $2\frac{1}{2}$ in.
G 3 in. **J** 2 in.

7. Last week Alex flew 1,562 miles. This week he flew 1,508 miles. What was the mean number of miles he flew?

A 1,502 **C** 1,575
B 1,535 **D** 1,613

8. There will be 8 children at a party. Mary bought 1 gallon of juice. Mary wonders if she bought enough juice to serve each child 2 glassfuls.

Explain What does Mary need to find out in order to solve her problem?

Safe Site

Internet Test Prep
Visit **www.eduplace.com/kids/mhm** for more *Test Prep Practice.*

LESSON 9

Integers and Absolute Value

You will learn how to find the absolute value of an integer.

New Vocabulary
absolute value

Learn About It

A temperature can be above, below, or equal to 0°. A land elevation can be above, below, or at sea level, which has an elevation of 0. Temperature and elevation measurements are often expressed as integers.

The set of integers consists of zero, the counting numbers (positive numbers), and their opposites (negative numbers).

A number line can be used to display integers.

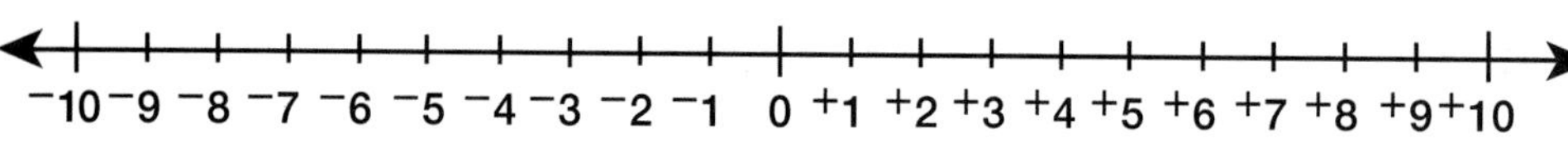

The distance from any number to zero is called the **absolute value**. To find the absolute value of an integer, find its distance from zero.

Finding Absolute Value

What is the absolute value of $^{+}5$?

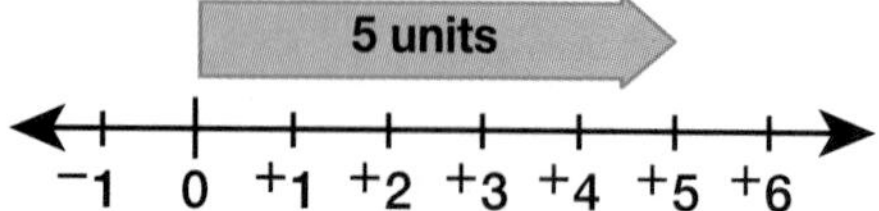

The absolute value of $^{+}5$ is 5.

What is the absolute value of $^{-}4$?

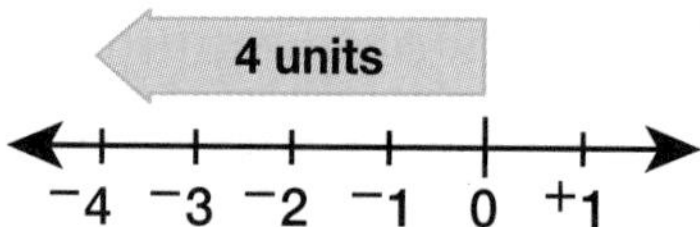

The absolute value of $^{-}4$ is 4.

The absolute value of zero is 0. The absolute value of every other number is greater than 0.

Explain Your Thinking

- ▶ Which two integers have the same absolute value? Is there more than one such pair of integers? Explain.
- ▶ Is the absolute value of an integer the same as the opposite of that integer? Explain.

Standards	NS 1.0, 1.5	AF 1.1	MR 1.0, 1.1

Guided Practice

Write the absolute value of each integer.

1. $^{+}3$ **2.** $^{-}1$ **3.** $^{-}8$ **4.** $^{+}11$

5. $^{-}2$ **6.** 0 **7.** $^{-}5$ **8.** $^{+}15$

> **Ask Yourself**
> - Do I need to change the sign?
> - Is the absolute value 0?

Independent Practice

Write the absolute value of each integer.

9. $^{+}7$ **10.** $^{-}6$ **11.** $^{+}1$ **12.** $^{-}7$ **13.** $^{-}16$ **14.** $^{-}9$

15. $^{-}10$ **16.** 0 **17.** $^{+}6$ **18.** $^{-}3$ **19.** $^{+}8$ **20.** $^{+}10$

21. $^{+}12$ **22.** $^{-}18$ **23.** $^{+}19$ **24.** $^{-}44$ **25.** $^{+}102$ **26.** $^{-}59$

Problem Solving • Reasoning

Use Data **Use the bar graph to solve Problems 27–32.**

The bar graph shows the elevation of selected places in meters. Some elevations are above sea level and some are below sea level.

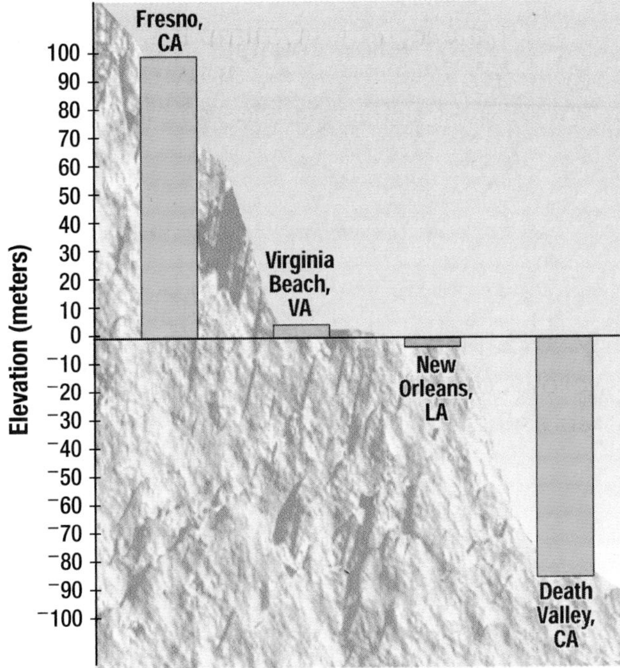

27. What elevation represents sea level?

28. **Compare** Which place has the greatest elevation above sea level?

29. Which place is closest to sea level?

30. Which place has the greatest elevation below sea level?

31. **Estimate** Estimate the difference in elevation between Fresno and Death Valley.

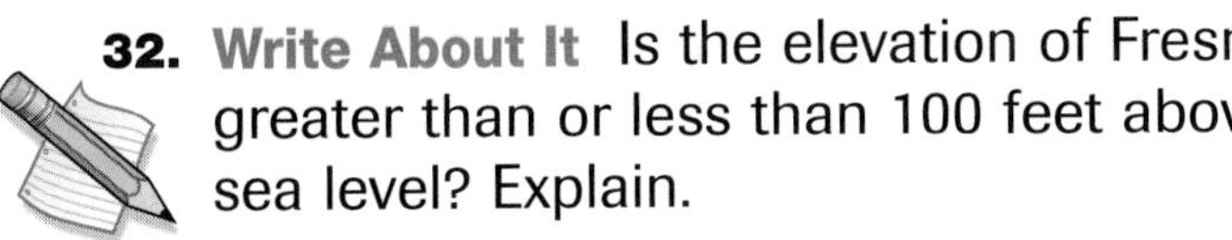

32. **Write About It** Is the elevation of Fresno greater than or less than 100 feet above sea level? Explain.

Mixed Review • Test Prep

Round each number to the underlined place. *(pages 8–9)*

33. $\underline{5}2{,}301$ **34.** $34{,}2\underline{4}0$ **35.** $1\underline{1}{,}585$ **36.** $9\underline{0}{,}621$ **37.** $79{,}\underline{0}50$

38 When rounded to the nearest hundred, what is the greatest possible number that rounds to 10,000? *(pages 8–9)*

A 9,949 **B** 9,950 **C** 10,049 **D** 10,050

Extra Practice See Set F on page 232.

Use Models to Add Integers

You will learn how to use counters to model addition of integers.

Learn About It

You can use two-color counters to add integers.

Find $^{-}3 + {}^{+}5$.

Materials

For each group:
10 yellow counters
10 red counters

Step 1 Use red counters to represent negative integers.

- Lay out 3 red counters to represent $^{-}3$.

Step 2 Use yellow counters to represent positive integers.

- Lay out 5 yellow counters to represent $^{+}5$.

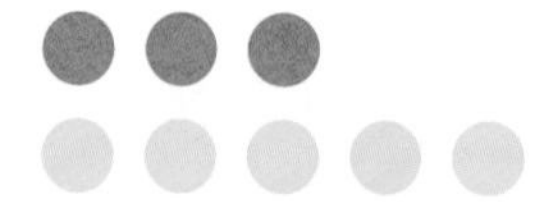

Step 3 Find all the pairs of red counters and yellow counters. Each pair of opposite counters represents 0.

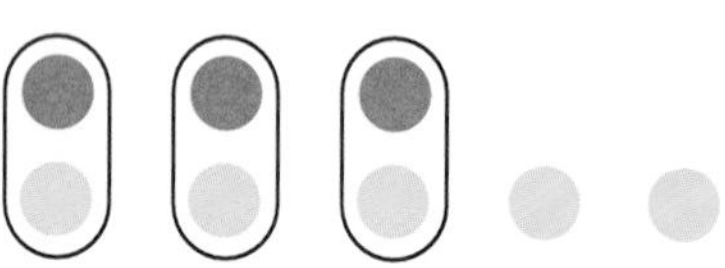

- How many pairs are there?

Step 4 The leftover counters represent the sum.

- How many counters are left over?
- What color are they?

Since there are 2 counters leftover and they are yellow,

$^{-}3 + {}^{+}5 = {}^{+}2$

 Standards NS **2.1** MR **2.0, 2.3, 3.0, 3.2, 3.3**

Try It Out

Write the addition expression shown by the counters and then find the answer.

1\.

2\.

3\.

4\.

5\.

6\.

7\.

8\.

Use two-color counters to find each sum.

9\. $^{+}7 + {}^{+}3$

10\. $^{-}6 + {}^{-}2$

11\. $^{-}9 + {}^{-}1$

12\. $^{-}4 + {}^{-}9$

13\. $^{-}7 + {}^{+}4$

14\. $^{-}2 + {}^{+}5$

15\. $^{+}3 + {}^{-}8$

16\. $^{-}5 + {}^{+}10$

17\. $^{-}5 + {}^{+}3$

18\. $^{+}7 + {}^{-}6$

19\. $^{+}8 + {}^{-}8$

20\. $^{-}4 + {}^{+}5$

Write about it! Talk about it!

Use what you have learned to answer these questions.

21\. If you were to combine two sets of yellow counters, what color counters would represent the answer? What does that tell you about the sum of two positive integers?

22\. If you were to combine two sets of red counters, what color counters would represent the answer? What does that tell you about the sum of two negative integers?

23\. When you combine a set of yellow counters and a set of red counters, how can you tell what color counters will represent the answer? What does this tell you about the sum of a positive integer and a negative integer?

24\. Why does it make sense that one red counter and one yellow counter represent zero?

LESSON 11 Add Integers on a Number Line

You will learn how to add integers by using a number line.

Learn About It

You can use a number line to add integers. You always start at 0, move left for negative integers and right for positive integers.

Suppose you are playing a game in which you can lose points (−) and gain points (+). On your first turn you lose 2 points. On your second turn you win 7 points. What is your score?

Add. $^{-}\mathbf{2} + {}^{+}\mathbf{7}$

Find $^{-}2 + {}^{+}7$.

Step 1 Start at 0. Move left 2 units to show $^{-}2$.

Step 2 Then, starting at $^{-}2$, move right 7 units to show $^{+}7$.

Step 3 The number of the point where you stop on the number line is the answer.

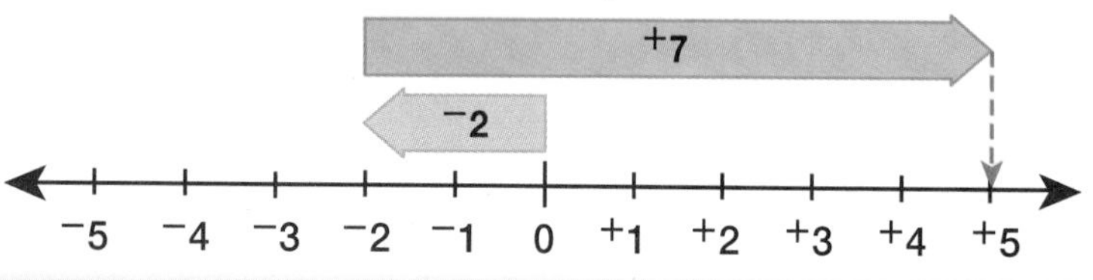

$^{-}2 + {}^{+}7 = {}^{+}5$

Solution: Your score is $^{+}5$ points.

Other Examples

A. Negative Sum

Find $^{-}5 + {}^{+}2$.

$^{-}5 + {}^{+}2 = {}^{-}3$

B. Sum of Two Negative Integers

Find $^{-}3 + {}^{-}1$.

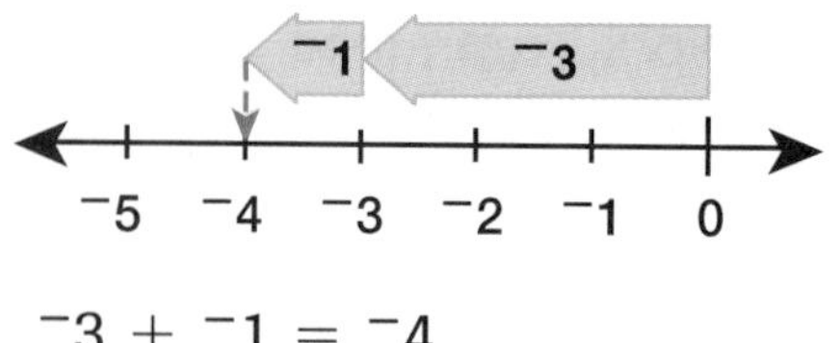

$^{-}3 + {}^{-}1 = {}^{-}4$

Explain Your Thinking

- Will the sum of two negative integers always be negative? Explain.
- When adding a negative and a positive integer, how can you tell if the sum will be negative or positive?

Standards NS 1.5, 2.1 MR 2.0, 2.3, 3.0, 3.2

Guided Practice

Use the number line to add.

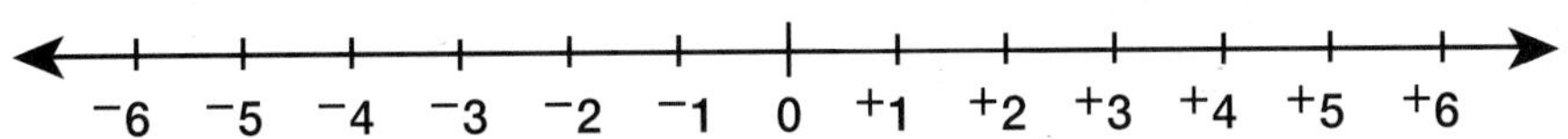

1. $^{+}2 + {}^{+}4$ **2.** $^{-}3 + {}^{-}2$ **3.** $^{+}4 + {}^{-}8$

4. $^{-}3 + {}^{+}7$ **5.** $^{-}6 + {}^{+}6$ **6.** $^{-}5 + 0$

Ask Yourself

- Where do I begin on the number line?
- Do I move left or right?

Independent Practice

Use a number line to add.

7. $^{+}11 + {}^{-}5$ **8.** $^{-}8 + {}^{-}5$ **9.** $^{+}8 + {}^{+}7$ **10.** $^{-}15 + {}^{+}15$

11. $^{+}12 + {}^{-}18$ **12.** $^{-}9 + {}^{-}3$ **13.** $^{+}10 + {}^{-}15$ **14.** $^{-}14 + {}^{+}5$

15. $^{-}10 + {}^{+}17$ **16.** $^{-}3 + {}^{+}16$ **17.** $^{-}8 + {}^{+}15$ **18.** $^{-}13 + {}^{+}6$

19. $^{-}12 + {}^{-}3$ **20.** $^{-}15 + {}^{+}3$ **21.** $^{+}9 + {}^{+}5$ **22.** $^{+}14 + {}^{-}8$

Algebra • Equations **Solve for *x*. Use a number line to help you.**

23. $^{-}11 + x = {}^{-}13$ **24.** $x + {}^{+}4 = {}^{-}8$ **25.** $^{+}8 + x = {}^{+}14$ **26.** $x + {}^{-}7 = {}^{+}8$

Solve. Choose a method.

Computation Methods

- **Mental Math**
- **Estimation**
- **Paper and Pencil**

27. During a game, Tim's team lost 5 points, won 4 points, won 3 points, and lost 3 points. What is his team's score so far?

28. **Compare** In the first 2 rounds, Pam's scores were $^{-}2$ and $^{-}6$. Jim's scores were $^{-}5$ and $^{-}4$. Who had the greater score after the first two rounds?

29. **Analyze** After 3 rounds of a game, Beth and Ken each have a score of $^{-}2$. The points they received in each round were different. What could their points in each round have been?

30. In a game tournament, Bill had 19 points. He lost 2 times that many points. Then he scored 31 more points. About how many points did Bill have in all? Explain your answer.

Mixed Review • Test Prep

Write each sum or difference. *(pages 54–55)*

31. 1,088 − 315 **32.** 237 + 91 **33.** 28 + 3,040 **34.** 2,455 − 129

35 Which expression can be simplified to $n + 8$? *(pages 66–67)*

A $n + n + 4$ **B** $(5 + 3) + n$ **C** $n + 4^2$ **D** $\frac{8}{n}$

Extra Practice See Set G on page 232.

Use Models to Subtract

You will learn how to use counters to model subtraction of integers.

Learn About It

You can use two-color counters to subtract integers.

Find $^{-}6 - {}^{-}4$.

Materials

For each group:
10 yellow counters
10 red counters

Step 1 Use red counters to represent $^{-}6$.

- What does each counter represent?
- How many counters will you lay out?

Step 2 Take away counters to subtract $^{-}4$.

- How many red counters will you take away?
- What is $^{-}6 - {}^{-}4$? How do you know?

Sometimes you may not have enough counters to take away the number being subtracted.

Find $^{-}5 - {}^{+}2$.

Step 1 Use red counters to represent $^{-}5$.

- How many counters will you lay out?

You need to subtract $^{+}2$, but there are no yellow counters to take away.

Step 2 Add pairs of red and yellow counters. Each pair represents 0. Adding 0 does not change the answer.

- How many pairs do you need to have 2 yellow counters to take away?

Step 3 Take away counters to subtract $^{+}2$.

- How many counters will you take away? What color will they be?

The counters that are left represent the answer.

- How many counters are left? What color are they?
- What is $^{-}5 - {}^{+}2$?

 Standards NS 2.1 MR 2.0, 2.3, 3.0, 3.2

Try It Out

Write a subtraction expression for each model. Then find the difference.

1. ●●●●●● Take away 4 reds.
2. ○○○○○ Take away 3 yellows.
3. ●●●● Take away 5 reds.
4. ○○○○ Take away 6 yellows.
5. ●●● Take away 2 yellows.
6. ○○○○○○ Take away 3 reds.
7. ●●●●● Take away 5 reds.
8. ○○○ Take away 3 yellows.

Use two-color counters to find each difference.

9. ${}^{+}3 - {}^{+}6$	**10.** ${}^{+}2 - {}^{-}8$	**11.** ${}^{-}2 - {}^{-}6$	**12.** ${}^{-}8 - {}^{-}3$
13. ${}^{-}8 - {}^{-}8$	**14.** ${}^{+}8 - {}^{+}4$	**15.** ${}^{+}8 - {}^{+}8$	**16.** ${}^{-}8 - {}^{+}8$
17. ${}^{-}4 - {}^{-}4$	**18.** ${}^{-}3 - {}^{-}7$	**19.** ${}^{+}5 - {}^{-}4$	**20.** ${}^{+}2 - {}^{+}7$

Write about it! Talk about it!

Use what you have learned to answer these questions.

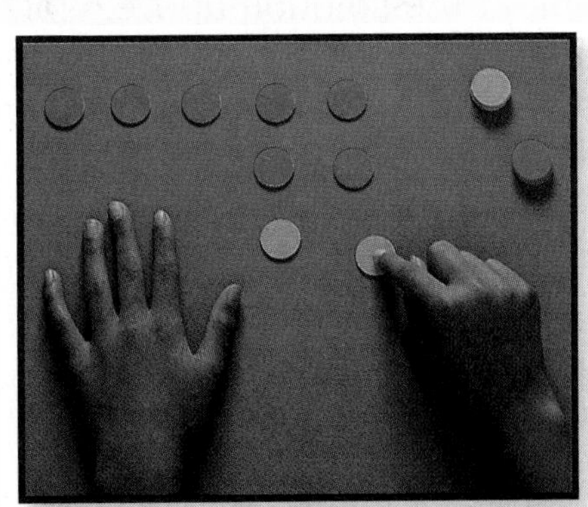

21. How can you tell when one integer is greater than another integer?
22. If the integer being subtracted is greater than the other integer, is the answer positive or is it negative?
23. If the integer being subtracted is less than the other integer, is the answer positive or is it negative?
24. Find ${}^{-}3 - {}^{+}4$ and ${}^{-}3 + {}^{-}4$. Did you get the same result adding the opposite of an integer instead of subtracting?

LESSON 13

Subtract Integers on a Number Line

You will learn how to subtract integers by using a number line.

Learn About It

You can use a number line to subtract integers.

Subtract. $^{-}\mathbf{7} - {}^{-}\mathbf{5} = \boldsymbol{n}$

Find $^{-}7 - {}^{-}5$.

Step 1 Begin at 0. Move to the left 7 units to show $^{-}7$.

Step 2 To add $^{-}5$, you would move 5 units to the left. So to subtract $^{-}\mathbf{5}$, move 5 units to the right.

Step 3 Your answer is where you stop on the number line.

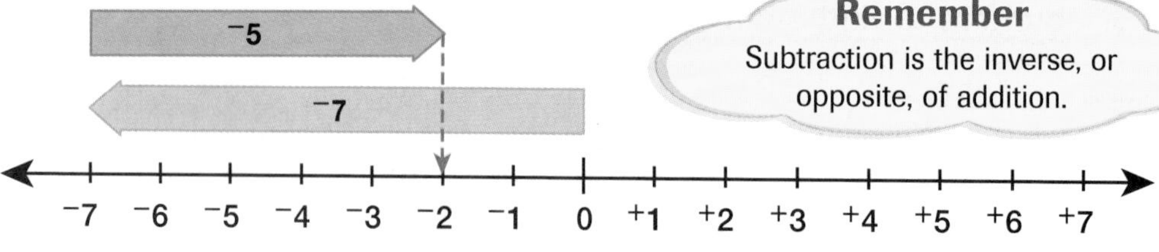

$7 - {}^{-}5 = {}^{-}2$

Solution: $^{-}7 - {}^{-}5 = {}^{-}2$

Look at the solution above. Notice that $^{-}7 - {}^{-}5$ is the same as $^{-}7 + {}^{+}5$. That is because subtracting an integer is the same as adding its opposite.

$(^{+}5) - (^{+}2) = 3$ $(^{+}5) + (^{-}2) = 3$	$(^{-}5) - (^{+}2) = {}^{-}7$ $(^{-}5) + (^{-}2) = {}^{-}7$
$(^{+}5) - (^{-}2) = 7$ $(^{+}5) + (^{+}2) = 7$	$(^{-}5) - (^{-}2) = {}^{-}3$ $(^{-}5) + (^{+}2) = {}^{-}3$

Remember
$^{+}2$ and $^{-}2$ are opposites

Explain Your Thinking

▶ Why do you end up at the same point on a number line whether you subtract an integer or add its opposite?

Standards NS **1.5, 2.1** AF **1.2** MR **2.0, 2.3, 3.0**

Guided Practice

Use a number line to complete each pair of number sentences.

1. $^{+}3 - ^{-}4 = \blacksquare$
$^{+}3 + ^{+}4 = \blacksquare$

2. $^{-}8 - ^{-}5 = \blacksquare$
$^{-}8 + ^{+}5 = \blacksquare$

3. $^{-}6 - ^{+}4 = \blacksquare$
$^{-}6 + ^{-}4 = \blacksquare$

Subtract. Write the related addition sentence that you used.

4. $^{+}5 - ^{+}5$ **5.** $^{-}6 - ^{+}1$ **6.** $^{-}5 - ^{-}2$

Ask Yourself

- Do I move left or right from 0 for the first integer?
- How do I move to subtract the second integer?

Independent Practice

Complete each pair of number sentences.

7. $^{-}9 - ^{-}9 = \blacksquare$
$^{-}9 + ^{+}9 = \blacksquare$

8. $^{+}8 - ^{+}3 = \blacksquare$
$^{+}8 + ^{-}3 = \blacksquare$

9. $^{+}7 - ^{-}2 = \blacksquare$
$^{+}7 + ^{+}2 = \blacksquare$

10. $^{+}10 - ^{-}3 = \blacksquare$
$^{+}10 + ^{+}3 = \blacksquare$

11. $^{-}9 - ^{+}4 = \blacksquare$
$^{-}9 + ^{-}4 = \blacksquare$

12. $^{-}12 - ^{-}5 = \blacksquare$
$^{-}12 + ^{+}5 = \blacksquare$

Subtract. Write the related addition sentence that you used.

13. $^{-}6 - ^{-}7 = \blacksquare$ **14.** $^{+}4 - ^{+}6 = \blacksquare$ **15.** $^{-}9 - ^{+}6 = \blacksquare$

16. $^{+}10 - ^{-}6 = \blacksquare$ **17.** $^{+}3 - ^{-}8 = \blacksquare$ **18.** $^{-}8 - ^{-}1 = \blacksquare$

Problem Solving • Reasoning

19. **Analyze** Monica borrows \$6 from Bob. Last month, she loaned Bob \$10. Who owes whom money and how much?

20. Harry has \$35. He owes his father \$22. Harry remembers that he had borrowed another \$9 dollars from his father. How much money will Harry have left after he pays his father the money he owes him?

21. **Write About It** Charles lends \$5 to a friend. Then Charles' sister gives him \$10. Charles now has \$20. How much did he have to begin with? Explain.

Solve for *n*.

A $n + ^{-}2 = ^{-}4$
B $n + ^{-}2 = ^{+}4$
C $n - ^{-}2 = ^{-}4$
D $n - ^{-}2 = ^{+}4$
E $n + ^{-}4 = ^{-}2$
F $n + ^{-}4 = ^{+}2$

Mixed Review • Test Prep

Write each decimal in word form. *(pages 24–25)*

22. 0.1 **23.** 3.5 **24.** 6.01 **25.** 10.67

26 What is another name for 10^0? *(pages 6–7)*

A $\frac{1}{10}$ **B** 1 **C** 10 **D** 100

Extra Practice See Set H on page 232.

LESSON 14

Add and Subtract Integers

You will learn how to use absolute value to find the sign of the sum or difference of two integers.

Learn About It

To help decide if the sum of two integers will be positive or negative, you can use these rules.

- **The sum of two positive integers is positive.**
- **The sum of two negative integers is negative.**
- **The sum of a positive integer and a negative integer will have the same sign as the integer with the greater absolute value.**

Adding Integers

$^{-}2 + {}^{+}7 = \blacksquare$

- Use the rules to decide if the sum will be positive or negative.

  Since $^{+}7$ has the greater absolute value, the sum will be positive.

- Add. **$^{-}2 + {}^{+}7 = {}^{+}5$**

$^{+}3 + {}^{-}10 = \blacksquare$

- Use the rules to decide if the sum will be positive or negative.

  Since $^{-}10$ has the greater absolute value, the sum will be negative.

- Add. **$^{+}3 + {}^{-}10 = {}^{-}7$**

Subtracting Integers

$^{-}13 - {}^{+}9 = \blacksquare$

- To subtract an integer, add its opposite.

  $^{-}13 - {}^{+}9 = {}^{-}13 + {}^{-}9$

- Use the rules to decide if the sum will be positive or negative.

  The sum of two negative integers is negative.

- Add. **$^{-}13 + {}^{-}9 = {}^{-}22$**

$^{+}1 - {}^{-}5 = \blacksquare$

- To subtract an integer, add its opposite.

  $^{+}1 - {}^{-}5 = {}^{+}1 + {}^{+}5$

- Use the rules to decide if the sum will be positive or negative.

  The sum of two positive integers is positive.

- Add. **$^{+}1 + {}^{+}5 = {}^{+}6$**

Standards NS **2.1** MR **2.0, 3.0, 3.2, 3.3**

Explain Your Thinking

► Can the rules for deciding the sign of the sum of two integers also be used for deciding the sign of the sum of three or more integers? Explain.

Guided Practice

Decide if each sum or difference will be positive or negative. Then add or subtract.

1. $^{+}1 + {}^{+}3$ **2.** $^{-}4 + {}^{+}2$ **3.** $^{-}9 - {}^{+}5$

4. $^{-}2 + {}^{-}6$ **5.** $^{+}7 - {}^{-}3$ **6.** $^{+}4 + {}^{-}8$

Ask Yourself

- Do I need to add the opposite?
- What is the sign of the integer with greatest absolute value?

Independent Practice

Decide if each sum or difference will be positive or negative. Then add or subtract.

7. $^{+}9 + {}^{-}2$ **8.** $^{+}5 + {}^{+}1$ **9.** $^{-}3 + {}^{+}4$ **10.** $^{-}6 + {}^{-}10$

11. $^{-}1 + {}^{+}3$ **12.** $^{+}8 - {}^{-}6$ **13.** $^{-}7 + {}^{-}9$ **14.** $^{+}2 + {}^{-}5$

15. $^{-}7 - {}^{-}2$ **16.** $^{-}10 + {}^{-}6$ **17.** $^{-}1 - 0$ **18.** $^{-}9 - {}^{-}9$

Problem Solving • Reasoning

Write and solve an equation for each Problem 19–23.

19. You have $20 and buy something for $5. How much do you have now?

20. You owe $7 and payback $5. How much do you still owe?

21. You have $7, earn $5 more, and then spend $10. How much do you have?

22. You owe $7 and borrow $5 more. How much do you owe?

23. You earn $6 and spend $5. Then you earn $4 more and spend $5. How much do you have?

24. **Write Your Own** Write a problem using addition or subtraction of integers. Give your problem to a partner to solve.

Mixed Review • Test Prep

Write the absolute value of each.

25. $^{+}2$ **26.** $^{-}3$ **27.** $^{-}9$ **28.** $^{+}8$ **29.** $^{-}13$ **30.** $^{+}7$

Write the letter of the correct answer. *(pages 18–19)*

31 Which number could have been rounded to the nearest million?

A 162,750,000 **C** 8,700,000

B 41,000,000 **D** 531,000

32 Which number could have been rounded to the nearest hundredth?

F 29.013 **H** 295

G 29.51 **J** 295.1

Extra Practice See Set I on page 232.

Problem-Solving Application: Use Integers

You will learn to solve problems that include integers.

You can use integers to solve problems.

Problem In football, the team with the ball tries to move the ball towards the other team's goal line by passing or running with it. (The other team, of course, tries to stop them!) Any forward movement is called a gain, and is recorded as a positive integer. Any backward movement is called a loss and is recorded as a negative integer.

On three consecutive plays, a team gained one yard, gained seven yards, and then lost five yards. How can you use integers to find the total yards the team gained or lost?

Understand

What is the question?
How can you use integers to find the total yards the team gained or lost?

What do you know?
- The team gained 1 yd, then gained 7 yds, then lost 5 yds.

Plan

How can you find the answer?
- Represent the team's movements using integers.
- Then find the sum of the integers by adding them two at a time.

Solve

1 yd gain = $^{+}1$; 7 yd gain = $^{+}7$; 5 yd loss = $^{-}5$

Add the first two integers. $^{+}1 + {}^{+}7 = {}^{+}\mathbf{8}$

Add the next integer. $^{+}\mathbf{8} + {}^{-}5 = {}^{+}3$

The team gained a total of 3 yards.

Look Back

Look back at the problem.
Did I check my work using a number line or counters?

Standards NS 2.1 MR 1.0, 1.2, 2.0, 3.0

Remember:
- Understand
- Plan
- Solve
- Look Back

Football is a very popular sport in the United States. Many people enjoy watching high school football games.

Guided Practice

Solve.

1. The set of integers ($^-3$, $^+4$, 0) represents the movement of a football in yards. What gain or loss of yards is represented by the set of integers?

   Think: How does 0 affect the sum of the first two integers?

2. Tyler ran with the ball on two plays. On one play he gained 8 yards. On the other he lost 12 yards. Did Tyler gain or lose yards altogether? How many yards?

   Think: How do you represent a gain or loss?

Choose a Strategy

Solve. Use these or other strategies.

Problem-Solving Strategies

- Find a Pattern
- Draw a Diagram
- Write an Equation

3. A football game is being played in an outdoor stadium. At the start, the temperature was $^-5$°F. At halftime, the temperature was $^-1$°F. At which time was the temperature higher?

4. Study these integers.

   $^-19$, $^-15$, $^-11$, $^-7$, $^-3$, ...

   Find a pattern. What is the next integer in your pattern?

5. On three consecutive plays, a quarterback passed for $^+9$, $^-2$, and $^+5$ yards. To earn a first down, the ball must move 10 or more yards. Did those plays earn a first down?

6. At 6:00 A.M., the temperature was $^-5$°F. By noon on the same day, the temperature was 6°F. How many degrees did the temperature rise in six hours?

7. At the beginning of a skiing competition, the temperature was $^+2$°F. By the end of the competition, the temperature was $^-2$°F. By how many degrees did the temperature rise or fall during the competition?

8. A football team scored a total of $(3 \times 6) + 2$ points. The opposing team scored $(5 \times 3) + 6$ points. How many points did each team score? Which team won the game? Explain how you got your answer.

Extra Practice See 9–12 on page 233.

Quick Check

Check Your Understanding of Lessons 9–15

Write the absolute value of each integer.

1. $^{-}8$ **2.** $^{+}6$ **3.** 0 **4.** $^{-}33$ **5.** $^{+}62$

Use a number line to add or subtract.

6. $^{+}6 + ^{-}4$ **7.** $^{-}9 + ^{-}3$ **8.** $^{-}5 + ^{+}2$ **9.** $^{-}4 + ^{+}7$

10. $^{-}1 - ^{-}5$ **11.** $^{+}8 - ^{-}2$ **12.** $^{-}7 - ^{+}4$ **13.** $^{+}6 - ^{+}6$

Decide if each sum or difference will be positive or negative. Then add or subtract.

14. $^{+}8 - ^{-}4$ **15.** $^{-}7 + ^{+}3$ **16.** $^{+}9 - ^{-}3$ **17.** $^{-}7 + ^{-}6$

18. $^{+}5 + ^{+}2$ **19.** $^{+}7 - ^{-}4$ **20.** $^{-}12 + ^{+}8$ **21.** $^{-}9 - ^{-}4$

Solve.

22. The temperature on a Celsius thermometer rose from $^{-}4$°C to $^{+}6$°C in one day. What was the increase in temperature?

How did you do?

If you had difficulty with any items in the Quick Check, you can use the following pages for review and extra practice.

California Standards	Items	Review These Pages	Do These Extra Practice Items
Number Sense: **1.5**	1–5	pages 214–215	Set F, page 232
Number Sense: **1.5, 2.1**	6–9	pages 218–219	Set G, page 232
Number Sense: **1.5, 2.1**	10–13	pages 222–223	Set H, page 232
Number Sense: **2.1**	14–21	pages 224–225	Set I, page 232
Math Reasoning: **1.0, 2.0**	22	pages 226–227	9–12, page 233

Test Prep • Cumulative Review

Maintaining the Standards

Choose the letter of the correct answer. If a correct answer is not here, choose NH.

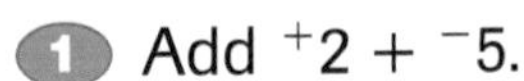

1. Add $^{+}2 + {}^{-}5$.

   Use this number line to help you.

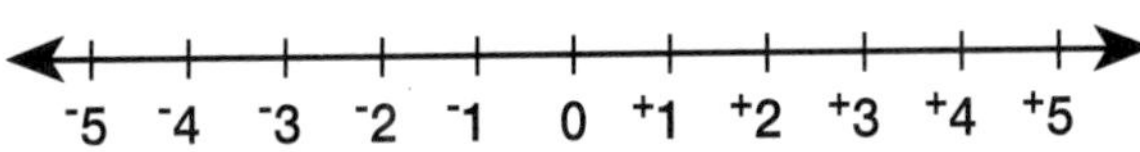

   A $^{-}7$
   B $^{-}3$
   C $^{+}3$
   D $^{+}7$

2. Which value for x makes this a true statement?

   $962 \div x = 37$

   F 42
   G 37
   H 26
   J 3

3. A set of 5 videos takes a long time to view. If you watch 25 minutes at each sitting, it will take 27 sittings to complete the set. How many sittings will it take if you watch 45 minutes at each sitting?

   A 25
   B 23
   C 16
   D 15

4. Which is the greatest number?

   F 3^5
   G 5^3
   H 10^0
   J 12^0

5. Marsha and 24 friends collected 850 pounds of aluminum cans. What is the mean number of pounds collected per person?

   A 34
   B 35
   C 36
   D 43

6. If it costs \$36 to buy 2 identical CDs, how much would it cost to buy 3 of them?

   F NH
   G \$48
   H \$54
   J \$72

7. Which number is farthest from zero on a number line?

   A 5
   B $^{-}3$
   C $^{-}5$
   D $^{-}8$

8. Virgil says that the first digit in the quotient of $2{,}592 \div 36$ is 8.

   Explain How do you know if 8 is correct, too great, or too small?

Safe Site

Internet Test Prep
Visit **www.eduplace.com/kids/mhm** for more *Test Prep Practice.*

Extra Practice

Set A (Lesson 2, pages 194–195)

Find the perimeter and area of each rectangle.

1. 3 in.

4 in.

2. 

3. 

4. 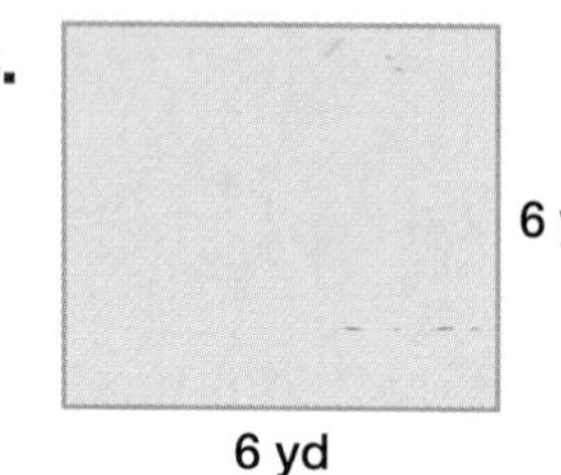

5. 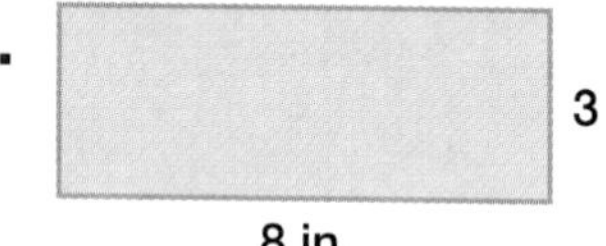

6. 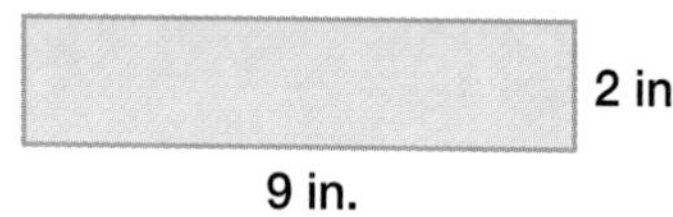

Complete.

7. 3 mi = ■ ft

8. ■ in. = 2 ft 7 in.

9. 21 ft = ■ yd

10. 5,900 ft = ■ mi ■ ft

11. ■ in. = 4 ft

12. 105 in. = ■ ft ■ in.

Set B (Lesson 3, pages 198–199)

Complete.

1. 48 oz = ■ lb

2. ■ lb = 3 T

3. ■ c = 4 pt

4. 16 qt = ■ gal

5. 8 pt = ■ qt

6. ■ pt = 80 fl oz

7. 5 T = ■ lb

8. ■ lb = 64 oz

9. 40 oz = ■ lb ■ oz

10. 7,250 lb = ■ T ■ lb

11. ■ c = 6 pt

12. ■ gal = 16 qt

13. 18 qt = ■ gal ■ qt

14. 19 c = ■ qt ■ c

15. 22 fl oz = ■ pt ■ fl oz

16. 15 gal = ■ pt

Extra Practice

Set C (Lesson 5, pages 202–204)

Complete.

1. ■ cm = 750 dm
2. 175 m = ■ cm
3. ■ m = 5 km
4. 4 m = ■ mm
5. ■ dm = 20 m
6. 5,200 cm = ■ m
7. 500 cm = ■ m
8. 650 mm ■ cm
9. 820 cm = ■ dm
10. 6,000 mm = ■ dm
11. 2 km = ■ cm
12. 4 m = ■ cm

Set D (Lesson 6, pages 206–207)

Complete.

1. 6,000 g = ■ kg
2. 23 g = ■ mg
3. 6 t = ■ kg
4. 3.6 kg = ■ g
5. 5 L = ■ dL
6. 6 L = ■ mL
7. 16,000 g = ■ kg
8. 8,000 mL = ■ L
9. 6,000 kg = ■ t

Complete. Write >, <, or = for each ●.

10. 2 L ● 2,000 mL
11. 1.5 kg ● 2 kg
12. 1,000 g ● 1 kg
13. 3.5 t ● 3,000 kg
14. 5 kg ● 4,000 g
15. 6 g ● 7,000 mg

Set E (Lesson 7, pages 208–209)

How many hours and minutes are there between these times?

1. 3:30 P.M. to 8:30 P.M.
2. 5:20 A.M. to 10:10 A.M.
3. 1:05 P.M. to 9:30 P.M.
4. 4:35 A.M. to 7:05 A.M.
5. 2:10 P.M. to 2:55 P.M.
6. 8:40 A.M. to 10:30 A.M.
7. 9:00 A.M. to 4:45 P.M.
8. 10:55 P.M. to 2:20 A.M.
9. 11:55 P.M. to 1:15 A.M.
10. 7:12 A.M. to 10:42 A.M.
11. 6:20 P.M. to 7:24 P.M.
12. 12:06 A.M. to 12:06 P.M.
13. 1:38 A.M. to 3:12 A.M.
14. 4:48 P.M. to 6:13 P.M.
15. 5:26 P.M. to 6:16 P.M.
16. 5:12 A.M. to 11:00 A.M.

Another Look

Use the numbers to solve each problem.
Show all your work.

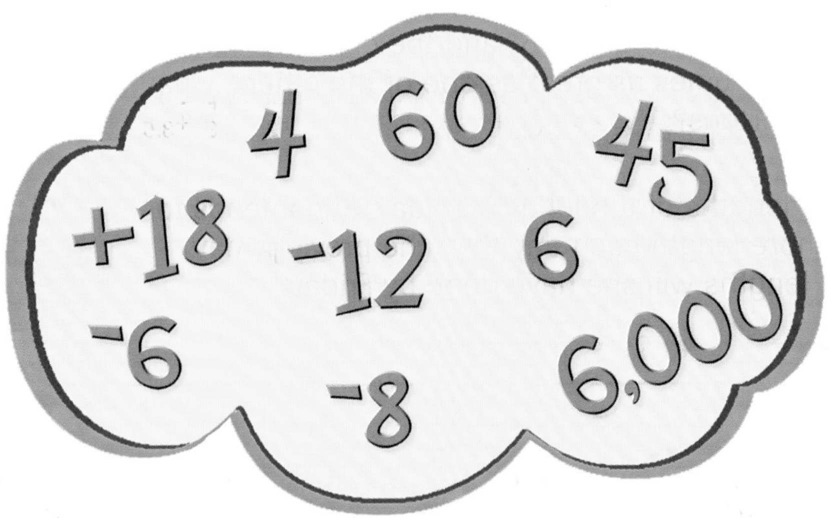

1. Find a number with an absolute value of 8.

2. Find the possible area of a book cover in square inches.

3. Find the possible area of a refrigerator magnet in square inches.

4. Find the number of pints in 3 quarts.

5. Find the number of minutes from 11:55 A.M. to 12:40 P.M.

6. Find two numbers whose sum is $^+6$.

7. Find two numbers whose difference is 26.

8. **Analyze** Find two numbers to complete this equation.
   ■ L = ■ mL

9. **Write Your Own** Create and solve a problem by using the numbers.

Standards	NS **1.0, 2.1** MR **2.0**

Enrichment

Negative Decimals

You can use a number line to add and subtract positive and negative decimals.

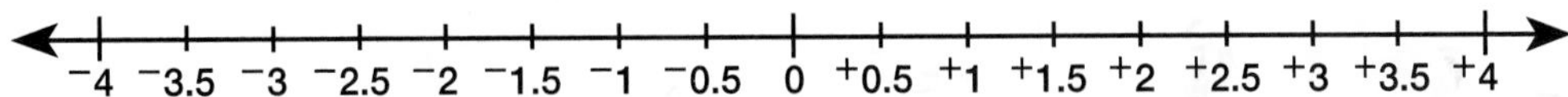

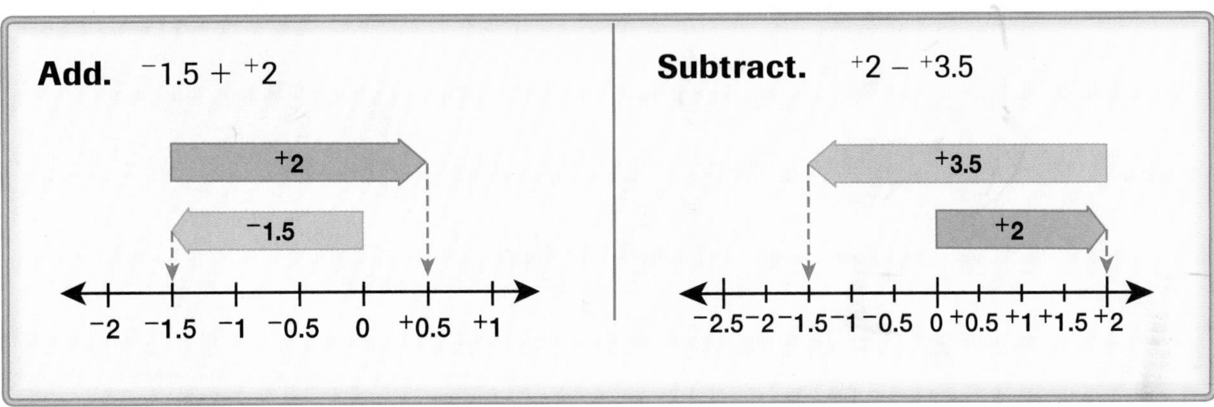

Use a number line to add.

1. $^{-}1.5 + {}^{+}2$ **2.** $^{+}1 + {}^{-}2.5$ **3.** $^{+}0.5 + {}^{+}4.5$

4. $^{+}2.5 + {}^{-}4.5$ **5.** $^{-}6.5 + {}^{+}3.5$ **6.** $^{-}5.5 + {}^{-}0.5$

7. One morning in winter, the temperature was $^{+}10.5$°F. By noon, it was 6.5 degrees higher. What was the temperature at noon?

Use a number line to subtract.

8. $^{+}4.5 - {}^{+}2$ **9.** $^{+}2.5 - {}^{+}2.5$ **10.** $^{-}3.5 - {}^{+}3.5$

11. $^{-}5.5 - {}^{+}1.5$ **12.** $^{+}8.5 - {}^{+}6$ **13.** $^{+}4.5 - {}^{-}2$

14. From 4 P.M. to 5 P.M., the temperature fell 4.5 degrees. If the temperature at 4 P.M. was 20°F, what was the temperature at 5 P.M.? If the temperature fell the same amount in the next hour, what was the temperature at 6 P.M.?

Explain Your Thinking

► How do you show subtraction of a negative number on a number line?

Standards Extends Grade 5 Standards

Data, Statistics, and Probability

Why Learn About Data, Statistics, and Probability?

Organizing data by making a graph makes the data easier to analyze and understand. Understanding probability helps you find the likelihood of a future event.

When you survey your classmates about their favorite movies and then display the results on a graph, you are collecting and organizing data. When you spin a spinner, you use probability to tell how likely it is to land on a particular color.

Meteorologists collect and analyze weather data from every part of the world. This woman is using many different kinds of data to prepare a local weather forecast.

Rain
0.00
29.94
Humidity
86%
Wind
Gusts
22
73
0.00
22
86%
29.94

Reading Mathematics

Reviewing Vocabulary

Understanding math language helps you become a successful problem solver. Here are some math vocabulary words you should know.

axis a horizontal or vertical line used to label a graph

range the difference between the greatest number and the least number in a set of data

median the middle number when an odd number of data are arranged in order (for an even number of data, it is the mean of the two middle numbers)

mode the number or numbers that occur most often in a set of data

mean the sum of a set of numbers divided by the number of addends

Reading Words and Symbols

When you read mathematics, sometimes you read only words, sometimes you read words and symbols, and sometimes you read only symbols.

Graphs use words, numbers, and visual images to present information in a way that people can readily understand.

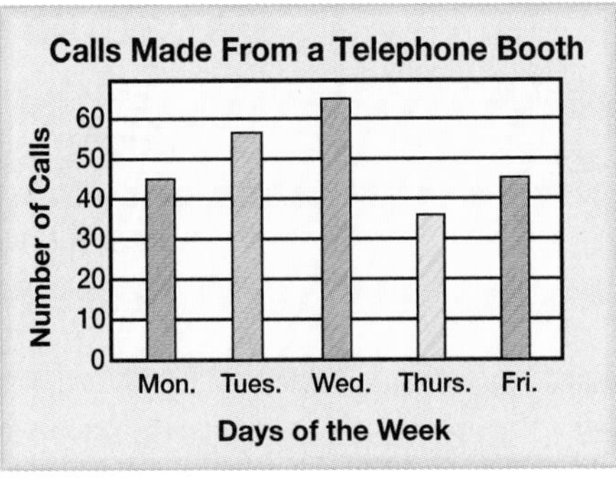

On a bar graph, the lengths of the bars allow people to compare amounts. Titles and axis labels help people interpret what they see.

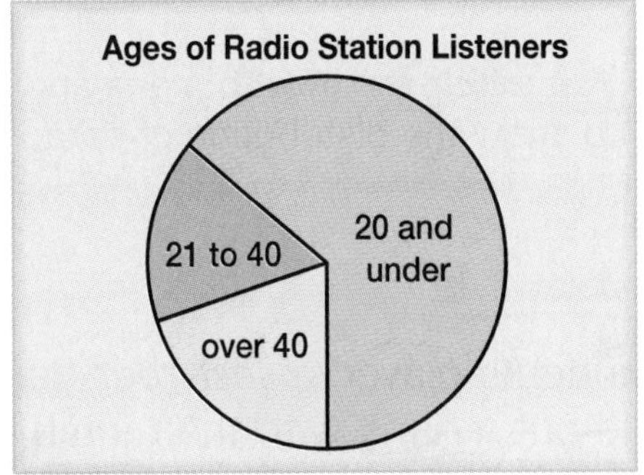

In a circle graph, parts of the circle show how parts of a set of data compare.

Try These

1. What information can you get from the bar graph?
2. Why do you think the vertical axis of the bar graph is labeled in tens instead of ones?
3. About how many calls were made from the telephone booth from Monday through Friday?
4. Do you think the number of calls shown on each bar is exact or estimated? Explain.
5. What information can you get from the circle graph?
6. Who listens to the radio station most, people 20 and under, people between 21 and 40, or people over 40? Explain how you know.

Upcoming Vocabulary

Write About It **Here are some other vocabulary words** you will learn in this chapter. Watch for these words. Write their definitions in your journal.

line graph	**histogram**	
double bar graph	**ordered pair**	**equally likely**
double line graph	**organized list**	**line plot**
frequency table	**tree diagram**	**certain event**
impossible event	**probability**	

Stem-and-Leaf Plots

You will learn how to make and use a stem-and-leaf plot to show the distribution of data.

New Vocabulary
gap
cluster
stem-and-leaf plot
stem
leaf

Learn About It

Pairs of students played a *Test Your Reflexes* game. One player held out a hand with the thumb and index finger about 2" apart. The other player held a pencil about 6" above the space between the first player's fingers. The pencil was dropped 100 times without warning. The list shows the number of catches for 14 players.

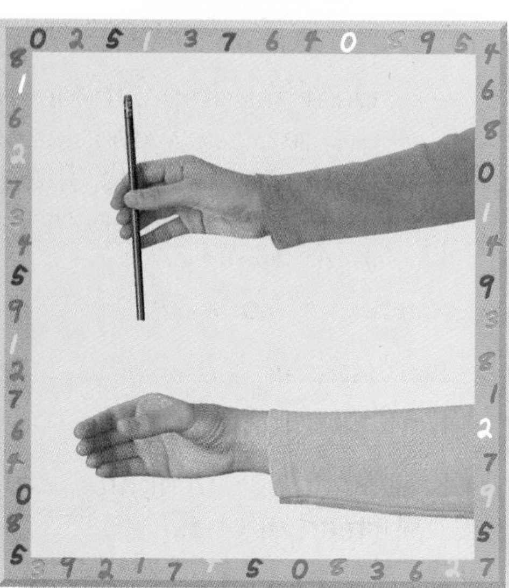

6, 65, 32, 39, 62, 20, 42, 27, 9, 27, 54, 28, 25, 33

When data are displayed, a **gap** is a part of the display that contains no data. A **cluster** is a part of the display that contains many data close together. What clusters or gaps can you find in these data?

One way to display data is to make a **stem-and-leaf plot**.

Making a Stem-and-Leaf Plot

Step 1 Write a title.

Step 2 Write the tens digits needed to represent the data, in order from least to greatest. These numbers form the **stem**.

Step 3 For each piece of data, write the ones digit next to its tens digit. Arrange these **leaves** in order from least to greatest.

Test Your Reflexes Results

Stem	Leaf
0	6 9
1	
2	0 5 7 7 8
3	2 3 9
4	2
5	4
6	2 5

5 | 4 means 54.

Solution: The data seem to cluster in the 20s. Since there are no leaves for the stem at 1, there is a gap from 10 to 19.

Explain Your Thinking

- ▶ Why is a stem-and-leaf plot a good way to organize this kind of data?
- ▶ What do the stems represent?
- ▶ Can all kinds of data be organized on a stem-and-leaf plot?
- ▶ What do the leaves represent?

Standards SDP **1.0** MR **1.0, 2.0, 2.3**

Guided Practice

Use the stem-and-leaf plot on page 244 for Problems 1–3.

1. How could you check that the data for all 14 players are included in the stem-and-leaf plot?
2. How many students caught the pencil 27 times?
3. How many students caught the pencil more than 27 times?

Ask Yourself

- How do I use the tens digits of the numbers?
- How do I use the ones digits of the numbers?

Independent Practice

Use the stem-and-leaf plot for Problems 4–7.

Science Books Borrowed From Library Each Week	
Stem	**Leaf**
0	5, 7, 7
1	2, 3, 6, 6, 6, 8, 8, 9
2	2, 4, 4, 8, 9
3	1, 3

4. What does 3 | 1 mean?
5. Which stem has 3 leaves? List them.
6. How many numbers are between 20 and 30?
7. For how many weeks is the data shown?
8. Make a stem-and-leaf plot for this set of data: 15, 8, 24, 36, 43, 43, 47, 44, 17, 29, 41, 34.

Problem Solving • Reasoning

Use Data Use the stem-and-leaf plot for Problems 9–12.

Game Score	
Stem	**Leaf**
0	4, 8
1	0, 5
2	5
3	3, 6, 6
4	0
5	
6	3, 6

9. How many students played the game?
10. What was the highest score for a player in this group?
11. **Analyze** Where do the data seem to cluster? Are there any gaps? If so, where?
12. What equation can you write to show the difference between the highest and lowest scores in this group?

Mixed Review • Test Prep

Write the value of the underlined digit. *(pages 4–5, 14–15)*

13. 2,$\underline{7}$60 **14.** 5$\underline{1}$4,689 **15.** 7$\underline{0}$8,963,532 **16.** 2$\underline{3}$,789,013,452

Write the letter of the correct answer. *(pages 54–55, 114–115)*

17 What is the difference between 902 and 689?

A 213 **C** 387
B 223 **D** 1,591

18 What is the product of 387 and 28?

F 3,096 **H** 3,870
G 9,086 **J** 10,836

Extra Practice See Set A on page 284.

Double Bar Graphs

You will learn how to use a double bar graph to compare sets of data.

New Vocabulary
double bar graph

Learn About It

Linda took a survey to find out how her classmates use their home computers. She recorded the girls' and boys' responses separately.

Follow the steps to make a **double bar graph** to compare the two sets of data.

Home Computer Use

Computer Use	Boys	Girls
Send E-mail	8	24
Web search	6	6
Games	36	10
Word processing	6	2

Making a Double Bar Graph

Step 1 Draw the axes.

Step 2 Label the vertical axis **Number of Students**. Choose an appropriate scale and mark equal intervals from 0 to 36.

Step 3 Label the horizontal axis **Computer Use** and list the uses.

Step 4 For each use, draw one bar for boys and one for girls. Use different colors for boys and girls.

Step 5 Make a key to show what each color represents. Then give the graph a title.

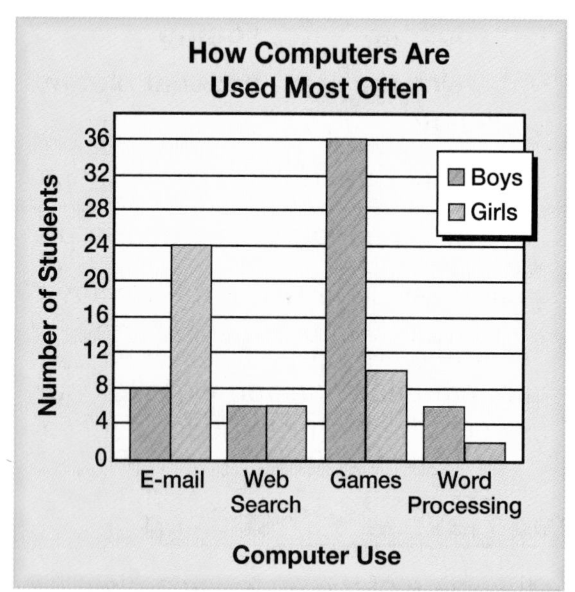

Explain Your Thinking

- Is it easier to tell which use is most popular for boys by looking at the double bar graph or at the table?
- Why is a double bar graph useful for displaying this data?

Standards AF **1.1** SDP **1.0** MR **1.0, 1.1, 2.0, 2.3**

Guided Practice

Use the graph on page 246 for Problems 1–3.

1. How many more girls use the computer for sending E-mail than boys?
2. For which computer use is there the greatest difference between boys and girls?
3. Which computer use is the same for boys and girls?

> **Ask Yourself**
> - Do I need to know the number the bar shows, or could I answer by looking at the bar length?
> - What scale did I use?
> - What labels did I use on the axes?

4. Five teachers surveyed the students in their classes to see how many used a computer every day. Make a double bar graph showing the data from the table at the right.

Do You Use a Computer Every Day?

Class	Mrs. Smith	Mr. Kaufman	Mr. Ross	Ms. Brown	Ms. Cruz
Yes	12	10	9	20	5
No	12	15	14	4	19

Independent Practice

Use the graph for Problems 5–8.

Five hundred households were surveyed in 1980 and again in 2000 about which electronic devices they had in their homes.

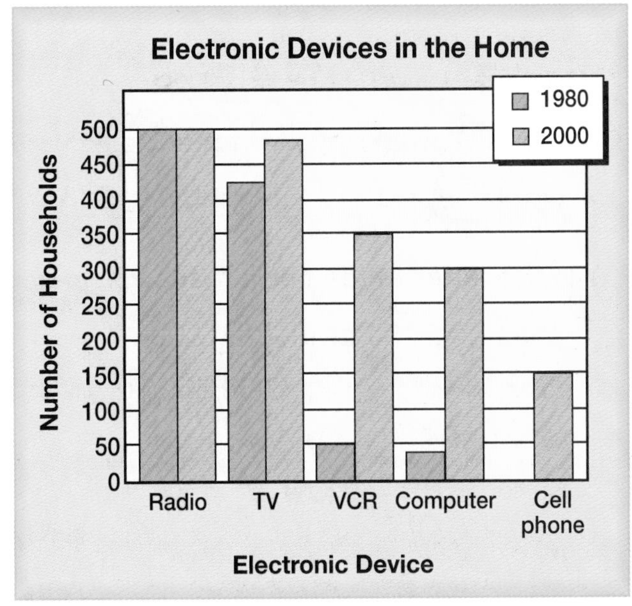

5. Which device was found in the most households in both 1980 and 2000?
6. About how many more households had computers in 2000 than in 1980?
7. In 1980, about how many more households had televisions than VCRs?
8. Why is there no bar to represent cell phones in 1980?
9. Use the table of students' telephone color preferences to make a double bar graph.
10. If you were designing a telephone for other students, which color would you choose? Explain your thinking.

Choices of Telephone Colors

	Purple	Orange	Blue	Green	Red
Like	12	6	18	14	10
Dislike	6	16	6	10	4

Problem Solving • Reasoning

Use the double bar graph to solve Problems 11–14.

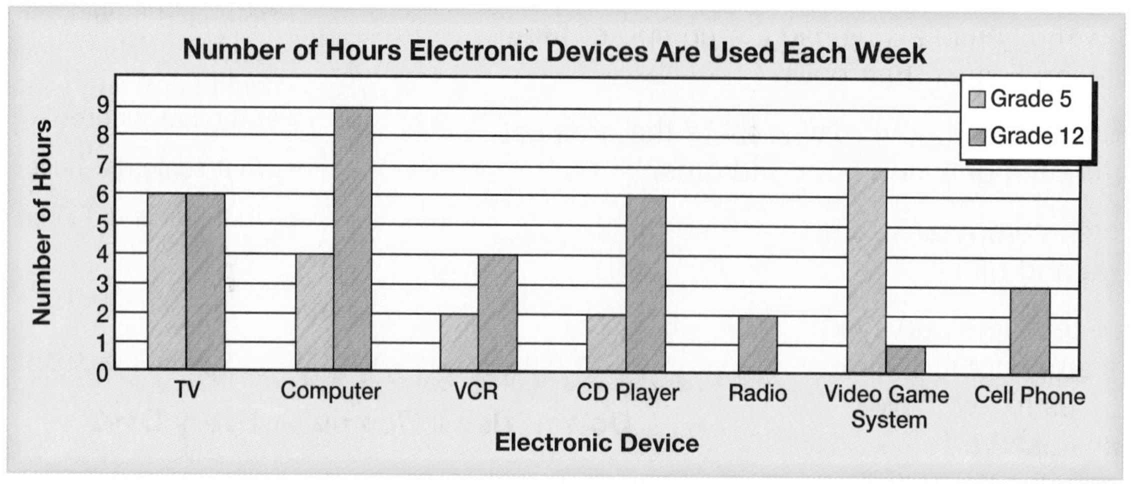

11. **Compare** For which device is there the greatest difference in hours of use between the two grades?

12. Overall, which device do the students use the most? In total, how many hours each week do they use this device?

13. **Analyze** How could you adjust the graph to make the differences between the age groups seem less obvious?

14. **Write About It** What are some reasons for the differences in hours of use between the two grades?

Mixed Review • Test Prep

Compare. Write >, <, or = for each ●. *(pages 8–9)*

15. 21,047 ● 21,087 **16.** 0.8 ● 3 **17.** 0.7 ● 0.700 **18.** 2.50 ● 2.09

Write the letter of the correct answer. *(pages 54–55, 148–149)*

19 What is 3,154 divided by 15?

A 3,139 **C** 208 R15

B 210 R4 **D** 15

20 What is the sum of 3,868 and 498?

F 3,256 **H** 4,266

G 4,366 **J** 7,848

Logical Thinking

Time

Between 8 P.M. and 10 P.M., Mr. Wilson used the VCR for 1 hour, the TV for 2 hours, and the cell phone and a video game system for half an hour each. Explain how this is possible.

Extra Practice See Set B on page 284.

Practice Game

Penny Drop

Partners can play this game and then make a double bar graph to compare their scores.

What You'll Need

- *5 pennies*
- *target and score cards (Teaching Tools 5 and 6)*
- *grid paper and ruler*

Players
2

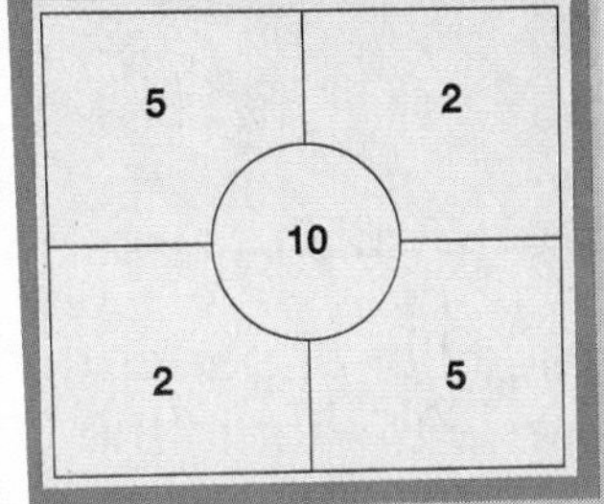

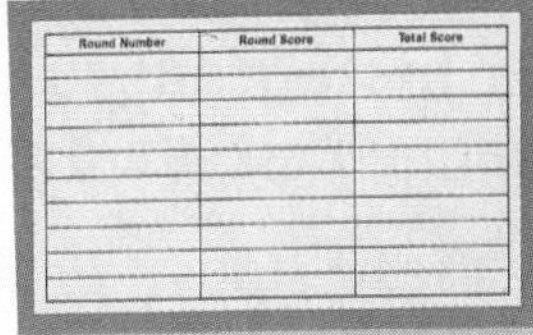

Here's What to Do

1. Make a target like the one shown or use Teaching Tool 5.
2. Players stand face to face with their toes just touching one long edge of the target. Players take turns dropping 5 pennies onto the target.
3. When a player has dropped all 5 pennies, he or she adds up their score and records it in a table (Teaching Tool 6).
   - A penny will score 0, 2, 5, or 10 points.
   - If a penny lands on the border between two areas of the target, it will score the lesser of the two values.
4. Repeat Steps 2 and 3. Players add the score to their score from the previous round. The player who has the highest score after 10 rounds wins.

Share Your Thinking Make a double bar graph showing your total score and your partner's for rounds 1 to 10. What information about the game can you get from the graph?

Histograms

You will learn how to make and use a histogram and how histograms are different from bar graphs.

New Vocabulary
histogram
frequency table

Learn About It

The ballet *The Nutcracker* is a holiday favorite for audiences and performers alike. One reason is that there are roles for performers of all ages. Look at this list of the ages of the performers for one ballet company last year.

10	11	35	38	55	28	32	46	57	69
58	14	8	9	10	11	7	12	8	13
11	12	25	19	45	52	35	42	62	27
31	29	15	17	16	18	20	19	22	34
29	30	20	25	13	14	15	16	15	17

How did the number of performers in the 20–29 age group compare with that in the 10–19 age group?

You can use a histogram to display and compare the data. A **histogram** is a graph that uses bars to display how frequently data occur within equal intervals.

Follow these steps to make a histogram. First, make a **frequency table** to organize the data in equal intervals.

Making a Frequency Table

Step 1 Decide what intervals to use. Look at the data. In this case, use equal intervals of 10.

Step 2 Use tally marks to record the frequency for each interval.

Step 3 Count the tally marks to record the frequency.

Intervals	Tally Marks	Frequency
0 – 9	IIII	4
10 – 19	~~IIII~~ ~~IIII~~ ~~IIII~~ ~~IIII~~ I	21
20 – 29	~~IIII~~ IIII	9
30 – 39	~~IIII~~ II	7
40 – 49	III	3
50 – 59	IIII	4
60 – 69	II	2

Standards AF 1.1 SDP 1.0, 1.2 MR 1.0, 1.1, 2.0, 2.3

Making a Histogram

Step 1 Give the graph a title.

Step 2 Draw the axes. Label the vertical axis. Choose an appropriate scale and mark equal intervals.

Step 3 Label the horizontal axis and list the age intervals.

Step 4 Draw a bar for each age interval. Don't leave spaces between the bars.

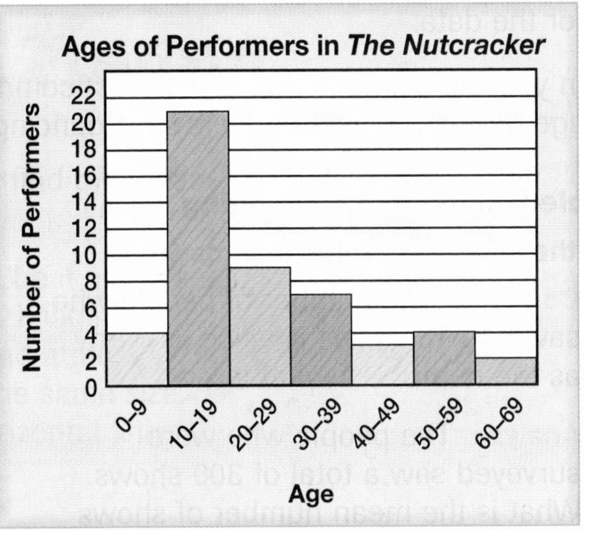

Solution: There are more than twice as many performers in the 10–19 age group as there are in the 20–29 age group.

Explain Your Thinking

▶ When you want to compare data, why is it easier to use a histogram than a table?

▶ How is a histogram different from a bar graph? How is it similar?

Guided Practice

Use the histogram above for Problems 1–3.

1. Which age group has the most performers? the fewest?
2. How many more performers are there in the 20–29 age group than in the 50–59 age group?
3. How many performers are less than 20 years old?

Ask Yourself

- Do I need to know the number the bar shows?

Independent Practice

Use the histogram for Problems 4–6.

4. How many more violinists have been in the orchestra for 8 to 11 years than for 0 to 3 years?
5. How many violinists have played in the orchestra for 4 to 15 years?
6. Have more violinists been in the orchestra for less than 8 years or for 8 years or more?

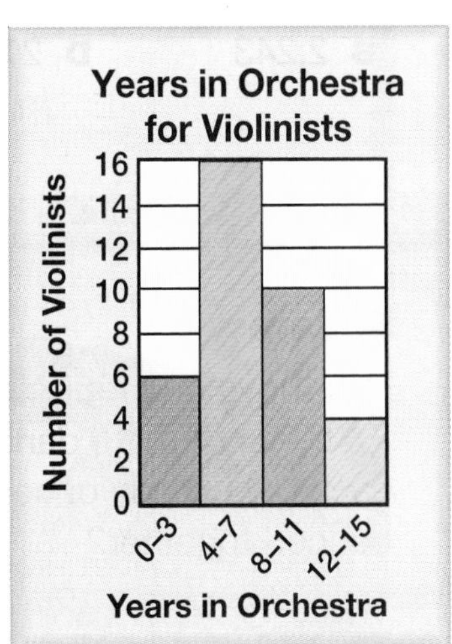

Quick Check

Check Your Understanding of Lessons 1–4

Use the stem-and-leaf plot for Problems 1–3.

Cost of Bake Sale Items (in Cents)	
Stem	**Leaves**
4	0 0 0 0 5 5 5 5
5	0 0 0 0 5 5 5 5 5 9
6	0 0 5 5

1. What are the lowest and highest prices shown?

2. How many items cost 60¢ or more?

3. Which price occurred most often?

Use the graph for Problems 4–6.

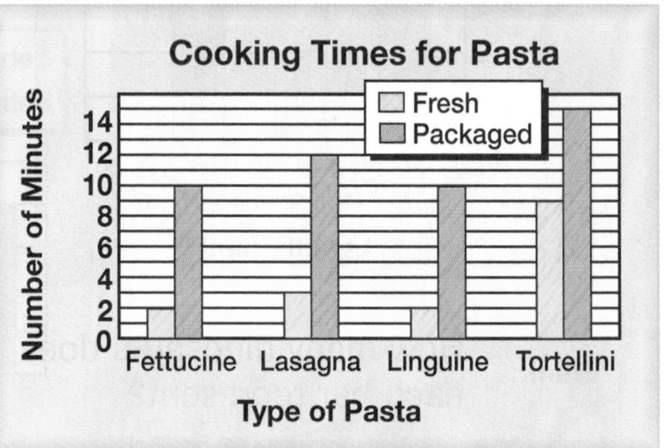

4. Does it take longer to cook fresh pasta or packaged pasta?

5. Which packaged pasta takes 5 minutes longer to cook than packaged linguine?

6. For which type of pasta is there the biggest difference in cooking times?

Make and use a histogram to solve.

7. The list shows the number of books read by each of 24 students. Make a frequency table and histogram for the data. Use intervals of 0–4, 5–9, 10–14, and 15–19 books.

Number of Books Read During Summer											
5	10	2	7	3	9	8	10	3	0	5	19
11	7	15	6	10	12	9	13	8	17	12	7

8. Using your histogram, how many students read 5–9 books?

9. Did most of the students read more than or less than 10 books? Explain.

How did you do?

If you had difficulty with any items in the Quick Check, you can use the following pages for review and extra practice.

California Standards	Items	Review These Pages	Do These Extra Practice Items
Statistics, Data, Probability: **1.0**	1–3	pages 244–245	Set A, page 284
Statistics, Data, Probability: **1.0**	4–6	pages 246–248	Set B, page 284
Statistics, Data, Probability: **1.0, 1.2**	7	pages 250–252	Set C, page 285
Statistics, Data, Probability: **1.0, 1.2** Math Reasoning: **1.1, 2.3**	8–9	pages 254–255	1–4, page 287

Test Prep • Cumulative Review

Maintaining the Standards

Choose the letter of the correct answer.

1 The stem-and-leaf plot shows the waist sizes of pants sold at a store. How many had a waist size of 31 inches?

A 1
B 2
C 3
D 4

Waist Size (inches)	
Stem	Leaves
2	2 3 4 4 5 7
3	0 1 1 1 2 2 3 4 5
4	0 0 1 1

2 What is the sum when it is rounded to the nearest tenth?

$$\begin{array}{r} 34.792 \\ +\ 61.85 \\ \hline \end{array}$$

F 96.6 **H** 50.0
G 96.7 **J** 27.1

3 There are 28 students in Lisa's math class. If the students work in groups of 5, how many complete groups can there be?

A 3 **C** 5
B 4 **D** 6

4 What is the area of this rectangle?

140 mm

8 cm

F 11,000 cm^2 **H** 1,120 mm^2
G 112 cm^2 **J** 112 mm^2

5 A rectangle has a length of 10 cm and a width of 3 cm. What is the area of the rectangle?

A 14 cm^2
B 20 cm^2
C 22 cm^2
D 30 cm^2

6 What value of *s* makes this statement true?

$$5 + s = 2$$

F 2 **H** $^-2$
G 1 **J** $^-3$

7 Use the number line to subtract $^-1 - {}^+4$.

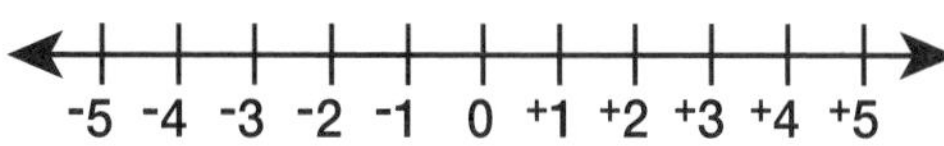

A $^+5$
B $^+3$
C $^-3$
D $^-5$

8 A cafeteria has square tables. One person can be seated on each side of a table. When two tables are pushed together, 6 people can be seated. How many people can be seated when 5 tables are pushed together?

Explain How did you find your answer?

Safe Site

Internet Test Prep
Visit **www.eduplace.com/kids/mhm** for more *Test Prep Practice.*

Line Plots

You will learn how to make and use a line plot to find the mean, median, and mode of a set of data.

New Vocabulary
line plot

Learn About It

What is the typical age at which a president of the United States is inaugurated?

The mean, median, and mode can help you describe a typical number from a set of data.

Using a **line plot** to organize the data makes it easier to find the mean, median, and mode. To make a line plot

- First create a number line that covers the range of numbers in your data set.
- Next put an X above each number as many times as the number appears in the list.

John F. Kennedy

Ronald W. Reagan

Inaugural Ages of Presidents from 1901-1993
42, 51, 56, 55, 51, 60, 62, 43, 55, 56, 61, 52, 64, 46, 69, 54, 51

The **mode** is 51.

40	41	42	43	44	45	46	47	48	49	50	51	52	53	54	55	56	57	58	59	60	61	62	63	64	65	66	67	68	69	70
		X	X			X					X X X	X		X	X X	X X				X	X	X		X					X	

The 17 numbers have a sum of 928, so the **mean** age is about 54.6.

There are 17 Xs, so the median is the 9th X, counting from left to right and bottom to top. The **median** is 55.

Solution: The mode is 51, the median is 55, and the mean is 54.6. Each of these is a good example of the typical age of a U.S. president at inauguration.

Franklin D. Roosevelt

Dwight D. Eisenho

Explain Your Thinking

- ▶ Why does a line plot make it easier to find the mean, median, and mode?
- ▶ What would happen to the median and mode if the data at 55 were removed?

Guided Practice

Make a line plot for the set of data. Find the mean, median, and mode.

> **Ask Yourself**
> - Did I use the line plot to find the median and mode?

1. history books borrowed
   6, 9, 6, 8, 9, 8, 10, 8, 11, 10, 10, 13

Independent Practice

Make a line plot for each set of data. Find the mean, median, and mode.

2. miles walked on tour
   8, 4, 5, 1, 3, 2, 3, 5, 1, 2, 1, 3, 2, 3, 2, 3, 5, 3, 5, 8, 5, 3, 5, 8, 10
3. number of visits to Washington
   0, 2, 4, 1, 2, 3, 2, 3, 1, 2, 3, 4, 2, 4, 5, 3, 5, 8
4. history test scores
   85, 80, 90, 95, 90, 100, 90, 75, 70, 80, 95, 100, 90, 90, 90
5. hours worked by tour guides in one month
   100, 120, 123, 113, 118, 111, 116, 115, 114, 119, 121, 122

Problem Solving • Reasoning

Use Data **Use the line plot on the right for Problems 6–8.**

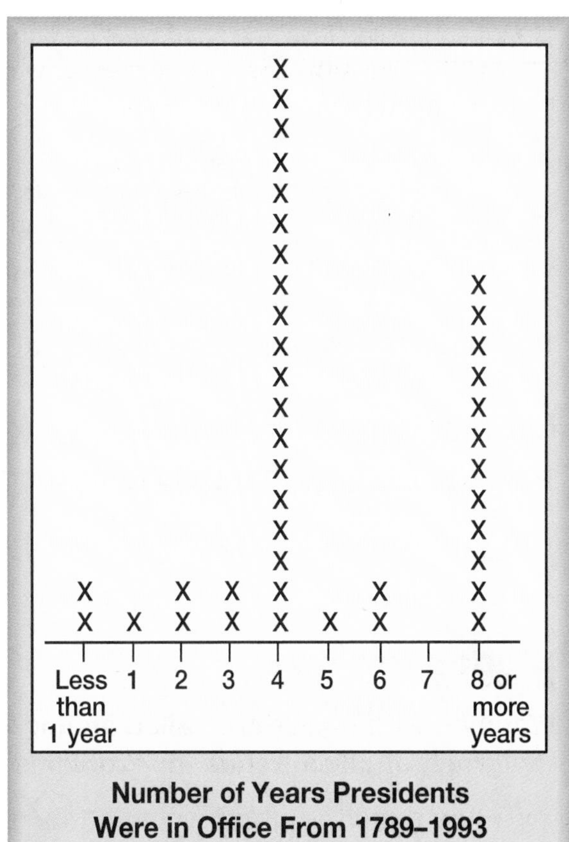

Number of Years Presidents Were in Office From 1789–1993

6. How many presidents served less than one year?
7. How many presidents served from 1789 to 1993?
8. **Analyze** What general conclusions can you draw from the line plot?
9. **Logical Thinking** George Washington served as president longer than John F. Kennedy. Jimmy Carter served longer than John F. Kennedy but not as long as George Washington. Franklin D. Roosevelt served longer than any other president. Name these presidents in order from longest term to shortest.

Mixed Review • Test Prep

Solve. *(pages 58–61, 110–111, 134–135)*

10. 4.534 + 3.68
11. 8.0 − 5.66
12. 7,805 × 30
13. 567 ÷ 7

14. How is 4 and 6 thousandths written in standard form? *(pages 24–25)*

A 4.6 **B** 4.06 **C** 4.006 **D** 4.0006

Extra Practice See Set D on page 285.

Interpret Line Graphs

You will learn how to analyze line graphs that do not have numbers.

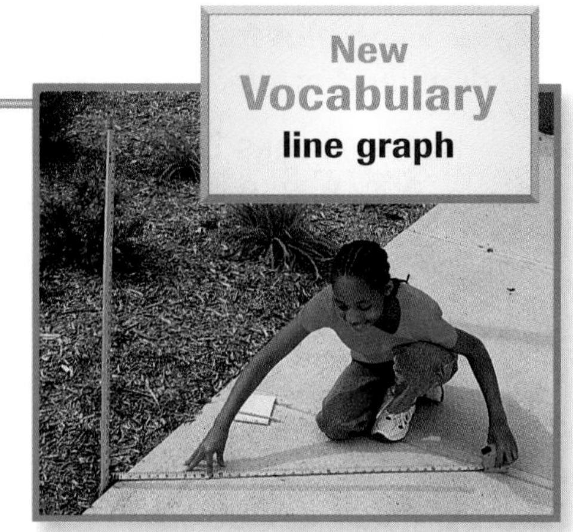

Learn About It

At one time people used a gnomon to tell time. A gnomon was a vertical stick or figure that cast a shadow on the ground. Pia made a gnomon by placing a stick in the ground. She measured its shadow every hour for 9 hours and made the **line graph** shown below. At what point was the shadow the shortest?

- The line shows the length of the shadow at hourly intervals through the day. The higher the point on the graph, the longer the shadow it represents.
- When the line falls, the shadow is getting shorter. When the line rises, the shadow is getting longer.
- The lowest point on the graph is point *E*, so this is when the shadow was shortest.

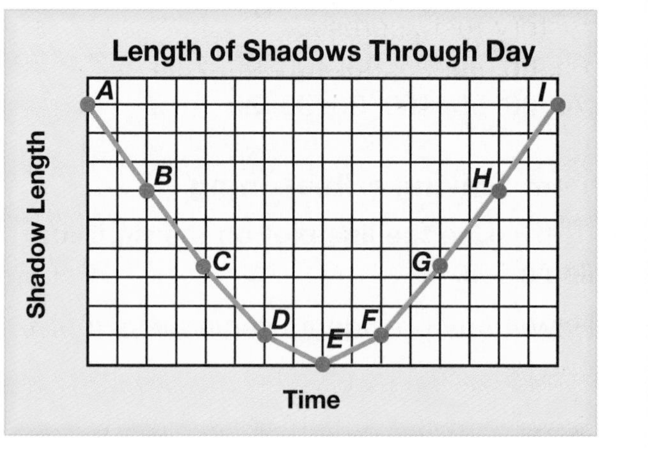

Solution: The shadow was shortest at the center of Pia's graph, after 5 hours.

Explain Your Thinking

► Is the shadow getting longer or shorter between points *A* and *B*? between points *E* and *F*? Explain.

► At which points on the graph is the length of the shadow about the same?

Guided Practice

Watches with hands are called analog watches. Use the graph of sales trends for Problems 1–4.

1. How does the graph show an increase in sales?
2. Did the sales grow steadily up to point *D*?
3. What happened between points *F* and *G*?
4. At which point do you think digital watches were introduced? Why?

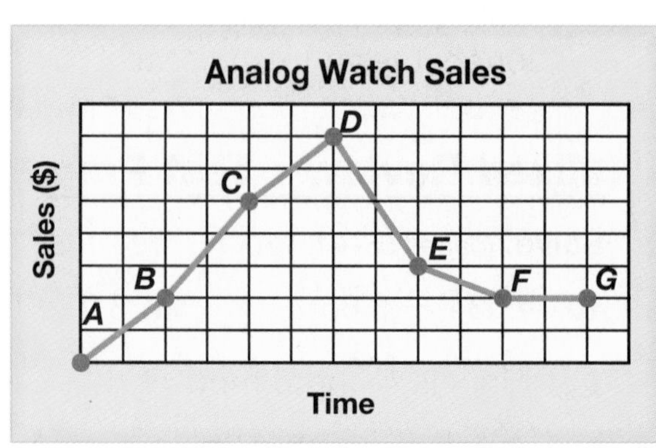

Standards AF 1.1 SDP 1.4 MR 1.0, 1.1

Independent Practice

Use the graph for Problems 5–8.

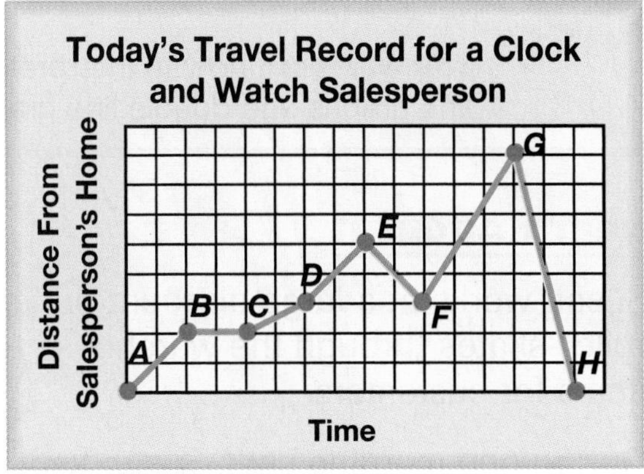

5. Which points represent the sales person's home?
6. What happened between points *G* and *H*?
7. What could have happened between points *B* and *C*?
8. Explain what happened between points *E* and *F*. Tell how you know.

Problem Solving • Reasoning

Use Data **Use the graph on page 262 for Problems 9 and 10.**

9. If point *E* on Pia's graph represents noon, what times do points *A* and *I* represent?
10. **Compare** Between which pair of points did the line change the most?
11. **Analyze** If Pia could continue her graph to show the shadow lengths after point *I*, what would the graph look like? Explain.
12. **Write About It** What information do you need to have in order to analyze a line graph? Explain.

SCIENCE Each time you cross into a new time zone while traveling from east to west, you need to set your watch 1 hour earlier.

Portland, Maine, is located three time zones east of California. When it is 1:30 P.M. in California, what time is it in Portland?

Mixed Review • Test Prep

Estimate. *(pages 138–139)*

13. $6\overline{)371}$ 14. $7\overline{)5{,}074}$ 15. $8\overline{)57{,}842}$ 16. $9\overline{)809{,}124}$

Write the letter of the correct answer. *(pages 60–61, 114–115)*

17. $\$20.00 - \$5.99 = m$
   - **A** $m = \$25.99$
   - **B** $m = \$15.01$
   - **C** $m = \$14.99$
   - **D** $m = \$14.01$

18. $28 \times 35 = n$
   - **F** $n = 63$
   - **G** $n = 140$
   - **H** $n = 224$
   - **J** $n = 980$

Extra Practice See Set E on page 285.

Line and Double Line Graphs

You will learn how to interpret and make line graphs and double line graphs.

New Vocabulary
double line graph
ordered pair

Learn About It

Susan works at a large discount outlet and roller-skates through the warehouse to find items for customers.

During one morning shift, Susan kept track of the distance she skated. Each half-hour she recorded the total number of miles she had traveled.

Make a line graph to show the data Susan collected.

Distance Skated

Time	8:00	8:30	9:00	9:30	10:00	10:30	11:00	11:30	12:00
Total Miles Skated	0	2	4	6	9	9	11	13	14

Making a Line Graph

Step 1 Draw the axes. Label the horizontal axis **Time** and the vertical axis **Total Miles Skated**. Choose an appropriate scale and mark equal intervals.

Step 2 Plot the ordered pairs. Join the points to make the line graph.

Step 3 Give the graph a title.

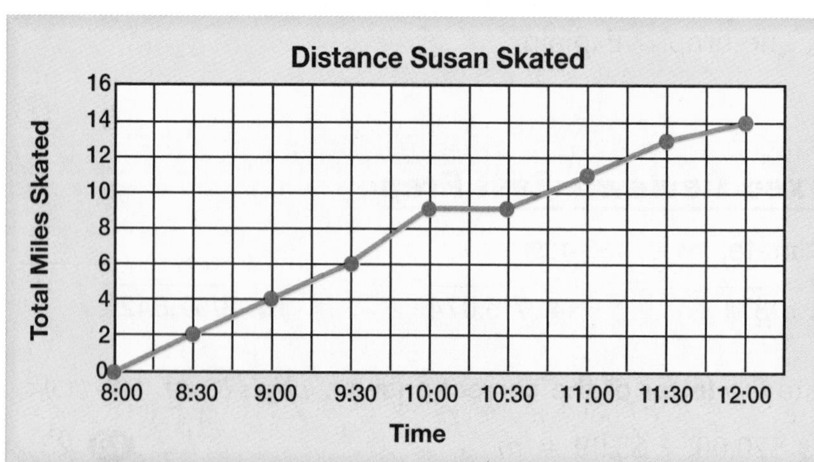

The point on the grid that corresponds to 8:00 on the horizontal axis and 0 on the vertical axis is represented by the **ordered pair** (8:00, 0).

Standards AF **1.1** SDP **1.0, 1.2, 1.4** MR **1.0, 1.1, 2.0**

To check sales, Jim takes monthly inventory of the pairs of in-line skates and roller skates at the discount store. Make a **double line graph** to compare the two sets of data over time.

Skate Inventory

	Dec.	Jan.	Feb.	Mar.	Apr.	May	June
In-Line Skates	60	35	35	25	20	15	0
Roller Skates	35	30	30	25	25	22	20

Making a Double Line Graph

Step1 Draw the axes. Label the horizontal axis **Month** and the vertical axis **Number in Stock**. Choose an appropriate scale and mark equal intervals.

Step 2 Plot the ordered pairs for in-line skates. Then connect the points to make a line graph for in-line skates.

Step 3 Repeat Step 3 for roller skates. Use a different color for this line.

Step 4 Make a key to show what each line represents. Then write a title for the graph.

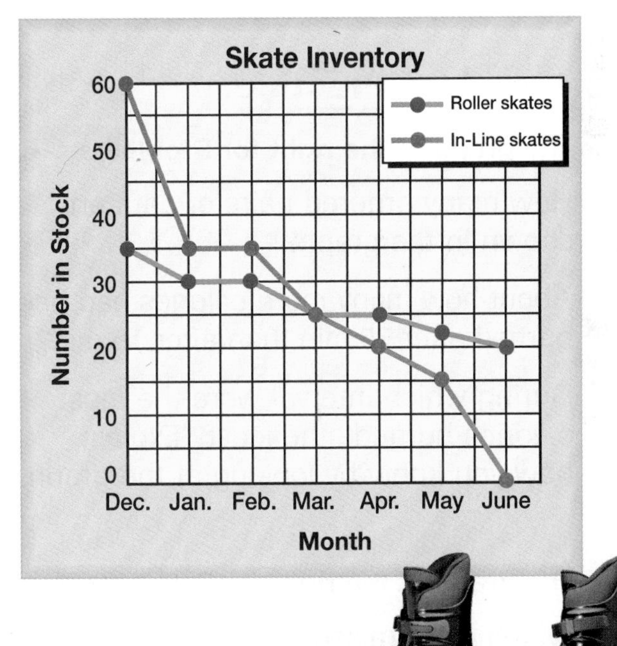

Explain Your Thinking

- Between what times do you think Susan took a break? Why?
- During which half-hour interval did Susan skate the farthest? How can you tell?
- Why are line graphs useful for showing data over time?
- Why is it easier to tell which skates are more popular by using the double line graph?

Guided Practice

Use the skate inventory graph on page 265 for Problems 1 and 2.

1. What does the graph tell you about the inventory of in-line skates and roller skates?
2. In what month was the inventory of in-line skates the greatest? the lowest?
3. Use the table below to make a line graph.

> **Ask Yourself**
> - What scale should I use?
> - How should I label the axes?
> - Did I include a title and a key?

Skateboard Sales

Year	1991	1992	1993	1994	1995	1996
Sales to date (in millions)	$40	$70	$90	$110	$120	$130

Independent Practice

Use the graph at the right for Problems 4–6.

4. How many ordered pairs of data are shown in the graph?
5. About how many more calories had been burned after 75 min than after 15 min?
6. During which interval were the most calories burned? the least? Explain how you know by looking at the graph.

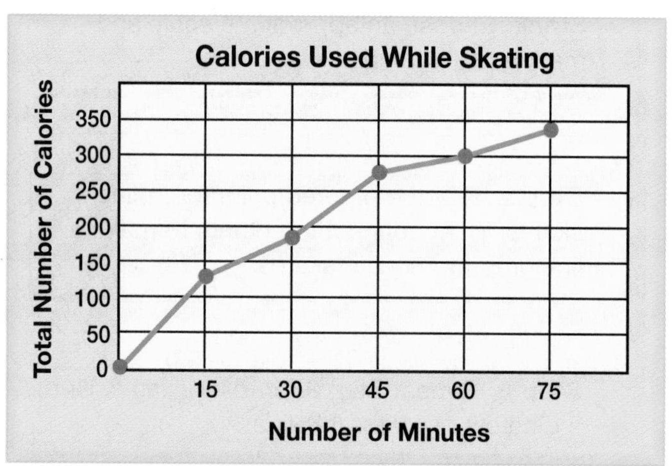

Use the graph at the right for Problems 7–10.

7. Which class raised more money from the skate-a-thon?
8. How much money had the sixth-graders raised after skating for 3 hours?
9. What do you notice about the amount of money raised between the first and second hours for both grades?
10. Are the skaters earning more money each hour near the beginning of the skate-a-thon or near the end? How do you know?

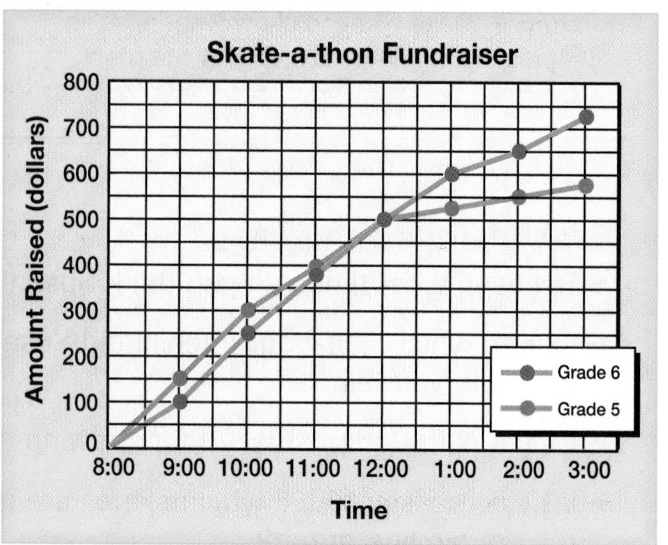

Use the tables below to make line graphs.

11. Make a double line graph of the safety helmet data.

Number of Safety Helmets Sold						
	May	**June**	**July**	**Aug.**	**Sept.**	**Oct.**
Brand X	60	35	35	25	20	15
Brand Y	35	30	30	25	25	22

12. Make a line graph of the Central Park data.

Afternoon Skating in Central Park								
Time	12:30	1:00	1:30	2:00	2:30	3:00	3:30	4:00
Distance From Start (mi)	0	1	2	2	1	2	3	0

Problem Solving • Reasoning

Use the graph for Problems 13–16.

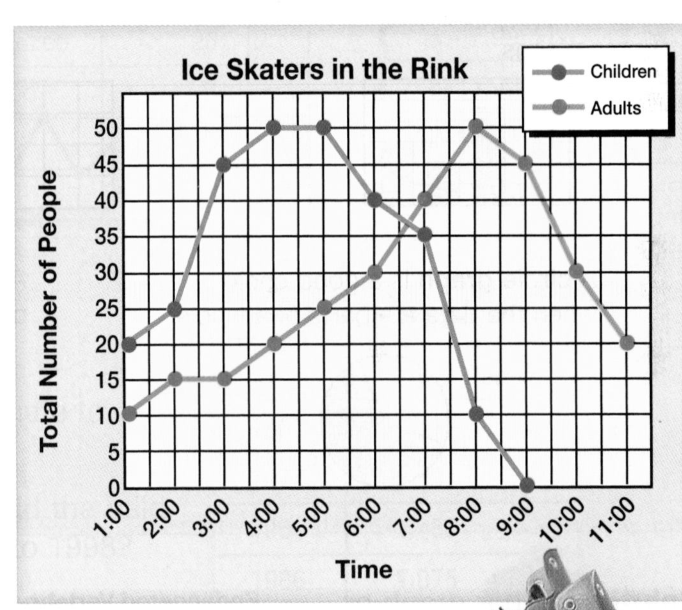

13. **Analyze** What conclusions can you draw from the graph?

14. Between what hours was there the greatest increase in the number of children skating in the park?

15. At what hour was there the greatest difference in the number of children and adults skating in the park?

16. **Write About It** Can you use the graph to find the total number of people skating in the park at a certain hour? Explain how or why not.

Mixed Review • Test Prep

Round the number to the underlined place. *(pages 28–29)*

17. $0.\underline{5}7$ **18.** $0.78\underline{8}5$ **19.** $2.3\underline{6}3$ **20.** $26.\underline{4}3$

21 What is $(6 \times 10^4) + (2 \times 10^3) + (1 \times 10^2) + (7 \times 10^1)$ in standard form? *(pages 6–7)*

A 6,217 **B** 60,217 **C** 62,170 **D** 60,000,217

Quick Check

Check Your Understanding of Lessons 11–14

Find all the possible choices.

1. Use an organized list.

Color	Footwear
brown	sneakers
red	slippers
black	boots
white	

2. Use a tree diagram.

Snack	Dip
chips	guacamole
crackers	onion
	cheese dip
	spinach dip

A number cube has sides labeled 2, 4, 6, 8, 6, and 8. Is each event very likely, unlikely, certain, or impossible?

3. a 4

4. a 6 or an 8

5. an even number

6. a number greater than 2

7. a prime number

8. an odd number

Use the spinner for Problems 9–12. What is the probability that you will spin the following?

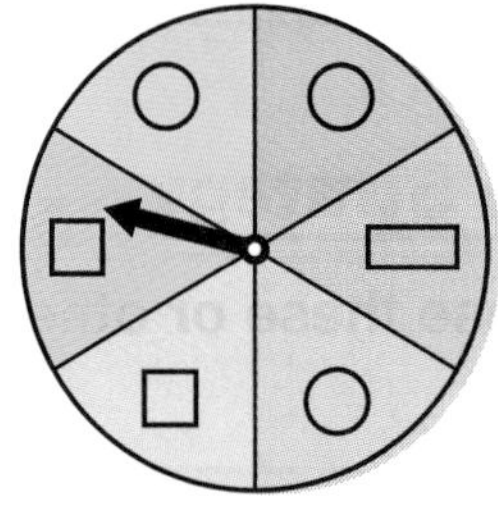

9. a square

10. a circle

11. a triangle

12. a geometric shape

Use the data in the table to solve.

13. The table shows the colors of all the marbles in a bag. Suppose you pick one marble from the bag. What is the probability of picking a green marble?

Marble Colors			
Red	Blue	Green	Black
11	8	12	9

How did you do?

If you had difficulty with any items in the Quick Check, you can use the following pages for review and extra practice.

California Standards	Items	Review These Pages	Do These Extra Practice Items
Math Reasoning: **1.1**	1–2	pages 274–275	Set G, page 286
Reviews Grade 4 Standards	3–12	pages 276–279	Set H, page 286
Math Reasoning: **1.1**	13	pages 280–281	8–9, page 287

Test Prep • Cumulative Review

Maintaining the Standards

Choose the letter of the correct answer.

1. Ben is making table decorations, using one candle and one bow. He has red, white, and blue bows and candles with either stars or stripes on them. In how many different ways can he choose a candle and a bow?

   A 3
   B 5
   C 6
   D 9

2. Measure the side lengths to the nearest millimeter to find the perimeter of the triangle.

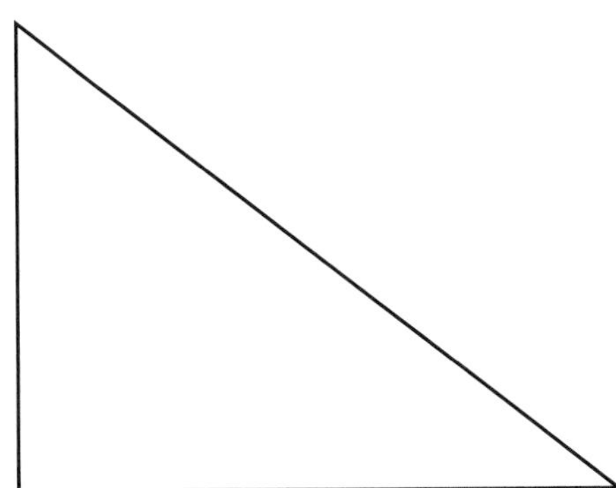

   F 750 mm **H** 180 mm
   G 190 mm **J** 126 mm

3. There will be 115 people at an awards banquet. If each table seats 8 people, what is the least number of tables needed?

   A 13 **C** 15
   B 14 **D** 16

4. Simplify $0.7 + (8 - 0.75)$.

   F 7.25 **H** 9.45
   G 7.95 **J** 14.25

5. Which is the next likely number in this sequence?

   $0.1, \frac{1}{5}, 0.3, \frac{2}{5}, 0.5, \frac{3}{5}, ■$

   A 0.8
   B $\frac{4}{5}$
   C 0.7
   D 0.9

6. In which experiment are the possible outcomes *not* equally likely?

   F tossing heads or tails with one coin
   G spinning a spinner with equal spaces for 1 to 5 to see if you land on an odd or even number
   H rolling a cube numbered 1 to 6 to see if you roll an odd or even number
   J choosing a red or blue chip from a bag with 4 red chips and 4 blue ones

7. A bus stops in front of a baseball stadium every 7 minutes, beginning at 5:22 P.M.

   Which of these times is *not* a time when a bus will stop in front of the baseball stadium?

   A 6:25 P.M. **C** 5:43 P.M.
   B 6:04 P.M. **D** 5:35 P.M.

8. Does $^{-}4 + {}^{+}3 = {}^{+}3 + {}^{-}4$?

   Explain Why or why not?

Safe Site

Internet Test Prep
Visit **www.eduplace.com/kids/mhm** for more *Test Prep Practice.*

Chapter Test

Make a line plot for each set of data. Then find the range, mean, median, and mode.

1. minutes spent on homework:
   15, 0, 35, 60, 40, 0, 30, 45, 45

Use the line graph to solve Problems 2–4.

2. On what day did Andrew receive the most calls? the fewest?
3. On which days did he receive more than six calls?
4. How many calls did Andrew receive in all during the week?

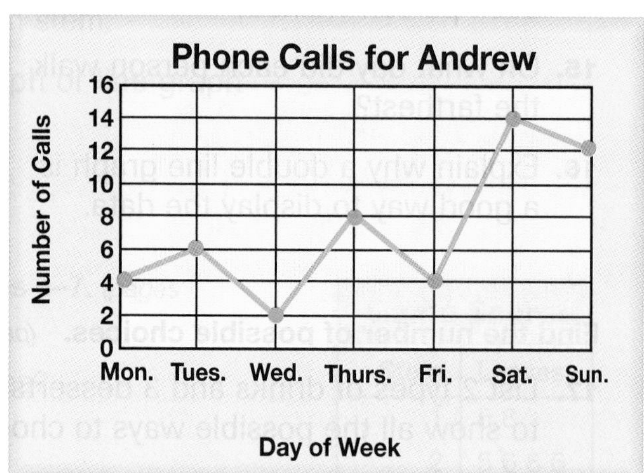

Choose an appropriate graph for the data given. Explain your choice.

5. a. ice cream flavors preferred by people in a survey group
   b. number of cars sold each month by a car dealership

Show all the possible choices for each table.

6. Use an organized list.

Pianos	
concert grand	black
baby grand	brown
upright	white

7. Use a tree diagram.

Hair	
straight	black
wavy	brown
curly	blond
	red

Solve.

8. Use the graph to find the number of zoo visitors who were 18 and under.
9. Were more visitors over 35 or 35 and under? How many more?
10. What is the probability that the next visitor to the zoo will be over 18?

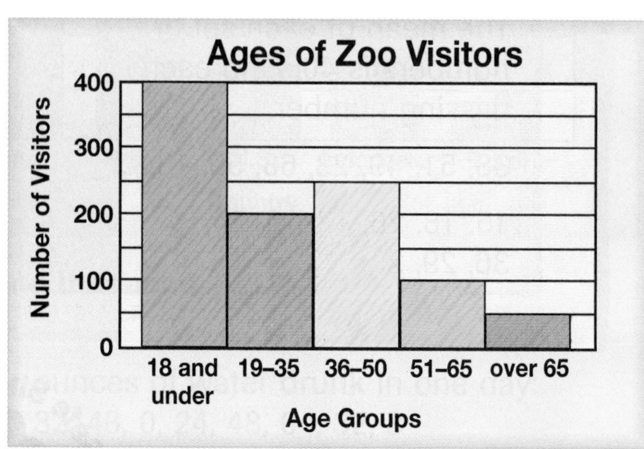

Write About It

Solve each problem. Use correct math vocabulary to explain your thinking.

1. Sketch an example of each type of graph. Include titles and axis labels where necessary.

   a. stem-and-leaf plot **b.** bar graph **c.** double bar graph

   d. histogram **e.** line plot **f.** line graph

2. What errors can you find in this graph?

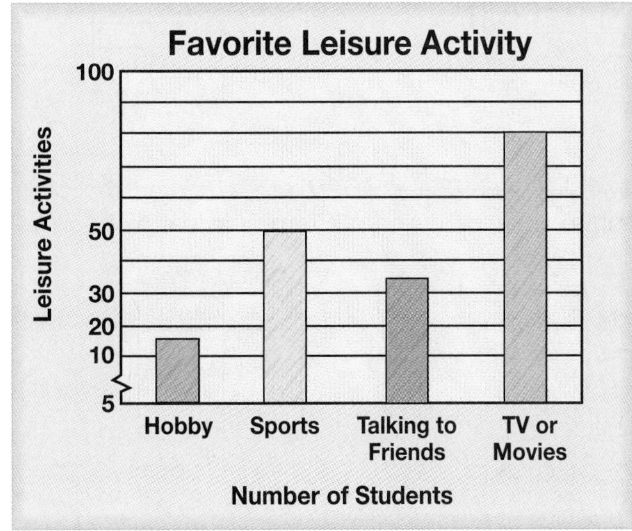

3. Define each term.

   a. mode **b.** mean

   c. median **d.** range

Use the graph at right for Problems 4–6.

4. Explain what is shown in the graph.
5. What is the range of the depths shown in this graph? Explain how you know.
6. Use the points on the graph to find the median and mode of the depths.

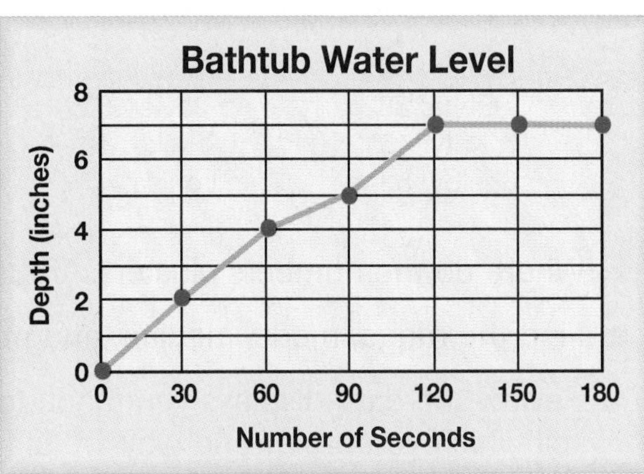

Another Look

Use what you have learned about different ways to present data to answer these questions.

Different Ways to Present Data

Double bar graph

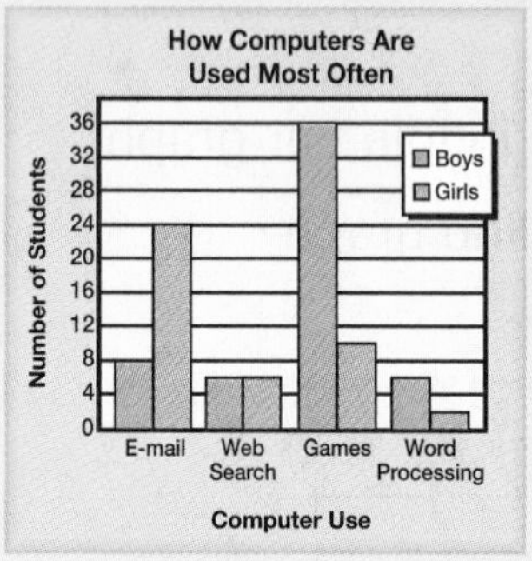

How Computers Are Used Most Often

Histogram

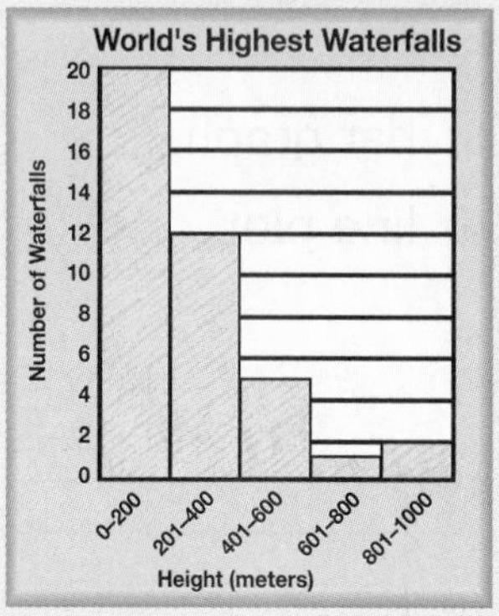

World's Highest Waterfalls

Double line graph

Skate Inventory

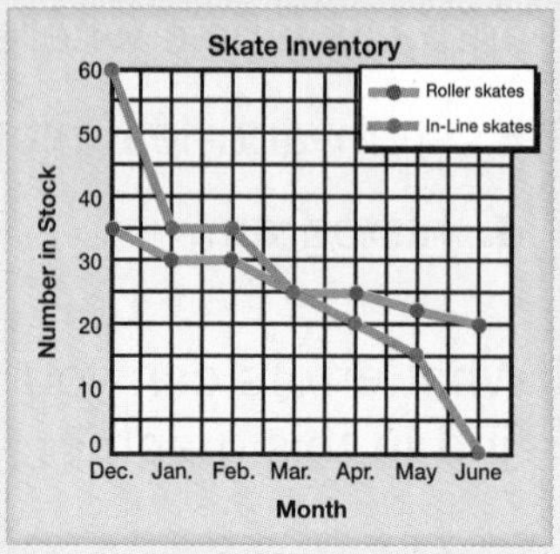

Table

Pianos	
concert grand	black
baby grand	brown
upright	white

Stem-and-leaf plot

Game Scores

Stem	Leaves
1	5 8
2	5 6 6 6
3	3 6 9
4	4 7 8
5	1

Line plot

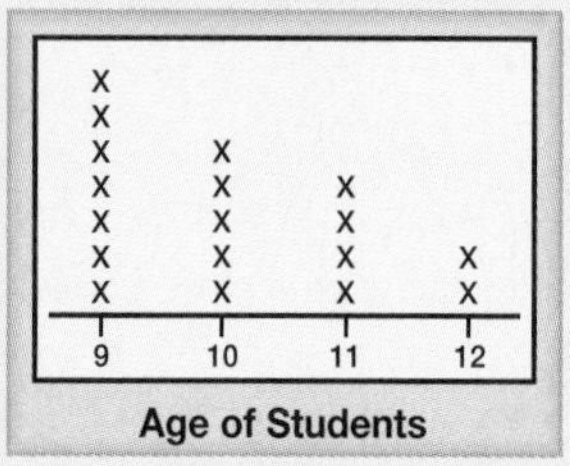

Age of Students

1. Make two different types of graphs or plots to display the data. Remember to include labels and titles.

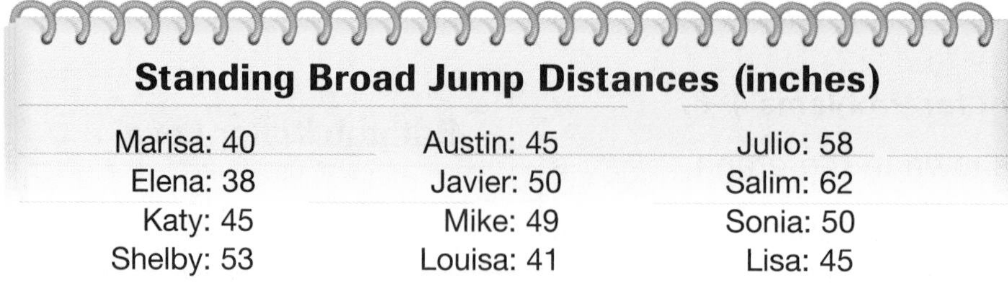

Standing Broad Jump Distances (inches)

Marisa: 40	Austin: 45	Julio: 58
Elena: 38	Javier: 50	Salim: 62
Katy: 45	Mike: 49	Sonia: 50
Shelby: 53	Louisa: 41	Lisa: 45

2. Where do the numbers cluster? Are there any gaps?
3. Find the range, mode, median, and mean for the data.
4. Review the data displays you made for Problem 1. Tell which you prefer and why.

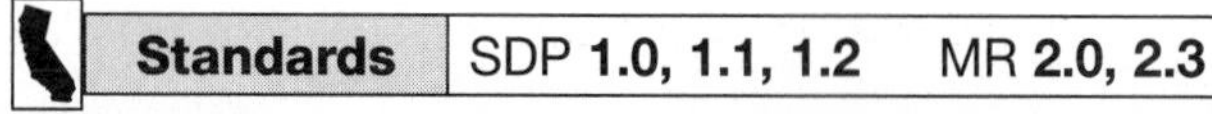

Enrichment

Choosing a Graph Scale

The scale you choose for a graph can affect the appearance of the data.

Here are two graphs that show the same data. What differences do you notice?

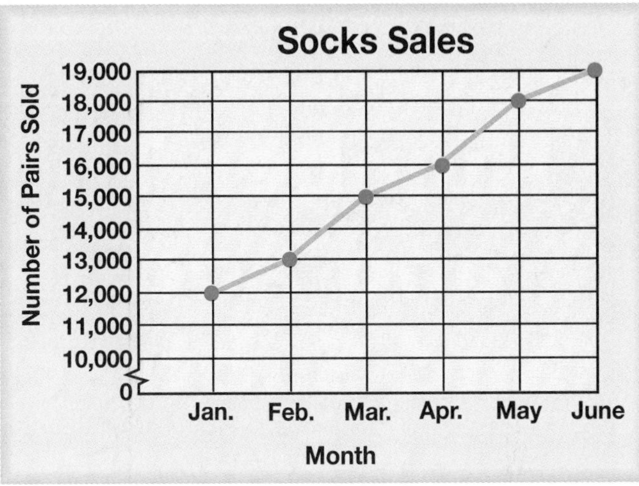

1. Which graph makes it look as though sales are increasing more? Why?
2. The zigzag line at the base of the vertical axis on the first graph shows that some numbers have been left out. How would the graph change if these numbers were included?
3. What do you notice when you compare the intervals used on the vertical axes of the two graphs? How do you think the appearance of the graph would change if intervals of 3,000 were used?
4. Make another graph that presents the same data. Adjust the vertical axis on your graph so sales appear to be increasing only a little bit each month.

Explain Your Thinking

- ► Why is it important to look at how the axes are numbered when you are interpreting a graph?
- ► When you are making a graph, what questions can help you decide on the best scale?

Standards	SDP **1.0, 1.2** MR **1.0, 2.0, 2.3**

CHAPTER 7

Number Theory and Addition and Subtraction of Fractions

Why Learn About Number Theory and Addition and Subtraction of Fractions?

Learning about number theory helps you understand base-ten numbers and their properties. Learning to add and subtract fractions helps you solve problems that involve parts of regions or sets.

This girl is taking violin lessons. She has to understand fractions in order to know when to play each note and how long to hold it.

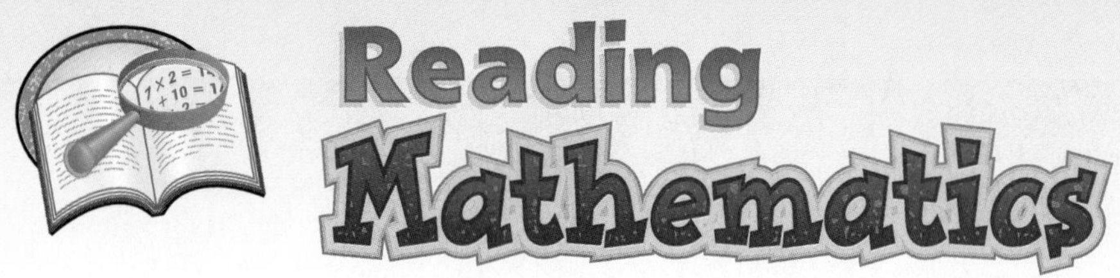

Reading Mathematics

Reviewing Vocabulary

Understanding math language helps you become a successful problem solver. Here are some math vocabulary words you should know.

factor of a number	a number that divides evenly into the number
divisible	a number is divisible by its factors
multiple	a number that is the product of the given number and a number
fraction	a number that describes part of a whole or part of a group
numerator	the number above the bar in a fraction
denominator	the number below the bar in a fraction

Reading Words and Symbols

When you read mathematics, sometimes you read only words, sometimes you read words and symbols, and sometimes you read only symbols.

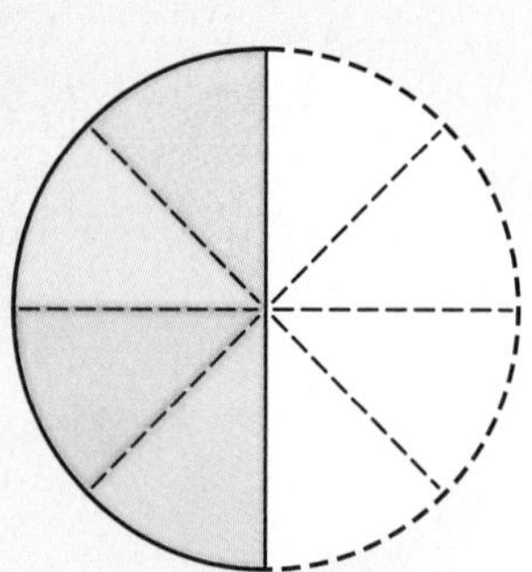

All of these statements represent the same number.

- one half
- $\frac{1}{2}$
- $\frac{4}{8}$
- 0.5
- $1 \div 2$

Try This

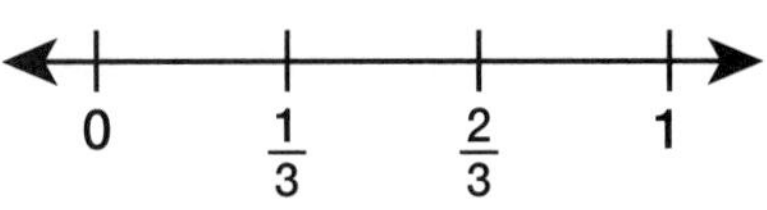

1. Use the number line to answer each question.
   a. How does the number line show that $\frac{1}{3}$ means the same as $1 \div 3$?
   b. What is the name of the fraction that falls half-way between 0 and $\frac{1}{3}$?
   c. How could the line show that $\frac{1}{3}$ is the same amount as $\frac{2}{6}$?

2. Write *true* or *false* for each statement.
   a. The product of 3×4 is 12, so 3 and 4 are factors of 12.
   b. The numbers 3 and 4 are the only factors of 12.
   c. Every number except 0 is divisible by itself and 1.
   d. If you multiply the numerator and denominator of a fraction by the same number, this gives the same result as multiplying the fraction by 1.
   e. If the numerator of a fraction is greater than the denominator, the fraction is less than one.

3. Explain how this diagram shows that 3 and 5 are factors of 15.

Upcoming Vocabulary

Write About It **Here are some other vocabulary words** you will learn in this chapter. Watch for these words. Write their definitions in your journal.

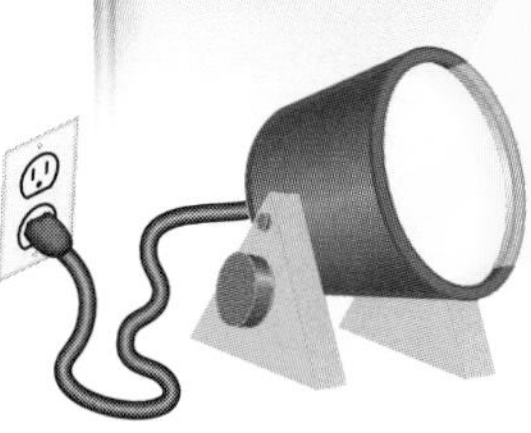

prime factorization

greatest common factor (GCF)

least common multiple (LCM)

equivalent fractions

common denominator

least common denominator (LCD)

Prime and Composite Numbers

You will learn how to identify prime and composite numbers.

New Vocabulary
prime number
composite number

Learn About It

When a number is written as a product of counting numbers, the numbers that are multiplied are called factors. Every counting number greater than 1 has at least two factors—1 and the number itself.

Since 10 can be written as 1 × 10 or 2 × 5, the numbers 1, 2, 5, and 10 are all factors of 10.

A **prime number** is a counting number greater than 1 whose only factors are 1 and the number itself.

A **composite number** is a counting number that has more than two factors.

Can Miriam arrange 11 butterflies in one or more rows with an equal number of butterflies in each row? To find out, decide whether 11 is prime or composite.

Is 11 a prime or a composite number?

Try to express 11 as the product of counting numbers from 1 to 11.

1 × 11 = 11

The only factors are 1 and 11. The number 11 is a prime number.

Solution: Miriam can arrange 11 butterflies only in 1 row of 11 or 11 rows of 1.

If Miriam adds one more butterfly, how can she arrange them in rows?

Is 12 a prime or composite number?

Try to express 12 as the product of counting numbers from 1 to 12.

1 × 12 = 12 **2 × 6 = 12** **3 × 4 = 12**

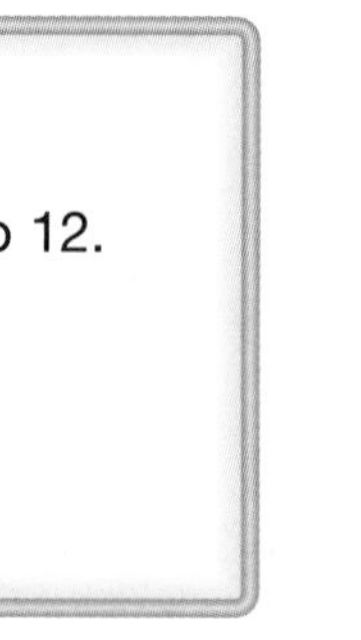

The factors of 12 are 1, 2, 3, 4, 6, and 12. The number 12 is a composite number because it has more than two factors.

Solution: Miriam can arrange 12 butterflies in rows of 1, 2, 3, 4, 6, or 12.

Explain Your Thinking

- ▶ Explain why the number 1 is neither prime nor composite.
- ▶ Is every number that is divisible by 2 a composite number? Explain.

Guided Practice

Identify each number as *prime* or *composite*. Write each composite number as a product of two factors that are either *prime* or *composite* numbers.

1. 4 **2.** 5 **3.** 6 **4.** 10

5. 13 **6.** 14 **7.** 16 **8.** 30

> **Ask Yourself**
> - How many factors does a prime number have?
> - How many factors does a composite number have?

Independent Practice

Identify each number as *prime* or *composite*. Write each composite number as a product of two factors that are either *prime* or *composite* numbers.

9. 2 **10.** 3 **11.** 7 **12.** 8 **13.** 9 **14.** 15

15. 24 **16.** 25 **17.** 26 **18.** 27 **19.** 28 **20.** 29

Problem Solving • Reasoning

21. **Patterns** Look at the pattern of butterflies. The pattern shows square numbers. A square number can be written as the product of two equal factors. Are any prime numbers also square numbers? Explain.

22. The public library has 4 times as many books on butterflies as the school library. The school library has 45 butterfly books. How many are in the public library?

23. **Analyze** How many different factors does 4 have? Find another number with the same number of factors.

24. **Write About It** Does a composite number always have at least one prime factor? Use examples to explain your thinking.

Mixed Review • Test Prep

Round each number to the nearest 10 and 100. *(pages 8–10)*

25. 481 **26.** 998 **27.** 3,458 **28.** 1,732

29 What is the sum of 215 and 94? *(pages 52–53)*

A 121 **B** 209 **C** 221 **D** 309

Extra Practice See Set A on page 352.

LESSON 2

Prime Factorization

You will learn how to write the prime factorization of a number.

New Vocabulary
prime factorization

Learn About It

Any composite number can be written as a product of prime factors. A factorization consisting of only prime factors is called a **prime factorization**.

A factor tree can be used to find the prime factorization of a number.

Find the prime factorization of 24.

Step 1 Write 24 as the product of two factors that are either prime or composite.

24
3×8

Step 2 Make a factor tree by writing each factor as a product of two factors until all factors are prime numbers.

24
3×8
$3 \times 2 \times 4$
$3 \times 2 \times 2 \times 2$

Step 3 Write all the prime factors from the bottom row of the factor tree in order. Then, use exponents to write the prime factorization.

$24 = 2 \times 2 \times 2 \times 3$
$= 2^3 \times 3$

The prime factorization of 24 is $2^3 \times 3$.

Another Example

No Repetition of Factors

30
6×5
$2 \times 3 \times 5$

The prime factorization of 30 is $2 \times 3 \times 5$. Exponents greater than 1 are not needed since no factors are repeated.

Explain Your Thinking

- If you used 3 and 10 for the first factor pair of 30, would the prime factorization be the same? Why?
- The number 1 is not used in a factor tree. Why not?

Guided Practice

What factor completes each factor tree?

1. 10
$2 \times$ ■

2. 18
2×9
$2 \times$ ■ $\times 3$

3. 30
6×5
■ $\times 3 \times 5$

Ask Yourself

- What basic fact can I use?
- What do I multiply to check if a prime factorization is correct?

 Standards NS 1.0, 1.3, 1.4 AF 1.0, 1.2

Independent Practice

Write the factors that complete each factor tree.
Then use exponents to write the prime factorization.

4. 12
3 × ■
3 × ■ × 2

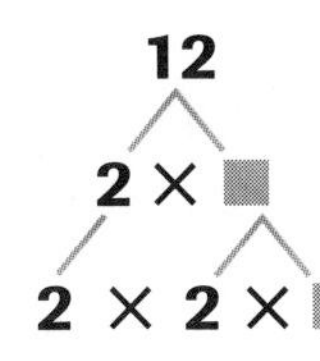

5. 40
■ × 8
■ × 2 × 4
■ × ■ × 2 × ■

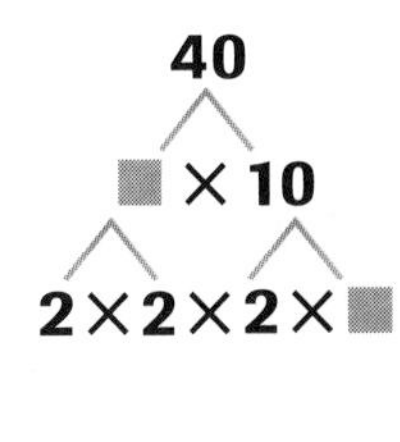

Write each prime factorization. Use exponents if possible.

6. 2	**7.** 3	**8.** 4	**9.** 5	**10.** 6	**11.** 7
12. 8	**13.** 9	**14.** 10	**15.** 11	**16.** 12	**17.** 13
18. 14	**19.** 15	**20.** 16	**21.** 17	**22.** 18	**23.** 19

Problem Solving • Reasoning

24. Show the prime factorization for numbers 20 through 50. Use exponents where possible.

25. **Compare** Each of two composite numbers has 2, 3, and 5 in its prime factorization, but one of the numbers is twice as large as the other. What might the numbers be?

26. **Analyze** How many different prime factors of 420 are there?

27. **Analyze** Given any number, what is the greatest possible factor? Why?

28. **Write About It** What does the factor tree of a prime number look like? For any counting number, why does the last row of its factor tree contain only prime numbers? Use an example to explain.

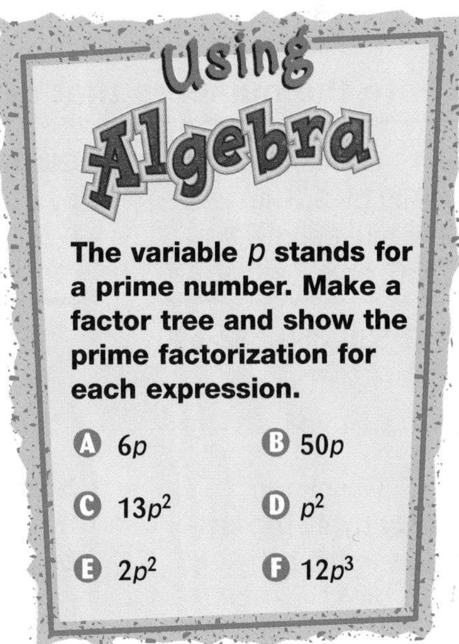

Mixed Review • Test Prep

Round each number to the nearest ten thousand. *(pages 8–10)*

29. 39,147 **30.** 203,562 **31.** 652,891 **32.** 21,538 **33.** 985,716

34 Which number rounded to the nearest thousand is 87,000? *(pages 8–10)*

A 86,491 **C** 86,450
B 86,498 **D** 86,791

Extra Practice See Set B on page 352.

Divisibility

You will learn how to determine when 2, 3, 4, 5, 9, or 10 is a factor of a number.

Review Vocabulary
divisible
factor

Learn About It

A number is **divisible** by another number when the quotient is a whole number and there is no remainder. Any **factor** of a given number divides that number evenly.

The first three digits of Amy's telephone number form one of the numbers listed. If the number formed is divisible by 2, 3, 4, 5, 9, and 10, what are the first three digits of Amy's telephone number?

Eliminate the numbers that are not divisible by 2, 3, 4, 5, 9, or 10.

Step 1 Check for divisibility by 2. The number must end with 0, 2, 4, 6, or 8.

~~725~~ 240 536 360 382 590

Step 2 Check for divisibility by 5. The number must end with 0 or 5.

~~725~~ 240 ~~536~~ 360 ~~382~~ 590

Step 3 Check for divisibility by 10. The number must end with 0.

All three remaining numbers are divisible by 10.

Step 4 Check for divisibility by 4. The last two digits must be divisible by 4.

240 → 40 ÷ 4 = 10
360 → 60 ÷ 4 = 15
590 → 90 ÷ 4 = 22 R2

~~725~~ 240 ~~536~~ 360 ~~382~~ ~~590~~

Step 5 Check for divisibility by 3. The sum of the digits must be divisible by 3.

240 → 2 + 4 + 0 = 6
6 ÷ 3 = 2
360 → 3 + 6 + 0 = 9
9 ÷ 3 = 3

Both remaining numbers are divisible by 3.

Step 6 Check for divisibility by 9. The sum of the digits must be divisible by 9.

240 → 2 + 4 + 0 = 6
6 ÷ 9 = 0 R6
360 → 3 + 6 + 0 = 9
9 ÷ 9 = 1

~~725~~ ~~240~~ ~~536~~ (360) ~~382~~ ~~590~~

Solution: The first three digits form the number 360.

Explain Your Thinking

▶ If a number is divisible by 9, must it be divisible by 3? Explain why or why not.

 Standards NS 1.0, 1.4, 2.2

Guided Practice

Test each number to see if it is divisible by 2, 3, 4, 5, 9, or 10.

	Number	Divisible by
1.	325	■
2.	540	■
3.	393	■
4.	632	■

	Number	Divisible by
5.	405	■
6.	990	■
7.	323	■
8.	3,000	■

Ask Yourself

- Did I check the final digit for divisibility by 2, 5, and 10?
- Did I check the last two digits for divisibility by 4?
- Did I add the digits to check divisibility by 3 and 9?

Independent Practice

Use the rules to test each number for divisibility by 2, 3, 4, 5, 9, and 10.

9. 118 **10.** 295 **11.** 177 **12.** 531 **13.** 236

14. 455 **15.** 7,100 **16.** 1,278 **17.** 6,765 **18.** 1,107

Problem Solving • Reasoning

Use Data **Use the map for Problems 19 and 20.**

19. Analyze The map shows the telephone area codes of several places in California. Lauren lives in a city shown on the map. Her area code forms a number that is divisible by 2, 3, and 5. Where does she live?

20. Many people use tricks to remember number combinations. How might you use divisibility to remember the arrangement of digits in your area code if you live in Fresno?

21. Logical Thinking Is a multiple of 2 always a multiple of 4? Is a multiple of 4 always a multiple of 2? Explain why or why not.

22. Write About It Gabriella says that if a number is divisible by both 2 and 3, then it must also be divisible by 6. Test some examples. Then explain why you think this rule does or does not work.

Mixed Review • Test Prep

Solve and check. *(pages 74–75)*

23. $c + 4 = 12$ **24.** $d - 3 = 11$ **25.** $7 + x = 35$ **26.** $22 = t - 5$

27 Which is the best estimate for $59.8 - 32.05$? *(pages 28–29, 60–61)*

A 26 **B** 28 **C** 30 **D** 92

Extra Practice See Set C on page 352.

Common Factors and Greatest Common Factor

You will learn how to find the common factors and greatest common factor of two or more numbers.

New Vocabulary
common factor
greatest common factor (GCF)
greatest common divisor (GCD)

Learn About It

If a number is a factor of two or more counting numbers, it is called a **common factor** of those numbers. The **greatest common factor (GCF)** of two or more numbers is the common factor that is greater than any other common factor.

Find the greatest common factor of 18 and 24.

Different Ways to Find the GCF

You can make a list.

Think about factor pairs. For example,
$18 = 1 \times 18$
$18 = 2 \times 9$
$18 = 3 \times 6$

Step 1 List all the factors of each number.

Factors of 18: 1, 2, 3, 6, 9, 18
Factors of 24: 1, 2, 3, 4, 6, 8, 12, 24

Step 2 Identify the common factors.

Factors of 18: **1**, **2**, **3**, **6**, 9, 18
Factors of 24: **1**, **2**, **3**, 4, **6**, 8, 12, 24

The common factors are 1, 2, 3, and 6.

Step 3 Compare to find the greatest factor.

The greatest common factor of 18 and 24 is 6.

You can use prime factorization.

Step 1 Make factor trees for 18 and 24.

18: 2×9 → $2 \times 3 \times 3$

24: 6×4 → $2 \times 3 \times 2 \times 2$

Step 2 Identify all the common prime factors.

$18 = \mathbf{2} \times \mathbf{3} \times 3$
$24 = 2 \times 2 \times \mathbf{2} \times \mathbf{3}$

Step 3 The product of the common prime factors is the GCF.

The GCF is 2×3 or 6.

 Standards NS 1.0, 1.3, 1.4 MR 2.0

Since each common factor of two or more numbers is a divisor of each number, the GCF is often called the **greatest common divisor (GCD)** of the numbers.

Other Examples

A. GCF is 1

Find the GCF of 21 and 26.

List the factors of each number.

Factors of 21: 1, 3, 7, 21

Factors of 26: 1, 2, 13, 26

The GCF is 1.

B. GCF of Larger Numbers

Find the GCF of 160 and 200.

First find the prime factorization of each number.

160 → 10 × 16 → 2 × 5 × 4 × 4 → 2 × 5 × 2 × 2 × 2 × 2

200 → 10 × 20 → 2 × 5 × 4 × 5 → 2 × 5 × 2 × 2 × 5

Then identify the common factors.

$160 = 2 \times 2 \times 2 \times 2 \times 2 \times 5$

$200 = 2 \times 2 \times 2 \times 5 \times 5$

Finally, find the GCF of 160 and 200.

The GCF is $2^3 \times 5$, or 40.

Explain Your Thinking

- ▶ Why is prime factorization a good way to find the GCF of two large numbers?
- ▶ Explain why two numbers always have at least one common factor.

Guided Practice

List the factors for each number. Then find the greatest common factor (GCF) for each pair of numbers.

1. 9, 27 **2.** 15, 22 **3.** 20, 28

Find the prime factorization of each number. Then find the greatest common factor (GCF) of each pair of numbers.

4. 10, 45 **5.** 45, 100 **6.** 16, 100

Ask Yourself

- What are the factors for each number?
- Did I find all the common factors?

Independent Practice

List the factors for each number. Then find the greatest common factor for each pair of numbers.

7. 14, 22 **8.** 30, 55 **9.** 10, 12 **10.** 9, 25 **11.** 15, 17

12. 20, 38 **13.** 26, 34 **14.** 13, 19 **15.** 12, 24 **16.** 32, 40

17. 15, 24 **18.** 25, 75 **19.** 42, 48 **20.** 11, 44 **21.** 30, 45

Find the prime factorization of each number. Then find the greatest common factor (GCF) of each pair of numbers.

22. 10, 24 **23.** 6, 15 **24.** 9, 28 **25.** 10, 55 **26.** 12, 42

27. 24, 64 **28.** 18, 54 **29.** 21, 30 **30.** 16, 72 **31.** 28, 70

32. 75, 120 **33.** 20, 125 **34.** 35, 105 **35.** 10, 240 **36.** 30, 150

Problem Solving • Reasoning

Solve. Choose a method.

Computation Methods

- Mental Math
- Estimate
- Paper and Pencil

37. **Analyze** Is 8 times 1,258 greater than or less than 10,000? Explain your thinking.

38. **Analyze** The GCF of an odd number and an even number is 17. The greater number is 51. Find the other number.

39. Ed has 45 cherries and 60 cashews. What is the greatest number of cakes he can decorate if he must use all of the cherries and cashews and if each cake must have the same numbers of cherries and cashews?

40. **Write About It** The number 24 has more factors than the number 9. Does the greater of two composite numbers always have more factors than the lesser composite number? Support your answer with several examples?

Mixed Review • Test Prep

Solve. *(pages 98–99, 114–115, 148–149)*

41. $48\overline{)576}$ **42.** 31×21 **43.** $85\overline{)765}$ **44.** 77×8

Write the letter of the correct answer. *(pages 258–259)*

45 Choose the median for the data: 12, 14, 17, 19, 19, 21.

A 9 **C** 18

B 17 **D** 19

46 Choose the mode for the data: 12, 14, 17, 19, 19, 21.

F 9 **H** 18

G 17 **J** 19

Extra Practice See Set D on page 352.

Show What You Know

Using Vocabulary

Give an example of each.

1. prime number

2. composite number

3. two numbers with a common factor greater than 1

4. the prime factorization of a composite number

5. the greatest common factor of two composite numbers

6. the greatest common divisor of two prime numbers

True or False

Check each statement by dividing both numbers by the GCF. If the statement is true, the two new numbers should have no common factors.

1. The GCF of 126 and 45 is 9.

2. The GCF of 126 and 70 is 7.

3. The GCF of 357 and 102 is 3.

4. The GCF of 260 and 308 is 4.

Prime Numbers

Make a table of numbers from 1 to 50.

Cross out 1.

Circle 2 and cross out the other multiples of 2.

Repeat the process for 3.

Continue the process starting with the next number that isn't crossed out.

~~1~~	(2)	3	~~4~~	5	~~6~~	7	~~8~~	9	~~10~~
11	~~12~~	13	~~14~~	15	~~16~~	17	~~18~~	19	~~20~~
21	~~22~~	23	~~24~~	25	~~26~~	27	~~28~~	29	~~30~~
31	~~32~~	33	~~34~~	35	~~36~~	37	~~38~~	39	~~40~~
41	~~42~~	43	~~44~~	45	~~46~~	47	~~48~~	49	~~50~~

Make a list of the circled numbers.
Explain how you know they are prime numbers.

Common Multiples and Least Common Multiple

You will learn how to find common multiples and the least common multiple.

New Vocabulary
multiple
common multiple
least common multiple (LCM)

Learn About It

A **multiple** of a counting number is the product of the number and any counting number. If a number is a multiple of two or more numbers, it is called a **common multiple** of the numbers.

The **least common multiple (LCM)** of two or more numbers is the common multiple that is less than all other common multiples.

A radio station has 12 logo hats and 9 T-shirts for prizes. Every 6th caller wins a logo hat. Every 10th caller wins a T-shirt. Which caller will be the first to win both prizes?

Find the LCM of 6 and 10.

Which callers win hats?
List the first twelve multiples of 6.

6: 6, 12, 18, 24, 30, 36, 42, 48, 54, 60, 66, 72

Which callers win T-shirts?
List the first nine multiples of 10.

10: 10, 20, 30, 40, 50, 60, 70, 80, 90

Which callers win both prizes?
List the common multiples.

30, 60

Which caller will be the first to win both prizes?
Find the least common multiple (LCM). The LCM is 30.

Solution: The 30th caller will be the first to win both prizes.

Other Examples

A. LCM is One of the Numbers Itself

Find the LCM of 2 and 6.

Multiples of 2: 2, 4, **6,** 8, 10, **12,** 14, . . .

Multiples of 6: **6, 12, 18, 24, 30,** . . .

The LCM of 2 and 6 is 6.

B. LCM of Greater Numbers

Find the LCM of 10 and 25.

Multiples of 10: 10, 20, 30, 40, **50,** . . .

Multiples of 25: 25, **50,** 75, **100,** . . .

The LCM of 10 and 25 is 50.

Sometimes it is easier to use prime factorizations to find the LCM.

Find the LCM of 35 and 63.

Step 1 Use factor trees to find the prime factorizations of the two numbers.

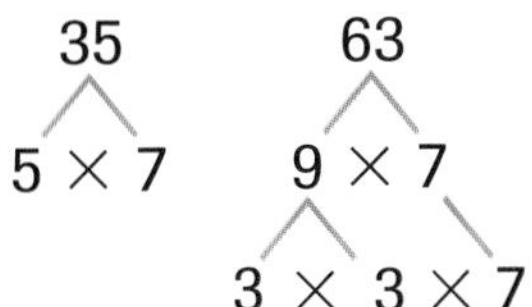

Step 2 List all the prime factors of the two numbers. Be sure to include repeated primes.

35: 5, 7
63: 3, 3, 7

repeated factors

The number 7 is a common factor of 35 and 63.

Step 3 Determine the LCM. Find the product of all the factors, *using the common factors only once.*

Think: Any multiple of 35 must have one 5 and one 7 in its prime factorization. Any multiple of 63 must have two 3s and one 7 in its prime factorization. So, the common factor, 7, is used only once.

The LCM of 35 and 63 is $3 \times 3 \times 5 \times 7$ or 315.

Solution: The LCM of 35 and 63 is 315.

Other Examples

A. No Common Prime Factors

Find the LCM of 6 and 49.

Prime factors of 6: 2, 3

Prime factors of 49: 7, 7

$\text{LCM} = 2 \times 3 \times 7 \times 7 = 294$

The LCM of 6 and 49 is 294.

B. LCM of Greater Numbers

Find the LCM of 84 and 120.

$84 = 2 \times 2 \times 3 \times 7$

$120 = 2 \times 2 \times 2 \times 3 \times 5$

$\text{LCM} = 2 \times 2 \times 2 \times 3 \times 5 \times 7 = 840$

The LCM of 84 and 120 is 840.

Explain Your Thinking

- ▶ Why must any multiple of 35 have at least one 5 and one 7 in its prime factorization?
- ▶ How can you use division to check if a number is a common multiple of two numbers?

Guided Practice

List multiples to find the LCM. Then use the prime factorization method.

1. 5, 20
2. 12, 30
3. 18, 24
4. 21, 28

Ask Yourself

- Did I list enough multiples of both numbers?
- Is my answer a multiple of both numbers?

Independent Practice

Write the first five multiples of each number.

5. 8	**6.** 14	**7.** 7	**8.** 25	**9.** 15
10. 12	**11.** 11	**12.** 30	**13.** 18	**14.** 24

Write the prime factorization of each number.

15. 9	**16.** 6	**17.** 4	**18.** 8	**19.** 10
20. 15	**21.** 20	**22.** 12	**23.** 25	**24.** 16

Find the LCM of each pair of numbers. Use either method.

25. 5, 9	**26.** 4, 10	**27.** 2, 11	**28.** 3, 15	**29.** 10, 12
30. 15, 20	**31.** 16, 32	**32.** 12, 18	**33.** 18, 27	**34.** 7, 13
35. 16, 18	**36.** 24, 72	**37.** 36, 48	**38.** 16, 80	**39.** 40, 50

Problem Solving • Reasoning

Use Data **Use the chart for Problems 40–42.**

Radio Station Commercial Schedule	
Radio Station	**Commercial Plays**
WJAZ	Every 12 minutes
KLAU	Every 8 minutes
WTAM	Every 6 minutes
WFUN	Every 5 minutes

40. If radio stations WJAZ and KLAU have commercials at 10:00 A.M., when will they both have a commercial at the same time again?

41. **Analyze** Which station plays more commercials per hour, WTAM or WFUN? How many more? Explain how you reached your decision.

42. **Write About It** If WJAZ, KLAU, and WTAM have commercials at 10 A.M., when will the three stations have a commercial at the same time again?

Mixed Review • Test Prep

Evaluate each expression for $a = 12$. *(pages 70–72, 162–164)*

43. $a + 15$ **44.** $60 \div a$ **45.** $a \times a$ **46.** $a - a$

Choose the letter of the correct answer. *(pages 166–167, 298–299)*

47 One number is twice another number. The sum of the numbers is 24. What are the numbers?

A 12, 12 **C** 6, 18
B 12, 24 **D** 8, 16

48 One number is a prime factor of the other number. What are the numbers?

F 18, 9 **H** 18, 5
G 18, 6 **J** 18, 3

Extra Practice See Set E on page 352.

Using Exponents

To find the GCF or LCM by prime factorization, you can use exponents as a shortcut.

Find the GCF of 72 and 108.

Find the prime factorizations of 72 and 108.

72
8 × 9
2 × 4   3 × 3
2   2

108
4 × 27
2 × 2   3 × 9
3   3

$72 = 2^3 \times \mathbf{3^2}$ $108 = \mathbf{2^2} \times 3^3$

To find the GCF, use each prime factor raised to the **smaller** exponent of that prime number in either prime factorization.

The GCF is $2^2 \times 3^2 = 4 \times 9$, or 36.

Solution: The GCF of 72 and 108 is 36.

Find the LCM of 80 and 100.

Find the prime factorizations of 80 and 100.

$80 = \mathbf{2^4} \times 5$

$100 = 2^2 \times \mathbf{5^2}$

To find the LCM, use each prime factor raised to the **greater** exponent of that prime number in either prime factorization.

The LCM is $2^4 \times 5^2 = 16 \times 25$, or 400.

Solution: The LCM of 80 and 100 is 400.

Explain Your Thinking

- Why is 2^3 the GCF of 2^3 and 2^5?
- Why is 2^5 the LCM of 2^3 and 2^5?

Problem-Solving Strategy: Use Logical Thinking

You will learn how to solve a problem by logical thinking.

210
10 × 21
2 × 5 × 3 × 7

Using logic requires thinking in an organized way to find an answer or conclusion.

Problem The LCM of two numbers, x and y, is 210. Their GCF is 3. The numbers differ by 9. What are the numbers?

Understand

What is the question?

What are the two unknown numbers?

What do you know?

The LCM is 210. The GCF is 3.
The numbers differ by 9.

Remember:
The GCF must be a factor of both numbers.
The LCM must contain all the prime factors of both numbers.

Plan

How can you find the answer?

Use logic to analyze the information you have.

Solve

Make a Venn diagram to represent the factors of the two numbers, x and y.

Write the common factor 3 in both circles.

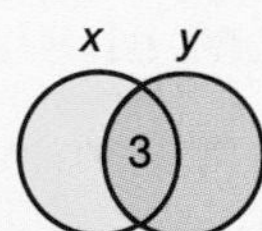

Factor the LCM to find all the factors of both numbers, x and y.

$$210 = 2 \times \mathbf{3} \times 5 \times 7$$

If 3 is the GCF, then 2, 5, and 7 cannot be common factors.

Try different arrangements of factors.

Look for the pair of numbers with a difference of 9.

The numbers are 21 and 30.

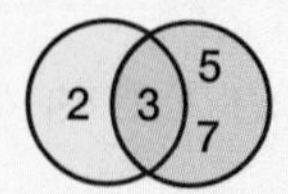

$x = 3 \times 2 = 6$
$y = 3 \times 5 \times 7 = 105$

5 | 3 | 2, 7

$x = 15$
$y = 42$

7 | 3 | 2, 5

$x = 21$
$y = 30$

Look Back

Look back at the problem.

Check that 21 and 30 fit all the requirements of the problem.

Standards MR **1.0, 1.1, 2.0, 2.3, 2.4, 3.0**

Gocarting is one of the most popular forms of auto racing in the world.

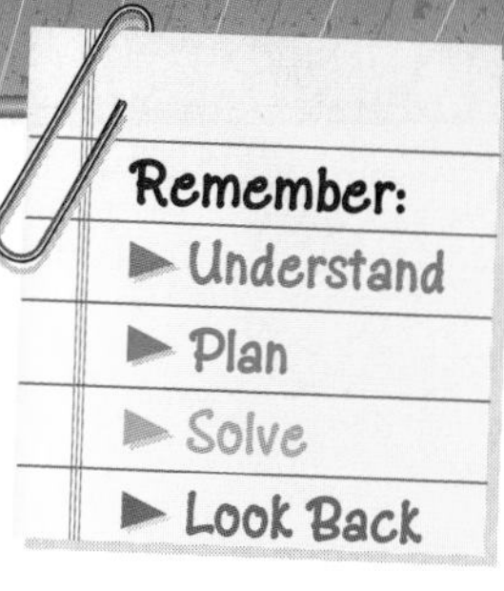

Guided Practice

Solve these problems, using the Logical Thinking strategy.

1. The LCM of two numbers is 60. One of the numbers is 20. The other number is even and has only two prime factors. What is the other number?

   Think: What do you know about the LCM?

2. The GCF of two numbers is 12. Both of these numbers are greater than 12 and both are less than 40. What are the numbers?

   Think: What do you know about prime factors of the numbers?

Choose a Strategy

Solve. Use these or other strategies.

Problem-Solving Strategies

- **Guess and Check**
- **Use Logical Thinking**
- **Draw a Diagram**
- **Find a Pattern**

3. The LCM of two numbers is 120. The GCF of the same two numbers is 4. The sum of the numbers is 44. What are the numbers?

4. Twin primes are a pair of prime numbers that differ by 2. 3 and 5 are twin primes, and so are 5 and 7. What are the next two pairs of twin primes?

5. A perfect number equals the sum of all its factors except the number itself.
   Factors of 6: 1, 2, 3, 6; $1 + 2 + 3 = 6$
   Find all perfect numbers greater than 0 and less than 30.

6. List the factors of each number.
   4 9 16 25
   If a number has an odd number of factors, why can the number always be represented by the expression n^2?

7. At a gocart racetrack, drivers on the pro track must be at least 54 in. tall. Rookie-track drivers must be at least 44 in. tall. If Deborah is 4 ft 4 in. tall, on which track can she drive?

8. In a gocart race, cars 28, 29, and 30 were the top three finishers. The prime-number car came second. The car with the number divisible by 4 did not win. Which car won the race?

9. Two racecars start at the same time. One car finishes a lap in 60 seconds. The other car takes 72 seconds. How many minutes will elapse before the faster car passes the slower car? (Hint: Find the LCM of 60 and 72.)

Extra Practice See 1–4 on page 355.

Quick Check

Check Your Understanding of Lessons 1–6

Identify each number as *prime* or *composite*.

1. 14 **2.** 47 **3.** 23 **4.** 33

Write each prime factorization. Use exponents if possible.

5. 20 **6.** 27 **7.** 42 **8.** 50

Test each number to see if it is divisible by 2, 3, 4, 5, 9, or 10.

9. 340 **10.** 615 **11.** 225 **12.** 5,580

Find the GCF of each pair of numbers.

13. 20, 30 **14.** 15, 45 **15.** 18, 27 **16.** 42, 60

Find the LCM of each pair of numbers.

17. 6, 5 **18.** 8, 4 **19.** 12, 9 **20.** 30, 50

Solve.

21. The LCM of two numbers is 200. The GCF of the same two numbers is 10. One number is 10 more than the other. What are the numbers?

How did you do?

If you had difficulty with any items in the Quick Check, you can use the following pages for review and extra practice.

California Standards	Items	Review These Pages	Do These Extra Practice Items
Number Sense: **1.4**	1–4	pages 298–299	Set A, page 352
Number Sense: **1.3, 1.4** Math Reasoning: **2.4**	5–8	pages 300–301	Set B, page 352
Number Sense: **1.3, 1.4** Math Reasoning: **2.4**	9–12	pages 302–303	Set C, page 352
Math Reasoning: **2.3**	13–16	pages 304–306	Set D, page 352
Math Reasoning: **2.3**	17–20	pages 308–310	Set E, page 352
Math Reasoning: **1.1**	21	pages 312–313	1–4, page 355

Test Prep • Cumulative Review

Maintaining the Standards

Choose the letter of the correct answer.

1 What is the prime factorization of 36?

A $2^3 \times 2^3$ **C** $2^2 \times 3^2$

B $2^2 \times 3^3$ **D** 6^2

2 Which number has two ones and twenty-four hundredths?

F 2,402 **H** 2.24

G 2.4 **J** 2.024

3 Divide.

$7\overline{)14{,}602}$

A 208 R6

B 286

C 2,086

D 2,860

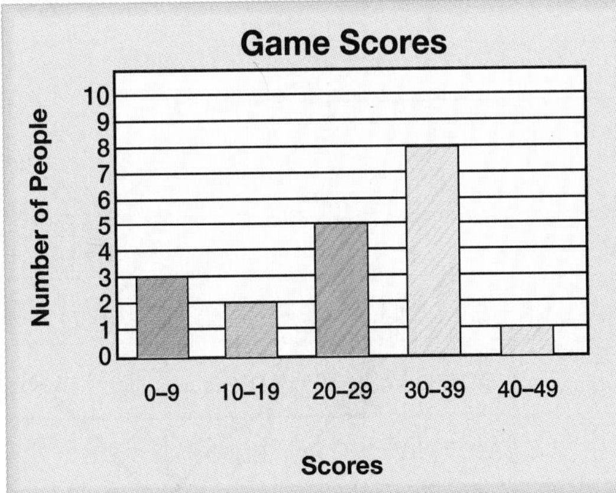

4 How many people scored from 20 to 29 points?

F 2

G 3

H 5

J 8

5 Which number is prime?

A 49

B 47

C 33

D 27

6 Which product is not equal to 32×9?

F $32 \times 3 \times 3$

G $8 \times 4 \times 3$

H 9×32

J 16×18

7 Which is a true statement?

A $^{-}3 < {}^{-}4$

B $4.5 < 3.29$

C $\frac{1}{3} > \frac{3}{4}$

D $^{-}18 < {}^{+}2$

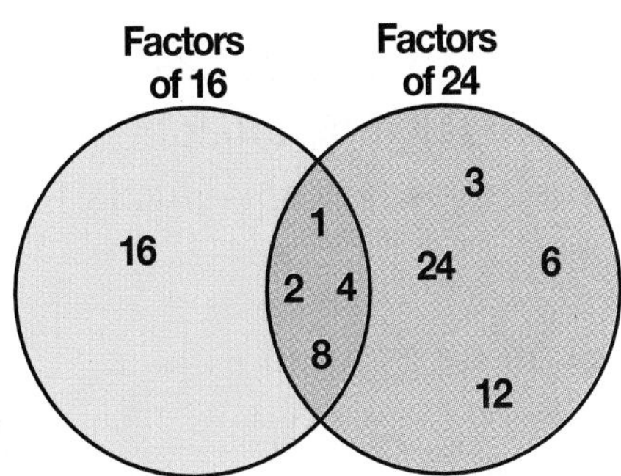

8 **Explain** How does this Venn diagram show the GCF of 16 and 24?

Safe Site

Internet Test Prep
Visit **www.eduplace.com/kids/mhm** for more *Test Prep Practice.*

Write Fractions

You will learn that a fraction represents some part of a whole amount or part of a group of objects.

New Vocabulary
unit fraction

Learn About It

A **unit fraction** has a numerator of 1. The fractions $\frac{1}{2}$, $\frac{1}{3}$, $\frac{1}{4}$, $\frac{1}{5}$, and $\frac{1}{6}$ are all unit fractions.

The unit fraction $\frac{1}{3}$ represents 1 piece of a whole pizza that has been cut in 3 pieces.

You can represent fractions on a number line.

If intervals of length 1 on the number line are divided into 3 equal pieces, the length of any one of the pieces represents $\frac{1}{3}$.

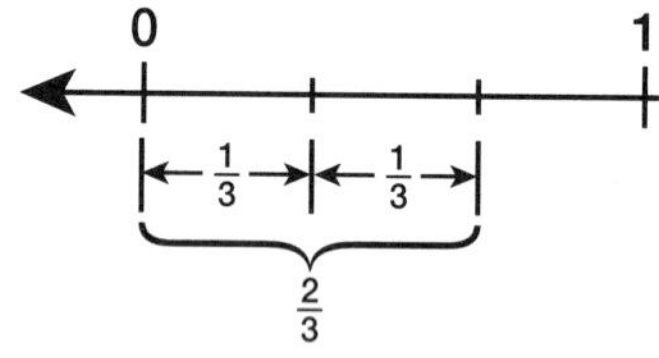

A fraction is written $\frac{a}{b}$ where a and b are whole numbers and $b \neq 0$. The fraction $\frac{2}{3}$ means 2 unit fractions of $\frac{1}{3}$.

Fractions can be used to label many points on a number line. Each unit interval on the number line can be cut into pieces of equal length. This number line is labeled with $\frac{0}{3}$, $\frac{1}{3}$, $\frac{2}{3}$, ... The number line shows that $\frac{0}{3} = 0$, $\frac{3}{3} = 1$, $\frac{6}{3} = 2$, and $\frac{9}{3} = 3$.

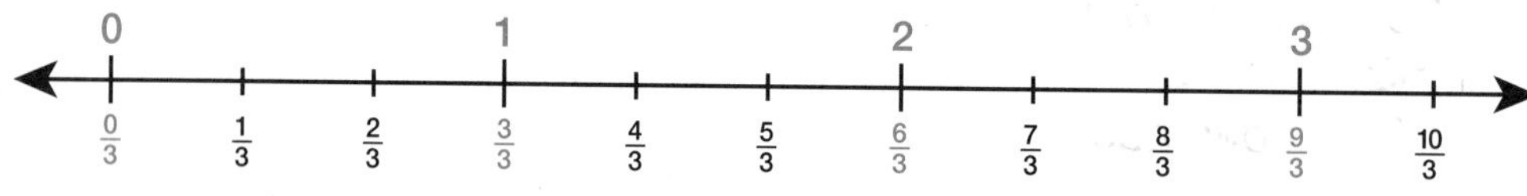

The unit fraction $\frac{1}{3}$ can be thought of as $1 \div 3$ since the unit interval is divided into 3 equal parts.

Any fraction can be thought of as a division problem. For example, when 2 units are divided into 3 equal parts, each part is $\frac{2}{3}$ of 1 unit: $2 \div 3 = \frac{2}{3}$.

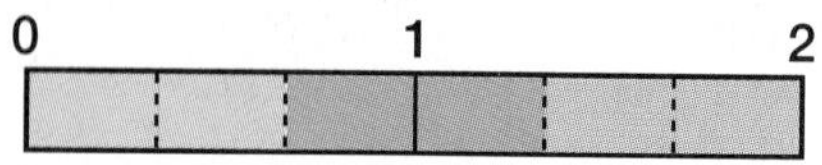

Fraction	In Words	In Symbols
$\frac{1}{3}$	one divided by three	$1 \div 3$
$\frac{2}{3}$	two divided by three	$2 \div 3$
$\frac{3}{3}$	three divided by three	$3 \div 3$
$\frac{4}{3}$	four divided by three	$4 \div 3$
$\frac{5}{3}$	five divided by three	$5 \div 3$
$\frac{6}{3}$	six divided by three	$6 \div 3$

Explain Your Thinking

▶ If the numerator is greater than the denominator, is the fraction less than 1, equal to 1, or greater than 1? Tell why.

Standards NS 1.0, 1.5 AF 1.0, 1.2

Guided Practice

Study this number line.

1. Write each missing fraction. Then draw a picture to represent each missing fraction.

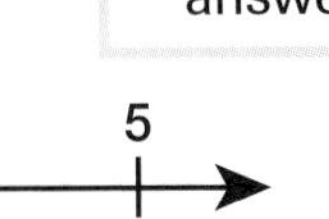

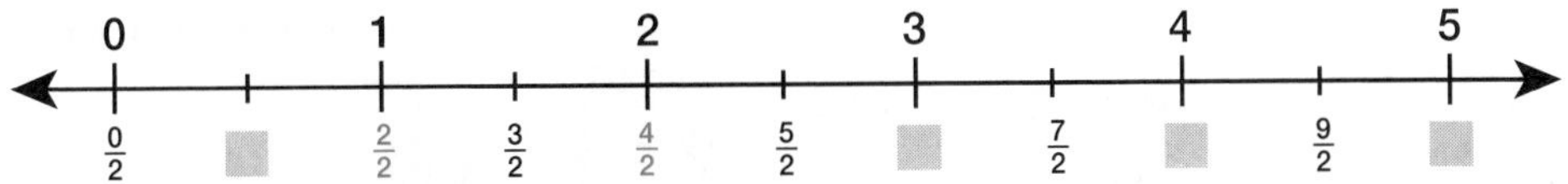

> **Ask Yourself**
>
> - How can I use division to find or check my answers?

Independent Practice

Study this number line.

2. Write each missing fraction. Then draw a picture to represent each missing fraction.

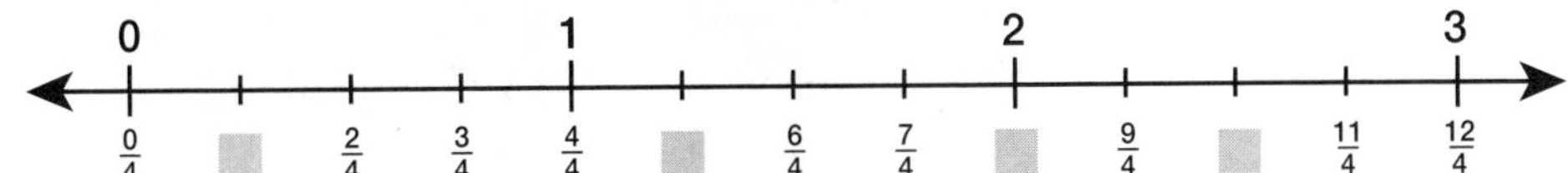

Rewrite each term or expression using a fraction bar or the ÷ symbol. For Exercises 3–5, locate each fraction on a number line.

3. $1 \div 5$ **4.** $9 \div 5$ **5.** $\frac{4}{5}$ **6.** $x \div y$ **7.** $\frac{7}{2}$

8. $\frac{a}{b}$ **9.** $\frac{m}{n}$ **10.** $7 \div 12$ **11.** $\frac{3}{16}$ **12.** $d \div c$

13. $\frac{10}{4}$ **14.** $25 \div 12$ **15.** $q \div h$ **16.** $\frac{r}{s}$ **17.** $\frac{11}{9}$

Problem Solving • Reasoning

18. Analyze The picture shows how much pizza is left. Write a fraction to show how much pizza was eaten.

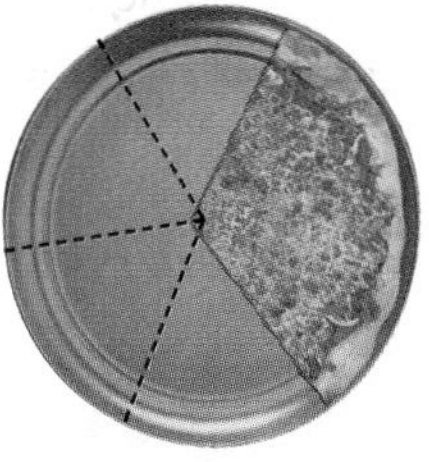

19. Show each fraction on a number line.

a. $\frac{3}{8}$ **b.** $\frac{5}{12}$ **c.** $\frac{3}{4}$ **d.** $\frac{7}{4}$

20. Analyze Two pizzas each had 8 slices. $\frac{3}{8}$ of a pepperoni pizza and $\frac{7}{8}$ of a cheese pizza were eaten. How much was left over?

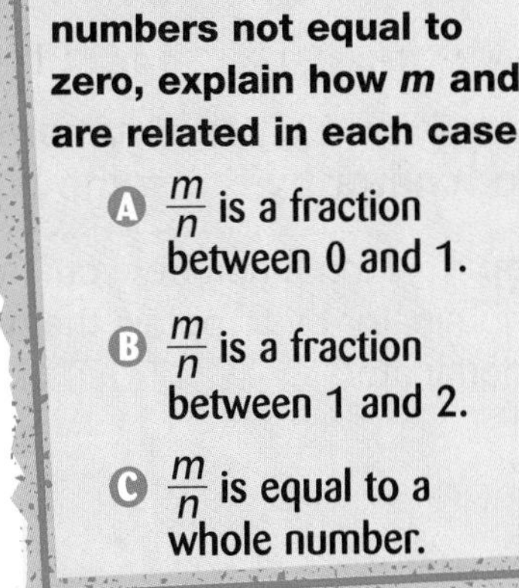

Using Algebra

If *m* and *n* are whole numbers not equal to zero, explain how *m* and *n* are related in each case.

A $\frac{m}{n}$ is a fraction between 0 and 1.

B $\frac{m}{n}$ is a fraction between 1 and 2.

C $\frac{m}{n}$ is equal to a whole number.

Mixed Review • Test Prep

Solve. *(pages 106–108, 146–147)*

21. 50×1 **22.** $8{,}000 \div 10$ **23.** 40×40 **24.** $6{,}000 \div 20$

25 Choose the correct way to check $188 \div 12 = 15$ R8. *(pages 148–149)*

A $15 \times 12 + 8$ **B** $12 \times 15 - 8$ **C** $8 \times 12 + 15$ **D** $8 \times 15 + 12$

Extra Practice See Set F on page 353.

Equivalent Fractions

You will learn how to use multiplication to find equivalent fractions.

New Vocabulary
equivalent fractions

Learn About It

Two fractions that name the same number are called **equivalent fractions**. If the numerator and the denominator of a fraction are each multiplied by the same counting number, then the new fraction is equivalent to the original fraction.

Only $\frac{3}{4}$ of 8 band members were present at band practice. How many band members were at the practice?

Find a fraction equivalent to $\frac{3}{4}$ with a denominator of 8.

Different Ways to Find Equivalent Fractions

You can use number lines.

The first number line shows fourths. 3 parts of the first line represents $\frac{3}{4}$.

The second number line shows eighths. 6 parts of the second line represents $\frac{6}{8}$. The fractions $\frac{3}{4}$ and $\frac{6}{8}$ are at the same position, so $\frac{3}{4} = \frac{6}{8}$.

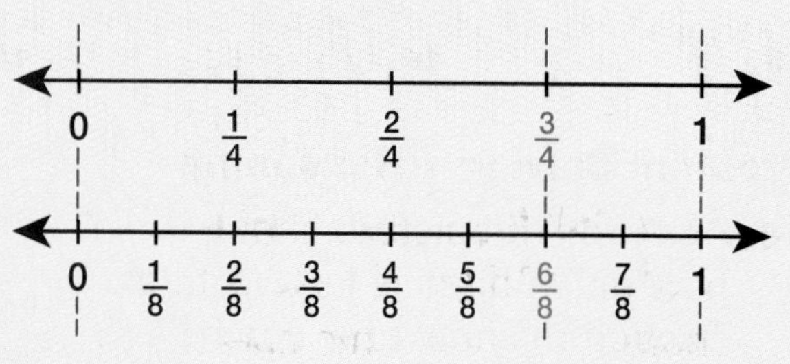

You can multiply the numerator and the denominator by the same number.

Step 1 Find a number you can multiply the denominator by to obtain the new denominator.

$\frac{3}{4} \xrightarrow{\times ?} \frac{■}{8}$, $\times ? = \times 2$

Step 2 Multiply the numerator by that number.

$\frac{3}{4} \xrightarrow{\times 2} \frac{6}{8}$, so $\frac{3}{4} = \frac{6}{8}$

If $\frac{6}{8}$ of the band members are at practice, the numerator 6 must be the number of people who practiced.

Solution: There were 6 band members at band practice.

Another Example

Use Division

Find a fraction equivalent to $\frac{12}{16}$.

$\frac{12}{16} \xrightarrow{\div 2} \frac{6}{8}$ (numerator ÷ 2, denominator ÷ 2): $\frac{12}{16} = \frac{6}{8}$

You can divide by any common factor of the numerator and the denominator.

Explain Your Thinking

▶ Use a number line to explain why $\frac{2}{3} = \frac{8}{12}$.

Guided Practice

Ask Yourself

- Did I multiply the numerator and denominator by the same number?

Complete.

1. $\frac{2}{5} = \frac{4}{10}$ (× ■, × ■)

2. $\frac{7}{42} = \frac{1}{6}$ (÷ ■, ÷ ■)

3. $\frac{4}{9} = \frac{■}{54}$

Independent Practice

Complete.

4. $\frac{1}{3} = \frac{2}{6}$ (× ■, × ■)

5. $\frac{3}{7} = \frac{■}{35}$ (× ■, × ■)

6. $\frac{3}{10} = \frac{9}{■}$

7. $\frac{6}{9} = \frac{2}{■}$

For each fraction, write three equivalent fractions.

8. $\frac{1}{5}$ **9.** $\frac{8}{12}$ **10.** $\frac{6}{36}$ **11.** $\frac{3}{5}$ **12.** $\frac{7}{10}$ **13.** $\frac{2}{9}$

Compare. Are the fractions in each pair equivalent? Write *yes* or *no*.

14. $\frac{5}{6}$ $\frac{10}{16}$ **15.** $\frac{6}{4}$ $\frac{3}{2}$ **16.** $\frac{5}{2}$ $\frac{2}{5}$ **17.** $\frac{2}{3}$ $\frac{12}{18}$ **18.** $\frac{70}{80}$ $\frac{7}{8}$

Problem Solving • Reasoning

19. There are 15 girls in the fifth-grade chorus. If $\frac{5}{6}$ of the members are girls, how many members are boys?

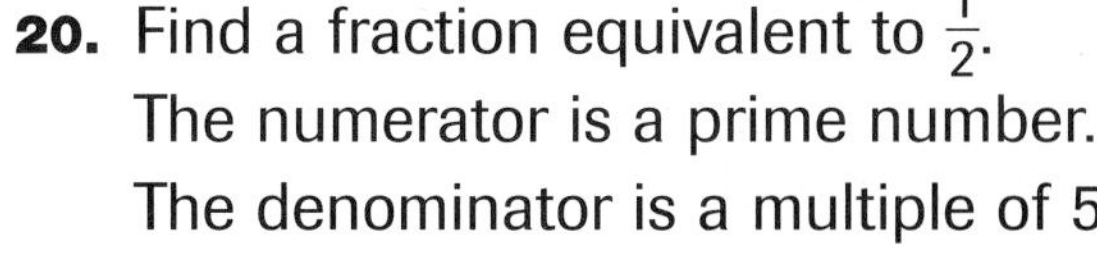

20. Find a fraction equivalent to $\frac{1}{2}$. The numerator is a prime number. The denominator is a multiple of 5.

21. Analyze Using the same number of quarters and dimes and half the number of nickels, how can you make $1.50?

22. Write About It How many equivalent fractions can be written for any given fraction? Give examples to support your thinking.

Mixed Review • Test Prep

Add or subtract. *(pages 52–55)*

23. 6,923 − 750 **24.** 2,088 + 6,745 **25.** 10,919 − 2,844 **26.** 32,863 + 25,137

27 Round 610,304 to the nearest hundred thousand. *(pages 8–10)*

A 6,000 **B** 60,000 **C** 600,000 **D** 6,000,000

Extra Practice See Set G on page 353.

LESSON 9

Simplest Form

You will learn how to use division and prime factorization to write fractions in simplest form.

New Vocabulary
simplest form

Learn About It

A fraction is in **simplest form** when the GCF of the numerator and denominator of the fraction is 1.

Bobbie earned $18 from baby-sitting. On Saturday she bought a CD for $12. She knows that she spent $\frac{12}{18}$ of her earnings, but she wants to express this fraction in simplest form.

Find the simplest form of the fraction $\frac{12}{18}$.

Different Ways to Find Simplest Form

You can use division by the greatest common factor.

Step 1 Find the greatest common factor (GCF) of the numerator and denominator.

$12 = 2 \times 2 \times 3$
$18 = 2 \times 3 \times 3$

The GCF of 12 and 18 is 2×3, or 6.

Step 2 Use the GCF to write an equivalent fraction.

$$\frac{12}{18} \xrightarrow{\div 6} \frac{2}{3}$$

$$\frac{12}{18} = \frac{2}{3}$$

You can cancel common factors.

Step 1 Use prime factorization to factor the numerator and the denominator.

$$\frac{12}{18} = \frac{2 \times 2 \times 3}{2 \times 3 \times 3}$$

Step 2 Cancel pairs of common factors that equal 1.

$$\frac{12}{18} = \frac{\overset{1}{\cancel{2}} \times 2 \times \overset{1}{\cancel{3}}}{\underset{1}{\cancel{2}} \times 3 \times \underset{1}{\cancel{3}}}$$

$$\frac{12}{18} = \frac{2}{3}$$

Think: $\frac{2}{2} = 1$ and $\frac{3}{3} = 1$

Solution: Bobbie spent $\frac{2}{3}$ of her earnings.

Explain Your Thinking

▶ How is canceling common factors like dividing by the GCF?

 Standards NS **1.0, 1.4, 2.0, 2.3**

Guided Practice

Simplify each fraction.

1. $\frac{2}{4}$ **2.** $\frac{3}{18}$ **3.** $\frac{18}{24}$ **4.** $\frac{10}{12}$

5. $\frac{5}{15}$ **6.** $\frac{8}{10}$ **7.** $\frac{14}{49}$ **8.** $\frac{15}{25}$

Ask Yourself

- Did I use the GCF to find an equivalent fraction?

Independent Practice

Simplify each fraction. If a fraction is already in simplest form, just write the fraction.

9. $\frac{4}{6}$ **10.** $\frac{5}{10}$ **11.** $\frac{9}{15}$ **12.** $\frac{8}{14}$ **13.** $\frac{2}{16}$ **14.** $\frac{7}{21}$

15. $\frac{3}{27}$ **16.** $\frac{5}{18}$ **17.** $\frac{15}{18}$ **18.** $\frac{28}{30}$ **19.** $\frac{5}{20}$ **20.** $\frac{19}{38}$

21. $\frac{6}{21}$ **22.** $\frac{28}{42}$ **23.** $\frac{22}{30}$ **24.** $\frac{15}{32}$ **25.** $\frac{36}{50}$ **26.** $\frac{48}{60}$

Problem Solving • Reasoning

Answer using the simplest form of each fraction.

27. What fraction of 25¢ is 10¢?

28. What fraction of \$2 is 25¢?

29. What fraction of \$10 is 50¢?

30. What fraction of \$4 is 75¢?

31. **Analyze** Remember, Bobbie had \$18 and spent \$12. If Bobbie spends another \$2 of her earnings, what fraction of her earnings does she still have?

32. **Write About It** Why can it be useful to show a fraction in its simplest form? Give examples to support your thinking.

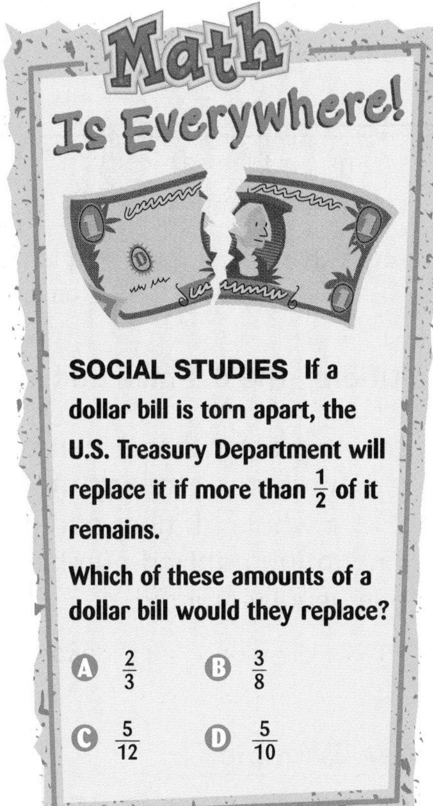

SOCIAL STUDIES If a dollar bill is torn apart, the U.S. Treasury Department will replace it if more than $\frac{1}{2}$ of it remains.

Which of these amounts of a dollar bill would they replace?

A $\frac{2}{3}$ **B** $\frac{3}{8}$

C $\frac{5}{12}$ **D** $\frac{5}{10}$

Mixed Review • Test Prep

Order the numbers in each set from least to greatest. *(pages 8–10, 30–31)*

33. 12, 9, 19 **34.** 0.75 0.67 0.5

35. 0.04 0.5 1.0 **36.** 2.01 2.0 2.001

37 The sum of two numbers is 0.4. One number is 0.16. What is the other number? *(pages 58–61)*

A 0.12 **B** 0.24 **C** 0.34 **D** 0.4

Extra Practice See Set H on page 353.

Fractions, Decimals, and Mixed Numbers

You will learn how to compare fractions with like denominators, decimals, and mixed numbers

New Vocabulary
mixed number

Learn About It

A bicycle trail in a park is 0.8 mile long. Another trail is $\frac{3}{5}$ mile long. Which trail is longer?

To compare two numbers, you need to write them in the same form.

Different Ways to Write Numbers

You can write the decimal as a fraction.

$$0.8 = \frac{8}{10} = \frac{8 \div 2}{10 \div 2} = \frac{4}{5}$$

Number line: 0, $\frac{1}{5}$, $\frac{2}{5}$, $\frac{3}{5}$, $\frac{4}{5}$, 1

$\frac{4}{5} > \frac{3}{5}$

$\frac{4}{5}$ is to the right of $\frac{3}{5}$ on the number line.

You can write the fraction as a decimal.

$$\frac{3}{5} = \frac{3 \times 2}{5 \times 2} = \frac{6}{10} = 0.6$$

Think: The denominator of a decimal fraction must be a power of 10.

Number line: 0, 0.2, 0.4, 0.6, 0.8, 1

$0.6 < 0.8$

Solution: The 0.8-mile trail is longer.

Fractions greater than 1 can be written as mixed numbers. A **mixed number** is the sum of a whole number and a fraction. When writing a mixed number, the addition sign is usually omitted.

$2\frac{3}{4}$ is a mixed number.

$$\frac{11}{4} = \frac{4}{4} + \frac{4}{4} + \frac{3}{4} = 2\frac{3}{4}$$

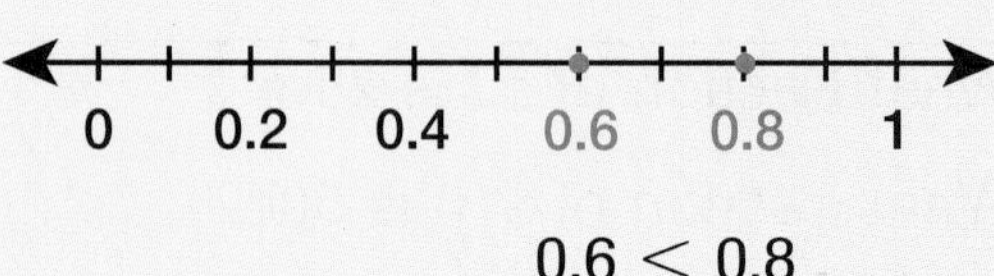

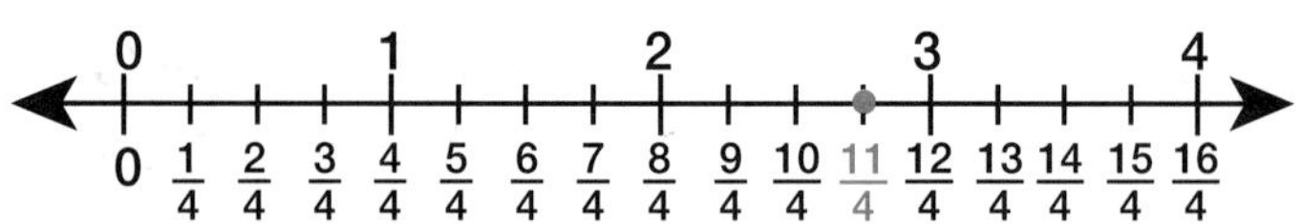

Other Examples

A. Two Fractions With Like Denominators

Compare $\frac{5}{8}$ and $\frac{7}{8}$. $5 < 7$ So $\frac{5}{8} < \frac{7}{8}$.

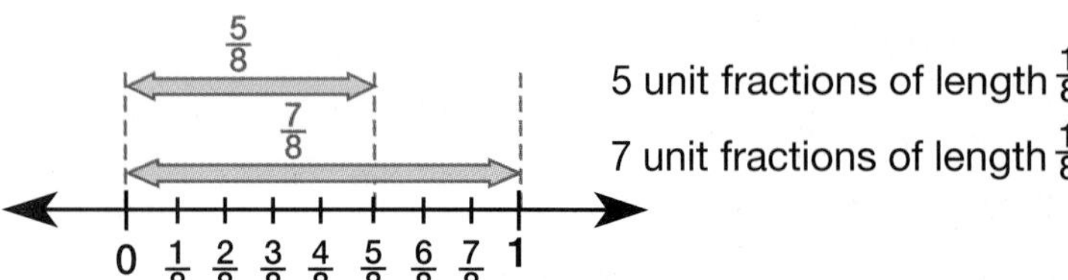

5 unit fractions of length $\frac{1}{8}$

7 unit fractions of length $\frac{1}{8}$

B. Mixed Numbers

Compare $2\frac{3}{5}$ and 2.5.

$2\frac{3}{5} = 2\frac{6}{10}$ $\quad \frac{3}{5} = \frac{6}{10}$

$= 2 + 0.6$

$= 2.6$

$2\frac{3}{5} > 2.5$

Standards NS **1.0, 1.2, 1.5**

Explain Your Thinking

► When comparing numbers, why does it help to express them in the same form?

Ask Yourself

- Did I write each fraction or mixed number in simplest form?
- Did I write the numbers in the same form to compare them?

Guided Practice

Write each as a fraction or mixed number.

1. 0.7 **2.** 1.2 **3.** $\frac{5}{4}$ **4.** $\frac{31}{10}$

Write each fraction as a decimal.

5. $\frac{4}{10}$ **6.** $\frac{3}{2}$ **7.** $1\frac{3}{4}$ **8.** $\frac{2}{1}$

Compare. Write >, <, or = for each ⬬.

9. $\frac{11}{12}$ ⬬ $\frac{5}{12}$ **10.** $\frac{1}{4}$ ⬬ 0.5 **11.** $2\frac{3}{5}$ ⬬ 2.1 **12.** $\frac{1}{4}$ ⬬ 0.25

Independent Practice

Compare. Write >, <, or = for each ⬬.

13. $\frac{3}{10}$ ⬬ 0.15 **14.** $\frac{1}{5}$ ⬬ 0.08 **15.** $\frac{7}{2}$ ⬬ 3.25 **16.** 0.4 ⬬ $\frac{2}{5}$

Order each set of numbers from least to greatest.

17. $\frac{1}{2}$, 0.55, 2.5, 0.4 **18.** $\frac{4}{5}$, $\frac{1}{100}$, $2\frac{3}{4}$, 2.1 **19.** $\frac{1}{3}$, 0.3, $\frac{7}{20}$, $1\frac{1}{5}$, $\frac{2}{3}$

Problem Solving • Reasoning

Use the number lines to answer Problems 20–22.

20. Analyze A park is surrounded by four fences. Each fence measures either 0.5 mi or $\frac{4}{8}$ mi. What shape is the park?

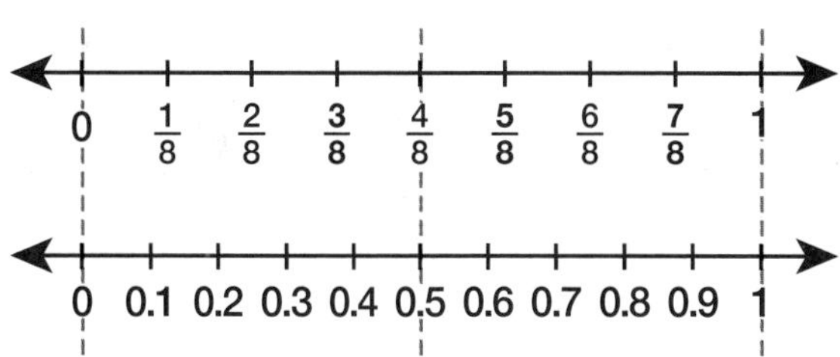

21. Analyze One hiking trail is 0.75 mi long and another is $\frac{7}{8}$ mi long. Which trail is longer?

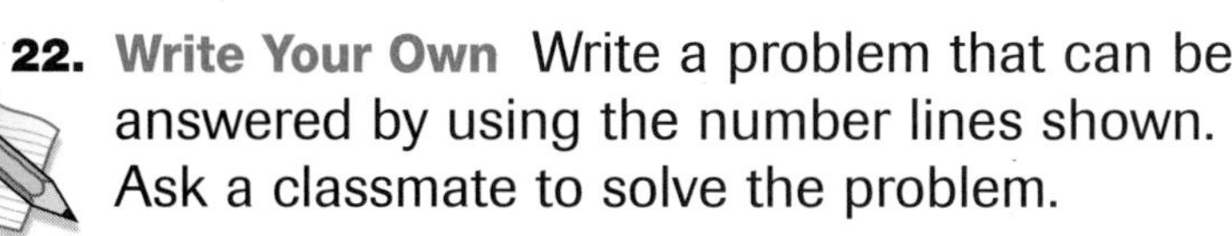

22. Write Your Own Write a problem that can be answered by using the number lines shown. Ask a classmate to solve the problem.

Mixed Review • Test Prep

Simplify. *(pages 6–7)*

23. 3^3 **24.** 2^6 **25.** 4^3 **26.** 5^1 **27.** 1^5 **28.** 0^2

29 What is the prime factorization of 60? *(pages 300–301)*

A 60^1 **B** $2 \times 3 \times 10$ **C** $2^2 \times 3 \times 5$ **D** $2^4 \times 5$

Compare Fractions

You will learn how to compare fractions using like, or common, denominators.

New Vocabulary
common denominator

Two fractions with the same, or like, denominators are said to have a **common denominator**. You can compare them by comparing the numerators.

Fractions with different, or unlike, denominators can also be compared.

Compare $\frac{2}{3}$ and $\frac{3}{4}$.

Different Ways to Compare Unlike Fractions

You can think about distance on a number line.

When the numerators are the same, a fraction with a greater denominator is less than the other fraction.

$\frac{1}{4} < \frac{1}{3}$ **Think:** The length $\frac{1}{4}$ is shorter than the length $\frac{1}{3}$.

Since $\frac{1}{4} < \frac{1}{3}$, the fraction $\frac{3}{4}$ is closer to 1 than the fraction $\frac{2}{3}$. The distance of $\frac{3}{4}$ is greater than the distance of $\frac{2}{3}$ on a number line.

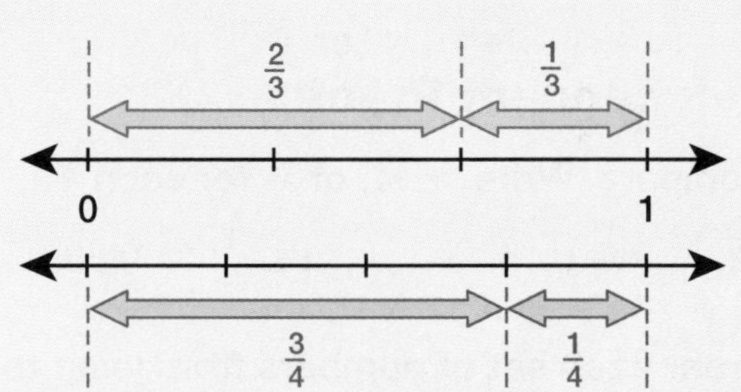

Think: 2 unit fractions of length $\frac{1}{3}$ are shorter than 3 unit fractions of length $\frac{1}{4}$.

You can find equivalent fractions with a common denominator.

Step 1 Find a common denominator by finding the product of the denominators of the fractions.

$3 \times 4 = 12$, so 12 is a common denominator for $\frac{2}{3}$ and $\frac{3}{4}$.

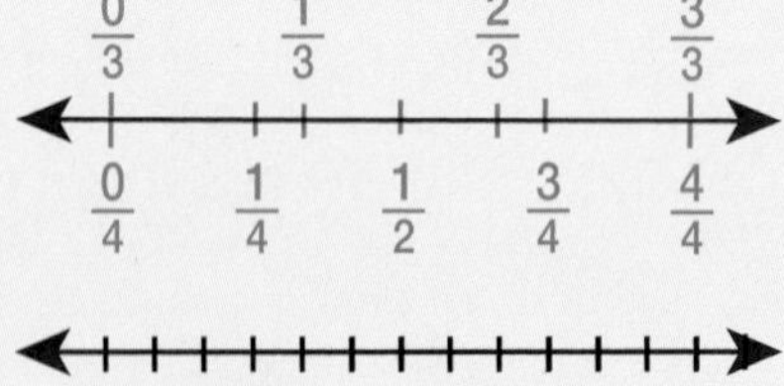

Step 2 Use the common denominator to find equivalent fractions.

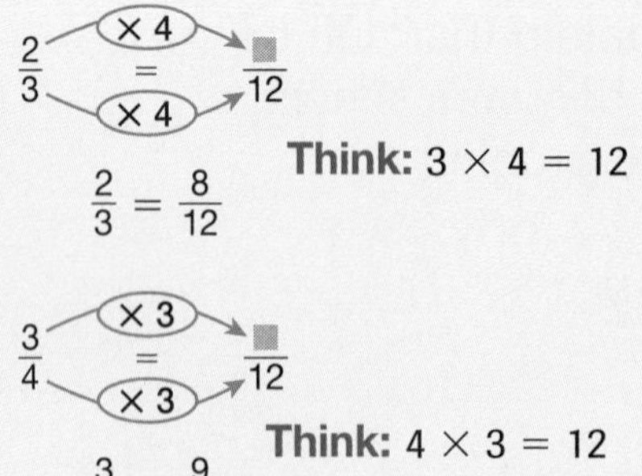

$\frac{2}{3} = \frac{8}{12}$ **Think:** $3 \times 4 = 12$

$\frac{3}{4} = \frac{9}{12}$ **Think:** $4 \times 3 = 12$

Step 3 To compare the fractions, compare the numerators.

Since $8 < 9$, $\frac{8}{12} < \frac{9}{12}$.

So, $\frac{2}{3} < \frac{3}{4}$

 Standards NS 1.0, 1.5

Another Example

Use Cross Multiplication

Compare $\frac{12}{15}$ and $\frac{7}{10}$.

$\frac{12}{15} \times \frac{7}{10}$ Cross multiply to compare fractions.

$12 \times 10 = 120 \quad 15 \times 7 = 105$

$120 > 105$, So, $\frac{12}{15} > \frac{7}{10}$

Why this works!
$15 \times 10 = 150$,
a common denominator.
So, $\frac{12}{15} = \frac{120}{150}$ and
$\frac{7}{10} = \frac{105}{150}$

Explain Your Thinking

► How does knowing that $\frac{1}{9} < \frac{1}{8}$ help you know that $\frac{7}{8} < \frac{8}{9}$ without using a common denominator?

Guided Practice

Compare. Write >, <, or =for each ⬬.

1. $\frac{5}{7}$ ⬬ $\frac{3}{4}$
2. $\frac{8}{9}$ ⬬ $\frac{12}{13}$
3. $\frac{6}{7}$ ⬬ $\frac{13}{15}$
4. $3\frac{1}{4}$ ⬬ $3\frac{2}{5}$
5. $3\frac{5}{17}$ ⬬ $4\frac{1}{8}$
6. $2\frac{3}{10}$ ⬬ $\frac{7}{3}$

Ask Yourself

- Did I find a common denominator?
- Is there an easier way to compare any of the fractions?

Independent Practice

Compare. Write >, <, or = for each ⬬.

7. $\frac{9}{10}$ ⬬ $\frac{5}{6}$
8. $\frac{3}{5}$ ⬬ $\frac{7}{12}$
9. $\frac{2}{3}$ ⬬ $\frac{7}{11}$
10. $\frac{3}{4}$ ⬬ $\frac{11}{15}$
11. $\frac{8}{15}$ ⬬ $\frac{3}{5}$
12. $\frac{8}{25}$ ⬬ $\frac{3}{10}$
13. $\frac{3}{8}$ ⬬ $\frac{5}{12}$
14. $1\frac{9}{10}$ ⬬ $\frac{5}{2}$

Problem Solving • Reasoning

15. **Compare** The length of one ribbon is $3\frac{1}{2}$ yd. The length of another is $3\frac{1}{8}$ yd. Which is longer?

16. **Analyze** Order the numbers and find the median and mode.
$\frac{3}{4}, \frac{7}{12}, \frac{3}{4}, \frac{1}{2}, \frac{11}{12}, \frac{2}{3}, \frac{5}{6}$

17. Order the numbers and find the median.
$1, 3, 4, \frac{7}{8}, \frac{33}{8}, 0, 3\frac{1}{3}, \frac{2}{3}$

18. **Write About It** Explain how you know $\frac{12}{25} < \frac{7}{13}$ without using equivalent fractions.

Mixed Review • Test Prep

Solve for *n*. *(pages 74–75)*

19. $n - 4 = 10$
20. $n + 1 = 3$
21. $n - 12 = 17$
22. $n + 9 = 25$

23. Which represents the phrase "a number subtracted from 10"? *(pages 70–75)*

A $n - 10$ **B** $10 - n$ **C** $n = 10$ **D** $n - 10 = n$

Extra Practice See Set J on page 353.

Problem-Solving Skill: Is the Answer Reasonable?

You will learn how to decide whether the answer to a problem you have solved is reasonable.

After you have solved a problem, look back at the problem and decide whether the answer is reasonable.

Sun

Mars

Look at the situations below.

Some answers are unreasonable because the problem is misinterpreted.

Joe knows that it takes 365 days for Earth to orbit the Sun, and it takes 687 days for Mars to orbit the Sun.

He said "A Mars year is about half as long as an Earth year."

Joe's answer is unreasonable. It takes more days for Mars to orbit the Sun than it takes Earth, so the Mars year must be longer.

Sometimes an answer doesn't make sense.

Ms. Rick's class of 25 students went on a field trip to a planetarium. They traveled in three groups.

Petra calculated that there were $8\frac{1}{3}$ students in each group.

Petra's answer is unreasonable because you cannot have $\frac{1}{3}$ of a student in a group.

Sometimes the calculations are incorrect.

Fred used a ten-dollar bill to pay for souvenirs that cost \$6.65 at the planetarium.

He calculated that \$10 – \$6.65, or \$4.45, should be his change.

Fred's answer is unreasonable. Since he spent more than \$6, his change should be less than \$4.

Look Back Why does thinking about the original question help you decide whether an answer is reasonable?

Standards NS **1.0** MR **1.0, 2.0, 2.1, 2.6, 3.0**

Because the length of a day on Mars is about the same as that on Earth, some scientists believe that it may someday be possible to transform Mars into a more Earth-like environment.

Earth

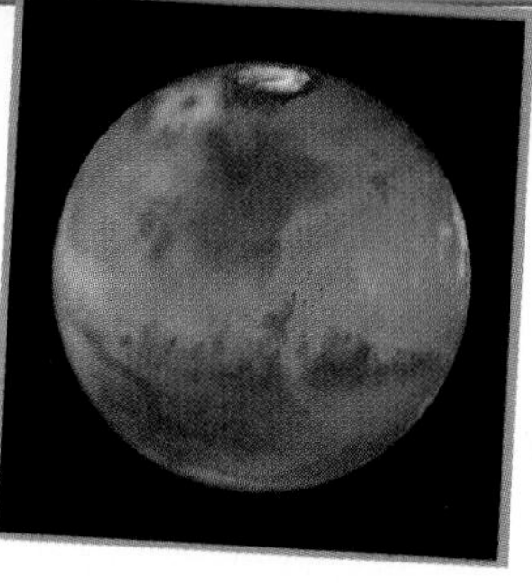

Mars

Guided Practice

Tell whether each statement is reasonable or unreasonable. Explain your answer.

1. In Ms. Rick's social studies class of 25 students, 12 are girls. Therefore, $\frac{1}{3}$ of the students in Ms. Rick's class are boys.

Think: How many boys are in the social studies class?

2. An astronaut in training can run 10 miles in one hour. There are 168 hours in a week. Therefore, an astronaut can run 1,680 miles in a week.

Think: Can an astronaut run for 7 days without stopping?

Choose a Strategy

Solve. Use these or other strategies.

Problem-Solving Strategies

- **Guess and Check**
- **Work Backward**
- **Use Logical Thinking**

Tell whether each statement in blue is reasonable or unreasonable and explain why you think so.

3. The radius of Earth is about 3,950 miles. The diameter of Mars is about 4,200 miles. Earth's radius is about double that of Mars.

4. A space station can accommodate 19 astronauts. A shuttle can deliver 6 astronauts at a time. Three shuttle trips are needed to fill the station.

The table shows the relative mass of each planet compared to Earth. Jupiter is the largest planet and Pluto is the smallest. Use the data for Problems 5–8.

Planet	Mass (Earth = 1)
Mercury	0.055
Venus	0.815
Mars	0.107
Jupiter	319
Saturn	95
Uranus	15
Neptune	17
Pluto	0.002

5. The total mass of all the planets is about 9 times the mass of Earth.

6. Earth and Venus have about the same mass.

7. Mercury has about half the mass of Earth.

8. Mercury, Venus, and Mars together have less mass than Earth.

Extra Practice See 5–8 on page 355.

Quick Check

Check Your Understanding of Lessons 7–12

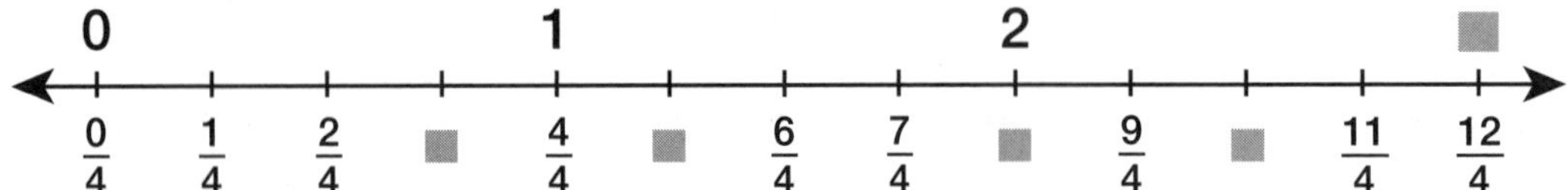

1. Write each missing fraction or whole number.

For each fraction, write three equivalent fractions.

2. $\frac{1}{5}$ **3.** $\frac{3}{4}$ **4.** $\frac{1}{6}$ **5.** $\frac{5}{8}$

Simplify each fraction.

6. $\frac{2}{8}$ **7.** $\frac{5}{20}$ **8.** $\frac{16}{24}$ **9.** $\frac{25}{30}$

Write each as a mixed number in simplest form.

10. $\frac{13}{4}$ **11.** 3.2 **12.** 4.5 **13.** $\frac{8}{3}$

Compare. Write $>$, $<$ or $=$.

14. $\frac{2}{3}$ ● $\frac{3}{5}$ **15.** $\frac{5}{12}$ ● $\frac{1}{3}$ **16.** $\frac{7}{10}$ ● $\frac{5}{9}$

Tell whether the blue statement is reasonable or unreasonable. Explain.

17. Maria said that she answered $\frac{4}{5}$ of the questions on a multiple choice test correctly. If there were 20 questions on the test, then she must have answered 6 incorrectly.

How did you do?

If you had difficulty with any items in the Quick Check, you can use the following pages for review and extra practice.

California Standards	Items	Review These Pages	Do These Extra Practice Items
Number Sense: **1.5**	1	pages 316–317	Set F, page 353
Number Sense: **1.4, 2.3**	2–5	pages 318–319	Set G, page 353
Number Sense: **2.3**	6–9	pages 320–321	Set H, page 353
Number Sense: **1.2**	10–13	pages 322–323	Set I, page 353
Number Sense: **1.2**	14–16	pages 324–325	Set J, page 353
Number Sense: **2.1** Math Reasoning: **2.1, 3.1**	17	pages 326–327	5–8, page 355

Test Prep • Cumulative Review

Maintaining the Standards

Choose the letter of the correct answer.

1 Between which two numbers on a number line would you find $2\frac{3}{5}$?

A 0 and 1
B 1 and 2
C 2 and 3
D 3 and 4

2 How many 📖s should Ms. Tipton use to represent the 270 letters received on Friday?

Letters to the Editor

Day	Letters
Monday	📖📖📖📖
Tuesday	📖📖
Wednesday	📖
Thursday	📖📖📖📖
Friday	

Each 📖 stands for 30 letters

F 5
G 7
H 9
J 11

3 Which type of graph would you use to compare the populations in the years 1900 and 2000 for four states?

A histogram
B double bar graph
C line graph
D circle graph

4 Carmen is going to pay $0.02 a page to have her 370-page report photocopied. What is a reasonable amount for her to expect to pay?

F $74.00
G $7.40
H $3.70
J $0.74

5 Marco's house is $\frac{4}{5}$ of a mile from his bus stop. Which decimal is equivalent to this distance?

A 0.8
B 0.54
C 0.45
D 0.2

6 Mona has 3 long-sleeved shirts, *x* short-sleeved shirts, and 2 T-shirts. She has a total of 9 shirts. How many short-sleeved shirts does she have?

F 2
G 3
H 4
J 5

7 So far this year Frank has scored 74, 87, 91, 88, 91, 76, and 95 on spelling tests. Which of the measures below is greatest?

A mean
B mode
C median
D range

8 A fraction has a numerator of 4 and a denominator that is a prime number greater than 3.

Explain Why is such a fraction in its simplest form?

Internet Test Prep
Visit **www.eduplace.com/kids/mhm** for more *Test Prep Practice.*

Add and Subtract Fractions With Like Denominators

You will learn how to add and subtract fractions with like denominators.

Learn About It

Marlene cut a pan of corn bread into 8 equal pieces. Her friends ate $\frac{5}{8}$ of it. Her brother ate 2 pieces. What fraction of the corn bread was eaten?

Add. $\frac{5}{8} + \frac{2}{8} = n$

How much more corn bread was eaten by Marlene's friends than by her brother?

Subtract. $\frac{5}{8} - \frac{2}{8} = m$

Find $\frac{5}{8} + \frac{2}{8}$.

To add fractions with like denominators, add the numerators and keep the same denominator.

The sum of 5 unit fractions of $\frac{1}{8}$ and 2 unit fractions of $\frac{1}{8}$ is 7 unit fractions of $\frac{1}{8}$.

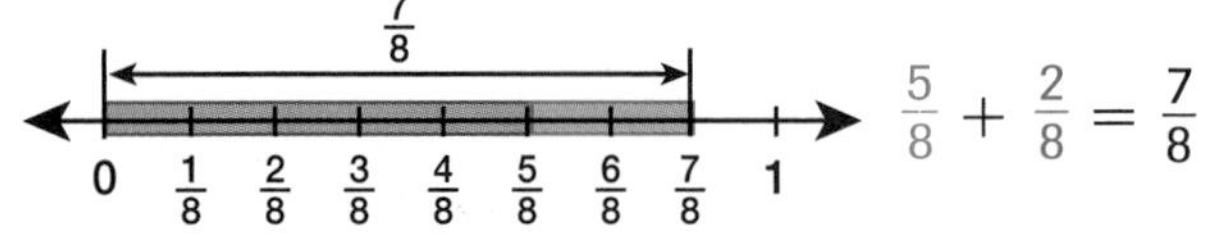

$\frac{5}{8} + \frac{2}{8} = \frac{7}{8}$

Find $\frac{5}{8} - \frac{2}{8}$.

To subtract fractions with like denominators, subtract the numerators and keep the same denominator.

The difference between 5 unit fractions of $\frac{1}{8}$ and 2 unit fractions of $\frac{1}{8}$ is 3 unit fractions of $\frac{1}{8}$.

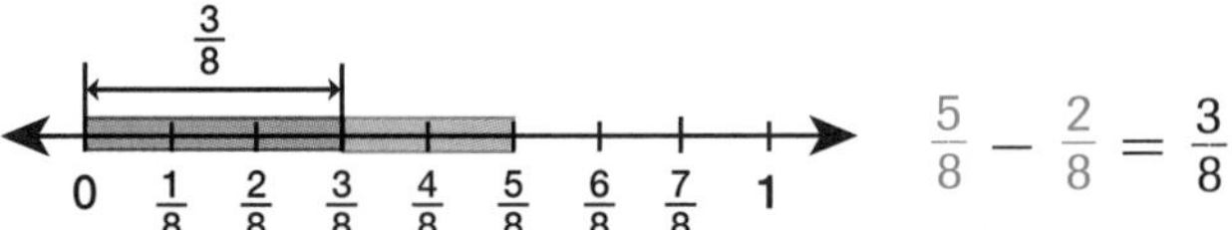

$\frac{5}{8} - \frac{2}{8} = \frac{3}{8}$

Solution: $\frac{7}{8}$ of the corn bread was eaten. Marlene's friends ate $\frac{3}{8}$ more of the corn bread than Marlene's brother ate.

Other Examples

A. Simplify the Answer

$\frac{8}{9} - \frac{5}{9} = \frac{3}{9}$

$\frac{3}{9} = \frac{3 \div 3}{9 \div 3} = \frac{1}{3}$

B. Sum Greater Than 1

$\frac{3}{8} + \frac{7}{8} = \frac{10}{8}$

$\frac{10}{8} = \frac{10 \div 2}{8 \div 2} = \frac{5}{4} = \frac{4}{4} + \frac{1}{4} = 1\frac{1}{4}$

Standards NS 1.0, 2.0, 2.3 MR 2.0, 2.3, 3.0

Explain Your Thinking

▶ To add or subtract fractions with like denominators, why can you add or subtract the numerators and keep the same denominator?

Guided Practice

Ask Yourself

- Did I check that these are fractions with like denominators?

Add or subtract. Show each answer in simplest form.

1. $\frac{2}{4} + \frac{1}{4}$ **2.** $\frac{2}{6} + \frac{4}{6}$ **3.** $\frac{5}{8} - \frac{1}{8}$

Independent Practice

Add or subtract. Show each answer in simplest form.

4. $\begin{array}{r} \frac{2}{6} \\ + \frac{2}{6} \\ \hline \end{array}$ **5.** $\begin{array}{r} \frac{3}{10} \\ - \frac{1}{10} \\ \hline \end{array}$ **6.** $\begin{array}{r} \frac{4}{9} \\ + \frac{3}{9} \\ \hline \end{array}$ **7.** $\begin{array}{r} \frac{5}{12} \\ - \frac{3}{12} \\ \hline \end{array}$ **8.** $\begin{array}{r} \frac{1}{7} \\ + \frac{3}{7} \\ \hline \end{array}$

9. $\frac{3}{10} + \frac{4}{10}$ **10.** $\frac{1}{2} + \frac{2}{2}$ **11.** $\frac{1}{16} + \frac{9}{16}$ **12.** $\frac{5}{9} + \frac{7}{9}$ **13.** $\frac{3}{4} + \frac{3}{4}$

14. $\frac{15}{16} - \frac{3}{16}$ **15.** $\frac{5}{8} + \frac{7}{8}$ **16.** $\frac{2}{3} - \frac{1}{3}$ **17.** $\frac{3}{16} + \frac{3}{16}$ **18.** $\frac{11}{12} - \frac{5}{12}$

Problem Solving • Reasoning

Solve. Write each answer in simplest form.

19. A block of cheese is broken into 12 equal pieces. Five pieces are melted to make macaroni and cheese, and five pieces are grated to sprinkle on top. What fraction of the block has been used?

20. **Analyze** Max has to deliver $1\frac{1}{4}$ tons of fruit in his $\frac{3}{4}$-ton truck. If he takes a full load on the first trip, how much fruit will be delivered the second trip?

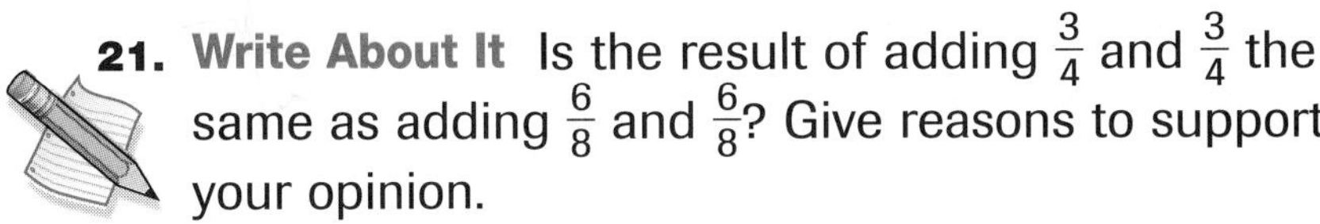

21. **Write About It** Is the result of adding $\frac{3}{4}$ and $\frac{3}{4}$ the same as adding $\frac{6}{8}$ and $\frac{6}{8}$? Give reasons to support your opinion.

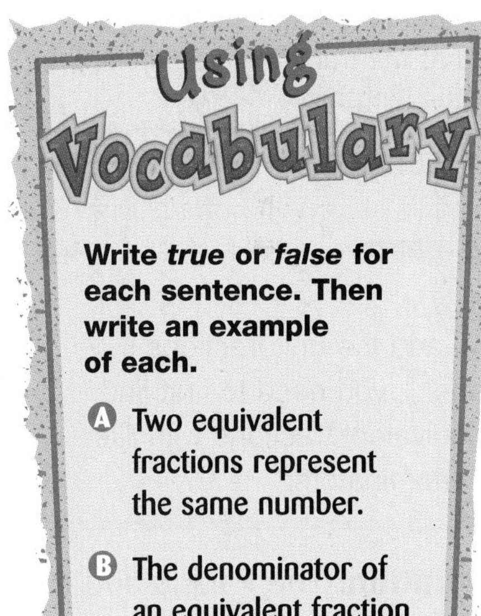

Mixed Review • Test Prep

Write each number in word form and standard form. *(pages 4–5)*

22. 400 + 9 **23.** 1,000 + 50 **24.** 70,000 + 2,000 + 100 **25.** 200,000 + 60,000

26 What is the standard form for thirty-four thousand, two? *(pages 4–5)*

A 3,402 **B** 34,002 **C** 340,002 **D** 340,020

Add Fractions With Unlike Denominators

You will learn how to add fractions that have different denominators.

Review Vocabulary
equivalent fraction

Learn About It

Most of Earth's surface is covered by water. The Pacific Ocean covers about $\frac{1}{3}$ of Earth's surface, and the Atlantic Ocean covers about $\frac{1}{5}$. What fractional part of Earth's surface is covered by these two oceans?

Add. $\frac{1}{3} + \frac{1}{5} = n$

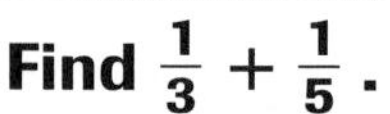

Find $\frac{1}{3} + \frac{1}{5}$.

Use the product of the denominators to write **equivalent fractions** with a common denominator.

Step 1 Use number lines to model the fractions. Notice that the fractions are different unit lengths.

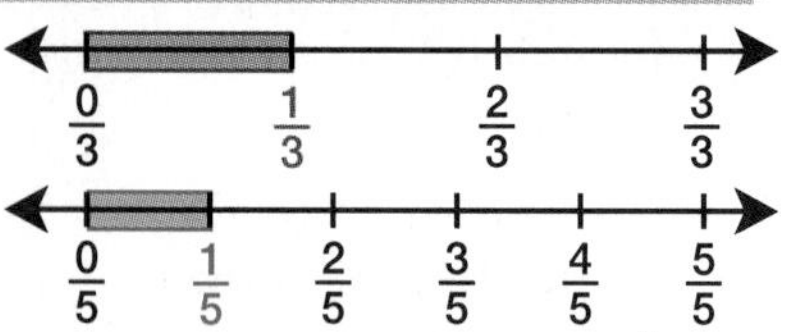

To add the unit fractions $\frac{1}{3}$ and $\frac{1}{5}$, you need to first find equivalent fractions with like denominators.

Step 2 Use the product of the denominators to write equivalent fractions with like denominators.

$3 \times 5 = 15$ ← common denominator

Think: Multiply by the denominator of the other fraction.

$\frac{1}{3} \xrightarrow{\times 5} \frac{5}{15}$ $\quad$ $\frac{1}{5} \xrightarrow{\times 3} \frac{3}{15}$

Step 3 Rewrite the problem using fractions. Then add.

$$\frac{1}{3} + \frac{1}{5} = \frac{5}{15} + \frac{3}{15} = \frac{8}{15}$$

Solution: The Pacific and Atlantic oceans cover $\frac{8}{15}$ of Earth's surface.

Another Example

Sums Greater Than 1

Find $\frac{3}{4} + \frac{5}{6}$.

$\frac{3}{4} \xrightarrow{\times 6} \frac{18}{24}$ $\quad$ $\frac{5}{6} \xrightarrow{\times 4} \frac{20}{24}$

$$\frac{3}{4} = \frac{18}{24}$$
$$+\frac{5}{6} = +\frac{20}{24}$$
$$\frac{38}{24} = \frac{24}{24} + \frac{14}{24} = 1 + \frac{7}{12} = 1\frac{7}{12}$$

Think: Write $\frac{14}{24}$ in simplest form.

$\frac{14}{24} \xrightarrow{\div 2} \frac{7}{12}$

Explain Your Thinking

► Why do you need to find equivalent fractions with the same denominator before adding fractions?

 Standards NS **1.0, 2.0, 2.3** MR **1.0, 1.1**

Guided Practice

Add. Write each sum in simplest form.

1. $\frac{1}{2} + \frac{1}{3}$

2. $\frac{2}{3} + \frac{4}{5}$

3. $\frac{11}{20} + \frac{1}{4}$

4. $\frac{3}{25} + \frac{2}{5}$

5. $\frac{1}{4} + \frac{1}{16}$

6. $\frac{2}{3} + \frac{3}{8}$

7. $\frac{3}{4} + \frac{1}{2}$

8. $\frac{7}{10} + \frac{3}{5}$

Ask Yourself

- Did I find equivalent fractions with unlike denominators?
- Is each sum in its simplest form?

Independent Practice

Add. Write each sum in simplest form.

9. $\frac{1}{6} + \frac{2}{3}$

10. $\frac{5}{8} + \frac{1}{2}$

11. $\frac{3}{16} + \frac{1}{8}$

12. $\frac{1}{10} + \frac{3}{8}$

13. $\frac{1}{16} + \frac{3}{4}$

14. $\frac{5}{8} + \frac{3}{16}$

15. $\frac{5}{12} + \frac{1}{2}$

16. $\frac{1}{3} + \frac{1}{6}$

17. $\frac{7}{10} + \frac{2}{5}$

18. $\frac{1}{3} + \frac{8}{9}$

Problem Solving • Reasoning

Use Data **Use the table to answer Problems 19–21.**

Water Use	Ground Water	Surface Water
Industry	$\frac{4}{25}$	$\frac{3}{50}$
Livestock	$\frac{3}{100}$	$\frac{1}{100}$
Irrigation	$\frac{16}{25}$	$\frac{33}{100}$
Household	$\frac{1}{25}$	$\frac{1}{100}$
Power	$\frac{1}{100}$	$\frac{1}{2}$
Other	$\frac{3}{25}$	$\frac{9}{100}$

19. **Patterns** Add the fractions in each column. What do you notice?

20. What fraction of ground water is used for livestock and irrigation combined?

21. **Analyze** Does irrigation use more ground water than each of the other categories? Does irrigation use more surface water than each of the other categories?

Mixed Review • Test Prep

Round to the nearest tenth. *(pages 28–29)*

22. 0.051 **23.** 0.126 **24.** 0.86 **25.** 0.003 **26.** 0.18

Choose the letter of the correct answer. *(pages 74–75)*

27 The sum of two numbers is 24. The smaller number is 2 less than the larger number. What are the numbers?

A 8, 16 **B** 10, 12 **C** 11, 13 **D** 11, 15

Extra Practice See Set L on page 354.

LESSON 15

Use the LCD to Add Fractions

You will learn how to use the LCD to add fractions that have different denominators.

New Vocabulary

least common denominator (LCD)

Learn About It

Jim spent $\frac{3}{8}$ of his birthday money at a baseball game and $\frac{5}{12}$ on new clothes. What fraction of his birthday money did Jim spend?

Add. $\frac{3}{8} + \frac{5}{12} = n$

Find $\frac{3}{8} + \frac{5}{12}$.

Step 1 Find the least common multiple (LCM) of the denominators. This is the **least common denominator (LCD).**

8: 8, 16, (24), 32
12: 12, (24), 36
The LCM is 24.

Step 2 Use the LCM as a common denominator to find equivalent fractions.

$\frac{3}{8} = \frac{■}{24}$ $\frac{5}{12} = \frac{■}{24}$

$\frac{3}{8} = \frac{9}{24}$ $\frac{5}{12} = \frac{10}{24}$

Step 3 Add the equivalent fractions. Check that the sum is in simplest form.

$\frac{9}{24} + \frac{10}{24} = \frac{19}{24}$

Solution: Jim spent $\frac{19}{24}$ of his birthday money.

Other Examples

A. One Denominator Is the LCD

Find $\frac{5}{16} + \frac{3}{8}$.

The LCM of 16 and 8 is 16.

So the LCD is 16.

$$\begin{array}{rcr} \frac{5}{16} & = & \frac{5}{16} \\ +\frac{3}{8} & = & +\frac{6}{16} \\ \hline & & \frac{11}{16} \end{array}$$

Think: $\frac{3}{8} \xrightarrow{\times 2} \frac{6}{16}$ (× 2 = × 2)

B. Simplify the Answer

Find $\frac{2}{3} + \frac{1}{12}$.

$\frac{2}{3} + \frac{1}{12} = \frac{8}{12} + \frac{1}{12}$

$= \frac{9}{12}$

Simplify.

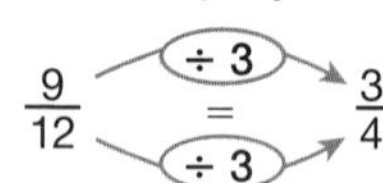

$\frac{9}{12} \xrightarrow{\div 3} \frac{3}{4}$ (÷ 3 = ÷ 3)

Explain Your Thinking

► Why is it usually best to use the least common denominator to add fractions, instead of another common denominator?

Guided Practice

Add. Write each sum in simplest form.

1. $\frac{1}{6} + \frac{1}{3}$

2. $\frac{2}{3} + \frac{5}{6}$

3. $\frac{1}{8} + \frac{1}{4}$

4. $\frac{1}{3} + \frac{2}{5}$

5. $\frac{2}{3} + \frac{5}{9}$

6. $\frac{7}{8} + \frac{1}{12}$

7. $\frac{2}{5} + \frac{1}{10}$

Ask Yourself

- Do I need to find the LCD?
- Did I use equivalent fractions?
- Is each sum in its simplest form?

Independent Practice

Add. Write each sum in simplest form.

8. $\frac{1}{6} + \frac{1}{4}$

9. $\frac{1}{10} + \frac{3}{4}$

10. $\frac{5}{6} + \frac{3}{4}$

11. $\frac{9}{16} + \frac{1}{12}$

12. $\frac{1}{2} + \frac{9}{10}$

13. $\frac{1}{2} + \frac{1}{4}$

14. $\frac{3}{8} + \frac{9}{16}$

15. $\frac{11}{12} + \frac{5}{6}$

16. $\frac{7}{16} + \frac{7}{8}$

17. $\frac{3}{4} + \frac{5}{6}$

Algebra • Expressions **Evaluate each expression if $a = \frac{1}{2}$, $b = \frac{2}{5}$, and $c = \frac{3}{4}$.**

18. $a + b$

19. $c + a$

20. $b + c$

21. $a + a + b$

Problem Solving • Reasoning

22. Barbara spent $\frac{5}{8}$ of her allowance on Monday and $\frac{1}{10}$ on Tuesday. What fraction of her allowance did she spend?

23. Fredrick bought a postcard for a quarter and a souvenir pencil for a dime. What fraction of a dollar did he spend on them?

24. **Analyze** Choose two numbers from 1 to 9. Multiply each number by 24. Add 12. Divide the sum by 8. What do you notice about the remainder?

25. **Write About It** Without adding, decide if each sum is greater than or less than $\frac{1}{2}$. Explain your decision.

a. $\frac{1}{3} + \frac{1}{4}$ **b.** $\frac{1}{3} + \frac{1}{8}$ **c.** $\frac{3}{8} + \frac{1}{5}$

Mixed Review • Test Prep

Evaluate each expression when $n = 10$. *(pages 162–164)*

26. $n \div 2$

27. $3 \times (n + 9)$

28. $(n \times 2) - 10$

29. $(n - 2) \times n$

30 What is the least whole number that is 90,000 when rounded to the nearest 10,000? *(pages 8–10)*

A 99,500 **B** 99,499 **C** 85,000 **D** 84,999

Extra Practice See Set M on page 354.

Add Mixed Numbers

You will learn how to add mixed numbers.

Learn About It

A hippopotamus weighs about $2\frac{3}{4}$ tons and a giraffe weighs about $1\frac{3}{4}$ tons. The combined weights of these animals is about the weight of one rhinoceros. About how much does the rhinoceros weigh?

Sometimes mixed numbers have like denominators.

Add. $\mathbf{1\frac{3}{4} + 2\frac{3}{4} = n}$

Find $1\frac{3}{4} + 2\frac{3}{4}$.

Step 1 Add the fractions.

$$\begin{array}{r} 1\frac{3}{4} \\ +\ 2\frac{3}{4} \\ \hline \frac{6}{4} \end{array}$$

Step 2 Add the whole numbers.

$$\begin{array}{r} 1\frac{3}{4} \\ +\ 2\frac{3}{4} \\ \hline 3\frac{6}{4} \end{array}$$

Step 3 Simplify the sum, if possible.

$$\begin{array}{r} 1\frac{3}{4} \\ +\ 2\frac{3}{4} \\ \hline 3\frac{6}{4} = 4\frac{1}{2} \end{array}$$

Think: $\frac{6}{4} = 1\frac{2}{4} = 1\frac{1}{2}$

$3\frac{6}{4} = 3 + 1\frac{1}{2} = 4\frac{1}{2}$

Solution: A rhinoceros weighs about $4\frac{1}{2}$ tons.

Sometimes mixed numbers have unlike denominators.

Add. $\mathbf{3\frac{5}{8} + 1\frac{1}{3} = n}$

Find $3\frac{5}{8} + 1\frac{1}{3}$.

Step 1 Write equivalent fractions for $\frac{5}{8}$ and $\frac{1}{3}$ by using the LCD, which is 24.

$$\begin{array}{rcr} 3\frac{5}{8} & = & 3\frac{15}{24} \\ +\ 1\frac{1}{3} & = & +\ 1\frac{8}{24} \\ \hline \end{array}$$

$\frac{5}{8} = \frac{5 \times 3}{8 \times 3} = \frac{15}{24}$

$\frac{1}{3} = \frac{1 \times 8}{3 \times 8} = \frac{8}{24}$

Step 2 Add. Simplify the sum, if possible.

$$\begin{array}{rcr} 3\frac{5}{8} & = & 3\frac{15}{24} \\ +\ 1\frac{1}{3} & = & +\ 1\frac{8}{24} \\ \hline & & 4\frac{23}{24} \end{array}$$

Standards NS **1.0, 1.4, 2.0, 2.3** MR **1.0, 1.1**

Other Examples

A. Mixed and Whole Numbers

$$\begin{array}{r} 3\frac{7}{8} \\ +\ 10 \\ \hline 13\frac{7}{8} \end{array}$$

B. Simplify the Answer

$$\begin{array}{r} 12\frac{1}{3} \\ +\ 15\frac{1}{6} \\ \hline \end{array} = \begin{array}{r} 12\frac{2}{6} \\ +\ 15\frac{1}{6} \\ \hline 27\frac{3}{6} \end{array} = 27\frac{1}{2}$$

C. Add Three Numbers

$$\begin{array}{r} 4\frac{1}{16} \\ 2\frac{9}{16} \\ +\ 5\frac{7}{16} \\ \hline 11\frac{17}{16} \end{array} = 12\frac{1}{16}$$

Think: $\frac{17}{16} = 1\frac{1}{16}$

Explain Your Thinking

▶ How can you use mental math to check a sum of mixed numbers?

Guided Practice

Ask Yourself

- Do I need to find the LCD?
- Do I add the whole numbers and fractions separately?
- Did I add only the numerators?
- Is my answer in simplest form?

Write each mixed number in simplest form.

1. $3\frac{4}{3}$ **2.** $5\frac{2}{8}$ **3.** $6\frac{10}{5}$

Add. Write each sum in simplest form.

4. $1\frac{1}{2} + 1\frac{1}{4}$

5. $2\frac{1}{4} + 3\frac{1}{6}$

6. $2\frac{4}{5} + 4\frac{1}{2}$

7. $3\frac{5}{12} + 7\frac{5}{6}$ **8.** $8\frac{9}{16} + 5\frac{1}{2}$ **9.** $1\frac{3}{4} + 6\frac{1}{3}$

Independent Practice

Write each mixed number in simplest form.

10. $2\frac{4}{3}$ **11.** $3\frac{13}{8}$ **12.** $1\frac{2}{4}$ **13.** $5\frac{9}{6}$ **14.** $4\frac{14}{10}$

Add. Write each sum in simplest form.

15. $3\frac{5}{6} + 1\frac{1}{6}$

16. $2\frac{1}{4} + 8\frac{3}{8}$

17. $1\frac{1}{2} + 2\frac{3}{4}$

18. $4\frac{3}{5} + 5\frac{7}{10}$

19. $2\frac{5}{6} + 3\frac{1}{3}$

20. $4\frac{3}{5} + 2\frac{1}{2}$

21. $3\frac{1}{4} + 7\frac{5}{6}$

22. $9\frac{11}{12} + 6\frac{2}{3}$

23. $2\frac{5}{8} + 6\frac{2}{3}$

24. $5\frac{3}{4} + 4\frac{1}{3}$

Add. Write each sum in simplest form.

25. $8\frac{1}{2} + 9\frac{3}{5}$ **26.** $10\frac{7}{8} + 2\frac{3}{4}$ **27.** $4\frac{1}{6} + 7\frac{1}{12}$ **28.** $3\frac{1}{2} + 1\frac{7}{8}$

29. $6\frac{2}{5} + 3\frac{1}{6}$ **30.** $7\frac{1}{3} + 4\frac{7}{12}$ **31.** $5\frac{3}{10} + 2\frac{1}{2}$ **32.** $5\frac{2}{3} + 3\frac{4}{5}$

33. $8\frac{2}{3} + 10\frac{11}{16}$ **34.** $2\frac{9}{16} + 12\frac{1}{4}$ **35.** $2\frac{2}{5} + 2\frac{5}{6}$ **36.** $1\frac{1}{2} + 9\frac{5}{8}$

Algebra • Expressions

Evaluate. Let $x = \frac{1}{2}$, $y = \frac{2}{5}$, and $z = \frac{3}{4}$.

37. $y + z$ **38.** $z + x$ **39.** $y + x$ **40.** $x + y + z$ **41.** $x + y + y$

Problem Solving • Reasoning

Use the table for Problems 42 and 43.

42. **Compare** Add the heights of the rhinoceros, the hippopotamus, and the elephant. Are the three heights combined greater than the height of the giraffe? Explain.

43. If you added the heights of all five animals, what would be the total height?

44. **Analyze** If you think you found a pattern in a sequence of numbers, how could you test the pattern to see if it continues?

45. The sum of two numbers is 72. One number is 6 less than the other. What is the smaller number?

46. **Write Your Own** Use the data in the table to write an addition problem. Give your problem to a partner to solve.

Animal	Average Height in Feet
Rhinoceros	$5\frac{3}{5}$
Hippopotamus	$4\frac{7}{8}$
Elephant	$9\frac{3}{4}$
Giraffe	$17\frac{5}{9}$
Bison	$5\frac{1}{2}$

Mixed Review • Test Prep

Find the product or quotient. *(pages 110–111, 146–149)*

47. 11×10 **48.** $850 \div 25$ **49.** 53×20 **50.** $32{,}000 \div 40$

Choose the letter of the correct answer. *(pages 258–259)*

51 What is the mean of 12, 18, 24?

A 12

B 24

C 18

D 30

52 21 is the mean of which set of numbers?

F 21, 19, 35

G 23, 21, 30

H 18, 20, 25

J 21, 19, 34

Extra Practice See Set N on page 354.

Number Sense

Compare and Order Rational Numbers

Rational numbers are numbers that can be expressed in the form $\frac{a}{b}$, where a and b are integers and b is not zero.

On a horizontal number line, a rational number is greater than any rational number to its left.

$^{-}\frac{6}{2}$ $^{-}\frac{5}{2}$ $^{-}\frac{4}{2}$ $^{-}\frac{3}{2}$ $^{-}\frac{2}{2}$ $^{-}\frac{1}{2}$ 0 $^{+}\frac{1}{2}$ $^{+}\frac{2}{2}$ $^{+}\frac{3}{2}$ $^{+}\frac{4}{2}$ $^{+}\frac{5}{2}$ $^{+}\frac{6}{2}$

$^{-}3$ $^{-}2.5$ $^{-}2$ $^{-}1.5$ $^{-}1$ $^{-}0.5$ 0 $^{+}0.5$ $^{+}1$ $^{+}1.5$ $^{+}2$ $^{+}2.5$ $^{+}3$

Order $^{-}1.5$, $^{+}\frac{1}{2}$, and $^{-}2$ from least to greatest.

Step 1 Locate each number on a number line.

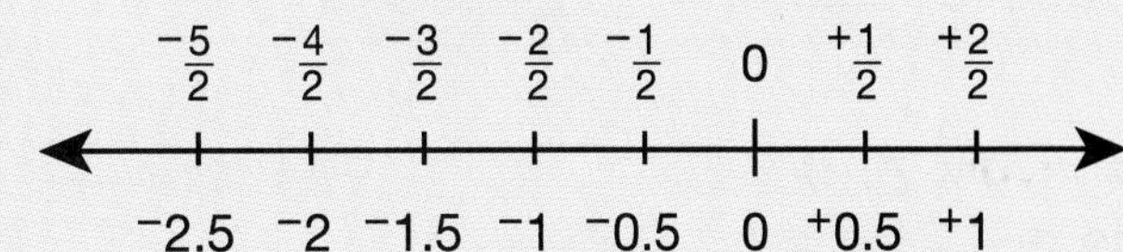

Step 2 Compare the numbers. Use $>$ and $<$.

- Since $^{-}2$ is farthest to the left, $^{-}2$ is the least number.
- Since $^{+}\frac{1}{2}$ is farthest to the right, $^{+}\frac{1}{2}$ is the greatest number.

$$^{-}2 < {}^{-}1.5 < {}^{+}\frac{1}{2}$$

Step 3 Write the numbers in order from least to greatest.

$$^{-}2,\ {}^{-}1.5,\ {}^{+}\frac{1}{2}$$

Explain Your Thinking

- ▶ Does every positive number have an opposite?
- ▶ Does every integer have an opposite?
- ▶ Is it true that the greatest number is always the one farthest from zero?

Rename Before You Subtract

You will learn how to use renaming to subtract fractions and mixed numbers.

Learn About It

Sometimes when you subtract, you must first rename 1 as a fraction. Any fraction with the same numerator and denominator is an equivalent fraction for 1.

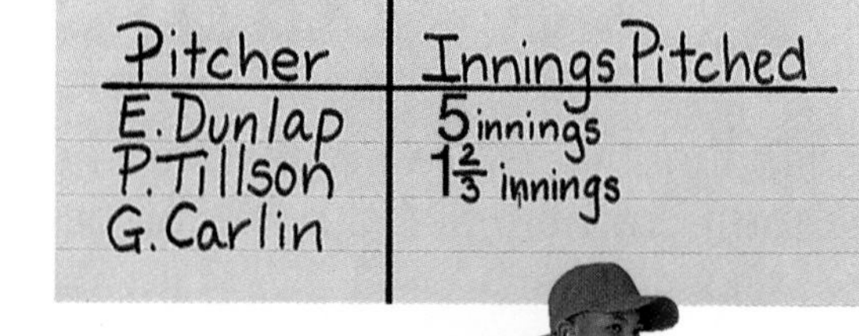

For example,

$\mathbf{1 = \frac{2}{2}}$ $\mathbf{1 = \frac{3}{3}}$ $\mathbf{1 = \frac{4}{4}}$ $\mathbf{1 = \frac{5}{5}}$

In a baseball game, the starting pitcher pitched 5 innings. The relief pitcher pitched another $1\frac{2}{3}$ innings before the closer came in to finish the game. How many more innings did the starting pitcher pitch than the relief pitcher?

Subtract. $\mathbf{5 - 1\frac{2}{3} = n}$

Find $5 - 1\frac{2}{3}$.

Step 1 Rename 5 as 4 + 1. Then rename 1, using 3 for the denominator.

$5 = 4 + 1$

$5 = 4 + \frac{3}{3}$

Step 2 Subtract the fractions.

$$\begin{array}{rcr} 5 & = & 4\frac{3}{3} \\ -\,1\frac{2}{3} & = & -\,1\frac{2}{3} \\ \hline & & \frac{1}{3} \end{array}$$

Step 3 Subtract the whole numbers.

$$\begin{array}{rcr} 5 & = & 4\frac{3}{3} \\ -\,1\frac{2}{3} & = & -\,1\frac{2}{3} \\ \hline & & 3\frac{1}{3} \end{array}$$

Check your work.

Use addition.

$$\begin{array}{r} 3\frac{1}{3} \\ +\,1\frac{2}{3} \\ \hline 4\frac{3}{3} \end{array} = 5$$

Solution: The starting pitcher pitched $3\frac{1}{3}$ more innings than the relief pitcher pitched.

Standards NS **1.0, 2.0, 2.3** MR **1.0, 1.1**

You can also rename a mixed number.

Find $7\frac{1}{4} - 1\frac{3}{4}$.

Step 1 Rename $7\frac{1}{4}$.

$$7\frac{1}{4} = 7 + \frac{1}{4}$$
$$= 6 + 1 + \frac{1}{4}$$
$$= 6 + \frac{4}{4} + \frac{1}{4}$$
$$= 6 + \frac{5}{4}$$

Step 2 Subtract the fractions.

$$\begin{array}{rcr} 7\frac{1}{4} & = & 6\frac{5}{4} \\ -\ 1\frac{3}{4} & = & -\ 1\frac{3}{4} \\ \hline & & \frac{2}{4} \end{array}$$

Step 3 Subtract the whole numbers. Simplify.

$$\begin{array}{rcr} 7\frac{1}{4} & = & 6\frac{5}{4} \\ -\ 1\frac{3}{4} & = & -\ 1\frac{3}{4} \\ \hline & & 5\frac{2}{4} = 5\frac{1}{2} \end{array}$$

Check your work.

Use addition.

$$\begin{array}{r} 5\frac{1}{2} \\ +\ 1\frac{3}{4} \\ \hline 6\frac{5}{4} = 7\frac{1}{4} \end{array}$$

Explain Your Thinking

▶ When you subtract a fraction from a whole number, why do you need to rename the whole number?

▶ How many different ways can you rename a whole number? Explain.

Guided Practice

Subtract. Write each difference in simplest form.

1. $4 - 1\frac{1}{4}$

2. $8\frac{3}{8} - 2\frac{5}{8}$

3. $2 - 1\frac{1}{3}$

4. $3\frac{1}{3} - 1\frac{2}{3}$

5. $6 - 4\frac{1}{5}$

6. $10\frac{1}{9} - 9\frac{4}{9}$

7. $5 - 2\frac{1}{6}$

8. $4\frac{1}{9} - 1\frac{8}{9}$

9. $58\frac{9}{20} - 19\frac{9}{20}$

Ask Yourself

- Do I need to rename?
- Is my answer in simplest form?
- Did I check my work?

Independent Practice

Write each difference in simplest form. Check your work.

10. $2\frac{2}{8} - 1\frac{5}{8}$

11. $5 - 3\frac{3}{4}$

12. $2\frac{1}{6} - 1\frac{5}{6}$

13. $8 - 5\frac{2}{5}$

14. $4\frac{1}{8} - 2\frac{1}{8}$

Write each difference in simplest form. Check your work.

15. $2 - 1\frac{5}{8}$ **16.** $8 - 4\frac{1}{5}$ **17.** $5\frac{2}{9} - 3\frac{8}{9}$ **18.** $3 - 2\frac{4}{6}$

19. $14\frac{5}{9} - 12\frac{7}{9}$ **20.** $27 - 11\frac{3}{10}$ **21.** $64 - 62\frac{7}{8}$ **22.** $32\frac{1}{5} - 21\frac{4}{5}$

Problem Solving • Reasoning

23. **Logical Thinking** In a city baseball league, the Cubs are $1\frac{1}{2}$ games behind the Cardinals, and the Cardinals are 4 games ahead of the Dodgers. How many games separate the Cubs and the Dodgers?

24. Softball bats are $2\frac{2}{4}$ in. in diameter. If a softball is $3\frac{3}{4}$ in. in diameter, how much wider is the softball than the bat?

25. **Analyze** If a baseball game lasted $3\frac{1}{4}$ hours and ended at 10 P.M., at what time did it start?

Mixed Review • Test Prep

Evaluate each expression if $p = 20$, $q = 5$, and $r = 10$. *(pages 162–164)*

26. $p \div r$ **27.** $r \div (p - 10)$ **28.** $(q \div p) \times 10$ **29.** $r \times (p + 40)$

Choose the letter of the correct answer. *(pages 298–299)*

30 Which composite number is divisible by 2, 3, and 4? *(pages 298–299)*

A 72 **C** 32

B 40 **D** 18

31 Which number is not a composite or prime number?

F 5 **H** 2

G 3 **J** 1

Averages

A good batting average is 0.300 or more. In this case, we say that a player is "batting three hundred." That means the batter would probably get about 300 hits out of every 1,000 times at bat. Write a fraction, in simplest form, equivalent to $\frac{300}{1,000}$. If a player gets a hit once in every 3 times at bat, is that player "batting more or less than 300"?

Extra Practice See Set O on page 354.

Practice Game

Fraction Dominoes

Play this game with a partner or in a small group to practice matching equivalent fractions.

Players
2–4

What You'll Need

- *Teaching Tool 7*

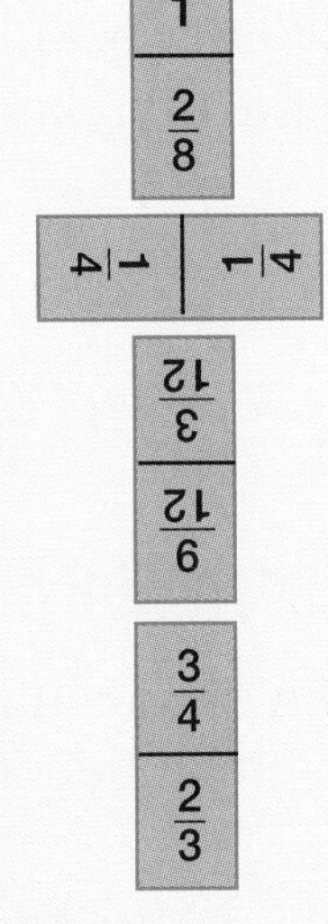

Here's What to Do

1. Shuffle the domino cards and place them facedown on the table. Each player draws 7 cards from the stack.
2. The player who draws the doubles card with the highest value begins the game by placing a domino card on the table.
3. Players take turns placing domino cards end to end, matching the equivalent fractions. Doubles cards are placed sideways.
4. Players who don't have a domino with a matching equivalent fraction must wait a turn. The player who first uses all his or her domino cards is the winner.

Share Your Thinking After you have played for a while, tell what strategies you have developed.

LESSON 18

Subtract Fractions With Unlike Denominators

You will learn how to subtract fractions and mixed numbers with different denominators.

Review Vocabulary
least common multiple (LCM)

Learn About It

The population of the world is about 6 billion. In 1990 the world had $\frac{5}{6}$ of today's population. In 1980 it had about $\frac{3}{4}$ of today's population. By what fraction of today's population did the world's population grow between 1980 and 1990?

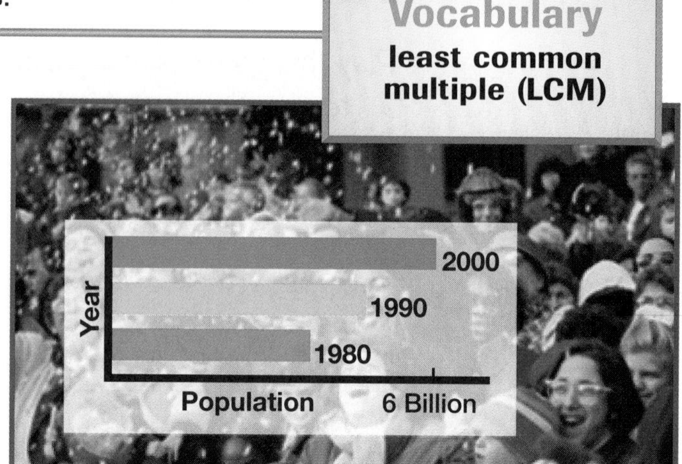

Subtract. $\frac{5}{6} - \frac{3}{4} = n$

Different Ways to Subtract Fractions

You can use any common denominator.

Use the product of the denominators, $6 \times 4 = 24$ as the common denominator.

$$\frac{5}{6} = \frac{5 \times 4}{6 \times 4} = \frac{20}{24} \qquad \frac{3}{4} = \frac{3 \times 6}{4 \times 6} = \frac{18}{24}$$

$$\frac{20}{24} - \frac{18}{24} = \frac{2}{24}$$

$\frac{2}{24} = \frac{1}{12}$ in simplest form.

You can use the least common multiple.

The LCM of 6 and 4 is 12.
So the LCD is 12.

$$\frac{5}{6} = \frac{5 \times 2}{6 \times 2} = \frac{10}{12} \qquad \frac{3}{4} = \frac{3 \times 4}{4 \times 4} = \frac{9}{12}$$

$$\frac{10}{12} - \frac{9}{12} = \frac{1}{12}$$

The answer is already in simplest form.

Solution: Between 1980 and 1990, the population increased by $\frac{1}{12}$ of today's population.

Another Example

Two Mixed Numbers

$$\begin{array}{rcr} 4\frac{7}{10} & = & 4\frac{21}{30} \\ -\,1\frac{7}{15} & = & -\,1\frac{14}{30} \\ \hline & & 3\frac{7}{30} \end{array}$$

Check:

$$\begin{array}{r} 3\frac{7}{30} \\ +\,1\frac{14}{30} \\ \hline 4\frac{21}{30} \end{array} = 4\frac{7}{10}$$

Explain Your Thinking

- ▶ Why does multiplying the numerator and the denominator of a fraction by the same number produce an equivalent fraction?
- ▶ Why can you use addition to check answers to subtraction questions?

Guided Practice

Subtract. Write the difference in simplest form.

1. $\frac{7}{8} - \frac{1}{2}$

2. $4\frac{1}{3} - 2\frac{1}{5}$

3. $\frac{3}{4} - \frac{1}{2}$

4. $9\frac{9}{10} - 4\frac{2}{5}$

5. $\frac{11}{12} - \frac{1}{3}$

6. $8\frac{3}{4} - 5\frac{1}{2}$

Ask Yourself

- Do I need to find the LCD?
- Did I write equivalent fractions?
- Did I subtract only the numerators?

Independent Practice

Write the difference in simplest form. Check your work.

7. $\frac{7}{10} - \frac{2}{5}$

8. $\frac{11}{12} - \frac{2}{3}$

9. $9\frac{6}{8} - 2\frac{1}{2}$

10. $\frac{1}{3} - \frac{1}{8}$

11. $\frac{8}{15} - \frac{2}{5}$

12. $\frac{2}{3} - \frac{2}{10}$

13. $1\frac{3}{4} - 1\frac{1}{3}$

14. $\frac{1}{4} - \frac{1}{10}$

15. $7\frac{1}{2} - 3$

16. $3\frac{1}{5} - 1\frac{4}{20}$

17. $\frac{7}{12} - \frac{2}{4}$

18. $\frac{4}{5} - \frac{3}{10}$

19. $\frac{9}{18} - \frac{3}{6}$

20. $7\frac{3}{16} - 6\frac{1}{8}$

21. $37\frac{3}{4} - 28\frac{1}{5}$

Problem Solving • Reasoning

22. **Compare** Suppose $\frac{5}{8}$ of Americans watch television and $\frac{1}{2}$ listen to radio. How much more of the population watches television than listens to radio?

23. **Analyze** In 1930 the U.S. population was about half the population in the 1990 census. By 1950 it had risen to $\frac{3}{5}$ of the 1990 level. By what fraction of the 1990 population did the population grow in those 20 years?

24. The Pacific Coast states, including Alaska and Hawaii, have a land area of almost 900,000 square miles. This is about $\frac{1}{4}$ the total land area of the U.S. The land area of Alaska is $\frac{4}{25}$ that of the U.S. What fractional part of the U.S. land area do the other Pacific states cover?

Television sets on display in a department store.

Mixed Review • Test Prep

Compare. Use >, <, or = for each ●. *(pages 8–10)*

25. 371 ● 378

26. 6,018 ● 5,180

27. 8.010 ● 8.101

28 The mean of four numbers is 88. The sum of three of the numbers is 80. What is the fourth number? *(pages 140–141)*

A 8 **B** 24 **C** 168 **D** 272

Subtract Mixed Numbers

You will learn how to rename when you subtract mixed numbers.

Learn About It

A horse can run a quarter mile in $21\frac{2}{5}$ seconds. A car can go a quarter mile in $7\frac{9}{10}$ seconds. If a horse raced a car for a quarter mile, how much longer than the car would it take the horse to reach the finish line?

Subtract. $\mathbf{21\frac{2}{5} - 7\frac{9}{10} = n}$

Find $21\frac{2}{5} - 7\frac{9}{10}$.

Step 1 Find the LCD of the fractions.

$$\begin{array}{rcr} 21\frac{2}{5} & = & 21\frac{}{10} \\ -\ 7\frac{9}{10} & = & -\ 7\frac{}{10} \\ \hline \end{array}$$

Step 2 Write equivalent fractions.

$$\begin{array}{rcr} 21\frac{2}{5} & = & 21\frac{4}{10} \\ -\ 7\frac{9}{10} & = & -\ 7\frac{9}{10} \\ \hline \end{array}$$

Step 3 Rename a mixed number if necessary.

$$\begin{array}{rcrcr} 21\frac{2}{5} & = & 21\frac{4}{10} & = & 20\frac{14}{10} \\ -\ 7\frac{9}{10} & = & -\ 7\frac{9}{10} & = & -\ 7\frac{9}{10} \\ \hline \end{array}$$

Step 4 Subtract and simplify.

$$\begin{array}{rcrcrl} 21\frac{2}{5} & = & 21\frac{4}{10} & = & 20\frac{14}{10} & \\ -\ 7\frac{9}{10} & = & -\ 7\frac{9}{10} & = & -\ 7\frac{9}{10} & \\ \hline & & & & 13\frac{5}{10} & = 13\frac{1}{2} \end{array}$$

Solution: It would take the horse $13\frac{1}{2}$ seconds longer to reach the finish line.

Another Example

Rename Both Numbers

Find $9\frac{1}{12} - 3\frac{7}{8}$.

$$\begin{array}{rcrcr} 9\frac{1}{12} & = & 9\frac{2}{24} & = & 8\frac{26}{24} \\ -\ 3\frac{7}{8} & = & -\ 3\frac{21}{24} & = & -\ 3\frac{21}{24} \\ \hline & & & & 5\frac{5}{24} \end{array}$$

Explain Your Thinking

▶ The *value* of a number does not change when it is renamed correctly. Tell why.

Standards NS 1.0, 2.0, 2.3

Guided Practice

Subtract. Write each difference in simplest form.

1. $5\frac{1}{4} - 2\frac{1}{2}$

2. $4\frac{1}{2} - 2\frac{7}{10}$

3. $3\frac{6}{8} - 1\frac{3}{4}$

4. $8\frac{5}{12} - 6\frac{7}{8}$

5. $8\frac{1}{2} - 7\frac{3}{5}$

6. $7\frac{4}{9} - 1\frac{2}{3}$

Ask Yourself

- Did I rename when necessary?
- Did I simplify the difference?

Independent Practice

Write each difference in simplest form. Check your work.

7. $2\frac{1}{2} - 1\frac{2}{3}$

8. $4\frac{1}{5} - 3\frac{3}{10}$

9. $8\frac{1}{6} - 5\frac{2}{3}$

10. $4\frac{1}{3} - 1\frac{3}{4}$

11. $8\frac{1}{3} - 3\frac{5}{6}$

12. $7\frac{5}{6} - 5\frac{9}{10}$

13. $6\frac{5}{8} - 3\frac{3}{4}$

14. $9\frac{1}{4} - 6\frac{5}{6}$

Problem Solving • Reasoning

Use Data **Use the table to answer Problems 15 and 16.**

15. **Analyze** When horses compete in show jumping, the horse with the fewest faults wins. Horses get 4 faults for knocking down a barrier, 3 faults for refusing a jump, and $\frac{1}{4}$ fault for each second over the time limit. Which horse won? By how many faults did the winner beat the horse that came in second?

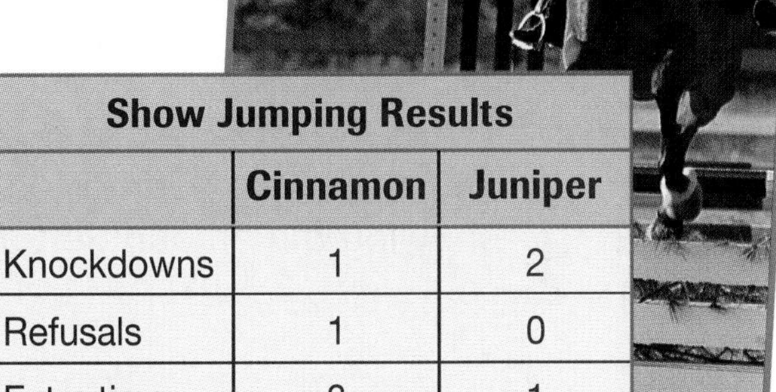

Show Jumping Results

	Cinnamon	Juniper
Knockdowns	1	2
Refusals	1	0
Extra time	3	1

16. **Write About It** Look back at Problem 15. How could you decide the winner without subtracting mixed numbers? Use the information in the table to support your opinion.

17. A horse's height is measured in hands. One hand equals $\frac{1}{3}$ ft. Cinnamon is 14 hands tall. Juniper is $5\frac{1}{2}$ ft tall. Find the difference in their heights in feet.

Mixed Review • Test Prep

Solve. *(pages 166–167)*

18. $n \times 5 = 25$

19. $a \div 8 = 7$

20. $x \div 2 = 11$

21. $b \times 7 = 49$

22 What is the mode of these values: 2, 2.5, 2.5, 3, 10? *(pages 258–259)*

A 2.5 **B** 4 **C** 8 **D** There is no mode.

Extra Practice See Set Q on page 354.

Problem-Solving Application: Use Patterns

You will learn to use patterns to solve fraction problems.

Patterns often can help you solve problems.

Problem For the fifth-grade picnic, Matt and Allison placed 32 pounds of ice in a tub to cool the soft drinks. Every 20 minutes during the picnic, $\frac{1}{2}$ of the remaining ice melted. How much ice was left after 2 hours?

Understand

What is the question?
How much ice was left after 2 hours?

What do you know?
The amount of ice is reduced by $\frac{1}{2}$ every 20 minutes. There are 60 minutes in an hour. They started with 32 pounds of ice.

Plan

What can you do to find the answer?
You can use a pattern to solve this problem. Make a table showing the amount left after every 20-minute period.

Solve

Two hours equals 120 minutes. The pattern shows that every 20 minutes, the amount of ice is divided by 2.

Time (min)	0	20	40	60	80	100	120
Ice left (lb)	32	16	8	4	2	1	$\frac{1}{2}$

After 2 hours, $\frac{1}{2}$ pound of the ice remains.

Look Back

Look back at the problem.
How does making a table help you find a pattern?

Standards NS 1.0 MR 1.0, 1.1, 2.0, 2.3, 3.0

Watermelon is not only delicious, it's also a good source of fiber, potassium, and vitamins A and C.

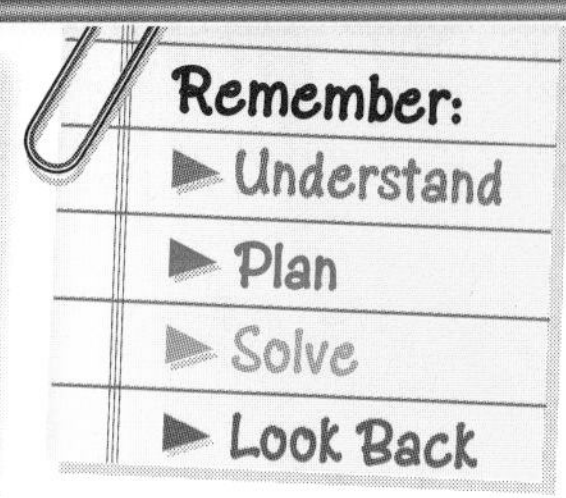

Guided Practice

Solve.

1. Kevin and Linda are getting ready for the water-balloon toss. For every 3 balloons, they need $\frac{1}{3}$ cup of water. How many cups of water will they need for 36 balloons?

   Think: Would a table help solve this problem? Is 36 divisible by 3?

2. Nancy and Warner are filling snack bags with trail mix. For every 4 bags, $\frac{1}{4}$ box of trail mix is used. How many bags can be filled from one box of trail mix?

   Think: How could a table help solve this problem?

Choose a Strategy

Solve. Use these or other strategies.

Problem-Solving Strategies

- **Find a Pattern**
- **Guess and Check**
- **Work Backward**
- **Use Logical Thinking**

3. There were 24 girls at a picnic. Two fifths of the students at the picnic were boys. How many students were at the picnic altogether?

4. In the "triple race," students had to run $\frac{1}{2}$ of the race, swim $\frac{1}{3}$ of it, and crawl the rest. If they crawled for 30 feet, how long was the race?

5. Anne, Ned, Eric, and Fiona are the four members of a team competing in the balloon toss. Ned is the first to toss. Eric is between Fiona and Anne. Fiona is not the last. In what order did the students toss their balloons?

6. It takes 4 minutes to bake one potato in a microwave oven. Baking more than one potato takes an extra 3 minutes for each potato. How long would it take to bake 4 potatoes in a microwave oven?

7. Write the next three likely fractions in the pattern. Explain your answer.

   $\frac{1}{2}, \frac{2}{3}, \frac{3}{4}, \frac{4}{5}, \ldots$

8. Use a calculator to find a fraction that is not equivalent to $\frac{2}{3}$.

   a. $\frac{122}{183}$ **b.** $\frac{134}{201}$ **c.** $\frac{131}{197}$ **d.** $\frac{116}{174}$

Extra Practice See 9–12 on page 355.

Quick Check

Check Your Understanding of Lessons 13–20

Add or subtract. Write each answer in simplest form.

1. $\frac{1}{4} + \frac{3}{4}$ **2.** $\frac{2}{5} + \frac{2}{5}$ **3.** $\frac{7}{8} - \frac{1}{8}$ **4.** $\frac{4}{5} - \frac{3}{5}$ **5.** $\frac{3}{4} + \frac{1}{8}$

6. $\frac{2}{5} + \frac{3}{10}$ **7.** $\frac{5}{6} + \frac{1}{8}$ **8.** $2\frac{2}{3} + 4\frac{1}{3}$ **9.** $5\frac{1}{2} + 3\frac{3}{8}$ **10.** $2\frac{1}{5} + 6\frac{1}{3}$

Subtract. Write each difference in simplest form.

11. $5 - 2\frac{5}{6}$ **12.** $4\frac{1}{3} - 2\frac{2}{3}$ **13.** $5\frac{3}{8} - 1\frac{7}{8}$

14. $\frac{3}{4} - \frac{1}{12}$ **15.** $\frac{5}{6} - \frac{1}{3}$ **16.** $4\frac{3}{4} - 1\frac{2}{3}$

17. $6\frac{1}{3} - 2\frac{7}{9}$ **18.** $9\frac{1}{10} - 3\frac{5}{6}$ **19.** $7\frac{3}{8} - 4\frac{3}{12}$

Solve.

20. A pancake recipe uses $1\frac{1}{3}$ cups of flour to make one dozen pancakes. How many cups of flour would be needed to make four dozen pancakes?

How did you do?

If you had difficulty with any items in the Quick Check, you can use the following pages for review and extra practice.

California Standards	Items	Review These Pages	Do These Extra Practice Items
Number Sense: **1.0, 2.0, 2.3**	1–4	pages 330–331	Set K, page 353
Number Sense: **1.0, 2.0, 2.3**	5–7	pages 332–333, 334–335	Set L, page 354 Set M, page 354
Number Sense: **1.0, 2.0, 2.3**	8–10	pages 336–338	Set N, page 354
Number Sense: **1.0, 2.0, 2.3**	11–13	pages 340–342	Set O, page 354
Number Sense: **1.0, 2.0, 2.3**	14–16	pages 344–345	Set P, page 354
Number Sense: **1.0, 2.0, 2.3**	17–19	pages 346–347	Set Q, page 354
Number Sense: **1.1, 1.2, 2.2, 2.6**	20	pages 348–349	9–12, page 355

Test Prep • Cumulative Review

Maintaining the Standards

Choose the letter of the correct answer.

1. The fifth grade had completed $\frac{1}{3}$ of their math book by November. By April they had completed another $\frac{7}{12}$ of the book. What fraction of the book had they completed by April?

   A $\frac{11}{12}$ **C** $\frac{8}{15}$
   B $\frac{8}{12}$ **D** $\frac{8}{36}$

2. A company ordered 450 boxes of paper that cost $7.95 each. What was the total cost of the paper?

   F $357.75 **H** $3,755.50
   G $3,577.50 **J** $3,777.50

3. In a sample, 10 out of 25 marbles are green. Predict how many green marbles would be in a bag of 100 marbles.

   A 25 **C** 50
   B 40 **D** 60

4. Seth wants to make a circle graph to show how he spent his time on Children's Day. He spent $\frac{3}{8}$ of the time making a clay pot, $\frac{1}{6}$ of the time watching a magic show, and the rest of the time swimming. What fraction of the time did he spend swimming?

   F $\frac{13}{24}$ **H** $\frac{11}{24}$
   G $\frac{5}{6}$ **J** $\frac{5}{7}$

5. When you divide a mystery number by 45, the result is 170. What is the mystery number?

   A 680 **C** 7,650
   B 850 **D** 8,500

6. Which statement is true?

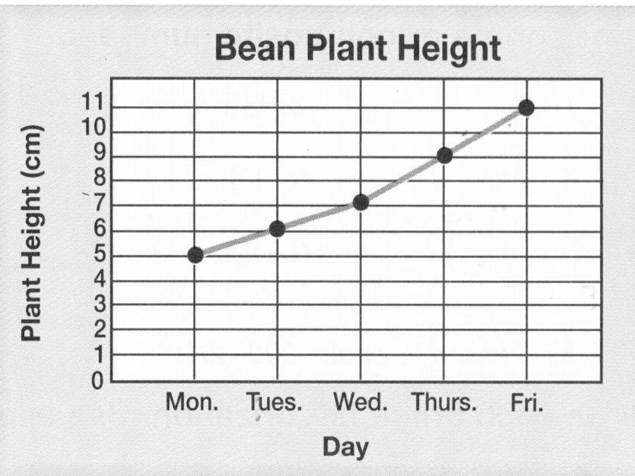

   F The plant doubled in height from Tuesday to Wednesday.
   G The plant was 9 cm high on Friday.
   H The plant tripled in height from Wednesday to Thursday.
   J The plant grew 2 cm from Thursday to Friday.

7. Which type of graph would you use to show how the population of bald eagles has changed over the last 10 years?

   A histogram
   B double bar graph
   C line graph
   D circle graph

8. Ken lives $5\frac{2}{5}$ miles from school and $9\frac{1}{3}$ miles from his dad's office. Ken says he lives $4\frac{1}{2}$ miles closer to school than to his dad's office.

   Explain Is Ken right? If not, what might he have done wrong in his calculations?

Safe Site

Internet Test Prep
Visit **www.eduplace.com/kids/mhm** for more *Test Prep Practice.*

Extra Practice

Set L *(Lesson 14, pages 332–333)*

Add. Write each sum in simplest form.

1. $\frac{1}{4} + \frac{1}{8}$ **2.** $\frac{2}{3} + \frac{2}{9}$ **3.** $\frac{3}{5} + \frac{3}{15}$ **4.** $\frac{1}{6} + \frac{7}{12}$

5. $\frac{3}{4} + \frac{1}{5}$ **6.** $\frac{1}{6} + \frac{7}{9}$ **7.** $\frac{2}{5} + \frac{7}{15}$ **8.** $\frac{7}{9} + \frac{3}{4}$

Set M *(Lesson 15, pages 334–335)*

Add. Write each sum in simplest form.

1. $\frac{1}{3} + \frac{1}{5}$ **2.** $\frac{1}{4} + \frac{3}{8}$ **3.** $\frac{3}{4} + \frac{1}{6}$ **4.** $\frac{1}{5} + \frac{3}{10}$

5. $\frac{5}{6} + \frac{1}{3}$ **6.** $\frac{7}{8} + \frac{1}{6}$ **7.** $\frac{11}{12} + \frac{2}{3}$ **8.** $\frac{3}{5} + \frac{7}{12}$

Set N *(Lesson 16, pages 336–338)*

Add. Write each sum in simplest form.

1. $2\frac{1}{5} + 3\frac{2}{5}$ **2.** $3\frac{5}{8} + 2\frac{3}{8}$ **3.** $4\frac{3}{4} + 5\frac{3}{4}$ **4.** $2\frac{1}{6} + 3\frac{1}{6}$

5. $4\frac{1}{2} + 5\frac{3}{4}$ **6.** $3\frac{3}{4} + 3\frac{7}{8}$ **7.** $2\frac{1}{5} + 3\frac{1}{8}$ **8.** $6\frac{3}{4} + 7\frac{5}{6}$

Set O *(Lesson 17, pages 340–342)*

Subtract. Write each difference in simplest form.

1. $2\frac{1}{3} - \frac{2}{3}$ **2.** $6\frac{3}{5} - 2\frac{4}{5}$ **3.** $5\frac{1}{6} - 2\frac{5}{6}$ **4.** $7 - 6\frac{3}{4}$

5. $5\frac{3}{8} - 4\frac{7}{8}$ **6.** $10\frac{3}{10} - 5\frac{7}{10}$ **7.** $4\frac{5}{12} - 2\frac{7}{12}$ **8.** $8\frac{1}{8} - 5\frac{7}{8}$

Set P *(Lesson 18, pages 344–345)*

Subtract. Write each difference in simplest form.

1. $\frac{3}{4} - \frac{1}{8}$ **2.** $\frac{5}{12} - \frac{1}{6}$ **3.** $\frac{11}{12} - \frac{5}{8}$ **4.** $\frac{5}{6} - \frac{1}{2}$

5. $3\frac{2}{5} - 2\frac{1}{10}$ **6.** $4\frac{2}{3} - 2\frac{4}{9}$ **7.** $5\frac{11}{12} - 3\frac{5}{6}$ **8.** $8\frac{2}{3} - 6\frac{1}{5}$

Set Q *(Lesson 19, pages 346–347)*

Subtract. Write each difference in simplest form.

1. $3\frac{1}{4} - 1\frac{3}{8}$ **2.** $9\frac{3}{8} - 4\frac{3}{4}$ **3.** $3\frac{1}{12} - 1\frac{5}{6}$ **4.** $4\frac{1}{8} - 2\frac{7}{16}$

5. $5\frac{2}{15} - 1\frac{2}{3}$ **6.** $9\frac{1}{2} - 4\frac{7}{8}$ **7.** $8\frac{1}{9} - 2\frac{1}{6}$ **8.** $7\frac{1}{9} - 3\frac{5}{6}$

Extra Practice • Problem Solving

Solve each problem, using the Logical Thinking strategy. *(Lesson 6, pages 312–313)*

1. The LCM of two numbers is 120. The GCF is 6. One number is 6 more than the other. What are the numbers?

2. The GCF of two numbers is 9. Both the numbers are greater than 50 and less than 70. What are the numbers?

3. The LCM of two numbers is 100. The GCF of the same two numbers is 10. The sum of the numbers is 70. What are the numbers?

4. The GCF of two numbers is 30. The sum of the digits in each number is 6. Both numbers are less than 200. What are the numbers?

Tell whether each statement is reasonable or unreasonable. Explain your answer. *(Lesson 12, pages 326–327)*

5. Mount Whitney, in California, is 4,417 m high. This is about $\frac{1}{3}$ as high as the tallest mountain in the world, Mount Everest, which rises to a height of 8,850 m.

6. Walking burns about 140 calories each hour while skiing burns about 480. You would burn more calories in 1 hour of skiing than in 3 hours of walking.

7. La Paz, Bolivia, is the world's highest capital at an altitude of 3,636 m. At 2,309 m, Mexico City is about 300 m lower.

8. Alicia used a $20-dollar bill to pay for a cable-car ride that cost $12.75. She calculated that her change should be $8.25.

Solve. *(Lesson 20, pages 348–349)*

9. A recipe calls for $1\frac{3}{4}$ cups of flour and $1\frac{1}{3}$ cups of milk. How much more flour is used than milk?

10. One fluid ounce is equal to $\frac{1}{8}$ of a cup. How many fluid ounces would it take to fill 6 cups?

11. One teaspoon is equal to $\frac{1}{3}$ of a tablespoon. How many teaspoons equals 5 tablespoons?

12. There are 10 tablespoons in $\frac{5}{8}$ of a cup. How many tablespoons would it take to fill 5 cups?

Chapter Review

Review Vocabulary

Write *always, sometimes,* or *never* for each statement. Give an example to support your answer.

1. A whole number that ends in 3 is divisible by 2.
2. To compare two mixed numbers, you need to express the fraction parts using the same denominator.
3. To add or subtract two fractions, you need to express both fractions using the same denominator.

Write the definition for each.

4. prime number
5. greatest common factor
6. equivalent fractions

Reviewing Concepts and Skills

Write whether each number is prime or composite. *(pages 298–299)*

7. 25 **8.** 7 **9.** 39 **10.** 42

Write each prime factorization. Use exponents if possible. *(pages 300–301)*

11. 32 **12.** 18 **13.** 40 **14.** 72

Test each number to see if it is divisible by 2, 3, 4, 5, 9, or 10. *(pages 302–303)*

15. 51 **16.** 183 **17.** 540 **18.** 3,645

Find the GCF of each pair of numbers. *(pages 304–306)*

19. 24, 28 **20.** 30, 60 **21.** 108, 63

Find the LCM of each pair of numbers. *(pages 308–310)*

22. 4, 5 **23.** 6, 10 **24.** 8, 12

Rewrite each expression as a fraction. *(pages 316–317)*

25. $7 \div 8$ **26.** $1 \div 5$ **27.** $8 \div 3$ **28.** $49 \div 100$

For each fraction, write three equivalent fractions. *(pages 318–319)*

29. $\frac{2}{3}$ **30.** $\frac{3}{4}$ **31.** $\frac{1}{5}$ **32.** $\frac{5}{8}$

Simplify each fraction. *(pages 320–321)*

33. $\frac{9}{27}$ **34.** $\frac{6}{10}$ **35.** $\frac{12}{30}$ **36.** $\frac{35}{42}$

Write a mixed number in simplest form for each. *(pages 322–323)*

37. $\frac{11}{5}$ **38.** $\frac{15}{4}$ **39.** 6.8 **40.** 9.09

Compare. Write >, < or = for each ●. *(pages 324–325)*

41. $\frac{7}{8}$ ● $\frac{13}{16}$ **42.** $\frac{4}{5}$ ● $\frac{8}{15}$ **43.** $\frac{5}{6}$ ● $\frac{9}{10}$ **44.** $\frac{3}{4}$ ● $\frac{15}{20}$

Add or subtract. Show each result in simplest form. *(pages 330–347)*

45. $\frac{1}{8} + \frac{5}{8}$ **46.** $\frac{3}{4} - \frac{1}{2}$ **47.** $\frac{3}{5} + \frac{5}{6}$ **48.** $\frac{11}{15} - \frac{2}{5}$

49. $7\frac{1}{3} - 4\frac{2}{3}$ **50.** $4\frac{5}{6} + 2\frac{5}{6}$ **51.** $2\frac{2}{3} + 3\frac{5}{6}$ **52.** $7\frac{1}{2} - 4\frac{7}{8}$

Solve. *(pages 312–313, 326–327, 348–349)*

53. The GCF of two numbers is 8. Both of the numbers are greater than 45 and less than 60. What are the numbers?

54. The Seikan railroad tunnel in Japan is $33\frac{1}{2}$ miles long. The Lötschberg tunnel in Switzerland is $9\frac{1}{10}$ miles long. What is the difference in length between the two tunnels?

55. The St. Gotthard tunnel in Switzerland is $10\frac{1}{5}$ miles long. This is 7 miles longer than the Mount Royal tunnel in Montreal, Canada. Would the combined length of the two tunnels be about 17 miles? Explain your reasoning.

Brain Teasers Math Reasoning

Twin Primes

Prime numbers with a difference of 2 are called twin primes. The numbers 3 and 5 are twin primes. What other pairs of twin primes can you find between 1 and 99?

Factor Parade

A three-digit number has five consecutive numbers as factors. What could the three-digit number be?

Internet Brain Teasers
Visit **www.eduplace.com/kids/mhm** for more *Brain Teasers.*

Chapter Test

Write whether each number is prime or composite.

1. 31 **2.** 46 **3.** 13 **4.** 81

Write each prime factorization. Use exponents if possible.

5. 12 **6.** 30 **7.** 45 **8.** 81

Test each number to see if it is divisible by 2, 3, 4, 5, 9, or 10.

9. 39 **10.** 180 **11.** 264 **12.** 612

Find the GCF of each pair of numbers.

13. 35, 15 **14.** 36, 48 **15.** 125, 75 **16.** 144, 54

Find the LCM of each pair of numbers.

17. 6, 8 **18.** 5, 12 **19.** 2, 30 **20.** 18, 27

Rewrite each expression as a fraction.

21. $11 \div 12$ **22.** $5 \div 9$ **23.** $63 \div 100$ **24.** $14 \div 8$

For each fraction, write three equivalent fractions.

25. $\frac{2}{5}$ **26.** $\frac{1}{8}$ **27.** $\frac{7}{10}$ **28.** $\frac{11}{12}$

Simplify each fraction.

29. $\frac{18}{36}$ **30.** $\frac{15}{20}$ **31.** $\frac{16}{24}$ **32.** $\frac{20}{32}$

Write a mixed number in simplest form for each.

33. $\frac{6}{5}$ **34.** $\frac{15}{8}$ **35.** 9.3 **36.** 1.02

Compare. Write $>$, $<$ or $=$ for each ⬬.

37. $\frac{1}{4}$ ⬬ $\frac{3}{8}$ **38.** $\frac{2}{5}$ ⬬ $\frac{8}{20}$ **39.** $\frac{4}{5}$ ⬬ $\frac{3}{10}$

Add or subtract. Show the result in simplest form.

40. $\frac{2}{5} + \frac{1}{5}$ **41.** $\frac{7}{8} - \frac{3}{8}$ **42.** $\frac{4}{5} + \frac{1}{6}$ **43.** $\frac{11}{12} - \frac{3}{4}$

44. $5\frac{1}{4} - 1\frac{3}{4}$ **45.** $4\frac{2}{5} + 6\frac{7}{8}$ **46.** $10 - 4\frac{3}{4}$ **47.** $7\frac{1}{2} - 3\frac{5}{6}$

Solve.

48. The LCM of two numbers is 24. The GCF is 4. One number is 4 more than the other. What are the numbers?

49. It takes $14\frac{2}{5}$ hours to fly from Auckland, New Zealand, to Chicago. This is 6 hours longer than it takes to fly from Madrid, Spain, to Miami. How long does it take to fly from Madrid to Miami?

50. It takes $9\frac{7}{10}$ hours to fly from Copenhagen, Denmark, to Los Angeles. It takes $8\frac{3}{5}$ hours to fly from Copenhagen to Montreal, Canada. Would it be reasonable to say that the flight to Montreal is about one hour longer than the flight to Los Angeles? Explain.

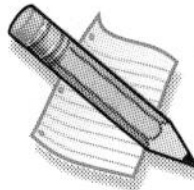

Write About It

Solve each problem. Use correct math vocabulary to explain your thinking.

1. Explain.

a. How can you use prime factorization to find the GCF of two numbers?

b. How can you use prime factorization to find the LCM of two numbers?

2. Mandy added $\frac{3}{5}$ and $\frac{12}{15}$ incorrectly.

$$\frac{3}{5} + \frac{12}{15} = \frac{3 + 12}{5 + 15} = \frac{15}{20} = \frac{3}{4}$$

a. Explain what she did wrong.

b. Show how to find the correct sum.

3. Explain how you would compare each set of numbers. Then give an example for each situation.

a. Compare a negative fraction with a positive one.

b. Compare two negative mixed numbers.

c. Compare a positive fraction with a positive decimal.

4. How can you tell if the sum or difference of two mixed numbers is in simplest form?

Another Look

The fifth-grade class held a vote to decide what they wanted to do for their class trip. The circle graph shows the results.

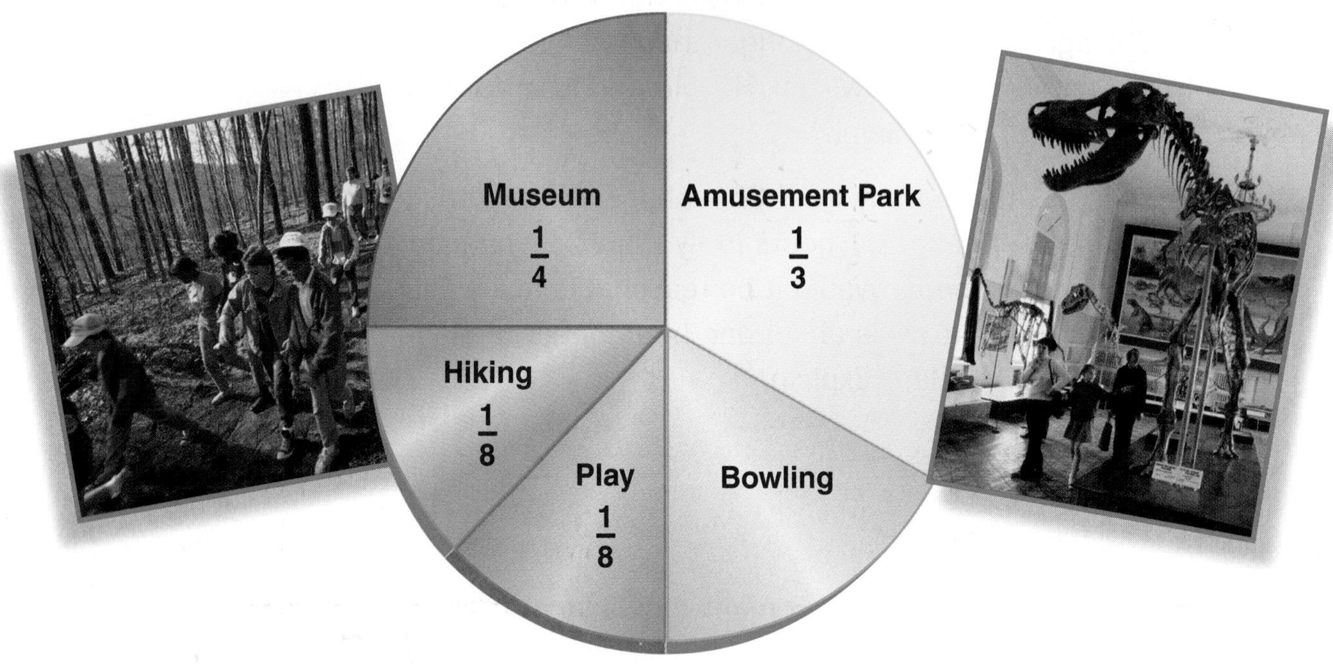

Use the circle graph to solve each problem. Show all your work.

1. What fraction of the class wanted to go bowling?
2. What fraction of the class chose either hiking or the amusement park?
3. List three equivalent fractions for the part of the class that voted to go to a play.
4. What fraction of the class chose either bowling or the museum?
5. Arrange all the activities in order from least to greatest number of voters.
6. **Analyze** How could you find the sum of all the sections without adding the fractions?
7. **Analyze** How many people do you think might be in the class? Why?
8. **Write Your Own** Create and solve three fraction problems about the information in the graph.

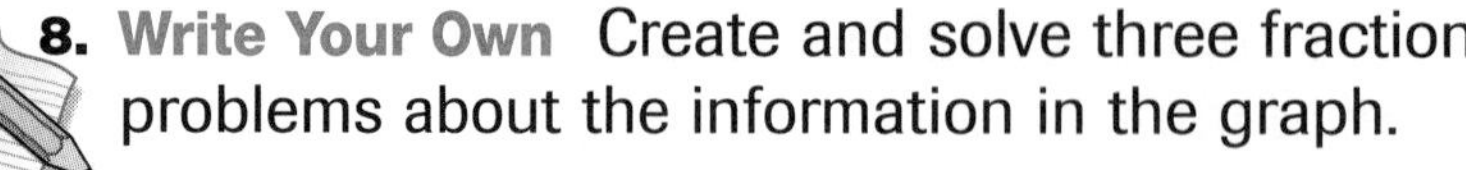

Enrichment

Prime Numbers

When you organize counting numbers in rows of six and mark the prime numbers, a pattern appears.

1	[2]	[3]	4	[5]	6
[7]	8	9	10	[11]	12
[13]	14	15	16	[17]	18
[19]	20	21	22	[23]	24
25	26	27	28	[29]	30
[31]	32	33	34	35	36

After the first row, every prime number is either 1 less than or 1 more than a multiple of 6.

Continue the chart to 100 to see if the pattern is the same for greater numbers. Use divisibility rules to find as many primes as you can.

Explain Your Thinking

- ▶ Why can numbers in the last column never be prime?
- ▶ Why can numbers in the third column except for 3 never be prime?
- ▶ Why will the numbers in the second and fourth columns always be even?

Standards NS **1.0, 1.4** MR **1.1**

Multiplication and Division of Fractions

Why Learn About Multiplication and Division of Fractions?

Multiplying and dividing fractions and mixed numbers are important for many practical things and for solving equations in algebra.

If you have a recipe that makes 4 servings, but you need 6 servings, you can multiply the amount of each ingredient by $1\frac{1}{2}$ to change the recipe to make 6 servings.

Since the gravity on the moon is $\frac{1}{6}$ the gravity on Earth, astronauts have to move around in a very different way than they do on Earth.

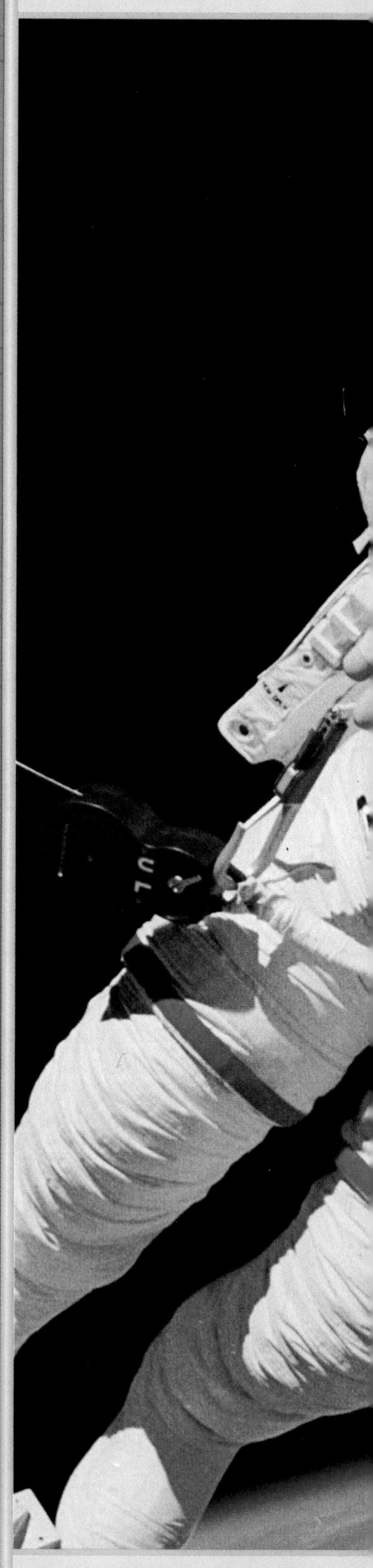

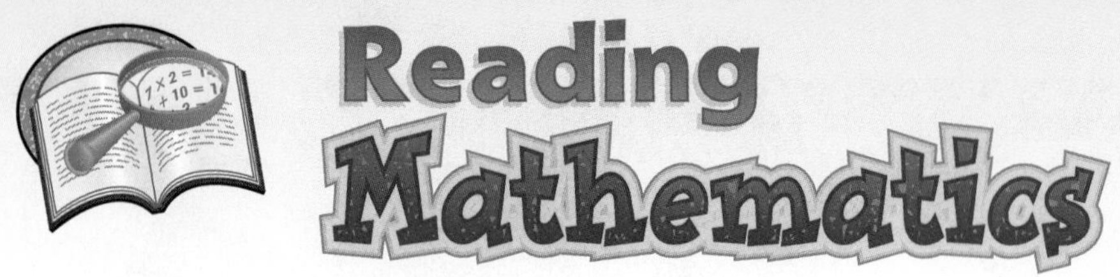

Reviewing Vocabulary

Understanding math language helps you become a successful problem solver. Here are some math vocabulary words you should know.

product	the answer in multiplication
factor of a number	a number that divides evenly into the number
greatest common factor (GCF)	the greatest counting number that is a common factor of two or more counting numbers
prime factorization	factoring a number into its prime factors only
mixed number	a number that is written as a sum of a counting number and a fraction
unit fraction	a fraction in which the numerator is 1

Reading Words and Symbols

When you read mathematics, sometimes you read only words, sometimes you read words and symbols, and sometimes you read only symbols.

The diagram can be used to model each of these statements.

- $\frac{1}{3}$ of $\frac{3}{4}$ is $\frac{1}{4}$
- You can make $\frac{3}{4}$ from 3 unit fractions of $\frac{1}{4}$.
- $3 \times \frac{1}{4} = \frac{3}{4}$
- $\frac{3}{4} \div 3 = \frac{1}{4}$

Try These

1. Use the number strip to answer each question.

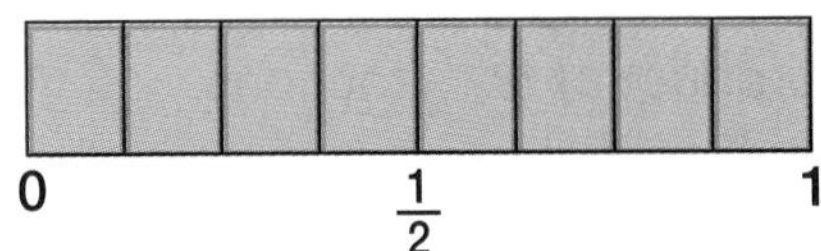

   a. How can you use the number strip to show that $3 \times \frac{1}{4}$ is $\frac{3}{4}$?

   b. How can you use the number strip to show that $\frac{1}{4}$ of $\frac{1}{2}$ is $\frac{1}{8}$?

   c. What is $\frac{1}{4} \div 2$?

   d. What is $\frac{3}{4} \div 2$?

2. Write *true* or *false* for each statement.

   a. Finding $\frac{1}{4}$ of any amount is the same as dividing the amount by 4.

   b. Finding the number of thirds in any counting number is the same as dividing the number by 3.

   c. Finding $\frac{3}{8}$ of any amount is the same as multiplying the amount by 3 and dividing the result by 8.

   d. If the numerator and denominator of a fraction have a common factor, then the fraction is in simplest form.

Upcoming Vocabulary

Write About It **Here are some other vocabulary words** you will learn in this chapter. Watch for these words. Write their definitions in your journal.

reciprocal

improper fraction

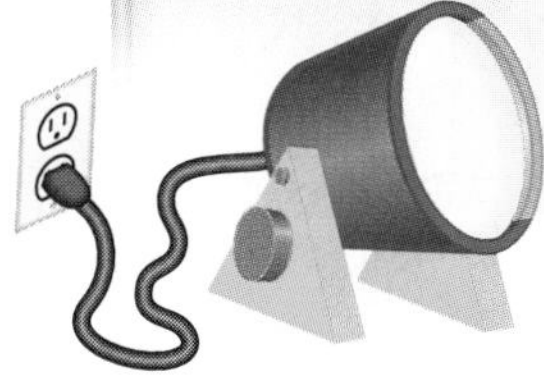

Model Multiplication of Fractions

You will learn how to use area to find the product of two fractions.

Learn About It

Use area to model the multiplication of two fractions.

You know that the area of a rectangle is the product of its length and width.

This window is 2 feet high and 3 feet wide. It has an area of 2×3, or 6 square feet.

The smaller window is $\frac{2}{3}$ ft high and $\frac{4}{5}$ ft wide.

Draw a model to show that the area of the small window is $\frac{8}{15}$ square feet.

Find $\frac{2}{3} \times \frac{4}{5}$.

Draw a square 1 unit by 1 unit.

- Divide the square into 3 congruent parts as shown. Label each third.
- Then divide the square into 5 congruent parts as shown. Label each fifth.
- The square has been divided into 15 congruent rectangles. What fraction of the area of the square does each rectangle represent?
- Shade a rectangle that is $\frac{2}{3}$ unit by $\frac{4}{5}$ unit. How many small rectangles are shaded?
- Complete: $\frac{2}{3} \times \frac{4}{5} = \frac{■}{■}$ ← number of small shaded rectangles / ← total number of small rectangles

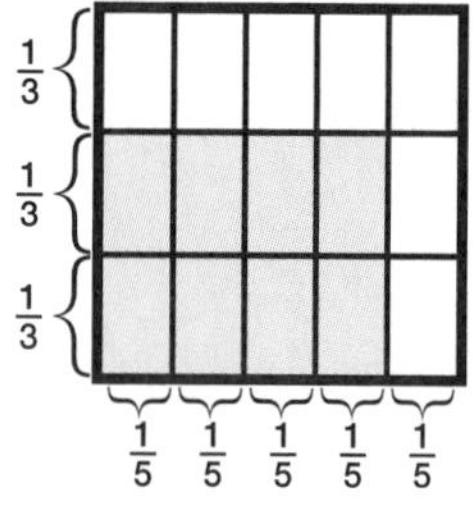

Find $2 \times \frac{3}{4}$.

Draw a rectangle 2 units by 1 unit.

- Divide the rectangle into 4 congruent parts and label.
- Shade a rectangle that is 2 units by $\frac{3}{4}$ unit. How many small rectangles did you shade?
- Complete: $2 \times \frac{3}{4} = \frac{■}{■}$ ← number of small shaded rectangles / ← total number of small rectangles

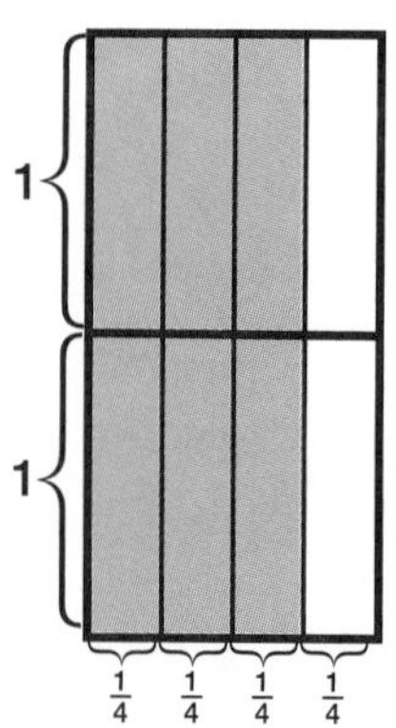

 Standards NS 1.0, 2.0, 2.4, 2.5 MR 2.3

Try It Out

1. Draw and label a square 1 unit by 1 unit. In one direction, divide the square into 5 congruent parts. Label each fifth. In the other direction, divide the square into 4 congruent parts. Label each fourth.

a. What fraction of the area of the square does each small rectangle represent?

b. Shade a rectangle that is $\frac{2}{5}$ unit by $\frac{3}{4}$ unit. How many small rectangles are shaded?

c. Complete: $\frac{2}{5} \times \frac{3}{4} = \frac{\blacksquare}{\blacksquare}$

Write the factors and the product represented by each model.

2.

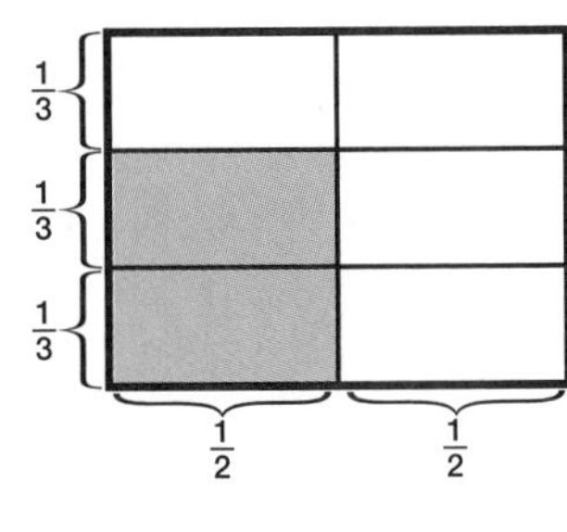

$\blacksquare \times \blacksquare = \blacksquare$

3.

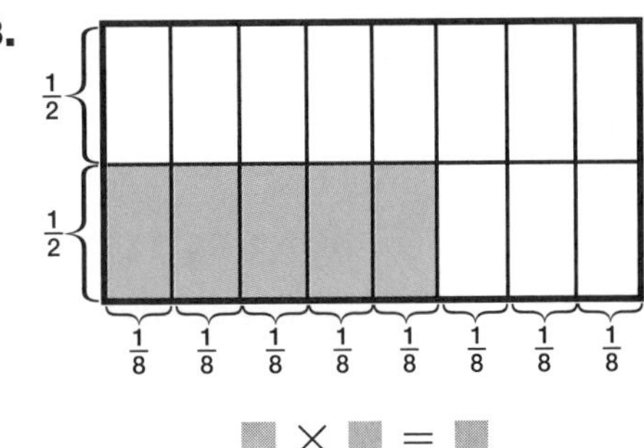

$\blacksquare \times \blacksquare = \blacksquare$

Use models to find each product.

4. $\frac{1}{3} \times \frac{3}{4} = \blacksquare$ **5.** $\frac{3}{4} \times \frac{4}{5} = \blacksquare$ **6.** $\frac{1}{2} \times \frac{1}{3} = \blacksquare$ **7.** $\frac{1}{4} \times \frac{3}{5} = \blacksquare$

8. $\frac{2}{3} \times \frac{3}{4} = \blacksquare$ **9.** $\frac{1}{3} \times \frac{3}{5} = \blacksquare$ **10.** $\frac{1}{3} \times \frac{1}{6} = \blacksquare$ **11.** $\frac{3}{4} \times \frac{2}{5} = \blacksquare$

12. $\frac{2}{3} \times 9 = \blacksquare$ **13.** $\frac{3}{4} \times 12 = \blacksquare$ **14.** $\frac{2}{5} \times 10 = \blacksquare$ **15.** $\frac{1}{2} \times 8 = \blacksquare$

Write about it! Talk about it!

Use what you have learned to answer each question.

16. How can you use area to explain why $3 \times 4 = 12$?

17. If two fractions are both less than 1, what can you say about their product?

18. Use two squares with equal sides to explain why $\frac{2}{3} \times \frac{3}{4} = \frac{3}{4} \times \frac{2}{3}$.

LESSON 2

Multiply Fractions

You will learn how to find the product of two fractions.

Review Vocabulary
product

Learn About It

The result in a multiplication is called a **product**. To find a fraction of a fraction, you need to find the product of the fractions.

Find $\frac{5}{6} \times \frac{3}{4}$.

Different Ways to Multiply Fractions

You can use a model.

Step 1 Draw a square 1 unit by 1 unit and mark off sixths and fourths.

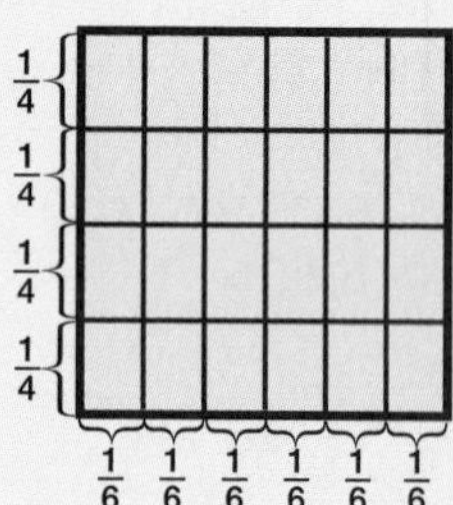

Step 2 Shade a rectangle that is $\frac{5}{6}$ unit by $\frac{3}{4}$ unit.

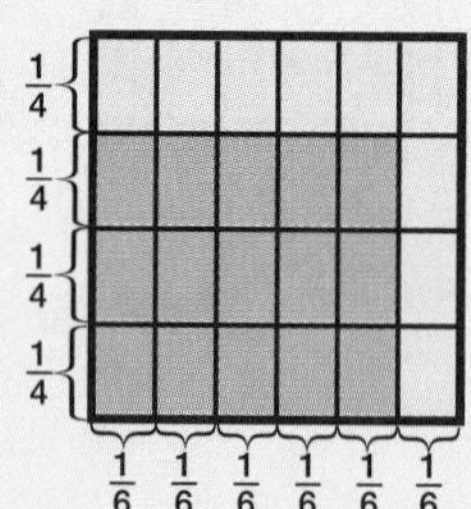

Step 3 Write a fraction that represents the shaded area. Then simplify the product.

$$\frac{5}{6} \times \frac{3}{4} = \frac{\blacksquare}{\blacksquare}$$

$$\frac{5}{6} \times \frac{3}{4} = \frac{15}{24}$$

$$\frac{15 \div 3}{24 \div 3} = \frac{5}{8}$$

You can multiply first, then simplify.

Step 1 Multiply the numerators. Multiply the denominators.

$$\frac{5}{6} \times \frac{3}{4} = \frac{5 \times 3}{6 \times 4} = \frac{15}{24}$$

Step 2 Simplify the product if necessary.

$$\frac{15 \div 3}{24 \div 3} = \frac{5}{8}$$

You can simplify first, then multiply.

Step 1 Rewrite the problem using factors.

$$\frac{5}{6} \times \frac{3}{4} = \frac{5 \times 3}{3 \times 2 \times 4}$$

Step 2 Cancel common factors in the numerator and the denominator.

$$\frac{5}{6} \times \frac{3}{4} = \frac{5 \times \overset{1}{\cancel{3}}}{\underset{1}{\cancel{3}} \times 2 \times 4}$$

Step 3 Multiply. Simplify further, if possible.

$$\frac{5 \times 1}{1 \times 2 \times 4} = \frac{5}{8}$$

Solution: $\frac{3}{4}$ of $\frac{5}{6}$ is $\frac{5}{8}$.

Standards NS **1.0, 2.0, 2.4, 2.5** AF **1.0** MR **1.1**

Other Examples

A. Use Prime Factorization

$$\frac{9}{10} \times \frac{2}{3} = \frac{9 \times 2}{10 \times 3}$$
$$= \frac{3 \times 3 \times 2}{2 \times 5 \times 3}$$
$$= \frac{3}{5} \times \frac{2}{2} \times \frac{3}{3}$$
$$= \frac{3}{5}$$

B. Use Algebra

$$\frac{ad}{b} \times \frac{c}{d} = \frac{a \times \overset{1}{\cancel{d}} \times c}{b \times \cancel{d}_1}$$
$$= \frac{ac}{b}$$

Notice that $\frac{2}{2} = 1$ and $\frac{3}{3} = 1$. The product of 1 and any number is that number.

Explain Your Thinking

- ▶ Suppose the product of two fractions is $\frac{a \times b}{b}$. Explain why it is possible to simplify the product.
- ▶ Explain why you can cancel common factors in the numerator and denominator to find an equivalent fraction.

Guided Practice

Multiply. Write each answer in simplest form.

1. $\frac{2}{3} \times \frac{3}{5}$ **2.** $\frac{3}{8} \times \frac{4}{5}$ **3.** $\frac{5}{6} \times \frac{3}{10}$

4. $\frac{4}{9} \times \frac{3}{4}$ **5.** $\frac{3}{25} \times \frac{2}{5}$ **6.** $\frac{3}{5} \times \frac{4}{7}$

7. $\frac{4}{9} \times \frac{3}{2}$ **8.** $\frac{3}{35} \times \frac{25}{42}$ **9.** $\frac{3}{8} \times \frac{4}{11}$

Ask Yourself

- Did I find the prime factorization of the numerator and denominator?
- Did I find fractions equal to 1 or did I cancel common factors in the numerator and denominator?

Independent Practice

Multiply. Write each answer in simplest form.

10. $\frac{1}{5} \times \frac{5}{8}$ **11.** $\frac{2}{5} \times \frac{5}{8}$ **12.** $\frac{3}{5} \times \frac{5}{9}$ **13.** $\frac{4}{5} \times \frac{5}{12}$

14. $\frac{1}{8} \times 6$ **15.** $\frac{1}{8} \times \frac{6}{7}$ **16.** $\frac{5}{8} \times \frac{6}{15}$ **17.** $\frac{1}{6} \times \frac{2}{3}$

18. $\frac{1}{12} \times \frac{3}{5}$ **19.** $\frac{7}{12} \times \frac{2}{7}$ **20.** $\frac{7}{12} \times \frac{2}{3}$ **21.** $\frac{1}{9} \times \frac{3}{4}$

22. $\frac{4}{9} \times \frac{1}{6}$ **23.** $\frac{1}{6} \times \frac{9}{10}$ **24.** $\frac{8}{9} \times \frac{1}{12}$

25. $\frac{7}{10} \times \frac{4}{5}$ **26.** $\frac{4}{9} \times \frac{6}{7}$ **27.** $\frac{5}{6} \times \frac{9}{10}$

28. $\frac{8}{9} \times \frac{5}{6}$ **29.** $\frac{7}{10} \times \frac{4}{7}$ **30.** $\frac{5}{12} \times \frac{4}{5}$

31. $\frac{9}{10} \times \frac{2}{3}$ **32.** $\frac{3}{10} \times \frac{5}{12}$ **33.** $\frac{7}{8} \times \frac{6}{7}$

Algebra • Expressions **Multiply. Write each answer in simplest form.**

34. $\frac{a}{6} \times \frac{2}{b}$ **35.** $2n \times \frac{2}{n}$ **36.** $\frac{p}{q} \times \frac{q}{p}$

Problem Solving • Reasoning

Use Data **Use the table for Problems 37–39.**

37. Two thirds of both the fourth- and fifth-grade classes are in the school choir. What fraction of the students in the school are in the choir?

38. Three fourths of the kindergarten students are five-year-olds. What fraction of the student population is this?

39. Analyze The third- and fourth-grade classes put on a play. What fraction of the student population is this?

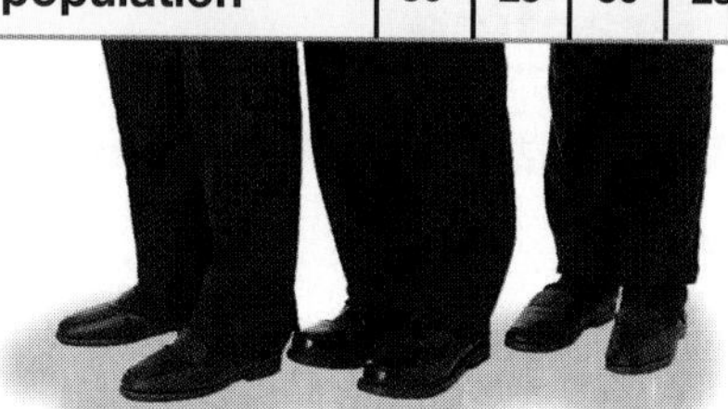

School Population by Grade

Grade	K	1	2	3	4	5
Part of student population	$\frac{9}{50}$	$\frac{4}{25}$	$\frac{9}{50}$	$\frac{4}{25}$	$\frac{4}{25}$	$\frac{4}{25}$

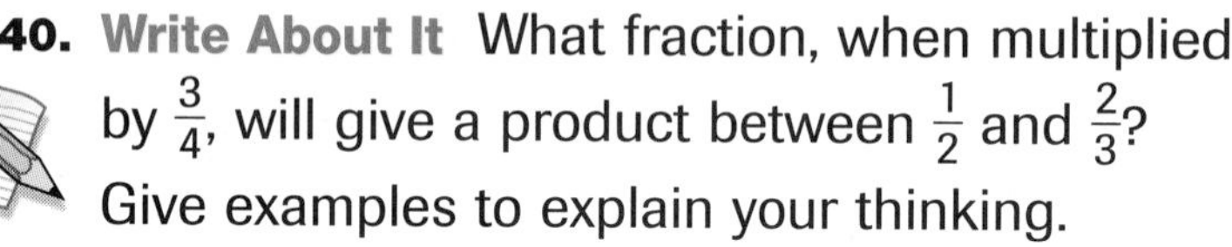

40. Write About It What fraction, when multiplied by $\frac{3}{4}$, will give a product between $\frac{1}{2}$ and $\frac{2}{3}$? Give examples to explain your thinking.

Mixed Review • Test Prep

Compare. Write >, <, or = for each ●. *(pages 8–10, 30–31, 322–323)*

41. 1.02 ● 2.01 **42.** $\frac{1}{2}$ ● $\frac{1}{8}$ **43.** 3,055 ● 989 **44.** $\frac{1}{4}$ ● 0.25

45 What must be true about two numbers if their LCM is the product of the two numbers? *(pages 324–325)*

A The numbers are both composite.

B The numbers are both prime.

C The numbers have no common prime factors.

D One number is a multiple of the other.

Logical Thinking

Musical Fractions

Some musical notes are described by using the words we use for fractions.

1. How many quarter notes are equivalent to 1 whole note?

2. How many sixteenth notes are equivalent to 3 quarter notes?

3. How many sixteenth notes are equivalent to 1 half note?

Extra Practice See Set A on page 394.

Show What You Know

Using Vocabulary

Use the fractions listed to answer each question.

$\frac{1}{3}$ $\frac{7}{12}$ $\frac{3}{4}$ $\frac{1}{6}$ $\frac{4}{10}$ $\frac{1}{12}$

1. Which two fractions have an **LCD** of 6?
2. Which two fractions have a **product** of $\frac{1}{4}$?
3. Which two fractions have a **difference** of $\frac{1}{4}$?
4. Which two fractions have a **sum** of $\frac{1}{4}$?
5. Which fraction is not in **simplest form**?
6. Which two fractions have a **product** of $\frac{1}{15}$?

Check It Out

Change one number or the operation sign in each number sentence to make it true.

1. $\frac{3}{4} \times \frac{5}{6} = \frac{9}{10}$
2. $\frac{7}{8} - \frac{3}{5} = \frac{21}{40}$
3. $\frac{2}{3} + \frac{1}{4} = \frac{1}{6}$
4. $\frac{2}{5} \times \frac{5}{6} = \frac{1}{6}$

Fraction Detective

Use the fractions at the right to answer Exercises 1–4.
Find two fractions to fit each description.

$\frac{1}{2}$ $\frac{1}{3}$ $\frac{1}{4}$ $\frac{2}{3}$ $\frac{3}{4}$

1. The product is $\frac{1}{8}$, and the sum is $\frac{3}{4}$.
2. Both the product and the difference are equal to $\frac{1}{12}$.
3. The product is $\frac{1}{2}$, and the difference is $\frac{1}{12}$.
4. The product is $\frac{1}{6}$, and the sum is less than 1.

LESSON 3

Multiply Fractions and Mixed Numbers

You will learn how to find products of fractions and whole or mixed numbers.

Review Vocabulary
mixed number
improper fraction

Learn About It

Factors in a multiplication expression may be **mixed numbers,** such as $2\frac{3}{4}$, or **improper fractions,** such as $\frac{11}{4}$.

A recipe for stuffed chilies serves 6 people and uses $1\frac{3}{4}$ cups of cream cheese. Cheryl needs to make enough for 4 people. She decides to make $\frac{2}{3}$ of the recipe. How much cream cheese should she use?

Multiply. $\frac{2}{3} \times 1\frac{3}{4} = n$

Find $\frac{2}{3} \times 1\frac{3}{4}$.

Step 1 Write the mixed number as an improper fraction.

$1\frac{3}{4} = \frac{4}{4} + \frac{3}{4} = \frac{7}{4}$

$\frac{2}{3} \times 1\frac{3}{4} = \frac{2}{3} \times \frac{7}{4}$

Step 2 Look for common factors to cancel.

$\frac{2}{3} \times \frac{7}{4} = \frac{\overset{1}{\cancel{2}} \times 7}{3 \times 2 \times \underset{1}{\cancel{2}}}$

$= \frac{1 \times 7}{3 \times 2}$

$= \frac{7}{6}$

Step 3 Simplify if possible. Write the fraction as a mixed number if necessary.

$\frac{7}{6} = \frac{6}{6} + \frac{1}{6} = 1\frac{1}{6}$

$\frac{2}{3} \times 1\frac{3}{4} = 1\frac{1}{6}$

Solution: She will need $1\frac{1}{6}$ cups of cream cheese.

Other Examples

A. Two Mixed Numbers

$1\frac{2}{3} \times 3\frac{1}{4} = \frac{5}{3} \times \frac{13}{4}$

$= \frac{65}{12}$

$= 5\frac{5}{12}$

Think: $65 \div 12 = ■$

B. A Mixed Number and a Whole Number

$2\frac{1}{8} \times 4 = \frac{17}{8} \times \frac{4}{1}$

$= \frac{17 \times \overset{1}{\cancel{2}} \times \overset{1}{\cancel{2}}}{2 \times \underset{1}{\cancel{2}} \times \underset{1}{\cancel{2}}}$

$= \frac{17}{2}$

$= 8\frac{1}{2}$

Explain Your Thinking

- Why is the product of two mixed numbers always greater than 1?
- To write $3\frac{1}{4}$ as $\frac{13}{4}$, why do you multiply the whole number part, 3, by the denominator, 4, before adding the numerator, 1?

Standards NS 1.0, 2.0, 2.4, 2.5

Guided Practice

Ask Yourself

- Did I use improper fractions?

Write each product in simplest form.

1. $\frac{4}{5} \times 1\frac{2}{3}$ **2.** $2\frac{3}{4} \times 1\frac{1}{2}$ **3.** $1\frac{3}{8} \times 4$

Independent Practice

Write each product in simplest form.

4. $1\frac{5}{6} \times \frac{1}{3}$ **5.** $\frac{3}{4} \times 2\frac{1}{3}$ **6.** $3\frac{1}{2} \times \frac{2}{5}$ **7.** $\frac{3}{8} \times 1\frac{1}{4}$

8. $1\frac{7}{9} \times \frac{1}{12}$ **9.** $2\frac{3}{4} \times \frac{5}{6}$ **10.** $1\frac{7}{9} \times 2$ **11.** $5 \times 4\frac{1}{5}$

12. $3 \times 4\frac{1}{6}$ **13.** $\frac{3}{4} \times 1\frac{1}{3}$ **14.** $2\frac{1}{3} \times 3\frac{3}{4}$ **15.** $2\frac{5}{6} \times 2\frac{1}{4}$

Compare. Write >, <, or = for each ●.

16. $2\frac{3}{4} \times \frac{1}{2}$ ● $2\frac{7}{8} \times \frac{1}{2}$ **17.** $\frac{11}{12} \times 1\frac{5}{8}$ ● $1\frac{3}{8} \times 1\frac{1}{12}$

Problem Solving • Reasoning

18. **Logical Thinking** Carl has 9 guests coming to dinner. If $1\frac{3}{4}$ cups of rice serves 6 people, will $1\frac{1}{2}$ times that amount be enough for Carl and all of his guests? Explain.

19. A 2-serving recipe for chicken mole calls for $3\frac{1}{2}$ teaspoons of chili powder and $1\frac{1}{2}$ tablespoons of olive oil. How much of each ingredient is needed to make 3 servings?

20. **Analyze** If 1 cup of orange juice fills $1\frac{1}{3}$ small glasses, how many small glasses can you fill with 10 cups of juice?

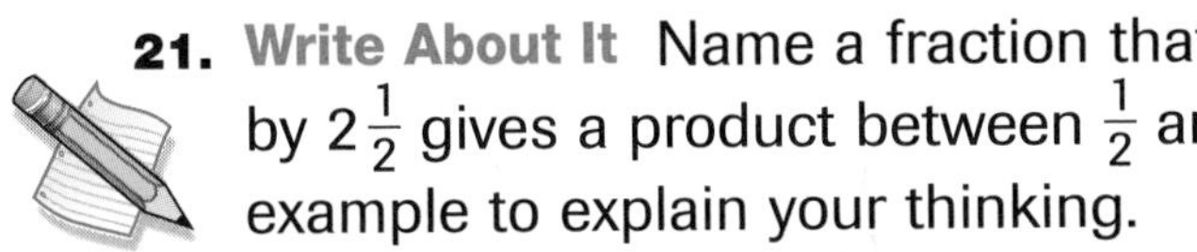

21. **Write About It** Name a fraction that when multiplied by $2\frac{1}{2}$ gives a product between $\frac{1}{2}$ and 1. Give an example to explain your thinking.

SCIENCE If a recipe shows a temperature in °C, you can convert that temperature to °F using this formula.

$F = \frac{9}{5}C + 32.$

Change these cooking temperatures to degrees Fahrenheit.

A 190°C **C** 235°C

B 150°C **D** 100°C

Mixed Review • Test Prep

Solve. *(pages 52–55, 98–99)*

22. 83 + 192 **23.** 705 − 167 **24.** 343 × 6 **25.** 2 + 106 + 55

26 What is *one thousand sixteen* written in standard form? *(pages 4–5)*

A 116 **B** 1,016 **C** 10,160 **D** 100,016

Extra Practice See Set B on page 394.

Problem-Solving Skill: Choose the Operation

You will learn how to choose the operation that will help you solve a problem.

To solve a problem, you need to read the problem carefully to understand which operation or operations to use.

Look at the situations below.

Look for key words in the problem.

On its first few bounces, a ball reaches $\frac{4}{5}$ **of the height** of its previous bounce. How high will it go on its second bounce?

- The height of the first bounce is $\frac{4}{5}$ of the original height.
- The second bounce is $\frac{4}{5}$ of the height of the first bounce.

To find a fraction of a number, you need to multiply.

$$\frac{4}{5} \times \frac{4}{5} = \frac{16}{25}$$

The ball will reach $\frac{16}{25}$ of its original height on its second bounce.

Sometimes more than one operation is needed.

The ball is dropped from a height of 1 meter. Find the difference between the heights of the first two bounces.

First, you need to multiply to find the height of each bounce.

After finding the heights of the two bounces, you need to subtract to find the difference between the heights.

$\frac{4}{5} \times 1 = \frac{4}{5}$ m $\quad \frac{16}{25} \times 1 = \frac{16}{25}$ m

$\frac{4}{5} - \frac{16}{25} = \frac{20}{25} - \frac{16}{25} = \frac{4}{25}$ m

The difference between the heights of the first two bounces is $\frac{4}{25}$ meter.

Look Back How does reading a problem carefully help you choose the correct operation to use?

Standards NS **1.0, 2.0, 2.4, 2.5** MR **1.0, 2.0, 3.0, 3.2**

This picture of a bouncing ball was taken using a flashing light, or stroboscope.

Guided Practice

Solve.

1. On each bounce, a ball reaches $\frac{4}{5}$ of the height of its previous bounce. How high will the ball bounce on its third bounce?

   Think: When you know the height of a bounce, what numbers do you use to calculate the height of the next bounce?

2. How many bounces will it take the ball in Problem 1 to bounce to a height that is less than $\frac{1}{2}$ of the height of the first bounce?

   Think: Which operation or operations do you need to use to solve the problem?

Choose a Strategy

Solve. Use these or other strategies.

Problem-Solving Strategies

- **Draw a Diagram**
- **Use Logical Thinking**
- **Work Backward**
- **Find a Pattern**

3. A different ball reaches $\frac{2}{3}$ of its previous height on each bounce. How many bounces will it take to reach less than half of its original height?

4. On Earth, a 1-kilogram mass weighs $2\frac{1}{5}$ pounds. After losing 5 pounds, Jo's mass is 55 kilograms. In pounds, what was Jo's original weight?

5. It takes about $29\frac{1}{2}$ days for the moon to orbit Earth. A space station orbits Earth about 15 times each day. How many orbits does the space station make during one moon orbit?

6. In a non-leap year, the average month is about $30\frac{2}{5}$ days long. What is the difference between the time it takes the moon to orbit Earth—$29\frac{1}{2}$ days—and the length of an average month?

7. Look at the table at the right. The data represent the distances a ball falls over a 4-second time period as the ball is dropped from the top of a high building. How far do you think the ball will have fallen after 5 seconds? Explain your thinking.

Time (seconds)	Distance (feet)
1	$16 \times 1 = 16$
2	$16 \times 4 = 64$
3	$16 \times 9 = 144$
4	$16 \times 16 = 256$

Extra Practice See 1–4 on page 397.

Quick Check

Check Your Understanding of Lessons 1–4

Multiply. Write each answer in simplest form.

1. $\frac{1}{6} \times \frac{4}{5}$ **2.** $\frac{4}{7} \times \frac{2}{3}$ **3.** $\frac{1}{3} \times \frac{5}{7}$ **4.** $\frac{5}{6} \times \frac{3}{7}$

5. $\frac{3}{4} \times \frac{8}{9}$ **6.** $\frac{5}{6} \times \frac{3}{5}$ **7.** $\frac{12}{13} \times \frac{2}{3}$ **8.** $\frac{4}{5} \times \frac{10}{11}$

Write each product in simplest form.

9. $1\frac{1}{3} \times \frac{5}{6}$ **10.** $\frac{1}{4} \times 1\frac{1}{5}$ **11.** $3\frac{1}{3} \times \frac{2}{5}$ **12.** $2\frac{2}{9} \times 1\frac{3}{5}$

13. $1\frac{5}{8} \times \frac{2}{9}$ **14.** $4 \times 2\frac{2}{11}$ **15.** $2\frac{1}{4} \times 5\frac{1}{2}$ **16.** $2\frac{3}{4} \times 1\frac{3}{11}$

Solve.

17. A recipe for oatmeal cookies makes two and one half dozen cookies. How many dozen cookies will be made if the recipe is tripled?

How did you do?

If you had difficulty with any items in the Quick Check, you can use the following pages for review and extra practice.

California Standards	Items	Review These Pages	Do These Extra Practice Items
Number Sense: **1.0, 2.0, 2.4, 2.5** Algebra and Functions: **1.0** Math Reasoning: **1.1**	1–8	pages 368–370	Set A, page 394
Number Sense: **1.0, 2.0, 2.4, 2.5**	9–16	pages 372–373	Set B, page 394
Number Sense: **1.0, 2.0, 2.4, 2.5** Math Reasoning: **1.0, 2.0, 3.0, 3.2**	17	pages 374–375	1–4, page 397

Test Prep • Cumulative Review

Maintaining the Standards

Choose the letter of the correct answer.

1. Which is the least product?
   - **A** $8 \times \frac{1}{2}$
   - **B** $\frac{1}{2} \times 2\frac{1}{8}$
   - **C** $2 \times \frac{1}{8}$
   - **D** $2\frac{1}{2} \times \frac{1}{8}$

2. Which drawing below shows $\frac{5}{8} \times \frac{1}{2}$?

F 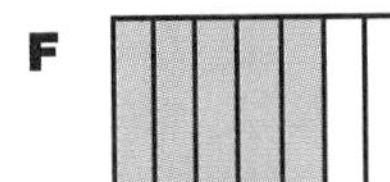

H 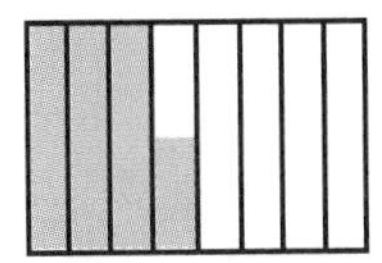

G 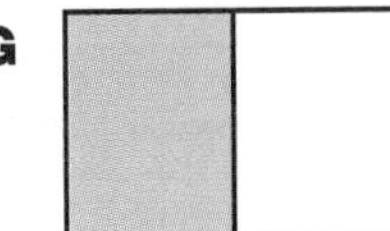

J 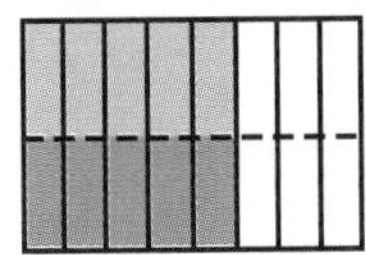

3. Natu cut an apple into s equal slices. He ate 7 slices and had 3 left. Which equation correctly represents the problem?
   - **A** $s - 7 = 3$
   - **B** $s + 7 = 3$
   - **C** $7 - s = 3$
   - **D** $7s = 3$

4. What is the number *ninety-three million, four thousand, twenty-eight* written in standard form?
   - **F** 93,400,280
   - **G** 93,400,028
   - **H** 93,004,028
   - **J** 9,304,028

5. Mr. Barco plans to have 54 students line up in equal rows. The number of students in each row is a prime number.
   How many different arrangements are possible?
   - **A** 4
   - **B** 3
   - **C** 2
   - **D** 1

6. Which estimate is closest to the actual difference?

$$\begin{array}{r} 248.172 \\ -\ 32.099 \\ \hline \end{array}$$

   - **F** 200
   - **G** 216
   - **H** 218
   - **J** 220

7. Use the stem-and-leaf plot below. What is the median score?

Test Scores

Stem	Leaf
7	2 4 5
8	0 5 5 7 9
9	0 0 2 3 7

   - **A** 90
   - **B** 89
   - **C** 87
   - **D** 85

8. Multiply any whole number by a fraction less than 1. Repeat with two more examples.

   Explain How does each product compare to each whole number?

Safe Site

Internet Test Prep
Visit **www.eduplace.com/kids/mhm** for more *Test Prep Practice.*

LESSON 5

Divide by a Unit Fraction

You will learn how to divide by a fraction with a numerator of 1.

Review Vocabulary
unit fraction

Learn About It

Mr. Perez has 6 oranges. He cuts each one in half and offers half an orange each to some students. To how many students can Mr. Perez give each half an orange?

Find how many halves are in 6 oranges.

Divide. $6 \div \frac{1}{2} = n$

Find $6 \div \frac{1}{2}$.

There are 2 halves in 1 whole.
So there are 12 halves in 6 wholes.

$6 \div \frac{1}{2} = 12$

Since $6 \times 2 = 12$, dividing by $\frac{1}{2}$ gives the same result as multiplying by 2.

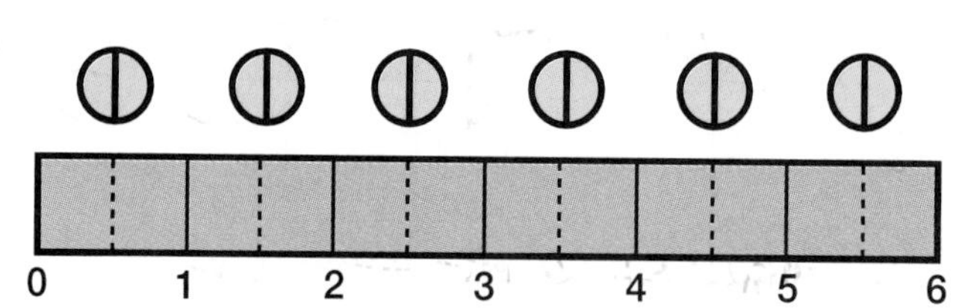

This number strip also shows that $6 \div \frac{1}{2} = 12$.

Solution: Mr. Perez can give half an orange to each of 12 students.

Check your answer using multiplication.

$12 \times \frac{1}{2} = 6$

To divide a number by a **unit fraction** like $\frac{1}{n}$, multiply the number by the denominator, n.

Another Example

What is $1\frac{1}{2}$ divided by $\frac{1}{4}$?

$1\frac{1}{2} \div \frac{1}{4} = \frac{3}{2} \times 4$

$= 6$

The number strip shows that there are 6 fourths in $\frac{3}{2}$.

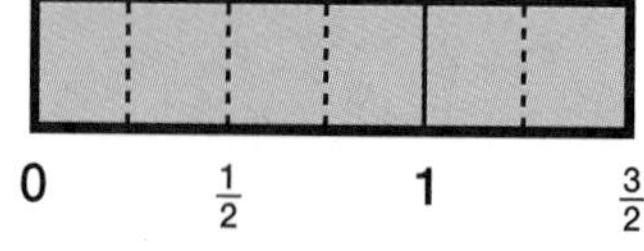

Explain Your Thinking

- Why does dividing by a unit fraction result in a quotient that is always greater than the number divided?
- Use number strips to explain how $10 \div \frac{1}{2}$ and 10×2 are related.

Standards NS 1.0, 2.0, 2.4, 2.5 MR 2.3

Guided Practice

Divide. Use a number strip to show the answer. Check your answer with multiplication.

1. How many thirds are in 2?
2. How many fifths are in 2?

> **Ask Yourself**
> - Did I write the dividend and the divisor in the correct order?
> - Did I multiply by the denominator of the unit fraction?

Divide. Check your answers.

3. $1 \div \frac{1}{4}$ 4. $\frac{2}{3} \div \frac{1}{6}$ 5. $2\frac{2}{5} \div \frac{1}{10}$

Independent Practice

Match each question with a number strip. Then write division sentence to answer the question.

6. What is 3 divided by $\frac{1}{4}$?
7. What is 3 divided by $\frac{1}{2}$?
8. What is 3 divided by $\frac{1}{6}$?

a 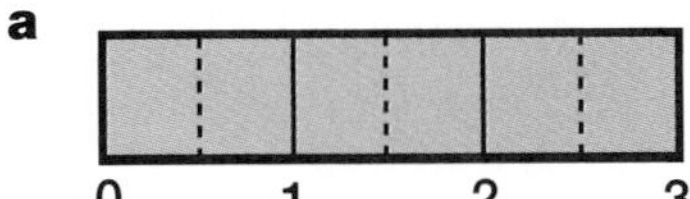

b. 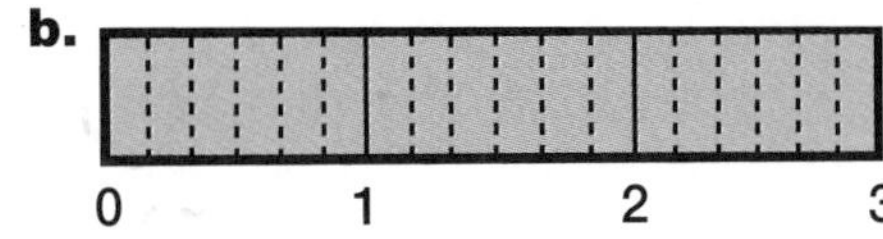

c. 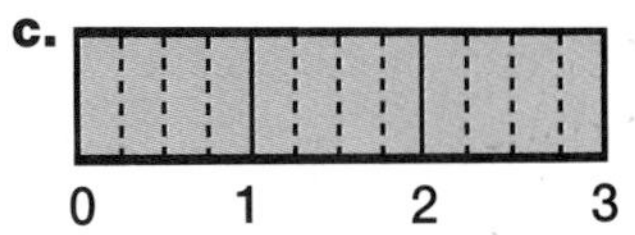

Find each quotient. Check your answers.

9. $4 \div \frac{1}{3}$ 10. $3 \div \frac{1}{8}$ 11. $\frac{4}{5} \div \frac{1}{5}$ 12. $2\frac{3}{4} \div \frac{1}{4}$ 13. $1\frac{1}{4} \div \frac{1}{4}$

Problem Solving • Reasoning

14. If each section of three oranges is about $\frac{1}{12}$ of one orange, how many sections are there?

15. **Analyze** If a dozen oranges produce about 16 oz of juice, how much juice does one orange produce?

16. **Logical Thinking** The U.S. produces more oranges than Spain but fewer than Brazil. China produces more than Spain but fewer than the U.S. List the countries from greatest to least by production of oranges.

17. **Write About It** If freezing rain destroyed $\frac{1}{9}$ of an orange grove and 100 trees were destroyed, how many trees were in the orange grove? Use a drawing to explain your thinking.

Mixed Review • Test Prep

Compare. Write >, <, or = for each ⬬. *(pages 66–68, 162–164, 336–338)*

18. $12 + 3$ ⬬ $3 + 14$ 19. $1.4 - 0.6$ ⬬ $2 - 1.5$ 20. $10 \div 4$ ⬬ $2 + \frac{1}{2}$

21. How many decimal places would you expect to find in the product $7 \times 0.7 \times 0.07$? *(pages 408–413)*

A 4   **B** 3   **C** 1   **D** none

Extra Practice See Set C on page 395.

Divide by a Counting Number

You will learn how to use unit fractions to divide by a counting number.

Learn About It

Bella uses $5\frac{1}{2}$ cups of dry food to feed her cat for a week. How much dry food does Bella use each day if she uses the same amount each day?

Divide. $5\frac{1}{2} \div 7 = n$

Find $5\frac{1}{2} \div 7$.

Step 1 Write the mixed number as a fraction.

$$5\frac{1}{2} = (5 \times \frac{2}{2}) + \frac{1}{2}$$
$$= \frac{10}{2} + \frac{1}{2}$$
$$= \frac{11}{2}$$

Think: $\frac{11}{2}$ means 11 unit fractions of $\frac{1}{2}$.

Step 2 Write an equivalent fraction with a numerator divisible by the counting number.

$$\frac{11}{2} = \frac{11}{2} \times \frac{7}{7} = \frac{77}{14}$$

Think: 11 is not divisible by 7 but 77 is, since 7 is a factor of 77.

Step 3 Divide the number of unit fractions by the counting number.

$$77 \div 7 = 11$$

So $\frac{77}{14} \div 7 = \frac{11}{14}$

and $5\frac{1}{2} \div 7 = \frac{11}{14}$

Check by using multiplication.

$$\frac{11}{14} \times 7 = \frac{77}{14} = 5\frac{7}{14} = 5\frac{1}{2}$$

Solution: Bella feeds her cat $\frac{11}{14}$ cup of dry food each day.

You know that to divide by a unit fraction, $\frac{1}{n}$, you can multiply by n. Similarly, to divide a number by a counting number, n, you can multiply by the unit fraction $\frac{1}{n}$.

$$5\frac{1}{2} \div 7 = \frac{11}{2} \times \frac{1}{7}$$
$$= \frac{11}{14}$$

Other Examples

A. Numerator Is a Multiple of the Counting Number

Find $\frac{9}{10} \div 3$.

$$\frac{9}{10} \div 3 = \frac{9}{10} \times \frac{1}{3}$$
$$= \frac{9}{30}$$
$$= \frac{3}{10}$$

B. Dividend Is a Whole Number

Find $3 \div 6$.

$$3 \div 6 = 3 \times \frac{1}{6}$$
$$= \frac{3}{6}$$
$$= \frac{1}{2}$$

Standards NS **1.0, 2.0, 2.4, 2.5** AF **1.2**

Explain Your Thinking

▶ Why is $3 \div 6$ equal to $\frac{1}{2}$ and not 2?

Guided Practice

Divide by multiplying by a unit fraction. Simplify your answer.

1. $6 \div 8$ **2.** $\frac{1}{2} \div 7$ **3.** $\frac{4}{3} \div 12$ **4.** $\frac{3}{4} \div 10$

Ask Yourself

- Did I multiply by the correct unit fraction?
- Did I write my answer in simplest form?

Independent Practice

Divide by multiplying by a unit fraction. Simplify your answer.

5. $\frac{3}{2} \div 7$ **6.** $\frac{7}{3} \div 21$ **7.** $\frac{8}{3} \div 2$ **8.** $7 \div 8$ **9.** $15 \div 18$

10. $\frac{4}{3} \div 3$ **11.** $\frac{4}{3} \div 4$ **12.** $9 \div 15$ **13.** $\frac{4}{7} \div 2$ **14.** $\frac{5}{8} \div 15$

Problem Solving • Reasoning

15. A recipe calls for 6 cups of oatmeal to make 24 dog biscuits. How much oatmeal is in one dog biscuit?

16. **Logical Thinking** Yesterday, Joy walked her dog three times for a total of 55 minutes. She walked the dog for 15 minutes in the morning and for a half-hour in the afternoon. If she started the evening walk at 7:00 P.M., what time did she get home?

17. **Write About It** A bag of cat food contains 35 cups of food. Each day, a pet store uses 3 cups of food. How many days will one bag of cat food last? Explain your answer.

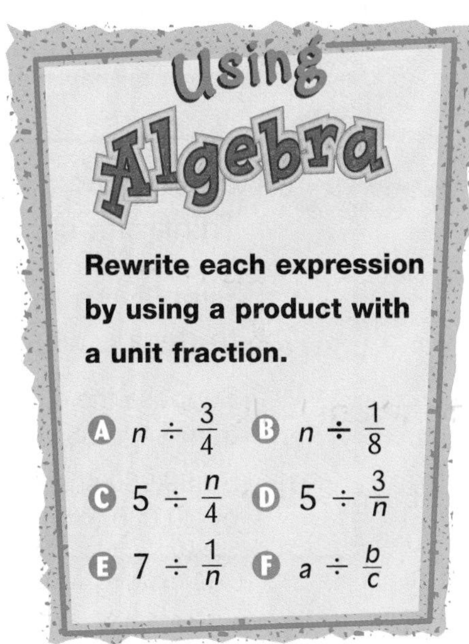

Mixed Review • Test Prep

Add or subtract. *(pages 52–55)*

18. 1,066 + 1,017 **19.** 6,239 − 726 **20.** 308 + 245 **21.** 5,401 − 900

22 What is the prime factorization of 45? *(pages 300–301)*

A $4 \times 10 + 5 \times 1$ **C** 5×9

B $40 + 5$ **D** $3 \times 3 \times 5$

Extra Practice See Set D on page 395.

Problem-Solving Strategy: Solve a Simpler Problem

You will learn how to solve a problem by solving a simpler problem first.

Simplifying the facts can help you solve a problem.

Problem The value of a company's stock increased from $\$4\frac{7}{8}$ to $\$5\frac{1}{16}$ per share in one day. There are 80,000 shares of stock in the company altogether. By how much did the value of the company increase?

Understand

What is the question?
What is the increase in the value of the company?

What do you know?
- Each share increased from $\$4\frac{7}{8}$ to $\$5\frac{1}{16}$.
- There are 80,000 shares.

Plan

How can you find the answer?
Think of a simpler problem.

Simplifying the numbers makes it easier to decide what operations to use.

Suppose the share value increased from \$4 to \$5. Then each share increased by \$1.

So 80,000 shares increased the value of the company by 80,000 × \$1, or \$80,000.

Solve

The actual increase was $\$5\frac{1}{16} - \$4\frac{7}{8}$.

$$5\frac{1}{16} - 4\frac{7}{8} = \frac{3}{16}$$

Now multiply $\frac{3}{16} \times 80{,}000 = 15{,}000$

The company's value increased by \$15,000.

Find the increase in the value of one share. Then multiply by the total number of shares.

Look Back

Look back at the problem.
Is your answer reasonable?

Standards NS 2.0, 2.3 MR 1.0, 1.2, 2.0, 2.2, 3.1, 3.2

Guided Practice

Solve each problem, using the Solve a Simpler Problem strategy.

1. The value of a company's stock decreases by $15,000. If each share decreased in value from $\$8\frac{1}{16}$ to $8.00, how many shares are there in the company?

How is the decrease in the value of one share related to the total decrease in the value in all the shares?

2. David's uncle bought him a $100 bond for his tenth birthday. At the end of each year, the bond's value increases by $\frac{1}{10}$. How much will it be worth on David's twelfth birthday?

How much will the bond increase in value after 1 year? What is the total value of the bond after 1 year?

Choose a Strategy

Solve. Use these or other strategies.

Problem-Solving Strategies

- **Guess and Check**
- **Solve a Simpler Problem**
- **Write an Equation**
- **Find a Pattern**

3. Vic owns 550 shares of a company. There are 77,000 shares altogether. What fraction of the company does Vic own? Simplify the answer.

4. Would you rather collect 50¢ a day for every day in May and June, or get $30 on July 1? Give reasons to support your decision.

5. Jamie had $48.35 in his savings account. He deposited $10 of his allowance and $14.60 that he earned. He withdrew $15 for pocket money. The bank took a service charge of $2.35 from his account. How much does Jamie have in his account?

6. Rosa's grandmother bought her a $100 bond for her tenth birthday. On her eleventh birthday, it was worth $106. By what fraction did the bond's value increase? If this pattern continues, how much would the bond be worth on Rosa's twelfth birthday?

7. Darlene needs to buy some Canadian dollars for a skiing vacation. If an American dollar is worth about $\frac{3}{2}$ of a Canadian dollar, about how many Canadian dollars will she get for $50?

8. A newspaper sells 6 square inches of advertising space for $60. It also sells 9 square inches of space for $75. Which is the better rate? Give examples to explain your thinking.

Extra Practice See 5–8 on page 397.

Divide by a Fraction

You will learn how to use a reciprocal to divide a fraction by a fraction.

New Vocabulary
reciprocal

Learn About It

The **reciprocal** of a fraction is the fraction inverted. For example, the fraction $\frac{4}{3}$ is the reciprocal of $\frac{3}{4}$. If neither a nor b is zero, then the fraction $\frac{b}{a}$ is the reciprocal of $\frac{a}{b}$.

The product of a fraction and its reciprocal is always 1. $\frac{3}{4} \times \frac{4}{3} = \frac{\overset{1}{\cancel{3}} \times \overset{1}{\cancel{4}}}{\underset{1}{\cancel{4}} \times \underset{1}{\cancel{3}}} = 1$ $\quad \frac{a}{b} \times \frac{b}{a} = 1$

Hannah and her family have 3 hours of family videos. If each tape is $\frac{3}{4}$ of an hour long, how many videos do they have?

Find $\mathbf{3 \div \frac{3}{4}}$.

Different Ways to Divide by a Fraction

You can draw a diagram.

Step 1 Draw a number strip to represent the hours. Then divide the strip into fourths.

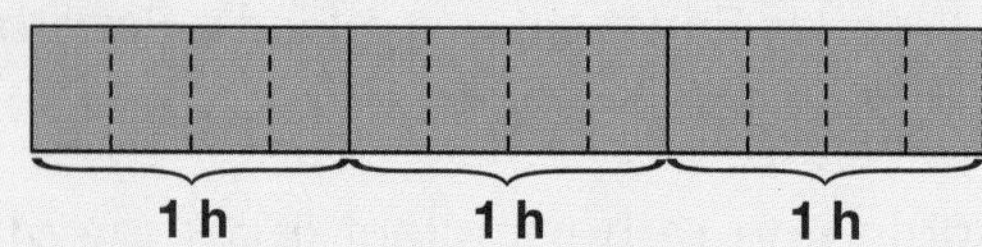

Think: How many fourths are in 3?

$3 \div \frac{1}{4} = 3 \times 4 = 12$

Step 2 Divide the number strip into groups of 3 fourths. Then count the number of groups.

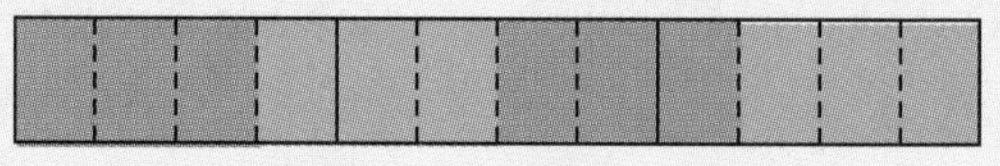

12 fourths ÷ 3 fourths = 4

$12 \div 3 = 4$

You can multiply by the reciprocal.

Step 1 Rewrite as a multiplication problem using the reciprocal of the divisor. Remember to invert to find the reciprocal.

$3 \div \frac{3}{4} = 3 \times \frac{4}{3}$

Step 2 Look for common factors to cancel.

Think: $\frac{3}{3} = 1$ and $\frac{3}{3} \times 4 = 4$

$3 \times \frac{4}{3} = \frac{\overset{1}{\cancel{3}} \times 4}{\underset{1}{\cancel{3}}}$

$= 4$

Check your work.

$4 \times \frac{3}{4} = \frac{\overset{1}{\cancel{4}} \times 3}{\underset{1}{\cancel{4}}} = 3$

Solution: The family has 4 videos.

To divide a number by a fraction, multiply the number by the reciprocal of the divisor.

 Standards NS **1.0, 2.0, 2.4, 2.5**

Another Example

Answer Is a Mixed Number

$$\frac{3}{4} \div \frac{5}{8} = \frac{3}{4} \times \frac{8}{5} = \frac{3 \times 8}{4 \times 5}$$

$$= \frac{3 \times \overset{1}{\cancel{2}} \times \overset{1}{\cancel{2}} \times 2}{\underset{1}{\cancel{2}} \times \underset{1}{\cancel{2}} \times 5} = \frac{6}{5} = 1\frac{1}{5}$$

Explain Your Thinking

- ▶ Why does multiplying by 2 give the same answer as dividing by $\frac{1}{2}$?
- ▶ Why are the reciprocals of $\frac{2}{3}$ and $\frac{4}{6}$ equivalent?

Guided Practice

Ask Yourself

- Did I multiply by the reciprocal of the divisor?

Divide. Multiply by the reciprocal of the divisor. Write answers in simplest form.

1. $\frac{1}{2} \div \frac{7}{12}$ **2.** $1\frac{5}{6} \div \frac{2}{3}$ **3.** $3\frac{3}{8} \div \frac{3}{4}$ **4.** $\frac{5}{12} \div \frac{1}{4}$

Divide. Write answers in simplest form.

5. $\frac{1}{2} \div \frac{3}{4}$ **6.** $\frac{1}{4} \div \frac{2}{3}$ **7.** $\frac{5}{6} \div \frac{5}{12}$ **8.** $\frac{1}{3} \div \frac{1}{4}$ **9.** $\frac{11}{12} \div \frac{3}{8}$

10. $\frac{7}{12} \div \frac{3}{4}$ **11.** $\frac{3}{4} \div \frac{1}{3}$ **12.** $\frac{1}{2} \div \frac{3}{6}$ **13.** $\frac{2}{3} \div \frac{1}{6}$ **14.** $1\frac{1}{8} \div \frac{1}{8}$

15. $\frac{7}{12} \div \frac{1}{12}$ **16.** $\frac{7}{8} \div \frac{1}{2}$ **17.** $\frac{3}{4} \div \frac{3}{5}$ **18.** $2\frac{3}{4} \div \frac{1}{2}$ **19.** $5\frac{1}{5} \div \frac{1}{5}$

Problem Solving • Reasoning

20. Last night in a small town, $\frac{3}{8}$ of the people watched television. If 600 people watched television, how many people live in the town?

21. **Analyze** In one city, $\frac{7}{8}$ of the households have cable television. One-third of those households use the most popular cable company. What fraction of cable users use the most popular cable company?

22. **Estimate** Find a number that, when divided by $\frac{3}{4}$, gives a quotient between $\frac{1}{2}$ and $\frac{2}{3}$.

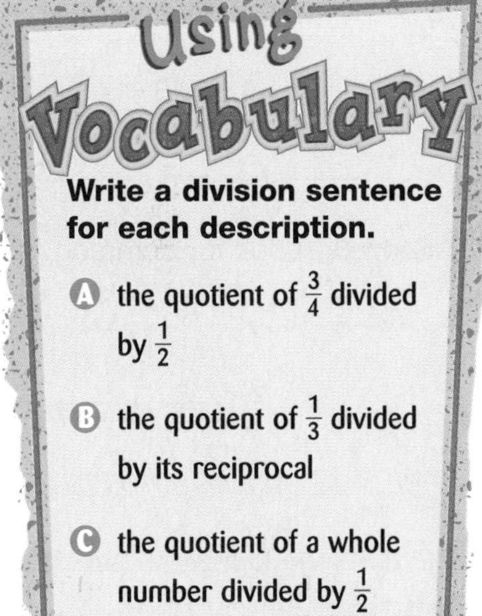

Write a division sentence for each description.

Ⓐ the quotient of $\frac{3}{4}$ divided by $\frac{1}{2}$

Ⓑ the quotient of $\frac{1}{3}$ divided by its reciprocal

Ⓒ the quotient of a whole number divided by $\frac{1}{2}$

Mixed Review • Test Prep

Divide. Write remainders as fractions. *(pages 134–135)*

23. $12 \div 5$ **24.** $27 \div 2$ **25.** $21 \div 9$ **26.** $46 \div 4$ **27.** $34 \div 6$

28 Mario is four years older than his sister Elena. If *a* represents Elena's age, which expression represents Mario's age? *(pages 66–72, 162–164)*

A $a + 4$ **B** $4 - a$ **C** $a - 4$ **D** $a \div 4$

Extra Practice See Set E on page 396.

Divide With Mixed Numbers

You will learn how to solve division problems involving mixed numbers.

Review Vocabulary
mixed number

Learn About It

A snowmobile tank holds $8\frac{1}{2}$ gallons of gas. Marty used $1\frac{1}{4}$ gallons today. What fraction of the gas in the tank did he use?

Think: $\dfrac{1\frac{1}{4} \text{ gal used}}{8\frac{1}{2} \text{ gal total}}$ ← divided by

You can write **mixed numbers** as improper fractions to divide.

Divide. $1\frac{1}{4} \div 8\frac{1}{2} = n$

Find $1\frac{1}{4} \div 8\frac{1}{2}$.

Step 1 Write the mixed numbers as improper fractions.

$$1\frac{1}{4} \div 8\frac{1}{2} = \frac{5}{4} \div \frac{17}{2}$$

Step 2 Rewrite as a multiplication problem using the reciprocal of the divisor.

$$\frac{5}{4} \div \frac{17}{2} = \frac{5}{4} \times \frac{2}{17}$$

Step 3 Look for common factors to cancel.

$$\frac{5}{4} \times \frac{2}{17} = \frac{5 \times 2}{\mathbf{4 \times 17}}$$
$$= \frac{5 \times \cancel{2}^{1}}{2 \times \cancel{2}_{1} \times 17}$$

Step 4 Multiply. Write the answer in simplest form.

$$\frac{5 \times \cancel{2}^{1}}{2 \times \cancel{2}_{1} \times 17} = \frac{5}{34}$$

Check your work.

$$\frac{5}{34} \times 8\frac{1}{2} = \frac{5}{34} \times \frac{17}{2} = 1\frac{1}{4}$$

Solution: Marty used $\frac{5}{34}$ of the gas in the tank.

Other Examples

A. Divide by a Whole Number

$$\frac{3}{4} \div 2 = \frac{3}{4} \div \frac{2}{1}$$
$$= \frac{3}{4} \times \frac{1}{2}$$
$$= \frac{3 \times 1}{4 \times 2}$$
$$= \frac{3}{8}$$

B. Simplify After Multiplying

$$\frac{8}{9} \div 4 = \frac{8}{9} \times \frac{1}{4}$$
$$= \frac{2 \times \cancel{4}^{1}}{9 \times \cancel{4}_{1}}$$
$$= \frac{2}{9}$$

Standards | NS 1.0, 2.0, 2.4, 2.5 | AF 1.0 | MR 2.0

Explain Your Thinking

- When dividing by a fraction less than 1, why is the quotient greater than the dividend?
- When dividing by a fraction greater than 1, why is the quotient less than the dividend?
- Explain how to find the reciprocal of a mixed number.
- What is the related multiplication expression for any number divided by a mixed number?

Guided Practice

Rewrite each expression as a multiplication expression using the reciprocal of the divisor.

1. $\frac{2}{3} \div 4\frac{2}{5}$ **2.** $11 \div 1\frac{1}{2}$ **3.** $8\frac{2}{3} \div 12\frac{1}{2}$

Write each quotient in simplest form.

4. $\frac{1}{4} \div 1\frac{1}{4}$ **5.** $\frac{5}{8} \div 5$ **6.** $1\frac{5}{9} \div \frac{7}{8}$

7. $\frac{4}{7} \div 2$ **8.** $7\frac{1}{3} \div 2\frac{3}{4}$ **9.** $\frac{9}{10} \div 1\frac{4}{5}$

Independent Practice

Rewrite each expression as a multiplication expression using the reciprocal of the divisor.

10. $\frac{3}{4} \div 1\frac{2}{3}$ **11.** $10 \div 3\frac{1}{5}$ **12.** $\frac{7}{4} \div 7\frac{3}{4}$ **13.** $1\frac{1}{5} \div 3\frac{7}{8}$

Write each quotient in simplest form.

14. $\frac{2}{3} \div 1\frac{1}{3}$ **15.** $\frac{3}{5} \div 6$ **16.** $\frac{3}{4} \div 2\frac{1}{2}$ **17.** $\frac{1}{6} \div 2\frac{1}{3}$

18. $\frac{2}{3} \div 2\frac{2}{3}$ **19.** $\frac{4}{5} \div 1\frac{1}{2}$ **20.** $\frac{5}{6} \div 3\frac{1}{3}$ **21.** $\frac{2}{5} \div 4\frac{2}{5}$

22. $\frac{1}{8} \div 1\frac{1}{2}$ **23.** $\frac{5}{6} \div 1\frac{5}{6}$ **24.** $\frac{7}{8} \div 2\frac{1}{2}$ **25.** $\frac{7}{10} \div 1\frac{3}{7}$

26. $6 \div 3\frac{1}{3}$ **27.** $1\frac{1}{4} \div 2\frac{1}{2}$ **28.** $\frac{3}{4} \div 2\frac{3}{8}$ **29.** $7\frac{1}{2} \div 2\frac{5}{8}$

n **Algebra • Expressions** **Rewrite each expression as a fraction in simplest form.**

30. $n \div 2$ **31.** $2 \div n$ **32.** $a \div b$ **33.** $b \div a$

34. $3n \div 3m$ **35.** $6xy \div 3x$ **36.** $\frac{1}{a} \div \frac{1}{a}$ **37.** $5ab \div \frac{a}{2}$

Problem-Solving Application: Use Circle Graphs

Sometimes using a circle graph can be helpful when solving word problems.

Problem The circle graph shows the fraction of 1 fifth-grade class that voted for different foods for a year-end party. If 10 students prefer pizza, how many students are in the class?

Understand

What is the question?
How many students are in the class?

What do you know?

- Ten students chose pizza.
- $\frac{5}{12}$ of the class chose pizza.

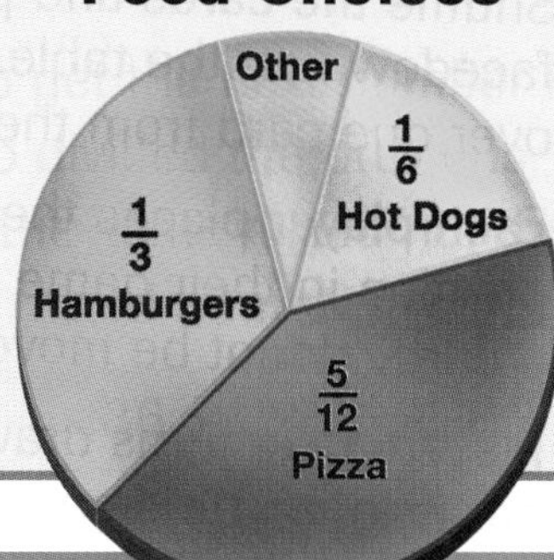

Plan

What can you do to find the answer?
Use n to represent the number of students in the class. Write and solve an equation.

Think:
$\frac{5}{12}$ of the class is 10 students. $\frac{5}{12}$ of what number is 10?

Solve

$$\frac{5}{12} \times n = 10$$

$$n = 10 \div \frac{5}{12}$$

$$n = 24$$

Use an inverse operation to solve the equation.

There are 24 students in the class.

Look Back

Look back at the question. Is your answer reasonable?
How does knowing a circle graph represents 1 whole help you solve the problem?

 Standards NS **2.0, 2.5** AF **1.1** MR **1.0, 2.0, 3.0, 3.1, 3.2**

Remember:
- ▶ Understand
- ▶ Plan
- ▶ Solve
- ▶ Look Back

Left: A woman uses a ballot box to cast her vote in an election.
Right: Using a mechanical voting machine is another way to vote.

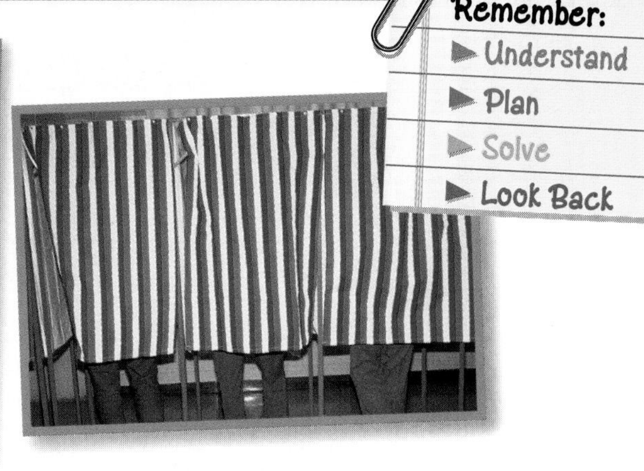

Guided Practice

Solve. Use the information and circle graph from page 390.

1. If $\frac{5}{12}$ of the students are boys and $\frac{2}{5}$ of the boys chose hamburgers, how many boys chose hamburgers?

   Think: How will the fraction $\frac{5}{12}$ help you find the number of boys who chose hamburgers?

2. What fraction of the students chose something other than pizza, hamburgers, or hot dogs?

   Think: What is the sum of all the fractions in the circle graph?

Choose a Strategy

Use these or other strategies. Use the circle graph below.

Problem-Solving Strategies

- **Write an Equation**
- **Work Backward**
- **Draw a Diagram**
- **Use Logical Thinking**

3. The circle graph shows the movie choices of another fifth-grade class. What fraction of the class would like to watch an animated movie?

4. Will any movie choice please more than half of the fifth-grade students? Explain.

5. If 5 students chose an action movie, how many students are in the class?

6. Three fifths of those who chose an animated movie would like to see *Tarzan*. What fraction of the students would like to see *Tarzan*?

7. How many of the students do not want to see *Tarzan*?

Movie Choices

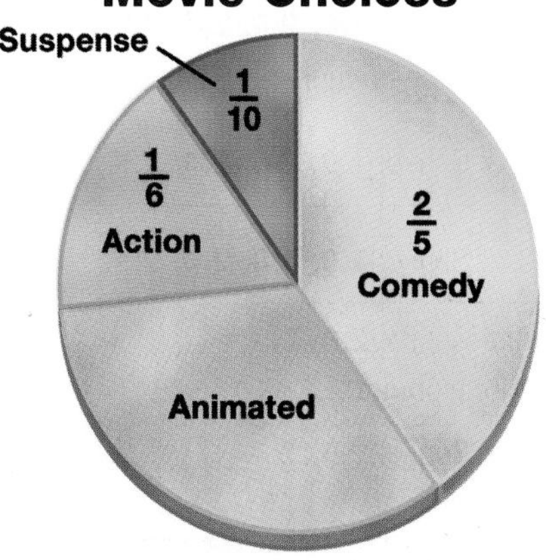

Extra Practice See 9–11 on page 397.

Quick Check

Check Your Understanding of Lessons 5–10

Divide.

1. $3 \div \frac{1}{4}$ **2.** $1\frac{1}{4} \div \frac{1}{4}$ **3.** $\frac{3}{5} \div \frac{1}{5}$ **4.** $\frac{2}{3} \div \frac{1}{6}$

5. $2\frac{1}{2} \div 5$ **6.** $\frac{3}{8} \div 2$ **7.** $\frac{3}{10} \div 8$ **8.** $\frac{6}{7} \div 3$

9. $\frac{1}{3} \div \frac{2}{5}$ **10.** $\frac{3}{4} \div \frac{2}{3}$ **11.** $4\frac{3}{7} \div \frac{1}{2}$ **12.** $2\frac{1}{2} \div \frac{3}{5}$

13. $\frac{2}{3} \div 1\frac{2}{5}$ **14.** $5 \div 2\frac{2}{3}$ **15.** $2\frac{3}{4} \div \frac{4}{5}$ **16.** $\frac{7}{10} \div 2\frac{5}{6}$

Solve.

17. Cara deposited $50.55 from babysitting in her savings account. Cara's father promised to give her $\frac{1}{5}$ of the deposit every 3 months. How much money did Cara's father give her after 6 months?

18. Use the circle graph shown. If 12 students prefer to read mysteries, how many students prefer adventure stories?

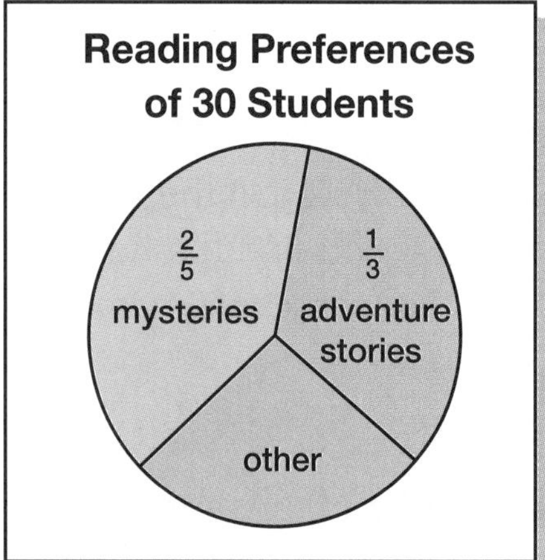

How did you do?

If you had difficulty with any items in the Quick Check, you can use the following pages for review and extra practice.

California Standards	Items	Review These Pages	Do These Extra Practice Items
Number Sense: **1.0, 2.0, 2.4, 2.5** Math Reasoning: **2.3**	1–4	pages 378–379	Set C, page 395
Number Sense: **1.0, 2.0, 2.4, 2.5** Algebra and Functions: **1.2**	5–8	pages 380–381	Set D, page 395
Number Sense: **1.0, 2.0, 2.4, 2.5**	9–12	pages 384–385	Set E, page 396
Number Sense: **1.0, 2.0, 2.4, 2.5**	13–16	pages 386–388	Set F, page 396
Number Sense: **2.0, 2.3** Math Reasoning: **2.2, 3.1, 3.2**	17	pages 382–383	5–8, page 397
Number Sense: **2.0, 2.3** Math Reasoning: **2.2, 3.1, 3.2**	17	pages 390–391	9–11, page 397

Test Prep • Cumulative Review

Maintaining the Standards

Choose the letter of the correct answer. If a correct answer is not here, choose NH.

1 Complete this statement. Dividing by $2\frac{1}{4}$ gives the same results as multiplying by ______.

A $2\frac{1}{4}$ **C** $\frac{9}{4}$

B $4\frac{1}{2}$ **D** $\frac{4}{9}$

2 Simplify $(^{-}4 + {}^{-}5) + (^{+}3 + {}^{+}6)$.

F $^{+}18$ **H** 0

G $^{+}10$ **J** $^{-}6$

3 Once a week for 5 weeks, Lydia measured her plant. She recorded its height in the table below. If the plant continues to grow at this same rate, how tall will it be when Lydia measures it during Week 6?

Week	Height (in.)
1	$\frac{1}{8}$
2	$\frac{3}{8}$
3	$\frac{5}{8}$
4	$\frac{7}{8}$
5	$1\frac{1}{8}$

A 1 in. **C** $1\frac{3}{8}$ in.

B $1\frac{1}{8}$ in. **D** $1\frac{1}{2}$ in.

4 A wall is 205 feet long. How many people with arms outstretched could stand against the wall, if each person's arm span is about $5\frac{1}{3}$ feet?

F 45 **H** 34

G 41 **J** NH

5 Today three friends meet at the pool. Brett goes to the pool every 2 days. Alex goes to the pool every 3 days. Josh goes to the pool every 4 days. In how many days will all three be at the pool again?

A 6 days **C** 10 days

B 8 days **D** 12 days

6 Which type of graph would be best to use to show what part of Alice's monthly allowance was spent on movies?

F histogram

G double bar graph

H line graph

J circle graph

7 Which fraction is equivalent to $\frac{15}{45}$?

A $\frac{5}{9}$ **C** $\frac{1}{3}$

B $\frac{3}{15}$ **D** $\frac{1}{5}$

8 Each side of a 6-sided number cube is marked A, B, or C. Only one side is labeled A. Of the remaining sides, $\frac{3}{5}$ are labeled B and all the other sides are labeled C. Write the fraction of the sides labeled C to all the sides on the cube.

Explain How did you find your answer?

Safe Site

Internet Test Prep
Visit **www.eduplace.com/kids/mhm** for more *Test Prep Practice.*

Extra Practice

Set A *(Lesson 2, pages 368–370)*

Multiply. Simplify each product.

1. $\frac{1}{4} \times \frac{8}{9}$ **2.** $\frac{5}{9} \times \frac{3}{5}$ **3.** $\frac{12}{13} \times \frac{1}{2}$

4. $\frac{7}{8} \times \frac{6}{13}$ **5.** $\frac{5}{6} \times \frac{9}{10}$ **6.** $\frac{4}{7} \times \frac{5}{2}$

7. $\frac{1}{3} \times \frac{9}{11}$ **8.** $\frac{4}{5} \times \frac{5}{11}$ **9.** $\frac{3}{4} \times \frac{2}{3}$

10. $\frac{8}{13} \times \frac{2}{7}$ **11.** $\frac{1}{4} \times \frac{4}{7}$ **12.** $\frac{6}{7} \times \frac{5}{8}$

13. $\frac{2}{3} \times \frac{1}{12}$ **14.** $\frac{1}{5} \times \frac{10}{11}$ **15.** $\frac{3}{10} \times \frac{7}{9}$

16. $\frac{10}{13} \times \frac{1}{10}$ **17.** $\frac{2}{3} \times \frac{5}{7}$ **18.** $\frac{2}{7} \times \frac{7}{12}$

Set B *(Lesson 3, pages 372–373)*

Write each product in simplest form.

1. $1\frac{4}{5} \times \frac{5}{6}$ **2.** $\frac{1}{3} \times 2\frac{3}{9}$ **3.** $3\frac{1}{4} \times \frac{2}{9}$

4. $\frac{4}{9} \times 1\frac{3}{4}$ **5.** $1\frac{1}{8} \times \frac{4}{7}$ **6.** $3\frac{2}{5} \times \frac{5}{7}$

7. $2\frac{7}{8} \times 1$ **8.** $4 \times 6\frac{1}{9}$ **9.** $10\frac{2}{3} \times 3\frac{6}{7}$

10. $2\frac{1}{6} \times \frac{8}{9}$ **11.** $1\frac{12}{13} \times \frac{1}{2}$ **12.** $2\frac{3}{7} \times \frac{5}{9}$

13. $3\frac{3}{8} \times \frac{7}{9}$ **14.** $\frac{3}{4} \times 4\frac{3}{5}$ **15.** $5\frac{1}{5} \times 2\frac{5}{8}$

16. $7\frac{1}{2} \times 1\frac{3}{8}$ **17.** $1\frac{3}{5} \times 2$ **18.** $2\frac{1}{7} \times \frac{7}{15}$

Extra Practice

Set C *(Lesson 5, pages 378–379)*

Divide.

1. $1 \div \frac{1}{5}$ **2.** $2 \div \frac{1}{5}$ **3.** $3 \div \frac{1}{5}$

4. $4 \div \frac{1}{5}$ **5.** $5 \div \frac{1}{5}$ **6.** $1\frac{1}{5} \div \frac{1}{5}$

7. $2\frac{4}{5} \div \frac{1}{5}$ **8.** $1\frac{3}{5} \div \frac{1}{5}$ **9.** $2\frac{1}{5} \div \frac{1}{5}$

10. $3\frac{1}{5} \div \frac{1}{5}$ **11.** $1 \div \frac{1}{8}$ **12.** $3 \div \frac{1}{4}$

13. $2 \div \frac{1}{6}$ **14.** $1 \div \frac{1}{10}$ **15.** $10 \div \frac{1}{10}$

16. $1\frac{1}{2} \div \frac{1}{3}$ **17.** $2\frac{1}{4} \div \frac{1}{2}$ **18.** $3\frac{2}{3} \div \frac{1}{3}$

Set D *(Lesson 6, pages 380–381)*

Divide by multiplying by a unit fraction. Simplify your answer.

1. $\frac{1}{3} \div 9$ **2.** $\frac{2}{5} \div 10$ **3.** $\frac{2}{3} \div 4$

4. $\frac{2}{7} \div 14$ **5.** $\frac{5}{7} \div 15$ **6.** $\frac{4}{3} \div 4$

7. $\frac{3}{4} \div 27$ **8.** $\frac{3}{2} \div 16$ **9.** $\frac{3}{5} \div 5$

10. $\frac{3}{7} \div 21$ **11.** $\frac{5}{6} \div 100$ **12.** $\frac{2}{7} \div 8$

13. $\frac{2}{3} \div 6$ **14.** $\frac{3}{15} \div 5$ **15.** $\frac{6}{11} \div 66$

16. $\frac{11}{10} \div 11$ **17.** $\frac{8}{9} \div 32$ **18.** $\frac{5}{6} \div 3$

19. $\frac{3}{8} \div 72$ **20.** $\frac{4}{5} \div 20$ **21.** $\frac{2}{7} \div 4$

Extra Practice

Set E (Lesson 8, pages 384–385)

Divide. Use the reciprocal of the divisor.

1. $\frac{1}{3} \div \frac{7}{12}$ **2.** $\frac{1}{2} \div \frac{1}{8}$ **3.** $\frac{4}{7} \div \frac{4}{9}$

4. $\frac{1}{6} \div \frac{2}{11}$ **5.** $\frac{8}{9} \div \frac{2}{3}$ **6.** $\frac{1}{44} \div \frac{5}{12}$

7. $\frac{7}{8} \div \frac{3}{4}$ **8.** $\frac{3}{5} \div \frac{9}{10}$ **9.** $\frac{5}{6} \div \frac{11}{12}$

10. $1\frac{1}{4} \div \frac{1}{2}$ **11.** $\frac{3}{7} \div \frac{9}{11}$ **12.** $\frac{7}{10} \div \frac{4}{5}$

13. $\frac{1}{5} \div \frac{3}{10}$ **14.** $\frac{2}{3} \div \frac{5}{8}$ **15.** $\frac{5}{7} \div \frac{5}{14}$

16. $\frac{2}{7} \div \frac{4}{11}$ **17.** $\frac{3}{8} \div \frac{3}{12}$ **18.** $\frac{9}{10} \div \frac{2}{5}$

19. $\frac{3}{9} \div \frac{6}{7}$ **20.** $\frac{2}{3} \div \frac{4}{7}$ **21.** $\frac{3}{4} \div \frac{5}{8}$

Set F (Lesson 9, pages 386–388)

Divide. Write each quotient in simplest form.

1. $\frac{2}{5} \div 1\frac{1}{5}$ **2.** $\frac{2}{3} \div 6$ **3.** $\frac{3}{8} \div 2\frac{1}{4}$

4. $\frac{1}{2} \div 5$ **5.** $\frac{3}{4} \div 2\frac{5}{8}$ **6.** $\frac{5}{6} \div 1\frac{7}{9}$

7. $\frac{5}{9} \div 3\frac{1}{3}$ **8.** $\frac{5}{8} \div 2\frac{3}{4}$ **9.** $\frac{3}{5} \div 9$

10. $\frac{1}{8} \div 1\frac{3}{4}$ **11.** $\frac{1}{6} \div 1\frac{1}{3}$ **12.** $\frac{7}{8} \div 2\frac{1}{4}$

13. $\frac{9}{10} \div 3\frac{1}{5}$ **14.** $\frac{4}{5} \div 1\frac{2}{3}$ **15.** $8 \div 1\frac{5}{6}$

16. $1\frac{3}{4} \div 1\frac{3}{8}$ **17.** $\frac{2}{5} \div 1\frac{3}{5}$ **18.** $4 \div 2\frac{1}{4}$

19. $5 \div 2\frac{1}{2}$ **20.** $11 \div 3\frac{2}{3}$ **21.** $1\frac{1}{8} \div 1\frac{2}{7}$

Extra Practice • Problem Solving

Solve. *(Lesson 4, pages 374–375)*

1. Tara has $10\frac{1}{4}$ ounces of yarn. The sweater she plans to knit requires $8\frac{1}{2}$ ounces. How much yarn will she have left over?

2. A recipe for fruit salad makes $8\frac{1}{2}$ cups. If Dan doubles the recipe, how many cups of fruit salad will he make?

3. In a carton of 12 eggs, $\frac{3}{4}$ are brown. Helena buys $\frac{2}{3}$ of the brown eggs. What fraction of the carton did she buy? How many eggs is this?

4. Sonia walked $\frac{3}{4}$ mile to her friend's house. Later she walked $\frac{5}{8}$ mile to the store. Which distance is longer? How far did she walk in all?

Solve. *(Lesson 7, pages 382–383)*

5. How many $5\frac{1}{2}$-inch pieces can be cut from a length of ribbon that is 1 yard $\frac{2}{9}$ inches long?

6. Find a number that, when divided by $\frac{2}{3}$, gives a quotient between $\frac{1}{4}$ and $\frac{3}{4}$.

7. Clara spent $8.23 on cheese and grapes for a party. She bought 3 times as many pounds of grapes as cheese. A pound of cheese costs $5.98. A pound of grapes costs $0.75. How many pounds of cheese and grapes did she buy?

8. A gas tank on a truck can hold 26.4 gallons of gas. If the tank is half full, how much gas is in the tank? How much gas is in the tank if it is $\frac{1}{4}$ full? $\frac{3}{4}$ full? Explain how you found your answers.

Solve. *(Lesson 10, pages 390–391)*

Use the circle graph for Problems 9–11.

Diana made this circle graph to show the number of hours she spends on various activities each day.

DAILY ACTIVITIES

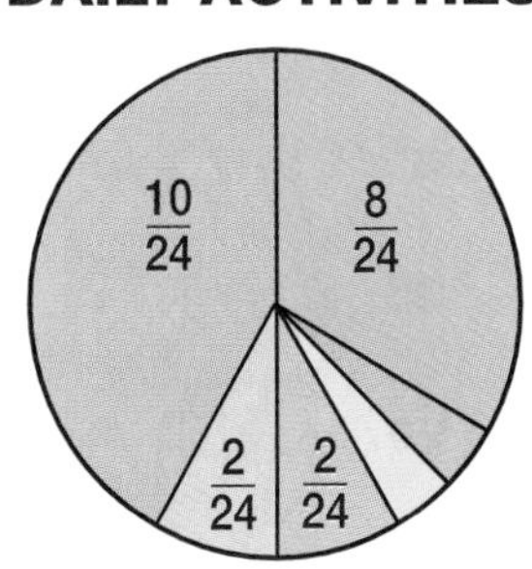

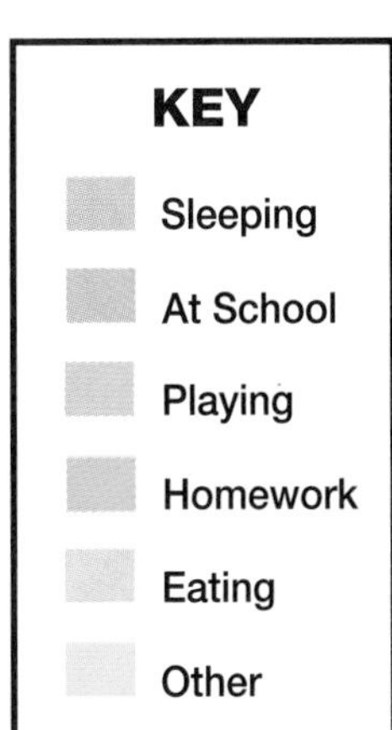

9. What fraction of Diana's day is spent sleeping? How many hours is that?

10. How many hours a day is Diana awake?

11. Which three activities take up half of Diana's day?

Chapter Review

Reviewing Vocabulary

Write *always, sometimes,* or *never* for each statement. Give an example to support your answer.

1. When two fractions less than 1 are multipled, the product is less than 1.
2. An improper fraction is a fraction in which the denominator is greater than or equal to the numerator.
3. When a whole number is divided by a fraction, the result is greater than the whole number.
4. When any whole number is divided by its reciprocal, the result is 1.

Match each word with a definition.

5. reciprocals
6. mixed number
7. improper fractions

a. fractions in which the numerators are greater than or equal to the denominators

b. two fractions whose product is 1

c. the sum of a counting number and a fraction

Reviewing Concepts and Skills

Multiply. Write each product in simplest form. *(pages 368–373)*

8. $\frac{1}{2} \times \frac{2}{5}$ **9.** $\frac{1}{4} \times \frac{7}{8}$ **10.** $\frac{5}{12} \times \frac{3}{10}$ **11.** $\frac{5}{6} \times \frac{12}{15}$

12. $2\frac{3}{4} \times \frac{2}{9}$ **13.** $2\frac{4}{5} \times 6$ **14.** $2\frac{7}{8} \times 1$ **15.** $4 \times 6\frac{1}{9}$

16. $10\frac{2}{3} \times 3\frac{6}{7}$ **17.** $4\frac{1}{6} \times \frac{1}{2}$ **18.** $3\frac{3}{7} \times \frac{7}{10}$ **19.** $4\frac{4}{5} \times 2\frac{3}{4}$

20. $2\frac{1}{7} \times 2\frac{3}{5}$ **21.** $3\frac{1}{8} \times 3\frac{2}{10}$ **22.** $1\frac{5}{16} \times 3\frac{1}{7}$ **23.** $4\frac{1}{5} \times \frac{10}{11}$

Divide. Use the reciprocal of the divisor. *(pages 380–388)*

24. $\frac{1}{4} \div \frac{5}{6}$ **25.** $\frac{1}{3} \div \frac{2}{9}$ **26.** $\frac{7}{12} \div \frac{2}{3}$ **27.** $\frac{1}{5} \div \frac{3}{10}$

28. $\frac{7}{8} \div \frac{3}{4}$ **29.** $\frac{1}{6} \div \frac{2}{3}$ **30.** $\frac{3}{4} \div 1\frac{1}{4}$ **31.** $\frac{3}{8} \div 8$

32. $\frac{4}{7} \div 2\frac{1}{7}$ **33.** $\frac{1}{3} \div 7$ **34.** $\frac{4}{5} \div 2\frac{3}{10}$ **35.** $\frac{1}{9} \div 1\frac{2}{3}$

36. $\frac{3}{5} \div \frac{12}{15}$ **37.** $6 \div 2\frac{1}{6}$ **38.** $7 \div 3\frac{1}{3}$ **39.** $15 \div 4\frac{1}{5}$

Write the reciprocal of each number. *(pages 384–385)*

40. $\frac{1}{6}$ **41.** $\frac{2}{3}$ **42.** $\frac{7}{2}$ **43.** $\frac{11}{5}$ **44.** $\frac{9}{4}$ **45.** 5

Write yes or no. Which of the following numbers are improper fractions? Explain how you know. *(pages 386–388)*

46. $\frac{7}{12}$ **47.** $\frac{12}{7}$ **48.** $\frac{7}{2}$ **49.** $\frac{2}{7}$ **50.** $\frac{7}{1}$ **51.** $\frac{2}{7}$

Solve. *(pages 374–375, 382–383, 390–391)*

52. Rita works 2 shifts every week. Each shift lasts $4\frac{1}{2}$ hours. How many hours does she work in one week?

53. Brad has $2\frac{1}{4}$ rolls of tape and needs $\frac{3}{4}$ of a roll to tape each hockey stick. How many hockey sticks can he tape?

54. It takes $3\frac{3}{4}$ cups of flour to make 12 dinner rolls. How many cups of flour would you need to make 18 dinner rolls?

Use the circle graph at the right.

55. What fraction of the students in the survey chose hockey as the favorite sport?

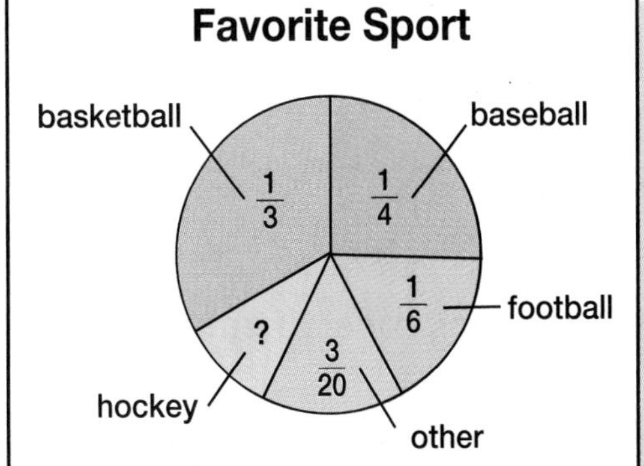

Brain Teasers Math Reasoning

What Number Am I?

My denominator is 3.

My numerator is an odd number.

I am greater than 7 and less than 8.

Number Puzzle

Put the digits 1, 2, 3, and 4 in the boxes so that the result is 6.

$$\frac{\square}{\square} \div \frac{\square}{\square} = 6$$

Safe Site

Internet Brain Teasers

Visit **www.eduplace.com/kids/mhm** for more *Brain Teasers.*

Chapter Test

Write each product in simplest form.

1. $\frac{1}{3} \times \frac{3}{7}$

2. $\frac{4}{9} \times \frac{3}{4}$

3. $\frac{1}{2} \times \frac{3}{5}$

4. $\frac{5}{6} \times \frac{9}{10}$

5. $2\frac{5}{6} \times \frac{8}{9}$

6. $2\frac{1}{2} \times \frac{4}{5}$

7. $4\frac{1}{3} \times \frac{3}{5}$

8. $4\frac{1}{6} \times \frac{4}{5}$

9. $7 \times \frac{3}{8}$

10. $6 \times \frac{2}{3}$

11. $5 \times \frac{3}{4}$

12. $2 \times \frac{4}{7}$

13. $2\frac{3}{5} \times 4\frac{1}{2}$

14. $1\frac{2}{3} \times 3$

15. $3\frac{1}{3} \times \frac{1}{10}$

16. $4\frac{6}{7} \times 6$

17. $5\frac{2}{3} \times 4\frac{1}{2}$

18. $3\frac{3}{5} \times 2\frac{1}{4}$

19. $3\frac{1}{6} \times 1\frac{6}{11}$

20. $2\frac{3}{4} \times 2\frac{3}{7}$

21. $3\frac{1}{2} \times \frac{2}{7}$

Write the reciprocal of each number.

22. $\frac{1}{3}$

23. $\frac{4}{5}$

24. $\frac{13}{6}$

25. 8

Divide, using the reciprocal of the divisor. Write each quotient in simplest form.

26. $8 \div \frac{1}{3}$

27. $16 \div \frac{3}{4}$

28. $9 \div \frac{2}{3}$

29. $30 \div \frac{5}{6}$

30. $21 \div \frac{7}{9}$

31. $8 \div \frac{2}{3}$

32. $\frac{1}{2} \div \frac{1}{4}$

33. $\frac{3}{5} \div \frac{2}{7}$

34. $\frac{2}{7} \div \frac{6}{11}$

35. $\frac{1}{4} \div \frac{1}{6}$

36. $2\frac{1}{5} \div \frac{7}{10}$

37. $1\frac{2}{3} \div \frac{4}{9}$

38. $\frac{1}{5} \div 2\frac{1}{5}$

39. $\frac{2}{3} \div 1\frac{1}{9}$

40. $4 \div 1\frac{3}{8}$

41. $2\frac{3}{4} \div 2\frac{5}{8}$

42. $\frac{3}{10} \div 1\frac{3}{10}$

43. $2 \div 1\frac{1}{2}$

44. $6 \div 3\frac{1}{3}$

45. $14 \div 3\frac{1}{2}$

46. $\frac{3}{4} \div 2\frac{1}{2}$

Solve.

47. Find three pairs of fractions that each have a product of $\frac{1}{4}$.

48. Carl boiled $\frac{3}{4}$ dozen eggs. How many eggs did he boil? Carl then used $\frac{2}{3}$ of the hard-boiled eggs to make sandwiches. How many eggs did he use?

49. In a display case, $\frac{3}{4}$ of the trophies are baseball trophies. If $\frac{1}{4}$ of the baseball trophies are silver and none of the other trophies is silver, what fraction of all the trophies are silver?

50. Look at the circle graph. What fraction of the students have a dog as a pet?

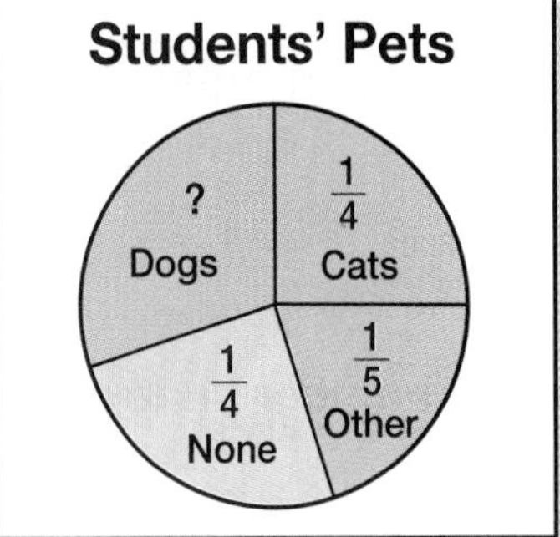

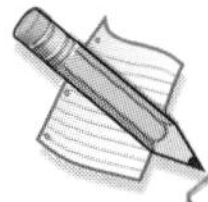

Write About It

Solve each problem. Use correct math vocabulary to explain your thinking.

1. Jason drew the diagram at right to show the following.

$$\frac{3}{4} \times \frac{5}{6} = \frac{3 \times 5}{4 \times 6} = \frac{15}{24}$$

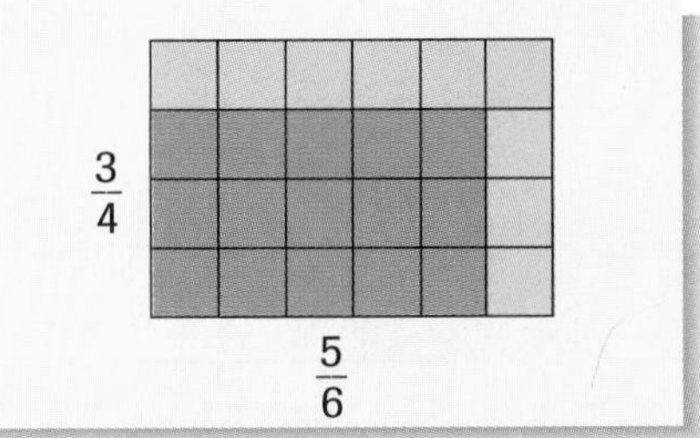

a. How is 3×5 shown in the diagram of $\frac{3}{4} \times \frac{5}{6}$?

b. How is 4×6 shown in the diagram of $\frac{3}{4} \times \frac{5}{6}$?

c. How can the product be written in simplest form?

2. Explain how multiplying by $\frac{1}{5}$ is the same as dividing by 5.

3. Use an example to help you explain.

a. When a fraction less than 1 is multiplied by a whole number, the product is less than the whole number. Why?

b. When dividing a whole number or fraction by a fraction, you can multiply by the reciprocal of the divisor. Why?

Another Look

You can use models to describe expressions and number sentences.

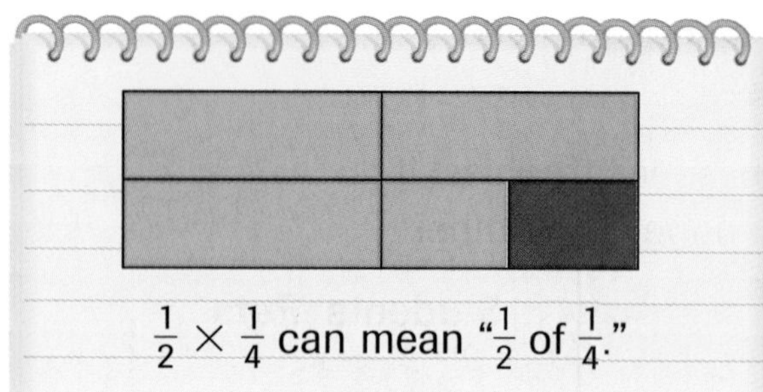

$\frac{1}{2} \times \frac{1}{4}$ can mean "$\frac{1}{2}$ of $\frac{1}{4}$."

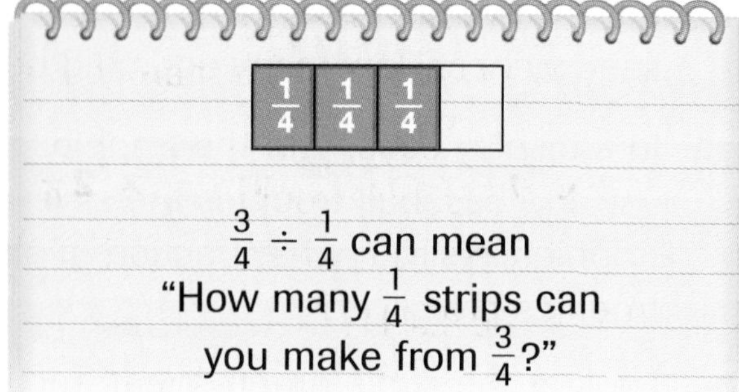

$\frac{3}{4} \div \frac{1}{4}$ can mean "How many $\frac{1}{4}$ strips can you make from $\frac{3}{4}$?"

Match each number sentence to the model that represents it.

1. $\frac{1}{3} \div 2 = \frac{1}{6}$ **2.** $2 \div \frac{1}{5} = 10$ **3.** $3 \times \frac{1}{8} = \frac{3}{8}$ **4.** $\frac{2}{3} \div \frac{1}{3} = 2$

a.

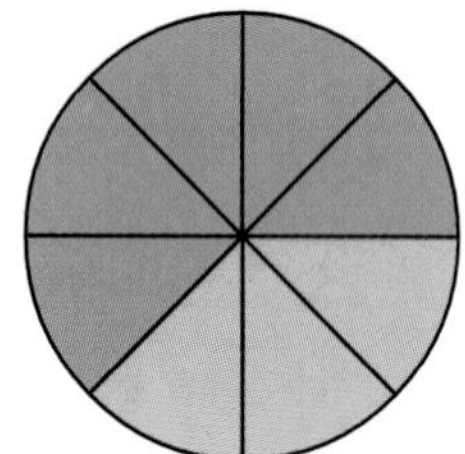

b.

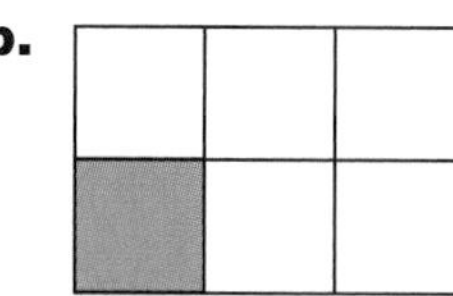

c.

d.

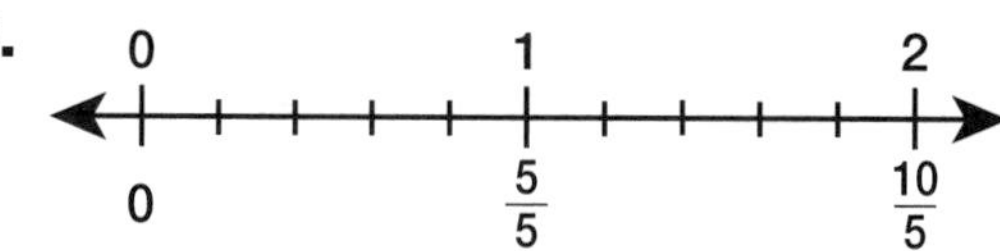

Draw a picture to illustrate each expression. Write each product or quotient.

5. $\frac{1}{2} \times \frac{4}{5}$ **6.** $3\frac{1}{2} \div \frac{1}{2}$ **7.** $4 \times \frac{5}{8}$

8. $3 \div \frac{3}{5}$ **9.** $\frac{1}{3} \times \frac{1}{4}$ **10.** $\frac{3}{4} \div 2$

11. Compare Without calculating, decide which is greater, $\frac{2}{3} \times \frac{3}{4}$ or $\frac{2}{3} \div \frac{3}{4}$. Explain how you know.

12. Write About It Explain the relationship between these two expressions.

$\frac{1}{2} \times \frac{3}{8}$ and $\frac{3}{8} \div 2$

Standards	NS **2.4, 2.5** MR **2.3, 2.4**

Enrichment

Estimating Products

You can estimate the product of any two fractions by rounding the factors to the nearest $\frac{1}{2}$.

Estimate the product of $1\frac{1}{3} \times 2\frac{1}{6}$.

Step 1 Round the first factor.	**Step 2** Round the second factor.	**Step 3** Multiply to estimate the product.
$1\frac{1}{3}$ rounds to $1\frac{1}{2}$.	$2\frac{1}{6}$ rounds to 2	Estimate: $1\frac{1}{2} \times 2 = 3$

Now find the product and compare it to the estimate.

Solution: The actual product $2\frac{8}{9}$ is close to the estimate of 3. The answer is reasonable.

Multiply. Estimate to check that your answer is reasonable.

1. $3\frac{1}{9} \times 2\frac{5}{11}$

2. $2\frac{3}{7} \times 2\frac{1}{4}$

3. $4\frac{7}{8} \times 3\frac{1}{6}$

4. $2\frac{1}{6} \times 4\frac{9}{10}$

5. $7\frac{2}{3} \times 5\frac{1}{5}$

6. $2\frac{1}{4} \times 3\frac{1}{3}$

7. $1\frac{1}{7} \times 2\frac{3}{8}$

8. $3\frac{2}{3} \times 1\frac{1}{6}$

9. $7\frac{1}{5} \times 2\frac{5}{6}$

10. How would you estimate $4 \times \frac{2}{3}$? What would be a good estimate? Find the product and use your estimate to check your work. Did your method of estimating the product give a useful estimate? Explain.

11. How could you use this method for $2\frac{3}{4} \times 1\frac{3}{4}$? $2\frac{1}{6} \times 2\frac{1}{8}$?

Explain Your Thinking

- Do you think this method of estimating would help when dividing fractions?

Standards NS **1.0, 2.0, 2.4, 2.5** MR **2.1**

Multiplication and Division of Decimals

Why Learn About Multiplication and Division of Decimals?

It is important to know how to multiply and divide decimals when you go shopping.

You divide decimals when you find the unit cost of ketchup in different-sized bottles. You multiply a decimal and a whole number when you find the cost of three bottles of ketchup.

This woman and her daughter are buying several plants that have the same price. The salesperson will use the cash register to multiply the price of a plant by the number of plants.

Reviewing Vocabulary

Understanding math language helps you become a successful problem solver. Here are some math vocabulary words you should know.

decimal a number that is written with a decimal point

round to find out how much or how many by expressing a number to the nearest hundredth, tenth, unit, ten, hundred, and so on

estimate a number close to an exact amount that tells about how much or about how many

factor one of two or more numbers that are multiplied to get a product

exponent a number that tells how many times the base is used as a factor

power of 10 10 raised to an exponent—10^2 and 10^3 are powers of ten

expression a statement that may contain a number, a variable, numbers and operation symbols; variables and operation symbols, or numbers, variables, and operation symbols

Reading Words and Symbols

When you read mathematics, sometimes you read only words, sometimes you read words and symbols, and sometimes you read only symbols.

All of these statements represent the same situation.

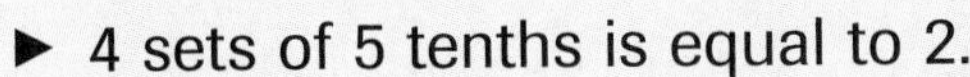

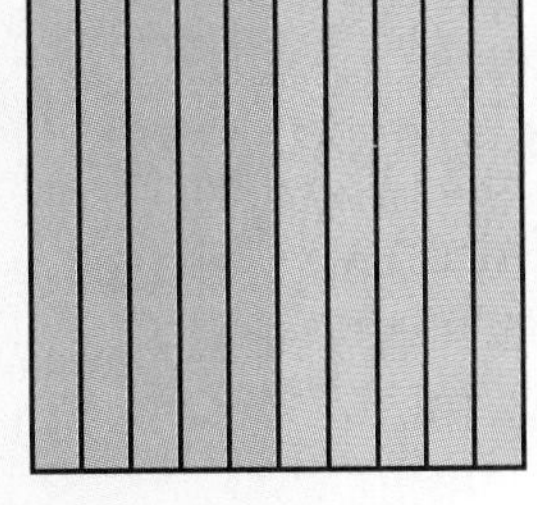

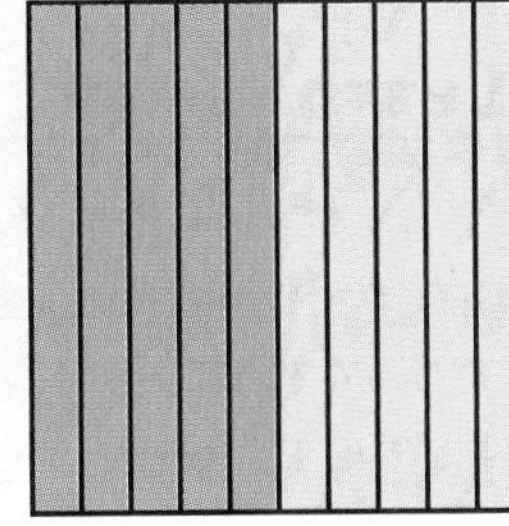

- 4 sets of 5 tenths is equal to 2.
- 5 tenths multiplied by 4 is equal to 2.
- $0.5 \times 4 = 2$
- You can make 4 sets of 5 tenths from 2.
- $2 \div 0.5 = 4$
- When you divide 2 into 4 equal parts, each part equals 5 tenths.
- $2 \div 4 = 0.5$

Try These

1. What fraction of each grid does the shaded part represent? Write the answer in fraction form and in decimal form.

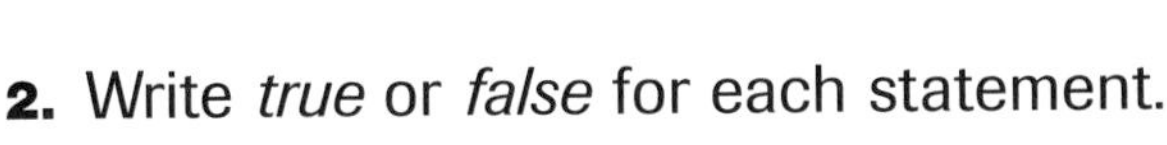

2. Write *true* or *false* for each statement.
   a. Ten times one tenth equals one hundredth.
   b. One tenth of one tenth equals one hundredth.
   c. One tenth divided by ten equals one hundredth.
   d. One hundredth times ten equals one whole.
   e. When the factors are 0.1 and 10, the product is 1.

3. Rewrite each decimal operation using fractions.
   a. 0.5×0.8 b. 0.2×0.03 c. $0.8 \div 0.2$ d. $1 \div 0.01$

LESSON 1

Multiply Whole Numbers and Decimals

You will learn how to find the product of a whole number and a decimal.

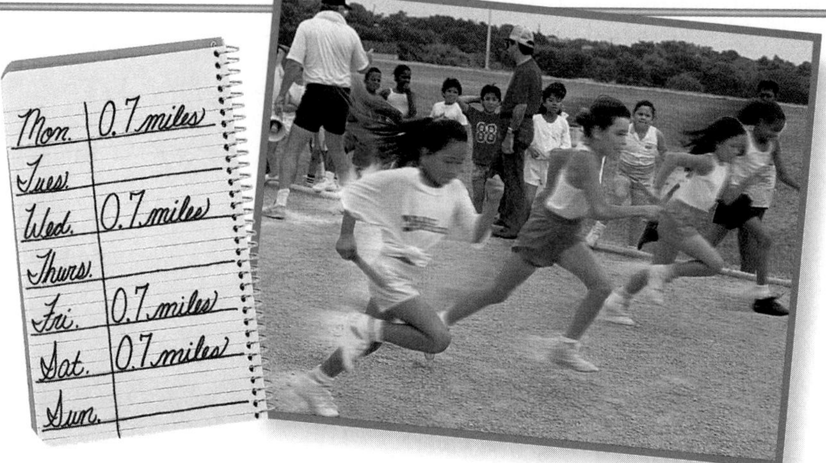

Learn About It

As part of their "Keep Fit" program, students at one school run 0.7 miles a day, 4 days a week. How far does each student run in one week?

Multiply. $\mathbf{4 \times 0.7 = n}$

Different Ways to Multiply Whole Numbers and Decimals

You can write the factors as fractions.

Step 1 Write each factor as a fraction.

$4 \times 0.7 = \frac{4}{1} \times \frac{7}{10}$

Step 2 Multiply.

$\frac{4}{1} \times \frac{7}{10} = \frac{28}{10}$

Step 3 Simplify.

$2\frac{8}{10}$ or 2.8

You can multiply and place the decimal point.

Step 1 Multiply the factors, disregarding the decimal points.

4 × 7 tenths = 28 tenths

Step 2 Place a decimal point in the product. The number of decimal places in the product must equal the total number of decimal places in the factors.

0.7	←	1 decimal place
× 4	←	+ 0 decimal places
2.8	←	1 decimal place

Solution: Each student runs 2.8 miles in one week.

Explain Your Thinking

► When you multiply a number in tenths by a whole number, why do you get an answer in tenths?

Standards NS **1.0, 2.0, 2.1, 2.4, 2.5**

Guided Practice

Find each product.

1. 4 × 0.3 **2.** 8 × 5.9 **3.** 6 × 1.82 **4.** 7 × 0.515

Ask Yourself

- Did I use the correct number of decimal places in the product?

Independent Practice

Write the number of decimal places you expect in each product. Then solve.

5. 9 × 5.622 **6.** 6 × 2.4 **7.** 9.647 × 8 **8.** 3.88 × 2 **9.** 0.135 × 5

Insert a decimal point to make each product correct.

10. 2.056 × 4 = 8224 **11.** 6 × 61.77 = 37062 **12.** 0.215 × 9 = 1935

Multiply.

13. 3 × 3.4 **14.** 9 × 0.18 **15.** 13 × 0.1 **16.** 3 × 31.44 **17.** 8 × 10.8

18. 7 × 7.7 **19.** 4 × 20.5 **20.** 11 × 0.9 **21.** 50.2 × 6 **22.** 9 × 1.23

23. 4 × 8.121 **24.** 7 × 5.291 **25.** 25.43 × 6 **26.** 4.412 × 8 **27.** 23.11 × 5

Problem Solving • Reasoning

28. **Compare** Paul runs 1.25 miles each day, while David runs 2.25 miles each day. How much farther will David run than Paul in 4 days?

29. For exercise, Candace runs around a jogging path 3 times a day. If the path is 1.2 miles long, how far does she run each day?

30. **Analyze** Jan walks 1.5 miles each day. Shirley walks twice as far as Jan. Altogether, how many miles will Jan and Shirley walk in 5 days?

31. **Write About It** Find two numbers that have a product of 7.2 and a sum of 5.8. Explain your thinking.

SPORTS In 1991 Arturo Barrios set a new world record by running 20,000 m in 56 min, 55.6 sec.

If 1,000 m is about 0.62 mi, about how many miles did Barrios run?

Mixed Review • Test Prep

Use an exponent to simplify each expression. *(pages 6–7)*

32. 3 × 3 × 3 **33.** 6 × 6 **34.** 1 × 1 × 1 × 1 × 1 **35.** 10 × 10 × 10

36 If 19 + n = 354, what is n? *(pages 74–75)*

A 335 **B** 345 **C** 363 **D** 373

Extra Practice See Set A on page 440.

LESSON 2

Estimate Products

You will learn how to use rounding to estimate products of decimal factors.

Review
Vocabulary
estimate
round

Learn About It

Emmeline and her family took a trip to Europe. As they drove through France, they saw a sign showing the distance to Paris. If 1 km is about 0.62 mi, **estimate** the distance in miles.

Estimate the product. **328 × 0.62**

Estimate 328 × 0.62.

Step 1 Round each factor.	**Step 2** Multiply the rounded factors, disregarding the decimal points.	**Step 3** Place a decimal point in the estimated product.
328 rounds to 300 × 0.62 rounds to × 0.6	300 × 0.6 1800	300 ⟵ 0 decimal places × 0.6 ⟵ + 1 decimal place 180.0 ⟵ 1 decimal place

Solution: The distance to Paris is about 180 miles.

When you estimate a product, you can **round** each factor to a greater or lesser number depending on whether you want a high or low estimate.

Other Examples

A. Round to Greater Numbers

Estimate 96 × 2.907.

$$\begin{array}{r} 96 \\ \times 2.907 \\ \hline \end{array} \begin{array}{c} \rightarrow \\ \rightarrow \end{array} \begin{array}{r} 100 \\ \times \quad 3 \\ \hline 300 \end{array}$$

Since both factors were rounded to a greater number, the actual product must be less than 300.

B. Round to Greater and Lesser Numbers

Estimate 0.34 × 359.

$$\begin{array}{r} 359 \\ \times 0.34 \\ \hline \end{array} \begin{array}{c} \rightarrow \\ \rightarrow \end{array} \begin{array}{r} 400 \\ \times 0.3 \\ \hline 120.0 \end{array}$$

Since one factor was increased and the other was decreased, it's hard to predict whether the actual product will be more or less than 120.

Explain Your Thinking

- ▶ How does the actual product compare to the estimate when both factors are rounded to lesser numbers?
- ▶ When might you want a high estimate?

Standards NS **1.0, 1.1, 2.0, 2.1** AF **1.0**

Guided Practice

Estimate each product by rounding each factor.

1. 6.572×18

2. 185×0.24

3. 532×1.7

4. 87×3.12

5. 32×0.43

6. 2.5×351

> **Ask Yourself**
> - How do I round each factor?

Independent Practice

Estimate the products by rounding each factor.

7. 0.29×41

8. 8×0.119

9. 12.7×32

10. 209×1.467

11. 6.6×27

12. 2.105×80

13. 3.5×58

14. 25×7.92

Algebra • Expressions **Find a value of *n* to make each statement true. Multiply to check your estimate.**

15. $13 \times n$ is between 55 and 65.

16. $n \times 138$ is between 200 and 250.

17. $n \times 11$ is between 135 and 140.

18. $n \times 25$ is between 40 and 45.

Problem Solving • Reasoning

Use Data **Use the table for Problems 19–21.**

Equivalent Measures	
1 km	0.62 mi
1 kg	2.205 lb
1 L	0.264 gal

19. Emmeline's family saw the auto race in Le Mans, France. One lap is 13.6 km long. Estimate the distance of one lap in miles.

20. At the airport, Emmeline found she had 14 kg of luggage. Estimate the weight of her luggage in pounds.

21. While in France, Emmeline's family used two full tanks of gas. One tank holds 43 L of gas. About how many gallons of gas did they use?

Mixed Review • Test Prep

Compare. Write >, <, or = for each ●. *(pages 8–9, 30–31)*

22. 2×7 ● 3×6

23. 15×3 ● 5×9

24. 1.2×4 ● 2.1×2

25. 13×9 ● 12×10

26 What is the value of *b* in the expression $\frac{7}{b} = 3\frac{1}{2}$? *(pages 318–319)*

A 2 **B** 3 **C** 4 **D** 12

Extra Practice See Set B on page 440.

LESSON 3

Multiply Decimals

You will learn how to find the product of two decimal factors.

Learn About It

Last year a mine produced 0.3 ton of silver. This year the production was only 0.9 times as much as last year. How much will be produced this year?

Multiply. $\mathbf{0.9 \times 0.3 = n}$.

Different Ways to Multiply Decimals

You can write the factors as fractions.

Step 1 Write each factor as a fraction.

$$0.9 \times 0.3 = \frac{9}{10} \times \frac{3}{10}$$

Step 2 Multiply and simplify.

$$\frac{9}{10} \times \frac{3}{10} = \frac{27}{100} = 0.27$$

You can multiply the factors and then place the decimal point.

Step 1 Multiply the factors, disregarding the decimal points.

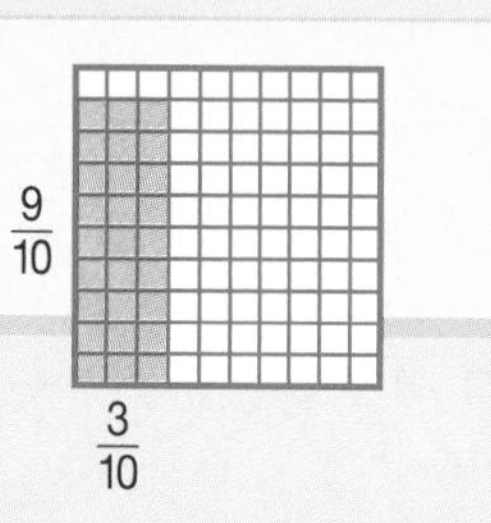


```
   3 tenths
 × 9 tenths
27 hundredths
```

Step 2 Place the decimal point. The number of decimal places in the product must equal the total number of decimal places in the factors.

```
  0.3 ←     1 decimal place
× 0.9 ←   + 1 decimal place
 0.27 ←     2 decimal places
```

Solution: This year the mine will produce 0.27 tons of silver.

Other Examples

A. One Factor in Hundredths

```
  0.71 ←     2 decimal places
×  0.9 ←   + 1 decimal place
 0.639 ←     3 decimal places
```

B. Factors Greater Than 1

```
  1.43 ←  2 decimal places
×  3.2 ←  1 decimal place
   286
  4290
 4.576 ←  3 decimal places
```

Explain Your Thinking

▶ Why would 27 be an unreasonable answer to 0.9 × 0.3?

▶ Why is it important to count the correct number of decimal places?

Standards NS **1.0, 2.0, 2.1, 2.4, 2.5** MR **1.0**

Guided Practice

Ask Yourself

- Did I count the number of decimal places in the product correctly?

Multiply.

1. 2 × 0.46 **2.** 0.6 × 0.5 **3.** 0.6 × 0.4

4. 0.8 × 0.34 **5.** 4.28 × 1.2 **6.** 0.23 × 0.7

Independent Practice

Find each product.

7. 0.5 × 0.5 **8.** 0.9 × 0.2 **9.** 0.4 × 0.7 **10.** 0.7 × 0.3

11. 0.7 × 0.5 **12.** 0.21 × 0.9 **13.** 0.94 × 0.2 **14.** 4.2 × 0.1

15. 0.8 × 0.02 **16.** 0.68 × 0.5 **17.** 0.4 × 0.44 **18.** 0.8 × 0.62

19. 0.92 × 0.3 **20.** 8.34 × 4.7 **21.** 12.3 × 5.4 **22.** 1.66 × 2.2

Problem Solving • Reasoning

Use Data **Use the table for Problems 24–26.**

Precious Metal Values

Precious Metal	Price (1 oz)
gold	$300.00
silver	$5.25
platinum	$500.00

23. The term 14-karat gold means that every ounce consists of 0.58 oz of pure gold and 0.42 oz of other metals. How many ounces of pure gold would there be in a 14-karat gold bracelet that weighs 7.5 oz?

24. **Compare** Which is worth more?

a. 50 oz of silver or 0.6 oz of platinum

b. 95 oz of silver or 1 oz of platinum

c. 60 oz of silver or 1 oz of gold

d. 0.5 oz of platinum or 75 oz of gold

25. The table shows the cost of 1 oz of each precious metal. How much would it cost to buy 3.8 oz of silver?

26. **Write About It** How many ounces of gold could be traded for 400 oz of silver? Explain how you know.

Mixed Review • Test Prep

Write each number in word form. *(pages 4–5, 14–15)*

27. 1,054 **28.** 3,100,049 **29.** 20,065 **30.** 815,022

31 Tickets cost $2.00 for children and $4.00 for adults. If 80 tickets were sold, which amount could not represent the ticket sales? *(pages 326–327)*

A $212 **B** $236 **C** $314 **D** $330

Extra Practice See Set C on page 440.

LESSON 4

Zeros in the Product

You will learn why you sometimes need to write zeros in the products of decimal factors.

Learn About It

Sometimes you need to write one or more zeros in the product before you can place the decimal point.

The fat content of a fruit bar is $\frac{3}{100}$ or 0.03. How much fat would a 0.2-kg fruit bar contain?

Multiply. $\mathbf{0.03 \times 0.2 = n}$

Find 0.03 × 0.2.

Step 1 Multiply the factors, disregarding the decimal points.

$$\begin{array}{r} 0.2 \\ \times\ 0.03 \\ \hline 6 \end{array}$$

Step 2 Count the number of decimal places needed for the product.

0.2 ←	1	decimal place
× 0.03 ←	+ 2	decimal places
0.006 ←	3	decimal places

Step 3 Write as many zeros as you need to place the decimal point correctly.

$$\begin{array}{r} 0.2 \\ \times\ 0.03 \\ \hline 0.006 \end{array}$$

Solution: A 0.2 kg fruit bar would contain 0.006 kg of fat.

Other Examples

A. Tenths and Hundredths as Factors

0.17 ←	2	decimal places
× 0.5 ←	+ 1	decimal place
0.085 ←	3	decimal places

B. Thousandths as a Factor

0.001 ←	3	decimal places
× 9 ←	+ 0	decimal places
0.009 ←	3	decimal places

Explain Your Thinking

► Why is it sometimes necessary to write zeros in a product?

Guided Practice

Multiply. Write as many zeros as you need to place the decimal point correctly.

1. $\begin{array}{r} 0.1 \\ \times\ 0.7 \\ \hline \end{array}$ **2.** $\begin{array}{r} 0.04 \\ \times\ \ 2 \\ \hline \end{array}$ **3.** $\begin{array}{r} 0.34 \\ \times\ 0.1 \\ \hline \end{array}$

4. 0.06 × 1.3 **5.** 0.3 × 0.02 **6.** 0.004 × 3

Ask Yourself

- Did I multiply the factors as if they were whole numbers?
- Did I write the correct number of zeros?

Independent Practice

Multiply.

7. 3×0.3 **8.** 0.3×0.3 **9.** 0.03×0.3 **10.** 0.03×0.03 **11.** 7×0.2

12. 0.7×0.2 **13.** 0.7×0.02 **14.** 0.07×0.02 **15.** 0.2×0.06 **16.** 0.5×0.06

17. 0.04×0.06 **18.** 0.06×0.25 **19.** 0.8×0.1 **20.** 0.03×0.7

21. 0.5×0.3 **22.** 0.01×0.9 **23.** 0.09×0.05 **24.** 0.7×0.06

25. 0.02×0.04 **26.** 0.04×0.45 **27.** 0.06×0.02 **28.** 0.002×0.6

Problem Solving • Reasoning

29. Apple chips are $\frac{4}{100}$, or 0.04, sugar. If a small bag contains 0.075 kg of chips, how much sugar does it contain?

30. **Compare** The product of two decimal factors is 0.0012. One factor is $\frac{1}{100}$ greater than the other. What are the two decimal factors?

31. A carob bar has four equal pieces. If the whole bar contains 0.014 kg of fat, how much fat would 0.25 of the bar contain?

32. **Write About It** Which decimal is greater: 0.18 or 0.018? Give an example to explain your thinking.

A If you know one factor and the product, how can you find the other factor?

B If you divide one of two factors by 10, what will happen to the product?

C If you divide both of two factors by 10, what will happen to the product?

Mixed Review • Test Prep

Compute. Estimate to check your answers. *(pages 52–53, 54–55, 114–115)*

33. 41×26 **34.** $\$32 \times 15$ **35.** $804 - 94$ **36.** 258×36 **37.** $86 + 12$

Choose the letter of the correct answer. *(pages 162–164)*

38 Which value of n makes the equation true?

$10 \times 15 = 10 \times (10 + n)$

A 150 **C** 15

B 50 **D** 5

39 Which value of x makes the equation true?

$100 \div 2 = (90 + x) \div 2$

F 10 **H** 50

G 45 **J** 180

Extra Practice See Set D on page 441.

Problem-Solving Strategy: Find a Pattern

You will learn how to solve problems by looking for a pattern.

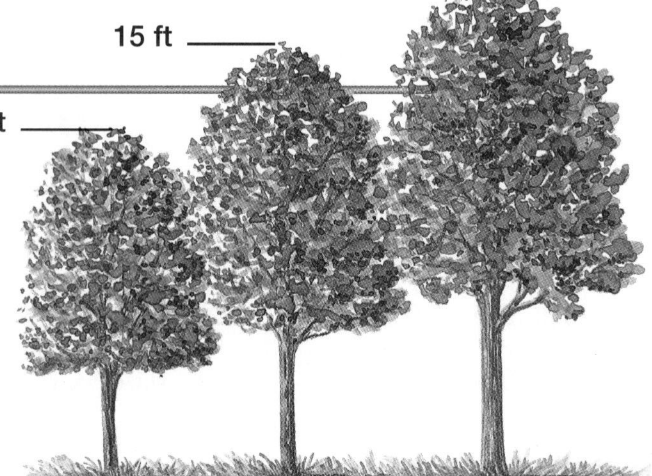

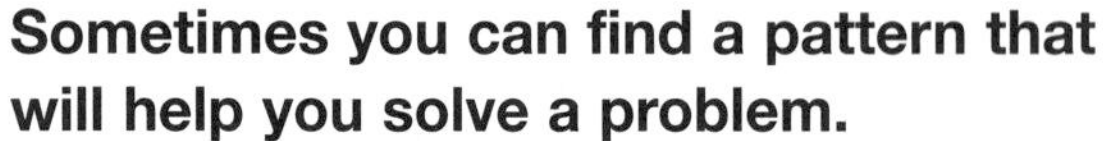

Sometimes you can find a pattern that will help you solve a problem.

Problem Jack's family planted a silver maple tree when it was 10 ft tall. It will grow about the same amount every year for the next 10 years. It was 12.5 ft tall after one year, 15 ft tall after two years, and 17.5 ft tall after three years. How tall is the tree likely to be after 6 years?

Understand

What is the question?
How tall is the tree likely to be after 6 years?

What do you know?
- The tree was 10 ft tall when planted.
- It grows the same amount every year.

Plan

How can you find the answer?
Make a table. Look for a pattern and then use the pattern.

Solve

Make a table to look for a pattern.
When you look at the difference in height from year to year, you see that the tree is growing 2.5 ft every year.

Use the pattern to find the height after 6 years.

The pattern shows that the tree is likely to be 25 ft tall after 6 years.

Year	Height (ft)	
0	10.0	2.5
1	12.5	2.5
2	15.0	2.5
3	17.5	
4	20.0	
5	22.5	
6	25.0	

Look Back

Look back at the problem.
How did finding a pattern help you solve the problem?

Standards NS 2.0, 2.1 MR 1.0, 1.1, 2.0, 2.3, 3.0, 3.2

Remember:
- Understand
- Plan
- Solve
- Look Back

Guided Practice

Solve each problem, using the Find a Pattern strategy.

1. A bakery doubled its first-year sales of bread in its second year. If this pattern continues and sales double every year, how large are the bakery's sales likely to be in its fifth year of business?

   Think: Is there a pattern to how much the sales increase every year?

2. Sasha's hair was 6.2 cm long. After 6 months it was 12.0 cm long, after 12 months it was 17.8 cm long, and after 18 months it was 23.6 cm long. Look for a pattern to predict how long Sasha's hair is likely to be after 2 years?

   Is there a pattern that can be used to find how long Sasha's hair will be after 2 years?

Choose a Strategy

Solve. Use these or other strategies.

- Work Backward
- Write an Equation
- Make a Table
- Find a Pattern

3. To estimate how tall a man was at age 12, you can divide his adult height by 1.19. If a 12-year-old boy is 63 in., calculate how tall he may be when he reaches adulthood.

4. In a study to determine growth rates, an ironwood tree grew about 0.8 ft each year. How much did the tree grow altogether during the 10 years of the study?

5. A sycamore tree grew 30 ft in 20 years. An American elm tree grew 1.6 ft each year over the same 20 years. If both trees were 5 ft tall when they were planted, which tree was taller at the end of 20 years?

6. Beamsville's population grew by 4,100 people in 12 years. During the same 12 years, Newton's population grew by 350 each year. Now both towns have a population of 15,000 each. What town had more people 10 years ago?

7. Find a pattern in the designs. How many squares will there be in the eighth design of your pattern?

   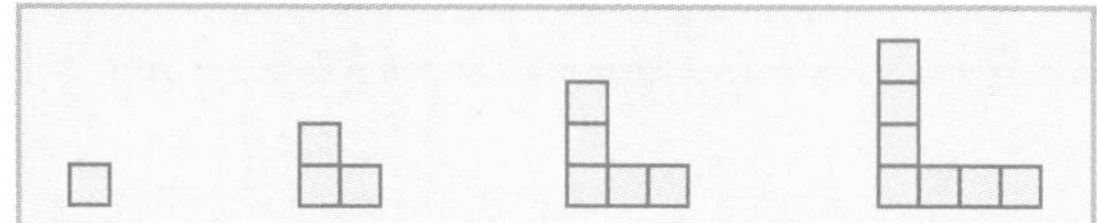

8. Mia measured a plant to be 34 in. tall. The next week, it was 41 in. tall. The following week, it was 48 in. tall. Find a pattern. If your pattern continues, how tall will the plant be in another two weeks?

Extra Practice See 1–4 on page 443.

Quick Check

Check Your Understanding of Lessons 1–5

Multiply.

1. 2×0.8 **2.** 7×0.4 **3.** 8×2.03 **4.** 6×4.51

Estimate the product by rounding each factor.

5. 0.83×6 **6.** 5.22×4 **7.** 3×7.95 **8.** 7×6.14

Multiply. Estimate to check.

9. 0.7×0.2 **10.** 0.4×0.5 **11.** 3.2×1.5 **12.** 5.28×7.5

13. 0.3×0.04 **14.** 0.6×0.05 **15.** 0.09×0.8 **16.** 0.07×0.04

Solve.

17. Alex performed the same operation on each starting number. What was the operation? What would the result be if Alex started with 10?

Starting Number	2	3	4	5	6	10
Result	2.4	3.6	4.8	6	7.2	?

How did you do?

If you had difficulty with any items in the Quick Check, you can use the following pages for review and extra practice.

California Standards	Items	Review These Pages	Do These Extra Practice Items
Number Sense: **1.0, 2.0, 2.1**	1–4	pages 408–409	Set A, page 440
Number Sense: **1.0, 2.0, 2.1**	5–8	pages 410–411	Set B, page 440
Number Sense: **1.0, 2.0, 2.1**	9–12	pages 412–413	Set C, page 440
Number Sense: **1.0, 2.0, 2.1**	13–16	pages 414–415	Set D, page 441
Math Reasoning: **1.1, 1.2**	17	pages 416–417	1–4, page 443

Test Prep • Cumulative Review

Maintaining the Standards

Choose the letter of the correct answer.
If a correct answer is not here, choose NH.

1 One ball bearing has a mass of 3.54 grams. What is the mass of 24 ball bearings?

A 8.496 g
B 84.96 g
C 849.6 g
D 8,496 g

2 What is the result when 7.109 is rounded to the nearest tenth?

F 7.0
G 7.1
H 7.11
J 7.2

3 A piece of sheet metal is 0.057 inches thick. How tall is a stack of 100 pieces of sheet metal?

A 5,700 in.
B 57 in.
C 5.7 in.
D NH

4 Which set of data has the greatest range?

F 18, 9, 6, 23, 45
G 23, 45, 64, 73, 18
H 45, 36, 24, 18, 63
J 100, 104, 95, 82, 100

5 Kim wants to write $\frac{24}{42}$ in simplest form. By what number should she divide the numerator and the denominator?

A 3 **C** 6
B 4 **D** 12

6 Which unit would be the best one to use to measure the area covered by a computer mouse pad?

F centimeters **H** feet
G meters **J** square inches

7 Which sign would give the greatest result?

$$\frac{7}{8} \bullet \frac{3}{4}$$

A $+$ **C** $-$
B $\times$ **D** $\div$

8 Look at the line graph.

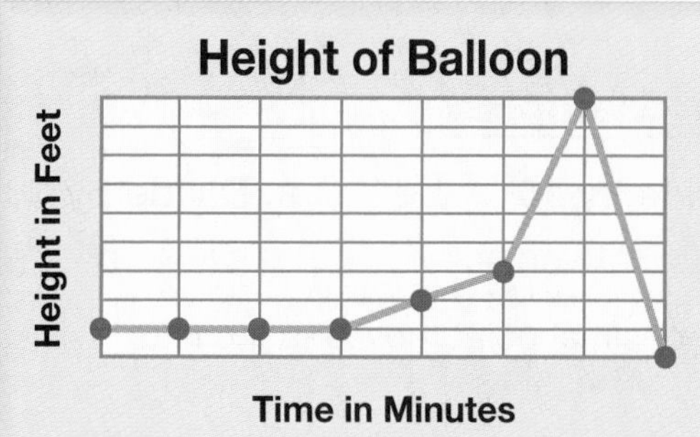

Explain Describe what happened to the balloon.

Safe Site

Internet Test Prep
Visit **www.eduplace.com/kids/mhm** for more *Test Prep Practice.*

Multiply and Divide Decimals by Powers of 10

You will learn how to use patterns to multiply and divide decimals by powers of 10.

Review Vocabulary
power of 10
exponent

Learn About It

When you multiply a number by 10^n, or a **power of 10**, you are multiplying by 10 n times. n is called the **exponent**. The decimal point moves n places to the right. You may need to insert or eliminate zeros.

Brain cells are among the smallest cells in the human body, measuring 0.005 mm across. Microscopes can make objects appear 10^1 times, 10^2 times, or 10^3 times larger using different lenses.

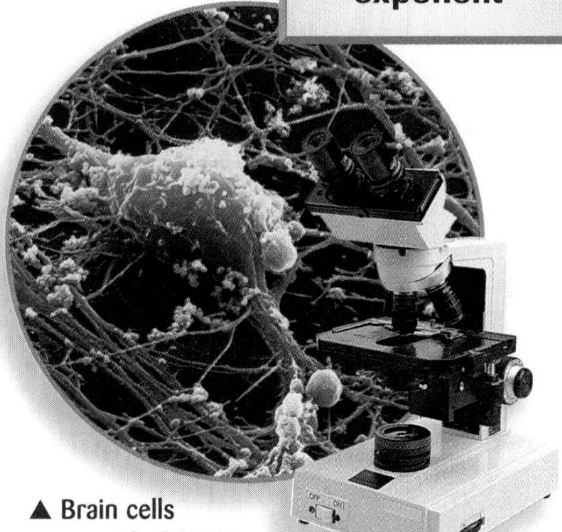

▲ Brain cells magnified 3,700×.

How large would a brain cell appear at each magnification level?

Multiply 0.005 mm by 10^1, 10^2, and 10^3.

10^1 level	10^2 level	10^3 level
0.005×10^1	0.005×10^2	0.005×10^3
$0.005 \times 10 = 0.05$	$0.005 \times 100 = 0.5$	$0.005 \times 1{,}000 = 5$
The cell appears to be 0.05 mm long.	The cell appears to be 0.5 mm long.	The cell appears to be 5 mm long.

Solution: The cell can be enlarged to appear 0.05 mm, 0.5 mm, and 5 mm.

Other Examples

A. Divide by 10^1

$6.5 \div 10^1 = 0.65$

B. Divide by 10^2

$6.5 \div 10^2 = 0.065$

The decimal point moves to the left.

Explain Your Thinking

▶ Why is the expression 4.2×10^3 equal to the expression 42×10^2?

Guided Practice

Multiply or divide by using patterns.

1. 0.5×10^2 **2.** $0.2 \div 10$ **3.** 3.8×100

4. $159 \div 10^3$ **5.** 0.04×10^3 **6.** $6.1 \div 10^2$

Ask Yourself

- Do I move the decimal point to the right or to the left?

Standards NS **1.0, 1.3, 2.0, 2.1, 2.2** AF **1.2**

Independent Practice

Multiply or divide.

7. 5.34×10^1 **8.** 5.34×10^2 **9.** $5.34 \div 10^1$ **10.** $5.34 \div 10^2$

11. 13.187×10^2 **12.** $3{,}240.27 \div 10^2$ **13.** 0.99×10^1 **14.** $0.6 \div 10^3$

15. 2.0×10^3 **16.** $75 \div 10^2$ **17.** 0.68×10^3 **18.** $4.72 \div 10^1$

19. 0.045×10^2 **20.** $8{,}274 \div 10^3$ **21.** $3{,}456 \times 10^2$ **22.** $0.04 \div 10^2$

Algebra • Equations **Solve for *a*.**

23. $100 = 10^a$ **24.** $1{,}000 = 10^a$ **25.** $10 = 10^a$ **26.** $10{,}000 = 10^a$

Problem Solving • Reasoning

Use Data **Use the table for Problems 27–29.**

27. **Analyze** Binoculars "zoom in" on objects that are far away, making them seem closer than they really are. If a set of binoculars can make an object appear $\frac{1}{10}$ as far away as it really is, how far away would the ant, bird, and tree appear to be?

28. **Analyze** How far away would the ant, bird, and tree seem if the binoculars made them appear 10 times farther away than they really are?

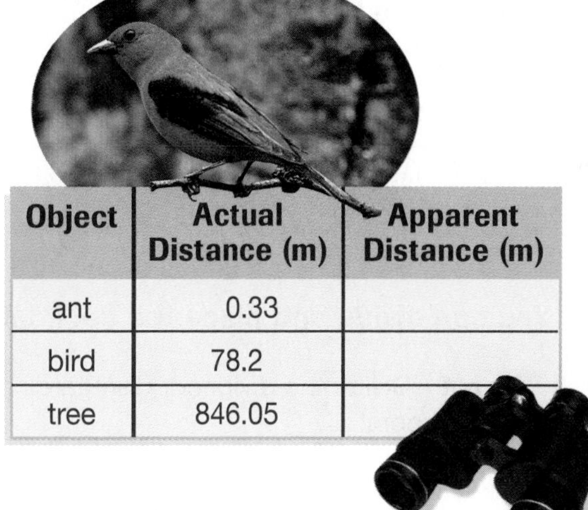

Object	Actual Distance (m)	Apparent Distance (m)
ant	0.33	
bird	78.2	
tree	846.05	

29. **Write Your Own** Use the data in the table to write your own problem about magnification. Give your problem to a partner to solve.

30. Bob bought binoculars and a book. The binoculars cost $165. The book cost 0.1 as much as the binoculars. How much did both cost?

Mixed Review • Test Prep

What is the next number likely to be in each pattern? *(pages 416–417)*

31. 2, 5, 9, 14, 20, 27, ■, . . . **32.** 1, 4, 9, 16, 25, 36, ■, . . . **33.** 95, 84, 74, 65, 57, 50, ■, . . .

34 Which algebraic expression represents the phrase "thirty decreased by a number"? *(pages 70–72)*

A $(30 - x) - x$ **B** $x - (30 - x)$ **C** $x - 30$ **D** $30 - x$

Extra Practice See Set E on page 441.

Divide a Decimal by a Whole Number

You will learn how to divide a decimal by a whole number.

Learn About It

To practice for a bike-a-thon, Karyn rides 8 times around the track each day. If she rides a total of 9.6 km, how long is the track?

Divide. $\mathbf{9.6 \div 8 = n}$

Different Ways to Divide a Decimal by a Whole Number

You can use fractions.

Step 1 Write the dividend and the divisor as fractions.

$$\frac{96}{10} \div \frac{8}{1} \qquad 9.6 = \frac{96}{10}$$

Step 2 Multiply the dividend by the reciprocal of the divisor.

$$\frac{96}{10} \times \frac{1}{8} = \frac{96}{80}$$

Step 3 Write the quotient as a decimal.

$$\frac{96}{80} = \frac{12}{10} = 1.2$$

You can divide and place the decimal point in the quotient.

Step 1 Divide the dividend, disregarding the decimal point.

```
   12 tenths
 8)96 tenths
  − 8
    16
  − 16
     0
```

Step 2 Place a decimal point in the quotient above the decimal point in the dividend.

```
   1.2
 8)9.6
  − 8
  − 1 6
  − 1 6
      0
```

Check your work.

Multiply

$8 \times 1.2 = 9.6$

Solution: The track is 1.2 km long.

Another Example

Quotient Less Than 1

```
    0.92
 7)6.44
  −6 3
    14
   −14
     0
```

Check.

```
  0.92
×    7
  6.44
```

Explain Your Thinking

► Why is it important to align the quotient and the dividend correctly when you divide with decimal numbers?

Guided Practice

Divide and check.

1. $2\overline{)16.2}$ **2.** $5\overline{)9.75}$ **3.** $6\overline{)5.4}$

4. $22.8 \div 4$ **5.** $58.1 \div 7$ **6.** $0.63 \div 3$

Ask Yourself

- Would using fractions help?
- Did I place the decimal point correctly?

Independent Practice

Find each quotient. Check using multiplication.

7. $6\overline{)7.2}$ **8.** $7\overline{)41.3}$ **9.** $3\overline{)16.2}$ **10.** $7\overline{)11.9}$ **11.** $4\overline{)0.8}$

12. $42.8 \div 4$ **13.** $3.87 \div 9$ **14.** $9.75 \div 3$ **15.** $6.32 \div 8$ **16.** $0.84 \div 2$

17. $8\overline{)2.80}$ **18.** $2\overline{)3.46}$ **19.** $6\overline{)1.44}$ **20.** $7\overline{)26.25}$ **21.** $9\overline{)45.27}$

22. $5.5 \div 5$ **23.** $8.4 \div 4$ **24.** $0.8 \div 2$ **25.** $20.7 \div 3$ **26.** $75.6 \div 9$

27. $5\overline{)0.95}$ **28.** $8\overline{)6.48}$ **29.** $6\overline{)9.06}$ **30.** $4\overline{)51.28}$ **31.** $7\overline{)23.17}$

Problem Solving • Reasoning

32. A cross-country team of cyclists are planning a relay race. If the course is 58.24 mi long, and the 8 cyclists all ride the same distance, how many miles will each cyclist ride?

34. **Analyze** Tony and Jan are training for the bike-a-thon. Tony rode his bike 4.5 km in 9 min, and Jan rode her bike 3.6 km in 6 min. Which rider might go farther in 1 min?

35. **Write About It** Which will be greater: the quotient $6.56 \div 8$ or the quotient $656 \div 80$? Explain how you can tell without dividing.

33. **Compare** Rosa's uncle and sister, Ana, pledged to give Rosa a certain amount of money for each mile she rode on the 5-mile bike-a-thon.

a. How much did her uncle pledge per mile?

b. How much did her sister pledge per mile?

Rosa's Pledge List

Name	Pledge
Uncle Thomas	$16.25
Ana	$11.50

Mixed Review • Test Prep

Solve for *n*. *(pages 166–167)*

36. $24.3 = 8.1 \times n$ **37.** $10.5 = 21 \times n$ **38.** $n \div 4 = 4.2$ **39.** $n \div 7 = 6.06$

40 Which equation represents the Commutative Property of Addition? *(page 165)*

A $a \times (b + c) = (a \times b) + (a \times c)$

B $e + f = f + e$

C $m + 1 = m + \frac{2}{2}$

D $(r + s) + t = r + (s + t)$

Extra Practice See Set F on page 441.

Problem-Solving Skill: Interpret Remainders

You will learn how to solve problems involving remainders.

When you solve a division problem, sometimes you need to decide how to interpret the remainder.

Look at the situations below.

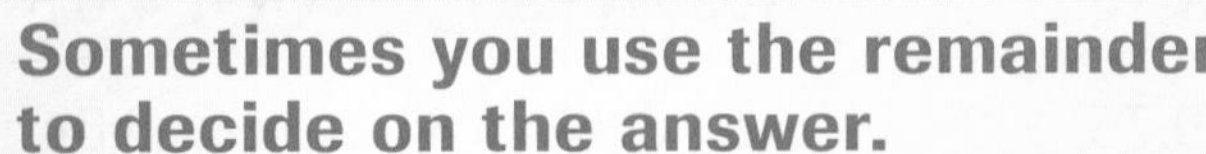

Sometimes you use the remainder to decide on the answer.

The craft club members made 19 puppets. They want to package the puppets 5 to a box. How many boxes will they need?

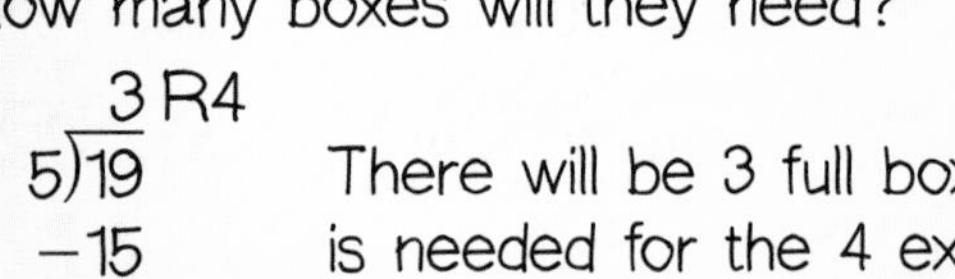

$$\begin{array}{r} 3\text{ R}4 \\ 5\overline{)19} \\ -15 \\ \hline 4 \end{array}$$

There will be 3 full boxes. Another box is needed for the 4 extra puppets. So 4 boxes are needed in all.

Sometimes you write the remainder as a fraction.

The craft club also made 4 picture frames. If they used 18 feet of framing material, how much material did each frame require?

$$\begin{array}{r} 4\text{ R}2 = 4\tfrac{2}{4} = 4\tfrac{1}{2} \\ 4\overline{)18} \\ -16 \\ \hline 2 \end{array}$$

Each frame required $4\frac{1}{2}$ feet of framing material.

Sometimes you write the quotient as a decimal.

The craft club spent $30.00 for materials. The 8 members want to share the cost. How much does each person owe?

$$\begin{array}{r} 3.75 \\ 8\overline{)30.00} \\ -24 \\ \hline 60 \\ -56 \\ \hline 40 \\ -40 \\ \hline 0 \end{array}$$

Each craft club member owes $3.75.

Look Back How does thinking about the question in each situation help you decide what to do with the remainder?

 Standards NS **2.2** MR **1.0, 2.0, 2.4, 2.6, 3.1**

Left: Traditional puppets for a "Punch and Judy" show.
Right: Indonesian leather puppet for a shadow play.

Guided Practice

Solve.

1. Large puppets require 2 yd of fabric each. How many large puppets can be made with 7 yd of fabric?

   Think: Can you make part of a puppet?

2. Eight tickets for a puppet show cost $42.00. How much did each ticket cost?

   Think: How many dollars and cents will each ticket cost?

Choose a Strategy

Solve. Use these or other strategies.

Problem-Solving Strategies

- **Make a Table**
- **Guess and Check**
- **Draw a Diagram**
- **Work Backward**

3. The puppet-making class has tables that seat 4 people. If 15 people attend the puppet-making class, how many tables will be needed?

4. Val spent four times as much money at the craft sale as Gary. Together, they spent $15. How much did each person spend?

5. Lynda made a puppet necklace with some red, white, and green beads. She used twice as many red beads as white ones. She used the same number of green beads as white beads. If she used 16 beads in all, how many of each type did she use?

6. The craft club members made refrigerator magnets. On Monday they made 20 magnets, 2 more than on Sunday. On Sunday they made 4 fewer than on Saturday. On Saturday they made twice as many as on Friday. How many did they make on Friday?

7. Yarn is used to make the puppets' hair by folding it in half and then cutting on the fold. If you start with one long piece of yarn, how many pieces will you have after 6 folds and cuts? How many times do you have to cut to get 128 pieces?

8. Bob, Nancy, and Kelly each made an item for the craft sale. They made a breadboard, a necklace, and a key chain. The name of the maker of the item does not start with same letter as the item. Bob did not make the key chain. Who made each item?

Extra Practice See 5–8 on page 443.

Write Zeros in the Dividend

You will learn how to write one or more zeros in the dividend to help you solve division problems.

Learn About It

Researchers in Antarctica make the trip from their main station to the telescope observatory three times each day. If they travel a total of 4.5 miles in the 3 trips there and back, how far is the main station from the observatory?

Divide. **4.5 ÷ 6 = *n***

Find 4.5 ÷ 6.

Step 1 Divide as though the dividend were a whole number.

Think: 45 ÷ 6 is about 7.

```
     7
  6)4.5
   -4 2
      3
```

Step 2 To continue the division, write a 0 in the hundredths place.

```
     75
  6)4.50
   -4 2↓
      30  ← Bring down the 0.
     -30    Continue dividing.
       0
```

Step 3 Place the decimal point in the quotient above the decimal point in the dividend.

```
  ↓ Write 0 in the ones place.
   0.75
  6)4.50
   -4 2
      30
     -30
       0
```

Solution: The main station is 0.75 mile from the observatory.

Another Example

Divide Whole Numbers

Write zeros after the decimal point to find the quotient to more decimal places.

```
     5.375
  8)43.000
   -40
     30
    -24
      60
     -56
       40
      -40
        0
```

Explain Your Thinking

▶ Why does writing zeros to the right of the least place digit in a decimal not change the value of that number?

▲ South Pole research station in Antarctica

 Standards NS 1.0, 2.0, 2.1, 2.2 AF 1.0, 1.2

Guided Practice

Divide and check.

1. $5\overline{)2.7}$
2. $5\overline{)24}$
3. $4\overline{)3.5}$
4. $6\overline{)0.75}$
5. $8\overline{)51}$
6. $2\overline{)39.77}$

Ask Yourself

- Did I place the first digit of the quotient correctly?
- Did I write zeros in the dividend until there was no remainder?

Independent Practice

Divide and check.

7. $2\overline{)9}$
8. $8\overline{)5.2}$
9. $4\overline{)19}$
10. $16\overline{)12.4}$
11. $18\overline{)0.9}$
12. $2.7 \div 4$
13. $0.38 \div 4$
14. $24.7 \div 5$
15. $6.11 \div 2$
16. $9.6 \div 5$
17. $46\overline{)16.1}$
18. $10\overline{)62.4}$
19. $5\overline{)24.72}$
20. $6\overline{)106.5}$
21. $8\overline{)474.8}$
22. $8\overline{)19}$
23. $24\overline{)15}$
24. $4\overline{)28.18}$
25. $12\overline{)4.2}$
26. $6\overline{)8.67}$

Problem Solving • Reasoning

27. **Analyze** The highest temperature ever recorded in Antarctica was 59°F. Over a five-day period, the following high temperatures were recorded at the researchers' station: 27.2°F, 24.6°F, 29°F, 22.4°F, and 28.1°F. What was the average high daily temperature?

28. The Antarctic Ice Prowler bicycle was specifically designed for the climate in Antarctica. It has a wheel diameter of about 20 inches. The tires are almost as wide as car tires, or about 8 inches. How many times greater is the diameter of a wheel than the width of a tire?

29. **Analyze** The Ice Prowler can travel about 11.1 miles in one hour. This is about three times as fast as a person can walk in Antarctic conditions. How far could a person walk in 1 hour in Antarctica?

Solve for x.

A. $\frac{x}{10} = 6$
B. $\frac{x}{100} = 6$
C. $\frac{x}{1{,}000} = 6$
D. $0.1x = 12$
E. $0.01x = 12$
F. $0.001x = 12$
G. $\frac{x}{10} = 15$
H. $\frac{x}{100} = 15$

Mixed Review • Test Prep

Find the value of each expression if $c = \frac{2}{3}$, $d = \frac{1}{2}$, and $e = \frac{3}{4}$. *(pages 70–72, 332–333, 344–345)*

30. $c + d$
31. $e - c$
32. $c - d$
33. $(c + e) - d$
34. $c + (d + e)$

35. In a class of 24 fifth-grade students, $\frac{5}{8}$ of the students are female. How many students in the class are male? *(pages 372–373)*

A 9 **B** 11 **C** 15 **D** 16

LESSON 10

Divide by a Decimal

You will learn how to divide with decimal divisors.

Learn About It

A fraction represents a quotient. Multiplying the numerator and the denominator of a fraction by the same number does not change the quotient.

For any division statement, the quotient does not change when you multiply the dividend and the divisor by the same number.

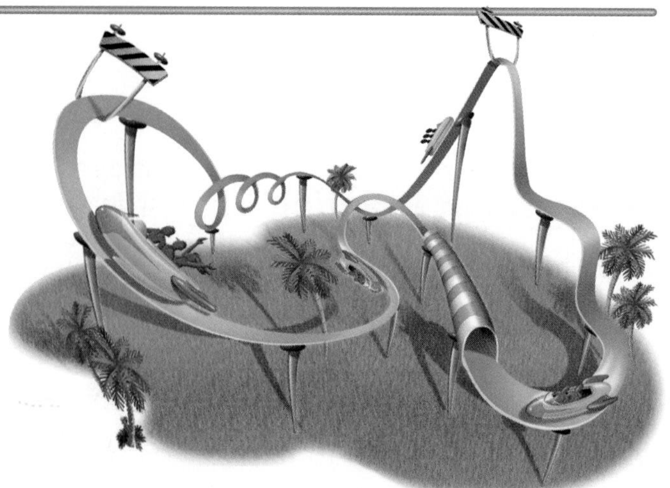

- Multiply the numerator (dividend) and the denominator (divisor) by 10.

$\frac{8}{2} = 4 \quad \frac{8}{2} \times \frac{10}{10} = \frac{80}{20} = 4$

- Multiply the dividend and the divisor by 10.

$2\overline{)8}$ = 4 $\quad 20\overline{)80}$ = 4

The *Lightning* roller coaster travels so fast that it completes its 3,300-foot long track in 2.5 min. If you could stay on the roller coaster for 15 min, how many times would you circle the track?

Divide. **15 ÷ 2.5 = *n***

Find 15 ÷ 2.5.

Step 1 To change the divisor to a whole number, multiply by 10.

$2.5 \times 10 = 25$

$25\overline{)15}$

Step 2 Multiply the dividend by the same number, 10, so the quotient will stay the same.

$15 \times 10 = 150$

$25\overline{)150}$

Step 3 Complete the division.

$25\overline{)150}$ = 6
−150
0

Check your work.

Multiply. 2.5 × 6 = 15.0

Solution: In 15 min you would circle the track 6 times.

Standards NS **1.0, 1.1, 2.0, 2.1, 2.2** MR **2.1, 2.4**

Another Example

Decimal Quotient

$10 \div 0.8 = \frac{10 \times 10}{0.8 \times 10}$

$= \frac{100}{8}$

$$\begin{array}{r} 12.5 \\ 8\overline{)100.0} \\ -8 \\ \hline 20 \\ -16 \\ \hline 4\,0 \\ -4\,0 \\ \hline 0 \end{array}$$

← There is a remainder of 4. Write a decimal point and a 0 in the dividend. Then bring down the 0 and continue dividing.

Explain Your Thinking

- ▶ Why does multiplying a decimal by 10 move the decimal point one place to the right?
- ▶ Why does the value of a fraction stay the same when both the numerator and the denominator are multiplied by the same number?

Guided Practice

Divide and check.

1. $1.2\overline{)6}$ **2.** $0.5\overline{)25}$ **3.** $0.7\overline{)28}$

4. $2.5\overline{)20}$ **5.** $3.5\overline{)490}$ **6.** $2.5\overline{)6}$

Ask Yourself

- Did I multiply the dividend and the divisor by the same number?
- Did I divide by a whole number?

Independent Practice

Divide and check.

7. $0.3\overline{)18}$ **8.** $0.6\overline{)18}$ **9.** $0.9\overline{)18}$ **10.** $1.8\overline{)18}$ **11.** $3.6\overline{)18}$

12. $0.4\overline{)24}$ **13.** $0.8\overline{)24}$ **14.** $1.6\overline{)24}$ **15.** $6.2\overline{)31}$ **16.** $2.5\overline{)140}$

17. $0.5\overline{)7}$ **18.** $1.5\overline{)90}$ **19.** $0.4\overline{)72}$ **20.** $9.9\overline{)198}$ **21.** $5.5\overline{)33}$

22. $1.2\overline{)9}$ **23.** $2.5\overline{)1}$ **24.** $7.5\overline{)3}$ **25.** $7.5\overline{)9}$ **26.** $0.8\overline{)30}$

Is each quotient reasonable? Check by rounding the divisor to the nearest whole number.

27. $90 \div 4.5 = 20$ **28.** $27 \div 1.2 = 2.25$ **29.** $85 \div 1.7 = 50$

30. $39 \div 2.6 = 1.5$ **31.** $9 \div 2.5 = 4$ **32.** $30 \div 3.75 = 8$

33. $18 \div 4.5 = 3$ **34.** $51 \div 1.7 = 30$ **35.** $48 \div 1.6 = 30$

Problem Solving • Reasoning

Solve. Choose a method.

Computation Methods

- Mental Math
- Estimation
- Paper and Pencil

36. The distance to the Moon is about 240,000 mi. The *Global Trek* ride has a track that is 0.6 mi long. How many times would you have to ride the *Global Trek* to travel the distance to the Moon?

37. **Predict** A passenger car begins the *Global Trek* ride every 0.6 min. How many cars start the ride during 9 min? 30 min? If each car can carry 24 passengers, how many people can ride the *Global Trek* in 1 hour?

38. **Analyze** A train travels 3,300 ft in 2.5 min. How many feet does it travel in 1 min? in 1 second?

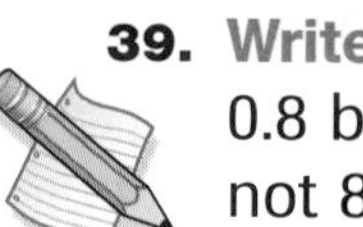

39. **Write About It** When you multiply 0.8 by 10, why is the product 8 and not 80?

Mixed Review • Test Prep

Compare. Write >, <, or = for each ●. *(pages 322–323, 324–325)*

40. $\frac{50}{75}$ ● $\frac{3}{5}$ **41.** 0.75 ● $\frac{3}{4}$ **42.** $2\frac{5}{6}$ ● 2.9 **43.** 0.5 ● $\frac{5}{8}$

44. 8.03 ● $\frac{83}{10}$ **45.** $\frac{1}{5}$ ● 0.15 **46.** 7.35 ● $7\frac{7}{35}$ **47.** $\frac{7}{9}$ ● 0.7

48 Each time an electric saw cuts a board, $\frac{1}{6}$ in. of material is lost. Suppose an 8-in. board is cut into 4 pieces of equal length. What is the length of each piece? *(pages 380–381)*

A $2\frac{1}{8}$ in. **C** $1\frac{29}{32}$ in.

B 2 in. **D** $1\frac{7}{8}$ in.

Patterns

Lisa is the 156th person in a line waiting to get on an amusement park ride. The first group of 24 passengers are boarding a ride now, and the next group will board in 0.6 min. If people keep boarding every 0.6 min, how long will it be until it is Lisa's turn?

Extra Practice See Set H on page 442.

Show What You Know

Using Vocabulary

Use the clues to solve.

1. The divisor is the reciprocal of $\frac{1}{2}$. The dividend is 25.5. What is the quotient?

2. I am 2 when you round me to my greatest place. I am 190 when you multiply me by 10^2. What am I?

3. I am the answer when you solve $43 \div 4$. How can you write me in three different ways?

4. The product of two numbers is 3.8. One factor is 2. What is the other factor?

Check It Out

Use division to check each product.
If a product is incorrect, find the correct answer.

1. $\begin{array}{r} 12.4 \\ \times \quad 5 \\ \hline 62 \end{array}$

2. $\begin{array}{r} 18.6 \\ \times \quad 3 \\ \hline 5.58 \end{array}$

3. $\begin{array}{r} 3.75 \\ \times \ 0.8 \\ \hline 30 \end{array}$

4. $\begin{array}{r} 71 \\ \times \ 0.2 \\ \hline 62 \end{array}$

Solution Hunt

Select one of the given numbers to make each statement true.

1. The quotient of $17.34 \div 34 = \blacksquare$.

2. The product of $0.06 \times 10^3 = \blacksquare$.

3. $0.4 \times 0.75 = \blacksquare$.

4. If $n \div 2.8 = 15$, then $n = \blacksquare$.

Divide a Decimal by a Decimal

You will learn how to divide one decimal by another.

Learn About It

A wheel-a-thon is like a walk-a-thon, except that the participants travel on anything with wheels. Matt wheeled 26.65 miles. If he traveled an average of 8.2 miles each hour, how long did it take him to travel this distance?

Divide. **26.65 ÷ 8.2 = *n***

Find 26.65 ÷ 8.2.

Step 1 Multiply both the divisor and the dividend by 10 to simplify the problem.

```
8.2)26.65
```

Step 2 Since there are not enough hundreds or tens to divide, begin dividing in the ones place.

```
      3
82)266.5
  -246
    20
```

Step 3 Bring down the tenths. Divide the tenths.

```
      32
82)266.5
  -246↓
    205
   -164
     41
```

Step 4 Write a zero after the final digit of the dividend. Place a decimal point in the quotient directly over the decimal point in the dividend.

```
     3.25
82)266.50
  -246
    20 5
   -16 4
     4 10
    -4 10
        0
```

Solution: It took Matt 3.25 hours to travel 26.65 miles.

Check your work. Reread the question to decide if your answer makes sense.

The problem states that Matt traveled more than 24 miles and that he traveled about 8 miles each hour, so the answer should be close to 3 hours.

Another Example

Write Zeros in the Dividend

Divide 45 ÷ 2.5.

$$2.5\overline{)45.0} \qquad \begin{array}{r} 18 \\ 25\overline{)450} \\ -25 \\ \hline 200 \\ -200 \\ \hline 0 \end{array}$$

45 ÷ 2.5 = 18

Explain Your Thinking

- ▶ Why do you sometimes need to write a 0 after the dividend?
- ▶ How can you tell when decimal division is complete?
- ▶ How did you decide what power of 10 to multiply by to simplify division by a decimal?

Guided Practice

Divide and check.

Ask Yourself

- Do I need to write a zero after the dividend?
- Did I place the decimal point correctly?

1. $0.8\overline{)1.6}$ **2.** $3.4\overline{)42.5}$ **3.** $0.8\overline{)1.5}$

4. $0.4\overline{)1.84}$ **5.** $9.5\overline{)10.07}$ **6.** $0.2\overline{)0.101}$

7. 9 ÷ 8 **8.** 30 ÷ 1.5 **9.** 1.44 ÷ 1.2

Independent Practice

Divide. Check each quotient by estimating, or by using multiplication.

10. $0.3\overline{)1.8}$ **11.** $0.3\overline{)0.18}$ **12.** $0.5\overline{)38.5}$ **13.** $0.5\overline{)3.85}$

14. $0.5\overline{)0.385}$ **15.** $0.2\overline{)0.178}$ **16.** $0.2\overline{)1.78}$ **17.** $0.2\overline{)1.618}$

18. $0.8\overline{)1.12}$ **19.** $0.08\overline{)11.2}$ **20.** $3.5\overline{)17.5}$ **21.** $3.5\overline{)1.75}$

22. $3.5\overline{)17.57}$ **23.** $0.9\overline{)4.86}$ **24.** $0.9\overline{)4.536}$ **25.** $0.04\overline{)4.3}$

26. $6.1\overline{)32.33}$ **27.** $0.7\overline{)4.032}$ **28.** $4.5\overline{)38.7}$ **29.** $4.5\overline{)36.27}$

30. $3.9\overline{)2.73}$ **31.** $6.9\overline{)5.175}$ **32.** $0.65\overline{)6.11}$ **33.** $7.8\overline{)36.27}$

n **Algebra • Equations** **For each equation, find values for *a* and *b* that make the equation true.**

34. $a \div b = 4$ **35.** $a \div b = 25$ **36.** $a \div b = 6$ **37.** $a \div b = 3$

38. $a \div b = 1$ **39.** $a \div b = 8$ **40.** $a \div b = 5$ **41.** $a \div b = 2$

Problem Solving • Reasoning

42. **Analyze** Marisol collected $11.83 from her uncle for the distance she rode in the wheel-a-thon. If her uncle pledged $0.65 for each mile, how far did Marisol ride?

43. In the wheel-a-thon, Ben rode 22.5 mi on his bicycle. Ben's mother pulled his sister Alexa in a wagon for 2.5 mi. How many times as far as Alexa did Ben go?

44. **Compare** Sue biked 28.6 mi. She biked 2.2 times as many miles as Crispin. How far did Crispin bike?

45. June drank 4.42 pints of water during her 22.1-mile bike ride. How much water did she drink for each mile?

46. In the wheel-a-thon, Josh raised $28.75. Josh raised 2.3 times as much as Tanya raised. How much more money did Josh raise than Tanya?

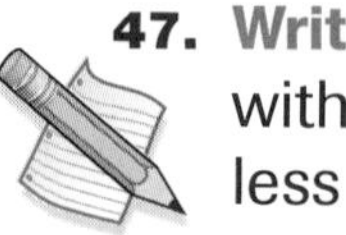

47. **Write About It** In a division problem with decimals, is the divisor always less than the dividend? Give an example to support your answer.

Mixed Review • Test Prep

Round each number to the underlined place. *(pages 8–9, 28–29)*

48. $4\underline{1}5$ **49.** $\underline{8}6$ **50.** $\underline{1},055$ **51.** $23\underline{4},634$ **52.** $\underline{9}75$

53. $\underline{1}.593$ **54.** $6.\underline{2}45$ **55.** $0.4\underline{0}5$ **56.** $12.0\underline{8}1$ **57.** $2\underline{0}.49$

Choose the letter of the correct answer. *(pages 304–306, 308–310)*

58 What are the GCF and the LCM of 9 and 15?

A GCF = 1; LCM = 135
B GCF = 3; LCM = 45
C GCF = 45; LCM = 9
D GCF = 135; LCM = 3

59 What are the GCF and LCM of 20 and 22?

F GCF = 1; LCM = 440
G GCF = 2; LCM = 410
H GCF = 2; LCM = 220
J GCF = 4; LCM = 220

Logical Thinking

Patterns

Continue the pattern for the next three divisions.

$8 \div 8$ $8 \div 4$ $8 \div 2$ $8 \div 1$ $8 \div \frac{1}{2}$ $8 \div \frac{1}{4}$ 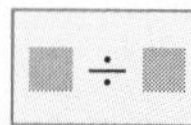 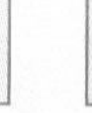 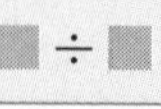 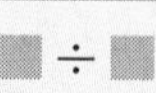

What is always true of the quotient you get when you divide by a fraction less than 1?

Extra Practice See Set I on page 442.

Number Sense

Changing Fractions to Decimals

To change a fraction to a decimal, you can divide the numerator of the fraction by the denominator.

$\frac{1}{2} = 1 \div 2$

$$\begin{array}{r} 0.5 \\ 2\overline{)1.0} \\ -\,1\,0 \\ \hline 0 \end{array}$$

$\frac{3}{4} = 3 \div 4$

$$\begin{array}{r} 0.75 \\ 4\overline{)3.00} \\ -\,2\,8 \\ \hline 20 \\ -\,20 \\ \hline 0 \end{array}$$

Sometimes the numerator can not be divided evenly by the denominator. The division will continue indefinitely and you will get a decimal that is called a repeating decimal.

Some fractions, like $\frac{1}{3}$, produce a single repeating digit.

$$\begin{array}{r} 0.33... \\ 3\overline{)1.00...} \\ -\;\;9 \\ \hline 10 \\ -\;9 \\ \hline 1 \end{array}$$

1 → The division pattern repeats because there will always be a remainder of 1.

$1 \div 3 = 0.333333...$

The decimal form of $\frac{1}{3}$ is $0.\overline{3}$. The bar over the 3 indicates a repeating digit.

Some fractions, like $\frac{5}{11}$, produce a repeating pattern of digits.

$$\begin{array}{r} 0.45... \\ 11\overline{)5.00...} \\ -\,4\,4 \\ \hline 60 \\ -\,55 \\ \hline 5 \end{array}$$

5 → The division pattern repeats each time the remainder is 5.

$5 \div 11 = 0.454545...$

The decimal form of $\frac{5}{11}$ is $0.\overline{45}$. The bar over the decimal indicates a repeating pattern of digits.

Change each fraction to decimal form.

1. $\frac{1}{8}$ **2.** $\frac{1}{5}$ **3.** $\frac{1}{6}$ **4.** $\frac{1}{4}$ **5.** $\frac{1}{9}$

Explain Your Thinking

► If you know the decimal for $\frac{1}{3}$, how can you find the decimal for $\frac{2}{3}$?

LESSON 12

Problem-Solving Application: Use Formulas

You will learn how to use a formula to solve a problem.

Sometimes you can use a formula to solve a problem.

Problem A soccer field can be between 100 yd and 130 yd long and between 50 yd and 100 yd wide. The center line divides a soccer field into two equal rectangular halves. If the field is 61 yd wide and each half has an area of 3,385.5 yd², what is the length of each half?

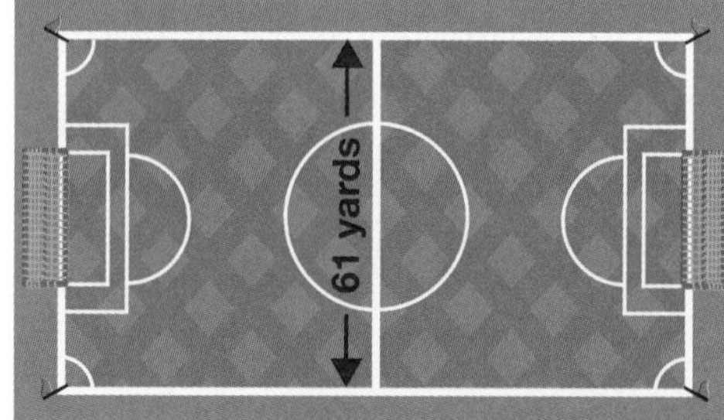

Understand

What is the question?

What is the length of each half of a soccer field?

What do you know?

Each half is a rectangle.
The area of each rectangle is 3,385.5 yd².
The width of each rectangle is 61 yd.

Plan

What can you do to find the answer?

Use the formula for finding the area of a rectangle.

Area = length × width = $l \times w$

Solve

Substitute the values you know into the formula.
Use l to represent the length of the rectangle.

$3{,}385.5 = l \times 61$

$3{,}385.5 \div 61 = l$

Remember:
You can divide a product by a known factor to find the other factor.

The length of each half of the soccer field is 55.5 yd.

Look Back

Look back at the question. Is your answer reasonable?

If each half of the field is 55.5 yd long, the field is 111 yd long. Since 111 is between 100 and 130, the answer is reasonable.

Standards MG **1.0, 1.4** MR **1.0, 1.1, 2.0, 2.6, 3.0**

Lacrosse is a game that originated with Native Americans. It is usually played on a field 60 yd by 110 yd.

Remember:
- ▶ Understand
- ▶ Plan
- ▶ Solve
- ▶ Look Back

Guided Practice

Solve.

1. Each half of a volleyball court is a square with a perimeter of 118 ft. How long is each side of half of a volleyball court?

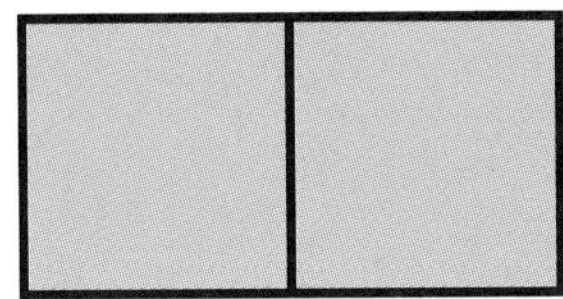

Think: What formula shows how the side length of a square is related to its perimeter?

2. A squash court is 18.5 ft wide. The service line is 6.5 ft above the floor. What is the area of the rectangle below the service line?

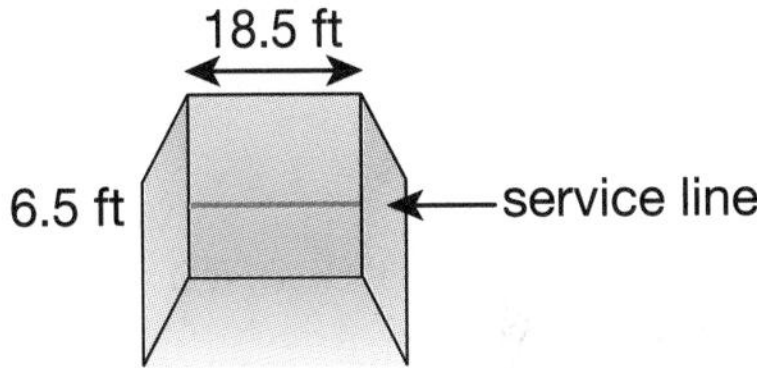

Think: How can you use the side lengths of a rectangle to find its area?

Choose a Strategy

Solve. Use these or other strategies.

Problem-Solving Strategies

- **Guess and Check**
- **Draw a Diagram**
- **Solve a Simpler Problem**
- **Write an Equation**

3. A handball court is divided into two squares with sides 20 ft long. What is the area of the full court?

4. The catcher's box in baseball is a rectangle 3 ft 7 in. wide and 8 ft long. What is its area in square inches?

5. A square field is divided across the center to create two soccer fields. If the side length of the square is 123 yd, what is the perimeter of one of the soccer fields?

6. A baseball diamond has an area of 900 yd^2. A line from home plate to second base would form two triangles. If the line is about 42 yd long, what is the area of each triangle?

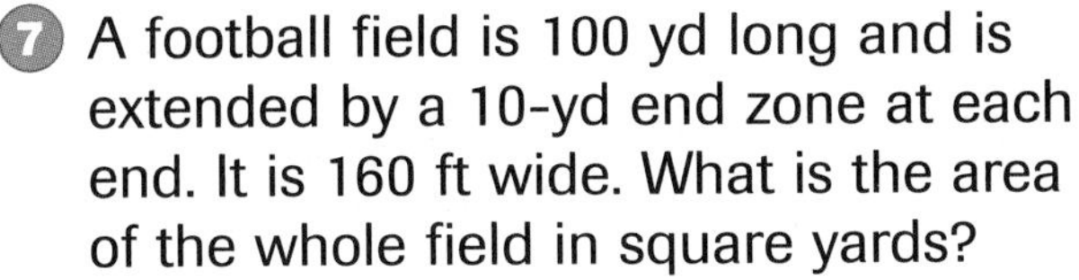

7. A football field is 100 yd long and is extended by a 10-yd end zone at each end. It is 160 ft wide. What is the area of the whole field in square yards?

8. The length of a rectangle is a multiple of 5 in. The width is 4.8 in. The area is between 80 in.^{2} and 100 in.^{2}. What is the length of the rectangle?

Extra Practice See 9–12 on page 443.

Quick Check

Check Your Understanding of Lessons 6–12

Multiply or divide by using patterns.

1. 7.2×10^2 **2.** $296.8 \div 10^3$ **3.** $4.9 \div 10^2$

Divide and check.

4. $5.4 \div 6$ **5.** $9.3 \div 3$ **6.** $12.35 \div 5$

7. $8\overline{)70}$ **8.** $5\overline{)10.2}$ **9.** $0.2\overline{)26}$

10. $0.3\overline{)78}$ **11.** $0.5\overline{)6.5}$ **12.** $6.3\overline{)15.12}$

Solve.

13. Four people shared the cost of gas for a car trip. If the gas cost $167, how much did each person pay?

14. If the area of the whole rectangle is 48.3 in.^{2}, what is the area of each of the smaller rectangles?

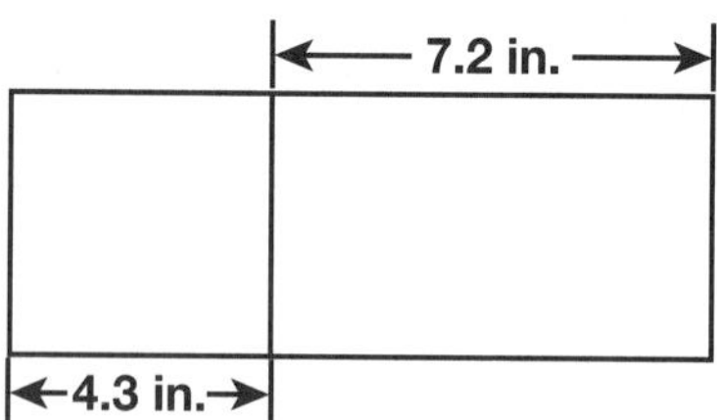

How did you do?

If you had difficulty with any items in the Quick Check, you can use the following pages for review and extra practice.

California Standards	Items	Review These Pages	Do These Extra Practice Items
Number Sense: **1.0, 2.0, 2.1, 2.2**	1–3	pages 420–421	Set E, page 441
Number Sense: **1.0, 2.0, 2.1, 2.2**	4–6	pages 422–423	Set F, page 441
Number Sense: **1.0, 2.0, 2.1, 2.2**	7–8	pages 426–427	Set G, page 442
Number Sense: **1.0, 2.0, 2.1, 2.2**	9–10	pages 428–430	Set H, page 442
Number Sense: **1.0, 2.0, 2.1, 2.2**	11–12	pages 432–434	Set I, page 442
Math Reasoning: **1.0, 1.1**	13	pages 424–425	5–8, page 443
Measurement and Geometry: **1.4** Math Reasoning: **1.1, 1.2, 2.3**	14	pages 436–437	9–12, page 443

Test Prep • Cumulative Review

Maintaining the Standards

Choose the letter of the correct answer. If a correct answer is not here, choose NH.

1 Divide.

8.0 ÷ 0.025

A 3,200 **C** 32
B NH **D** 0.32

2 Robert planted an oak seedling. It grew 10 inches the first year. Every year after that it grew $1\frac{1}{4}$ inches. How tall was the oak tree after 9 years?

F $22\frac{3}{4}$ in. **H** $20\frac{1}{4}$ in.
G $21\frac{1}{2}$ in. **J** 20 in.

3 Use the spinners below. Each spinner is spun once. How many possible outcomes have a sum of 5?

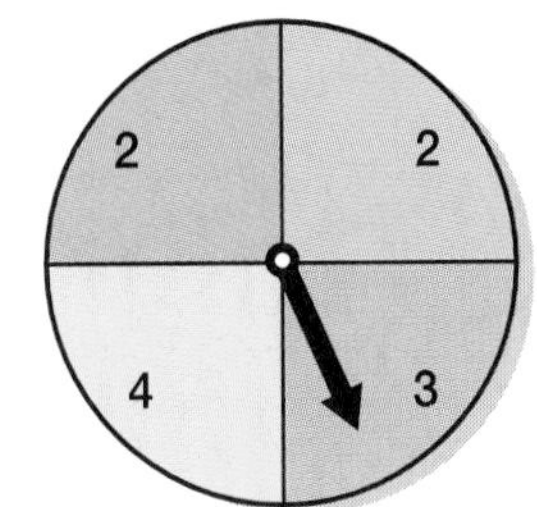

A 3 **C** 5
B 4 **D** 6

4 Multiply. Give your answer in simplest form.

$\frac{4}{15} \times \frac{9}{12}$

F $\frac{3}{15}$ **H** $\frac{3}{5}$
G $\frac{1}{5}$ **J** $\frac{1}{3}$

5 Add.

$$\begin{array}{r} 3\frac{1}{2} \\ +\ 5\frac{2}{5} \\ \hline \end{array}$$

A $8\frac{3}{5}$ **C** $8\frac{9}{10}$
B $8\frac{3}{7}$ **D** $8\frac{2}{7}$

6 Find the mean of the following measurements.

18.02 in., 13.4 in., 8.07 in., 14.35 in.

F 26.92 in. **H** 0.21 in.
G 13.46 in. **J** 32

7 Ms. Lincoln wants to divide each of her 4 gym classes into teams with no students left over. She wants to divide them into teams of first 2, then 3, then 6 students. With which class can this *not* be done?

A class of 18 students
B class of 24 students
C class of 26 students
D class of 30 students

8 Rosa found 3 red chips in a sample of 10 chips from a box. Thao found 8 red chips in a sample of 20 chips from the same box. The box contains 100 chips.

Explain Which sample would you use to predict how many red chips might be in the box?

Safe Site

Internet Test Prep
Visit **www.eduplace.com/kids/mhm** for more *Test Prep Practice.*

Extra Practice

Set A (Lesson 1, pages 408–409)

Multiply.

1. 6×0.2
2. 9×0.5
3. 8×0.61
4. 5×0.82
5. 2×5.47
6. 8×4.17
7. 6×7.08
8. 3×4.98
9. 6.5×4
10. 7.4×7
11. 5.69×3
12. 82.54×6
13. 1.02×9
14. 14.58×6
15. 23.04×8
16. 49.49×7

Set B (Lesson 2, pages 410–411)

Estimate the products by rounding each factor.

1. 0.17×4
2. 3.97×6
3. 7.22×70
4. 11.79×3
5. 82×0.58
6. 21×4.07
7. 48×9.39
8. 4×10.77
9. 0.42×300
10. 1.92×7
11. 4.25×6
12. 8.82×5
13. 2.46×50
14. 18.09×21
15. 25.5×4
16. 8.99×80

Set C (Lesson 3, pages 412–413)

Find each product.

1. 0.6×0.3
2. 0.5×0.7
3. 0.8×0.8
4. 0.5×0.8
5. 0.18×0.8
6. 5.75×0.5
7. 3.6×1.2
8. 6.14×3.5
9. 0.83×0.7
10. 5.16×6.1
11. 7.26×5.3
12. 10.75×3.2
13. 1.07×5.3
14. 0.91×2.4
15. 14.22×8.1
16. 8.59×0.3

Extra Practice

Set D (*Lesson 4, pages 414–415*)

Multiply. Write as many zeros as you need to place the decimal point correctly.

1. 4×0.6
2. 0.4×0.6
3. 0.4×0.06
4. 0.04×0.06
5. 9×0.8
6. 0.9×0.8
7. 0.9×0.08
8. 0.09×0.08
9. 0.5×7
10. 0.5×0.7
11. 0.5×0.07
12. 0.05×0.07
13. 0.01×0.8
14. 0.6×0.03
15. 0.04×0.05

Set E (*Lesson 6, pages 420–421*)

Multiply or divide by using patterns.

1. 6.2×10^1
2. 8.34×10^2
3. 27.456×10^3
4. $7.25 \div 10^1$
5. $8.67 \div 10^2$
6. $6.5 \div 10^3$
7. 11.546×10^2
8. $36.44 \div 10^2$
9. $0.8 \div 10^1$
10. $76 \div 10^3$
11. 27.621×10^3
12. 19.6×10^3
13. $3{,}246 \times 10^2$
14. $0.03 \div 10^1$
15. $1{,}215 \div 10^3$

Set F (*Lesson 7, pages 422–423*)

Find each quotient. Check using multiplication.

1. $4.8 \div 6$
2. $8.1 \div 9$
3. $1.44 \div 6$
4. $2.36 \div 2$
5. $21.7 \div 7$
6. $24.75 \div 3$
7. $9.04 \div 4$
8. $30.88 \div 8$
9. $3.85 \div 5$
10. $6\overline{)7.38}$
11. $4\overline{)21.84}$
12. $7\overline{)61.95}$
13. $5\overline{)4.65}$
14. $9\overline{)28.17}$
15. $4\overline{)51.6}$

Extra Practice

Set G *(Lesson 9, pages 426–427)*

Divide and check.

1. $8\overline{)4}$ **2.** $4\overline{)15}$ **3.** $15\overline{)63}$

4. $774 \div 10$ **5.** $4.2 \div 4$ **6.** $6.7 \div 5$

7. $24.6 \div 8$ **8.** $36.8 \div 5$ **9.** $34.8 \div 8$

10. $6\overline{)16.5}$ **11.** $5\overline{)235.9}$ **12.** $4\overline{)634.2}$

13. $38\overline{)13.3}$ **14.** $22\overline{)144.1}$ **15.** $24\overline{)15.6}$

Set H *(Lesson 10, pages 428–430)*

Divide and check.

1. $0.4\overline{)24}$ **2.** $0.9\overline{)36}$ **3.** $0.8\overline{)64}$

4. $1.2\overline{)84}$ **5.** $3.5\overline{)28}$ **6.** $7.6\overline{)190}$

7. $6.2\overline{)279}$ **8.** $3.4\overline{)255}$ **9.** $6.1\overline{)610}$

10. $6.5\overline{)39}$ **11.** $0.6\overline{)3}$ **12.** $0.9\overline{)18}$

13. $0.6\overline{)15}$ **14.** $8.4\overline{)252}$ **15.** $2.3\overline{)92}$

Set I *(Lesson 11, pages 432–433)*

Divide and check.

1. $1.5\overline{)1.5}$ **2.** $0.5\overline{)0.15}$ **3.** $0.6\overline{)3.6}$

4. $0.9\overline{)5.04}$ **5.** $0.8\overline{)5.84}$ **6.** $0.7\overline{)1.75}$

7. $0.4\overline{)0.864}$ **8.** $7.2\overline{)45.36}$ **9.** $5.7\overline{)4.56}$

10. $9.8\overline{)54.88}$ **11.** $8.3\overline{)48.97}$ **12.** $4.5\overline{)2.7}$

13. $3.1\overline{)16.43}$ **14.** $6.1\overline{)0.183}$ **15.** $5.2\overline{)3.016}$

Extra Practice • Problem Solving

Solve each problem, using the Find a Pattern Strategy. *(Lesson 5, pages 416–417)*

1. A seedling was 1.25 in. tall after one week, 2.5 in. tall after two weeks, and 3.75 in. tall after three weeks. If the pattern continues, how tall is the seedling likely to be after five weeks?

2. Erin saved \$2.50 one week, \$5 the second week, and \$7.50 the third week. If she continues her pattern, how much money is Erin likely to have saved after 6 weeks?

3. A cup of hot tea has a temperature of 180°F. The temperature of the tea is 169°F after two minutes, 158°F after four minutes, and 147°F after six minutes. If the tea continues to cool steadily, what will its temperature be after ten minutes?

4. Find a pattern in the designs below. How many circles will there be in the sixth design of your pattern?

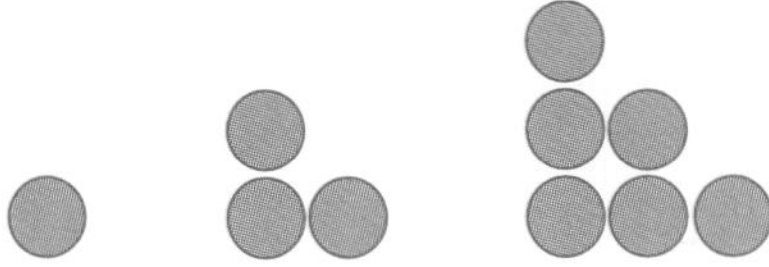

Solve. *(Lesson 8, pages 424–425)*

5. Jessie has 482 napkin rings to package in boxes of 12. How many boxes can she fill?

6. Fourteen boxes of napkin rings were sold for a total of \$91.00. What was the cost of one box?

7. A rectangular tabletop has an area of 14.25 square feet. If the tabletop is 3 feet wide, how long is the table?

8. Cloth napkins each require $\frac{2}{5}$ yard of fabric. How many napkins can be made from 9 yards of fabric?

Solve. *(Lesson 12, pages 436–437)*

9. A square with 3.2-cm long sides has an area of 10.24 cm^2. What is the area of a square whose sides are twice as long?

10. The perimeter of a rectangle is 19.8 inches. If the rectangle is 7.8 inches long, how wide is it?

11. The perimeter of a rectangle is 19.4 m. If its length is 6.2 m, what is its width? Is the area of the rectangle greater than the area of a square with a perimeter of 20.8 m?

12. A square with 3.5-cm long sides is cut from the corner of a rectangle. If the rectangle is 7 cm long and 5.2 cm wide, what is the area of the part that is left after the square is removed?

Chapter Review

Reviewing Vocabulary

Write *always, sometimes,* or *never* for each statement. Give an example to support your answer.

1. If you round both factors to a greater number to estimate a product, the actual product will be less than the estimate.
2. If you multiply a number of tenths by a number of hundredths, the result always has three decimal places.
3. When you divide a number by 10^2, the decimal point in the number moves two places to the right.
4. When you divide with decimals, the quotient is less than the dividend.

Explain how to perform each operation.

5. Multiply a number by 10^3.
6. Multiply one decimal by another.
7. Divide a decimal by a whole number.
8. Divide a whole number by a decimal.

Reviewing Concepts and Skills

Multiply. *(pages 408–409)*

9. 5×6.3 **10.** 11×4.9 **11.** 7.42×8 **12.** 0.559×4

Estimate the products by rounding each factor. *(pages 410–411)*

13. 0.68×72 **14.** 9×0.081 **15.** 18.2×58 **16.** 31.05×39

Find each product. *(pages 412–415)*

17. 0.8×0.4 **18.** 3.2×5.1 **19.** 4.27×2.4 **20.** 0.9×1.23

21. 0.02×0.6 **22.** 0.5×0.03 **23.** 0.08×0.6 **24.** 0.23×0.09

Multiply or divide. *(pages 420–421)*

25. 4.2×10^2 **26.** $6.43 \div 10^1$ **27.** $29.2 \div 10^2$ **28.** 0.451×10^3

Divide and check. *(pages 422–423, 426–430, 432–434)*

29. $6\overline{)4.8}$ **30.** $9\overline{)37.8}$ **31.** $5\overline{)7.5}$ **32.** $4\overline{)46.48}$

33. $4\overline{)6.5}$ **34.** $5\overline{)8.8}$ **35.** $8\overline{)12.6}$ **36.** $18\overline{)245.7}$

37. $42 \div 0.7$ **38.** $682 \div 3.1$ **39.** $336 \div 2.4$ **40.** $2 \div 1.6$

41. $5.6 \div 0.8$ **42.** $33.62 \div 4.1$ **43.** $3.92 \div 0.07$ **44.** $8.16 \div 0.05$

Solve. *(pages 416–417, 424–425, 436–437)*

45. Find a multiplication pattern. Write the next number in your pattern.

3, 0.6, 0.12, 0.024,. . .

46. Five people are sharing the cost of a gift for a friend. If the total cost is $42, how much does each person owe?

47. A rectangle has an area of 53.3 in.^{2}. If the rectangle is 8.2 in. long, how wide is it?

48. One square has 5.2-ft long sides. A second square has a perimeter of 25.6 ft. Which of the two squares has the greatest area?

Brain Teasers Math Reasoning

Find a Pattern

What rule would give this pattern? Use that rule to find the next three numbers in the pattern.

1.2	3	7.5	18.75

Target Two

1 2 3 4 5

Use these digits once each to create a decimal multiplication or division statement whose result is very close to 2.

Safe Site

Internet Brain Teasers
Visit **www.eduplace.com/kids/mhm** for more *Brain Teasers.*

Chapter Test

Multiply.

1. 7×6.2 **2.** 9×3.41 **3.** 2.6×4 **4.** 6.55×8

5. 6×21.3 **6.** 1.25×8 **7.** 12.6×8 **8.** 31.5×5

Estimate the products by rounding each factor.

9. 0.85×7 **10.** 3.82×5 **11.** 11.42×61 **12.** 48.23×49

13. 49×23.1 **14.** 18×31.25 **15.** 102×8.72 **16.** 81.41×79

Find each product.

17. 0.6×0.8 **18.** 7.1×6.4 **19.** 8.36×1.9 **20.** 4.72×4.9

21. 0.04×0.5 **22.** 0.8×0.07 **23.** 0.04×0.12 **24.** 0.56×0.05

Multiply or divide.

25. 4.6×10^1 **26.** 72.2×10^2 **27.** 6.23×10^3 **28.** 5.348×10^2

29. $8.6 \div 10^1$ **30.** $69.1 \div 10^2$ **31.** $267.9 \div 10^3$ **32.** $5.1 \div 10^3$

Divide and check.

33. $9\overline{)7.2}$ **34.** $8\overline{)20.8}$ **35.** $5\overline{)80.75}$

36. $4\overline{)3.5}$ **37.** $5\overline{)7.2}$ **38.** $8\overline{)15.6}$

39. $81 \div 0.9$ **40.** $65 \div 5.2$ **41.** $426 \div 0.8$

42. $6.4 \div 0.4$ **43.** $31.62 \div 6.2$ **44.** $4.65 \div 9.3$

45. $11.5 \div 0.8$ **46.** $8.84 \div 2.6$ **47.** $25.46 \div 3.8$

Solve.

48. Meg makes this number pattern: 1.1, 3.2, 4.3, 7.5, 11.8. If Meg continues her pattern, what number is likely to come next?

49. The students are making costumes for a school play. Each costume requires 2.5 yards of fabric. How many costumes can be made from 22 yards of fabric?

50. A rectangle is 6.7 in. wide and 12.4 in. long. What is its area?

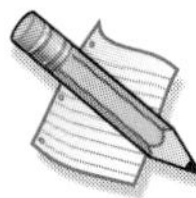

Write About It

Solve each problem. Use correct math vocabulary to explain your thinking.

1. Explain.
   a. How can you tell where to place the decimal point in a product?
   b. How can you tell where to place the decimal point in a quotient?

2. Josh divided these two decimals incorrectly.
   a. Explain what he did wrong.
   b. Show how to find the correct quotient.

$$\begin{array}{r} 5.45 \\ 0.5\overline{)27.25} \\ -\ 25 \\ \hline 2.2 \\ -\ 2\,0 \\ \hline 25 \\ -\ 25 \\ \hline 0 \end{array}$$

3. Complete each operation.

a.
$$\begin{array}{r} 2.4 \\ \times\ 6.5 \\ \hline 120 \end{array}$$

b.
$$\begin{array}{r} 1 \\ 0.4\overline{)42.6.} \end{array}$$

4. Why does the decimal point move two places to the right when you multiply a decimal by 100?

5. Why does the quotient in division remain the same if you multiply the dividend and the divisor by the same amount?

Another Look

Choose two numbers to solve each problem.
Show all your work.

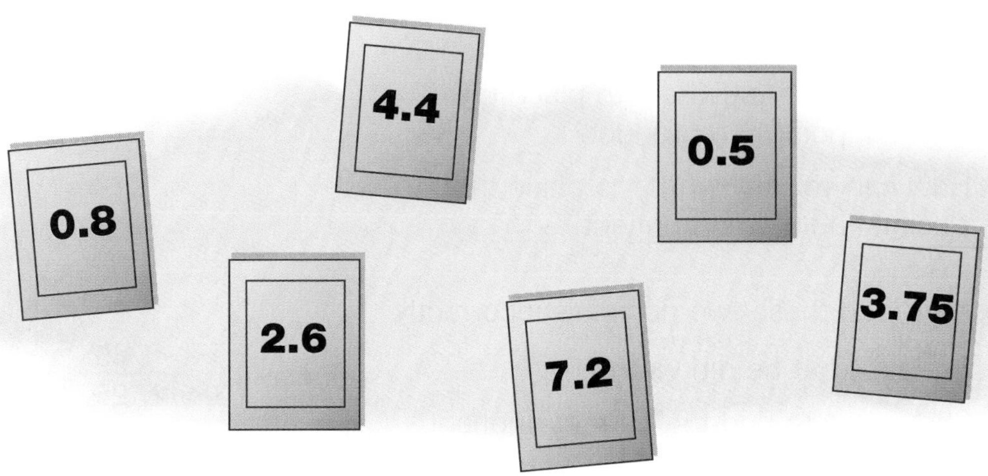

1. Find the greatest product.
2. Find the least product.
3. Find the greatest quotient.
4. Find two numbers with a product of 2.2.
5. Find two numbers with a quotient of 7.5.
6. **Look Back** Check Problems 1 to 3 to make sure that no greater or lesser results are possible.
7. **Analyze** What are the greatest and least numbers? How did these numbers help you find the answers to some of the problems?

Standards	NS **1.0, 2.0, 2.1, 2.2** MR **2.1**

Enrichment

Estimation Destination

Practice estimating and calculating decimal products and quotients by playing this game with a partner or small group.

What You'll Need

- *a number cube labeled 1 to 6*
- *pennies*
- *four sets of number cards labeled 0 to 9 or Teaching Tool 9.*

Players
2

Here's What to Do

1. One player rolls the number cube twice and writes the numbers rolled in order. This two-digit number is the target number.
2. Shuffle the number cards. Each player then draws 4 cards. Players use their cards in any order to make two decimal numbers, whose product or quotient is as close as possible to the target number. Players use pennies for decimal points.

   Note: When dividing decimals, players may need to round answers to the nearest tenth.
3. Players compare to see whose product or quotient comes closest to the target number. That player scores 2 points.

Repeat Steps 1 to 3. The first player to reach a total of 10 points wins.

Explain Your Thinking

- What ways have you found to combine your cards to get the results you want?
- What have you learned about decimal operations from playing this game?

Standards NS **1.0, 2.0, 2.1** MR **3.0, 3.3**

CHAPTER 10

Geometry and Measurement

Why Learn About Geometry and Measurement?

Geometry can help you measure and draw angles and identify the shapes that surround you. Measurement can help you find the areas of shapes such as circles, triangles, and parallelograms.

You can use geometry to draw a pattern for a box. You can use measurement to find the work space area of your desk.

Architects know that triangular structures are very strong. That is one of the reasons you often see many triangles in bridges.

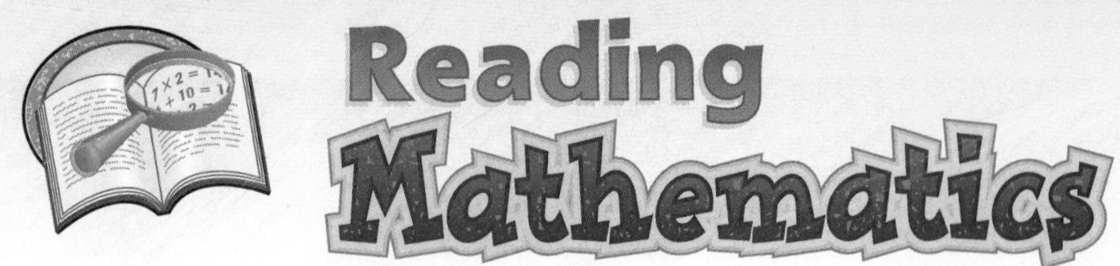

Reviewing Vocabulary

Understanding math language helps you become a successful problem solver. Here are some math vocabulary words you should know.

congruent plane figures that have the same size and shape

parallelogram a quadrilateral in which both pairs of opposite sides are parallel

rhombus a parallelogram with four congruent sides

trapezoid a quadrilateral with exactly one pair of parallel sides

Reading Words and Symbols

When you read mathematics, sometimes you read only words, sometimes you read words and symbols, and sometimes you read only symbols.

There are many different ways to use words and numbers to describe an object's shape and size.

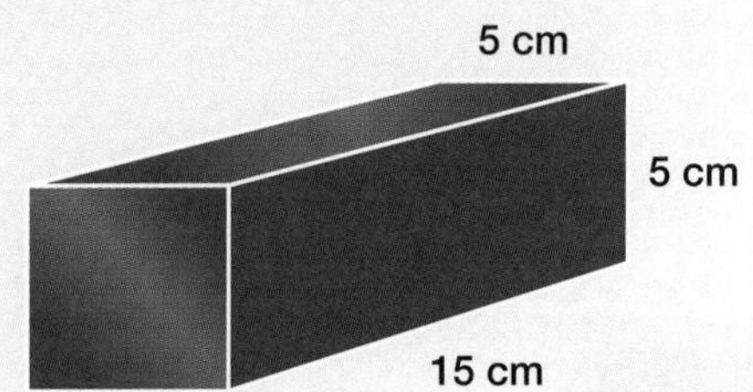

- This box has six faces.
- Two faces are congruent squares.
- Four faces are congruent rectangles.
- Each rectangular face has an area of 15×5 or 75 square centimeters.
- Each square face has an area of 5×5 or 25 square centimeters.
- The surface area of the box is the sum of the areas of all the faces:

  $(2 \times 25) + (4 \times 75) = 350 \text{ cm}^2$
- If you filled the box with centimeter cubes, it would take 5 rows of 15 to cover the bottom. You could make 5 layers this size, so the box would hold 375 centimeter cubes.

Try These

1. Describe the shape and size of this object in as many different ways as you can. Use the words *face*, *congruent*, *square*, *area*, *surface area*, and *centimeter cubes* in your description.

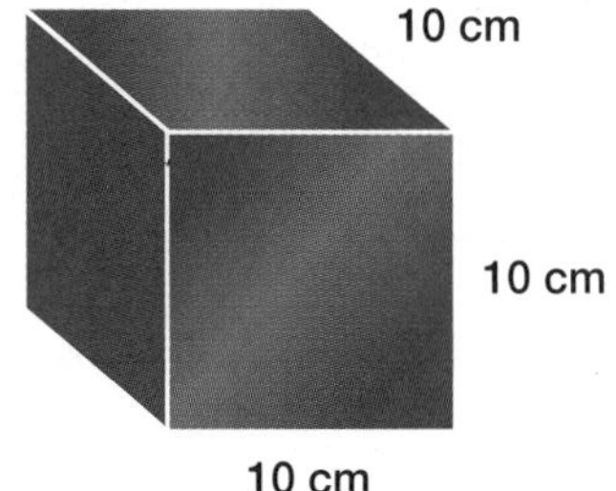

2. If you trace a figure and then turn the tracing upside down, are the two figures still congruent? Use the triangles shown to explain your answer.

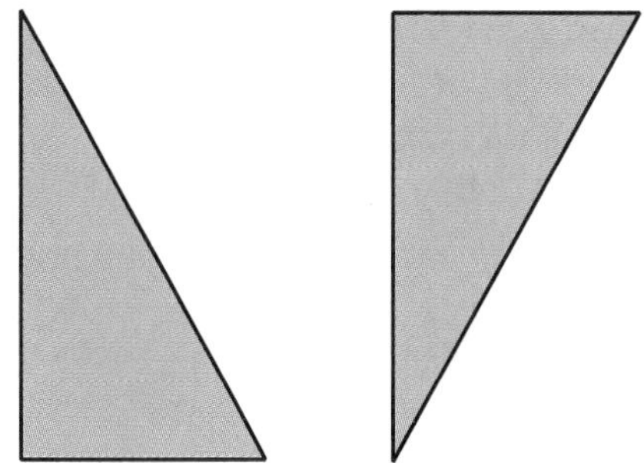

Upcoming Vocabulary

Write About It **Here are some other vocabulary words** you will learn in this chapter. Watch for these words. Write their definitions in your journal.

ray	**plane**	**parallel lines**
vertex	**right angle**	**acute angle**
radius	**diameter**	**chord**
central angle	**circumference**	**pi** π
prism	**base**	**cubic unit**
intersecting lines	**perpendicular lines**	

Points, Lines, and Rays

You will learn to identify and draw points, lines, line segments, and rays.

Learn About It

Geometry is the study of the position, shape, and size of figures. Lines are important in geometry. Many line segments are involved in the photograph of the airport.

The Language of Geometry

A **point** is a location in space that has no length, width, or height.

• C

Read: point *C*
Write: •*C*

A **line** is a straight, continuous, and unending path made up of a collection of points in a plane.

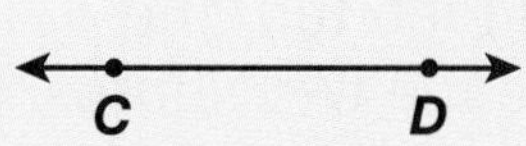

Read: line *CD* or line *DC*
Write: $\overleftrightarrow{CD}$ or $\overleftrightarrow{DC}$

A **line segment** is part of a line and has two endpoints.

Read: line segment *CD* or line segment *DC*
Write: $\overline{CD}$ or $\overline{DC}$

A **ray** is part of a line made up of one endpoint and all the points on one side of it.

Read: ray *CD*
Write: $\overrightarrow{CD}$

A **plane** is a flat surface made up of a continuous and unending collection of points.

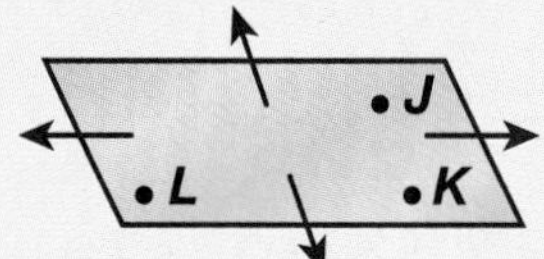

Read: plane *JKL* (The letters can be in any order.)

Here is how you can tell how pairs of lines are related.

Classifying Lines

Intersecting lines have one point in common.

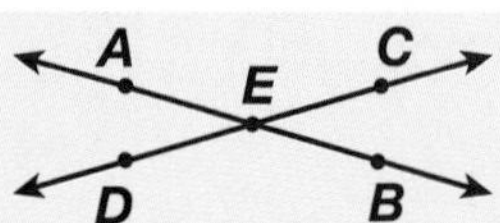

Read: Line *AB* intersects line *CD* at point *E.*

Perpendicular lines intersect at right angles.

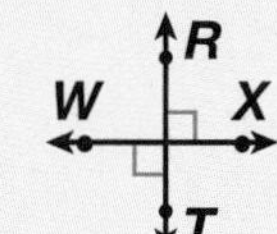

Read: Line *RT* is perpendicular to line *WX*.
Write: $\overleftrightarrow{RT} \perp \overleftrightarrow{WX}$

Parallel lines lie in the same plane but never intersect.

Read: Line *MN* is parallel to line *PQ.*
Write: $\overleftrightarrow{MN} \parallel \overleftrightarrow{PQ}$

Standards | MG **2.0, 2.1** MR **2.0, 2.3**

Explain Your Thinking

- ▶ What is the least number of points you need to determine a line? a plane? Explain.
- ▶ Why do $\overrightarrow{CD}$ and $\overrightarrow{DC}$ name different rays?

Guided Practice

Name each figure.

1. T

2. F E

3. S T

4. C M

> **Ask Yourself**
> - Which letters do I use to name each figure?
> - What letter goes first in the name of the ray?

Independent Practice

Describe each pair of lines. If possible, use the appropriate symbols to write the relationship.

5.

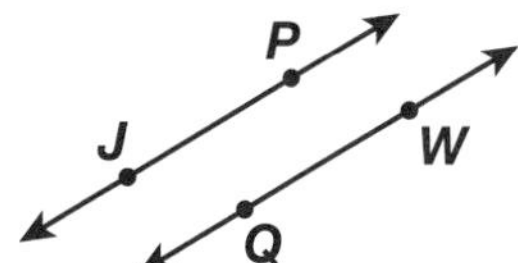

6.

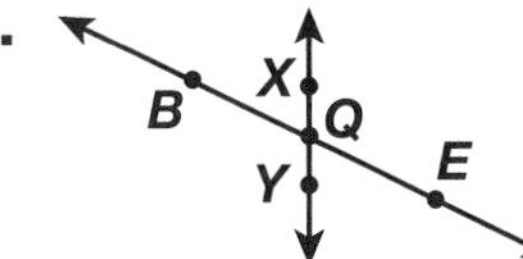

7.

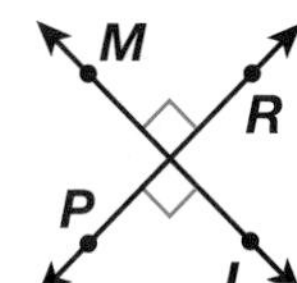

Draw and label a picture for each description.

8. point Y **9.** $\overline{AZ}$ **10.** $\overleftrightarrow{NV}$ **11.** $\overrightarrow{DR}$

12. $\overrightarrow{GN}$ and $\overrightarrow{GT}$ **13.** $\overleftrightarrow{DF} \perp \overleftrightarrow{LN}$ **14.** $\overleftrightarrow{CQ} \parallel \overleftrightarrow{DX}$ **15.** plane EBT

Problem Solving • Reasoning

16. Analyze How many intersecting points occur when 4 parallel lines are perpendicular to 5 other lines?

17. Analyze How many lines can intersect at a point? Use a diagram to explain your thinking.

18. Which of these—a line, line segment, or ray—can contain the other two figures?

19. Write About It How are perpendicular lines like intersecting lines? How are they different?

Mixed Review • Test Prep

Solve. *(pages 106–107, 114–115, 134–135, 154–155)*

20. $13\overline{)2,678}$ **21.** 105×60 **22.** $618 \div 6$ **23.** 102×14 **24.** $11\overline{)1,650}$

25 Which expression is equivalent to $3 \times (45 + 10)$? *(pages 96–97)*

A $(135 + 10)$ **C** $(3 \times 45) + 10$

B $(3 \times 55) + (3 \times 10)$ **D** 3×55

Extra Practice See Set A on page 504.

Measure and Draw Angles

You will learn how to name, measure, and draw angles.

New Vocabulary
vertex
protractor
degrees
right angle
acute angle
obtuse angle
straight angle

Learn About It

When two lines intersect to form rays, the rays become the sides of angles. A small arc is used to mark the angle. The rays' common end point is called the **vertex** of the angle.

An angle is named using the name of the vertex and the name of a point on each ray. The name of the vertex is always in the middle. You can also name an angle by the name of its vertex alone.

- The symbol ∠ is used to identify an angle. How could you use the symbol to write the name of ∠*MXH* in two other ways?

Materials

protractor

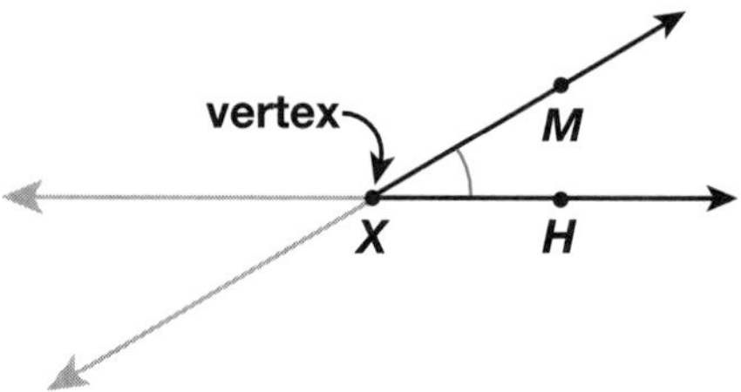

The diagram shows angle *MXH*, angle *HXM*, or angle *X*.

A **protractor** is a tool used to measure angles in **degrees**. Follow these steps to measure ∠*FDE* and ∠*BDC*.

What is the measure of ∠*FDE*? ∠*BDC*?

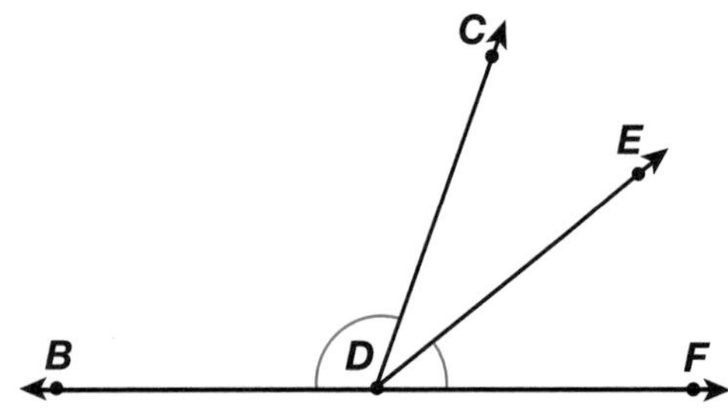

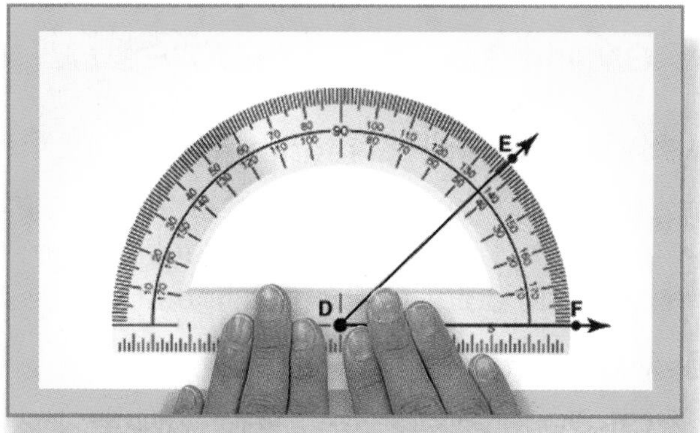

Step 1 Place the center mark of the protractor on the vertex, *D*.

Step 2 Align the 0° mark of one of the protractor scales with one ray of the angle to be measured.

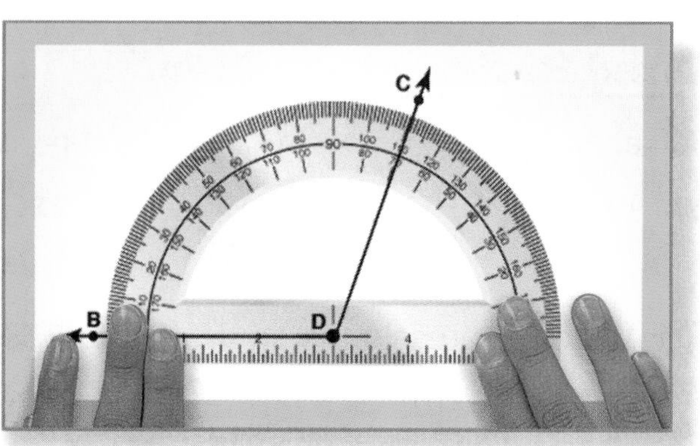

Step 3 Find where the other ray passes through the same scale. Read the measure of the angle on that scale.

- What is the measure of ∠*FDE*? ∠*BDC*?

Standards MG **2.0, 2.1** MR **3.0, 3.3**

You can also use a protractor to draw an angle with a given number of degrees.

Draw $\angle XYZ$ that measures 75°.

Drawing Angles

Step 1 On a sheet of paper, draw ray $\overrightarrow{YX}$ and label it.

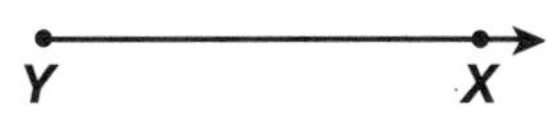

Step 2 Place the center mark of the protractor on the endpoint.

- What degree marks on the protractor are aligned with ray $\overrightarrow{YX}$?

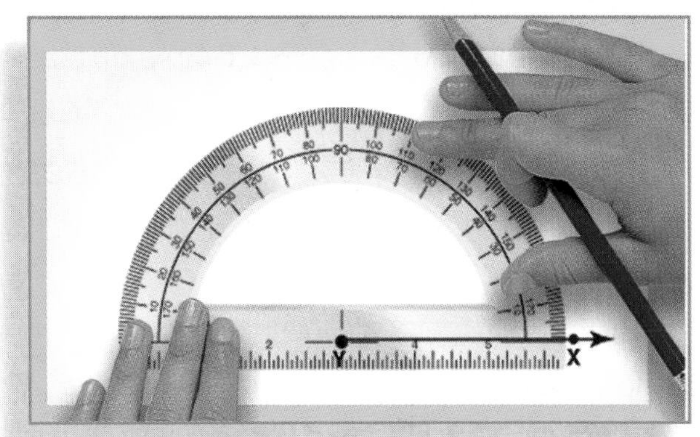

Step 3 Using the scale on which $\overrightarrow{YX}$ aligns with 0°, mark a point at 75°. Label the point.

- What letter is used to label the point?

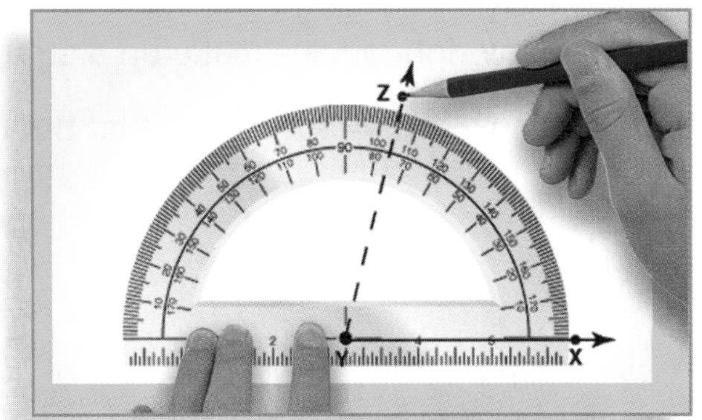

Step 4 Draw a ray from the vertex through the point you labeled.

- What is the measure of $\angle XYZ$?

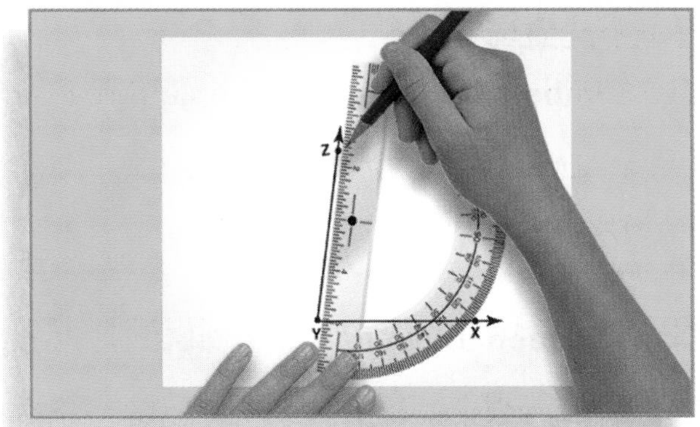

You can classify an angle by its measure.

Classifying Angles

The measure of a **right angle** is equal to 90°.

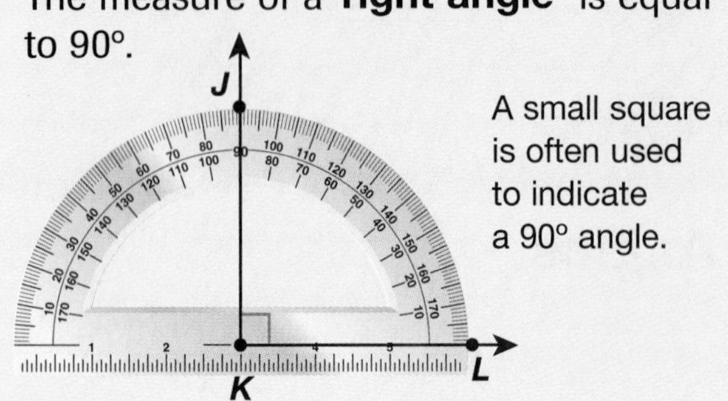

A small square is often used to indicate a 90° angle.

The measure of an **acute angle** is greater than 0° and less than 90°.

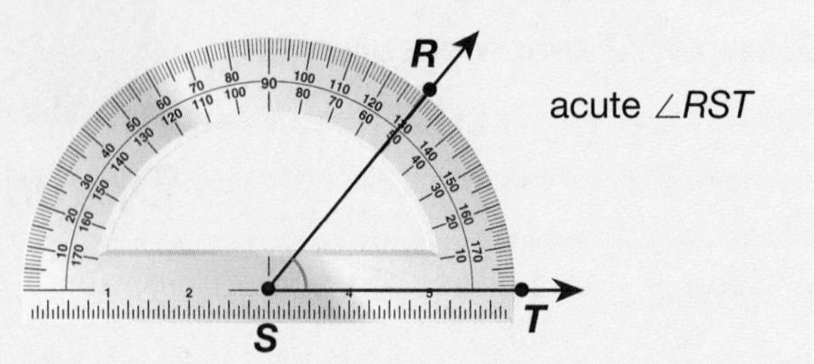

acute ∠*RST*

The measure of an **obtuse angle** is greater than 90° and less than 180°.

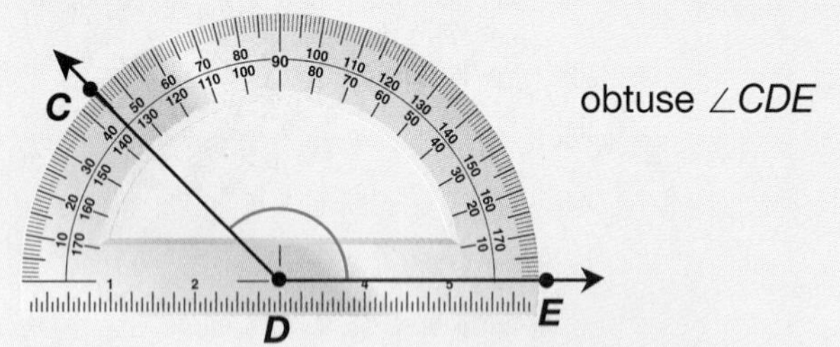

obtuse ∠*CDE*

The measure of a **straight angle** is equal to 180°.

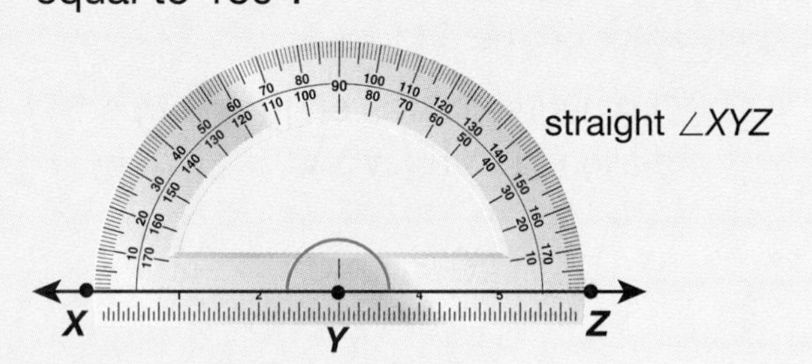

straight ∠*XYZ*

- How is a right angle different from an acute or an obtuse angle?
- What is another name for a straight angle?
- How many right angles make up a straight angle?

The equation $\angle JKL = 90°$ means that the measure of angle *JKL* is ninety degrees.

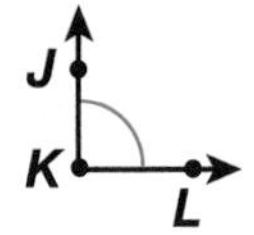

$\angle JKL = 90°$

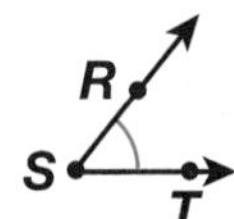

$\angle RST < 90°$

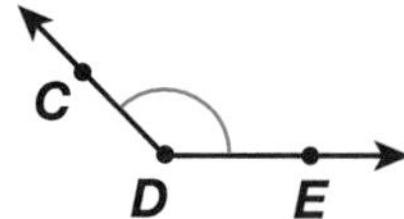

$90° < \angle CDE < 180°$

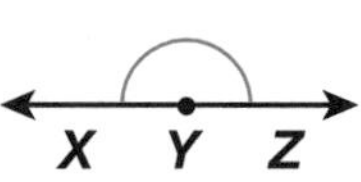

$\angle XYZ = 180°$

Try It Out

Use symbols to name each angle three different ways.

1. 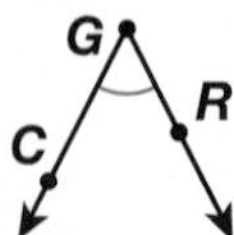

2. 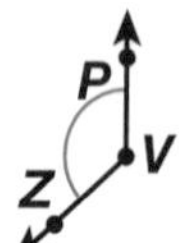

3. 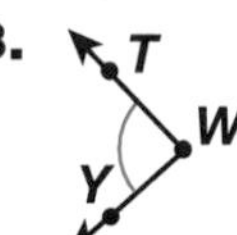

4. 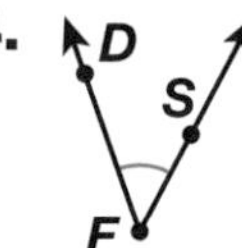

Classify each angle as acute, obtuse, straight, or right.

5. 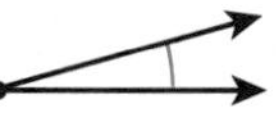

6. 

7. 

8. 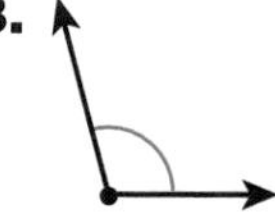

Use a protractor to measure each angle. Write the measure.

9.

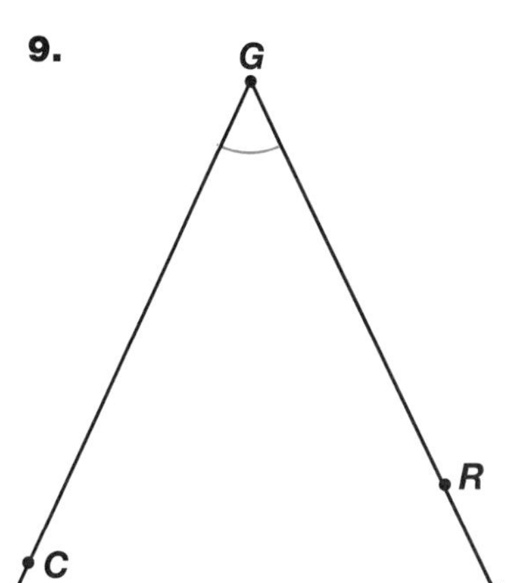

10.

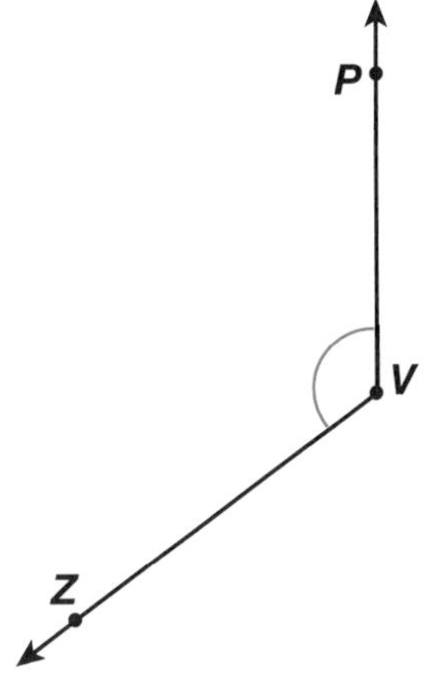

11.

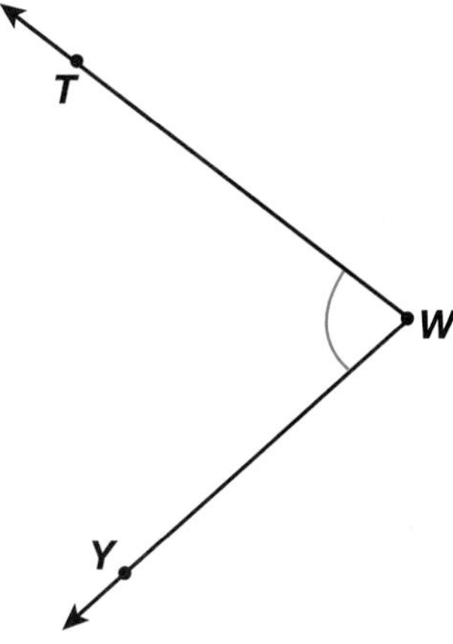

12.

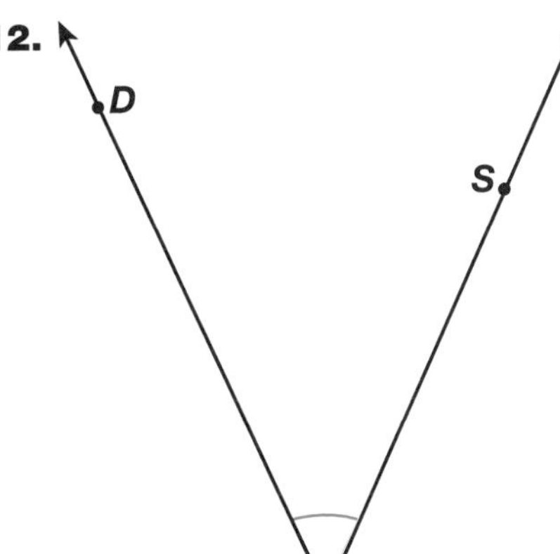

13.

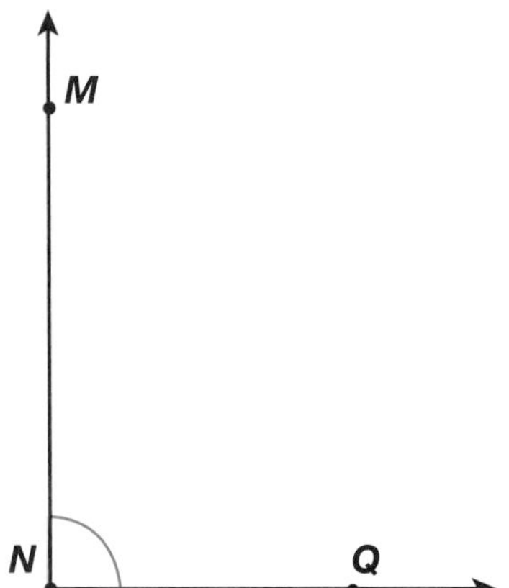

14.

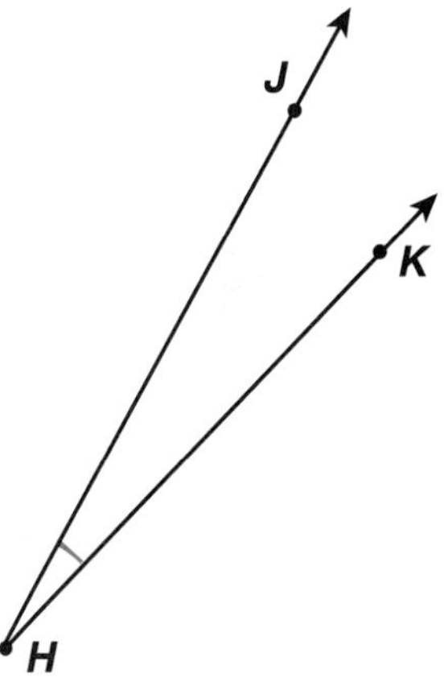

Use a protractor to draw an angle having each measure. Then classify the angle as *right*, *acute*, *obtuse*, or *straight*.

15. 165° **16.** 90° **17.** 20° **18.** 180° **19.** 85°

Write about it! Talk about it!

Use what you have learned to answer these questions.

20. **Analyze** A protractor has two scales. Describe how you decide which scale to use to measure an angle?

21. **Analyze** How can the outer scale of a protractor be used to measure an angle that opens to the right?

22. When an angle is named by using three letters, which letter indicates the vertex?

23. **Analyze** Is the sum of the measures of two acute angles always less than 90°? Explain.

24. How many angles are formed by two rays with a common endpoint? Use a diagram to explain.

25. Describe how you could use a protractor to draw an angle greater than 180°.

Extra Practice See Set B on page 504.

Triangles

You will learn how to classify triangles and find missing angle measures.

New Vocabulary
equilateral
isosceles
scalene

Learn About It

A triangle is made up of 3 line segments called sides. Each pair of sides has a common endpoint or vertex and forms an angle.

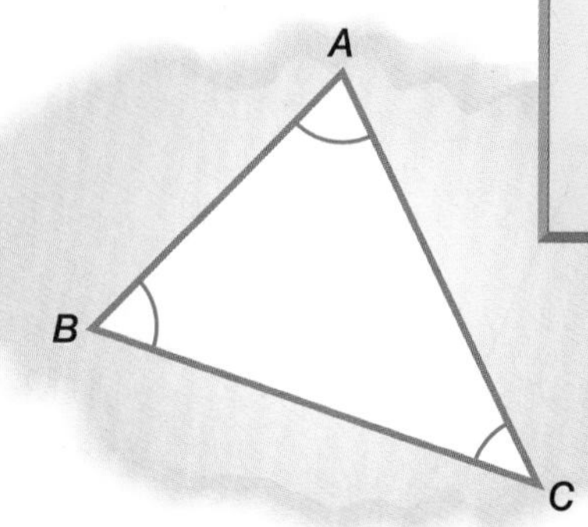

Different Ways to Classify Triangles

There are several different types of triangles. You can classify triangles by the length of their sides.

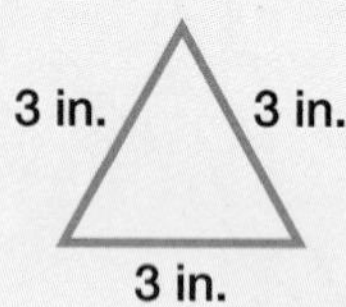

equilateral triangle
all sides are the same length

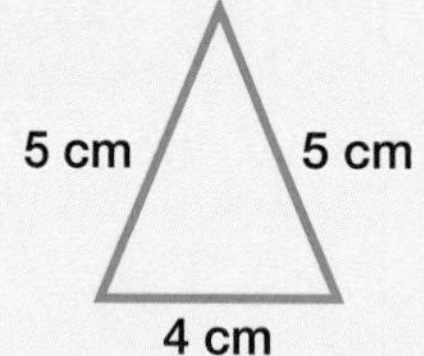

isosceles triangle
at least two sides are the same length

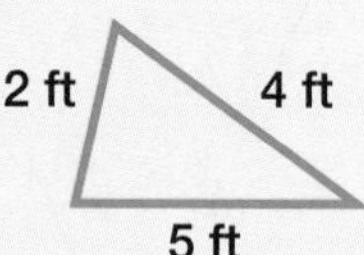

scalene triangle
no sides are the same length

You can classify triangles by their angle measures. The sum of the angle measures in any triangle is 180°.

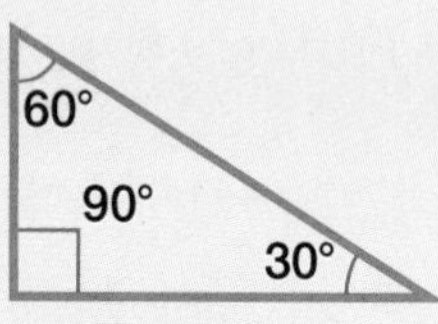

right triangle
one right angle

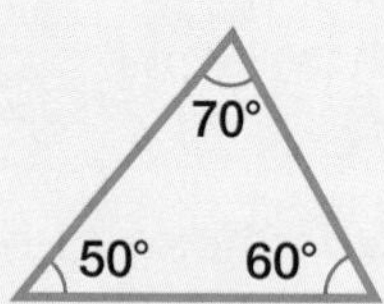

acute triangle
all acute angles

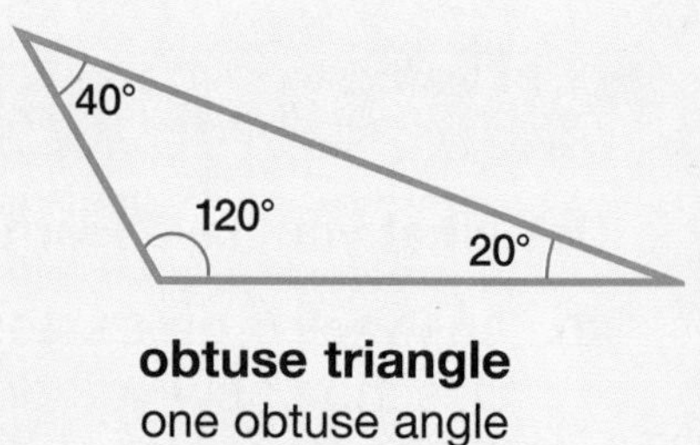

obtuse triangle
one obtuse angle

Another Example

Missing Angle Measure

$\angle T = 180° - (100° + 44°)$

$\angle T = 180° - 144°$

$\angle T = 36°$

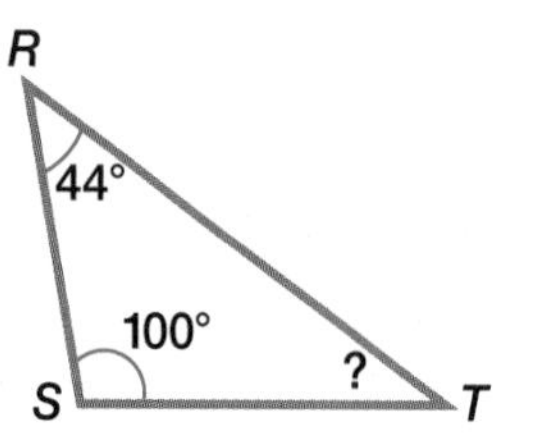

Explain Your Thinking

- ▶ Can a triangle have two right angles? Explain.
- ▶ Does every triangle have to have an obtuse angle? Explain why or why not.

Standards MG **2.0, 2.1, 2.2** MR **2.0, 2.3** AF **1.0**

Guided Practice

Find each missing angle measure. Then classify each triangle in two ways.

1. 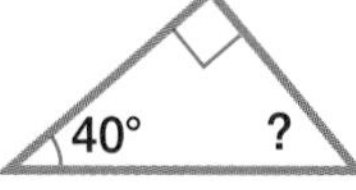

2. 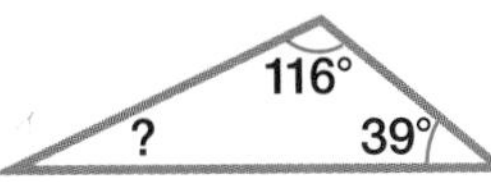

Ask Yourself

- What do I subtract from 180°?
- Are the angles acute? right? obtuse?

Independent Practice

Classify each triangle in two ways.

3. 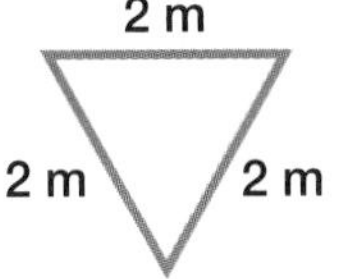

4. 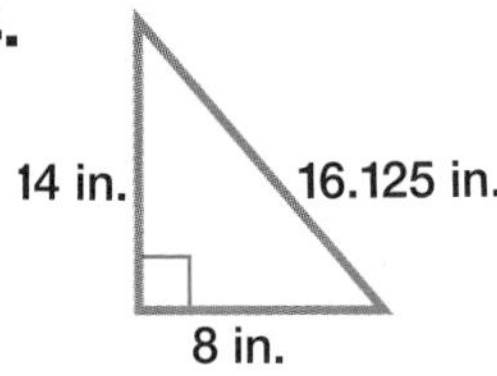

5. 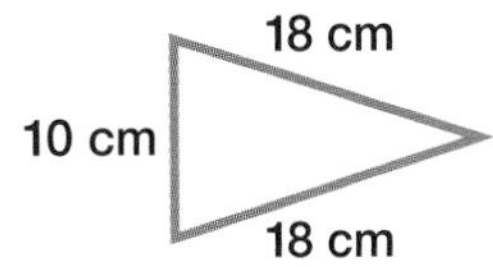

6. 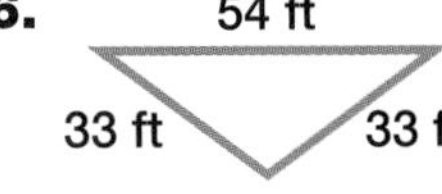

Find the missing angle measures.

7. 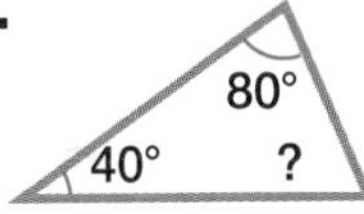

8. 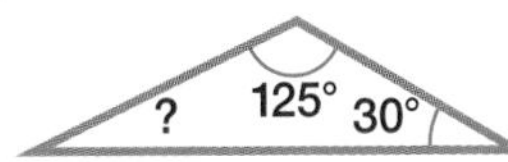

9. 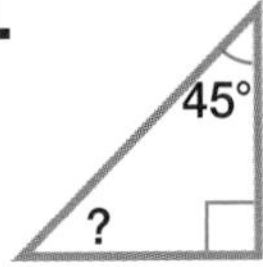

10. 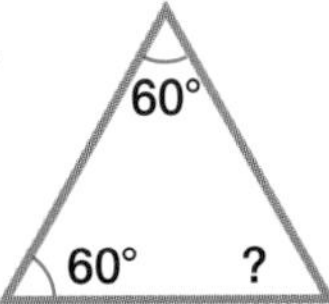

Problem Solving • Reasoning

11. **Analyze** In a right triangle, one of the acute angles is twice the size of the other. What is the measure of the smallest angle?

12. **Analyze** Can an isosceles triangle be obtuse? Use a diagram to explain.

13. **Write Your Own** Use the sum of the angles in a triangle to write your own triangle problem. Give your problem to a partner to solve.

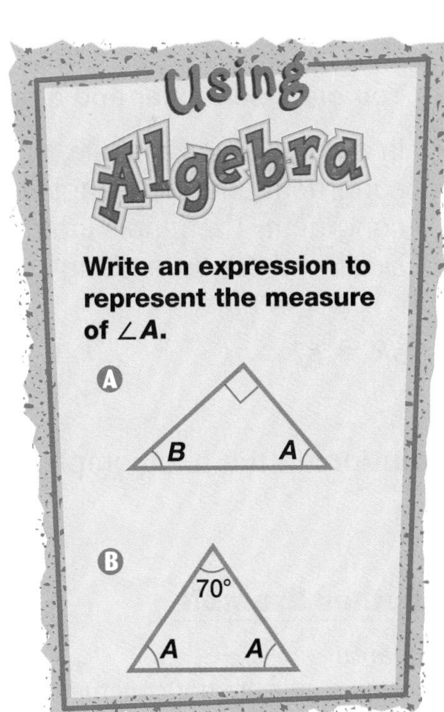

Mixed Review • Test Prep

Add or subtract. Perform the operation in parentheses first. *(pages 66–68)*

14. 94 − (18 + 32)

15. (49 − 27) + 33

16. (6 + 39) − 21

17. 10 + (82 − 75)

18 Five students are standing in line. Tamara is behind Andre. Shawna is in front of Nora and behind Lucia. Nora is in front of Andre. Who is second in line? *(pages 312–313)*

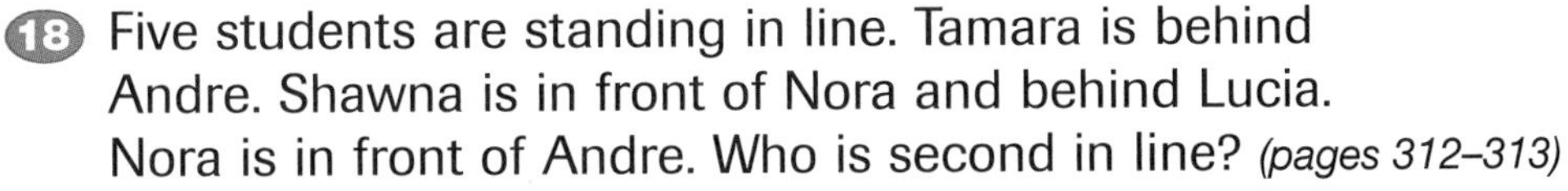

A Andre **B** Shawna **C** Nora **D** Tamara

Extra Practice See Set C on page 504.

Congruence

You will learn how to identify congruent figures and congruent parts of figures.

Review Vocabulary
congruent

Learn About It

Figures that are the same size and shape are called **congruent** figures. The symbol ≅ is used to indicate congruence. The symbol △ is used to identify triangles.

Which figures in this photograph appear to be congruent?

Different Ways to Check For Congruence

You can use a tracing.

If you trace triangle *ABC* and place the tracing on top of triangle *DEF*, you will find that the triangles are identical.

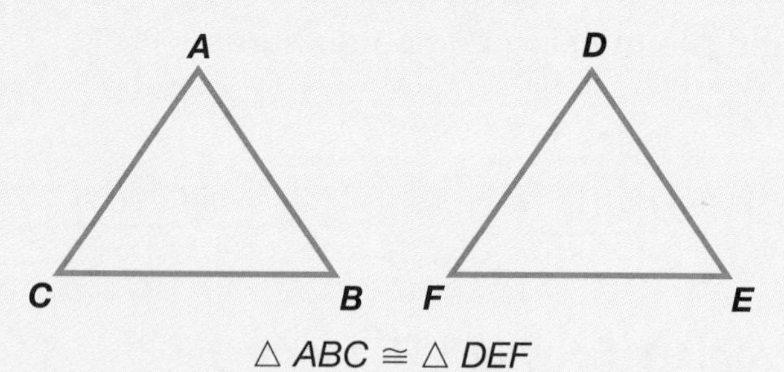

$\triangle ABC \cong \triangle DEF$

You can use a ruler and a protractor.

In an equilateral triangle, the 3 sides are congruent and the 3 angles are congruent. The marks indicate congruent sides and congruent angles.

$\overline{JK} \cong \overline{KL} \cong \overline{JL}$ $\quad \angle J \cong \angle K \cong \angle L$

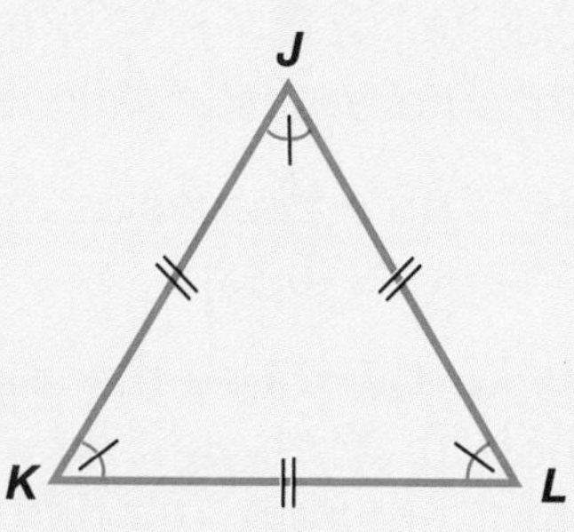

Solution: In the photograph, the sails are congruent triangles.

Another Example

Squares
These squares are not congruent. They have the same shape but they are not the same size.

Explain Your Thinking

- ▶ When are two line segments congruent?
- ▶ If two angles are the same measure, are they congruent? Explain.
- ▶ Can irregular figures be congruent? Use a diagram to explain.

 Standards MG 2.1 MR 2.3

Guided Practice

Trace these figures. Mark the sides and angles that appear to be congruent.

1.

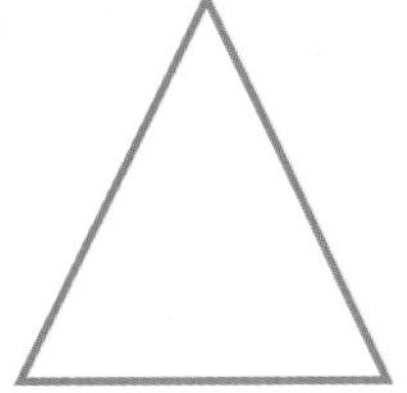

2.

> **Ask Yourself**
> - Which sides are the same length?
> - Which angles have the same measure?

Independent Practice

Trace each figure. Use a ruler to measure the sides and a protractor to measure the angles of each figure. Mark and name the congruent sides and congruent angles.

3.

4.

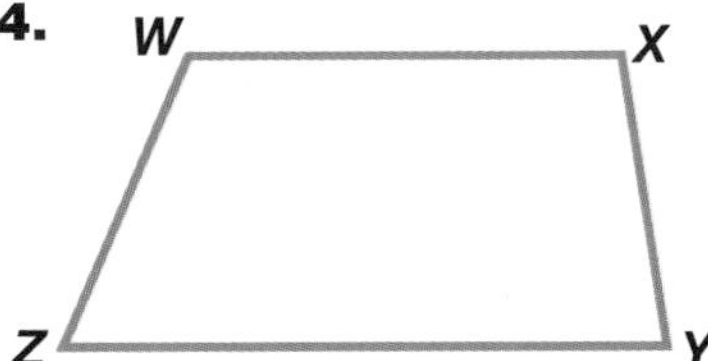

5.

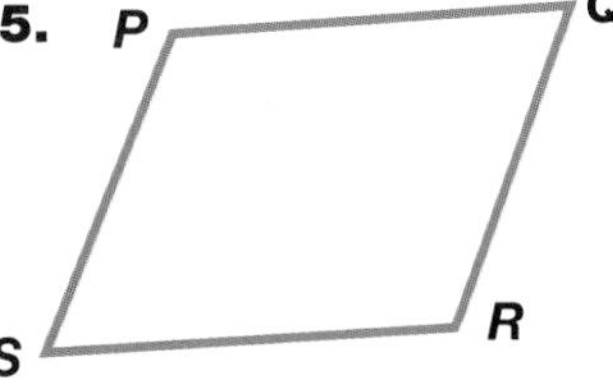

Problem Solving • Reasoning

Use the diagram to answer the questions.

$\triangle ABC \cong \triangle DEF$

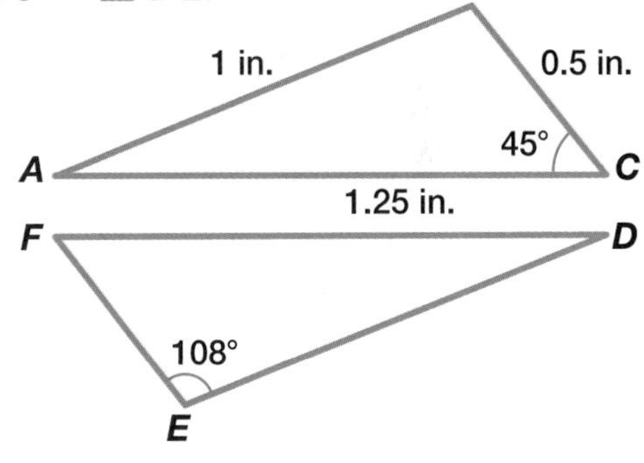

6. What is the length of side $\overline{DE}$?

7. What is the measure of $\angle F$?

8. What is the measure of $\angle A$?

9. What is the length of $\overline{DF}$?

10. What is the measure of $\angle D$?

Mixed Review • Test Prep

Write each fraction in simplest form. *(pages 320–321)*

11. $\frac{3}{6}$ **12.** $\frac{16}{24}$ **13.** $\frac{5}{25}$ **14.** $\frac{14}{42}$ **15.** $\frac{16}{18}$ **16.** $\frac{24}{9}$

17 Which two numbers have a sum of about 35,000? *(pages 52–53)*

A 915 and 3,544

B 19,675 and 1,530

C 29,848 and 5,399

D 251,491 and 101,721

Extra Practice See Set D on page 505.

Quadrilaterals

You will learn how to classify quadrilaterals and find missing angle measures.

Review Vocabulary
quadrilateral
rectangle
square
parallelogram
rhombus
trapezoid

Learn About It

A quadrilateral is a four-sided figure. The sum of the angle measures in any quadrilateral is 360°. You can use sides and angles to classify quadrilaterals.

Classifying Quadrilaterals

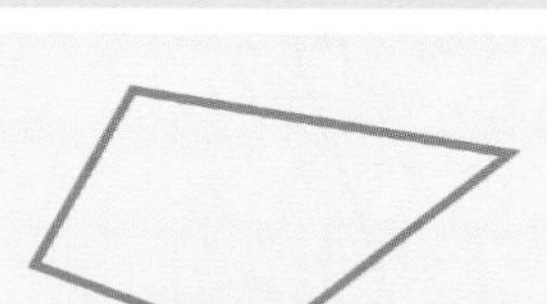

quadrilateral
four sides
four angles

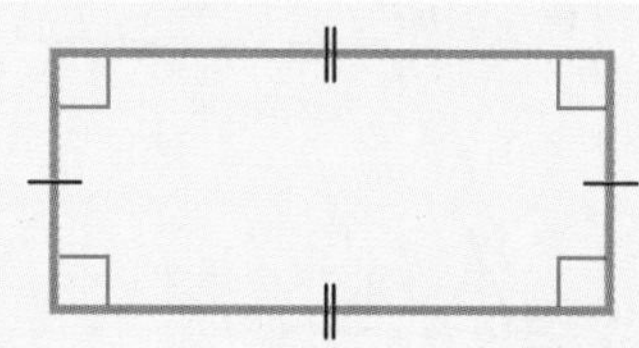

rectangle
opposite sides congruent
four right angles

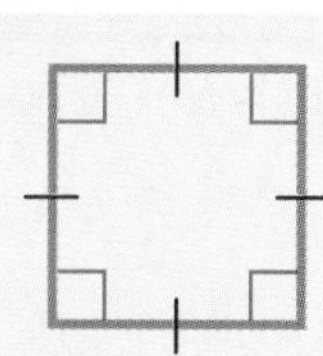

square
four congruent sides
four right angles

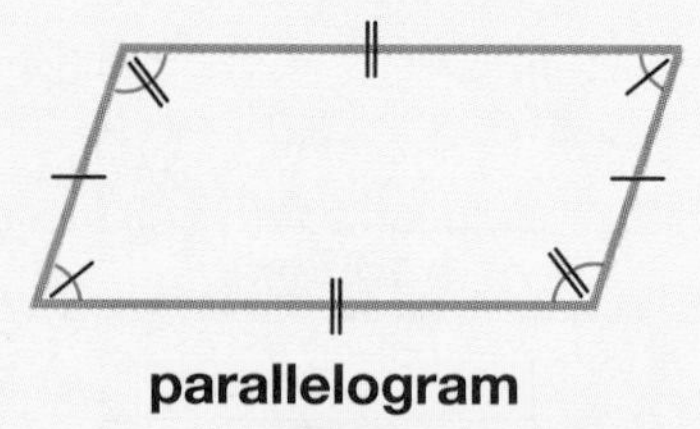

parallelogram
opposite sides congruent and parallel

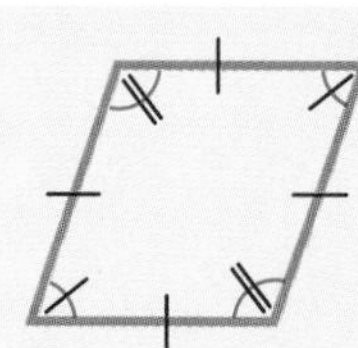

rhombus
four congruent sides
opposite sides parallel

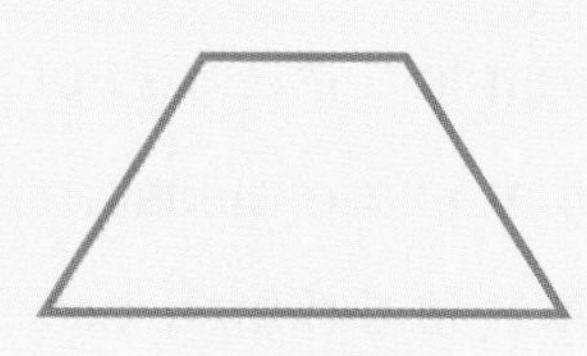

trapezoid
one pair of parallel sides

Another Example

Missing Angle Measure

Find the measure of $\angle MQP$.

Subtract the sum of the known angle measures from 360°.

$\angle MQP = 360° - (75° + 41° + 132°)$

$\angle MQP = 360° - 248°$ so, $\angle MQP = 112°$

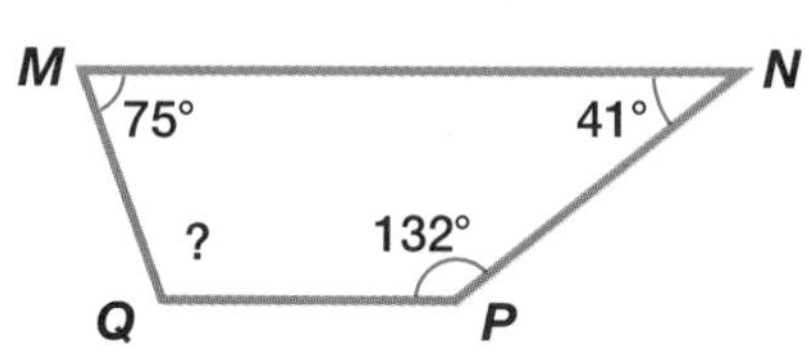

Explain Your Thinking

► Why can some quadrilaterals be classified in more than one way?

► Cut a quadrilateral into two triangles. Use them to explain why the angle sum for a quadrilateral is 360°.

Standards MG **2.0, 2.2** MR **2.0, 2.3**

Guided Practice

Classify each figure in as many ways as possible. Then find the missing angle measures.

1. 

2. 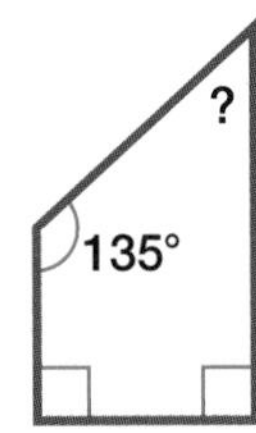

> **Ask Yourself**
> - Are the sides parallel? congruent?
> - Which angles measure 90°?

Independent Practice

Classify the figure in as many ways as possible.

3. 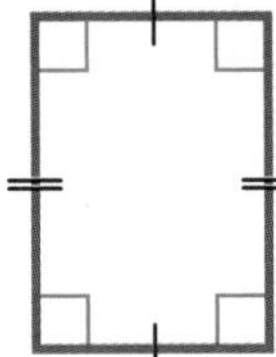

4. 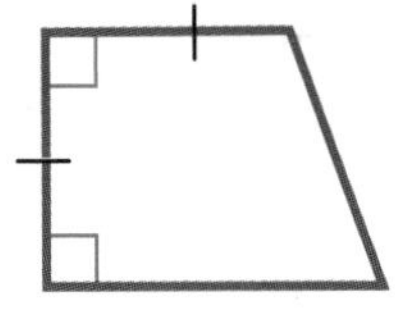

5. 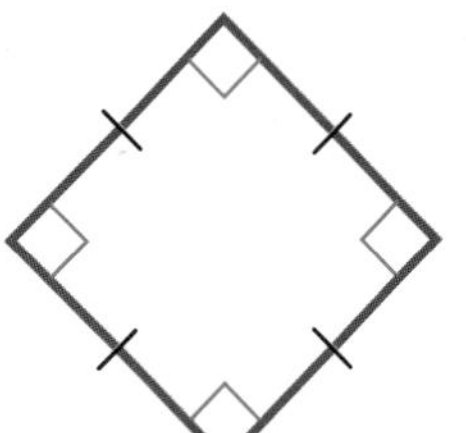

6. 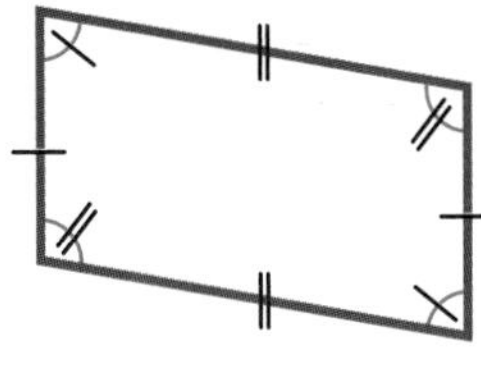

Use the figure to answer each question.

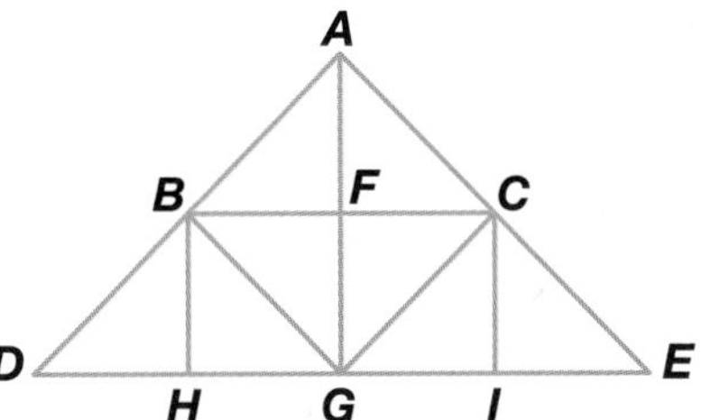

7. Name two different-sized triangles.

8. Name two congruent triangles.

9. Name a square.

10. Name a rectangle that is not a square.

11. Name a trapezoid.

Problem Solving • Reasoning

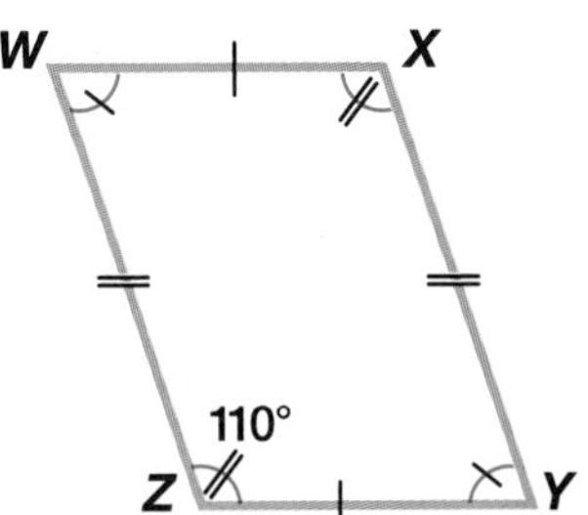

12. What is the measure of $\angle X$?

13. What is the measure of $\angle W$?

14. **Analyze** Is every square a rhombus? Is every rhombus a square? Explain.

Mixed Review • Test Prep

Write the sum and difference of each pair of fractions in simplest form. *(pages 330–331)*

15. $\frac{2}{3}$ and $\frac{1}{3}$ **16.** $\frac{4}{5}$ and $\frac{3}{5}$ **17.** $\frac{3}{4}$ and $\frac{1}{4}$ **18.** $\frac{3}{2}$ and $\frac{1}{2}$

19 Which set of numbers has the least median? *(pages 258–259)*

A 2, 3, 4 **C** 0, 1, 5, 9

B 1, 2, 3, 4 **D** 2, 4, 6

Extra Practice See Set C on page 504.

Problem-Solving Strategy: Solve a Simpler Problem

You will learn how to solve a problem by thinking about a simpler problem.

Sometimes you can solve a problem by solving a simpler problem.

Problem How many triangular pieces were used to make these four quilting blocks?

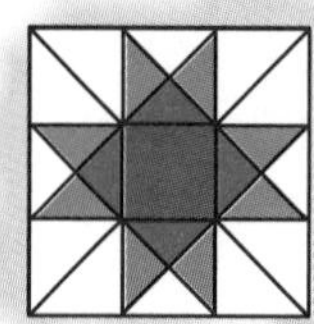

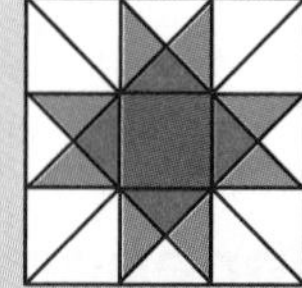

Understand

What is the question?

How many triangular pieces were used to make the four quilting blocks?

What do you know?

The squares and the different-colored triangles the quilt is made up of.

Plan

How can you find the answer?

Solve a simpler problem first by looking at the first block. Group the triangles by color. Find the number of green, red, and white triangles in one block. Multiply by the number of blocks.

Solve

Count the number of green, red, and white triangles in one quilting block.

8 green triangles   4 red triangles   12 white triangles

Calculate the number of triangles in one quilting block.

$8 + 4 + 12 = 24$

Now that you know the number of triangles for one block, it's easy to find the number for 4 blocks.

$24 \times 4 = 96$

There are 96 triangular pieces in the 4 quilting blocks.

Look Back

Look back at the problem.

For what kinds of problems is it helpful to solve a simpler problem?

Standards MG **2.0** MR **1.0, 1.1, 1.2, 2.0, 2.2, 3.0, 3.2, 3.3**

Remember:
- ▶ Understand
- ▶ Plan
- ▶ Solve
- ▶ Look Back

Guided Practice

Solve each problem by solving a simpler problem.

1. How many squares can you find in this figure?

   Think: How many sizes of squares can you find in the figure?

   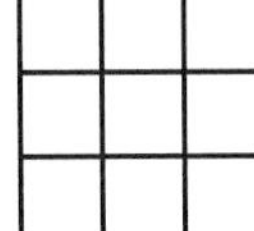

2. How many squares can you find in this quilting block?

   How does the answer to Problem 1 help with this problem?

   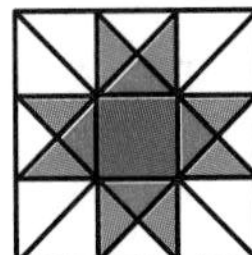

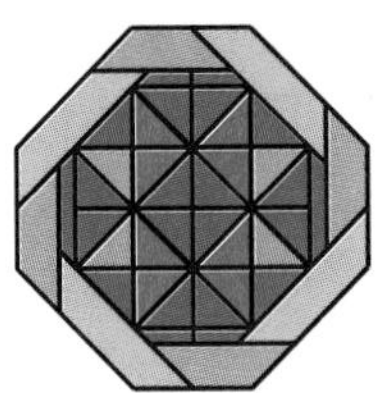

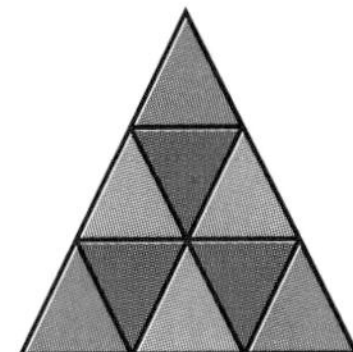

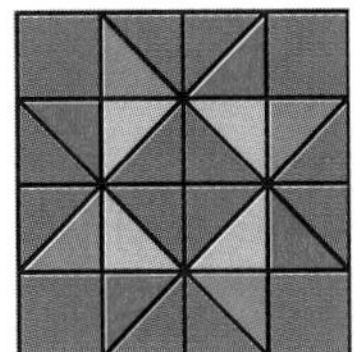

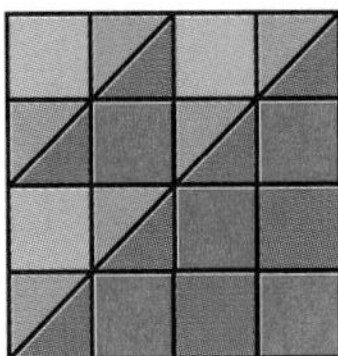

Choose a Strategy

Use these or other strategies.

Problem-Solving Strategies

- **Find a Pattern**
- **Draw a Diagram**
- **Solve a Simpler Problem**
- **Use Logical Reasoning**

3. The blocks in Sara's quilt are each a solid color. The color pattern is red, yellow, blue, yellow, red, yellow, blue, yellow. If this pattern continues as blocks are added to the quilt, what color will the twenty-fifth block be?

4. A pattern has four rectangles in a row. A green rectangle is to the left of a red rectangle. A yellow rectangle is in between the green and the red rectangle. A blue rectangle is first. What is the order of the rectangles?

5. Erica arranges triangular fabric pieces in the form of a larger triangle as shown. How many small fabric pieces will she need to make a triangle with 7 rows?

6. At an auction, four quilts sold for a total of $2,000. The Butterfly Quilt sold for $500. The Star Quilt was half that price. The Morning Quilt sold for three times the price of the Star Quilt. How much did the fourth quilt sell for?

7. A quilt is made up of a repeating pattern of five shapes: four squares and one rectangle. If every third square is blue, how many blue squares will be in a quilt of 45 pieces?

8. How many triangles are there in a quilt made of 24 of these quilting blocks? Explain.

   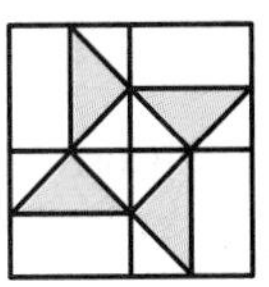

Extra Practice See 1–4 on page 507.

Check Your Understanding of Lessons 1–6

Use the figures below for Exercises 1–5.

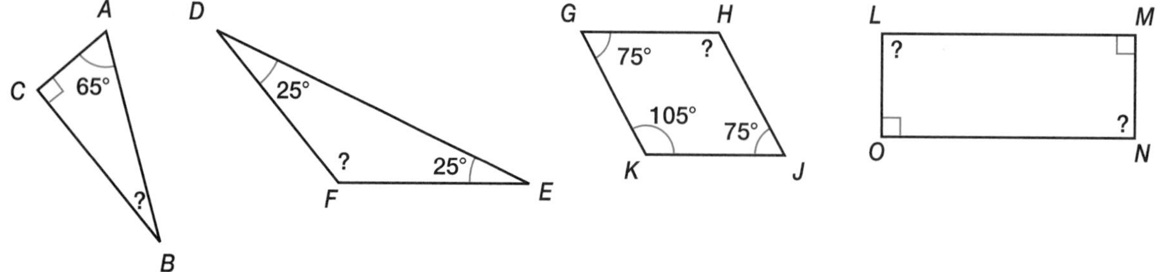

1. Name all the parallel line segments in each figure.
2. Name all the perpendicular line segments in each figure.
3. Classify each angle in each figure as right, acute, obtuse, or straight. Then find the missing angle measures.
4. Classify each figure in as many ways as possible.
5. Use a ruler to help you name the congruent sides in each figure.

Solve.

6. Tony is making a star pattern with pattern blocks. Each star uses 1 square and 4 triangles. If Tony has used 45 blocks, how many stars has he made?

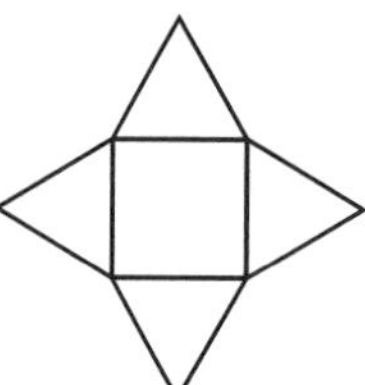

How did you do?

If you had difficulty with any items in the Quick Check, you can use the following pages for review and extra practice.

California Standards	Items	Review These Pages	Do These Extra Practice Items
Measurement and Geometry: **2.0, 2.1**	1–2	pages 454–455	Set A, page 504
Measurement and Geometry: **2.0, 2.1, 2.2**	3	pages 456–459	Set B, page 504
Measurement and Geometry: **2.0, 2.1, 2.2**	4	pages 460–461, 464–465	Set C, page 504
Measurement and Geometry: **2.0**	5	pages 462–463	Set D, page 505
Math Reasoning: **1.1, 3.2**	6	pages 466–467	1–4, page 507

Test Prep • Cumulative Review

Maintaining the Standards

Choose the letter of the correct answer.
If a correct answer is not here, choose NH.

1 Which lines are parallel?

A

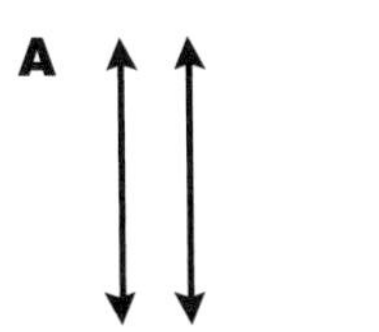

C

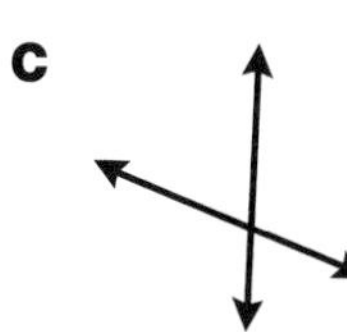

B

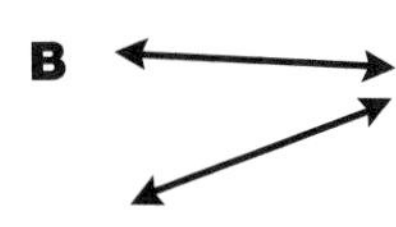

D

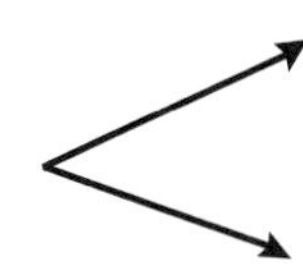

2 Find the digit that makes this statement true.

$$\begin{array}{r} 4\ 7\ 6.85 \\ -\ 2\ \blacksquare\ 8.63 \\ \hline 1\ 7\ 8.22 \end{array}$$

F 0   **H** 7
G 4   **J** 9

3 How many beads are needed to make a 12-inch necklace if the beads are $\frac{3}{4}$ of an inch long?

A 6   **C** NH
B 9   **D** 20

4 Mark worked $1\frac{3}{4}$ hours on one project. He worked $4\frac{1}{6}$ hours on another project. Which expression could you use to find how long Mark worked on both projects?

F $1\frac{9}{12} + 4\frac{2}{12}$

G $4\frac{1}{6} - 1\frac{3}{4}$

H $2\frac{5}{6} - \frac{7}{4}$

J $1\frac{3}{12} + 4\frac{1}{12}$

5 Find the missing angle measure.

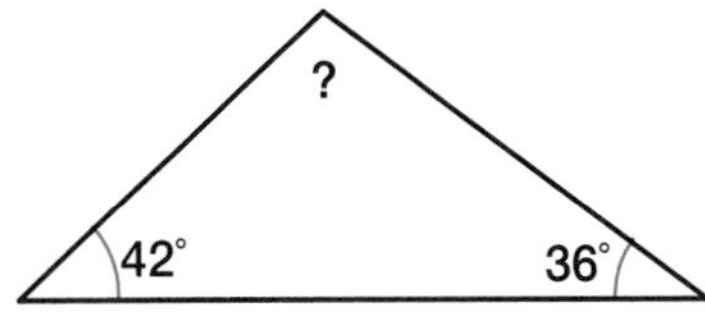

A 87°   **C** 106°
B 102°   **D** 258°

6 Which of the following can never be the product of two odd factors?

F an odd number
G a multiple of 3
H an even number
J a prime number

7 Find the missing angle measure.

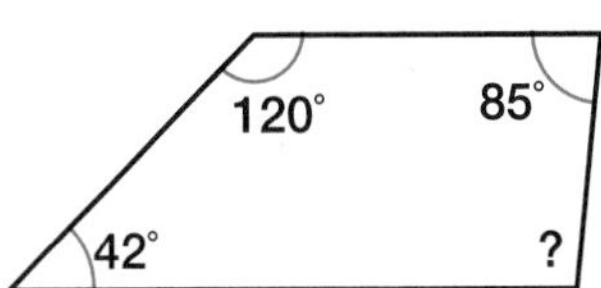

A 250°   **C** 113°
B 240°   **D** 50°

8 Suzy drew a triangle with a 90° angle.

Explain Could the triangle be acute? obtuse?

Safe Site

Internet Test Prep
Visit **www.eduplace.com/kids/mhm** for more *Test Prep Practice.*

Circles and Angles

You will learn how to draw circles and construct and identify parts of a circle.

New Vocabulary
center
radius
diameter
chord
central angle

Learn About It

A circle is the set of all points in a plane that are the same distance from a given point called the **center**. A safe drawing compass or a compass and straightedge can be used to draw a circle and the parts of that circle.

This girl has her finger on the pivot point.

Materials
safe drawing compass

To draw a circle with center *A* and measure and identify parts of the circle, follow these steps.

Step 1 To draw a circle:

- Draw a point and label it point *A*. This will be the center of your circle.
- Place the pivot point of the compass on point *A* and move the slider to any measure you choose.
- Insert your pencil in one of the holes in the slider and draw a circle.

Is every point on the circle the same distance from the center?

Step 2 To draw a radius:

- A **radius** is a segment that connects the center of a circle to any point on the circle.
- Label a point *B* on the circle.
- Connect *A* and *B* to draw radius $\overline{AB}$.

The plural of radius is *radii*. How many radii can a circle have?

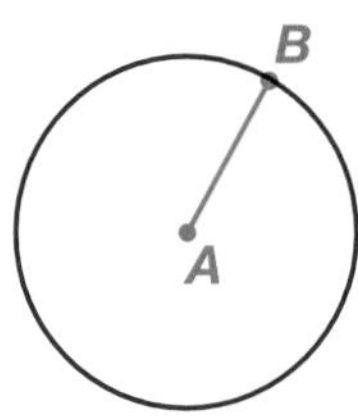

Step 3 To draw a diameter:

- A **diameter** is a segment that connects two points on a circle and passes through the center of the circle.
- Draw points *C* and *D* as shown.
- Connect the points to draw diameter $\overline{CD}$.

How many diameters can a circle have?

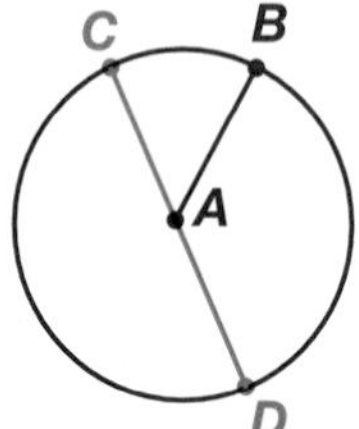

Step 4 To draw a chord:

- A **chord** is a segment that connects two points on a circle.
- Draw two points on the circle and label them *E* and *F*.
- Draw chord $\overline{EF}$.

Is a diameter of a circle also a chord of that circle? Explain.

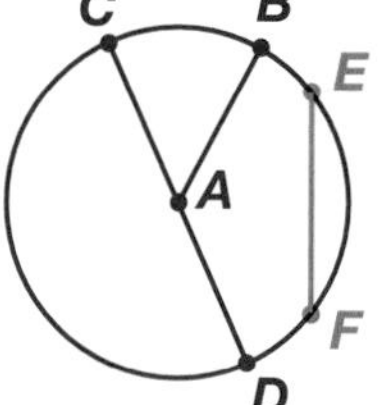

Standards Extends Grade 5 Standards

Step 5 **To identify a central angle:**

A **central angle** is an angle with its vertex at the center of a circle.

$\angle CAB$ is a central angle.

- Name another central angle of the circle.

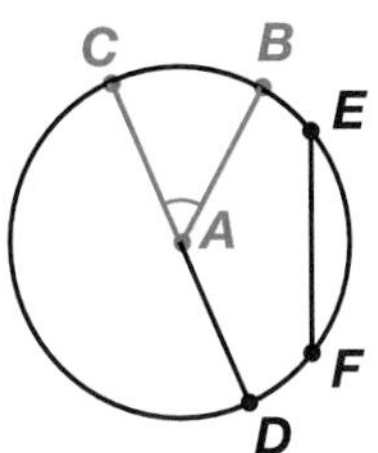

Try It Out

Use symbols to identify the following parts of this circle.

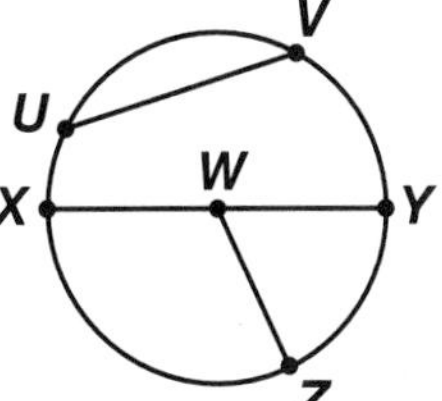

1. radii

2. diameter

3. chords

4. central angles

Classify each figure as a *radius, diameter, chord,* or *central angle*. Indicate if more than one term applies.

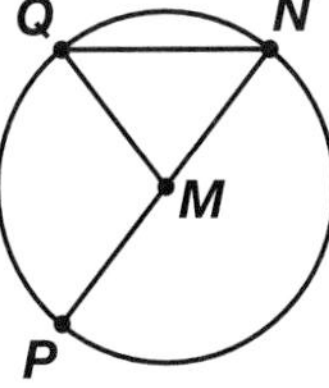

5. $\overline{MP}$

6. $\angle NMQ$

7. $\overline{NP}$

8. $\overline{MQ}$

9. $\overline{QN}$

10. $\angle QMP$

On a separate sheet of paper, construct a circle that contains all of the following.

11. center B

12. chord $\overline{CL}$

13. diameter $\overline{RL}$

14. radius $\overline{BC}$

15. central angle RBH

16. chord $\overline{RH}$

Write about it! Talk about it!

Use what you have learned to write about these questions.

17. What relationship does a radius of a circle share with a diameter? What relationship does a diameter of a circle share with a radius?

18. **Analyze** What is the sum of the measures of the two straight angles formed by a diameter of a circle?

Parallel and Perpendicular Lines

You will learn how to construct lines that are parallel or perpendicular to a given line.

Learn About It

Materials

safe drawing compass

Lines can be named by identifying two of their points or by using lowercase letters like *c* and *d*.

Perpendicular lines intersect at right angles. A compass and a straightedge can be used to construct a line that passes through a given point and is perpendicular to another line.

To construct line *d* perpendicular to line *c* through point *W*, follow these steps.

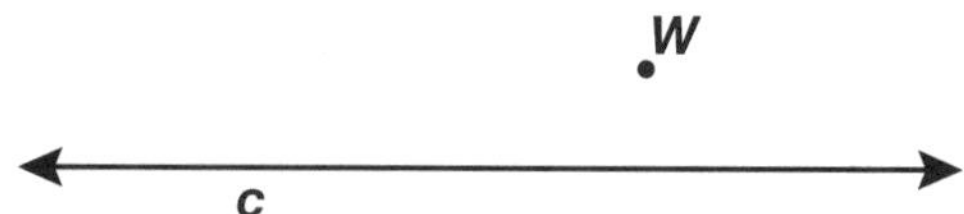

Constructing Perpendicular Lines

Step 1 Draw *c* and *W* as shown above. Put the point of the compass on *W*. Draw an arc that intersects line *c* twice. Label the intersecting points *X* and *Y*.

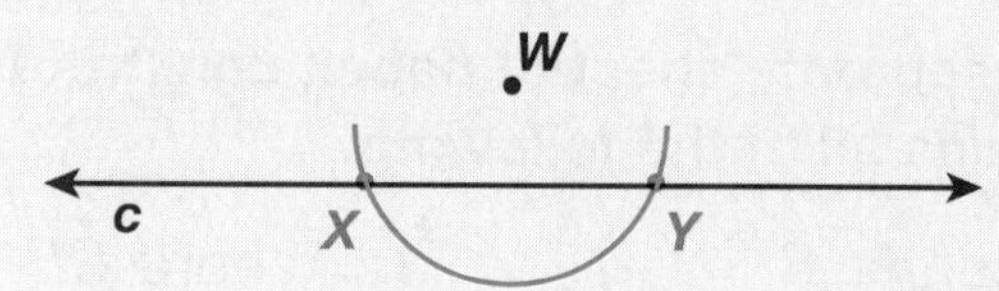

Step 2 Then, place the point of the compass at *X* and draw an arc. Using the same compass measure, draw an arc from *Y*. Label the point where the two arcs intersect *V*.

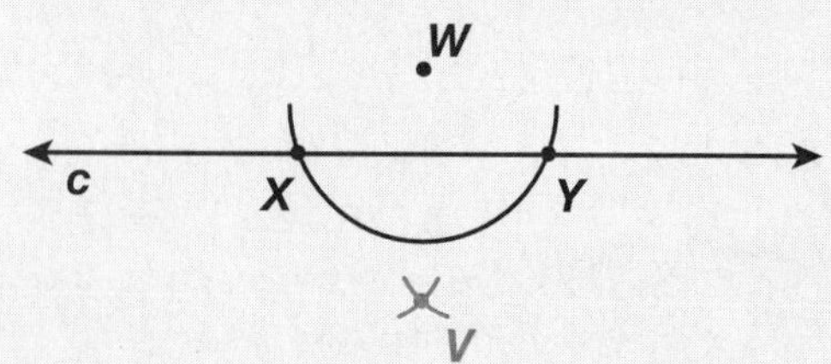

Step 3 Draw line *WV* and label it *d*. Line *d* is perpendicular to line *c*.

- How would you write that line *c* is perpendicular to line *d* using symbols?

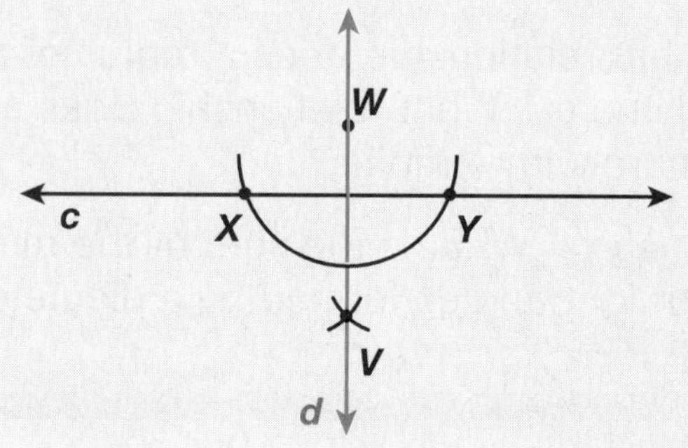

Standards MG **2.0, 2.1** MR **2.0, 2.3, 3.0, 3.3**

Parallel lines never intersect. They are always the same distance from each other. A compass and a straightedge can be used to construct a line that is parallel to another line.

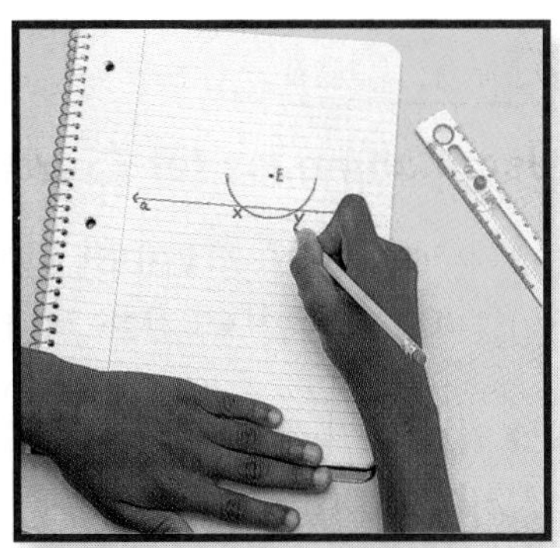

To construct line *e* parallel to a given line *f* through point *Q* that is not on line *f*, follow these steps.

Q

Constructing Parallel Lines

Step 1 Draw *f* and *Q* as shown above. Construct line *g* through point *Q* perpendicular to *f* where *Q* is not on *f*.

Q
f
g

Line *g* and line *f* are perpendicular. Write $g \perp f$.

Step 2 Construct line *e* through point *Q* perpendicular to *g* where *Q* is on *g*.

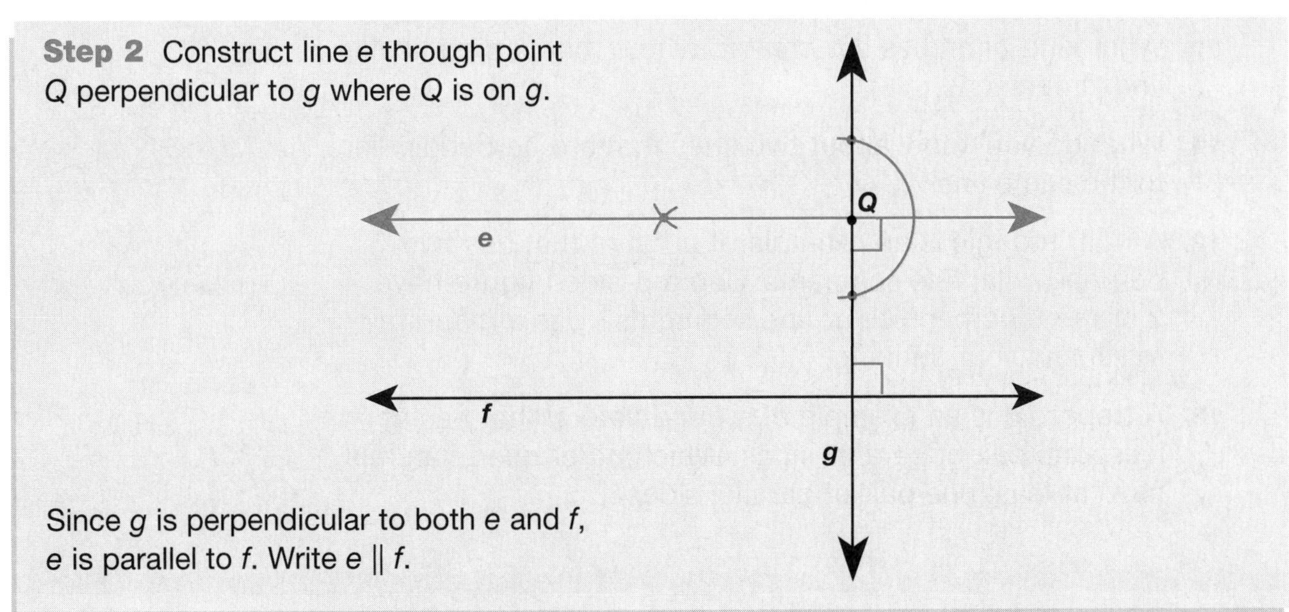

Since *g* is perpendicular to both *e* and *f*, *e* is parallel to *f*. Write $e \parallel f$.

Try It Out

Use a compass for Exercises 1–9.

1. Draw line r. Label a point Z that is not on r. Construct line h so that h is perpendicular to r and passes through Z.
2. Draw a line and label it m. Construct line n so that n is perpendicular to m.
3. Draw line x. Label a point A that is on x. Construct line y so that y is perpendicular to x and passes through A.
4. Draw a line and label it e. Construct line f so that line f is parallel to e.
5. Draw 3 line segments congruent to $\overline{AB}$.

6. Construct a right triangle with a right angle at A. Label it $\triangle ABC$.
7. Construct a rectangle. Label it $ABCD$.
8. Construct a square and label it $ABCD$.
9. Construct a rhombus that is not a square.

Below: Triangles are often used in structures, like this bridge, because they add strength to the structure.

Write about it! Talk about it!

Use what you have learned to answer each question.

10. What kind of angles are created where two perpendicular lines intersect?
11. What do you know about two lines that are perpendicular to the same line?
12. A right triangle is an example of a figure that has two perpendicular line segments. Can a 5-sided figure have 2 or more perpendicular line segments? Use a diagram to explain your thinking.
13. A trapezoid is an example of a quadrilateral that has at least one pair of parallel sides. Which other quadrilaterals have at least one pair of parallel sides?

Extra Practice See Set E on page 505.

Show What You Know

Using Vocabulary

Write *true* or *false* for each sentence. If a sentence is false, rewrite it to make it true.

1. If two lines intersect, they must be parallel.
2. A ray is a set of points in a straight path that extends in two directions without end.
3. A square is also a rhombus.
4. The measure of an acute angle is less than 90°.
5. A compass is a tool for measuring angles.
6. An equilateral triangle has only two congruent sides.

Check It Out

Find the measure of each angle.

1. ∠*BED*
2. ∠*ABE*
3. ∠*CBE*
4. ∠*ABC*

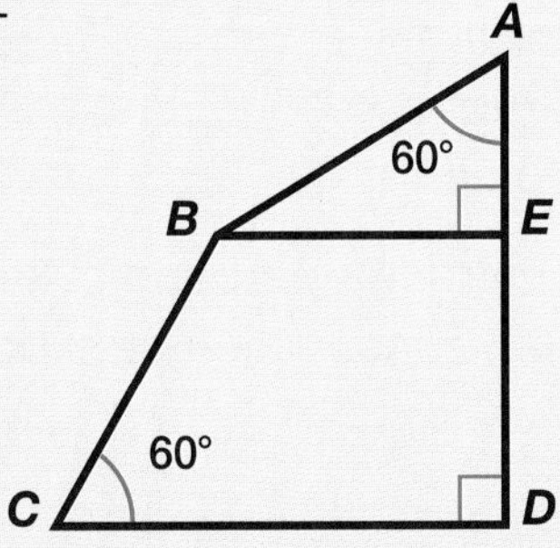

Match It Up

Use three letters to name each angle in the diagram at the right.

1. an acute angle
2. an obtuse angle
3. a 15° angle
4. a 45° angle

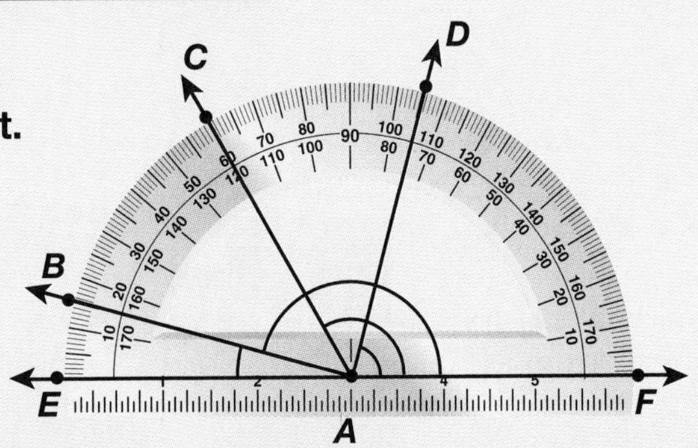

Triangles and Rectangles

You will learn how to construct various plane figures.

Learn About It

You can construct triangles and rectangles with a compass and a straightedge.

Construct a rectangle, *MNPQ*, congruent to rectangle *BCGH*.

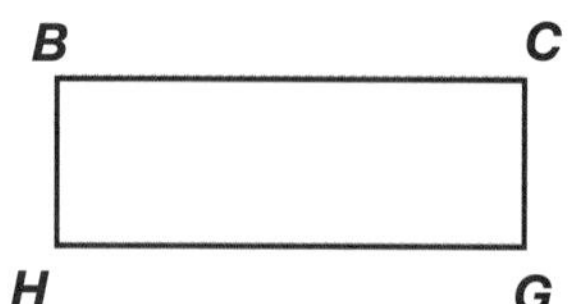

Materials

safe drawing compass (or compass and straightedge)

Drawing Congruent Rectangles

Step 1 Draw a line. Mark a point on the line. Label the point *Q*.

- What symbol on a line is used to indicate a point?

Step 2 Measure $\overline{HG}$. Move the slider to that measure. Using this measure, draw an arc from Q. Label point *P*.

- Which segment in *BCGH* is $\overline{QP}$ congruent to?

Step 3 Construct a line perpendicular to $\overline{QP}$ at *Q*. Construct a second line perpendicular to $\overline{QP}$ at *P*.

- When you construct a perpendicular line from a point on a line, which arcs do you draw first?

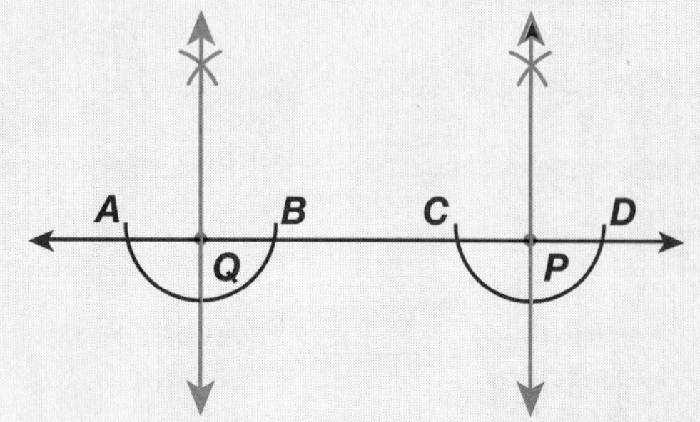

Step 4 Measure $\overline{GC}$. Using this measure, draw an arc from *P* and label point *N*. Draw an arc from *Q* and label point *M*. Use a straightedge to draw $\overline{MN}$.

- How do you know that rectangle *MNPQ* is congruent to rectangle *BCGH*?

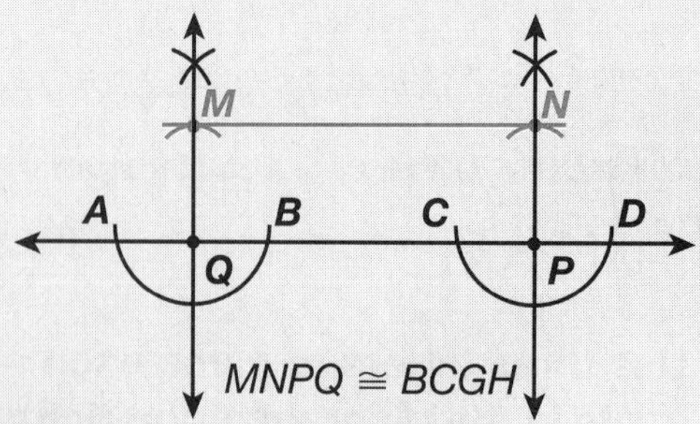

LEFT: You can see both triangles and rectangles in this Mayan pyramid located in Mexico.

RIGHT: The Great Pyramid in Egypt has 4 triangular faces.

Standards MG **2.0, 2.1** MR **2.0, 2.4, 3.0, 3.3**

Construct triangle *RST* congruent to equilateral triangle *JKL*.

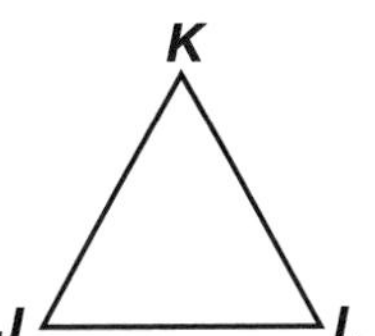

Drawing Congruent Triangles

Step 1 Draw a line. Mark a point on the line. Label the point *R*.

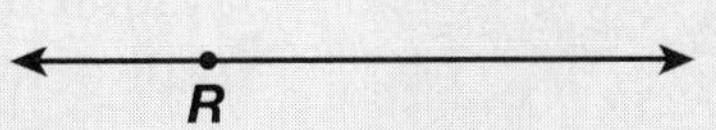

Step 2 Measure $\overline{JL}$ and move the slider. Using this measure, draw an arc from *R*. Label the point of intersection *T*.

Step 3 Without changing the compass measure, draw an arc from point *R* and an arc from point *T*. Label the point of intersection *S*.

- How do you know $\overline{RS}$ will be congruent to $\overline{JK}$?

Step 4 Use a straightedge to draw $\overline{RS}$ and $\overline{TS}$.

- Why do you keep the same compass measure?
- How do you know that $\triangle RST \cong \triangle JKL$?

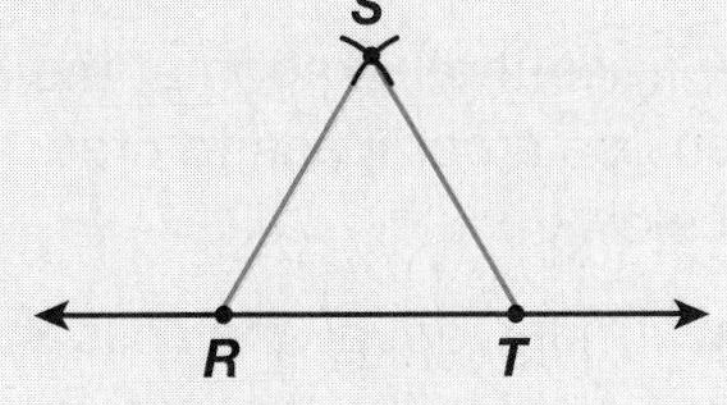

Try It Out

Complete each construction.

1. Construct triangle *PNR* congruent to equilateral triangle *BXY*.
2. Construct rectangle *AEIU* congruent to rectangle *CJNR*.

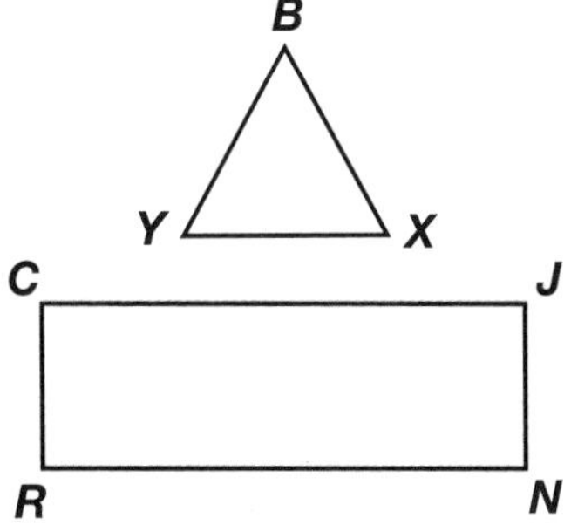

Write about it! Talk about it!

Use what you have learned to answer each question.

3. What does it mean to say two figures are congruent?
4. **Analyze** Suppose a rectangle is given. Explain how a congruent rectangle can be constructed at a given point. Use constructions to support your explanation.

Extra Practice See Set F on page 505.

Symmetry

You will learn how to identify rotational and line symmetry.

New Vocabulary
rotational symmetry
line symmetry

Learn About It

Suppose the blades of this windmill make a half turn. How will the appearance of the windmill compare to the way it looks in this picture?

If you can turn a figure less than a full turn about a fixed point and the figure looks exactly the way it did before the turn, that figure has **rotational symmetry** about the fixed point.

Materials
unlined paper
compass
scissors
straightedge
protractor

Test a figure for rotational symmetry.

Step 1 Trace the hexagon at the right and cut it out. Then use a compass to draw a circle as shown below.

- Into how many equal angles is the circle divided? What is the measure of each angle?

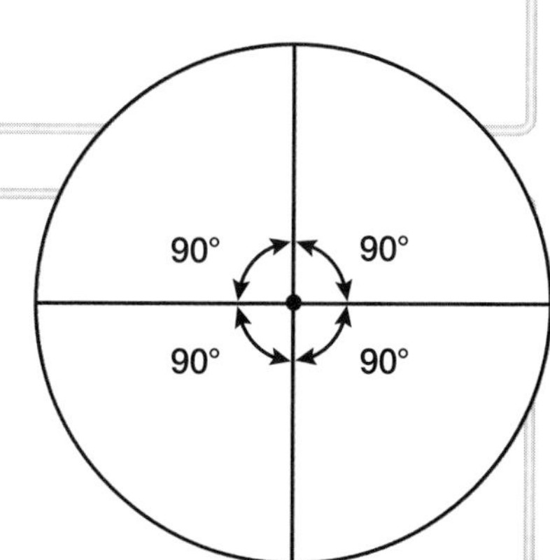

Step 2 Place the center point of the figure on the center of the circle. With the point of your pencil, hold the figure at the center point. With your other hand, slowly turn the figure.

- As you turn, why must you keep the center of the figure aligned with the center of the circle?

Step 3 Continue turning until the figure matches the original image.

- What kind of turn resulted in a figure that matched the original image? How many degrees is this?

Standards Reviews Grade 4 Standards

If a figure can be folded in half and the two halves are congruent, the figure has **line symmetry**. The fold is a line of symmetry.

Use a tracing to test a figure for line symmetry.

Step 1 Trace the square at the right and cut it out.

Step 2 Try to fold the square in as many ways as possible so that both halves are congruent.

- Can a figure have more than one line of symmetry? Explain.
- How many lines of symmetry does a square have?

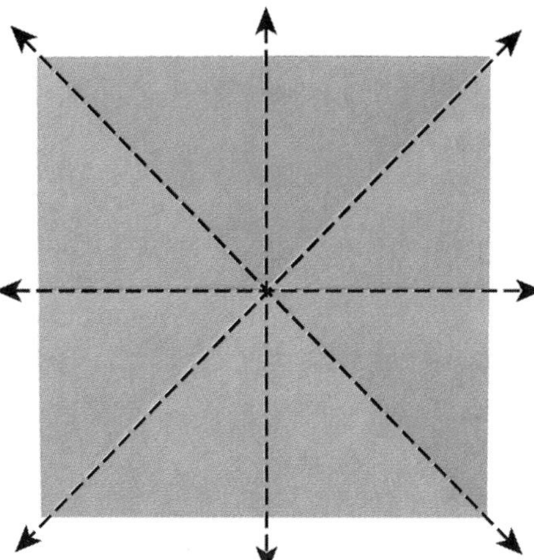

Try It Out

Trace each figure and turn it. Then, for each figure, write *yes* or *no* to tell if it has rotational symmetry. If it does, tell how many degrees you turned it.

1. 

2. 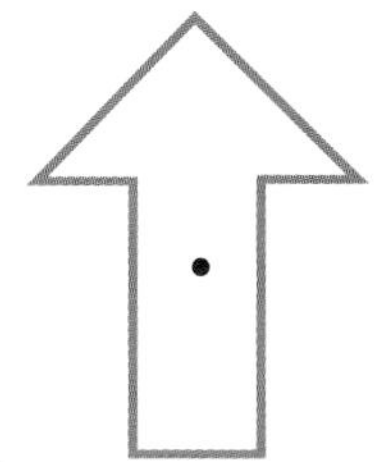

3. 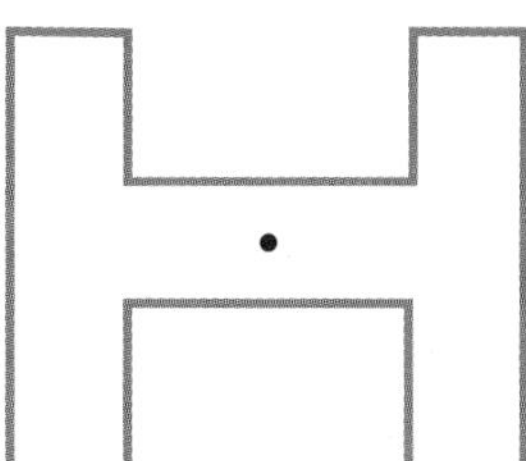

4. 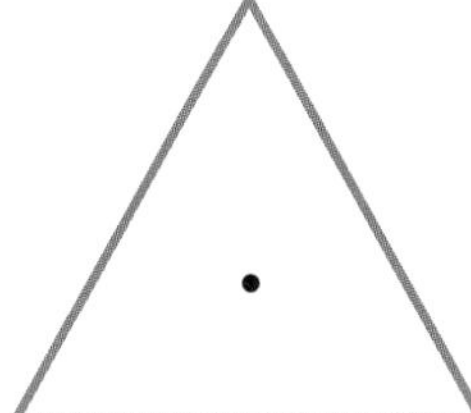

5. 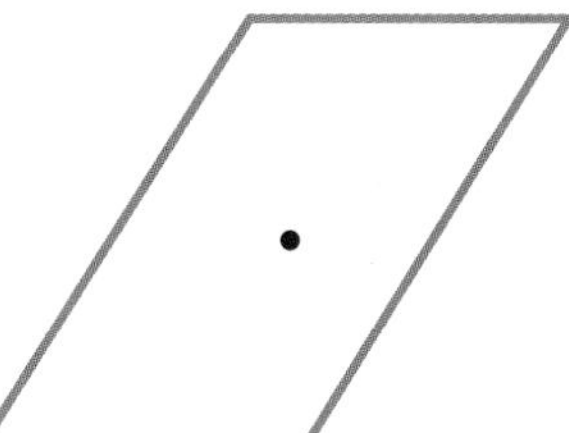

6. 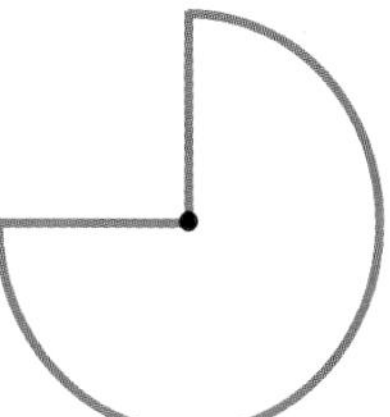

7. 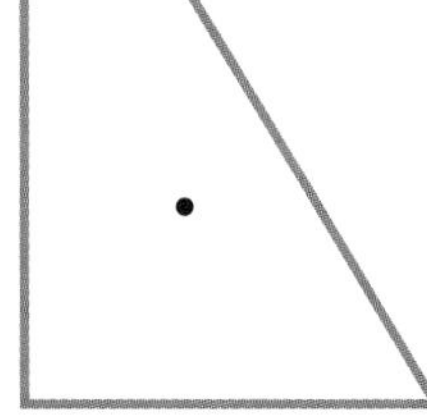

8. 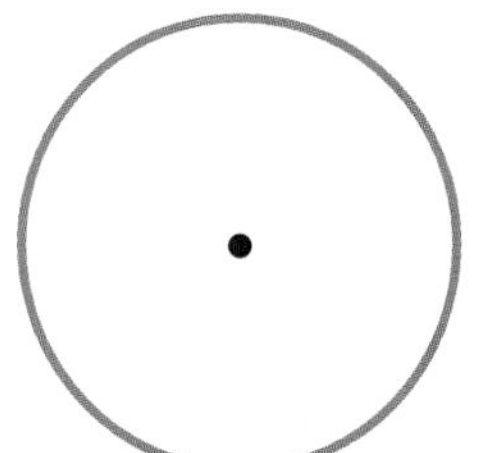

9. 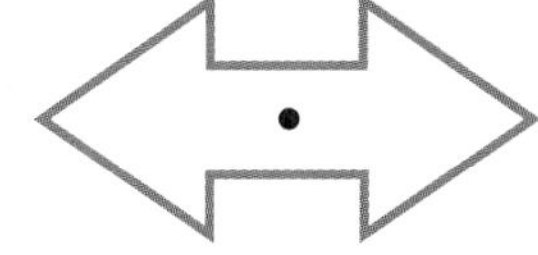

Trace each figure and fold it. Then, for each figure, write *yes* or *no* to tell if it has line symmetry. If it does, write the number of lines of symmetry that it has.

10. 

11. 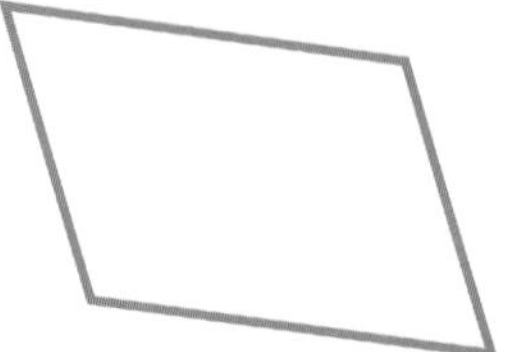

12. 

13. 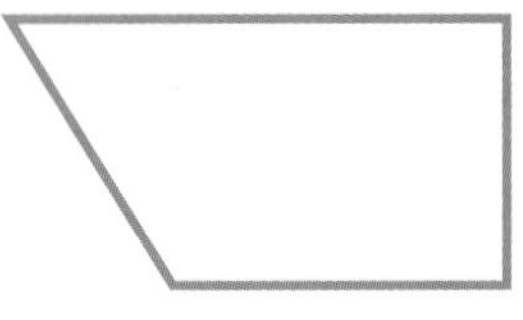

14. 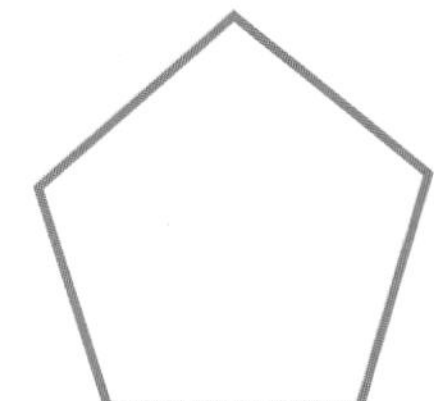

15. 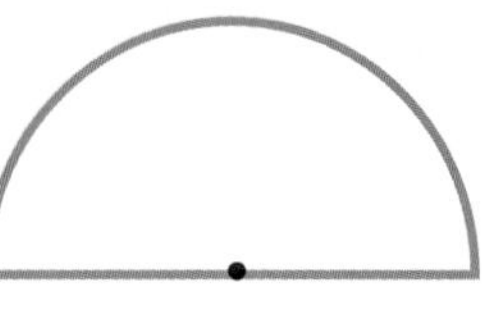

16. 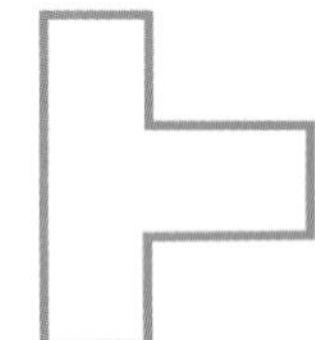

17. 

18. 

Use a compass, a protractor, and another sheet of paper to draw these figures.

19. a figure that has line symmetry but not rotational symmetry

20. a figure that has rotational symmetry but not line symmetry

21. a figure that has line symmetry and rotational symmetry

Write about it! Talk about it!

Use what you have learned to answer these questions.

22. **Analyze** Why is a full turn of 360° not included when describing rotational symmetry?

23. **Analyze** Is it possible for a figure to have line symmetry but not rotational symmetry? If so, draw such a figure.

24. What is the greatest number of lines of symmetry a figure may have?

25. What fraction of a full turn, is a turn of 90°? 180°? 270°?

Practice Game

Tangrams

Practice making two-dimensional figures by playing this game with a partner.

What You'll Need

- *a set of tangram pieces like the ones shown (Teaching Tool 10)*

Players 2

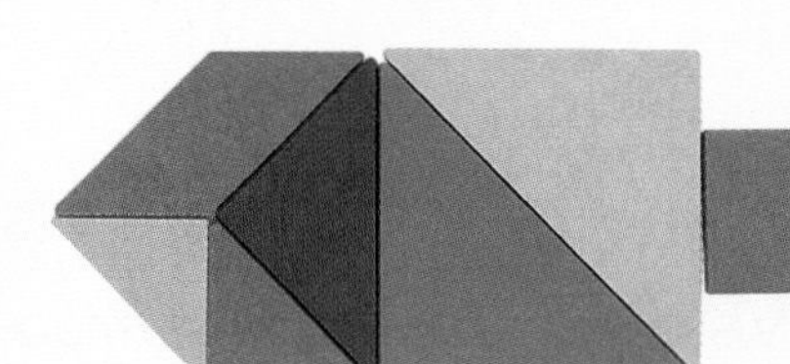

Here's What to Do

If you don't have tangrams or Teaching Tool 10, you can make your own pieces by tracing the ones on this page and cutting them out.

1. The first player makes a shape with the tangram pieces and traces its outline. The pieces should not overlap. At least some of them should be placed edge to edge.
2. The pieces are removed and mixed up. The second player must figure out how to arrange the pieces within the outline, without any overlapping pieces.

Take turns repeating Steps 1 and 2.

You may want to make a sketch of your design to help you remember it if your partner can't solve the puzzle.

Share Your Thinking Why might it be a good idea to place several pieces edge to edge when you make your puzzle?

Problem-Solving Skill: Visual Thinking

You will learn how to solve problems by thinking about them visually.

When you are solving a problem, it can help if you visualize the solution and work backward.

The figure shown is made up of 12 toothpicks.

Problem How can you move 4 toothpicks so that there will be exactly 3 small squares, all the same size with no toothpicks left over?

Sometimes you can visualize a problem.

Visualize three squares made up of toothpicks.

Squares have four sides, so three squares would use 12 toothpicks altogether only if no squares share a side.

Then you can manipulate a model.

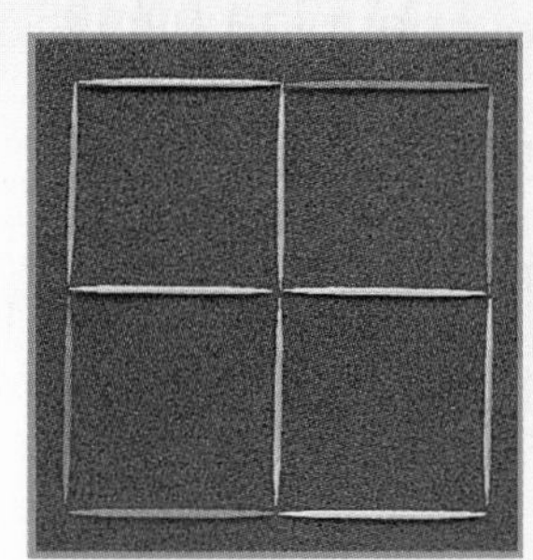

If you remove two toothpicks in opposite corners, you are left with two squares that don't share a side.

Then you can make a third square with the four toothpicks you removed.

Solution: 

Look Back Can you move different toothpicks to get the same result? How? Can you move 4 toothpicks and make exactly two squares? How?

 Standards MR **1.0, 2.0, 2.2, 2.3, 3.0, 3.2**

Chicago artist Wayne Kusy has been building large ships out of toothpicks since he was in fifth grade. Here he is shown with a model of the *Cutty Sark*.

Guided Practice

Solve.

1. How can you remove two toothpicks to leave two triangles?

Think: Do the triangles you leave have to be the same size?

2. How many different figures can you make with four congruent equilateral triangles placed edge to edge with no overlapping?

Think: How can you check to see if each figure is different?

Choose a Strategy

Solve. Use these or other strategies.
Use the figure at the right for Problems 3 and 4.

Problem-Solving Strategies

- **Write an Equation**
- **Draw a Diagram**
- **Guess and Check**

3. How can you remove six toothpicks to leave three squares?

4. How can you remove four toothpicks to leave five squares?

5. Wooden toothpicks can be packed in crates. A crate can hold about 400,000 toothpicks. If a toothpick company produced 34,000,000 toothpicks in one week, about how many crates would be needed to pack them?

6. Rearrange the numerals so that every row and column has a sum of 10.

1	2	3	4
1	2	3	4
1	2	3	4
1	2	3	4

7. Standard toothpicks are 2 in. long. If 400,000 toothpicks are placed end to end, about how long would the line be in miles?

8. A box of 100 toothpicks sells for $5.00. Five boxes sell for $23.50. How much money is saved by buying 5 boxes at a time?

Extra Practice See 5–6 on page 507.

Check Your Understanding of Lessons 7–11

Use a compass and a straightedge to construct each line.

1. Draw line *t*. Label point *B* on the line. Construct line *s* so that *s* is perpendicular to *t* and passes through *B*.
2. Draw line *p*. Construct line *q* so that *q* is parallel to *p*.

Use a compass and a straightedge to construct each figure.

3. Construct triangle *ABC* congruent to triangle *DEF*.

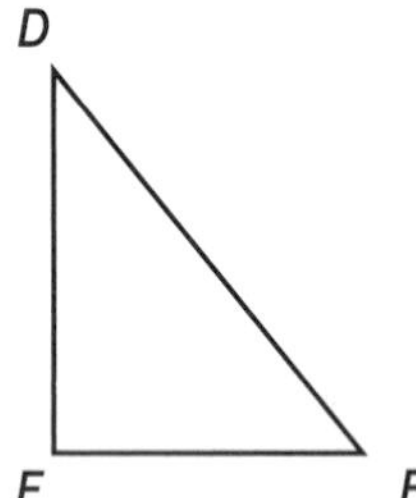

4. Construct rectangle *STUV* congruent to rectangle *MNOP*.

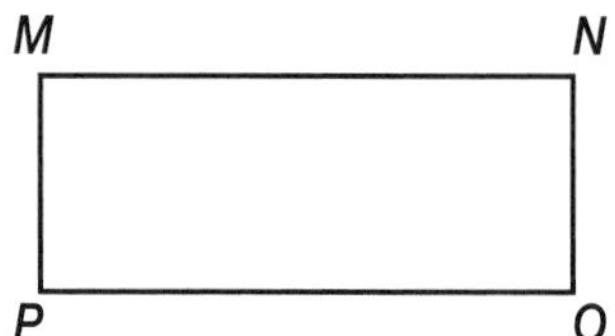

Solve.

5. How can you use seven toothpicks to make one square and two triangles?

How did you do?

If you had difficulty with any items in the Quick Check, you can use the following pages for review and extra practice.

California Standards	Items	Review These Pages	Do These Extra Practice Items
Measurement and Geometry: **2.1**	1–2	pages 472–474	set E, page 505
Measurement and Geometry: **2.1**	3–4	pages 476–477	set F, page 505
Math Reasoning: **1.0**	5	pages 482–483	5–6, page 507

Test Prep • Cumulative Review

Maintaining the Standards

Choose the letter of the correct answer.

1. How many lines of symmetry does an equilateral triangle have?

   A 1 **C** 3
   B 2 **D** 4

2. A population projection predicts that the population of the United States in 2028 will be 342,517,584. Round this figure to the nearest ten million.

   F 350,000,000
   G 342,000,000
   H 340,000,000
   J 300,000,000

3. If one chip is drawn from each bag, what is the probability that the sum of the numbers drawn will be 8?

   A $\frac{1}{8}$ **C** 4
   B $\frac{1}{6}$ **D** 8

4. Ramon is following a recipe for making 24 pancakes. The recipe calls for $3\frac{1}{4}$ cups of flour. How much flour should Ramon use if he wants to make only 12 pancakes?

   F $1\frac{5}{8}$ c **H** $2\frac{1}{4}$ c
   G $1\frac{3}{4}$ c **J** $6\frac{1}{2}$ c

5. Use the data to determine which of the choices below equals 37.

   Data: 12, 37, 32, 37, 18, 20

   A mean **C** median
   B mode **D** range

6. Which number is divisible by 3, 4, and 9?

   F 96 **H** 297
   G 168 **J** 324

7. Describe what is being constructed.

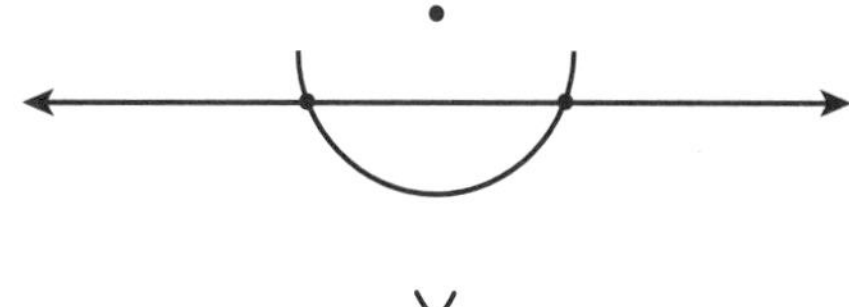

   A parallel lines
   B perpendicular lines
   C a triangle
   D a rectangle

8. Show how you could construct a line that is perpendicular to a given line.

   Explain What steps did you use?

Safe Site

Internet Test Prep
Visit **www.eduplace.com/kids/mhm** for more *Test Prep Practice.*

Perimeter and Area of Complex Figures

You will learn how to find the perimeter and the area of complex figures.

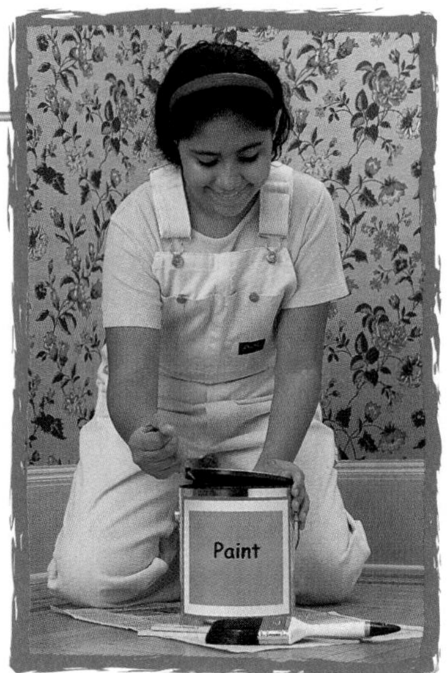

Learn About It

Suppose you are planning to paint the floor of a room. Then you plan to add baseboards around the edge of the floor. How can you find out how much paint and wood to buy?

The room is a complex figure since it can be divided into simple figures.

Find the area and perimeter of the room.

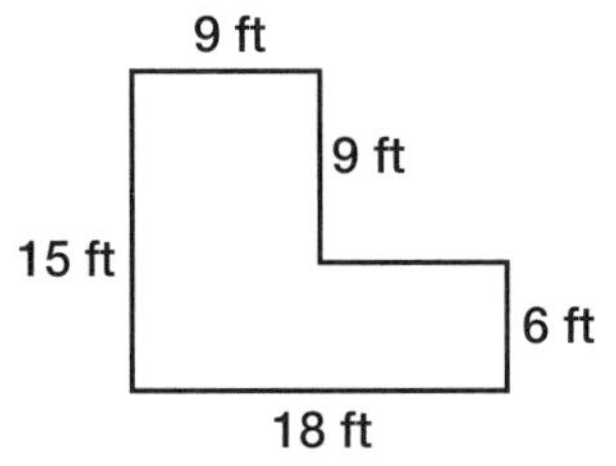

Find the area of the room.

Step 1 Divide the figure into simple figures. For example, draw a line that divides the figure into a square and a rectangle.

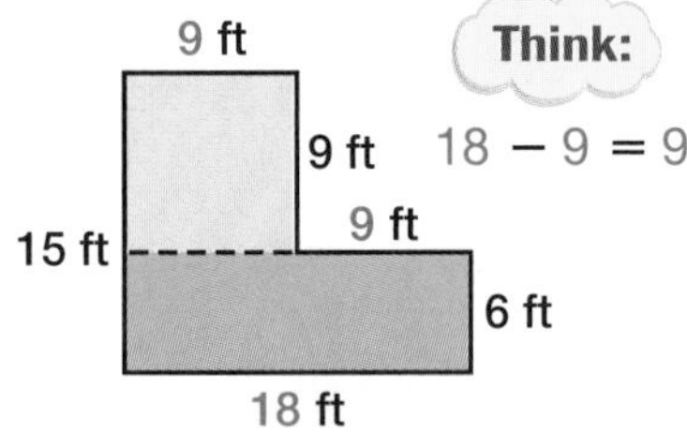

Think: $18 - 9 = 9$

Step 2 Use formulas to find the area of each figure.

square: $A = s^2$
$= (9 \text{ ft})^2$
$= 81 \text{ ft}^2$

rectangle: $A = lw$
$= (18)(6) \text{ ft}^2$
$= 108 \text{ ft}^2$

Step 3 Find the sum of the areas.

$A = 81 \text{ ft}^2 + 108 \text{ ft}^2$
$= 189 \text{ ft}^2$

Find the perimeter of the room.

You can find the perimeter of a complex figure by finding the sum of the lengths of the sides.

$P = 9 \text{ ft} + 9 \text{ ft} + 9 \text{ ft} + 6 \text{ ft} + 18 \text{ ft} + 15 \text{ ft}$
$P = 66 \text{ ft}$

Solution: You will need 66 ft of baseboard and enough paint to cover 189 ft^2 of floor.

Explain Your Thinking

- How could you use subtraction to find the area of the figure?
- Will dividing the figure a different way change its area or perimeter? Explain.

 Standards AF **1.0, 1.2** MG **1.0, 1.1** NS **2.0, 2.1, 2.3**

Guided Practice

Find the perimeter and area of each figure.

1.

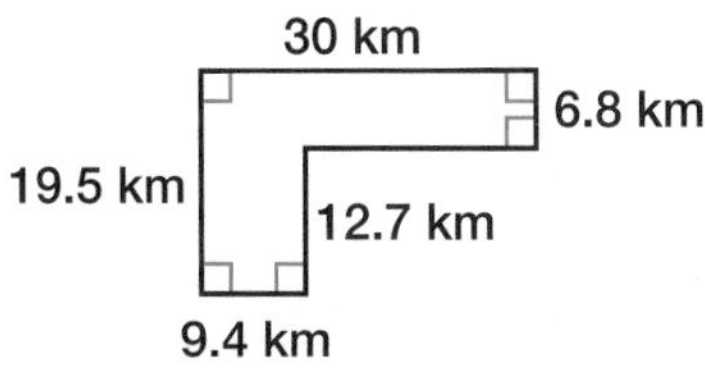

2.

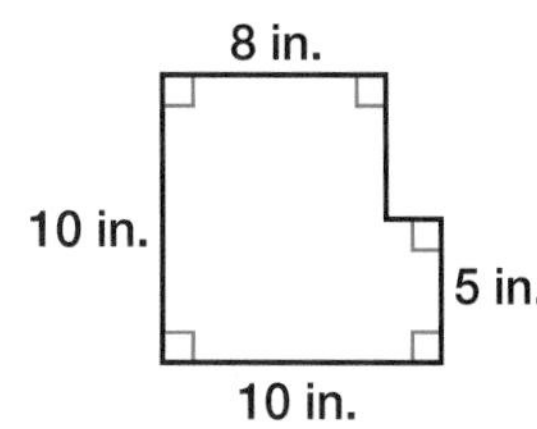

> **Ask Yourself**
> - Is there a measure missing?
> - How can the figure be divided?

Independent Practice

Find the perimeter and area of each figure.
All intersecting sides meet at right angles.

3.

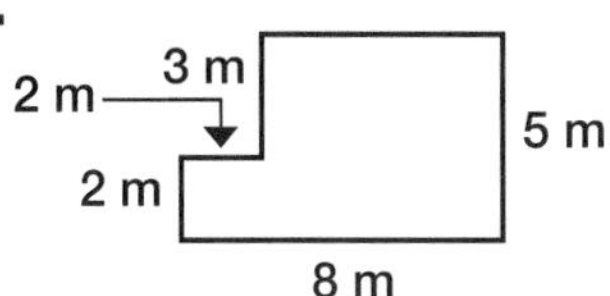

4.

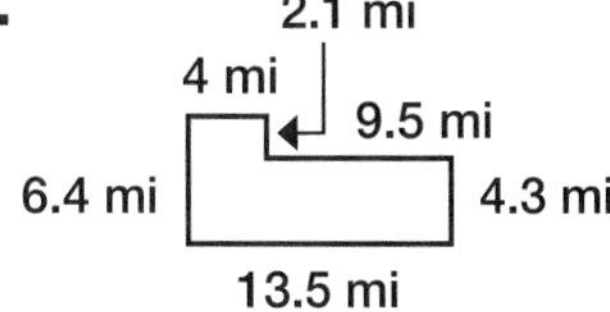

5.

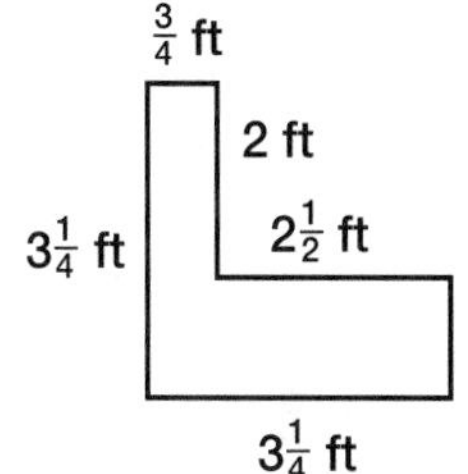

Algebra • Expressions **Write an expression to represent the perimeter of each figure.**

6.

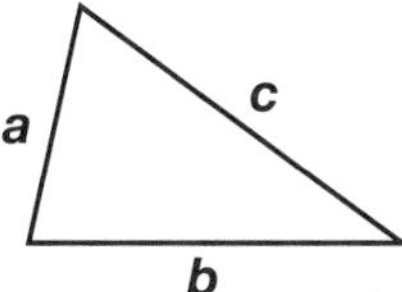

7.

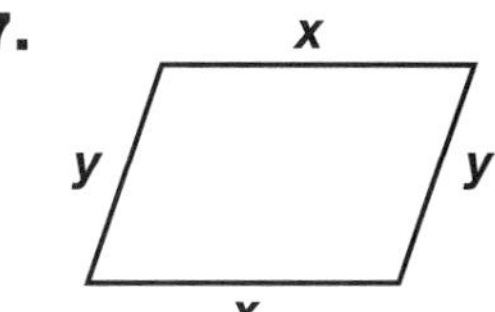

8.

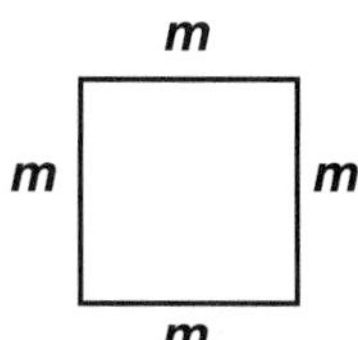

Problem Solving • Reasoning

Find the missing measures in each figure. Then calculate the area and perimeter. All intersecting sides meet at right angles.

9.

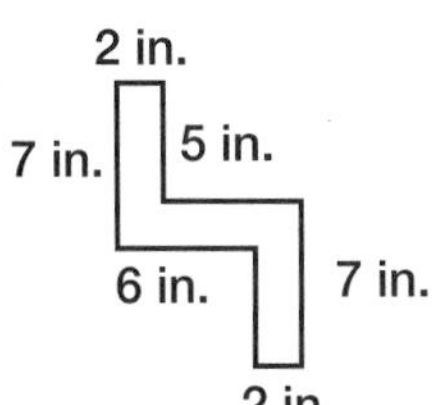

10.

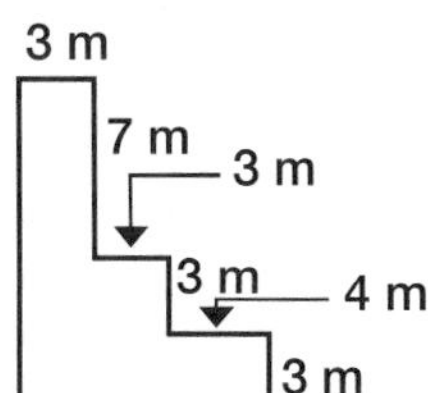

11.

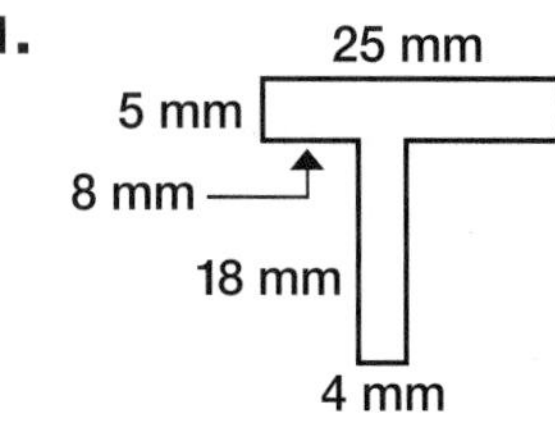

Mixed Review • Test Prep

Write the value of the digit 7 in each number. *(pages 4–5, 20–25)*

12. 1,171 **13.** 8.07 **14.** 32,716 **15.** 44.7 **16.** 5,709,818

17 What is the mode of this set of data? 9, 8, 8, 4, 4, 9, 4 *(pages 258–259)*

A 4 **B** 8 **C** 9 **D** none

Extra Practice See Set G on page 506.

Find the Area of a Parallelogram

You will learn how to find and use the formula for the area of a parallelogram.

Learn About It

A gardener is going to seed a lawn that is in the shape of a parallelogram. She needs to know the area to be seeded.

You can use what you know about the formula for the area of a rectangle to help you write a formula for the area of a parallelogram.

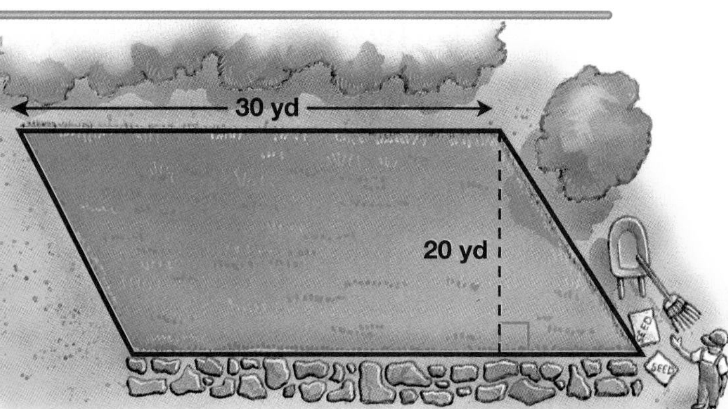

Step 1 Trace this parallelogram (including the dotted line) and cut out the tracing. The dotted line represents the height, h, (also called the perpendicular width) of the parallelogram. It is perpendicular to the base, b.

Remember
b = base
h = height

Step 2 Remove the right triangle from the tracing by cutting along the dotted line. Move the triangle to the other side of the parallelogram to form a rectangle.

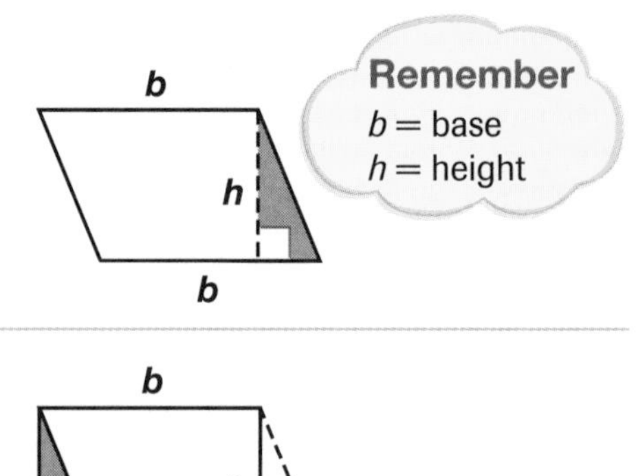

- The area of the rectangle is the same as the area of the parallelogram.
- The length of the rectangle is b.
- The width of the rectangle is h.
- So the area of the parallelogram is $b \times h$.

$A = b \times h$ or $A = bh$

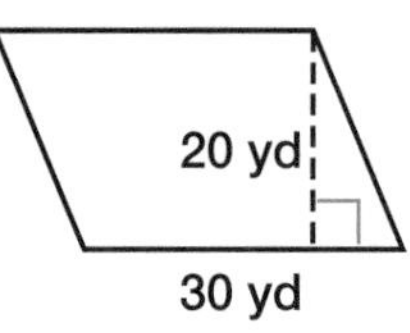

In the lawn, $b = 30$ yd and $h = 20$ yd.

$A = 30 \text{ yd} \times 20 \text{ yd}$
$= 600 \text{ yd}^2$

Solution: The area of the parallelogram-shaped lawn is 600 yd^2.

Explain Your Thinking

- ► Can the formula $A = bh$ be used to find the area of any rectangle? Explain.
- ► Why is 20 yd used for the height of the lawn and 30 yd used for the base?

Standards AF **1.0, 1.2** MG **1.0, 1.1** MR **2.0, 2.6**

Guided Practice

Find the area of each figure.

1.

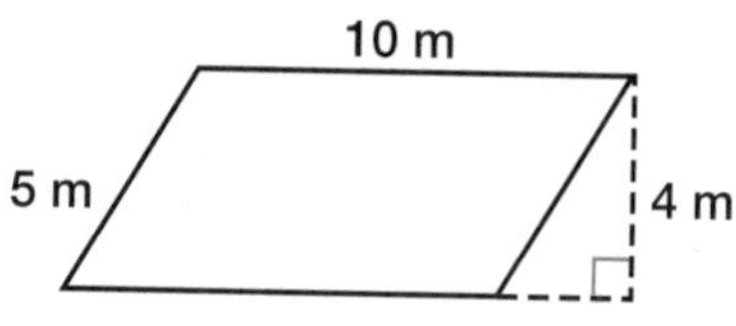

2.

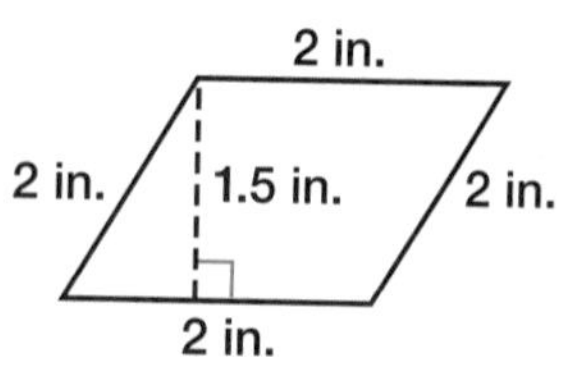

> **Ask Yourself**
> - Which measure is the height?
> - Which measures do I multiply?

Independent Practice

Find the area of each figure.

3.

4.

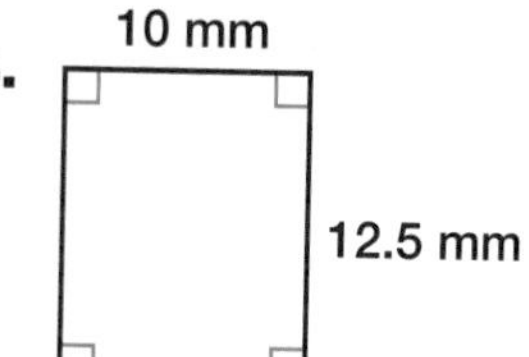

5.

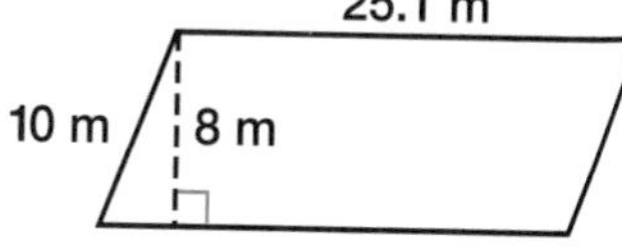

6.

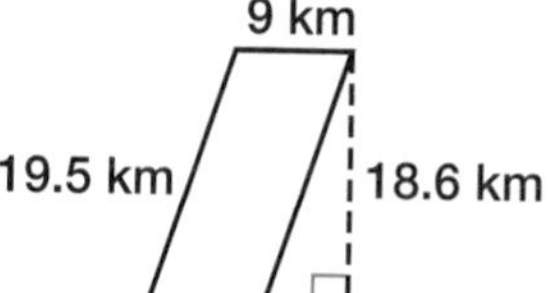

7.

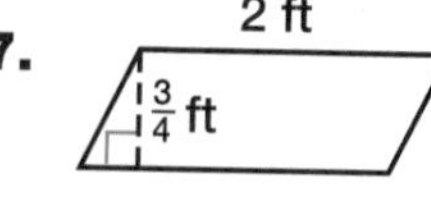

8.

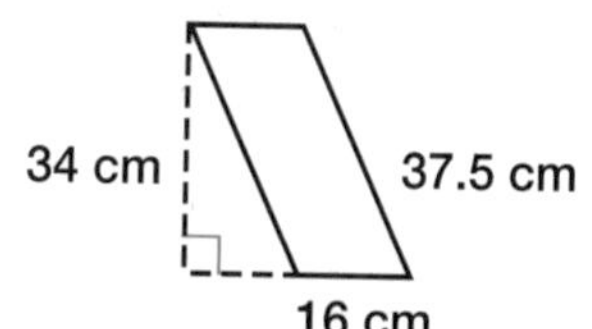

Problem Solving • Reasoning

9. A garden is planted in the shape of a rhombus and fenced with 40 ft of fencing. The perpendicular width of the garden is 8 ft. What is its area?

10. Analyze A parallelogram is 2 cm high and has an area of 14 cm^2. How long is its base?

11. Write About It Which has the greater area, a square with 3-cm sides or a non-square rhombus with 3-cm sides? Use a diagram to explain.

Mixed Review • Test Prep

Complete. *(pages 198–199)*

12. 2 T = ■ lb **13.** ■ oz = 9 lb **14.** 64 oz = ■ lb

15 The sum of an acute angle and an obtuse angle is equal to a straight angle. The acute angle measures 35°. What is the measure of the obtuse angle? *(pages 456–459)*

A 55° **B** 145° **C** 155° **D** 180°

Math Is Everywhere!

FARMING The area of a farm is measured in acres. An acre is 43,560 square feet.

A How large is an acre in square yards?

B If a rectangular piece of land is almost square, and is one acre in area, what could its dimensions be in feet?

Find the Area of a Triangle

You will learn how to find and use the formula for the area of a triangle.

Learn About It

A surveyor lays out building lots along a river. Some lots are rectangular and some are triangular. How can she find the area of a triangular lot?

Use what you know about the formula for the area of a parallelogram to help you write a formula for the area of the triangle.

15 yd

20 yd

Step 1 Trace this triangle and cut the tracing out.

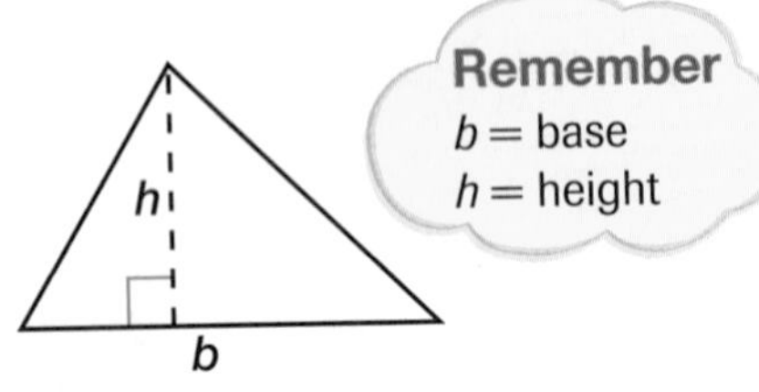

Remember
b = base
h = height

Step 2 Place the triangle you traced next to the one shown to make a parallelogram.

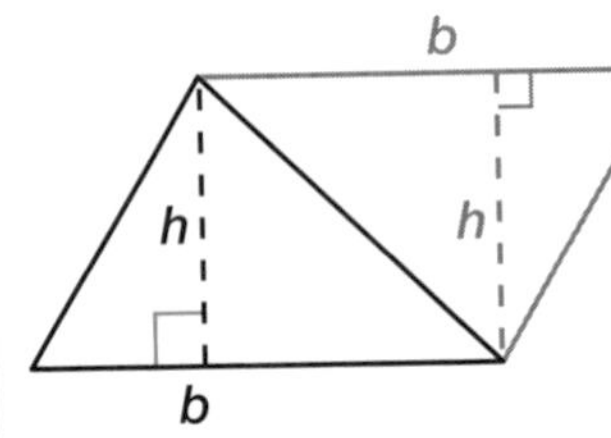

Remember
The formula for the area of a parallelogram is $b \times h$.

- The triangles are congruent so each triangle represents one half of the area of the parallelogram.
- The area of the triangle is $\frac{1}{2} \times b \times h$.

So, $A = \frac{1}{2} \times b \times h$ or $A = \frac{1}{2}\,bh$

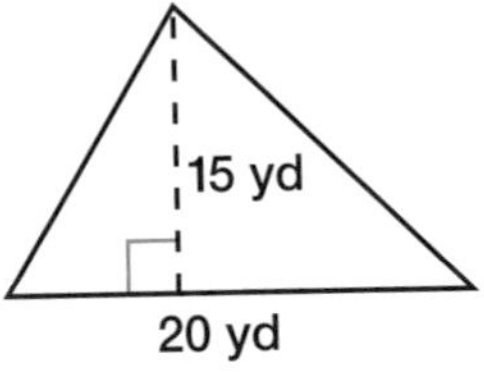

- In the building lot, b = 20 yd and h = 15 yd.

$A = \frac{1}{2} \times 20 \text{ yd} \times 15 \text{ yd}$

$A = 150 \text{ yd}^2$

Solution: The area of the building lot is 150 yd^2.

Explain Your Thinking

► If you know the lengths of the sides of a right triangle, can you find its area? Use a diagram to explain.

 Standards AF **1.0, 1.2** MG **1.0, 1.1** MR **2.0, 2.3, 2.6**

Guided Practice

Find the area of each triangle.

1. 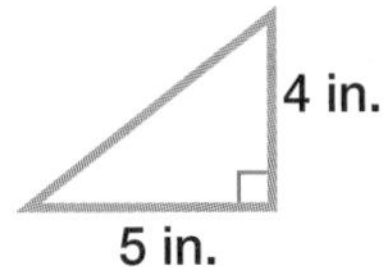

2. 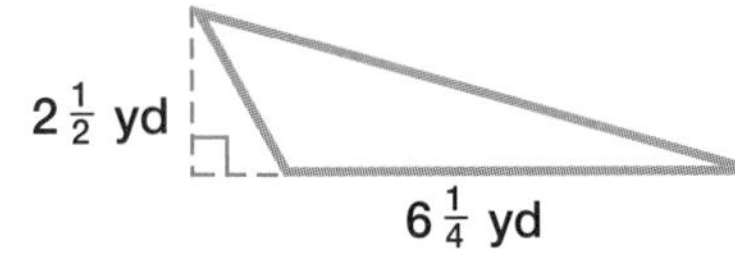

Ask Yourself

- What formula do I use?

Independent Practice

Find the area of each triangle.

3. 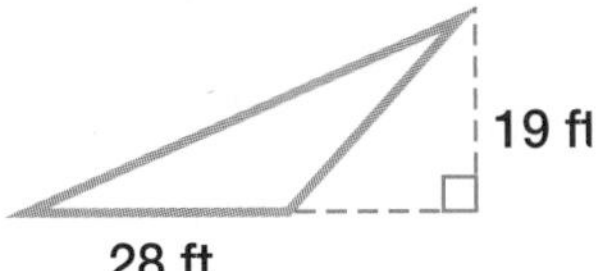

4. 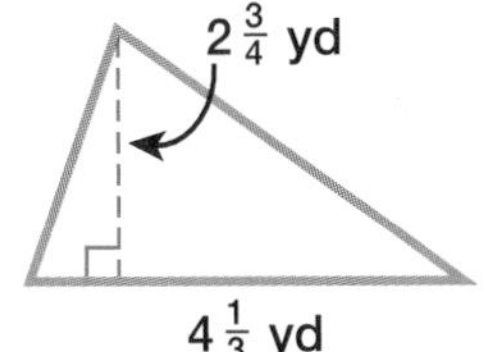

5. 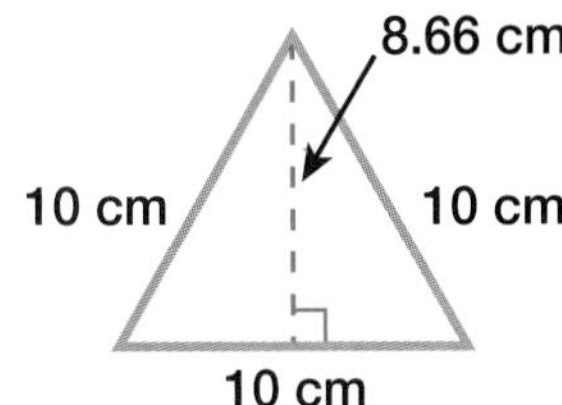

Algebra • Expressions Write an expression to represent the area of each triangle.

6. 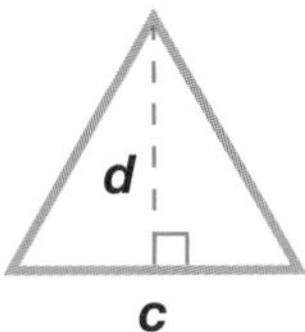

7. 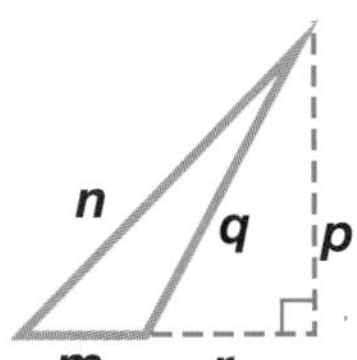

8. 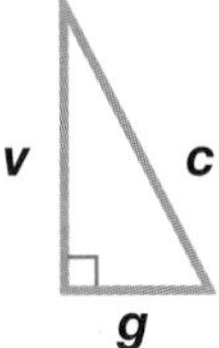

Problem Solving • Reasoning

9. A garden is fenced in the shape of an equilateral triangle. The fence is 48 ft long. The perpendicular width of the garden is 14 ft. What is the area?

10. **Analyze** A plot of land is in the shape of a right triangle. The sides are 30 ft, 40 ft, and 50 ft. What is the area? Use a diagram to explain.

11. **Write About It** What is the area of the unshaded part of the square? Is there more than 1 way to solve the problem? Explain.

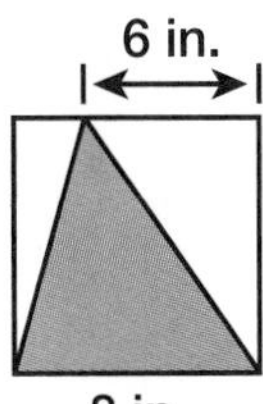

Mixed Review • Test Prep

Estimate. *(pages 98–99, 134–135)*

12. 235 ÷ 4
13. 6 × 183
14. 101 ÷ 2
15. 5 × 467

16. What is the remainder when 3,051,337,605 is divided by 10? *(pages 302–303)*

A 0 **B** 1 **C** 5 **D** 9

Extra Practice See Set G on page 506.

Find the Circumference of a Circle

You will learn about the value of pi (π) and how to use it to find the circumference of circles.

New Vocabulary
circumference
pi (π)

Learn About It

Jodi and Bob are designing a cat food label for a project. The can has a diameter of 3.25 in. About how long should the label be to go all the way around the can?

The word *diameter* is used to describe both a line segment and its length. The diameter of a circle is related to the circumference in a special way.

The distance around a circle is called the **circumference**. Find the distance around the can by finding its circumference.

Different Ways to Find Circumference

You can measure the can.

Wrap a string once around the can and use a ruler to find its length.

You can use a formula.

To find the approximate circumference, C, of any circle, multiply the diameter by a number that is slightly greater than 3. The name of the number is **pi**. The Greek letter π is its symbol.

$$C = \pi d$$

As a decimal, $\pi \approx 3.14$
As a fraction, $\pi \approx \frac{22}{7}$

$\approx$ means "is approximately equal to"

For the can: $C \approx 3.14d$ or $C \approx \frac{22}{7}d$.

$$3.14 \times 3.25 \text{ in.} = 10.205 \text{ in.}$$

Solution: The label of the can should be about 10.2 in long.

Explain Your Thinking

- How could you find the circumference of a circle given only the radius?
- When might you use 3.14 for π? When might you use $\frac{22}{7}$ for π?

 Standards Extends the Grade 5 Standards

Guided Practice

Find the circumference of each circle. Use 3.14 or $\frac{22}{7}$ for π.

1.

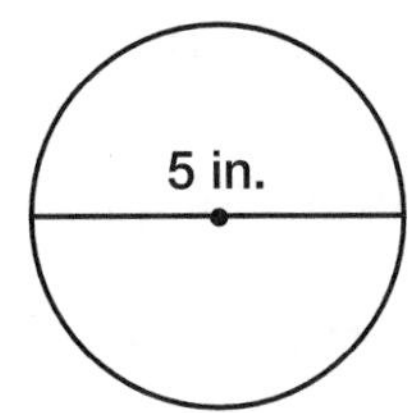

2.

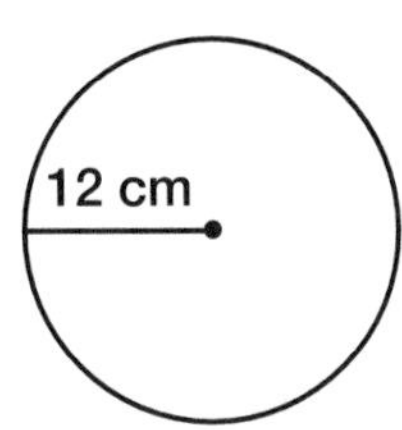

> **Ask Yourself**
> - Is the diameter given?
> - Should I use $\frac{22}{7}$ or 3.14 for π?

Independent Practice

Find each circumference. Use 3.14 for π.

3.

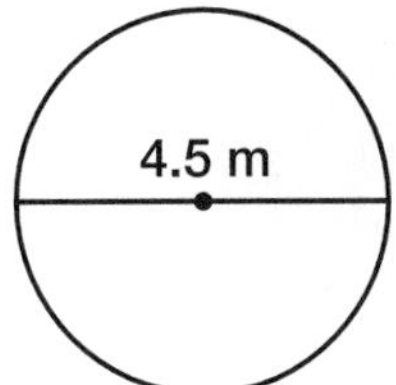

4.

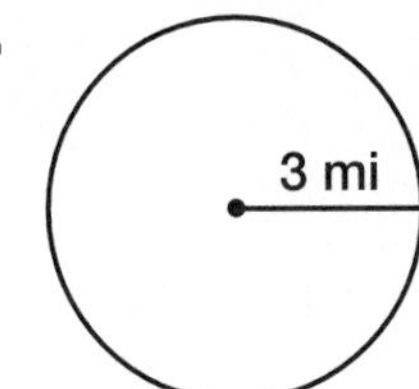

5.

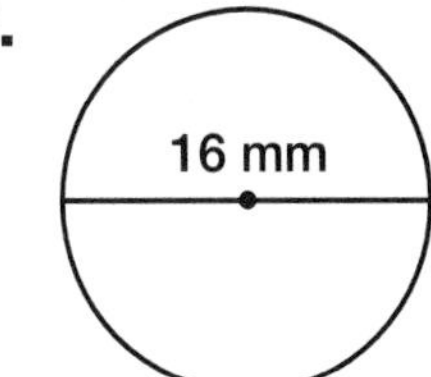

Express each circumference as a fraction in simplest form. Use $\frac{22}{7}$ for π.

6. radius $= \frac{2}{3}$ yd **7.** diameter $= \frac{1}{2}$ km **8.** radius $= 3\frac{3}{4}$ ft **9.** diameter $= \frac{7}{24}$ in.

Problem Solving • Reasoning

Use Data **Use the table for Problems 10 and 11.**

Can	Diameter
tomatoes	10 cm
fruit cocktail	7.5 cm
soup	2.5 in.
peas	85 mm

10. Calculate the length of the label around each can.

11. **Analyze** If the height of the label of the tomato can is 11 cm, what is the approximate area of the label?

12. Without calculating, explain which is greater, the perimeter of the square or the circumference of the circle. Check your answer by calculating both measurements.

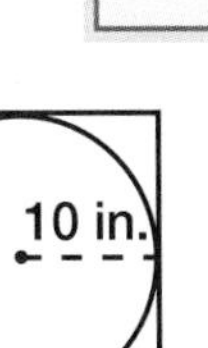

Mixed Review • Test Prep

Express each fraction as a decimal. *(pages 322–323, 422–423)*

13. $\frac{1}{2}$ **14.** $\frac{5}{4}$ **15.** $\frac{7}{10}$ **16.** $\frac{3}{8}$ **17.** $\frac{14}{10}$

18 The product of two numbers is the same as their quotient. What are the numbers? *(page 165)*

A 10 and 10 **B** 2.5 and 2.5 **C** 1 and 1 **D** $\frac{1}{2}$ and $\frac{1}{2}$

Extra Practice See Set H on page 506.

Solid Figures

You will learn how to identify solid figures from different perspectives and to find the surface area of rectangular prisms and cubes.

New Vocabulary
solid figure
prism
base
rectangular prism
cube
surface area

Learn About It

A figure that has length, width, and height is an example of a **solid figure**.

Which solid figures are shown in the photograph?

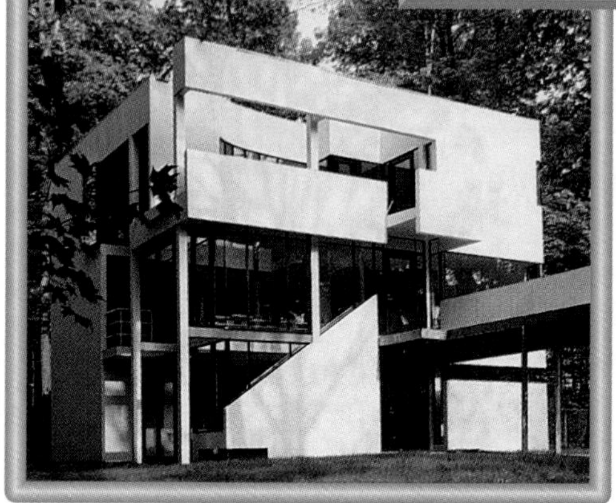

A **prism** is a solid figure that has two parallel congruent faces. These faces are called **bases**.

The other faces of a prism are parallelograms.

Solid Figures

A **rectangular prism** has rectangular faces.

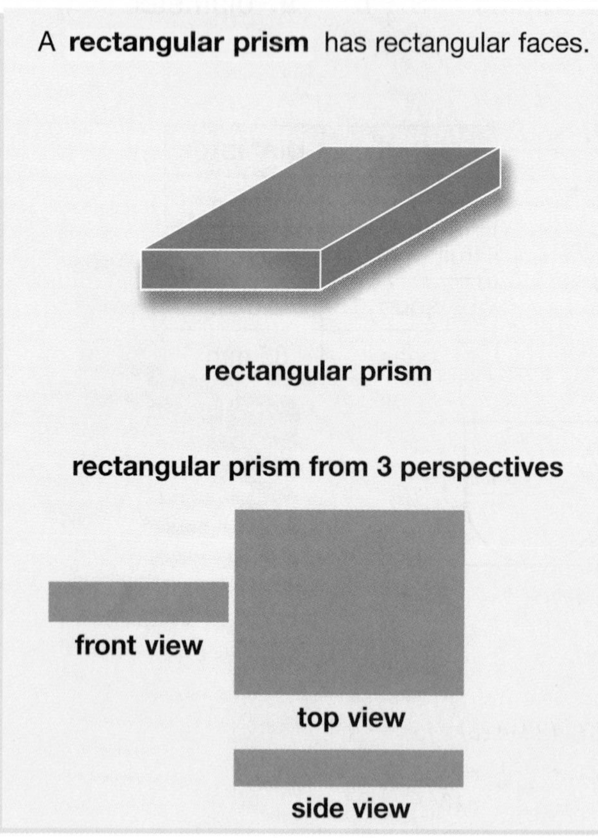

A **cube** is a special kind of rectangular prism. All the faces of a cube are squares.

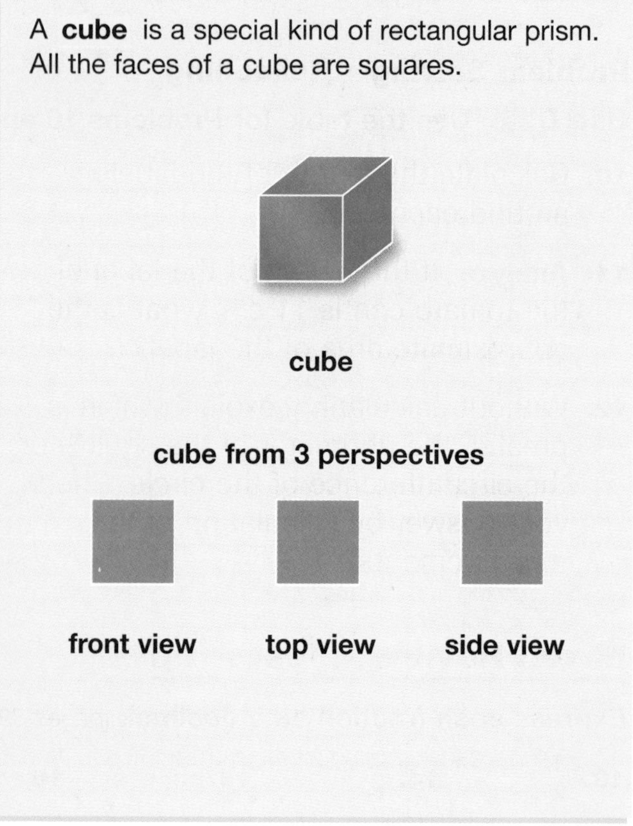

Solution: The house in the photograph is in the shape of a cube. There are many rectangular prisms inside this cube.

Standards | MG 1.0, 1.2, 1.4, 2.0, 2.3

The pattern shows the faces of the rectangular prism when it is cut apart and laid flat.

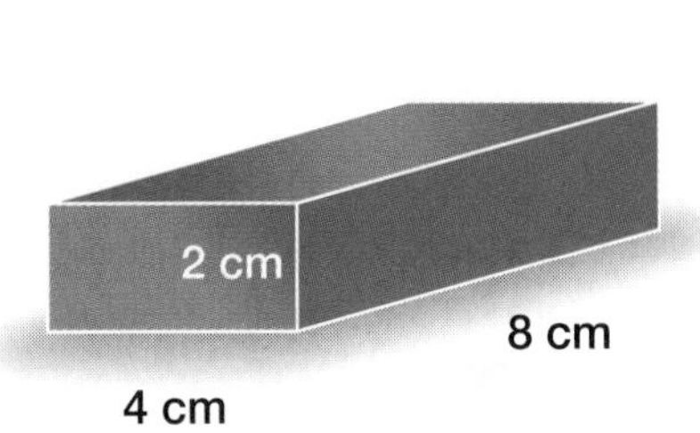

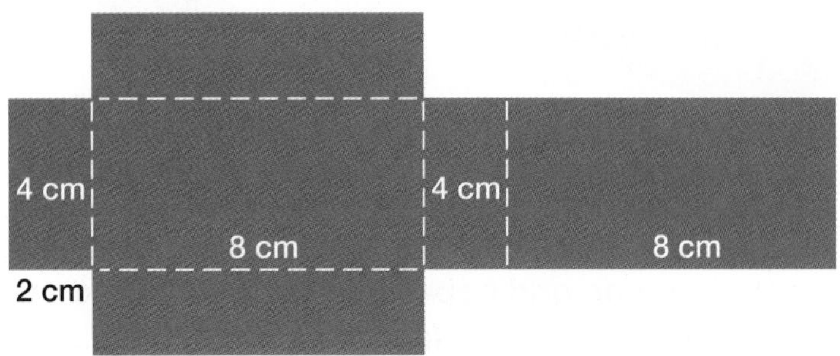

The sum of the areas of the faces is called the **surface area** of the solid figure. You can use a table to help determine the surface area.

The surface area of the rectangular prism is 112 cm^2.

Face	Length	Width	Area
top	8 cm	4 cm	32 cm^2
bottom	8 cm	4 cm	32 cm^2
front	4 cm	2 cm	8 cm^2
back	4 cm	2 cm	8 cm^2
left side	8 cm	2 cm	16 cm^2
right side	8 cm	2 cm	16 cm^2
		sum:	**112 cm^2**

Another Example

Surface Area of a Cube

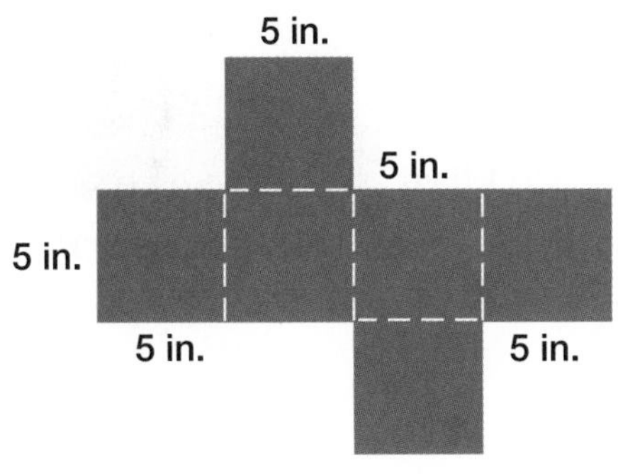

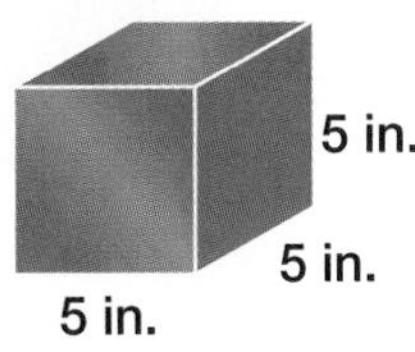

(5 in. × 5 in.) × 6 = 150 in.^{2}

Explain Your Thinking

- ► Why do you think rectangular prisms are sometimes called right rectangular prisms?
- ► How is finding the surface area of a cube different from finding the surface area of another rectangular prism?

Guided Practice

Identify each figure. Then determine its surface area.

1. 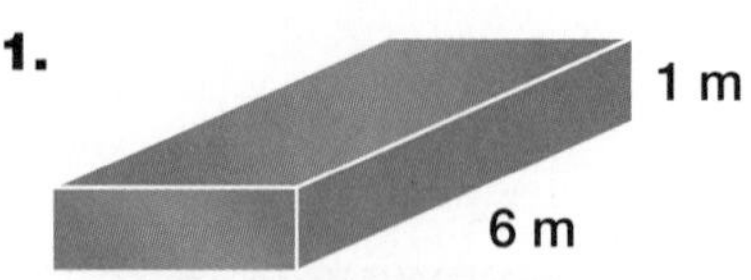

2. 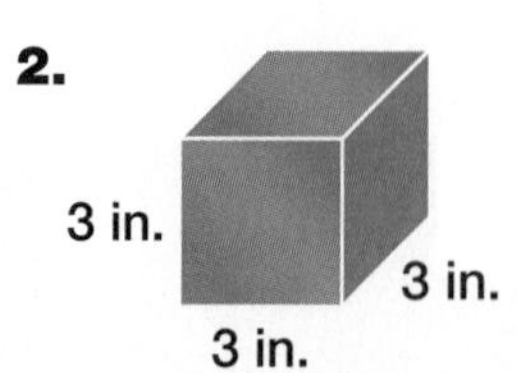

> **Ask Yourself**
>
> - Which numbers do I multiply?
> - What do I add?

Copy each figure on grid paper and cut it out. Fold and tape the figure to make a solid. Find the surface area of each solid.

3. 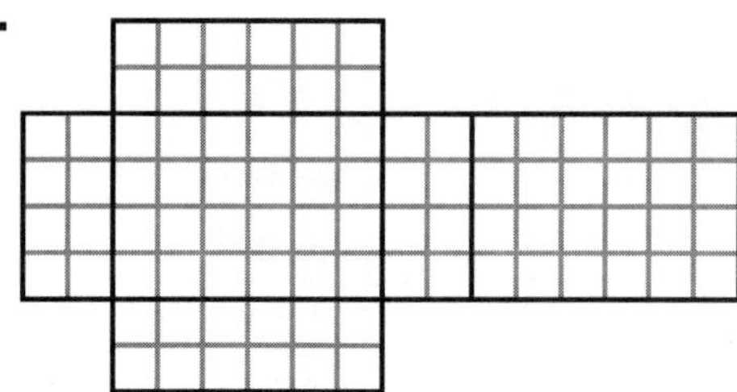

4. 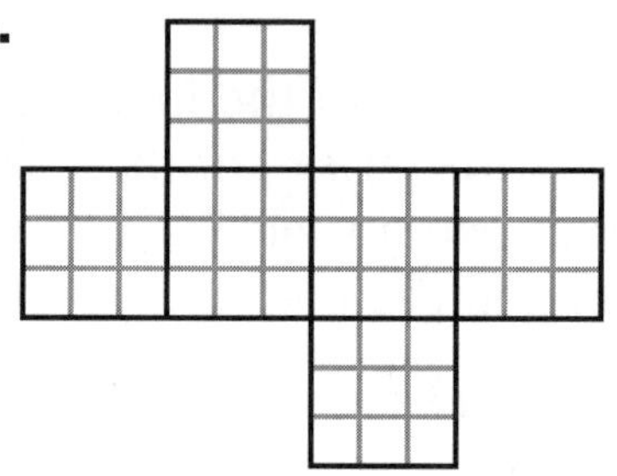

Independent Practice

Determine the surface area of each solid figure.

5. 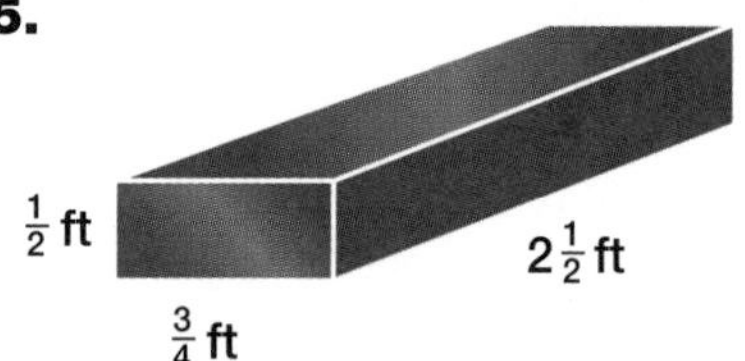

6. 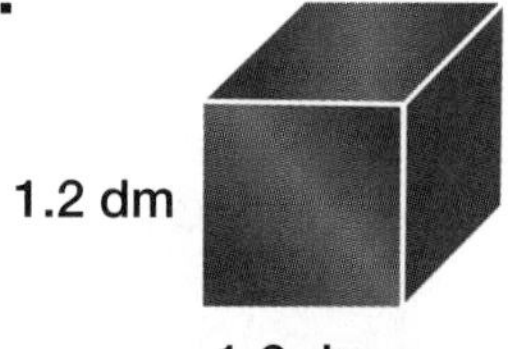

7. 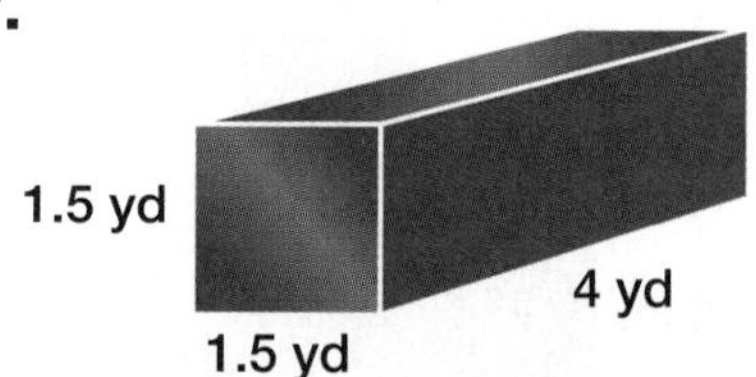

Copy each figure on grid paper and cut it out. Fold and tape the figure to make a solid. Find the surface area of each solid.

8. 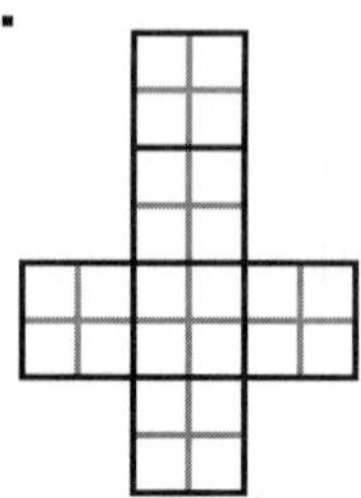

9. 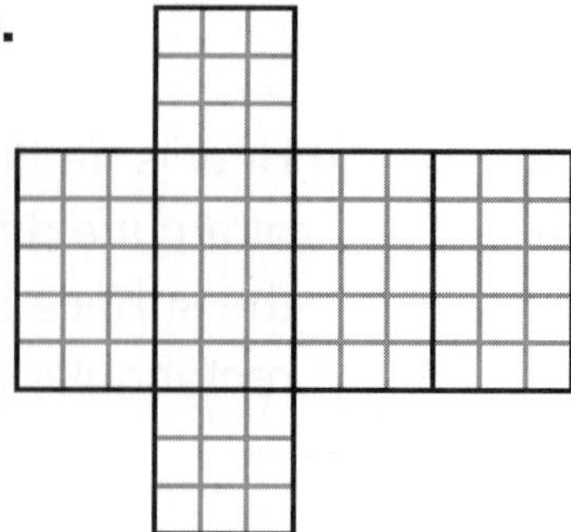

10. 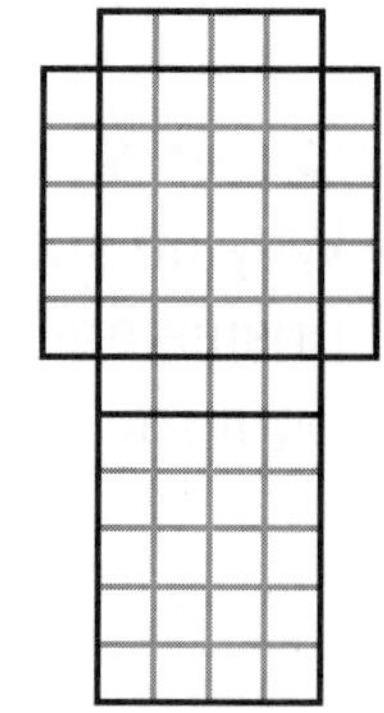

Problem Solving • Reasoning

Solve. Choose a method.

Computation Methods

- Pencil and Paper
- Mental Math
- Estimation

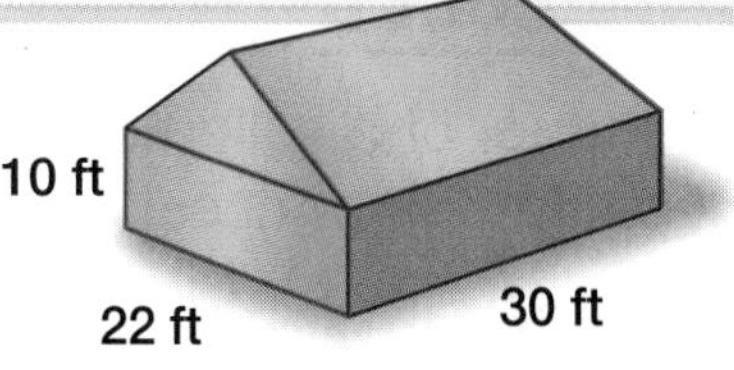

11. What is the area of the walls of the building?
12. **Analyze** A box with a surface area of 94 $in.^2$ is 3 in. high and 5 in. long. How wide is the box?
13. **Predict** A box measures 10.1 cm by 10.5 cm by 10.3 cm. Will 600 cm^2 of wrapping paper cover the surface of the box? Explain.

14. What is the total surface area of 8 cubes if each cube has 1-cm sides?
15. **Analyze** If 8 one-centimeter cubes are put together to make a large cube, what is the surface area of the large cube?
16. **Analyze** How is the surface area of the large cube related to the total surface area of the small cubes?

Mixed Review • Test Prep

Express each product or quotient in simplest form. *(pages 368–369, 384–385)*

17. $\frac{3}{8} \times \frac{8}{9}$ **18.** $\frac{1}{4} \div \frac{4}{5}$ **19.** $\frac{2}{3} \div \frac{9}{10}$ **20.** $\frac{7}{16} \times \frac{1}{2}$

21 Which represent the GCF and LCM of 4 and 6? *(pages 304–305, 308–309)*

A 2, 10 **B** 2, 12 **C** 4, 12 **D** 2, 24

Visual Thinking

Three-dimensional Slices

Match each solid figure to the face that will show when the figure is cut along the dotted line. Explain why they match.

1. 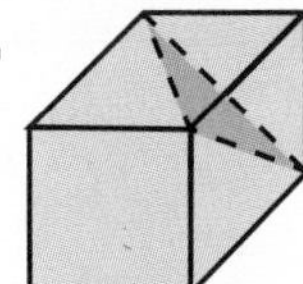

2. 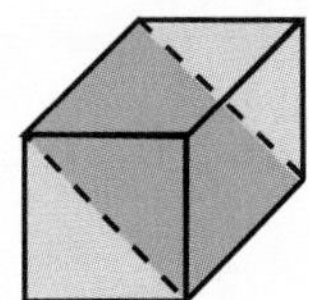
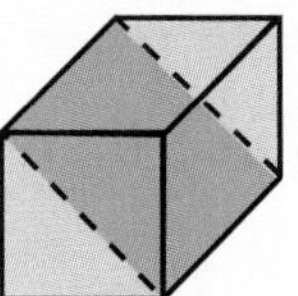

3. 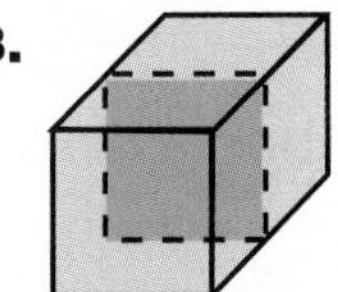

a. 

b.

c.

Extra Practice See Set I on page 506.

Volume

You will learn how to find the volume of rectangular prisms and cubes.

New Vocabulary
volume
cubic unit

Learn About It

The **volume** of a solid figure is a measure of the amount of space the figure occupies.

A cube measuring 1 unit on each side has a volume of 1 **cubic unit** or 1 unit^3.

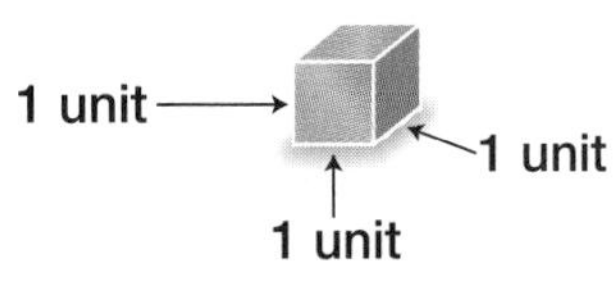

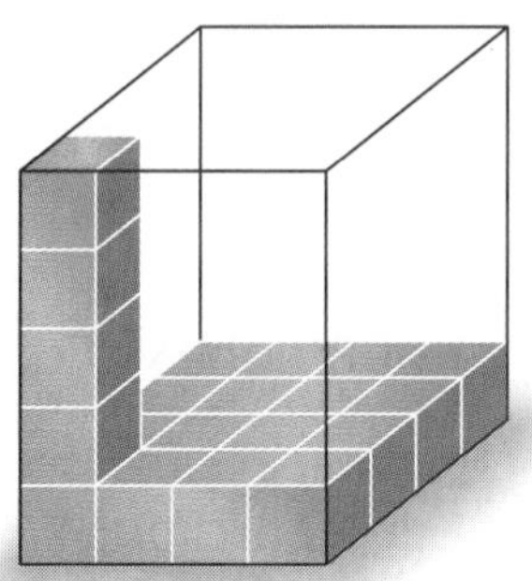

Volume can be measured using cubic units. For example, cubic inches (in.^{3}) and cubic centimeters (cm^3) are used to measure volume.

Sam is packing cardboard boxes. He has a choice of two sizes of boxes, and both sizes cost the same amount. He wants to know which box will hold more.

When you know the length, width, and height of a rectangular prism, you can multiply them to find the volume.

Use $V = l \times w \times h$ to find the volume of a rectangular prism.

$V = l \times w \times h$
$= 4 \text{ ft} \times 3 \text{ ft} \times 2 \text{ ft}$
$= 24 \text{ ft}^3$

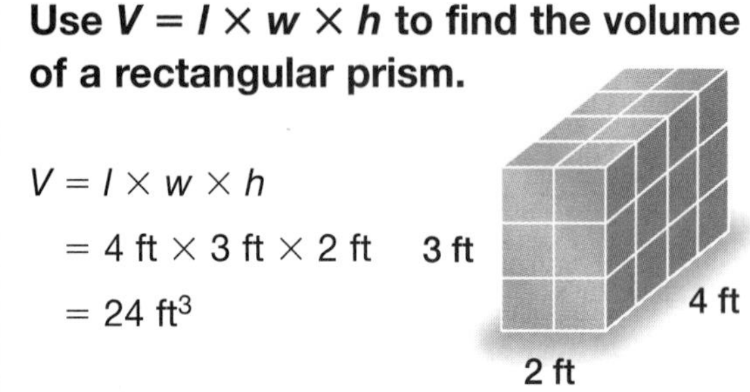

Use $V = s^3$ to find the volume of a cube.

$V = s^3$
$= (3 \text{ ft})^3$
$= (3 \text{ ft})(3 \text{ ft})(3 \text{ ft})$
$= 27 \text{ ft}^3$

3 ft
3 ft
3 ft

Solution: The box shaped like a cube will hold more.

Explain Your Thinking

- How is a unit of volume different from a unit of area?
- Why do you think 1,000 is called a cubic number?
- A rectangular prism and a cube have the same surface area. Which do you think has the greater volume?

 Standards AF **1.0, 1.2** MG **1.0, 1.2, 1.3, 1.4**

Guided Practice

Determine the volume of each solid figure.

1.

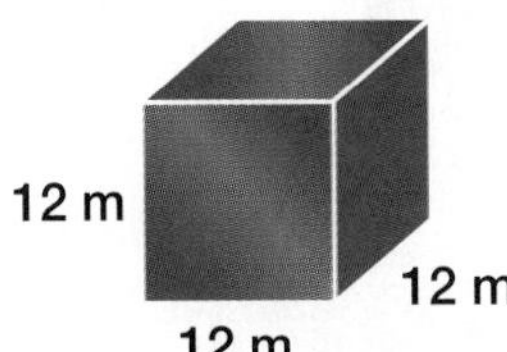

2.

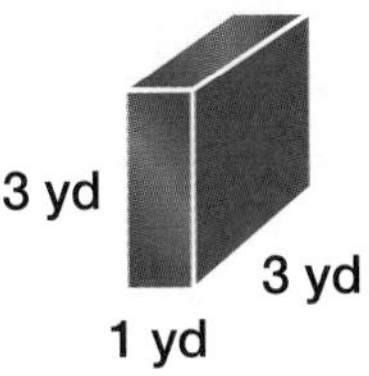

Ask Yourself

- Which numbers do I multiply?
- What unit symbol do I use?

Independent Practice

Determine the volume of each solid figure.

3.

4.

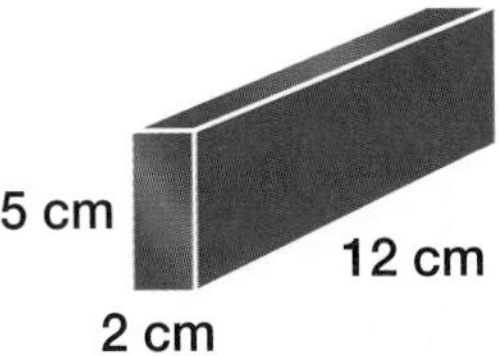

5.

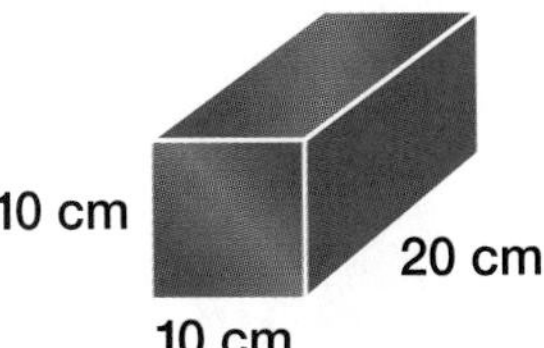

6.

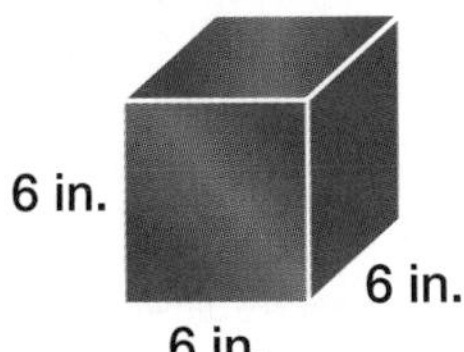

7.

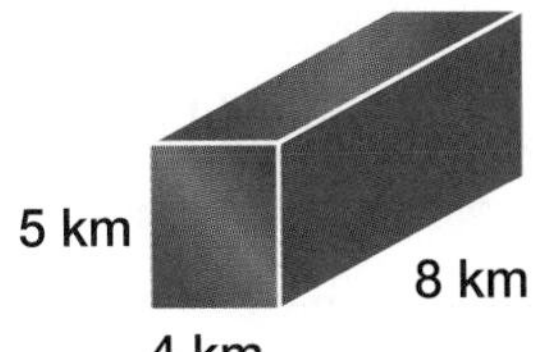

8.

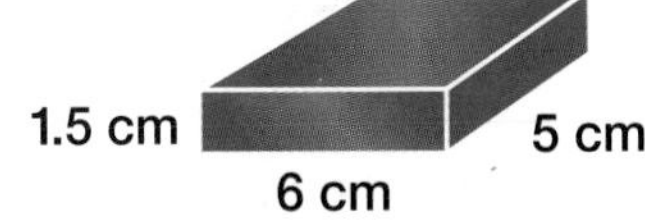

Problem Solving • Reasoning

Choose the most appropriate measure. Write *length, area,* or *volume*.

9. the height of a flagpole
10. carpeting needed to cover a floor
11. the size of a pencil
12. the amount of sand to fill a box
13. the amount of wall space one gallon of paint will cover

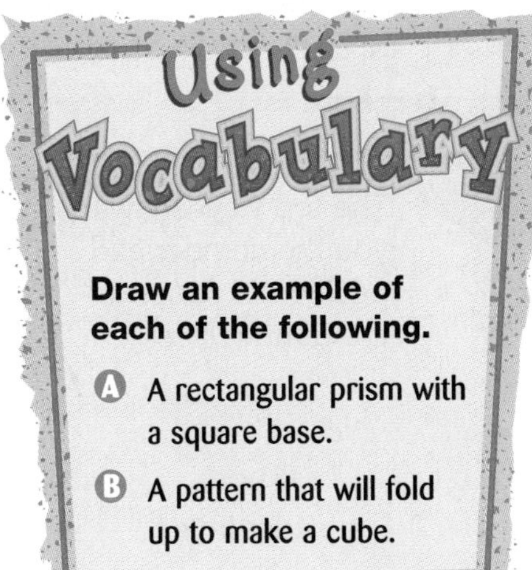

Draw an example of each of the following.

Ⓐ A rectangular prism with a square base.

Ⓑ A pattern that will fold up to make a cube.

Mixed Review • Test Prep

Simplify each expression given $n = 6$. *(pages 66–69, 70–73)*

14. $n - (5 + 1)$ **15.** $(15 - n) + 3$ **16.** $26 - (n + 1)$ **17.** $(n + 3) - n$

18 If Bessie built 5 ft 9 in. of fencing yesterday and 3 ft 7 in. today, how long is the fence so far? *(pages 192–193)*

A 12 ft 2 in. **B** 9 ft 4 in. **C** 8 ft 16 in. **D** 2 ft 2 in.

Extra Practice See Set I on page 506.

LESSON 18

Problem-Solving Application: Use Geometry

You will learn how to visualize the answer to a problem.

Sometimes you can use what you know about geometry to solve a problem.

Problem A solid figure is made up of centimeter cubes. If you are given three different two-dimensional views of the figure, how could you build the figure?

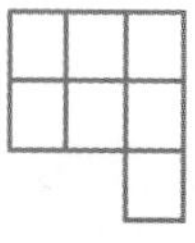

top

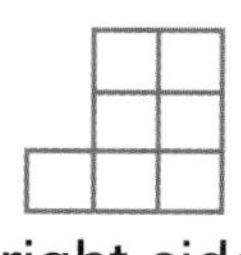

right side

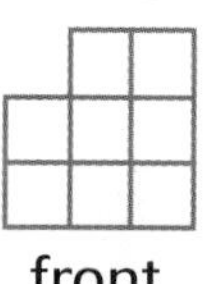

front

Understand

What is the question?

How can you build a solid figure given 3 different views?

What do you know?

You know what the figure looks like from the top, side, and front.

Plan

What can you do to find the answer?

Use the views to visualize the number of cubes in each layer of the figure.

Solve

The top view shows you the number and position of cubes in the bottom layer.

bottom layer

The side view shows you that there could be three layers of cubes in the two back rows.

middle layer

The front view shows you that there are no cubes in the left side of the top layer.

top layer

Put the layers together to show 1 figure that can be made that has these views.

Look Back

Look back at the problem.

Is there another possible answer? Explain.

Standards MG **1.0, 1.3** MR **1.0, 1.2, 3.0, 3.2**

This palace in Harbin, China, is constructed entirely of blocks of ice.

Remember:
- ▶ Understand
- ▶ Plan
- ▶ Solve
- ▶ Look Back

Guided Practice

Solve.

1. Sketch or build a three-dimensional figure with these views.

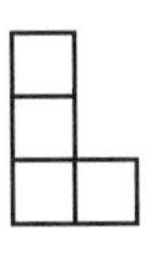
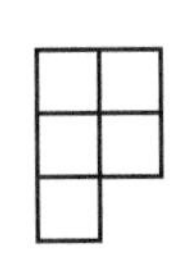
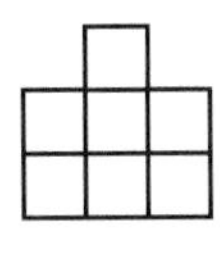

front **top** **right side**

Think: Which view tells you what must be in the bottom layer to support the other layers?

2. Sketch the front, top, and right-side views of this solid figure.

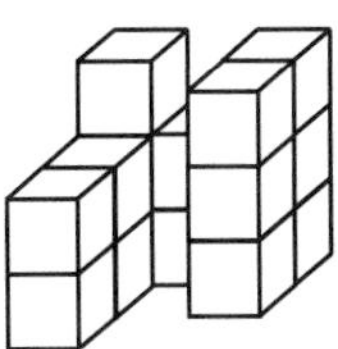

Think: How can you tell if there are cubes hidden from your view?

Choose a Strategy

Solve. Use these or other strategies.

Problem-Solving Strategies
- **Guess and Check**
- **Find a Pattern**
- **Make a Table**
- **Draw a Diagram**

3. How many pairs of perpendicular line segments can you draw by joining the points of a square?

4. What is the first capital letter of the alphabet that has no lines of symmetry?

A B C D E F G

5. Which figure covers the red figure when the square is folded along this diagonal?

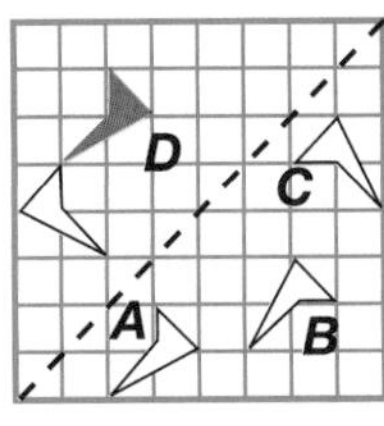

6. Which two figures will fit together to make a square?

A
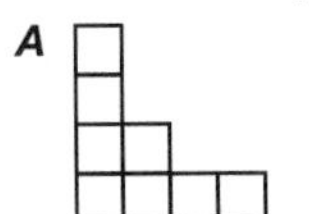
B
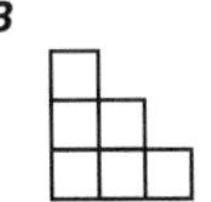
C
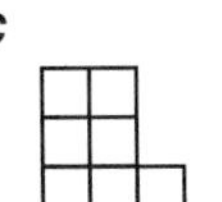
D
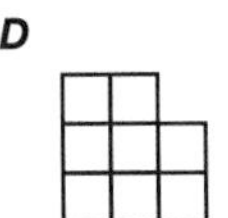

7. If each side of a rectangle is a whole number of inches long, how many different-shaped rectangles can you draw with an area of 18 in.^{2}? How many rectangles can you draw with a perimeter of 18 in.?

8. How many equilateral triangles will be in the eighth row of this pattern?

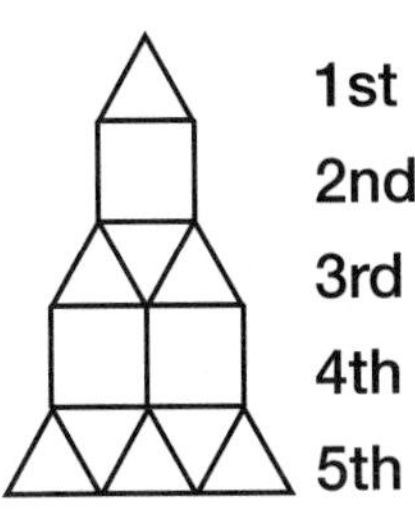

Extra Practice See 7–8 on page 507.

Quick Check

Check Your Understanding of Lessons 12–18

Find the perimeter and area of each figure.

1.

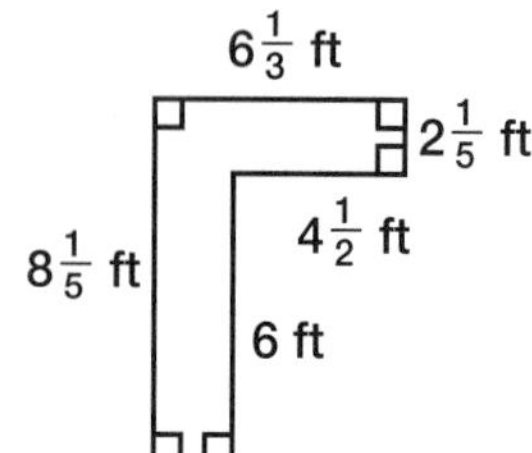

2.

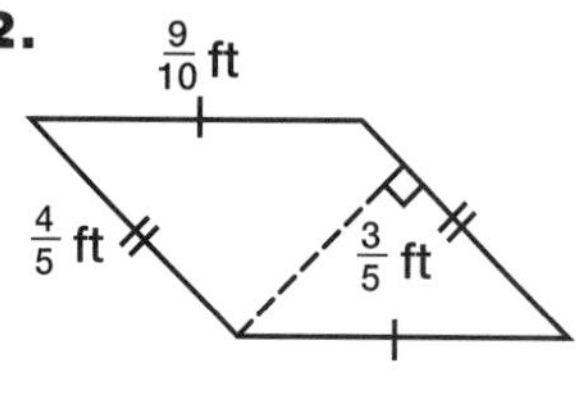

3.

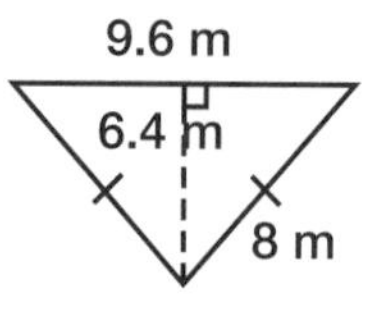

4.

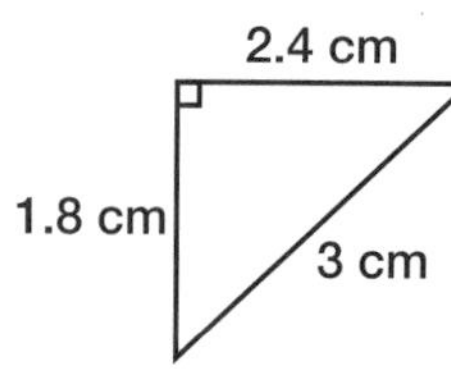

Find each circumference. Use $\frac{22}{7}$ or 3.14 for π.

5. diameter = 8 yd

6. radius = $6\frac{1}{4}$ in.

7. radius = 0.42 km

Determine each figure's surface area and volume.

8.

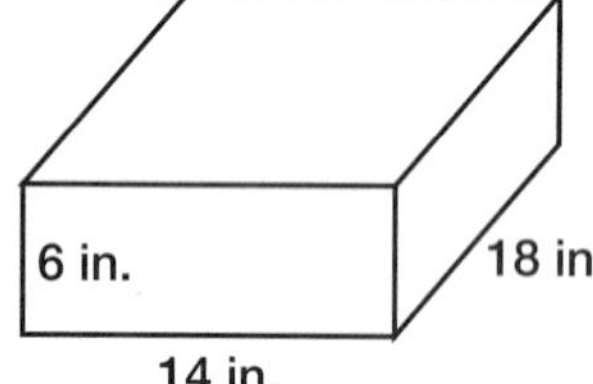

9.

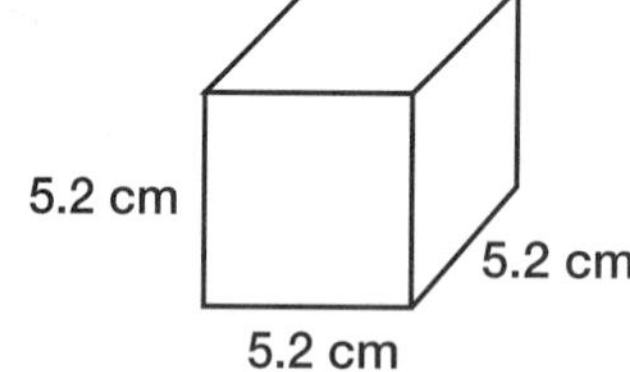

Solve. Sketch or build a three-dimensional figure with these views.

10.

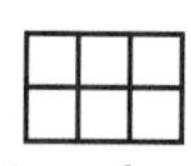
front view

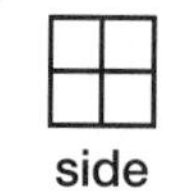
top view

side

How did you do?

If you had difficulty with any items in the Quick Check, you can use the following pages for review and extra practice.

California Standards	Items	Review These Pages	Do These Extra Practice Items
Measurement and Geometry: **1.0, 1.1**	1–4	pages 486–491	Set G, page 506
Algebra and Functions: **1.2**	5–7	pages 492–493	Set H, page 506
Measurement and Geometry: **1.3**	8–9	pages 494–499	Set I, page 506
Measurement and Geometry: **1.2**	10	pages 500–501	7–8, page 507

Test Prep • Cumulative Review

Maintaining the Standards

Choose the letter of the correct answer.

1. Find the area of this figure.

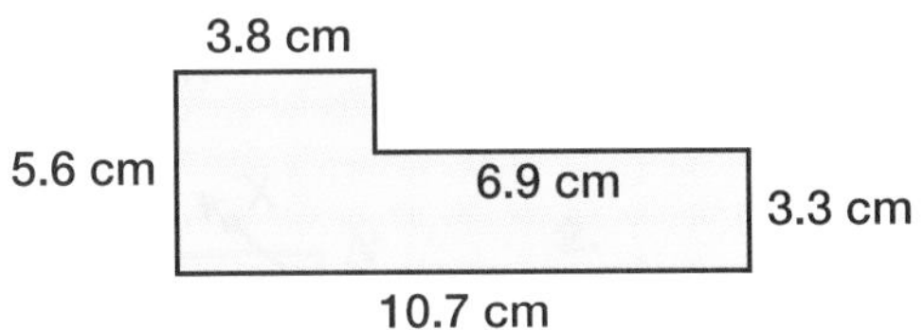

A 8.74 cm^2 **C** 44.05 cm^2
B 35.31 cm^2 **D** 59.92 cm^2

2. What is the volume of a cube whose sides are 3 feet long?

F 27 ft^2 **H** 27 ft^3
G 27 ft **J** 9 ft^3

3. Which expression has the greatest value when $n = 14.2$?

A $n - 12.8$
B $n + 26$
C $3n$
D $(n - 2) + 6.15$

4. Millie plans to buy 5 T-shirts. What is the least she could pay?

F \$40.00 **H** \$33.18
G \$37.77 **J** \$16.59

5. Divide. Give the answer in simplest form.

$$\frac{8}{15} \div \frac{5}{12}$$

A $1\frac{7}{25}$ **C** $\frac{32}{25}$
B $\frac{2}{9}$ **D** 2

6. What would you expect the price of this brand of jeans to be in the year 2010?

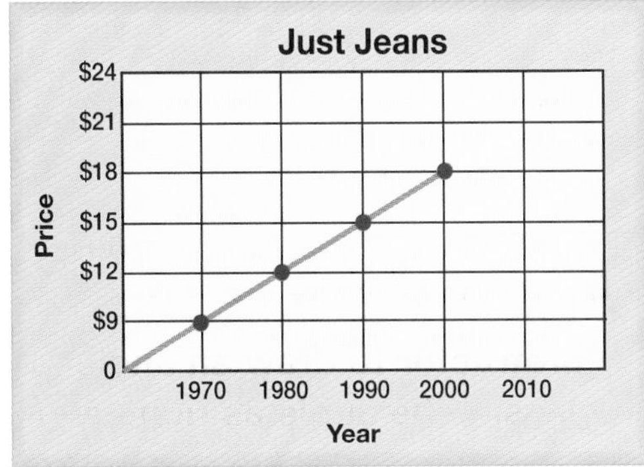

F \$15 **H** \$21
G \$18 **J** \$24

7. Which side lengths are *not* possible for a box with a volume of 270 cubic inches?

A 9 in., 10 in., 3 in.
B 3 in., 30 in., 30 in.
C 5 in., 9 in., 6 in.
D 18 in., 3 in., 5 in.

8. Marita said that the quotient of $15 \div 8$ to the nearest hundredth is 2.88.

Explain Is her answer reasonable?

Safe Site

Internet Test Prep
Visit **www.eduplace.com/kids/mhm** for more *Test Prep Practice.*

Chapter Review

Reviewing Vocabulary

Write *always, sometimes,* or *never* for each statement. Give an example to support your answer.

1. A quadrilateral contains four right angles.
2. The sum of the angles in a triangle equals 180°.
3. To find the circumference of a circle, multiply the radius by π.

List three different units that would be appropriate for each measurement.

4. the perimeter of a parking lot
5. the area of a parallelogram drawn on a sheet of paper
6. the volume of a packing case

Reviewing Concepts and Skills

Refer to the figures to answer Problems 7–11 *(pages 454–465, 472–474)*

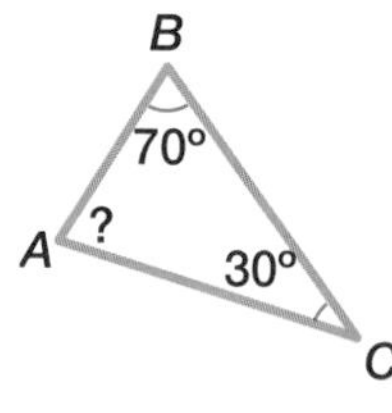

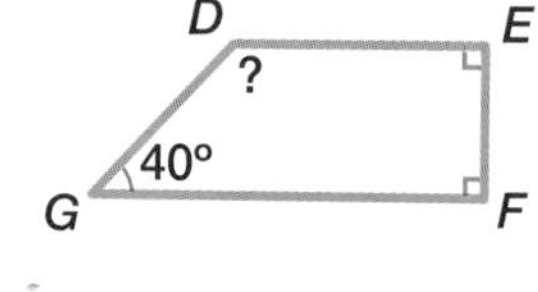

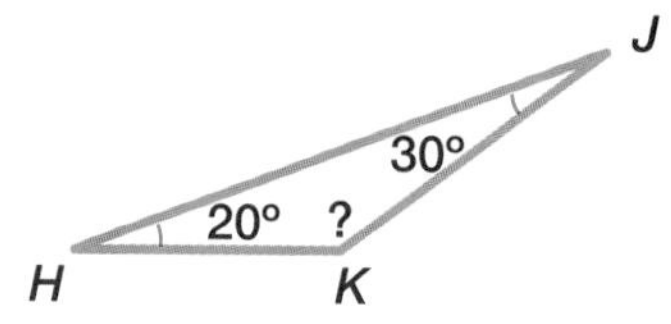

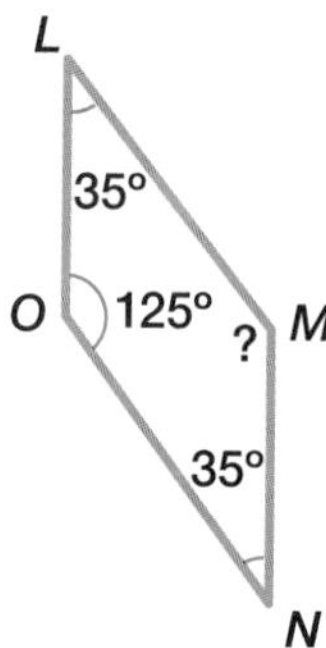

7. Name all the parallel line segments in each figure.
8. Name all the perpendicular line segments in each figure.
9. Classify each angle in each figure as right, acute, obtuse, or straight. Then find the missing angle measures.
10. Classify each figure in as many ways as possible.
11. Use a ruler to help you name the congruent sides in each figure.
12. Use a compass and a straightedge to construct parallel lines *a* and *b*, and line *c* which is perpendicular to lines *a* and *b*.

Find the perimeter and area of each figure.
(pages 486–487, 488–489, 490–491)

13.

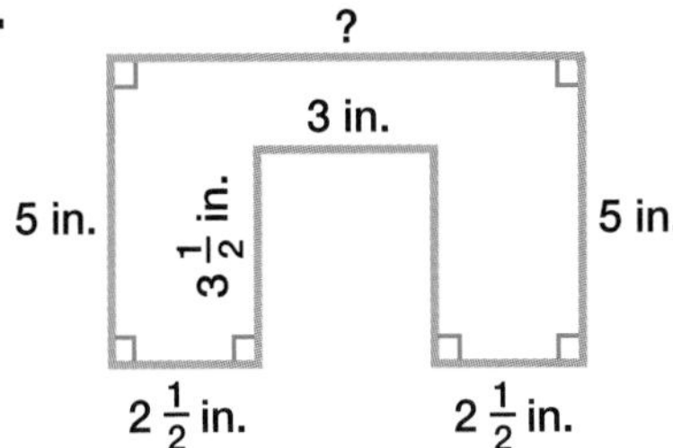

14.

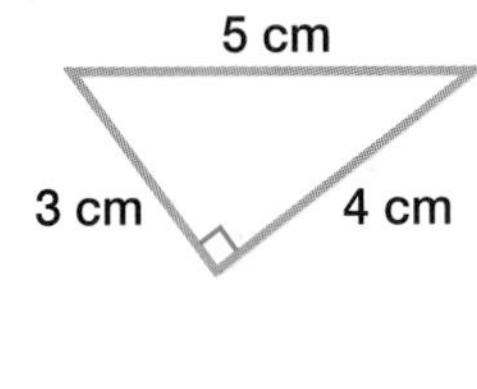

15.

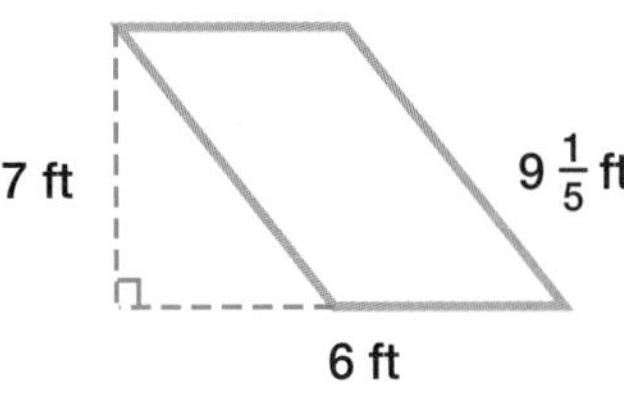

16. Use a compass and a straightedge to construct the triangle in Problem 14. *(pages 476–477)*

17. Find the diameter and the circumference of a circle with a radius of 3.5 m. *(pages 492–493)*

18. Identify the solid figure. Then determine its surface area and volume. *(pages 494–497, 498–499)*

7.2 cm

7.2 cm

6 cm

Solve. *(pages 466–467, 482–483, 500-501)*

19. Sketch three different rectangular prisms you could make using 27 centimeter cubes. Which one has the greatest surface area?

20. a. Sketch the front, top, and right-side views of this solid figure.

b. Look at the right-side view you drew. How many squares of any size would there be in five drawings like this?

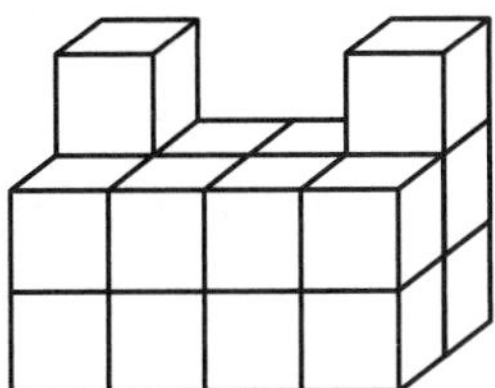

Brain Teasers Math Reasoning

Tetrominoes

This is a tetromino. It is made by joining squares side to side.

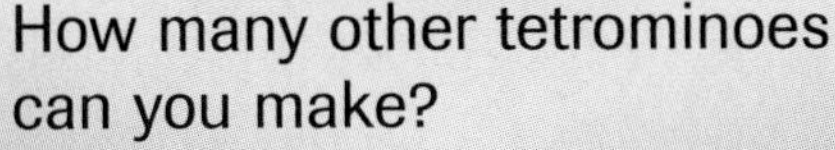

How many other tetrominoes can you make?

Circles and Squares

Which is greater, the circumference or the perimeter of a square? How are the two measurements related?

n *n*

Internet Brain Teasers
Visit **www.eduplace.com/kids/mhm** for more *Brain Teasers.*

Chapter Test

Refer to the figures at the right to answer Problems 1–6.

1. Name all the parallel line segments in each figure.
2. Name all the perpendicular line segments in each figure.
3. Find the missing angle measures in each figure.
4. Classify each angle in each figure as right, acute, obtuse, or straight.
5. Classify each figure in as many ways as possible.
6. Use a ruler to help you name the congruent sides in each figure.

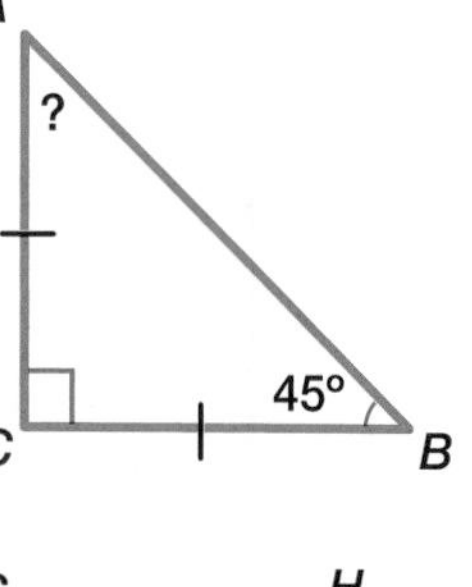

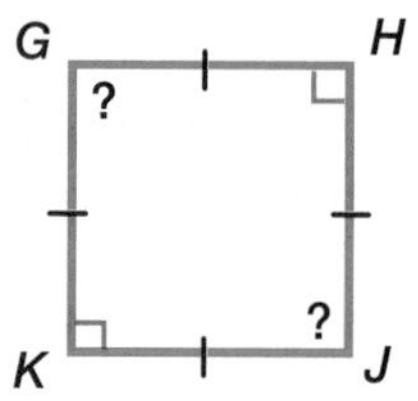

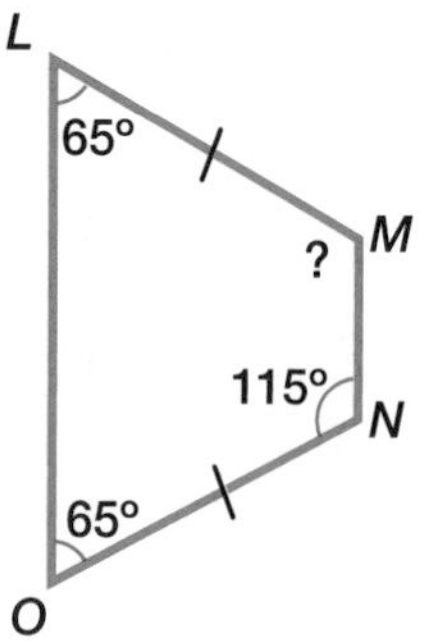

Use a compass and a straightedge to construct each line.

7. Draw line p. Construct line s parallel to line p.
8. Draw line t perpendicular to lines p and s.

Use a compass and a straightedge to construct each figure.

9. Construct a triangle congruent to triangle ABC.
10. Construct a rectangle congruent to rectangle $GHJK$.

Find the perimeter and area of each figure.

11.

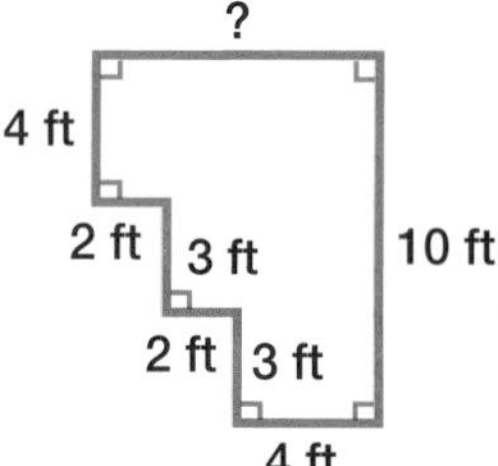

12.

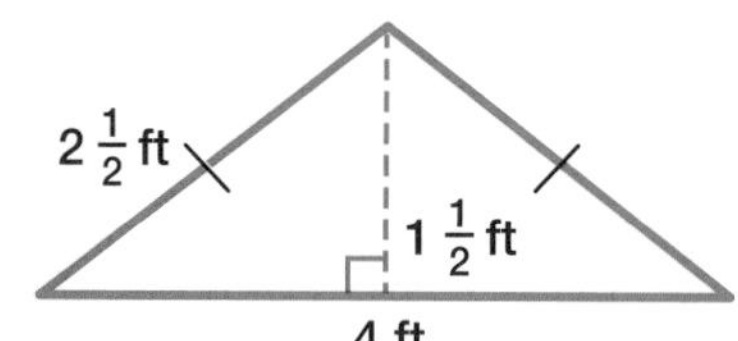

13.

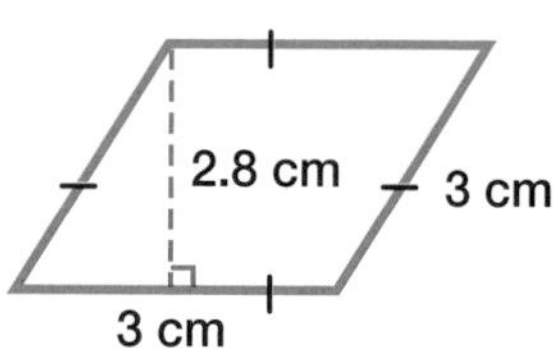

Find the missing measure for each rectangle described below.

14. $A = 24$ cm, $l = 8$ cm, $w = ?$

15. $P = 36$ in., $l = ?$, $W = 7$ in.

Use the solid figure for Problems 16–18.

16. Find its surface area.
17. Find its volume.
18. Sketch the front, top, and right-side views.

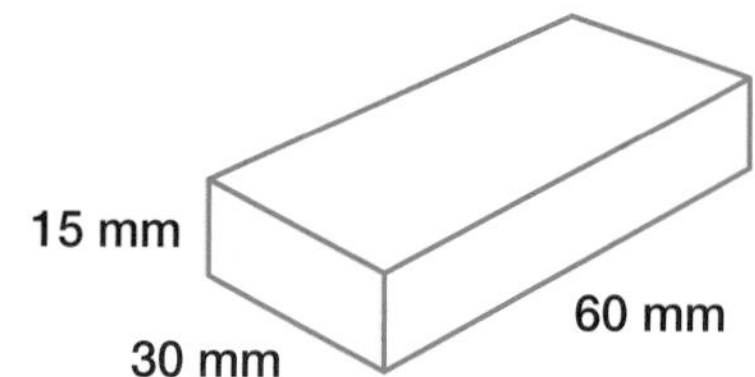

Solve.

19. In a right triangle, one of the smaller angles is 36°. What are the measures of the other two angles?

20. Sketch a cube with edges that are 3 cm long. Find the surface area and volume of the cube. How would the surface area and volume change if you extended each side length to 4 cm?

Write About It

Solve each problem. Use correct math vocabulary to explain your thinking.

1. List two different units that would be appropriate for each measurement. Write *length, area,* or *volume.*

a. the height of a tree

b. the size of a garden

c. the distance from one town to another

d. the space covered by the bottom of an eraser

e. the size of a jump rope

f. the amount you could pack inside a box

2. Krista made an error when she calculated the surface area of this solid figure.

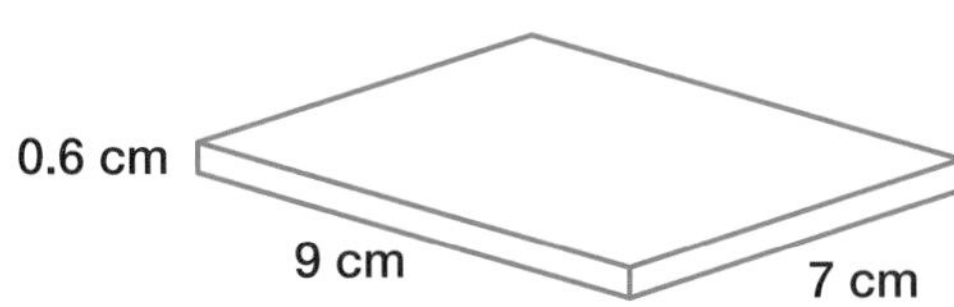

$(9 \times 0.6) + (0.6 \times 7) + (7 \times 9)$

$= 5.4 + 4.2 + 63$

$= 72.6$

The surface area is 72.6 cm^2

a. Explain what she did wrong.

b. Show how to find the correct surface area.

3. Draw a flat pattern that will fold to make a rectangular prism with a square base. Explain how you used congruent figures to make your pattern.

4. Draw the front, top, and side views of this solid figure.

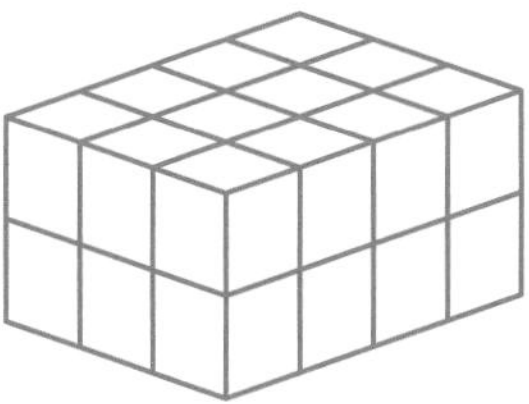

5. Construct a circle. Draw and label the radius, the diameter, a chord parallel to the diameter, and a 90° central angle.

Another Look

Trace the diagrams. Calculate and label any missing angles or side lengths.

A.

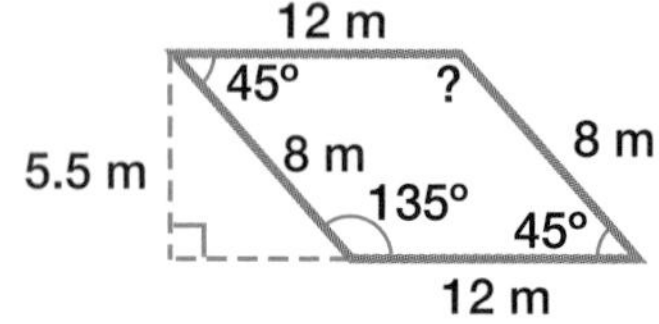

B.

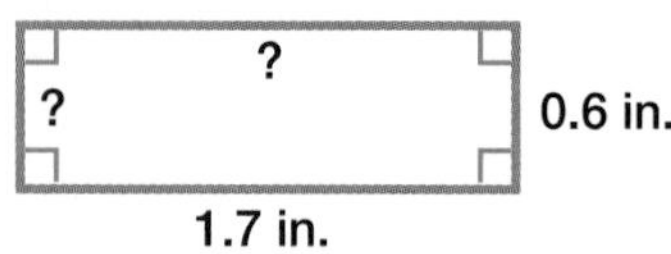

C.

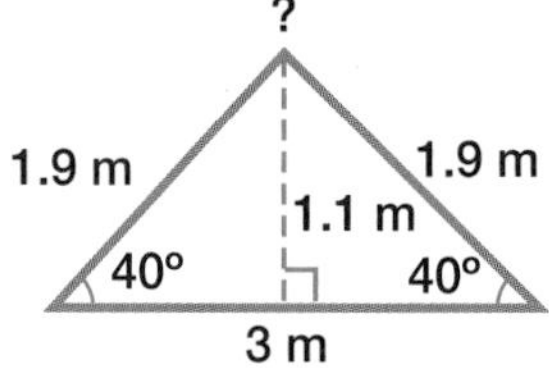

D.

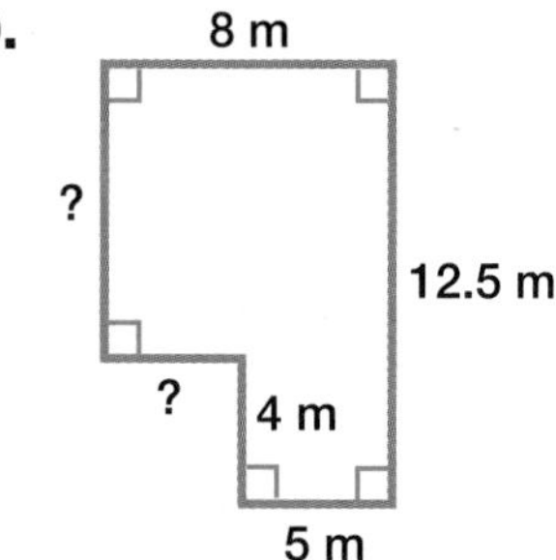

Use the diagrams to solve each problem.

1. Which figures have at least one pair of perpendicular sides?
2. Which figures are parallelograms?
3. Which figure has exactly two congruent sides and two congruent angles?
4. Which figure has an area of 66 m^2?
5. Which figure has a perimeter of 6.8 m?
6. Which figures are quadrilaterals?
7. **Compare** Which figure has the greatest area?
8. **Analyze** How can you find the area of figure *D* in two different ways, using addition or subtraction?

Standards MG **1.4, 2.1, 2.2**

Enrichment

Exploring Right Triangles

The sides of a right triangle have a special property. To explore this property, follow the steps below.

1. **a.** Construct a small right triangle near the center of a sheet of paper.

   b. Construct a square along each side of your triangle.

   c. Cut out the two smaller squares. Place one of them inside the largest square. Cut the remaining square into rectangular pieces and use it to cover the rest of the largest square.

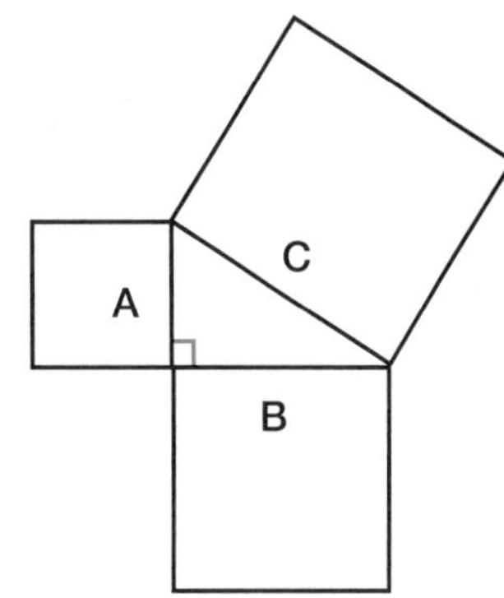

   d. What can you conclude about the areas of squares drawn on all three sides of a right triangle? Write an algebraic sentence to summarize your conclusion, using a^2 and b^2 to represent the areas of the smaller squares and c^2 to represent the area of the largest square.

Find the area of the square you could draw on each labeled side. Then find the area of the square you could draw on the third side.

2.

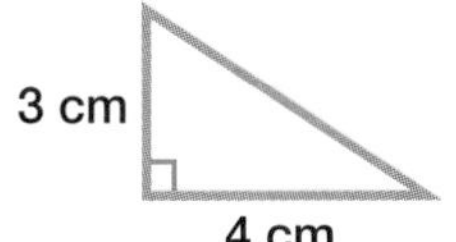

3.

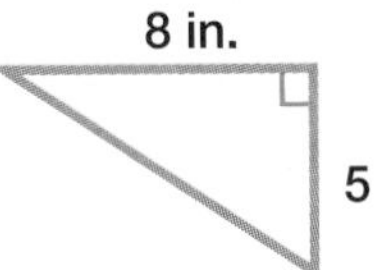

4.

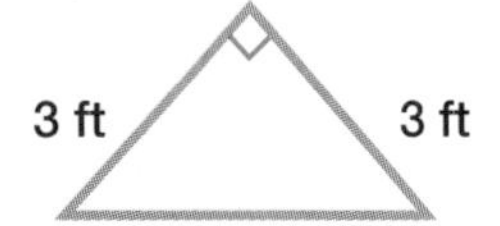

5.

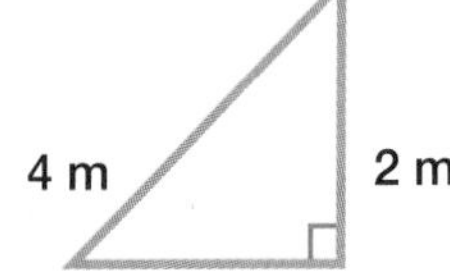

Explain Your Thinking

- ▶ If you know a side length of a triangle, how can you find the area of a square that has that side as its base?
- ▶ If you know the area of a square based on an unknown side length, how could you estimate the side length? Test your ideas with one of the triangles above.

Standards MG 1.1

Ratio and Percent

Why Learn About Ratio and Percent?

Ratio and percent can help you understand, describe, and compare relationships between quantities.

When you draw a map with a scale or make a scale drawing, you are using ratio. When you save 25% of your allowance each week, you are using percent.

Model railroading is a popular hobby. Model railroaders use ratios to build houses, trees, and all sorts of things for their railroad setups.

Reviewing Vocabulary

Understanding math language helps you become a successful problem solver. Here are some math vocabulary words you should know.

fraction	a number that describes part of a whole or part of a group
unit fraction	a fraction in which the numerator is 1, such as $\frac{1}{5}$
decimal	a number that is written with a decimal point
circle graph	a circular graph that shows data as parts of a whole

Reading Words and Symbols

When you read mathematics, sometimes you read only words, sometimes you read words and symbols, and sometimes you read only symbols.

Ratios and percents are ways of comparing one group with another.

All these statements represent the same situation.

- One out of eight crayons is yellow.
- For every seven crayons of other colors, there is one yellow crayon.
- There is one yellow crayon for every box this size.
- The ratio of yellow crayons to other colors is 1 to 7.

Try These

1. Which two situations are the same? Why?
   a. There are 2 sandwiches for each person.
   b. There are 3 sandwiches for 3 people.
   c. There are 5 sandwiches for 4 people.
   d. There are 8 sandwiches for 4 people.
   e. There are 6 sandwiches for 2 people.

2. Write *true* or *false* for each statement.
   a. The numerator in a fraction must always be greater than the denominator.
   b. A decimal is always less than one.
   c. You can find equivalents for any fraction by multiplying the numerator and denominator by the same amount.
   d. *one out of two* is equivalent to *two out of four.*
   e. $\frac{2}{5}$ represents the same amount as $\frac{40}{100}$.
   f. A mark of 7 out of 10 is better than a mark of 85 out of 100.

3. What other ways can you think of to use numbers to describe the crayons shown on page 516.

Upcoming Vocabulary

Write About It **Here are some other vocabulary words** you will learn in this chapter. Watch for these words. Write their definitions in your journal.

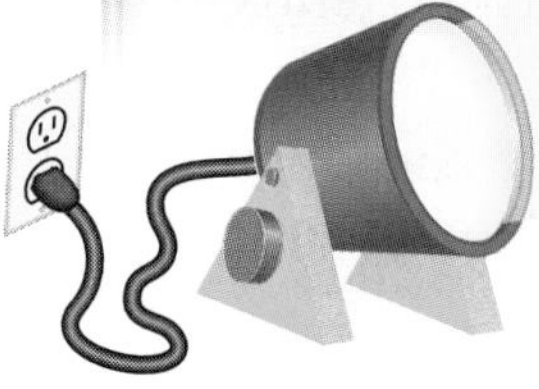

ratio
terms
equal ratio
rate
unit rate
per
scale
scale drawing
percent

Meaning of Ratios

You will learn how to read, write, and simplify ratios.

New Vocabulary
term
ratio

Learn About It

Olga finds 7 wooden tangram pieces in a box. Two of the shapes are quadrilaterals and 5 are triangles. One way to compare the number of quadrilaterals to the number of triangles is to write a ratio.

The **terms** of a ratio are the numbers you are comparing. You can write a **ratio** as a fraction, with the first term as the numerator and the second term as the denominator.

Compare the numbers of tangram pieces.

Step 1 Identify the terms of the ratio.

2 quadrilaterals
The first term is 2.

5 triangles
The second term is 5.

Step 2 Write the ratio of quadrilaterals to triangles.

The ratio can be written 3 ways.

Word form: **2 to 5**

Ratio form: **2:5**

Fraction form: $\frac{2}{5}$

To read all 3 forms, say, "2 to 5."

Solution: The ratio of quadrilaterals to triangles is 2 to 5, 2:5, or $\frac{2}{5}$.

Another Example

Reduce a Ratio

22 stickers to 4 sheets of paper

$$\frac{22}{4} = \frac{11 \times \overset{1}{\cancel{2}}}{2 \times \underset{1}{\cancel{2}}} = \frac{11}{2}, \text{ or } 11:2, \text{ or } 11 \text{ to } 2$$

If both terms have a common factor, you can cancel that factor to reduce the ratio.

Explain Your Thinking

► If you wanted to compare the number of triangles to the number of quadrilaterals, why would you use the ratio 5:2 instead of the ratio 2:5?

Guided Practice

Write each ratio three different ways.

1. 5 paints to 6 brushes

2. 16 beads to 7 sequins

3. 2 pens to 3 markers

4. 8 stamps to 2 stencils

5. 4 chalks to 5 slates

6. 4 books to 2 shelves

Ask Yourself

- Did I write the terms in the correct order?
- Did I write each ratio three different ways?

Standards Extends Grade 5 Standards

Independent Practice

Write each ratio three different ways.

7. squares to red rectangles
8. blue parallelograms to squares
9. blue parallelograms to red rectangles
10. squares to blue parallelograms
11. red rectangles to squares
12. red rectangles to blue parallelograms
13. squares to all figures
14. all rectangles to other figures

Problem Solving • Reasoning

Use the table at the right to answer Problems 15 and 16.

Number of Each Shape	
triangles	15
squares	3
parallelograms	3

15. Olivia emptied a box of wooden tangram pieces onto the desk. She counted the number of each shape and organized her findings in a chart. What is the ratio of triangles to squares?

16. **Analyze** A tangram is made up of 5 triangles, 1 square, and 1 parallelogram. In the puzzle box, Olivia found 15 triangles, 3 squares, and 3 parallelograms. If all the pieces are the right size, how many complete tangrams could be made from these shapes?

17. **Write About It** Seven tangram pieces, put together, make one large square. Write a ratio comparing the number of tangram pieces to the number of large squares. Write a second ratio comparing the number of large squares to the number of tangram pieces. Why are these two ratios different?

Mixed Review • Test Prep

Write an algebraic expression for each word phrase.
Use *n* as the variable. *(pages 70–72, 162–164)*

18. ten more than a number
19. seven less than a number
20. a number divided by fifteen
21. the sum of two and a number

22. Which number represents a reasonable estimate of the product 52 × 196? *(pages 114–115)*

A 1,000 **B** 10,000 **C** 100,000 **D** 1,000,000

Extra Practice See Set A on page 558.

LESSON 2

Equivalent Ratios

You will learn how to use multiplication and division to find equivalent ratios.

New Vocabulary
equivalent ratio

Learn About It

After you choose a paint color when buying paint, the clerk mixes the paint by adding small units of color to a base color.

Henry has chosen a color that requires 2 units of blue for every 6 units of yellow. If the clerk uses 6 units of blue for Henry's order, how many units of yellow will he need?

You can find an **equivalent ratio** that has 6 as its first term.

Different Ways to Find Equivalent Ratios

You can find an equivalent fraction.

Step 1 Write the first ratio as a fraction in simplest form.

$\frac{2}{6} = \frac{1}{3}$ (÷ 2, ÷ 2)

Step 2 Find a number to multiply by that gives 6 as the new first term.

$\frac{1}{3} = \frac{6}{■}$ (× ?, × ?)

Step 3 Multiply the numerator and denominator by 6.

$\frac{1}{3} = \frac{6}{18}$ (× 6, × 6)

You can make a list of equivalent ratios.

Step 1 Multiply or divide each term of the ratio by the same number to make a list of equivalent ratios.

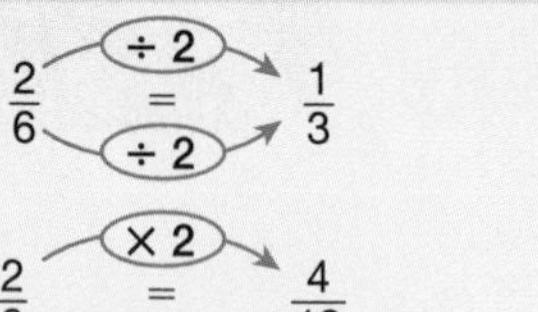

$\frac{2}{6} = \frac{1}{3}$ (÷ 2, ÷ 2)

$\frac{2}{6} = \frac{6}{18}$ (× 3, × 3)

$\frac{2}{6} = \frac{4}{12}$ (× 2, × 2)

$\frac{2}{6} = \frac{8}{24}$ (× 4, × 4)

Step 2 Find the ratio in the list that has 6 as its first term.

$\frac{6}{18}$

Solution: If the clerk uses 6 units of blue, he will need to add 18 units of yellow.

Explain Your Thinking

- Why is the ratio the same when you multiply the numerator and denominator by the same number?
- How many equivalent ratios are there for 1:2?

Standards NS **1.0, 2.0, 2.4, 2.5** AF **1.0, 1.2**

Guided Practice

Write 4 equivalent ratios for each.

1. $\frac{2}{6}$ **2.** 8 to 12 **3.** 6:15 **4.** $\frac{20}{25}$

> **Ask Yourself**
> - Did I multiply both terms by the same number?
> - Did I divide both terms by the same number?

Independent Practice

Write two equivalent ratios for each given ratio.

5. $\frac{1}{3}$ **6.** 3 to 4 **7.** 1:5 **8.** 2 to 3 **9.** $\frac{5}{6}$

Write each ratio as a fraction in simplest form.

10. $\frac{10}{40}$ **11.** 6:18 **12.** 24 to 42 **13.** 12:60 **14.** $\frac{16}{36}$

Complete each set of equivalent ratios.

15. $\frac{1}{4} = \frac{■}{12}$ **16.** $\frac{8}{24} = \frac{■}{6}$ **17.** $\frac{4}{5} = \frac{■}{30}$ **18.** $\frac{15}{25} = \frac{3}{■}$

19. $\frac{3}{5} = \frac{■}{10}$ **20.** $\frac{6}{9} = \frac{■}{12}$ **21.** $\frac{15}{18} = \frac{10}{■}$ **22.** $\frac{12}{18} = \frac{16}{■}$

Problem Solving • Reasoning

23. **Predict** One gallon of paint covers 400 square feet. Michelle wants to cover 1,200 square feet. Use equivalent ratios to find the number of gallons Michelle needs.

24. **Analyze** The ratio of boys to girls enrolled in a painting class is 4 to 5. If 12 boys are enrolled, how many students are there?

25. Paulo takes 10 days to paint the halls in a 15-story building. Write the ratio of days to stories as a fraction in simplest form. If Paulo works at the same pace, how long would it take him to paint the halls in a 24-story building?

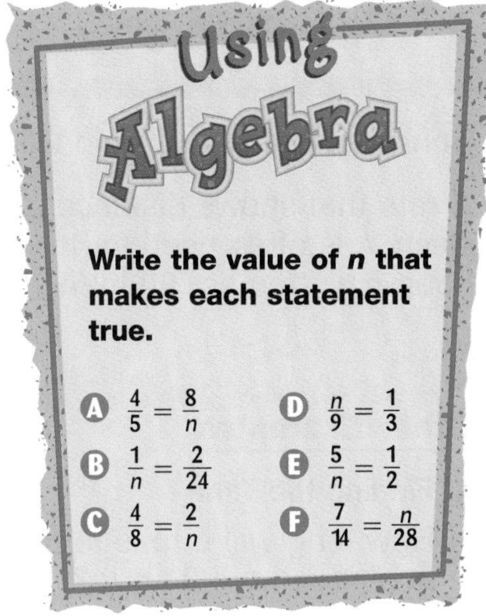

Mixed Review • Test Prep

Round each number to the underlined place. *(pages 8–9, 28–29)*

26. 1,06<u>5</u>.44 **27.** 61.9<u>5</u>1 **28.** <u>2</u>41.67 **29.** 3.<u>0</u>519 **30.** 55,9<u>3</u>6.3

31 What is true about the product of any two consecutive counting numbers? *(pages 298–299)*

A It is always less than the sum.
B It is always a prime number.
C It is always an even number.
D It is always a composite number.

Extra Practice See Set B on page 558.

Rates

You will learn about rates and how to use them to solve problems.

New Vocabulary
rate
per

Learn About It

A **rate** is a ratio that compares different units. A unit rate shows the amount of one quantity for each unit value of another quantity.

Mr. Roth's train travels 180 miles in 2 hours. At that rate, how far will the train travel in 8 hours?

To find out how far the train will travel, find the unit rate and multiply.

Step 1 Divide to find the rate in miles per hour. **Per** means *for each.*

$$\frac{180 \text{ mi}}{2 \text{ h}} = \frac{180}{2} = \frac{90}{1}$$

The rate is 90 miles per hour.

Step 2 Multiply by the number of hours.

$$\frac{90 \text{ mi}}{1 \text{ h}} \xrightarrow{\times 8} \frac{720 \text{ mi}}{8 \text{ h}}$$

Solution: Mr. Roth's train will travel 720 miles in 8 hours.

A rate that shows distance per unit of time is a speed. A slash, /, is often used for the word per. Ninety miles per hour is written as "90 mi/h."

Other Examples

A. Finding the Time

How long will it take to travel 450 km at a speed of 90 km/h?

$$90 \times n = 450$$
$$n = 5$$

It will take 5 hours.

B. Rates With Money

A worker receives $60 for 8 hours work. What is the rate of pay per hour?

$$\frac{60}{8} = 7\frac{1}{2}$$

The rate is $7.50 per hour.

Explain Your Thinking

- ▶ How is a rate different from other types of ratios?
- ▶ How can you find an unknown term in two equivalent rates?

 Standards NS 1.0, 2.0, 2.4, 2.5

Guided Practice

Find the rate per unit of time.

1. 15 miles in 3 hours
2. $20 in 4 hours
3. 60 meters in 5 seconds
4. $1,000 in 5 days
5. 100 miles in 4 hours
6. 50 km in 5 hours

Ask Yourself

- Did I write the units?
- Was my answer reasonable?

Independent Practice

Find the rate per unit of time.

7. 80 miles in 16 min
8. 72 mi in 9 seconds
9. 90 meters in 18 min
10. 75 cm in 15 seconds
11. $100 in 5 hours
12. $35 in 7 hours

Find the distance traveled in the given amount of time.

13. 5 hours at 50 mi/h
14. 3 min at 8 m/min
15. 12 seconds at 16 ft/s
16. 0.5 hour at 30 mi/h
17. 7 days at 25 mi/day
18. 2.5 hours at 40 km/h

Find the length of time for each trip.

19. 200 miles at 50 mi/h
20. 75 km at 25 km/h
21. 1,500 ft at 30 ft/s

Problem Solving • Reasoning

22. Bobbie took 2 hours to go 30 miles on a slow train. At that rate, how long will it take to complete her 90-mile trip?
23. Ms. Aikins has been on the train for 2 hours and has traveled 160 mi. At this rate, her entire trip will take 6 hours. How far will she travel in all?
24. **Write Your Own** A sightseeing train travels 36 mi through the Napa Valley. The trip takes 3 hours. Write a problem that can be solved using division to find equal ratios.

Math Is Everywhere!

6.07 in.

HOBBIES Many model trains use the HO Scale, which is 1 in.:87 in. The length of a scale model boxcar is 6.07 in. Find the actual length of the boxcar in inches.

Mixed Review • Test Prep

Estimate each sum or difference. *(pages 58–59)*

25. $2.05 − $1.98
26. $72.30 + $61.95
27. $14.01 − $0.75

28. A rectangular flower garden has a length of 20 ft and a perimeter of 56 ft. What is the width of the garden? *(pages 194–196)*

A 8 ft **B** 16 ft **C** 36 ft **D** 96 ft

Extra Practice See Set C on page 558.

Scale Drawing

You will learn how to use equal ratios to interpret scale drawings.

New Vocabulary
scale drawing
scale

Learn About It

In a **scale drawing**, every measure is enlarged or reduced by the same factor. A **scale** is a ratio that compares measurements in a drawing to measurements of real objects.

How tall is the chair that is shown in this scale drawing?

You can use the scale and equivalent ratios to find the height of the chair.

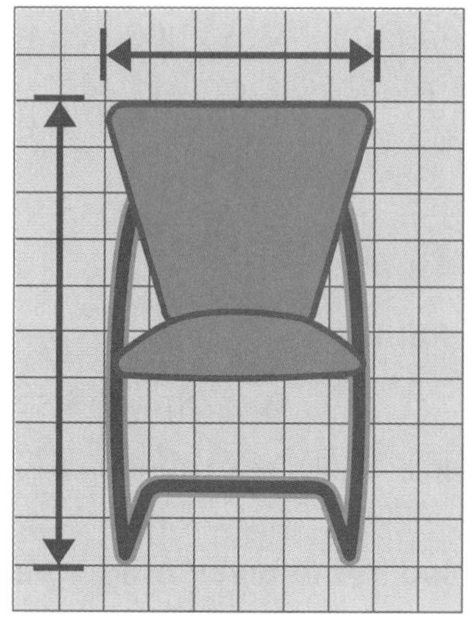

1 cm:20 cm

Materials

rulers marked in centimeters and inches

Step 1 Use a centimeter ruler to measure the height of the chair in the drawing.

- How tall is the chair in the drawing?

Step 2 Write the scale for the drawing in fraction form.

- How many centimeters does 1 cm in the drawing represent?

Step 3 Write the scale and equivalent ratios to show the relationship between the height of the chair in the drawing and the actual height, h, of the chair.

$$\frac{1}{20} = \frac{5}{h}$$

- Look at the scale. Does 1 cm represent a measurement on the drawing or the actual measurement?
- Why is 5 the first term of the second ratio?

Step 4 Find the height of the chair.

$$\frac{1}{20} \times \frac{5}{5} = \frac{5}{h}$$

- How tall is the chair?

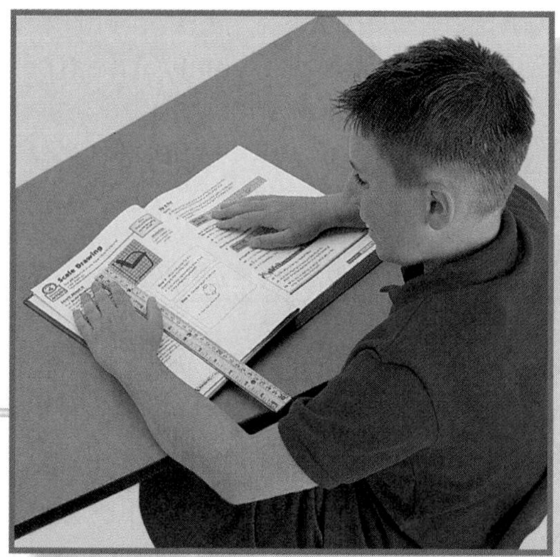

Standards AF **1.0, 1.2** MR **2.0, 2.3, 3.0, 3.3**

Try It Out

Solve.

1. Measure the width of the chair in the drawing. Use this measurement to find the actual width of the chair.
2. Complete the table and continue the pattern to see how the measurements would change if the drawing were enlarged.

Chair Height	5 cm	10 cm	15 cm	■	■	■	■	■
Chair Width	3 cm	■	■	12 cm	15 cm	18 cm	■	■

In a scale for a drawing of a building, 1 cm represents 5 m. The scale is 1 cm:5 m. Find *n* in each case.

3. 4 cm represents *n* m.
4. *n* cm represents 10 m.
5. *n* cm represents 50 m.
6. 0.5 cm represents *n* m.
7. *n* cm represents 1.25 m.
8. 1.5 cm represents *n* m.

Find the missing measurements.

9.

Drawing Size	$\frac{1}{2}$ in.	1 in.	■	2 in.	■	■	■	4 in.
Actual Size	1 ft	■	3 ft	■	5 ft	6 ft	7 ft	8 ft

A blueprint is made with a scale of $\frac{1}{8}$ in.:1 ft. Find *n* in each case.

10. *n* in. represents 5 ft.
11. $\frac{1}{4}$ in. represents *n* ft.
12. $\frac{3}{4}$ in. represents *n* ft.
13. *n* in. represents 12 ft.
14. *n* in. represents 1.5 ft.
15. $\frac{5}{16}$ in. represents *n* ft.

Write about it! Talk about it!

Use what you have learned to write about these questions.

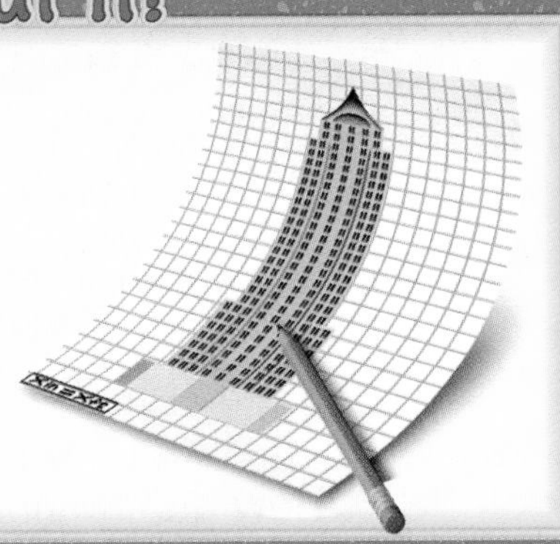

16. Explain why a scale is a special ratio.
17. How can equivalent ratios help you determine the actual distances represented in a scale drawing?
18. When you write two equivalent ratios, why is the order of the terms important?

Problem-Solving Skill: Choose a Computation Method

You will learn how to decide when to solve a problem mentally and when to use paper and pencil.

To solve a problem you need to begin by making a plan.

Look at the situations below.

Sometimes you can calculate mentally.

Angelo is drawing a floor plan of his classroom to scale so that 1 cm represents 100 cm. If his desk is 70 cm wide, how wide will it be on the plan?

Think: 100 cm is represented by 1 cm in the floor plan, so all the measurements in the plan will be $\frac{1}{100}$ of their actual size. Each real length is divided by 100.

$$70 \text{ cm} \div 100 = 0.7 \text{ cm}$$

The width of Angelo's desk in the floor plan will be 0.7 cm.

Sometimes you need to calculate on paper.

Kelsey lives in Fresno, California, and has an e-mail pal in Alice Springs, Australia. On a map, the distance from Fresno to Alice Springs is about 12 in. If 1 in. on the map represents 660 mi, what is the actual distance?

Write two equivalent ratios. The variable n represents the unknown distance.

1 in.:660 mi = 12 in.:n mi

$$\frac{1}{660} = \frac{12}{n}$$

$$\frac{1}{660} \xrightarrow{\times ?} \frac{12}{n}$$

$$\frac{1}{660} \xrightarrow{\times 12} \frac{12}{7{,}920}$$

$$n = 7{,}920$$

The distance from Fresno to Alice Springs is about 7,920 miles.

Look Back How did the numbers in each problem help you decide whether to calculate mentally or on paper?

 Standards MR **1.0, 2.0, 2.3, 2.4, 3.0, 3.2**

LEFT: Merced County, California is one of the world's most productive agricultural areas.
RIGHT: San Jose, California is an important center of the technology industry.

Guided Practice

Solve.

1. A map of California uses a scale of 1 cm:24 km. If the map distance between Merced and San Jose is 5 cm, what is the actual distance between the two places?

   Think: Can I solve this problem mentally?

2. A map of Laguna Beach uses a scale of $\frac{3}{4}$ in.:500 ft. If the part of the Pacific Coast Highway shown on the map is $4\frac{1}{2}$ in. long, what is the actual length of this part of the highway?

   Think: What equal ratios can I use to solve this problem?

Choose a Strategy

Solve. Use these or other strategies.

Problem-Solving Strategies

- **Draw a Diagram**
- **Solve a Simpler Problem**
- **Work Backward**
- **Make a Table**

3. On a map, Frog Creek is 1.5 in. long. The actual length is about 15 miles. What distance does 1 in. represent on the map scale?

4. A floor plan of a house has the scale 40 cm:20 m. On the floor plan, a room is 8 cm long. How long is the room?

5. On a map of Golden Gate Park, the distance between the golf course and the arboretum is 13.5 cm. What will this distance become if the map is enlarged so the ratio of enlargement to original is 2:1?

6. The distance from San Francisco, CA, to El Paso, TX, is 995 miles by air. If you wanted to draw a scale map of the area between San Francisco and El Paso on an 11-in.-wide sheet of paper, what scale would you use?

7. On a map, a bicycle path goes 6 cm in a straight line to a bridge, makes a 90° turn to the right, continues 8 cm to a playground, makes another turn, and returns straight to the starting point. If the map scale is 2 cm:0.5 km, what is the actual distance from the playground back to the starting point?

8. On a map of Bakersfield, California, the distance from the Kern County Museum to the Mesa Marin Raceway is about 8 cm. The distance from the museum to the fairgrounds is about 1.5 in. If 1 in. equals about 2.5 cm, is the raceway or the fairgrounds farther from the museum?

Extra Practice See 1–4 on page 561.

Quick Check

Check Your Understanding of Lessons 1–5

Write each ratio three different ways.

1. 7 stars to 8 squares
2. 9 circles to 15 squares
3. 12 squares to 8 stars

Complete each set of equivalent ratios.

4. 3 to 4 = ■ to 16
5. 6 to 24 = ■ to 8
6. 3 to 1 = ■ to 7
7. 6 to 9 = ■ to 36
8. 7 to 15 = ■ to 45
9. 22 to 28 = ■ to 14

Find the rate.

10. 160 miles in 4 hours
11. 6,000 feet in 12 seconds
12. 270 meters in 54 minutes

Solve.

13. Hailey is drawing a scale map of her apartment so 10 cm on the map represents 5 m in her apartment. If her living room is 4 m wide, how wide is it on the map?

How did you do?

If you had difficulty with any items in the Quick Check, you can use the following pages for review and extra practice.

California Standards	Items	Review These Pages	Do These Extra Practice Items
Statistics, Data Analysis and Probability: **1.3**	1–3	pages 518–519	Set A, page 558
Statistics, Data Analysis and Probability: **1.3**	4–9	pages 520–521	Set B, page 558
Statistics, Data Analysis and Probability: **1.3**	10–12	pages 522–523	Set C, page 558
Math Reasoning: **2.1, 2.4, 2.6**	13	pages 526–527	1–4, page 561

Test Prep • Cumulative Review

Maintaining the Standards

Choose the letter of the correct answer.

1. For a certain shade of green paint, the ratio of blue tint to yellow tint is 3 to 2. If 4 gallons of this shade require 6 units of blue tint, how many units of yellow tint would you need for 20 gallons?

   A 2 units **C** 20 units
   B 9 units **D** 40 units

2. There are 3 softballs for every 5 players on a softball team. Which expression does not show the softball to player ratio?

   F 3 to 5 **H** $\frac{3}{5}$
   G 3:5 **J** $3 < 5$

3. Divide.

   $5.3\overline{)45.58}$

   A 860 **C** 8.6
   B 86 **D** 0.86

4. Which of these is a geometric figure whose angle sum is 180°?

   F rectangle
   G square
   H triangle
   J circle

5. Find the area of this figure.

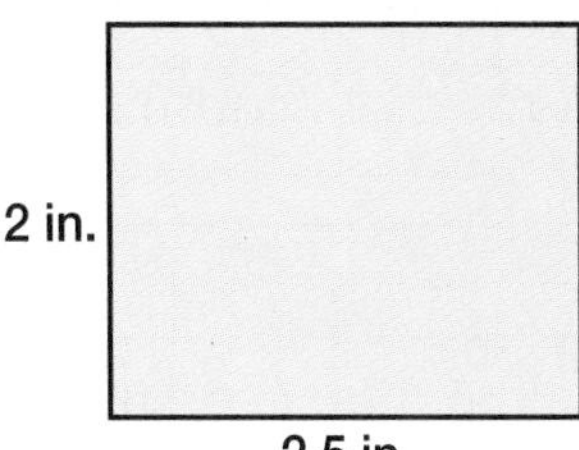

   A 5 in. **C** 9 in.
   B 5 in.^{2} **D** 9 in.^{2}

6. What value belongs in the box?

   $5(n + 6) = (5 \times \blacksquare) + (5 \times 6)$

   F 6 **H** 11
   G t **J** n

7. Mr. Ramirez told his class that the answer to one of their homework problems was a fraction equivalent to $\frac{3}{8}$. Which of these fractions could be the answer?

   A $\frac{9}{32}$ **C** $\frac{12}{40}$
   B $\frac{6}{24}$ **D** $\frac{12}{32}$

8. Find ratios equivalent to 5:6.

   Explain How can your knowledge of multiplying fractions help you? Give an example.

Safe Site

Internet Test Prep
Visit **www.eduplace.com/kids/mhm** for more *Test Prep Practice.*

Understand Percent

You will learn how to use ratios to write percents.

New Vocabulary
percent

Learn About It

Use grid paper to learn about percent.

A **percent** is a ratio of a number line to 100.

Fifty percent means $\frac{50}{100}$ and is written as 50%.	$50\% = \frac{50}{100}$	$\frac{50}{100} = 0.50$ or 0.5

Percent means "per hundred."

Materials

For each pair:
grid paper
ruler
colored pencils

Use the percent symbol (%) to write each ratio.

Step 1 On a sheet of grid paper, use a ruler to outline an area that measures 10 units by 10 units.

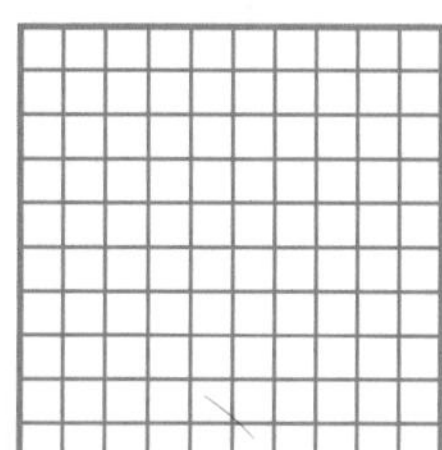

- Count the small squares in the figure.

Step 2 Color 40 small squares blue, 25 small squares yellow, and 15 green.

- What is the ratio of blue squares to the total number of squares?
- What is the ratio of yellow squares to the total number of squares?
- What is the ratio of colored squares to the total number of squares?

Step 3 Use the percent symbol to write each percent of the total number of squares.

- the percent of blue squares
- the percent of yellow squares
- the percent of green squares
- the percent of colored squares
- the percent of uncolored squares

Standards NS 1.0, 1.2 MR 3.3

Try It Out

Write the percent of each grid that is shaded.

1. 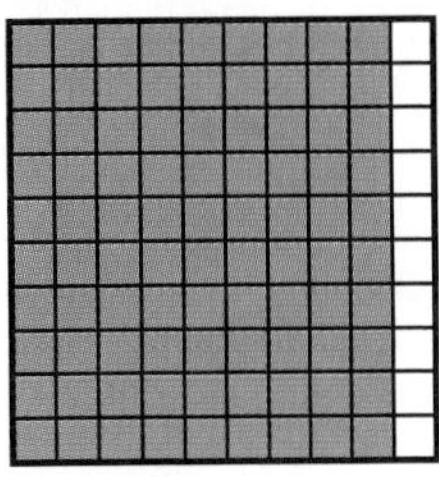

2. 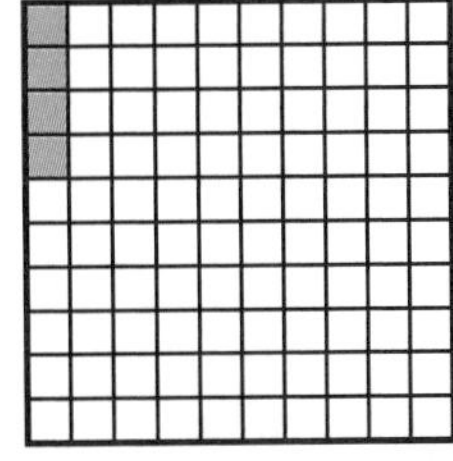

3. 

4. 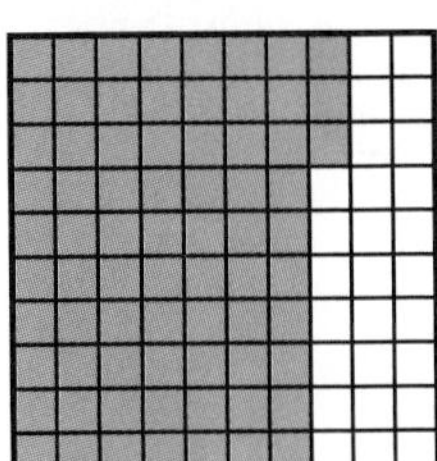

5. 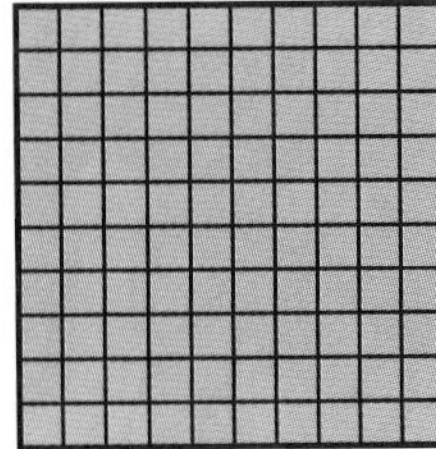

6. 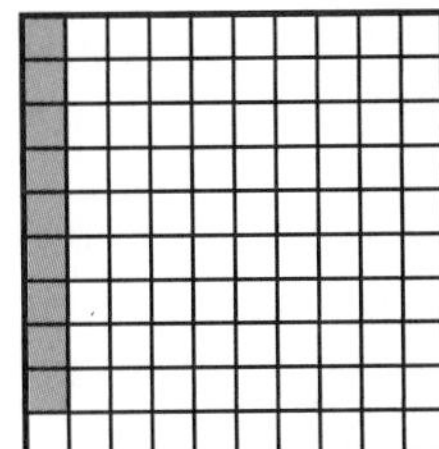

Write each ratio as a percent.

7. $\frac{55}{100}$ **8.** $\frac{2}{100}$ **9.** $\frac{31}{100}$ **10.** $\frac{79}{100}$

11. $\frac{48}{100}$ **12.** $\frac{16}{100}$ **13.** $\frac{91}{100}$ **14.** $\frac{63}{100}$

15. 35 parts out of 100 **16.** 6 parts out of 100 **17.** 15 parts out of 100

18. 1 part out of 100 **19.** 0 parts out of 100 **20.** 50 parts out of 100

Write each percent as a ratio in simplest form.

21. 10% **22.** 28% **23.** 81% **24.** 12%

25. 39% **26.** 53% **27.** 62% **28.** 98%

29. 70% **30.** 23% **31.** 40% **32.** 75%

33. 65% **34.** 17% **35.** 99% **36.** 100%

Write about it! Talk about it!

Use what you have learned to write about these questions.

37. What does ten percent mean on a 10-by-10 grid?

38. How would you show 100% on a 10-by-10 grid?

39. Why is percent a good name for this type of ratio?

LESSON 7

Ratio and Percent

You will learn how to write a ratio as a percent and a percent as a ratio.

New Vocabulary
percent
fraction

Learn About It

Two out of five students play soccer, and 20% of them play hockey.

What **percent** of the students play soccer? What **fraction** of them play hockey?

You can write a ratio as a percent. You can write a percent as a ratio in fraction form.

Write $\frac{2}{5}$ as a percent.

- Write the known fraction.

  $\frac{2}{5}$

- Write an equivalent ratio with a denominator of 100.

  $\frac{2 \times 20}{5 \times 20} = \frac{40}{100}$

- Write the equivalent ratio, using the percent symbol.

  $\frac{40}{100} = 40\%$

Write 20% as a ratio in fraction form.

- Express the percent as an equivalent ratio.

  20% means $\frac{20}{100}$

- Try to find an equivalent ratio with the smallest possible first term.

  $\frac{20}{100} = \frac{2}{10}$

  $= \frac{1}{5}$

Solution: 40% of the students play soccer and $\frac{1}{5}$ play hockey.

Explain Your Thinking

- ▶ Why is it easy to express a percent as a fraction in hundredths or a fraction in hundredths as a percent?
- ▶ How can you tell whether the terms of a ratio have common factors?
- ▶ When is a ratio in simplest form?

Standards NS **1.0, 1.2** AF **1.0, 1.2** SDP **1.3**

Guided Practice

Express each ratio as an equivalent percent and each percent as a ratio.

1. $\frac{4}{5}$ **2.** 10% **3.** $\frac{3}{10}$ **4.** $\frac{5}{5}$

5. 40% **6.** $\frac{1}{4}$ **7.** $\frac{3}{4}$ **8.** $\frac{3}{25}$

9. 97% **10.** 2% **11.** 8% **12.** 5%

Ask Yourself

- Did I write the percent sign when necessary?
- Did I write each fraction in simplest form?

Independent Practice

Match each percent in Column *A* to an equivalent ratio in Column *B*.

Column A	Column B
13. 40%	**a.** $\frac{1}{4}$
14. 25%	**b.** $\frac{9}{10}$
15. 80%	**c.** $\frac{1}{2}$
16. 75%	**d.** $\frac{3}{5}$
17. 20%	**e.** $\frac{3}{4}$
18. 30%	**f.** $\frac{1}{5}$
19. 90%	**g.** $\frac{3}{10}$
20. 60%	**h.** $\frac{2}{5}$
21. 50%	**i.** $\frac{4}{5}$

Write each ratio as a percent.

22. $\frac{4}{20}$ **23.** $\frac{4}{25}$ **24.** $\frac{7}{50}$ **25.** $\frac{18}{20}$ **26.** $\frac{9}{100}$

27. $\frac{7}{10}$ **28.** $\frac{33}{100}$ **29.** $\frac{3}{20}$ **30.** $\frac{11}{50}$ **31.** $\frac{4}{200}$

Write each percent as a ratio.

32. 6% **33.** 84% **34.** 15% **35.** 44% **36.** 62%

37. 45% **38.** 95% **39.** 52% **40.** 18% **41.** 67%

Algebra • Equations **Solve each equation for *n*.**

42. $\frac{25}{100} = \frac{1}{n}$ **43.** $\frac{n}{100} = \frac{1}{20}$ **44.** $\frac{36}{n} = \frac{9}{25}$ **45.** $\frac{16}{100} = \frac{8}{n}$

46. $12\% = \frac{n}{25}$ **47.** $13\% = \frac{26}{n}$ **48.** $2\% = \frac{1}{n}$ **49.** $n\% = \frac{19}{25}$

Problem Solving • Reasoning

Solve. Choose a method.

Computation Methods

- Mental Math
- Estimation
- Paper and Pencil

50. **Analyze** A goalie stopped 95% of the shots on goal during a soccer game. How many shots out of 20 did the goalie stop?

51. Karin took 5 shots on goal during a hockey game. Only one of her shots went into the net. What percent of her shots resulted in goals?

52. There are 25 students practicing soccer. Nine of them are girls. What percent of the students are girls? What percent of the students are boys?

53. **Estimate** Linda took 33 shots in a basketball game. She scored on 22 shots. Use equivalent ratios to estimate the percent of her shots that resulted in goals.

54. **Predict** Carlos scores an average of 22 points per basketball game. In one game, he scored 4 points in the first quarter, 7 in the second, and 5 in the third. What does he need to do in the fourth quarter to improve his average?

55. **Write About It** When you express ratios as percents, the results all have the same denominator, 100. Why is it useful to express two ratios with the same second term? Use examples to explain your answer.

Mixed Review • Test Prep

Write each decimal in word form. *(pages 24–25)*

56. 0.4 **57.** 0.41 **58.** 0.7 **59.** 0.08 **60.** 1.6 **61.** 25.01

62 Which of these has the least cost for one item? *(pages 422–423)*

A 2 for $0.28 **B** 5 for $0.45 **C** 6 for $0.72 **D** 12 for $1.20

Sorting

Skyla, Nicole, Josh, and Chris all play on sports teams.

- One plays baseball, one plays soccer, one plays ice hockey, and one plays basketball.
- Josh and Chris play sports that involve a ball.
- Chris is the goalie for his team.
- Skyla scores for her team when she makes a basket.

What sport does each person play?

Extra Practice See Set D on page 559.

Show What You Know

Using Vocabulary

Give an example of each.

1. a ratio
2. two equivalent ratios
3. a rate
4. a speed
5. a scale
6. a percent

On Your Own

Write each ratio as a fraction and a percent. Remember to write the fractions in simplest form.

7. 40:100
8. 5 to 10
9. 3:25
10. 2 to 2

Match Up

Find the matching numbers.

11. 20%	**a.** $\frac{3}{4}$
12. $\frac{1}{3}$	**b.** 55%
13. $\frac{6}{10}$	**c.** one to three
14. 75%	**d.** $\frac{5}{7}$
15. $\frac{11}{20}$	**e.** $\frac{1}{5}$
16. 5:7	**f.** 6:10
17. $\frac{2}{25}$	**g.** five to 4
18. 1:2	**h.** 7%
19. 5:4	**i.** $\frac{1}{2}$
20. $\frac{7}{100}$	**j.** 8:100

LESSON 8

Decimals and Percents

You will learn how to write percents as decimals and decimals as percents.

Review Vocabulary
decimal

Learn About It

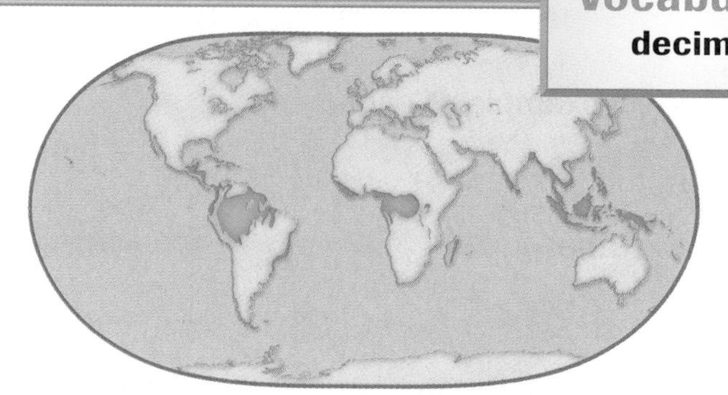

Tropical rain forests cover about 5% of Earth's surface.

You can also express this comparison in **decimal** form.

Write 5% in decimal form.

Step 1 Express the percent as a ratio in fraction form.

$5\% = \frac{5}{100}$

Step 2 Read the fraction in words. Then write it as a decimal.

$\frac{5}{100}$ means five hundredths.

$\frac{5}{100} = 0.05$

Solution: In decimal form, 5% is written as 0.05.

Other Examples

A. Write Tenths in Percent Form

$0.3 = \frac{3}{10}$

$\frac{3}{10} = \frac{30}{100}$

$\frac{30}{100} = 30\%$

B. Write Hundredths in Percent Form

$0.01 =$ one hundredth or $\frac{1}{100}$

$\frac{1}{100} = 1\%$

Explain Your Thinking

▶ Explain why 5% and $\frac{5}{100}$ represent the same ratio.

▶ Do 0.8 and 0.80 represent the same number? Explain.

▶ How many grid squares in a 10-by-10 grid would be shaded to show 0.3? to show 0.01?

Guided Practice

Write each percent in decimal form and each decimal in percent form.

1. 10% **2.** 0.04 **3.** 0.1

4. 42% **5.** 85% **6.** 0.31

Ask Yourself

- Did I write each percent or decimal as a ratio with a second term of 100?

Standards NS **1.0, 1.2** AF **1.1** MR **1.1, 2.3**

Independent Practice

Write each percent in decimal form and each decimal in percent form.

7. 91% **8.** 0.2 **9.** 15% **10.** 0.09 **11.** 49%

12. 0.52 **13.** 83% **14.** 0.25 **15.** 67% **16.** 0.5

How many units in a 10-by-10 grid should be shaded to represent each percent or decimal?

17. 23% **18.** 0.07 **19.** 18% **20.** 0.7 **21.** 0.11

22. 0.8 **23.** 64% **24.** 0.74 **25.** 39% **26.** 26%

Problem Solving • Reasoning

Use Data **Use the graph to answer Problems 27–29.**

27. Write a decimal that represents the percent of the world's tropical rain forests that are located in Brazil.

28. **Analyze** What percent of the world's rain forests are located outside Indonesia, Zaire, and Brazil?

29. **Estimate** Rain forests occur where more than 1,800 mm of rain falls in a year. If 1 in. is about 25.5 mm, about how many inches of rain is 1,800 mm?

30. **Write About It** Why must the sum of the percents in the graph be 100%? Use the data to explain your thinking.

Rain Forest Locations

Brazil 33%
Other
Zaire 10%
Indonesia 10%

Mixed Review • Test Prep

Use patterns to solve. *(pages 106–108, 134–135)*

31. $2\overline{)20}$ **32.** $2\overline{)200}$ **33.** $2\overline{)2{,}000}$ **34.** $2\overline{)20{,}000}$

35. 7×6 **36.** 70×6 **37.** 70×60 **38.** 700×60

39 On a map, the distance between two cities is 3 in. The actual distance between the cities is 180 mi. What is the scale of the map? *(pages 524–525)*

A 1 in.:6 mi **B** 1 in.:60 mi **C** 1 in.:540 mi **D** 1 in.:600 mi

Extra Practice See Set E on page 559.

Use Fractions, Decimals, and Percents for Comparisons

You will learn how to use fractions, decimals, and percents to compare numbers.

Learn About It

The fifth-grade class is selling tickets for the school concert. All the students have the same number of tickets to sell. Carl sold $\frac{2}{5}$ of his tickets. Tania sold 78% of hers. Ashley sold 0.55 of hers. Who sold the most tickets?

Compare $\frac{2}{5}$, **78%**, and **0.55** of the ticket sales.

Different Ways to Make Comparisons

You can use a number line to show parts of a unit.

$\frac{2}{5}$ is between $\frac{1}{4}$ and $\frac{1}{2}$

0.55 is a bit more than 50% of 1

78% of 1 is a bit more than 75% of 1

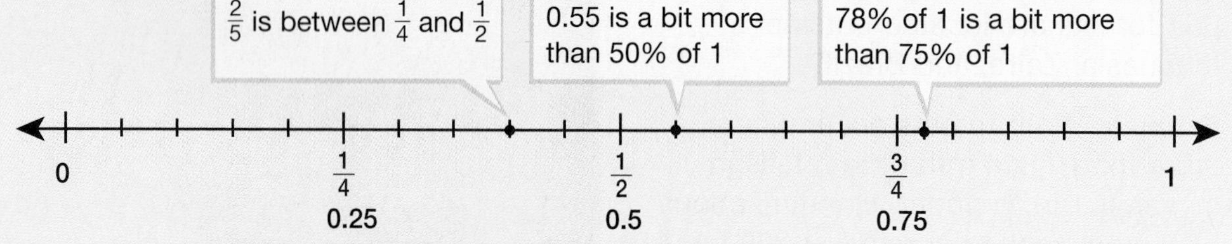

You can rewrite the ratios as decimals.

Step 1 To rewrite the fraction, divide the numerator by the denominator.

$$\begin{array}{r} 0.4 \\ 5\overline{)2.0} \\ -\,2\,0 \\ \hline 0 \end{array}$$

$\frac{2}{5} = 0.4$

Step 2 Think of the percent as a number of hundredths.

$78\% = \frac{78}{100} = 0.78$

Step 3 Compare 0.4, 0.78, and 0.55.

0.78 is greater than the other numbers.

Solution: 78% of the tickets is greater than 0.55 and $\frac{2}{5}$ of them, so Tania sold the most tickets.

Explain Your Thinking

- ▶ Why is it easier to make comparisons when the numbers or ratios are in the same form?
- ▶ Why is it easier to compare decimals than it is to compare fractions?

 Standards NS **1.0, 1.2, 1.5**

Guided Practice

Which represents the greatest part of a unit?

1. 0.4 $\frac{1}{2}$ 30% **2.** $\frac{1}{5}$ 30% 0.25 **3.** 70% 0.6 $\frac{2}{3}$

4. $\frac{1}{8}$ 0.2 40% **5.** $\frac{3}{10}$ 33% 0.35 **6.** $\frac{1}{20}$ 4% 0.3

Ask Yourself

- Did I write the numbers in the same form?
- Did I check the order to see if it's reasonable?

Independent Practice

Which represents the least part of a unit?

7. $\frac{4}{5}$ 0.2 60% **8.** $\frac{3}{5}$ 0.4 80% **9.** $\frac{4}{5}$ 0.9 85%

10. $\frac{1}{5}$ 0.1 25% **11.** $\frac{2}{5}$ 0.5 25% **12.** $\frac{7}{10}$ 0.6 3%

Order each set from the greatest to the least parts of a unit.

13. $\frac{3}{10}$ 0.25 20% **14.** $\frac{9}{10}$ 0.75 80% **15.** $\frac{7}{20}$ 0.3 40%

16. $\frac{12}{25}$ 0.3 50% **17.** $\frac{13}{20}$ 0.7 67% **18.** $\frac{3}{50}$ 0.6 3%

Problem Solving • Reasoning

19. Compare Orange juice and lemonade were sold during intermission. Three fifths of the sales were orange juice and 35% were lemonade. Which drink was less popular?

20. Analyze Fifty percent of the students performing in the concert are in Grade 5. Another 0.3 of the students are in Grade 4. The rest of the students are in Grade 6. What fraction of the students are in Grade 6?

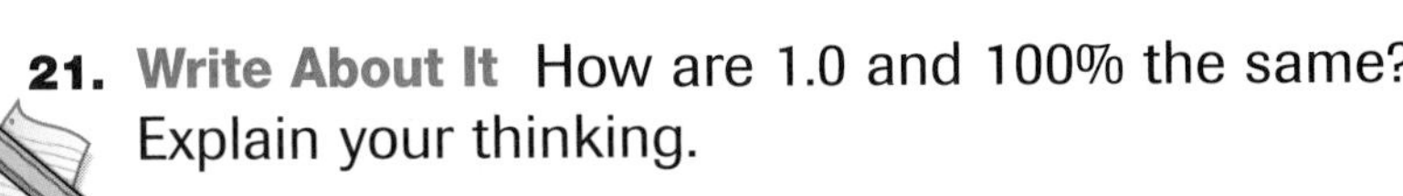

21. Write About It How are 1.0 and 100% the same? Explain your thinking.

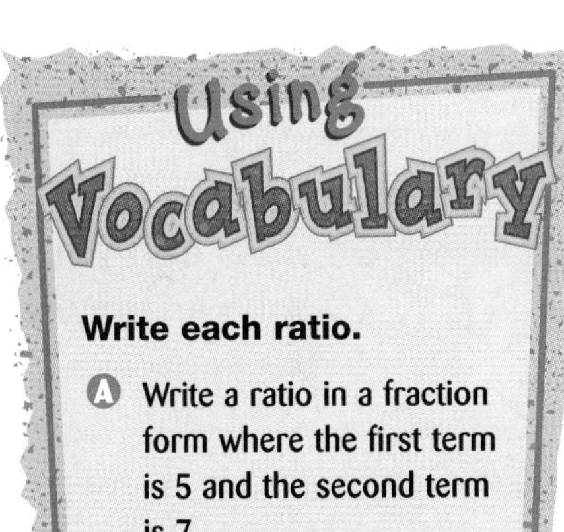

Write each ratio.

A Write a ratio in a fraction form where the first term is 5 and the second term is 7.

B Write a ratio as a fraction in simplest form in which the second term is twice the other.

Mixed Review • Test Prep

Use patterns to find the products and quotients. *(pages 98–99, 134–135)*

22. 3×10 **23.** 3×100 **24.** $3 \times 1{,}000$ **25.** $3 \times 10{,}000$

26. $21 \div 7$ **27.** $210 \div 7$ **28.** $2{,}100 \div 7$ **29.** $2{,}100 \div 70$

30 Which mixed number is equal to 1.125? *(pages 322–323)*

A $1\frac{1}{400}$ **B** $1\frac{1}{125}$ **C** $1\frac{1}{8}$ **D** $1\frac{1}{4}$

Extra Practice See Set F on page 559.

Problem-Solving Strategy: Choose a Strategy

You will learn how to choose a strategy that will help you solve a problem in an efficient way.

Sometimes different strategies can be used to solve a problem.

Problem A toy store offers a free mystery toy with every purchase. There are different toys you can get, and you are equally likely to get each one. If you have a 20% chance of getting the toy you want on a single visit, how many different toys are there?

Understand

What is the question?

How many different toys are there?

What do you know?

- You have only one chance to get a toy.
- The chance of getting each toy is 20%.

Plan

How can you solve this problem?

You can draw a diagram or write an equation.

Solve

Draw a Diagram

Draw a 10-by-10 grid.

- Color 20 squares to represent the 20% chance of getting each toy.
- Count the number of sets of 20.

There are 5 different mystery toys.

Write an Equation

Use equivalent ratios.

Let n represent the total number of toys.

$$\frac{20}{100} = \frac{1}{n}$$

$$\frac{20}{100} = \frac{1}{5}$$

$$n = 5$$

Look Back

Look back at the problem

Can you think of another way to solve the problem?

Standards NS **2.1** AF **1.2** MR **1.0, 1.1, 2.0, 2.3, 2.4, 3.0, 3.2**

Remember:
- ► Understand
- ► Plan
- ► Solve
- ► Look Back

Guided Practice

Solve. Choose the best strategy.

1. Brad collects toy action figures from his favorite cartoon series. The store sells packages of 2 figures for $3.75 and packages of 5 figures for $11.99. Which package offers the better unit price?

   Think: How can I find the price for 1 figure?

2. A toy store finds that about 65% of its customers are less than 18 years old. At an electronics store next door, about $\frac{5}{8}$ of the customers are under 18. Which store has a greater percent of customers who are under 18?

   Think: How can I express 65% as a fraction and compare it to $\frac{5}{8}$?

Choose a Strategy

Solve. Use these or other strategies.

Problem-Solving Strategies

- **Guess and Check**
- **Work Backward**
- **Find a Pattern**
- **Draw a Diagram**

3. When a new video game was released, a large toy store sold twice as many games on the 1st day as on the 4th day. On the 3rd day, they sold 134 games. On the 2nd day, they sold 27 more games than on the 3rd day and 52 less than on the 4th day. How many games were sold on the 1st day?

4. Sandi used triangular blocks to make this pattern. If she continues the pattern, how many blocks will there be in total by the 10th row? What fraction of the blocks will be facing point-up?

   Row 1
   Row 2
   Row 3

5. A rectangular game board is 40 cm long and 30 cm wide. What is the diagonal distance across the board?

6. Jonathan bought two toys for $5.00. One toy cost 3 times as much as the other. How much did each toy cost?

7. A toy store sells two different sizes of the Star Racer spaceship. The ratio of large size to small size is 5:2. How long is the small spaceship if the larger one is 12.5 in. long?

8. Angie has a $1.50 coupon she can use at the toy store. If she buys 6 party favors for 85¢ each and 6 sticker books for $1.35 each, how much will she have to pay after she uses the coupon?

Extra Practice See 5–7 on page 561.

Quick Check

Check Your Understanding of Lessons 6–10

Complete.

1. $\frac{4}{5} = \blacksquare\%$

2. $\frac{\blacksquare}{20} = 10\%$

3. $\frac{11}{25} = \blacksquare\%$

4. $\frac{3}{\blacksquare} = 75\%$

5. $\frac{\blacksquare}{50} = 66\%$

6. $\frac{1}{8} = \blacksquare\%$

Write each percent in decimal form and each decimal in percent form.

7. 95%

8. 0.56

9. 20%

10. 0.82

11. 63%

12. 0.7

Order each set from the greatest to the least parts of a unit.

13. 0.6, $\frac{6}{20}$, 32%

14. $\frac{3}{5}$, 0.3, 35%

Solve. Choose the best strategy.

15. Each student from Ms. Lowes' class made a name card and dropped it into a hat. If the chance that Rahel will choose her own card from the hat is 5%, how many students are there in the class?

How did you do?

If you had difficulty with any items in the Quick Check, you can use the following pages for review and extra practice.

California Standards	Items	Review These Pages	Do These Extra Practice Items
Number Sense: **1.2** Statistics, Data Analysis and Probability: **1.3**	1–6	pages 530–534	Set D, page 559
Number Sense: **1.0, 2.1** Statistics, Data Analysis and Probability: **1.3**	7–12	pages 536–537	Set E, page 559
Number Sense: **1.0, 1.2, 1.5** Statistics, Data Analysis and Probability: **1.3**	13–14	pages 538–539	Set F, page 559
Math Reasoning: **1.0, 2.2**	15	pages 540–541	5–7, page 561

Test Prep • Cumulative Review

Maintaining the Standards

Choose the letter of the correct answer. If a correct answer is not here, choose NH.

1. If $\frac{3}{8}$ is equal to 0.375, what is the equivalent for $\frac{6}{8}$?

   A 0.375×6
   B 0.375×2
   C 0.375×0.5
   D 0.375×0.375

2. What percent of this model is shaded?

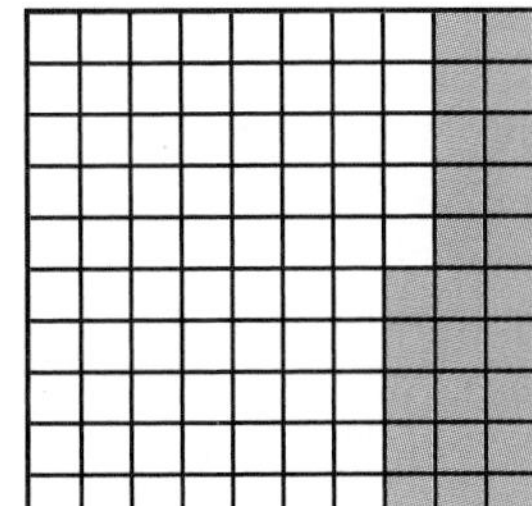

   F 25% **H** 75%
   G 50% **J** 100%

3. Mr. Mauer has $3\frac{1}{8}$ quarts of oil. He puts $\frac{5}{8}$ of a quart into his car. How much oil does he have left?

   A $2\frac{1}{4}$ qt **C** NH
   B $2\frac{1}{2}$ qt **D** $3\frac{1}{2}$ qt

4. Which type of angle is $\angle ABC$?

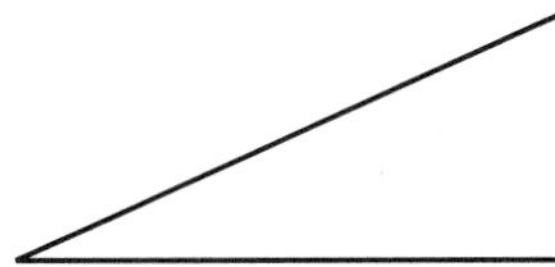

   F obtuse angle
   G right angle
   H acute angle
   J straight angle

5. Divide.

   $6.8 \div 10^3$

   A 6,800 **C** 0.229
   B 0.68 **D** 0.0068

6. Ryan measured 4 boards.The lengths were $3\frac{1}{2}$ ft, $4\frac{3}{8}$ ft, $1\frac{5}{12}$ ft, and $4\frac{1}{2}$ ft. Ryan put the shortest and longest boards end-to-end to make one long board. How long is this new board?

   F $4\frac{11}{12}$ ft **H** $5\frac{11}{12}$ ft
   G $5\frac{19}{24}$ ft **J** $7\frac{7}{8}$ ft

7. What value for p makes this statement true?

   $^{-}5 - {}^{+}8 = p$

   A $^{-}13$ **C** $^{+}3$
   B $^{-}3$ **D** $^{+}13$

8. Three-eighths of Jim's class researched the life of an animal for a science project. The cell structure of plants was researched by $\frac{9}{20}$ of Jim's class.

   Explain Describe two ways of determining which topic was studied by more students.

Safe Site

Internet Test Prep
Visit **www.eduplace.com/kids/mhm** for more *Test Prep Practice.*

LESSON 11

Mental Math: Find 10% of a Number

You will learn how to use mental math to find 10% and multiples of 10% of a number.

Learn About It

Lauren spends 24 hours per month practicing swimming. If she spends 10% of the time practicing the backstroke, for how many hours does she swim the backstroke each month?

Compute. **10% of 24 = *n***

Different Ways to Find 10% of a Number

You can multiply by $\frac{1}{10}$.

Finding 10% of a number is the same as finding $\frac{1}{10}$ of that number.

$$10\% \times 24 = \frac{1}{10} \times 24$$

$$\frac{1}{10} \times \frac{24}{1} = \frac{24}{10}$$

$$= 2\frac{4}{10}$$

$$= 2.4$$

You can move the decimal point to divide by 10.

An easy way to find 10% of any number is to divide the number by 10 by moving the decimal point one place to the left.

$$24 \div 10 = 2.4$$

Solution: Lauren spends 2.4 hours each month practicing the backstroke.

Other Examples

A. Find 10% of a Decimal

Find 10% of 3.29.

$$10\% \text{ of } 3.29 = 0.1 \times 3.29$$

$$= 0.329$$

B. Find 20% of a Number

Find 20% of 42. **Think:** 20% = 2 × 10%

$$10\% \times 42 = 0.1 \times 42$$

$$= 4.2$$

$$4.2 \times 2 = 8.4$$

$$20\% \text{ of } 42 = 8.4$$

Explain Your Thinking

- ► Name three different ways you can use to find 10% of a number.
- ► How could you use mental math to find 15% of a number?
- ► Why can you find 10% of a decimal by moving the decimal point one place to the left?

Standards NS **1.0, 1.2, 2.0, 2.1, 2.4, 2.5** AF **1.0, 1.2**

Guided Practice

Find 10% of each number. Use mental math.

1. 75 **2.** 19 **3.** 7

4. 162 **5.** 3.8 **6.** 0.4

Ask Yourself

- Did I move the decimal point one place to the left?

Independent Practice

Find 10% of each number. Use mental math.

7. 42 **8.** 25 **9.** 9 **10.** 3 **11.** 1 **12.** 216

13. 783 **14.** 4,012 **15.** 7.8 **16.** 100.5 **17.** 4.41 **18.** 0.13

Find 20% of each number.

19. 42 **20.** 9 **21.** 1 **22.** 312 **23.** 92 **24.** 3.42

Problem Solving • Reasoning

25. A diving board extends across 10% of the length of an 84-ft pool. How far does it extend?

26. **Analyze** A pool has 10 lanes. During a swim meet, 80% of the lanes are used. How many lanes are not used?

27. **Analyze** Erica's time for swimming the length of the pool was 22.5 s. Now that she has practiced for a month, she swims faster and has cut her time down by 10%. What is her new time?

28. Ten percent of the 440 people who came to a swim meet had free passes to get in. How many people had free passes? How many people had to pay to get in?

29. **Write About It** Why is it easy to find 100% of a number? Explain your thinking.

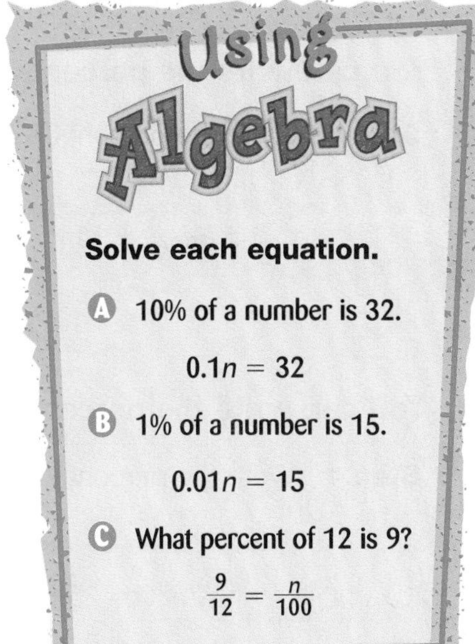

Mixed Review • Test Prep

Find the perimeter (P) of each rectangle with the given length (l) and width (w). *(pages 194–196)*

30. $l = 6$, $w = 1$ **31.** $l = 5$, $w = 0.4$ **32.** $l = 1.6$, $w = 0.8$ **33.** $l = 100$, $w = 300$ **34.** $l = 0.75$, $w = 3.5$

35 Given the base, b, and the height, h, of a triangle, what is the area? *(pages 490–491)*

A $A = bh$ **B** $A = 2 \times (b + h)$ **C** $A = \frac{bh}{2}$ **D** $A = \frac{b + h}{2}$

Extra Practice See Set G on page 560.

Percent of a Number

You will learn different ways to find a percent of a number.

Learn About It

Twenty kites are on display in a store window. If 25 percent of the kites are red, how many kites are red?

Compute. **25% of 20 = *n***

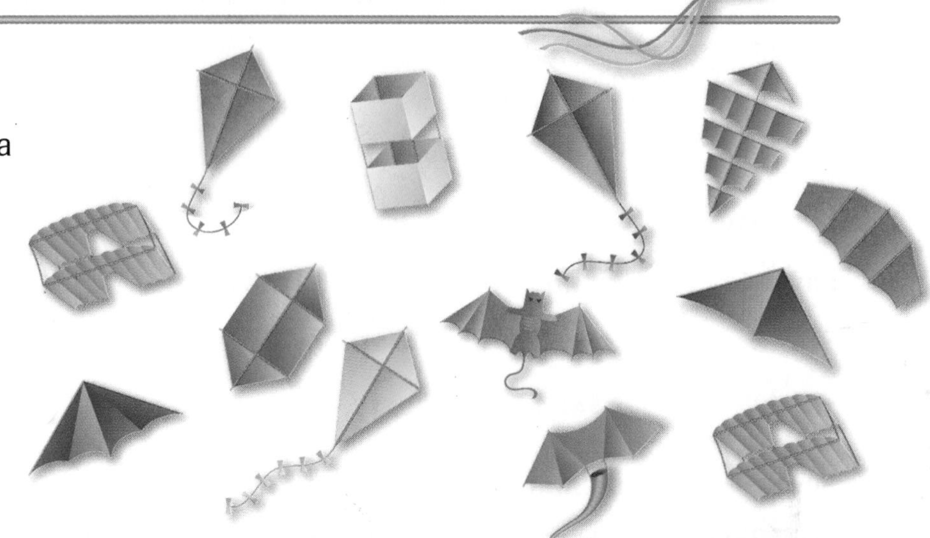

Different Ways to Find a Percent of a Number

You can write the percent as a fraction.

Step 1 Write the percent as a ratio.

$$25\% = \frac{25}{100}$$
$$= \frac{1}{4}$$

Step 2 Multiply.

$$\frac{1}{4} \times \frac{20}{1} = \frac{20}{4}$$
$$= 5$$

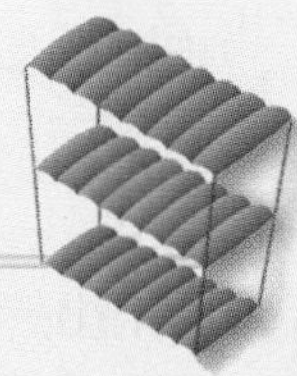

You can write the percent as a decimal.

Step 1 Write the percent in decimal form.

25% = 25 hundredths
= 0.25

Step 2 Multiply.

```
   20
× 0.25   ← 2 decimal places in the factors
  100
  400
 5.00    ← 2 decimal places in the product
```

You can use equivalent ratios.

Step 1 Write the percent as a ratio with the smallest possible first term.

$$25\% = \frac{25}{100}$$
$$= \frac{1}{4}$$

Step 2 Write an equivalent ratio with the original number as the second term.

$$\frac{1}{4} \overset{\times 5}{=} \frac{5}{20}$$ ← red kites / ← all kites

Solution: There are 5 red kites.

Standards NS **1.2, 2.0, 2.1, 2.5** AF **1.2, 1.5** MR **1.0**

Explain Your Thinking

- ▶ What are three different ways to find a percent of a number?
- ▶ Which method would you use to find 50% of 80? Why?
- ▶ Which method would you use to find 28% of 66? Why?

Guided Practice

Solve each problem three ways.

1. 70% of 90 **2.** 32% of 50

3. 40% of 20 **4.** 75% of 20

> **Ask Yourself**
> - Should I express the percent as a fraction? as a decimal?

Independent Practice

Solve by writing the percent as a fraction.

5. 90% of 30 **6.** 35% of 300 **7.** 20% of 45 **8.** 40% of 25

9. 75% of 80 **10.** 15% of 40 **11.** 50% of 36 **12.** 30% of 1,000

Solve by writing the percent as a decimal.

13. 25% of 44 **14.** 33% of 30 **15.** 16% of 15 **16.** 90% of 50

17. 7% of 20 **18.** 60% of 12 **19.** 37% of 20 **20.** 14% of 300

Solve using equal ratios.

21. 84% of 25 **22.** 55% of 20 **23.** 32% of 25 **24.** 45% of 20

25. 17% of 200 **26.** 29% of 300 **27.** 13% of 500 **28.** 51% of 2,000

Solve. Use any method.

29. 25% of 232 **30.** 20% of 20 **31.** 1% of 100 **32.** 65% of 40

33. 7% of 30 **34.** 19% of 200 **35.** 75% of 4 **36.** 49% of 300

Algebra • Functions **Use the rule to complete each function table.**

37. $y = x\%$ of 200

x	y
5	■
10	■
15	■
20	■

38. $y = 25\%$ of x

x	y
10	■
20	■
30	■
40	■

39. $y = 50\%$ of x

x	y
■	50
■	100
■	150
■	200

Problem Solving • Reasoning

Use Data Use the table to solve Problems 40–42.

Kite	Price	Discount
Parafoil	\$50.00	10%
Dragon	\$25.00	20%
Box	\$21.75	30%

40. How much tax will be charged for a parafoil kite if the sales tax is 8% of the price?

41. A discount is the amount of money deducted from the price of an item. Find the price of a box kite after a discount of 30%. Round to the nearest cent.

42. **Analyze** Elena has saved \$15. Does she have enough money to buy a dragon kite after the discount? Explain how you know.

43. **Estimate** About 8,000 children's tickets were sold at the Flying Kite Festival. If 20,000 tickets were sold in total, about what percent were children's tickets?

44. **Write Your Own** A newspaper reported that the attendance at this year's kite festival was 20% less than the year before. This year's attendance was 12,000. Use this information to write your own problem.

Mixed Review • Test Prep

Evaluate each expression for $x = 0.5$, $y = 2$, and $z = 10$. *(pages 70–72, 162–164)*

45. $x + y + z$ **46.** $z - (y + x)$ **47.** $(x)(y)$ **48.** $\frac{(x)(z)}{y}$ **49.** $(y)(\frac{z}{x})$

Choose the letter of the correct answer. *(pages 300–301, 308–310)*

50 What is the prime factorization of 45?

A $(4 \times 10) + (5 \times 1)$ **C** 5×9

B $(4^1)(5^1)$ **D** $3^2 \times 5$

51 What is the LCM of 12 and 21?

F 3 **H** 84

G 42 **J** 252

Properties

Allison thinks the numbers can be interchanged in a percent problem, and the answer will stay the same. For example, she says that since 50% of 30 is 15, 30% of 50 must also be 15. Is Allison correct? Explain.

Extra Practice See Set H on page 560.

Unit Fractions and Percents

When you need to estimate or calculate a percent of a number, it often helps to think of unit fractions and their related percents—especially if you want to find the answer mentally. Here are some relationships you should know.

Fraction	$\frac{1}{20}$	$\frac{1}{10}$	$\frac{1}{8}$	$\frac{1}{6}$	$\frac{1}{5}$	$\frac{1}{4}$	$\frac{1}{3}$	$\frac{1}{2}$
Percent	5%	10%	12.5%	$16\frac{2}{3}\%$	20%	25%	$33\frac{1}{3}\%$	50%

Use a unit fraction to estimate 35% of 48.

Find 35% of 48.

If you only need an estimate, you can find a unit fraction that converts to a percent close to 35%.

Estimate

$33\frac{1}{3}\% = \frac{1}{3}$, so 35% of 48 is about $\frac{1}{3}$ of 48.

$48 \div 3 = 16$

So, 35% of 48 must be a bit more than 16.

If you need an exact calculation, you can find unit fractions whose corresponding percents have a sum or difference of 35%.

Exact Calculation

$25\% + 10\% = 35\%$

25% of $48 = \frac{1}{4}$ of 48 $= 48 \div 4 = 12$

10% of $48 = \frac{1}{10}$ of 48 $= 4.8$

So, 35% of $48 = 12 + 4.8 = 16.8$.

Think: Add 25% of 48 and 10% of 48 to get 35% of 48.

$12 + 4.8 = 16.8$

35% of 48 is exactly 16.8.

Explain Your Thinking

- Why are unit fractions and their related percents helpful if you want to find a percent of a number using mental math?
- How could you use unit fractions to find 20% of 60? to find 45% of 90?

LESSON 13

Compare Data Sets

You will learn how to use mental math to compare data sets using fractions and percents.

Learn About It

Ted and Janine collect buttons. Twelve of the 16 buttons in Ted's collection are circular. Janine has collected 25 buttons and 20 are circular. Who has the greater percent of circular buttons?

Step 1 Write each set as a fraction in simplest form.

Ted: 12 of 16 buttons

$\frac{12}{16} = \frac{3}{4}$

Janine: 20 of 25 buttons

$\frac{20}{25} = \frac{4}{5}$

Step 2 Express each fraction as a percent.

$\frac{3}{4} \times \frac{25}{25} = \frac{75}{100} = 75\%$

75% of Ted's buttons are circular.

$\frac{4}{5} \times \frac{20}{20} = \frac{80}{100} = 80\%$

80% of Janine's buttons are circular.

Solution: Janine has the greater percent of circular buttons.

Other Examples

A. Compare Ratios

Which is greater: 15 out of 25 or 12 out of 16?

$\frac{15}{25} = \frac{3}{5}$ $\frac{12}{16} = \frac{3}{4}$

$\frac{1}{4} > \frac{1}{5}$, so $\frac{3}{4} > \frac{3}{5}$.

B. Compare to One Whole

Which is greater: 8 out of 9 or 6 out of 7?

$\frac{8}{9}$ is $\frac{1}{9}$ less than 1 whole.

$\frac{6}{7}$ is $\frac{1}{7}$ less than 1 whole.

Sevenths are larger than ninths, so $\frac{6}{7}$ is farther from 1 whole. $\frac{6}{7}$ is less than $\frac{8}{9}$.

Explain Your Thinking

- Which ratio/percent relationships have you memorized?
- Is it always necessary to use a common denominator to compare fractions? Explain.

Standards NS **1.0, 1.2** SDP **1.0, 1.3** MR **1.0, 1.1**

Guided Practice

Write each set as a fraction in simplest form and as a percent. Then order the percents from least to greatest.

1. 60 out of 75 **2.** 35 out of 50

3. 24 out of 32 **4.** 28 out of 56

5. 45 out of 75 **6.** 9 out of 24

Ask Yourself

- Did I check to make sure the fraction is in simplest form?
- Did I check each answer to make sure it is reasonable?

Independent Practice

Use the illustration to complete Problems 7–14.

7. What percent of the red buttons are small?

8. What fraction of all the buttons are green?

9. What percent of all the buttons are small?

10. What fraction of all the buttons are blue?

11. What percent of all the buttons are yellow?

12. What percent of the green, blue, and yellow buttons are yellow?

13. What percent of the small buttons are green?

14. What percent of the small buttons are red?

Compare. Use >, <, or = for each ⬬.

15. 10 out of 25 ⬬ 7 out of 28

16. 3 out of 30 ⬬ 1 out of 6

17. 30 out of 36 ⬬ 25 out of 40

18. 48 out of 60 ⬬ 12 out of 15

19. 11 out of 55 ⬬ 7 out of 42

20. 25 out of 30 ⬬ 4 out of 16

21. 5 out of 8 ⬬ 16 out of 24

22. 9 out of 12 ⬬ 12 out of 18

Compare these fractions. Write >, <, or =.

23. $\frac{3}{8}$ ⬬ $\frac{3}{10}$ **24.** $\frac{5}{12}$ ⬬ $\frac{5}{11}$ **25.** $\frac{2}{5}$ ⬬ $\frac{2}{7}$

26. $\frac{7}{8}$ ⬬ $\frac{9}{10}$ **27.** $\frac{11}{12}$ ⬬ $\frac{10}{11}$ **28.** $\frac{5}{6}$ ⬬ $\frac{6}{7}$

29. $\frac{4}{25}$ ⬬ $\frac{15}{100}$ **30.** $\frac{19}{50}$ ⬬ $\frac{38}{100}$ **31.** $\frac{7}{20}$ ⬬ $\frac{29}{100}$

n **Algebra • Equations** **Find each value of *n*.**

32. 6 out of 12 = 9 out of *n*

33. *n* out of 30 = 4 out of 6

34. 5 out of *n* = 6 out of 24

35. 7 out of 10 = *n* out of 50

Problem Solving • Reasoning

Use Data The table describes the buttons in two collections. Use the data to complete Problems 36–41.

Type of Buttons	Sandy's Collection	Mark's Collection
Metallic	350	200
Jewel-type	150	150
Fabric	50	90
Plastic	200	160
Total	750	600

36. Which collection contains a greater percent of jewel-type buttons?

37. **Analyze** Both collections contain 150 jewel-type buttons. Why are the percents different?

38. **Analyze** Both collections contain equal percents of one type of button. Which type is it?

39. In Sandy's collection, the ratio of one type of button to another is 3:1. What are the two types?

40. **Predict** Suppose Sandy added 30 wooden buttons to her collection. How would this affect the percent of fabric buttons in the collection? Why?

41. **Write Your Own** Create a problem about the buttons in the two collections. Give your problem to a partner to solve.

Mixed Review • Test Prep

Use a compass and a straightedge to construct each figure. *(pages 470–474)*

42. line segment *AB*

43. a circle with central angle *TYQ*

44. a circle with radius *EV*

45. perpendicular lines *JK* and *SD*

46 Order $\frac{3}{20}$, 45%, 0.3, $\frac{3}{4}$ from the least to the greatest part of a unit. *(pages 538–539)*

A 0.3, $\frac{3}{20}$, $\frac{3}{4}$, 45% **B** 45%, $\frac{3}{20}$, 0.3, $\frac{3}{4}$ **C** $\frac{3}{4}$, 45%, 0.3, $\frac{3}{20}$ **D** $\frac{3}{20}$, 0.3, 45%, $\frac{3}{4}$

Add Sets of Data

Taylor has 48 buttons. She says that half of them have 4 holes, $\frac{1}{3}$ of them have gold on them, $\frac{1}{4}$ are square, and $\frac{3}{8}$ are more than an inch wide. Her friend says that's impossible because $\frac{1}{2} + \frac{1}{3} + \frac{1}{4} + \frac{3}{8}$ adds to more than 1 whole. Is Taylor's friend right? Explain.

Extra Practice See Set I on page 560.

Practice Game

Percent Concentration

Practice matching percents, fractions, and decimals by playing this game in groups of up to 4 people.

What You'll Need

- *27 blank cards or Teaching Tool 11*

Players
2

Here's What to Do

1. Players prepare for the game by writing on a card each fraction shown. Then each player chooses one card and writes the matching percent and the matching decimal on separate blank cards. Continue until this has been done for all the fractions.
2. One player shuffles the cards and then lays them out, facedown, in a 10 × 3 array. Players take turns turning over three cards. If all three cards match, the player keeps the cards. If no match can be made, the cards are turned over in place and the next player gets a chance. Play continues until all the cards have been matched.

Share Your Thinking
How can you quickly tell whether a percent matches a decimal? whether a fraction matches a decimal?

Quick Check

Check Your Understanding of Lessons 11–14

Find 10% of each number. Use mental math.

1. 60 **2.** 3,200 **3.** 43 **4.** 172 **5.** 5.1

Solve.

6. Find 20% of 175.

7. What is 4% of 175?

8. What is 60% of 25?

9. Find 80% of 25.

Compare using > or <.

10. 35 out of 70 ● 52 out of 100

11. 6 out of 18 ● 30 out of 100

12. 5 out of 8 ● 5 out of 10

13. 30 out of 40 ● 50 out of 60

Solve.

14. On a survey about movie preferences, 40% of the people surveyed said that they prefer comedies. If you were making a circle graph to show the data, what angle would you use to represent the people who prefer comedies?

How did you do?

If you had difficulty with any items in the Quick Check, you can use the following pages for review and extra practice.

California Standards	Items	Review These Pages	Do These Extra Practice Items
Number Sense: **1.0, 1.2**	1–5	pages 544–545	Set G, page 560
Number Sense: **1.2, 2.0** Algebra and Functions: **1.2**	6–9	pages 546–548	Set H, page 560
Statistics, Data Analysis and Probability: **1,3**	10–13	pages 550–552	Set I, page 560
Algebra and Functions: **1.2** Statistics, Data Analysis and Probability: **1.0, 1.2, 1.3**	14	pages 554–555	8–10, page 561

Test Prep • Cumulative Review

Maintaining the Standards

Choose the letter of the correct answer. If a correct answer is not here, choose NH.

1. What is 10% of 23,000?

   A 2,300 **C** 23
   B 230 **D** NH

2. Elisa spent $\frac{2}{3}$ of an hour preparing a wall for painting. She spent $\frac{1}{4}$ of the time putting tape around a window. How much time did she spend putting tape around the window?

   A 2 hours **C** 20 minutes
   B $1\frac{1}{4}$ hours **D** 10 minutes

3. A survey asked 50 people what they eat for breakfast. This circle graph shows the results of that survey. How many of the people surveyed eat eggs and toast for breakfast?

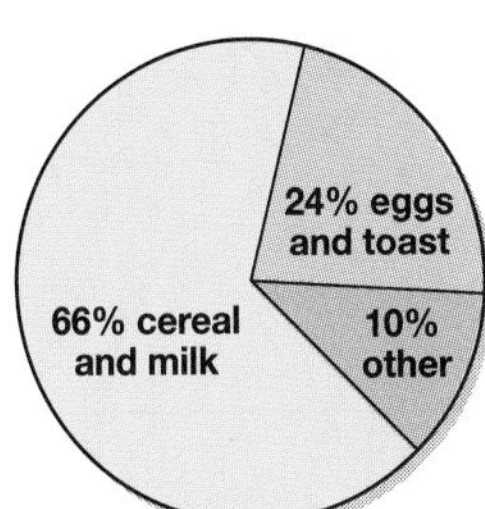

   A 5 **C** 24
   B 12 **D** 33

4. If 40% of a number is 18, what is the number?

   F 40 **H** 72
   G 45 **J** 180

5. What is the value of 3^5?

   A 15 **C** 243
   B 125 **D** 33,333

6. What is the measure of angle P?

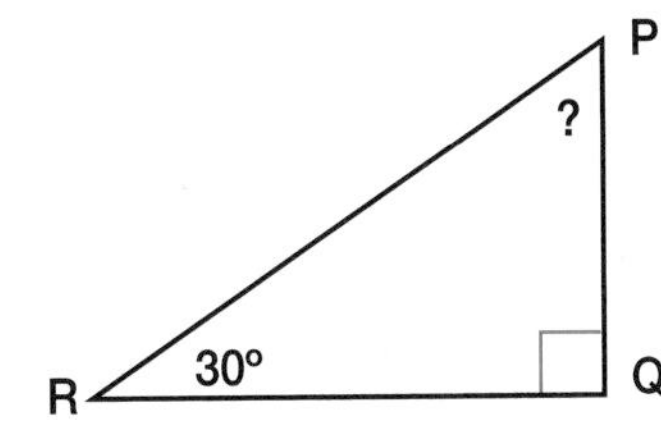

   F 30° **H** 90°
   G 60° **J** 240°

7. Which letter represents the number that is 3 greater than $^{-}6$?

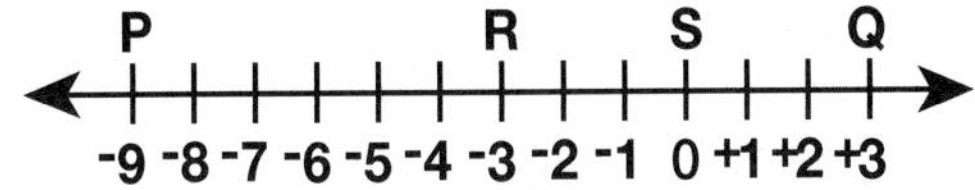

   A P **C** Q
   B S **D** R

8. Look at the triangle.

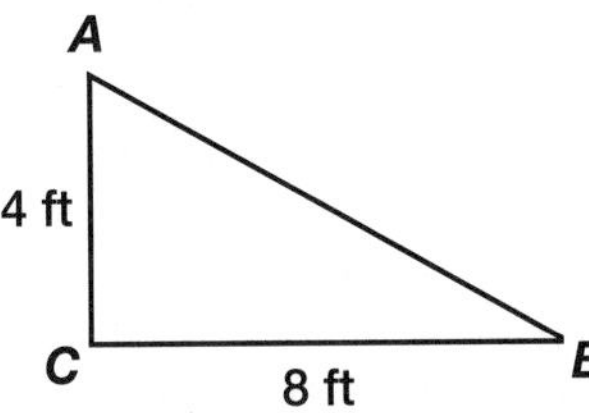

   Explain How can you show that the area of the triangle is equal to half the area of a rectangle with the same base and height? Use a diagram to explain. What is the area of the triangle?

Extra Practice

Set A (Lesson 1, pages 518–519)

Write each ratio three different ways.

1. 5 cards to 2 letters
2. 1 camera to 3 films
3. 20 pens to 5 pencils
4. 10 spoons to 5 forks
5. 14 rolls to 12 buns
6. 15 books to 3 shelves
7. 3 crayons to 7 pens
8. 12 nails to 3 boards
9. 8 lemons to 1 bowl
10. 1 foot to 12 inches
11. 9 buckets to 4 shovels
12. 15 holes to 5 pages
13. 50 sheets of paper to 1 note pad
14. 8 pens to 16 markers
15. 4 cups to 3 saucers

Set B (Lesson 2, pages 520–521)

Write two equivalent ratios for each.

1. $\frac{3}{9}$
2. $\frac{7}{14}$
3. $\frac{4}{12}$
4. $\frac{2}{10}$
5. $\frac{1}{25}$
6. 6 to 18
7. 5 to 20
8. 9 to 15
9. 12 to 14
10. 8 to 17
11. 1:4
12. 3:10
13. 1:5
14. 2:3
15. 4:8

Set C (Lesson 3, pages 522–523)

Find the rate per unit of time.

1. 60 miles in 15 seconds
2. 56 miles in 8 seconds
3. $64 in 4 hours
4. 270 km in 3 hours
5. $108 in 3 hours
6. 420 km in 7 hours

Find the distance traveled in the given amount of time.

7. 4 hours at 40 mi/h
8. 5 days at 35 mi/day
9. 15 seconds at 14 ft/s
10. 26 seconds at 19 ft/s
11. 0.5 hour at 50 mi/h
12. 8 days at 75 mi/day

Find the length of time for each trip.

13. 300 miles at 60 mi/h
14. 54 km at 18 km/h
15. 1,600 ft at 40 ft/s
16. 125 km at 25 km/h
17. 9,600 ft at 30 ft/s
18. 450 miles at 50 mi/h

Extra Practice

Set D *(Lesson 7, pages 532–534)*

Write each ratio as a percent and each percent as a ratio.

1. $\frac{3}{5}$	**2.** 20%	**3.** $\frac{7}{10}$	**4.** 30%	**5.** $\frac{4}{50}$
6. 42%	**7.** $\frac{1}{4}$	**8.** $\frac{16}{20}$	**9.** 75%	**10.** $\frac{50}{100}$
11. 37%	**12.** 61%	**13.** $\frac{1}{2}$	**14.** 8%	**15.** $\frac{2}{5}$

Set E *(Lesson 8, pages 536–537)*

Write each percent in decimal form and each decimal in percent form.

1. 72%	**2.** 55%	**3.** 0.31	**4.** 29%	**5.** 39%
6. 40%	**7.** 6%	**8.** 0.82	**9.** 0.75	**10.** 88%
11. 41%	**12.** 0.06	**13.** 1%	**14.** 0.73	**15.** 20.4

Set F *(Lesson 9, pages 538–539)*

Order each set from the greatest to the least parts of a unit.

1. $\frac{2}{5}$ 0.1 50%	**2.** $\frac{8}{10}$ 0.6 40%	**3.** $\frac{6}{10}$ 0.4 30%
4. $\frac{3}{20}$ 0.2 10%	**5.** $\frac{2}{10}$ 0.5 15%	**6.** $\frac{1}{5}$ 0.4 8%
7. $\frac{9}{10}$ 0.8 75%	**8.** $\frac{3}{5}$ 0.9 65%	**9.** $\frac{1}{2}$ 0.7 90%
10. $\frac{3}{4}$ 0.3 80%	**11.** $\frac{3}{10}$ 0.2 35%	**12.** $\frac{11}{20}$ 0.1 25%
13. $\frac{4}{5}$ 0.4 70%	**14.** $\frac{1}{4}$ 0.55 87%	**15.** $\frac{8}{50}$ 0.4 48%

Chapter Review

Reviewing Vocabulary

Write *always, sometimes,* or *never* for each statement. Give an example to support your answer.

1. To reduce a ratio, divide each term of the ratio by the same number.
2. To find 10% of any number, move the decimal point one place to the right.
3. Use the same units of measure when writing a scale ratio.
4. Thirty percent of a number is the same as $\frac{1}{3}$.

Match each word with a definition.

5. scale	a way of comparing two quantities
6. percent	a ratio that compares quantities in different units
7. ratio	a ratio that compares measurements in a drawing or model to the measurements of the actual objects
8. rate	a ratio of a number to 100

Reviewing Concepts and Skills

Write two equivalent ratios for each. *(pages 518–521)*

9. $\frac{1}{3}$ **10.** $\frac{4}{28}$ **11.** $\frac{6}{12}$ **12.** $\frac{2}{20}$

13. $\frac{2}{24}$ **14.** $\frac{9}{27}$ **15.** $\frac{10}{14}$ **16.** $\frac{8}{16}$

17. $\frac{1}{8}$ **18.** $\frac{9}{45}$ **19.** $\frac{3}{18}$ **20.** $\frac{12}{36}$

Complete each set of equivalent ratios. *(pages 520–521)*

21. $\frac{1}{3} = \frac{■}{12}$ **22.** $\frac{4}{6} = \frac{■}{3}$ **23.** $\frac{3}{8} = \frac{■}{32}$ **24.** $\frac{6}{14} = \frac{■}{7}$

25. $\frac{2}{5} = \frac{■}{20}$ **26.** $\frac{7}{35} = \frac{■}{5}$ **27.** $\frac{9}{27} = \frac{■}{54}$ **28.** $\frac{25}{125} = \frac{■}{5}$

Write each in percent form. *(pages 532–534, 536–537, 538–539)*

29. $\frac{53}{100}$ **30.** $\frac{3}{5}$ **31.** 0.35 **32.** 4 parts out of 100

33. $\frac{3}{20}$ **34.** 0.45 **35.** $\frac{49}{50}$ **36.** 0.79

Solve. *(pages 544–547)*

37. 10% of 350 **38.** 25% of 200 **39.** 10% of 17.5 **40.** 20% of 80

41. 5% of 76 **42.** 2% of 12 **43.** 90% of 300 **44.** 15% of 40

A map is drawn with a scale of 1 cm: 30 km. Find *n* in each. *(pages 524–525)*

45. 0.5 cm represents *n* km

46. *n* cm represents 90 km

Solve. Tell the method and strategy you used. *(pages 526–527, 540–541, 554–555)*

47. Andrew is buying school supplies. A package of 5 pens costs $1.75. A pair of other pens cost 69¢. Which is the better price for 10 pens?

48. Rachel put together a model airplane whose scale is 1 in.: 48 ft. If the actual length of the airplane is 624 ft, how long is the model?

49. Use the data in the table to make a circle graph. Calculate each central angle.

Favorite Ethnic Foods

Food	Number of People
Thai	30
Italian	50
Chinese	40

Brain Teasers Math Reasoning

What Decimal Am I?

I am greater than 0.75.

I am less than 1.0.

The fraction $\frac{39}{50}$ is equivalent to me.

Magic Square

Write the digits 1, 2, 3, 4, 6, 7, 8, and 9 in the squares so that the sum is the same in every column and every row.

	5	

Internet Brain Teasers
Visit **www.eduplace.com/kids/mhm** for more *Brain Teasers.*

Chapter Test

Write two equivalent ratios for each, using multiplication and division.

1. $\frac{1}{2}$ **2.** $\frac{3}{7}$ **3.** $\frac{5}{25}$ **4.** $\frac{8}{24}$

5. $\frac{4}{16}$ **6.** $\frac{2}{4}$ **7.** $\frac{6}{18}$ **8.** $\frac{14}{28}$

9. $\frac{9}{90}$ **10.** $\frac{10}{110}$ **11.** $\frac{12}{96}$ **12.** $\frac{7}{21}$

13. $\frac{1}{3}$ **14.** $\frac{33}{99}$ **15.** $\frac{22}{44}$ **16.** $\frac{10}{44}$

17. $\frac{33}{55}$ **18.** $\frac{8}{17}$ **19.** $\frac{2}{3}$ **20.** $\frac{1}{5}$

Complete each set of equivalent ratios.

21. $\frac{1}{4} = \frac{\blacksquare}{16}$ **22.** $\frac{2}{3} = \frac{\blacksquare}{9}$ **23.** $\frac{5}{10} = \frac{\blacksquare}{40}$

24. $\frac{4}{8} = \frac{\blacksquare}{4}$ **25.** $\frac{4}{5} = \frac{\blacksquare}{25}$ **26.** $\frac{7}{14} = \frac{\blacksquare}{2}$

27. $\frac{1}{6} = \frac{\blacksquare}{30}$ **28.** $\frac{2}{16} = \frac{\blacksquare}{80}$ **29.** $\frac{8}{80} = \frac{\blacksquare}{10}$

30. $\frac{3}{9} = \frac{\blacksquare}{18}$ **31.** $\frac{24}{48} = \frac{\blacksquare}{12}$ **32.** $\frac{8}{12} = \frac{\blacksquare}{3}$

Write each in percent form.

33. $\frac{21}{25}$ **34.** $\frac{3}{50}$ **35.** 0.75

36. $\frac{4}{20}$ **37.** 2 parts out of 100 **38.** 0.69

39. 0.4 **40.** 14 parts out of 100 **41.** $\frac{80}{100}$

Solve.

42. 10% of 95 **43.** 20% of 40 **44.** 75% of 200

45. 5% of 50 **46.** 2% of 800 **47.** 15% of 60

Solve. Tell what method and strategy you used.

48. A three-chapter book has 45 pages. What is the ratio of chapters to pages? If two more chapters are added and the ratio is equivalent to that for the first three chapters, how many pages will be in the book?

49. Math was selected by 20 of 60 students as their favorite subject. To make a circle graph of these students' favorite subjects, what central angle would be needed for math?

50. A room was drawn using the scale 1 cm:20 cm. If the actual length of the room is 6 m, what is the length of the room in the drawing?

Write About It

Solve each problem. Use correct math vocabulary to explain your thinking.

1. Explain.

a. How can you compare a decimal to a fraction and to a percent?

b. How can you compare a decimal to percent?

c. How can you tell whether a ratio is in simplest form?

2. Karenna completed this equivalent ratio.

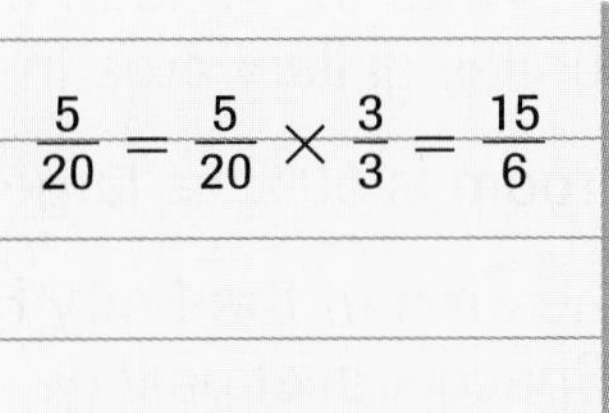

a. Explain what she did wrong.

b. Show how to find the correct ratio.

3. Explain the steps you would use to show that these ratios are equivalent.

a. $\frac{1}{3}$

b. 4:12

c. 10 to 30

Another Look

Use the map to solve each problem. Show all your work.

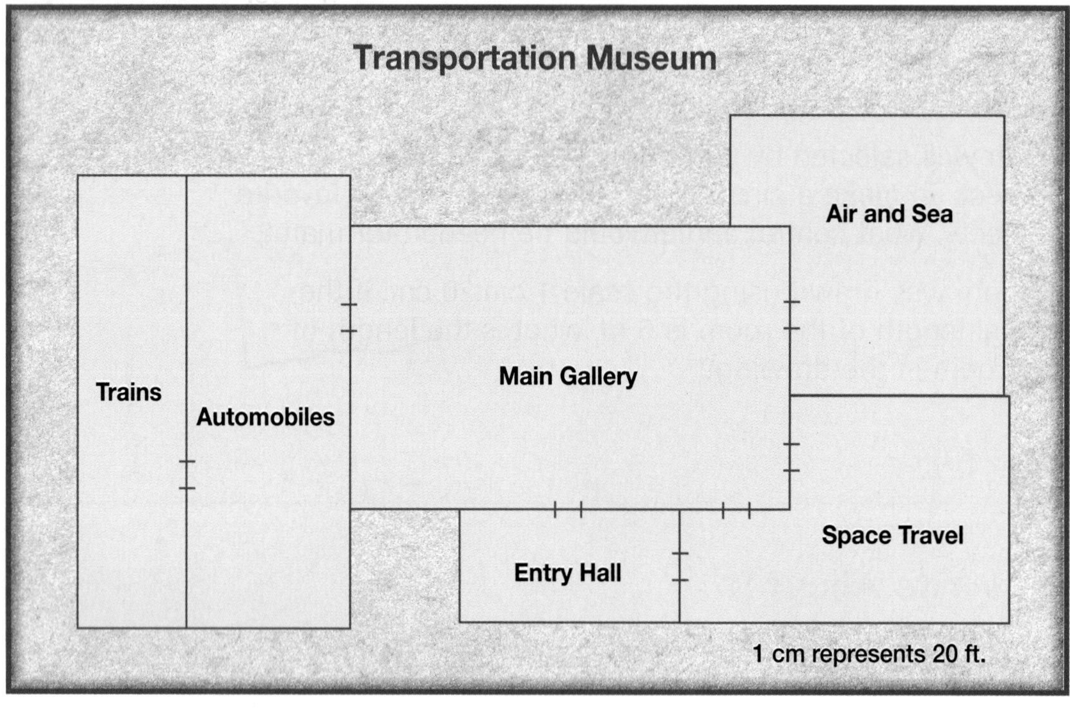

1. Trace the map. Measure the walls and mark their lengths on the diagram. Then use the scale to find the actual area of each room in the Transportation Museum.
2. **Compare** Which room has the greatest area? the least?
3. **Analyze** Write the ratio of the Trains gallery area to the Automobiles gallery area in simplest terms.
4. Which room is 50% as large as the Trains gallery?
5. Write the area of the Entry Hall as a percent of the area of the Space Travel gallery.
6. The Trains gallery is 80% as large as what room?
7. **Write About It** If you know the areas of the rooms on the diagram, can you find the actual areas by multiplying each one by 20? Explain why or why not.

Standards | MG **1.0, 1.1, 1.4, 2.0, 2.1**

Enrichment

Proportion

A playhouse was built in proportion to the Fernandes' house. The playhouse is 2 m tall and 4 m wide. If the height of the Fernandes' house is 6 m, how wide is it?

New
Vocabulary
proportion

A **proportion** shows equivalent ratios written as an equation.

Use equivalent ratios to find the proportion.

$$\frac{2}{4} = \frac{6}{■}$$

$$\frac{2 \times 3}{4 \times 3} = \frac{6}{12}$$

The Fernandes' house is 12 m wide.

Write = or ≠ to show that each pair of ratios is or is not a proportion.

1. $\frac{4}{6}$ ■ $\frac{8}{12}$

2. $\frac{3}{4}$ ■ $\frac{9}{12}$

3. $\frac{5}{20}$ ■ $\frac{4}{16}$

4. $\frac{8}{16}$ ■ $\frac{16}{32}$

5. $\frac{6}{12}$ ■ $\frac{9}{18}$

6. $\frac{3}{15}$ ■ $\frac{6}{30}$

7. $\frac{14}{20}$ ■ $\frac{7}{10}$

8. $\frac{5}{6}$ ■ $\frac{15}{18}$

9. $\frac{10}{20}$ ■ $\frac{1}{2}$

10. $\frac{32}{16}$ ■ $\frac{4}{2}$

11. $\frac{22}{24}$ ■ $\frac{10}{12}$

12. $\frac{7}{14}$ ■ $\frac{14}{28}$

13. Playhouse furniture is built in proportion to the Fernandes' furniture. What scale was used? If a bench in the house is 4.5 ft wide, how wide is the playhouse bench?

14. Connie is making a recipe for fruit punch. For every 2 cups of orange juice, she adds 3 cups of pineapple juice and 1 cup of grapefruit juice. If Connie wanted to make 12 cups of fruit punch, how much orange juice would she need? How much pineapple and grapefruit juice?

15. Explain why $\frac{4}{6}$ is proportional to $\frac{8}{12}$ but not to $\frac{16}{30}$.

Standards MR **2.0, 2.2, 3.0, 3.2, 3.3**

Integers and the Coordinate Plane

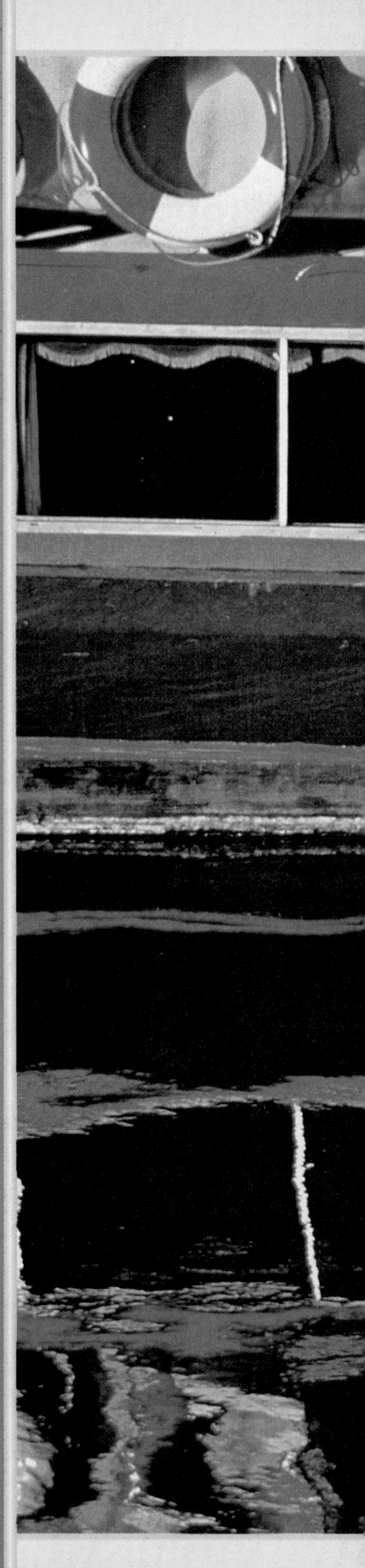

Why Learn About Integers and the Coordinate Plane?

Learning about integers and the coordinate plane can help you plot points that show a relationship between numbers.

When you plot points to make a graph of the equation $y = x - 4$, you are starting to understand that part of mathematics called algebra.

This boat and its reflection in the water are related in the same way as a geometric figure and its reflection in the coordinate plane.

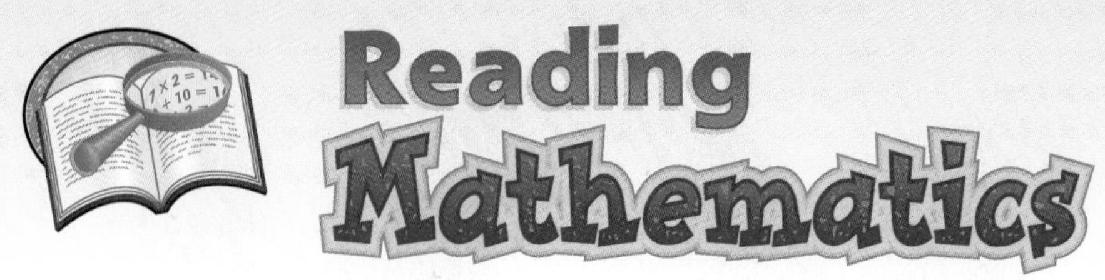

Reviewing Vocabulary

Understanding math language helps you become a successful problem solver. Here are some math vocabulary words you should know.

congruent figures that have the same size and shape

axis a horizontal or vertical line used to label a graph

integer the numbers that include zero, the counting numbers (positive whole numbers), and their opposites (negative whole numbers)

function a rule that gives exactly one value of y for every value of x

Reading Words and Symbols

When you read mathematics, sometimes you read only words, sometimes you read words and symbols, and sometimes you read only symbols.

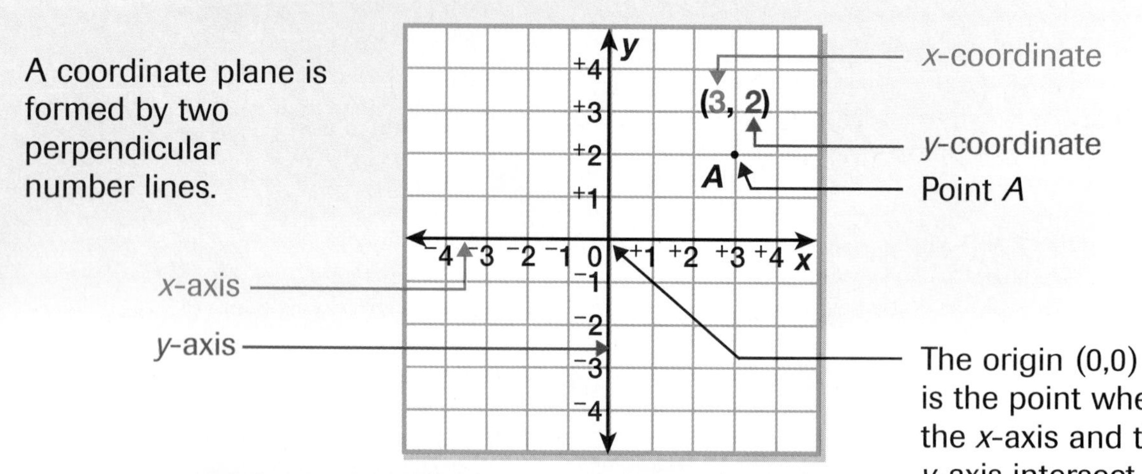

Try These

1. Write the coordinates for each point.

   a. Point *T* b. Point *O*

   c. Point *U* d. Point *R*

2. Make a coordinate grid like the one at the right. Plot each point.

   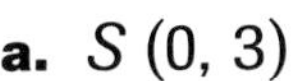

   a. *S* (0, 3) b. *H* (3, 1)

   c. *A* (2, $^{-}2$) d. *P* ($^{-}2$, $^{-}2$)

   e. *E* ($^{-}3$, 1)

3. Connect *S* to *H*, *H* to *A*, *A* to *P*, *P* to *E* and *E* to *S*. What shape did you make?

4. Use the coordinate graph above. Write *true* or *false* for each statement.

   a. The coordinates (3, 2) are an ordered pair.

   b. The first coordinate is the *y* coordinate.

   c. The point (3, 2) is to the right of the point (3, 4).

   d. The point ($^{-}1$, 1) is above the point ($^{-}1$, $^{-}1$).

Upcoming Vocabulary

Write About It **Here are some other vocabulary words** you will learn in this chapter. Watch for these words. Write their definitions in your journal.

transformation **coordinate plane** **ordered pair**

translation ***x*-axis** **origin**

reflection ***y*-axis** **coordinates**

rotation **quadrant**

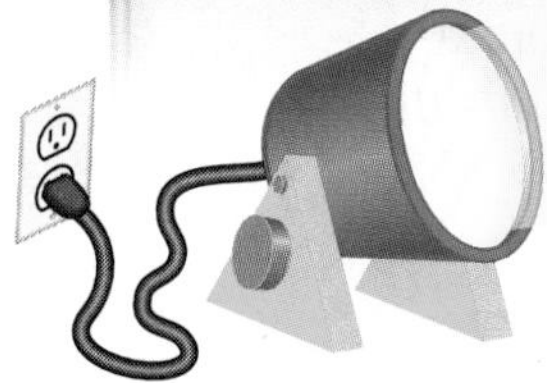

Transformations

You will learn to identify transformations such as translations, reflections, and rotations.

New Vocabulary
transformation
translation
reflection
rotation

Learn About It

The verb *to transform* means "to change." In geometry, a **transformation** changes the position of a plane figure.

Translation

A **translation** slides a figure a given distance in a given direction.

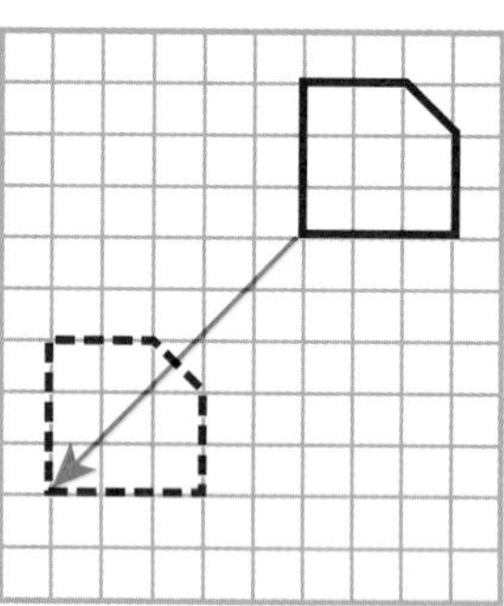

Reflection

A **reflection** flips a figure across a given line.

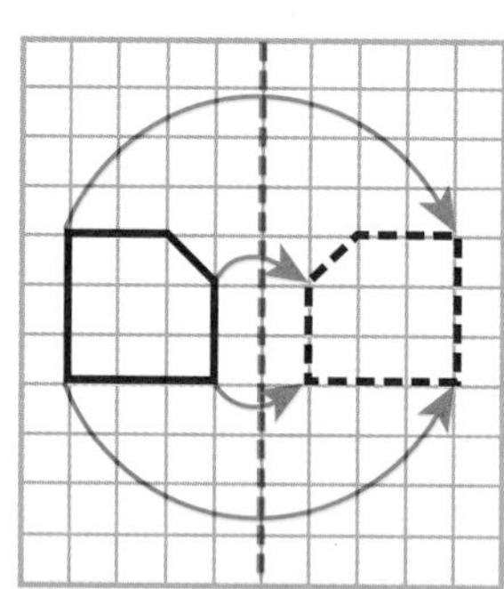

Rotation

A **rotation** turns a figure about a given point.

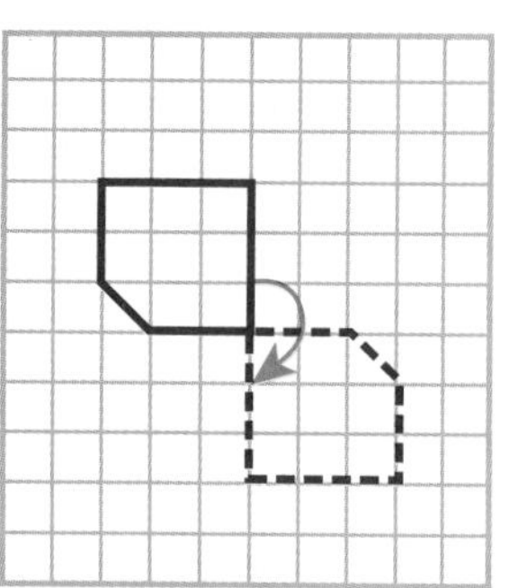

In these three transformations, the new figure is congruent to the original figure.

Explain Your Thinking

- Why does a figure remain congruent to itself after making a number of these transformations?
- Describe how a figure moves during a translation, during a reflection, and during a rotation.

Mountains reflecting on water at Tern Lake, AK

Guided Practice

Tell whether the transformation is a translation, reflection, or rotation.

1. 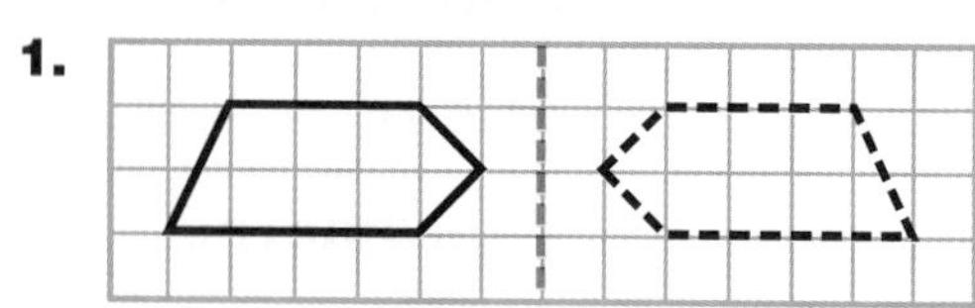

Ask Yourself

- How do I test the figure for a translation, a reflection, or a rotation?

Standards MG 2.1 MR 1.0, 2.3

Independent Practice

In each pair the figures are congruent. Tell whether the transformation shown is a translation, reflection, or rotation.

2. 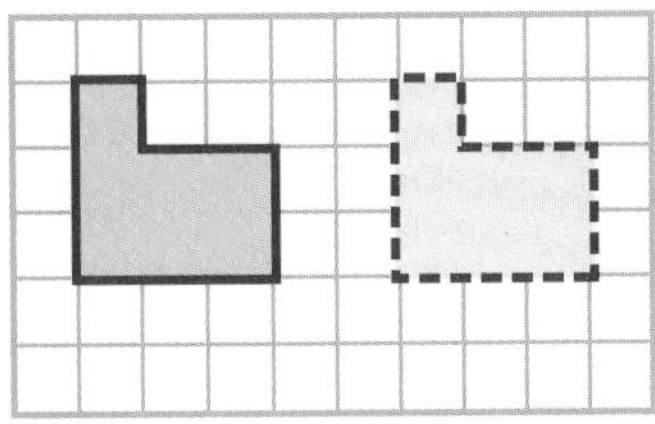

3. 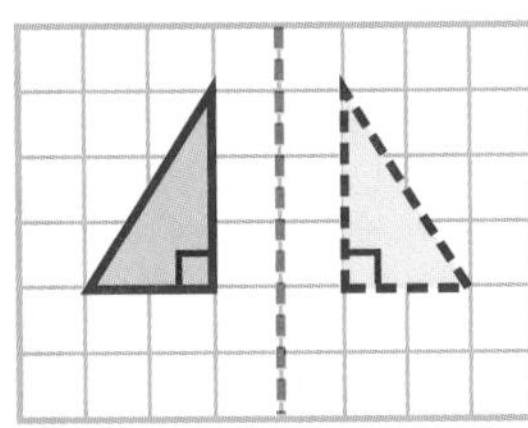

4. 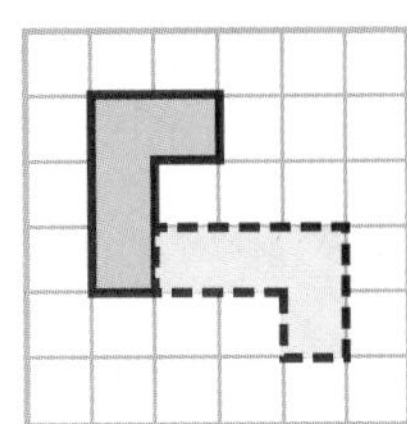

Copy each figure on grid paper. Then complete the given transformations.

5. 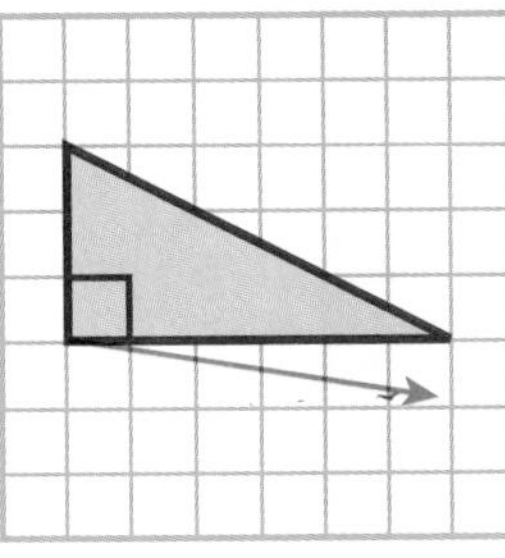

translation

6. 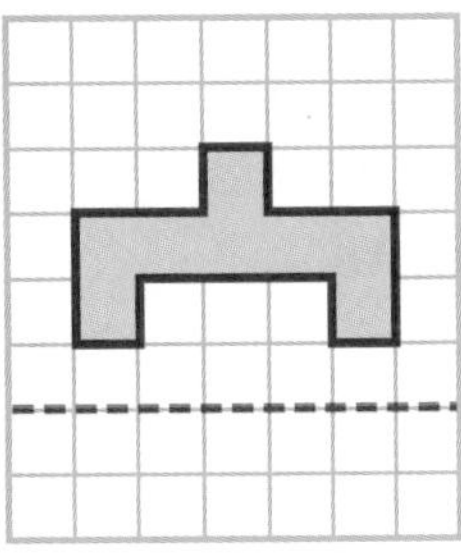

reflection

7. 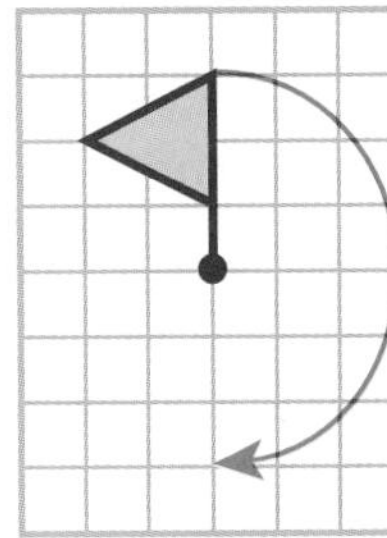

rotation

Problem Solving • Reasoning

8. Which lowercase letters of the alphabet can create a different letter with one or more transformations?

9. Which capital letters of the alphabet would remain unchanged by a reflection across a vertical line?

10. **Analyze** What happens when you reflect a figure twice across the same line?

11. **Write About It** What happens when you rotate a figure 360°? Use an example to explain your thinking.

Write *true* or *false* for each sentence. If a sentence is false, rewrite it to make it true.

A Congruent figures have the same shape and size.

B Intersecting lines form right angles.

C A diameter is a line of symmetry for a circle.

Mixed Review • Test Prep

Round each decimal to the underlined place. *(pages 28–29)*

12. $1.5\underline{4}1$ **13.** $0.\underline{8}59$ **14.** $34.\underline{6}4$ **15.** $0.\underline{0}65$

16 The mean of three fractions is $\frac{2}{5}$. One fraction is $\frac{1}{3}$. Another is $\frac{3}{10}$. What is the third fraction?
(pages 258–259, 332–333, 380–381)

A $\frac{7}{15}$ **B** $\frac{17}{30}$ **C** $\frac{7}{30}$ **D** $\frac{33}{40}$

Extra Practice See Set A on page 594.

Integers and the Coordinate Plane

You will learn how to locate and graph ordered pairs of integers on a coordinate plane.

New Vocabulary
coordinate plane
x-axis
y-axis
quadrant
ordered pair
origin
coordinates

Learn About It

Constellations are groups of stars that appear in the sky together. The constellation Cassiopeia is shown at the right. Constellations can be mapped on a grid called a **coordinate plane**.

In a coordinate plane, the horizontal axis is called the ***x*-axis**. The vertical axis is called the ***y*-axis**. These axes divide the grid into 4 **quadrants**.

Cassiopeia's five stars are mapped below.
How can you describe the location of point *A*?

You can describe any location on the grid by using an **ordered pair**. The point named by the ordered pair (0, 0) is called the **origin** of the graph.

- Point *A* can be described by the ordered pair ($^-1$, $^+3$).
- To reach point *A* from the origin, move left to $^-1$ and up to $^+3$.
- The numbers $^-1$ and $^+3$ are called the **coordinates** of the point.

point *A* is described by ($^-1$, $^+3$).

x coordinate (distance right or left of 0)

y coordinate (distance above or below 0)

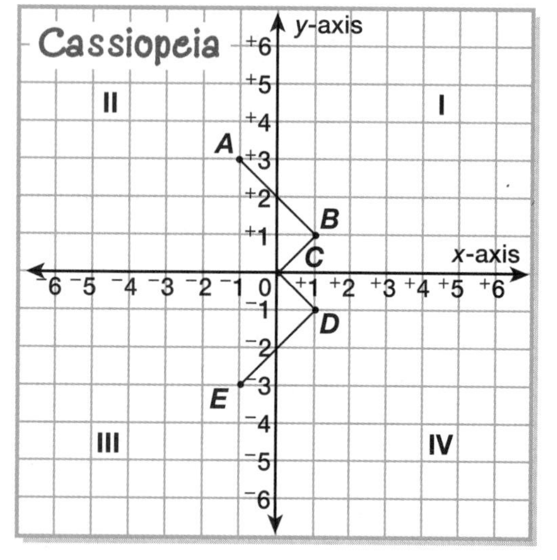

Other Examples

A. Point in Quadrant I
- Point *B* is in Quadrant 1.
- To reach point *B* from the origin (0, 0), move right 1 unit and up 1 unit.
- The coordinates of point *B* are ($^+1$, $^+1$).

B. Point in Quadrant IV
- Point *D* is in Quadrant IV.
- To reach point *D* from (0, 0), move right 1 unit and down 1 unit.
- The coordinates of point *D* are ($^+1$, $^-1$).

C. Point in Quadrant III
- Point *E* is in Quadrant III.
- To reach point *E* from (0, 0), move left 1 unit and down 3 units.
- The coordinates of point *E* are ($^-1$, $^-3$).

Standards AF **1.0, 1.1, 1.2, 1.4** SDP **1.4, 1.5**

You can also use coordinates to plot a point on a coordinate plane.

The points for the major stars in a constellation called Volans, or the Flying Fish, can be plotted using ordered pairs.

Plot the star located at point F $(^-8, ^+3)$.

- Start at (0, 0).
- Go left to $^-8$ and up to $^+3$.
- Mark a point at $(^-8, ^+3)$. Label it F.

To plot other stars in the Flying Fish, copy the grid and use these ordered pairs.

$(^+3, ^-3)$ ⟶ (right 3, down 3) ⟶ point K

$(^+6, ^+3)$ ⟶ (right 6, up 3) ⟶ point I

$(0, ^+2)$ ⟶ (no move, up 2) ⟶ point H

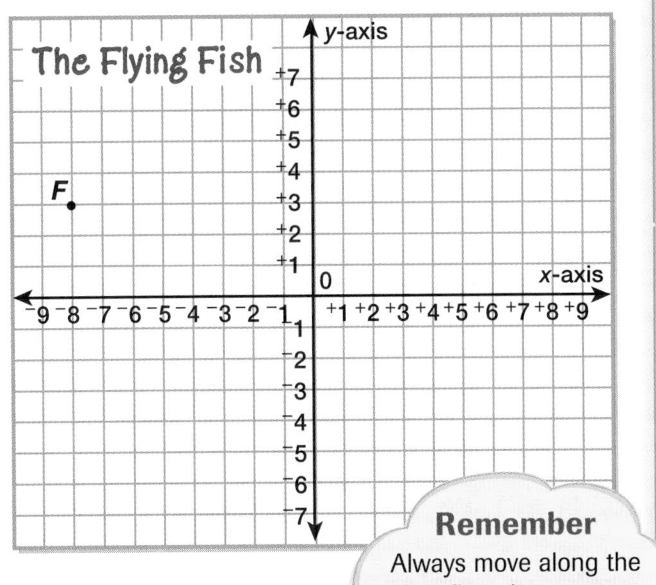

Remember
Always move along the x-axis first, then move up or down the y-axis.

Explain Your Thinking

▶ Is the location of $(^-2, ^+4)$ the same as $(^+4, ^-2)$? Why or why not?

▶ What is the x coordinate of any point on the y-axis?

Guided Practice

Use the grid showing the Big Dipper and the Little Dipper. Write the ordered pair for each point or the letter name of the ordered pair.

1. Q **2.** Z **3.** R

4. $(^+7, ^+6)$ **5.** $(^+2, ^-8)$ **6.** $(^+1, ^+4)$

Ask Yourself

- Do I move left or right from 0 to find the x coordinate?

Independent Practice

Write the ordered pair for each point.

7. B **8.** D **9.** H

10. I **11.** K **12.** L

Write the letter name of each point.

13. $(^-8, ^-1)$ **14.** $(^-3, ^-4)$

15. $(^-2, ^-7)$ **16.** $(^+3, ^-6)$

17. $(0, ^+6)$ **18.** $(^-7, ^+5)$

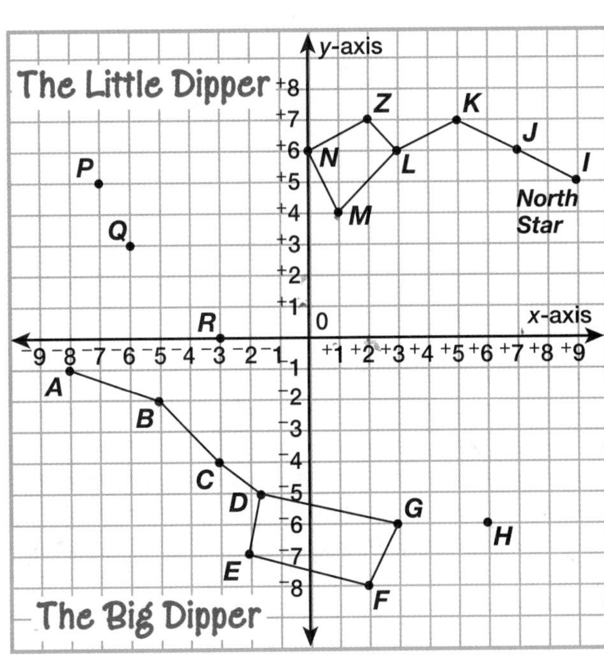

Draw a grid. Make a constellation called the Whale, or the Sea Monster.

19. Create a coordinate plane on grid paper and then plot and label each ordered pair to make the constellation.

Connect points A to J in order. Then connect K to F, F to L, L to M, and M to N. To see the part of the constellation that looks like a whale, connect M to G.

- $A\,(^{-}12, ^{+}5)$
- $B\,(^{-}11, ^{+}8)$
- $C\,(^{-}9, ^{+}8)$
- $D\,(^{-}9, ^{+}4)$
- $E\,(^{-}8, ^{+}2)$
- $F\,(^{-}4, 0)$
- $G\,(^{+}4, ^{-}4)$
- $H\,(^{+}6, ^{-}5)$
- $I\,(^{+}7, ^{-}9)$
- $J\,(^{+}10, ^{-}6)$
- $K\,(^{-}12, ^{-}6)$
- $L\,(0, ^{-}4)$
- $M\,(^{+}2, ^{-}6)$
- $N\,(^{-}3, ^{-}8)$

Algebra • Expressions Use $x = 2$ and $y = 3$ to find the coordinates of each point.

20. $(x + 1, y - 2)$

21. $(x - 5, y + 6)$

22. $(x - 8, y - 3)$

Problem Solving • Reasoning

23. Plot the points $(^{-}2, ^{+}5)$, $(^{+}4, ^{-}2)$, and $(^{-}2, ^{-}2)$. Connect them. What type of triangle did you make?

24. **Predict** What will happen if you add 1 to each y coordinate of the Whale?

25. **Patterns** What pattern can you find in this group of ordered pairs: $(0, 0)$, $(^{+}1, ^{+}2)$, $(^{+}2, ^{+}4)$, $(^{+}3, ^{+}6)$, $(^{+}4, ^{+}8)$, $(^{+}5, ^{+}10)$?

26. **Write Your Own** Draw your own constellation on grid paper. List the ordered pairs. Write instructions for drawing your constellation.

Mixed Review • Test Prep

Solve. *(pages 332–335, 346–347, 368–369, 384–385)*

27. $\frac{1}{2} + \frac{3}{4}$

28. $2\frac{1}{4} - 1\frac{3}{4}$

29. $\frac{3}{8} \times \frac{2}{3}$

30. $\frac{2}{3} \div \frac{1}{2}$

31 **Solve.** $2\frac{1}{2} \div \frac{5}{8} = n$ *(pages 386–387)*

A 4 **B** $3\frac{1}{5}$ **C** $1\frac{9}{16}$ **D** $\frac{1}{4}$

Sorting

Four constellations are called Taurus, Cygnus, Pegasus, and Draco. Each of these looks like a different creature–a swan, a winged horse, a dragon and a bull. Cygnus does not look like a bull or a dragon. Pegasus looks like a winged horse. Draco does not look like a swan. Taurus does not look like a dragon. Which animal does each constellation look like?

Extra Practice See Set B on page 594.

Practice Game

Where's the Spaceship?

Practice locating coordinates by playing this game with a partner. Try to be the first person to find four spacecraft.

What You'll Need

- *graph paper*
- *colored pencils*

Players
2

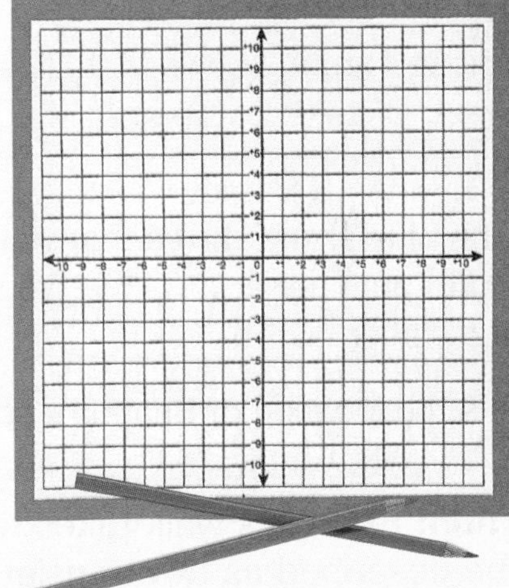

Here's What to Do

1. Each player draws a coordinate plane on a piece of grid paper and labels the x-axis from $^{-}10$ to $^{+}10$ and the y-axis from $^{-}10$ to $^{+}10$.
2. Each player marks the locations of 4 spacecraft on the grid. Each spacecraft is identified by a different pair of coordinates.
   - Satellite
   - Space shuttle
   - Spaceship
   - Space station
3. The object of the game is to find each other's spacecraft. Players take turns naming coordinates to try to locate the other player's spacecraft.
4. After each attempt, the player must be told whether a spacecraft was located or be given a hint telling whether the location of a spacecraft is left of, right of, above, or below the point.

The player who finds all of the other player's spacecraft first wins the game.

Share Your Thinking What strategies help you find the spacecraft?

Transformations in the Coordinate Plane

You will learn to use coordinates to describe transformations.

Learn About It

Brianna mapped her neighborhood on a grid with her home at point (0, 0). If she leaves her home, walks west 3 blocks and north 5 blocks, where will she be? What translations would take her to this location?

Find Brianna's location after she goes 3 blocks west and 5 blocks north.

- The red arrow shows that after walking 3 blocks west, Brianna is at point $(^-3, 0)$. You can describe this translation as $^-3$.
- The blue arrow shows that walking 5 blocks north puts her at $(^-3, ^+5)$. You can describe this translation as $^+5$.

This is the location of Brianna's school.

Solution: Brianna's walk takes her to school, and can be described as two translations: $^-3$ followed by $^+5$.

Other Examples

A. Reflection

Name the coordinates of points A and B after a reflection across the y-axis.

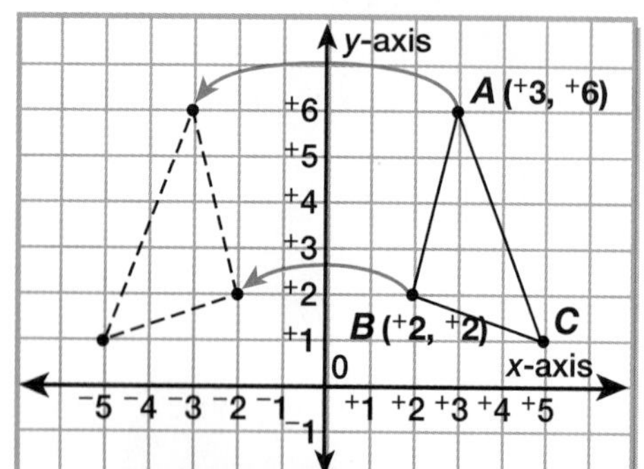

Reflect each vertex across the y-axis. The new points will be the same distances to the left of the axis as A and B are to the right of it.

The new points will be $(^-3, ^+6)$ and $(^-2, ^+2)$.

B. Rotation

Name the coordinates of point A after a half turn about the origin.

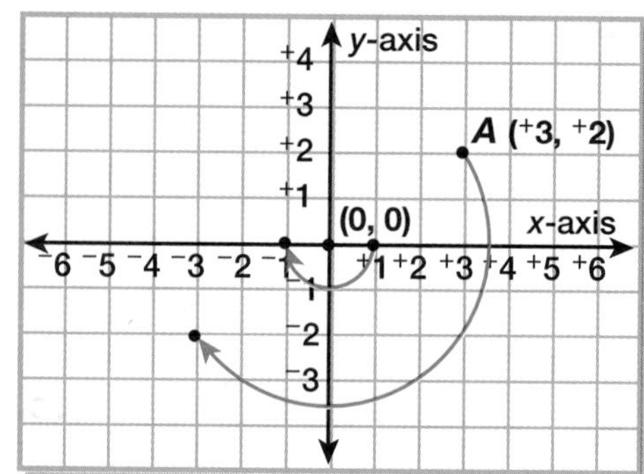

One complete turn is 360°. Trace the axes, mark point A, and turn the tracing 180°.

After the rotation the new point will be $(^-3, ^-2)$.

Standards AF 1.1, 1.4 SDP 1.4, 1.5

Explain Your Thinking

▶ What is another combination of two translations that will take Brianna from her home to school?

▶ When you describe a rotation, why do you have to name the point around which the figure is turning?

Guided Practice

Describe each combination of translations on Brianna's map.

1. from home to Jane's house
2. from home to the pharmacy
3. from the park to the grocery store
4. from the city hall to the restaurant

Ask Yourself

- Did I move each point in the correct direction?

Independent Practice

Use the diagram to name the coordinates of triangle *RST* after the transformations.

5. Translate right 4, then down 1.
6. Reflect over the *y*-axis.
7. Rotate a half turn about (0, 0).

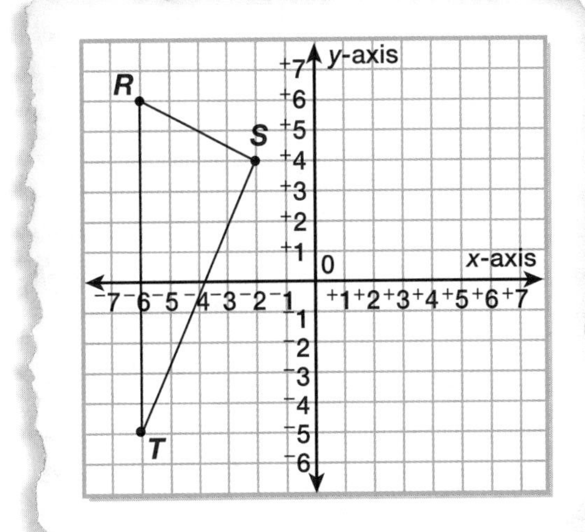

Find the result of the translations.

8. Translate point ($^-4$, $^-3$) right 3, then up 6.

Problem Solving • Reasoning

9. Describe a translation that moves point *A* to point *B*.
10. Describe a reflection that moves point *A* to point *B*.
11. Describe a rotation that moves point *A* to point *B*.

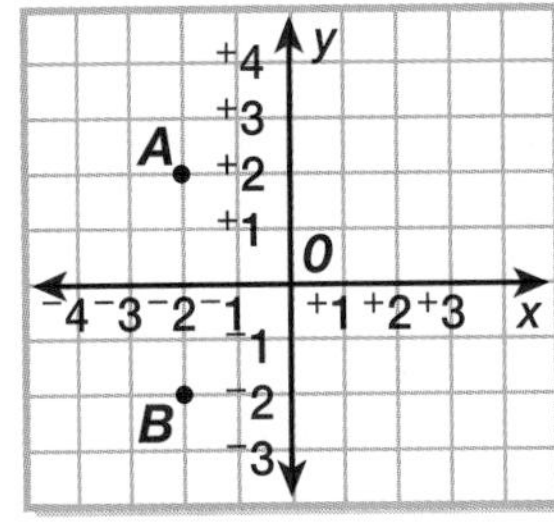

Mixed Review • Test Prep

Divide. *(pages 384–385, 386–387)*

12. $\frac{1}{2} \div \frac{1}{3}$ **13.** $\frac{3}{4} \div \frac{5}{8}$ **14.** $1\frac{1}{3} \div \frac{2}{9}$ **15.** $\frac{7}{10} \div 1\frac{3}{4}$ **16.** $2\frac{1}{4} \div 1\frac{1}{2}$

17 What is the median of the data? *(pages 258–259)*

2, 7, 6, 4, 7, 3, 8, 5, 6, 7, 9, 2

A 9 **B** 6 **C** 5.5 **D** 5

Problem-Solving Strategy: Draw a Diagram

You will learn how a diagram can help you think about and solve a problem.

Sometimes you can solve a problem by drawing a diagram.

Daniel made a geometry puzzle for his little sister Rose. Rose can finish the puzzle by putting one more piece in place. This piece is shaped like a parallelogram. The hole is congruent to the shape. How many different ways will the piece fit into the hole?

Understand

What is the question?

How many different ways will the piece shaped like a parallelogram fit into the hole of the same shape?

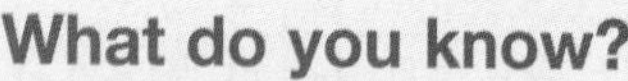

What do you know?

A parallelogram has two pairs of parallel sides.

Plan

How can you find the answer?

You can draw a diagram by tracing the parallelogram and trying different ways to fit it over the hole.

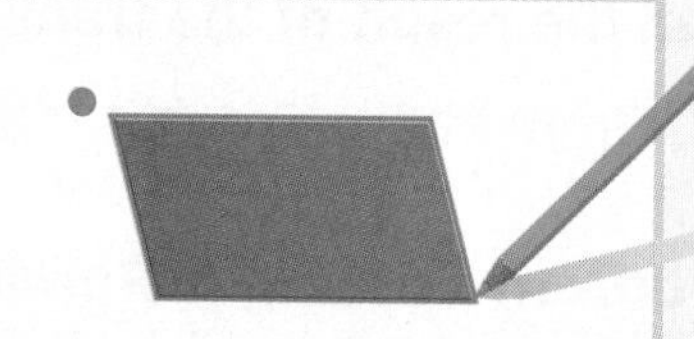

Solve

The tracing fits two ways because you can rotate it by a half turn.

There are two ways to fit the puzzle piece shaped like a parallelogram into the hole with the same shape.

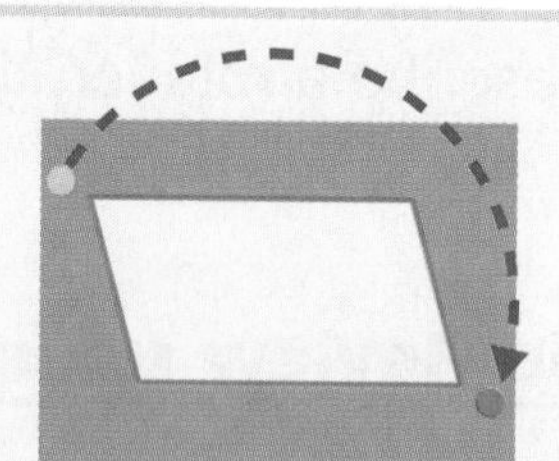

Look Back

Look back at the problem.

Is there another transformation of the parallelogram that would result in a different way to fit it in the hole?

Standards MR 1.0, 2.0, 2.2, 2.3, 3.0, 3.2

Remember:
- Understand
- Plan
- Solve
- Look Back

Guided Practice

Draw a diagram to solve each problem.

1. How many different ways will a piece in the shape of an equilateral triangle fit into a congruent hole?

   Think: How is this similar to the parallelogram problem? How is it different?

2. How many different ways will a square-shaped piece fit into a congruent hole?

   Think: Did I try flipping the square and turning it to check all possibilities?

Choose a Strategy

Solve. Use these or other strategies.

Problem-Solving Strategies

- Draw a Diagram
- Guess and Check
- Work Backward
- Find a Pattern

3. How many lines of symmetry are there on this game board?

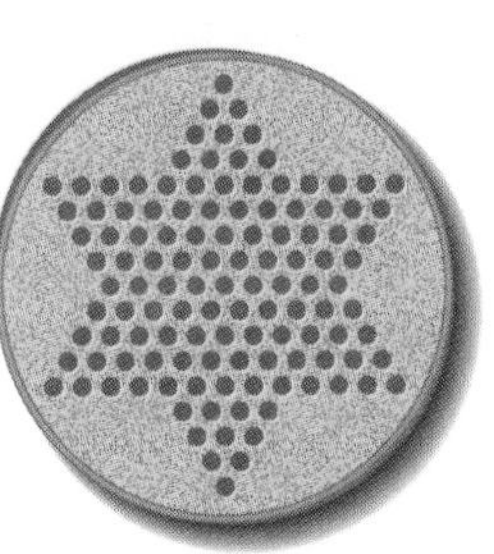

4. Describe a sequence of two transformations that will make triangle *ABC* cover triangle *DEF* exactly.

5. In the dart game 301, players start at 301 and subtract their scores. Players throw 3 darts on each turn. On her first turn, Anna scored 40, 17, and 39. What was her score after one turn?

6. Megan, Josh, and Brad roll two number cubes in a game. Megan will win with a sum from 1 to 4, Josh with a sum from 5 to 8, and Brad with a sum from 9 to 12. Who is most likely to win?

7. In chess, a knight can move one square left or right and then two squares up or down. It can also move two squares left or right and then one square up or down. A knight is on square 37 of this chess board. To what squares can this knight move?

Extra Practice See 1-2 on page 597.

Quick Check

Check Your Understanding of Lessons 1–4

Copy the figure on grid paper. Show an example of each transformation.

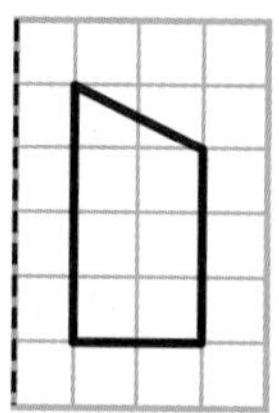

1. a translation
2. a rotation
3. a reflection

Draw a coordinate grid. Plot each point.

4. $G\ (^{+}4, {}^{+}1)$ 5. $R\ (^{-}3, {}^{+}1)$ 6. $I\ (^{-}3, {}^{-}1)$ 7. $D\ (^{+}4, {}^{-}1)$

Find the result of the transformations.

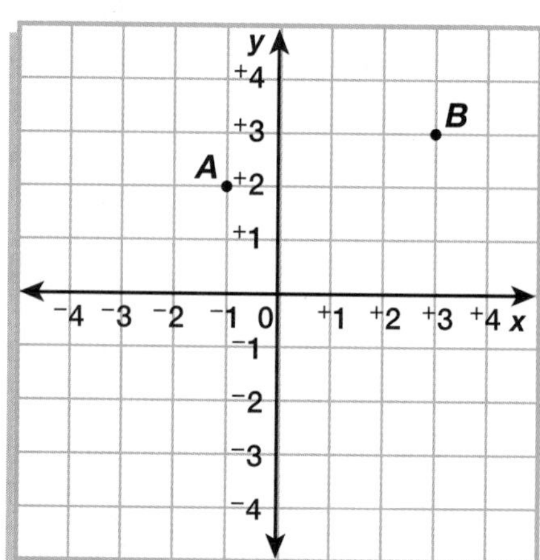

8. Translate *A* right 3, then down 3.
9. Reflect *B* over the *y*-axis.

Solve.

10. How many different ways will a block in the shape of a regular hexagon fit into a congruent hole?

How did you do?

If you had difficulty with any items in the Quick Check, you can use the following pages for review and extra practice.

California Standards	Items	Review These Pages	Do These Extra Practice Items
Measurement and Geometry: **2.0, 2.1**	1–3	pages 572–573	Set A, page 594
Algebra and Functions: **1.1, 1.4** Statistics, Data, Probability: **1.5**	4–7	pages 574–576	Set B, page 594
Algebra and Functions: **1.4** Statistics, Data, Probability: **1.4, 1.5**	8–9	pages 578–579	Set C, page 595
Math Reasoning: **1.1, 2.3, 3.2**	10	pages 580–581	1–2, page 597

Test Prep • Cumulative Review

Maintaining the Standards

Choose the letter of the correct answer.

1. In the first 24 days of April, $\frac{5}{24}$ of the days were sunny, $\frac{1}{6}$ were snowy, $\frac{3}{8}$ were cloudy, and $\frac{1}{4}$ were rainy. Which letter on the graph represents the cloudy days?

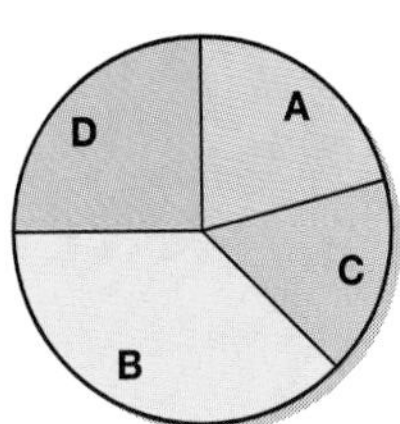

A section A **C** section C
B section B **D** section D

2. Name the point located at ($^+2$, $^-3$).

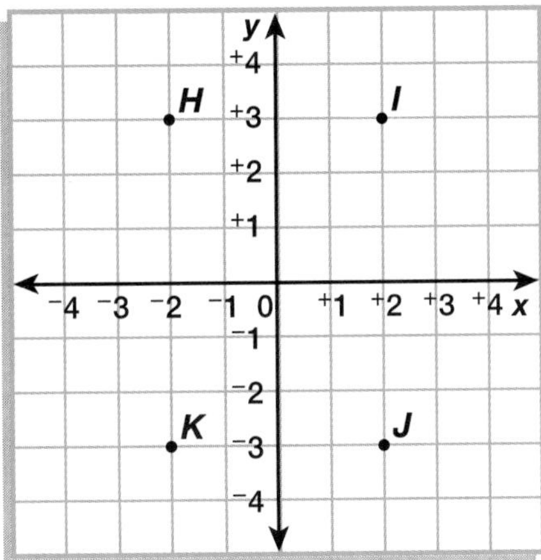

F *H* **H** *J*
G *I* **J** *K*

3. Name the ordered pair that is 3 units right and 1 unit up from the origin on a coordinate grid.

A (1, 3) **C** ($^-1$, $^-3$)
B (3, 1) **D** ($^-3$, $^-1$)

4. Find the missing angle measure.

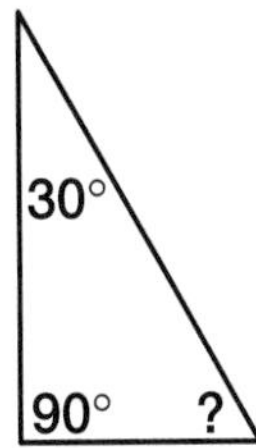

F 50° **H** 90°
G 60° **J** 150°

5. Classify this triangle.

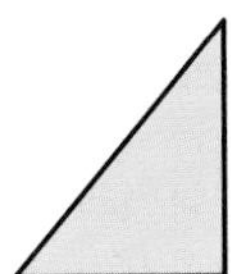

A acute **C** obtuse
B right **D** equilateral

6. Each serving of potato chips has 10.5 grams of fat. If a bag contains 3.5 servings, how many grams of fat are in one bag of potato chips?

A 367.5 g **C** 36.75 g
B 351.75 g **D** 14 g

7. Use the figure to show that the area of the parallelogram is the same as the area of a rectangle with the same base and height.

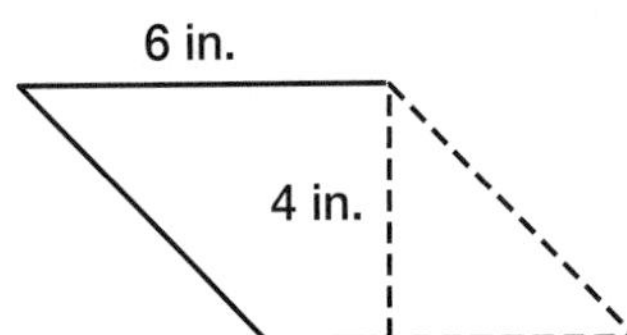

Explain What steps did you use?

Internet Test Prep
Visit **www.eduplace.com/kids/mhm** for more *Test Prep Practice*.

Integers and Functions

You will learn how to use a function to find ordered pairs and how to use ordered pairs to find a function.

Review
Vocabulary
function

Learn About It

Kalina's class made a giant integer number line for a game. Four players stand on the numbers from $^{-}2$ to $^{+}1$. These are the values of *x*. When the teacher spins a spinner to select a rule, each player follows the rule to move to a value of *y*. The teacher spins the **function** $y = x + 2$. Where will each player move?

Let *y* represent the final position. Find the value of *y* for each value of *x* from $^{-}2$ to $^{+}1$.

Find the values of *y*.

Step 1 Make a function table with an *x* column and a *y* column for the function $y = x + 2$.

$y = x + 2$

x	*y*

Step 2 Write the integers from $^{-}2$ to $^{+}1$ in the *x*-column. Then use the function to find a value of *y* for each value of *x*.

$y = x + 2$

x	*y*
$^{-}2$	0
$^{-}1$	$^{+}1$
0	$^{+}2$
$^{+}1$	$^{+}3$

Solution: The players will move to 0, $^{+}1$, $^{+}2$, and $^{+}3$.

Another Example

Find the Function

Find an addition rule that will produce these ordered pairs: ($^{+}3$, $^{+}2$), ($^{+}1$, 0), (0, $^{-}1$), ($^{-}1$, $^{-}2$).

Make a function table. In each row, you can subtract 1 from the value of *x* to get the value of *y*.

x	*y*
$^{+}3$	$^{+}2$
$^{+}1$	0
0	$^{-}1$
$^{-}1$	$^{-}2$

The function is $y = x - 1$.

Explain Your Thinking

► Why is it helpful to organize the *x*- and *y*-values in a function table?

► For the function $y = x - 1$, what will be the value of *y* if you have a value of 2 for *x*?

Standards AF **1.0, 1.1, 1.2, 1.5** SDP **1.5** MR **2.3**

Guided Practice

Complete the function table or find the function.

1. Function: $y = 3 - x$

x	y
$^-2$	$^+5$
$^-1$	■
0	■
$^+1$	■

2. Function: $y = x +$ ■

x	y
$^-2$	$^+2$
$^-1$	$^+3$
0	$^+4$
$^+1$	$^+5$

Ask Yourself

- Which value comes first in the ordered pair?
- Can I see a pattern that will help me find the rule?

Independent Practice

Complete each function table or find the function.

3. Function: $y = x + 5$

x	y
$^-2$	■
$^-1$	■
0	■
$^+1$	■

4. Function: $y = x - 3$

x	y
$^+3$	■
$^+4$	■
$^+5$	■
$^+6$	■

5. Function: $y = 1 - x$

x	y
$^-3$	■
$^-2$	■
$^-1$	■
0	■

Problem Solving • Reasoning

Solve. Choose a method.

Computation Methods

- **Mental Math**
- **Estimation**
- **Paper and Pencil**

6. If a player starts at 15, where will she be after the following moves?
$^+2$, $^-6$, $^+3$, $^-1$

7. **Logical Thinking** If Bob and Sid have 28 points and Bob has 4 more than Sid, what are their scores?

8. **Analyze** Who will win the game, Jodi with 20 points who loses 7 points and gains 3 or Sara with 11 points who gains 6 and loses 2?

9. **Predict** Ruth has 223 points and scores 31, 40, and 22 points on her last three turns. If she needed 310 points to tie the game, did she win?

Mixed Review • Test Prep

Find the mean, median, mode, and range. *(pages 258–259)*

10. 8, 4, 9, 5, 4

11. 88, 88, 89, 92, 94, 89

12. 300, 400, 500

13 What is the remainder in 645 ÷ 8? *(pages 134–135)*

A 0 **B** 5 **C** 80 **D** 80 R5

Extra Practice See Set D on page 595.

Problem-Solving Skill: Choose an Equation

You will learn how to choose an equation to represent a situation.

It is important to use the correct equation to solve a problem.

A skydiver jumping into Death Valley ($^-86$ m) opens his parachute at an elevation of 1,146 m. The table shows the skydiver's elevation during each minute of the jump.

Time After Chute Opens (min)	0	1	2	3	4
Elevation (m)	1,146	838	530	222	$^-86$

Three equations were written to try to represent the situation.

A	B	C
$e = 1{,}146 - t$	$e - 308 = t$	$e = 1{,}146 - (308 \times t)$

e represents elevation in meters. t represents time in minutes.

Which of these equations best represents the situation?

Test the equations to find the best one.

To do this, you can substitute the ordered pairs from the table into each equation to see which equation is true. Try (1, 838).

A	B	C
$e = 1{,}146 - t$	$e - 308 = t$	$e = 1{,}146 - (308 \times t)$
$838 = 1{,}146 - 1$	$838 - 308 = 1$	$838 = 1{,}146 - (308 \times 1)$
$838 \neq 1{,}145$	$530 \neq 1$	$838 = 838$
not a true statement	not a true statement	true statement

Equation C results in a true statement for the ordered pair.

Look Back Is equation C true for the 4 ordered pairs?

Standards AF 1.0, 1.2, 1.5 MR 1.0, 1.1 2.0, 3.0, 3.2

A circle of skydivers in freefall just before opening their parachutes.

Guided Practice

Choose the equation that describes each situation.

1. As a skydiver descends, the air temperature increases at a steady rate.

Time (min)	0	1	2	3	4	5
Temperature (°F)	40	47	54	61	68	75

Which equation describes the relationship between time (t) and air temperature (d)?

a. $d = t + 7$ **b.** $d = 40 + 7t$ **c.** $d = 40 - 7t$

Think: What happens to temperature as t increases by 1 min?

2. A hiker walks up a steady slope from the shore of the Dead Sea ($^{-}408$ m).

Time (min)	0	1	2	3	4	5
Elevation (m)	⁻408	⁻402	⁻396	⁻390	⁻384	⁻378

Which equation describes the relationship between time (t) and elevation in meters (e)?

a. $t = {}^{-}408 - 6e$ **b.** $e = {}^{-}408 - 6t$ **c.** $e = {}^{-}408 + 6t$

Think: What happens to the elevation as t increases by 1 min?

Choose a Strategy

Solve. Use these or other strategies.

Problem-Solving Strategies

- Write an Equation
- Draw a Diagram
- Find a Pattern
- Make a Table

3. Skydivers can jump from elevations up to about 4,000 m without oxygen. About what fraction of the height of Mount Everest (8,848 m) is this?

4. A skydiver can fall at a rate of about 126 mi/hr before opening his parachute. At this rate, how far would a skydiver fall in 20 seconds?

5. Gary spent $2,700 for equipment. Maria paid $\frac{2}{3}$ as much as Gary. Kiana bought used equipment for about 75% of Maria's cost. How much did Kiana pay for her equipment?

6. The table shows the cost of skydives. Which equation describes the relationship between the number of jumps (j) and the cost (c)?

Jumps	Cost ($)
1	16
2	32
3	48
4	64

a. $j + 16 = c$
b. $j \times 16 = c$
c. $j - 16 = c$
d. $j \div 16 = c$

7. A parachute has an area of about 963 ft^2. An emergency chute is $\frac{2}{3}$ of the area of the larger chute. How much parachute material are in both parachutes?

Extra Practice See 3–5 on page 597.

LESSON 7 Graph an Equation

You will learn how to graph an equation on a coordinate plane.

Learn About It

Latanya spins a number and adds 5 points to it to get her score. She can find all the possible scores by using the equation $y = x + 5$, where x is the number she spins and y is the score.

Make a graph to show all the possible scores. What does the graph look like? What is the best possible score Latanya can get?

Graph the equation $y = x + 5$ on a coordinate plane.

Step 1 Make a function table to find the ordered pairs.

Use values for x from $^-4$ to $^+3$, since these are the numbers on the spinner.

Rule: $y = x + 5$

x	y
$^-4$	$^+1$
$^-3$	$^+2$
$^-2$	$^+3$
$^-1$	$^+4$
0	$^+5$
$^+1$	$^+6$
$^+2$	$^+7$
$^+3$	$^+8$

Step 2 Graph each ordered pair on a coordinate plane.

For each ordered pair, go along the x-axis to the x coordinate, then up to the y coordinate.

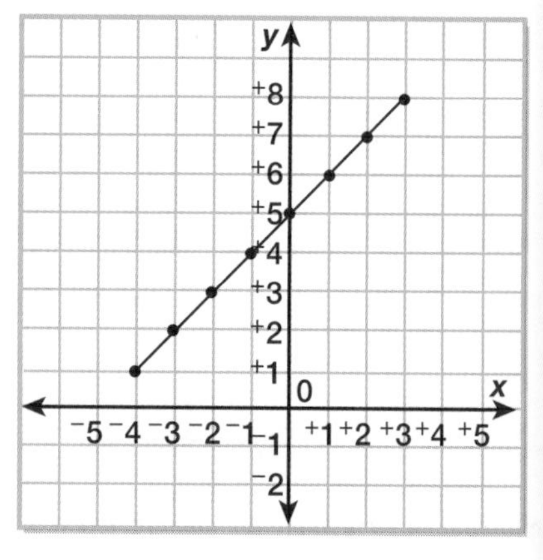

Solution: The points lie along a straight line. The greatest value of y is $^+8$, so the best possible score is 8 points.

Another Example

Graph a Two-Step Equation

Graph $y = 2x + 1$ where x is 0 or greater.

- Choose values of x that are 0 or greater.
- Find ordered pairs that make the equation true.
- Graph the ordered pairs.

x	y
0	$^+1$
$^+1$	$^+3$
$^+2$	$^+5$
$^+3$	$^+7$

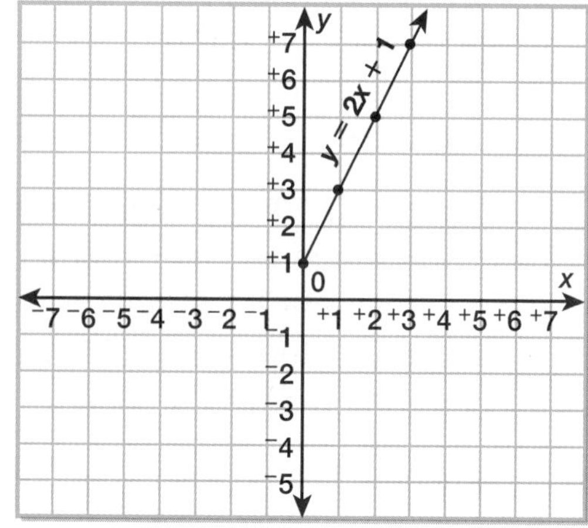

Explain Your Thinking

- ▶ For the first graph, could you add any more points to the line? Explain.
- ▶ Could you graph any more points for the second example? Explain.

Standards AF **1.0, 1.1, 1.2, 1.4, 1.5** SDP **1.4, 1.5**

Guided Practice

Find values of y to complete each table. Then graph the straight line equation.

1. $y = x - 2$

x	y
$^{-}1$	
0	
$^{+}3$	
$^{+}4$	

2. $y = x + 3$

x	y
$^{-}1$	
0	
$^{+}1$	
$^{+}2$	

3. $y = 2x - 1$

x	y
0	
$^{+}1$	
$^{+}2$	
$^{+}3$	

Ask Yourself

- Did I substitute each value of x into the equation to find y?
- Do I move right or left from (0, 0) to find the x coordinate or up or down to find the y coordinate?

Independent Practice

Find three ordered pairs for each equation. Then use them to graph the straight line equation.

4. $y = x + 1$ **5.** $y = x - 4$ **6.** $y = x + 6$ **7.** $x - 5 = y$

8. $y = 2x + 2$ **9.** $2x + 3 = y$ **10.** $y = 3x - 1$ **11.** $2x - 2 = y$

12. $1 - 3x = y$ **13.** $y = 2x - 5$ **14.** $y = 4 - 2x$ **15.** $2 - 4x = y$

Problem Solving • Reasoning

16. Graph $y = x + 2$ and $y = 2x$ on the same coordinate plane. What do you notice about the ordered pair ($^{+}2$, $^{+}4$)? What does this mean?

17. **Analyze** Graph the equations $y = 2x$ and $y = 3x$. Which line is steeper? Why do you think this happens?

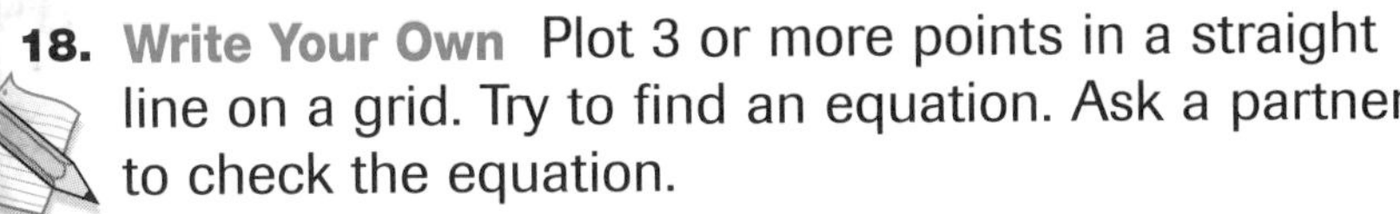

18. **Write Your Own** Plot 3 or more points in a straight line on a grid. Try to find an equation. Ask a partner to check the equation.

Math Is Everywhere!

SCIENCE Spinning a popular toy through the air lifts it higher and higher. Two record throws are shown below. Convert the records to feet using 1 m = 3.25 ft.

Ⓐ Boys under 11: 82.3 m

Ⓑ Girls under 11: 70.2 m

Mixed Review • Test Prep

Find each area. *(pages 476–477)*

19. 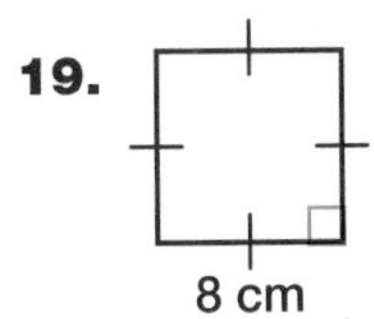

20. 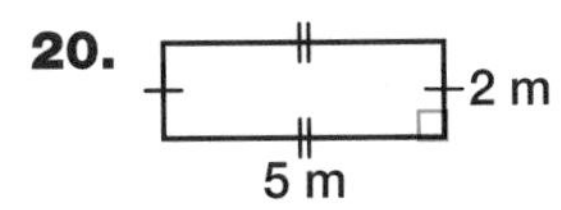

21. 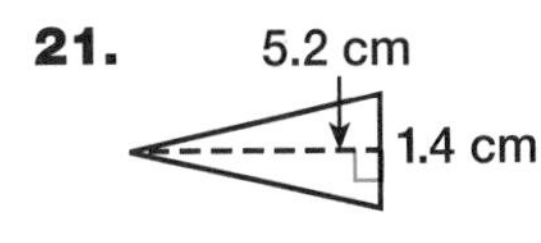

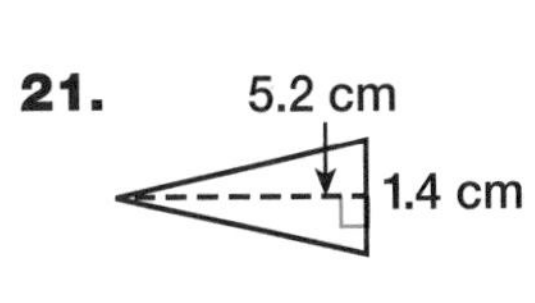

22 Which of these is an obtuse angle? *(pages 456–458)*

A 

B 

C 

D 

Extra Practice See Set E on page 596.

LESSON 8

Problem-Solving Application: Use a Graph

You will learn how to write an equation that describes information in a line graph.

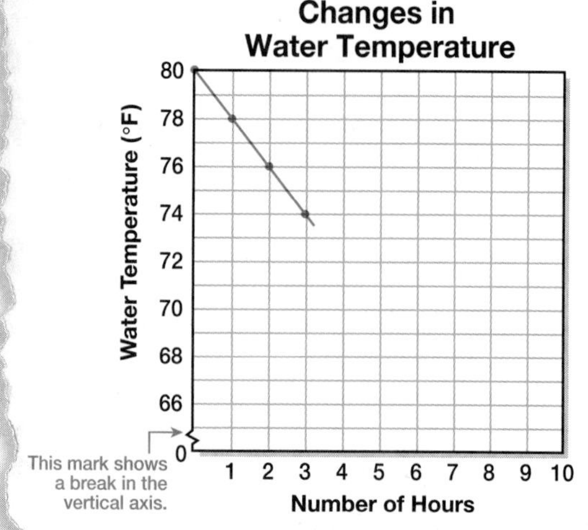

When the points of the graph of a function all lie along a straight line, you can use the equation of the function to find other points on the line.

Problem The water temperature in a swimming pool starts at 80°F and goes down 2°F every hour. If this pattern continues, what will the water temperature be after 7 hours?

Understand

What is the question?

If the pattern continues, what will the water temperature be after 7 hours?

What do you know?

The temperature starts at 80°F and decreases by 2°F each hour.

Plan

What can you do to find the answer?

Write ordered pairs in a function table. Look for a pattern and write an equation that describes the pattern. Then substitute 7 into the equation and solve to find the water temperature.

Solve

Use x to represent the number of hours and y to represent the temperature of the water.

x	y
0	80
1	78
2	76
3	74

To find the water temperature at any hour, multiply the number of hours by 2°F and subtract the product from 80°F. The equation that describes this pattern is $y = 80 - 2x$.

Substitute 7 for x to find the temperature after 7 hours.

$y = 80 - 2x$ or $y = 80 - 14 = 66$

After 7 hours, the water temperature will be 66°F.

Look Back

Look back at the question.

Is your answer reasonable?

 Standards AF **1.0, 1.1, 1.2, 1.4, 1.5** SDP **1.4, 1.5** MR **1.0, 2.0, 3.0**

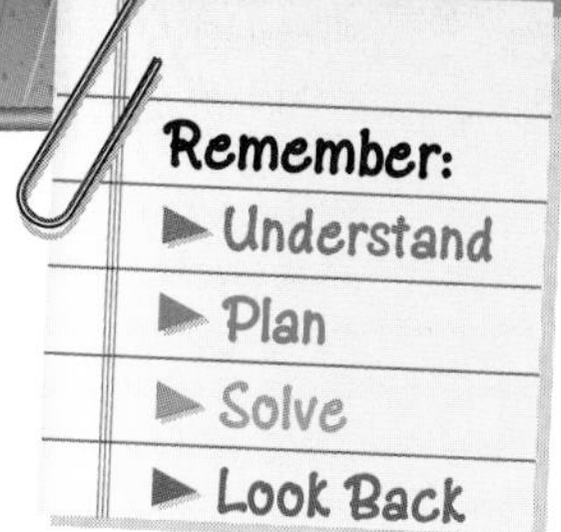

Guided Practice

Use a function table and an equation to solve each problem.

1. A heater warms the water in a pool by 3°F each hour. Write an equation to show how warm the water will be after a given number of hours if the starting temperature is 70°F.

   Think: If you start with the number of hours (x), what operation will you use to get temperature (y)?

2. The temperature of a cup of hot chocolate is 126°F. If the temperature drops by 2°F each minute, in how many minutes will its temperature be 104°F?

   Think: If you start with the number of minutes (x), how do you get the temperature (y)?

Choose a Strategy

Solve. Choose these or other strategies.

Problem-Solving Strategies

- Use a Graph
- Write an Equation
- Work Backward
- Guess and Check

3. The temperature of a bucket of water was 15°F. Its temperature rose by $\frac{1}{2}$°F every minute. What equation describes the relationship between the time (x) and the temperature (y)?

4. The highest outdoor temperature ever recorded was 136°F in Libya in 1922. The lowest ever recorded was $^{-}129$°F in Antarctica in 1983. What is the difference between these temperatures?

5. The Celsius thermometer was invented in a year containing the digits 1, 2, 4, and 7. The hundreds place has the greatest digit. The tens digit is twice the ones digit. In what year was the Celsius thermometer invented?

6. A bat has a higher body temperature than a whale but lower than a baboon. If a goat has a higher body temperature than a baboon, write the mammals in order from the highest to lowest body temperature.

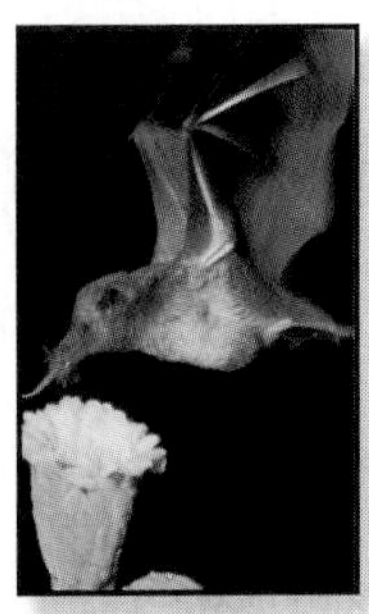

7. The equation $F = \frac{9}{5}C + 32$ relates temperatures in degrees Fahrenheit (F) to temperatures in degrees Celsius (C). Complete the function table to show the equivalent temperatures.

°C	°F
0	■
5	■
10	■
■	59

Extra Practice See 6–8 on page 597.

Quick Check

Check Your Understanding of Lessons 5–8

Complete each function table.

1. **Function: $y = x + 7$**

x	y
$^{+}1$	■
$^{-}1$	■

2. **Function: $y = (2x) - 8$**

x	y
$^{+}4$	■
0	■

Solve.

3. The table shows the cost of concert tickets. Which equation describes the relationship between the number of tickets (t) and the cost (c)?

Tickets	Total Cost ($)
1	15
2	30
3	45

a. $t + 15 = c$ **b.** $t \times 15 = c$

Find three ordered pairs for each equation. Then use them to graph the equation.

4. $y = x - 3$
5. $y = x + 6$
6. $y = 3x - 4$

7. The temperature of some hot water was 150°F. When the water was placed in a freezer, its temperature decreased by 20°F each hour. What equation describes the relationship between the time (x) and the temperature (y)?

How did you do?

If you had difficulty with any items in the Quick Check, you can use the following pages for review and extra practice.

California Standards	Items	Review These Pages	Do These Extra Practice Items
Algebra and Functions: **1.2** Statistics, Data, Probability: **1.5**	1, 2	pages 584–585	Set D, page 595
Algebra and Functions: **1.5** Statistics, Data, Probability: **1.5**	4–6	pages 588–589	Set E, page 596
Math Reasoning: **2.3**	3, 7	pages 586–587, 590–591	3–8, page 597

Test Prep • Cumulative Review

Maintaining the Standards

Choose the letter of the correct answer. If a correct answer is not here, choose NH.

1. Which ordered pair makes the equation $y = x + (^-3)$ true?

   A $(0, ^+3)$ **C** $(^+1, ^-2)$
   B $(^-3, 0)$ **D** $(^-2, ^+1)$

2. Which ordered pair makes the equation $y = 2x + 4$ true?

   F $(^+2, ^+4)$ **H** $(^-2, 0)$
   G $(^-2, ^+4)$ **J** $(^-1, ^-2)$

3. What is the rule for this function table?

x	y
1	-1
2	0
3	1
4	2
5	3

   A $y = x - 1$ **C** $y = {^-x}$
   B $y = x - 2$ **D** $y = 2x$

4. What is the area of this triangle?

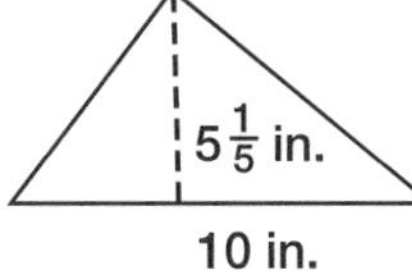

   F 55 in.^{2} **H** 26 in.^{2}
   G 52 in.^{2} **J** $15\frac{1}{5}$ in.^{2}

5. A package of 50 trash bags costs \$6.50. What is the cost of one trash bag?

   A \$0.13 **C** \$7.69
   B \$1.30 **D** \$13.00

6. A pill contains 0.705 milligrams of an active ingredient. How much active ingredient would be in 3 pills?

   F NH
   G 3.525 mg
   H 3.705 mg
   J 21.15 mg

7. The area of this rectangle is 2.0 km^2. What is the unknown side length?

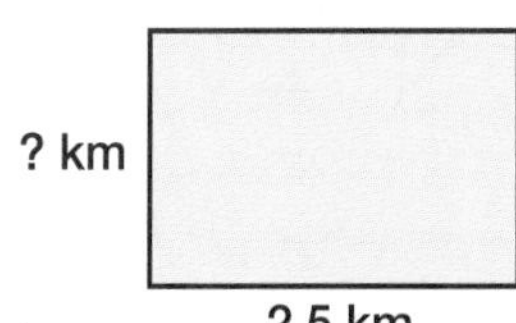

   A 0.08 km **C** 0.8 km
   B 0.5 km **D** 8 km

8. Draw a net you could use to make this solid. Label the side lengths. What is the surface area of the net?

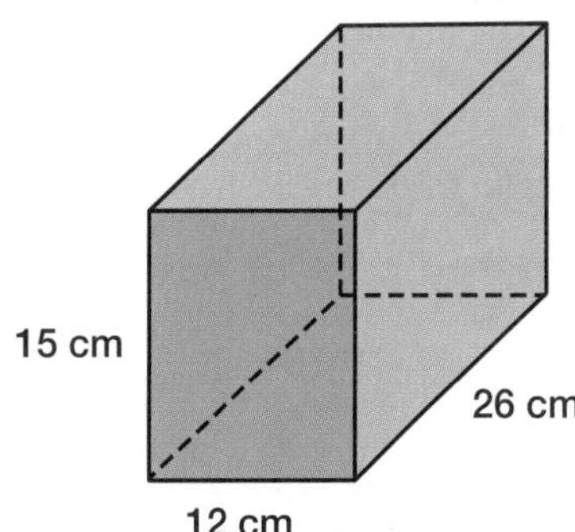

   Explain How did you find the surface area?

Safe Site

Internet Test Prep
Visit **www.eduplace.com/kids/mhm** for more *Test Prep Practice.*

Extra Practice

Set A (Lesson 1, pages 572–573)

The figures in each pair are congruent. Tell if the transformation is a translation, reflection, or rotation.

1. 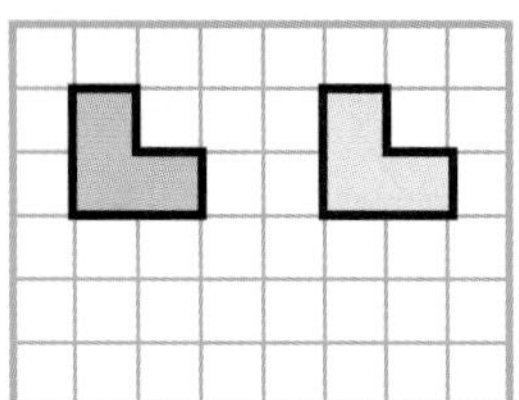

2. 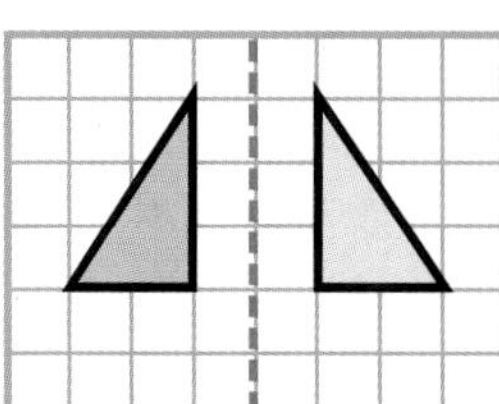

3. 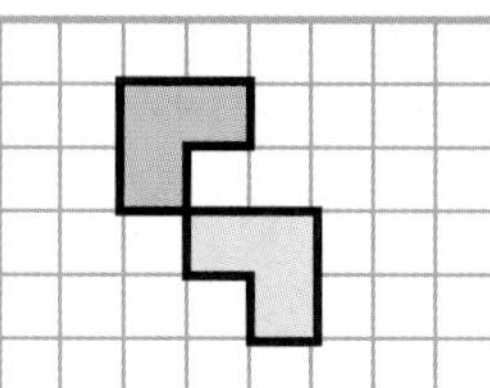

4. 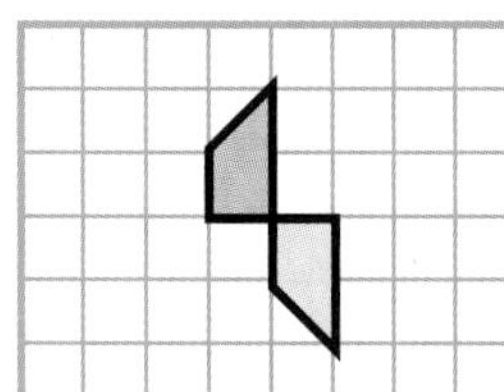

5. 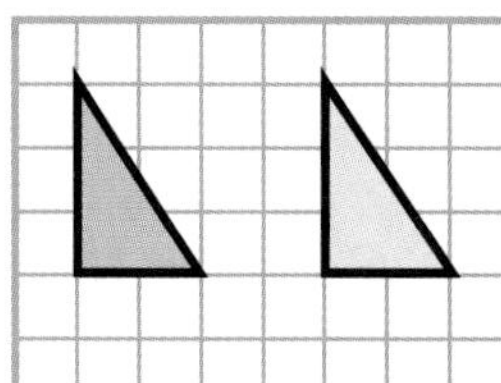

6. 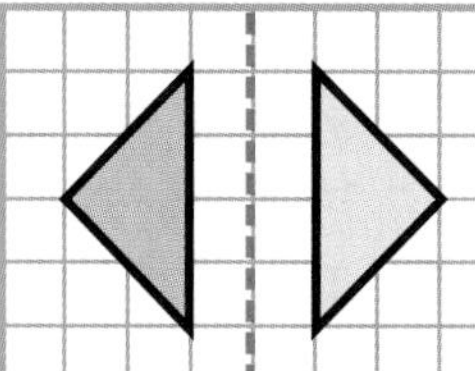

7. 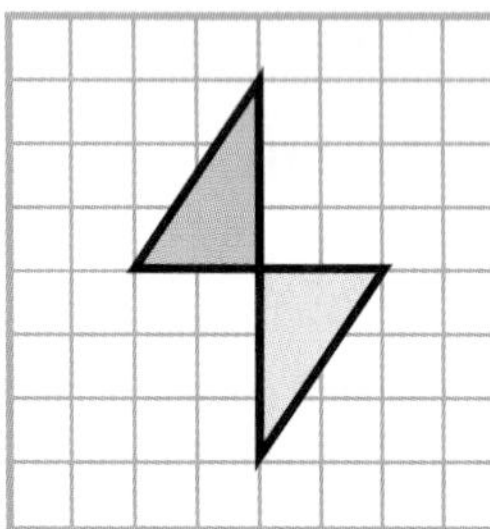

8. 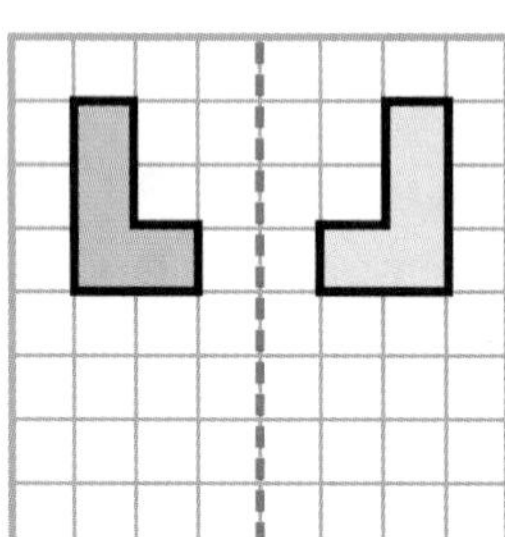

9. 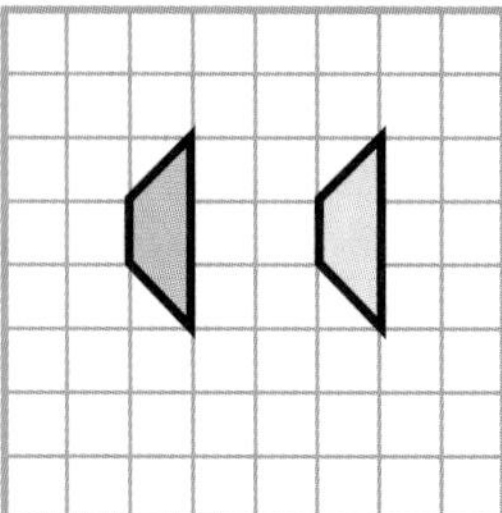

Set B (Lesson 2, pages 574–576)

Write the ordered pair for each point.

1. *A* **2.** *B*

3. *C* **4.** *D*

5. *E* **6.** *F*

7. *G* **8.** *H*

9. *I* **10.** *J*

11. *K* **12.** *L*

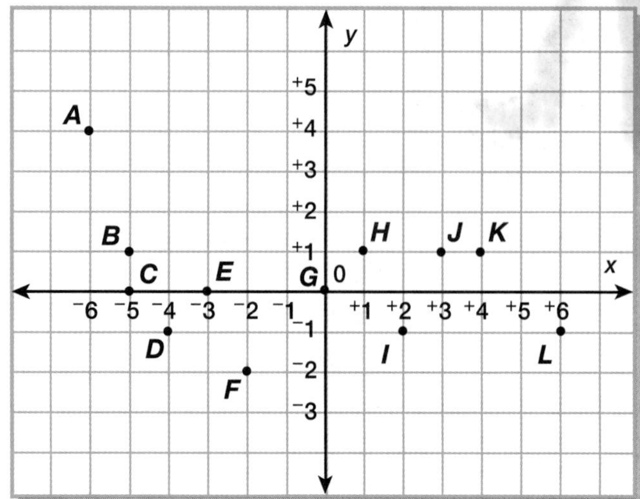

Extra Practice

Set C (Lesson 3, pages 578–579)

Use the diagram to name the coordinates of the triangle after each transformation.

1. Triangle *ABC*

- **a.** Translate right 3 and down 4.
- **b.** Reflect over the *x*-axis.
- **c.** Rotate a half turn about (0, 0).

2. Triangle *DEF*

- **a.** Translate down 4 and left 1.
- **b.** Reflect over the *y*-axis.
- **c.** Rotate a half turn about point *D*.

3. Triangle *GHI*

- **a.** Translate up 3 and right 2.
- **b.** Reflect over the *y*-axis.
- **c.** Rotate a half turn about point *G*.

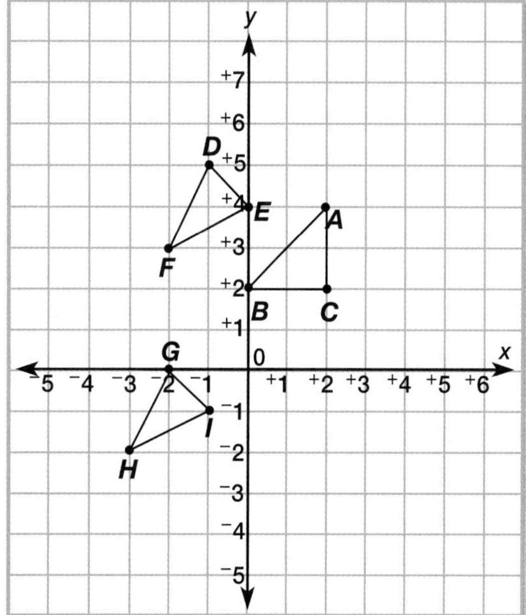

Set D (Lesson 5, pages 584–585)

Complete each function table.

1.

Rule: $y = x - 2$	
x	*y*
$^-1$	■
0	■
$^+3$	■
$^+4$	■

2.

Rule: $y = x + 4$	
x	*y*
$^+1$	■
0	■
$^-1$	■
$^-2$	■

3.

Rule: $y = 2x$	
x	*y*
$^-1$	■
0	■
$^+2$	■
$^+4$	■

4.

Rule: $y = 2 - x$	
x	*y*
$^+2$	■
$^+1$	■
0	■
$^-1$	■

5.

Rule: $y = 2x - 1$	
x	*y*
$^+1$	■
$^+2$	■
$^+3$	■
$^+4$	■

6.

Rule: $y = 2x + 2$	
x	*y*
$^-4$	■
$^-2$	■
0	■
$^+2$	■

Extra Practice

Set E *(Lesson 7, pages 588-589)*

Find values of y to complete each table. Then graph the equation.

1. $y = x - 1$

x	y
$^{-}1$	■
0	■
$^{+}2$	■
$^{+}3$	■

2. $y = x + 5$

x	y
$^{-}3$	■
0	■
$^{+}1$	■
$^{+}2$	■

3. $y = x - 4$

x	y
$^{+}2$	■
$^{+}3$	■
$^{+}4$	■
$^{+}5$	■

4. $y = 1 - x$

x	y
$^{+}1$	■
0	■
$^{-}1$	■
$^{-}2$	■

5. $y = 2x - 1$

x	y
0	■
$^{+}1$	■
$^{+}2$	■
$^{+}3$	■

6. $y = 3x - 10$

x	y
0	■
$^{+}2$	■
$^{+}4$	■
$^{+}6$	■

7. $y = 2 + 2x$

x	y
0	■
$^{+}1$	■
$^{+}2$	■
$^{+}3$	■

8. $y = 3x - 2$

x	y
$^{+}3$	■
$^{+}2$	■
$^{+}1$	■
0	■

9. $y = 2x - 5$

x	y
0	■
$^{+}5$	■
$^{+}6$	■
$^{+}7$	■

10. $y = 2x + 1$

x	y
0	■
$^{+}2$	■
$^{+}3$	■
$^{+}4$	■

11. $y = 2x + 4$

x	y
0	■
$^{+}1$	■
$^{+}2$	■
$^{+}3$	■

12. $y = 4x - 2$

x	y
0	■
$^{+}1$	■
$^{+}2$	■
$^{+}3$	■

Extra Practice • Problem Solving

Draw a diagram to solve each problem. *(Lesson 4, pages 580–581)*

1. Describe a sequence of transformations that will make triangle *CDE* cover triangle *FGH* exactly.

2. The diagram shows a series of transformations. Find a likely pattern. Describe how to find the next 3 figures in your pattern.

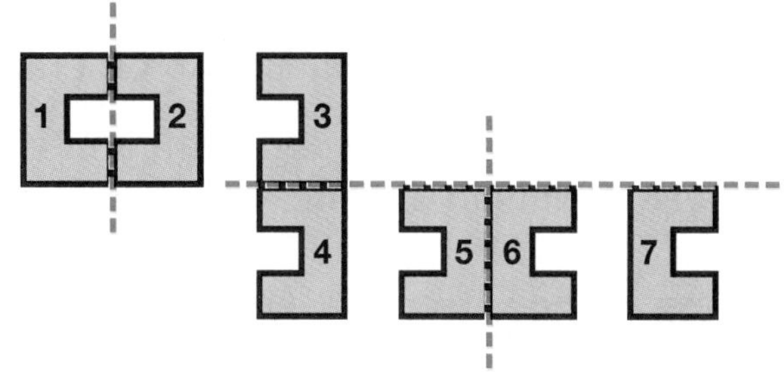

Use an equation to solve each problem. *(Lesson 6, pages 586–587)*

3. The table shows the cost of piano lessons. Which equation describes the relationship between the number of lessons (***L***) and the cost (***C***)?

   a. $L + 12 = C$ **b.** $L \times 12 = C$

Lessons	Cost ($)
1	12
2	24
3	36

4. Use the equation to find how much 6 lessons cost.

5. A piano lesson is 30 minutes long. Write and solve an equation to find how long 5 lessons are.

Solve. Use the graph to write an equation. *(Lesson 8, pages 590–591)*

6. The graph shows the number of milliliters of water that drips from a leaky tap. If this pattern continues, how many milliliters will drip in 5 minutes?

7. How long will it take for 12 mL of water to drip?

8. The leak was fixed after 6 minutes. How many milliliters of water had dripped from the tap?

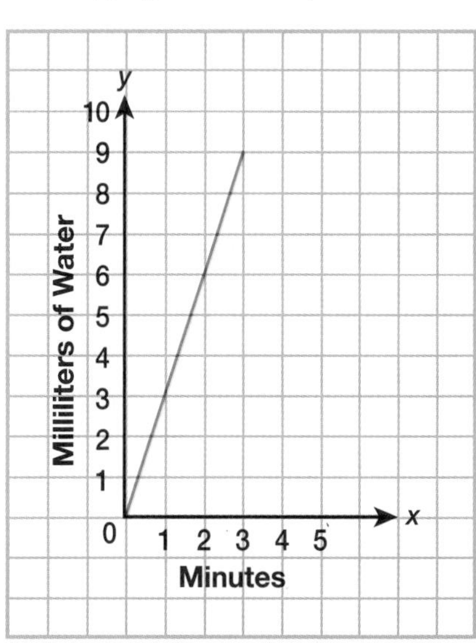

Chapter Review

Reviewing Vocabulary

Write *true* or *false* for each statement.

1. A reflection produces an image that is congruent to the original figure.
2. A translation involves turning points or figures.
3. The value of y appears first in an ordered pair.
4. A coordinate plane is a grid with number lines used to locate points in a plane.

Reviewing Concepts and Skills

Copy each figure on grid paper. Show an example of each transformation. *(pages 572–573)*

5. translation

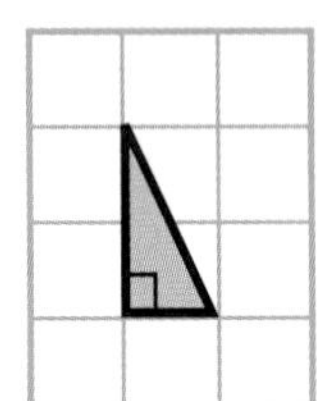

6. reflection

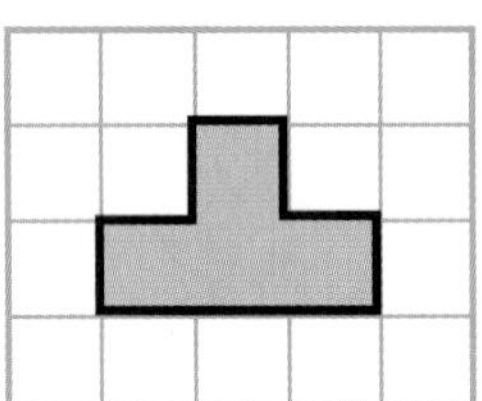

7. rotation

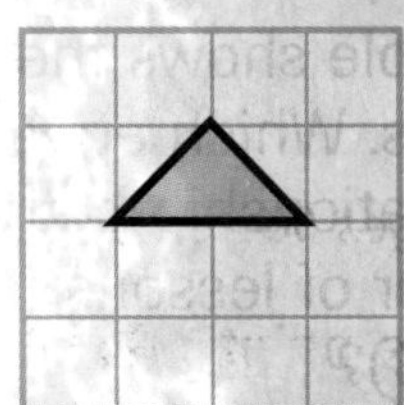

Write the letter name of the point at each location. *(pages 574–576)*

8. $(^-1, ^+1)$
9. $(^-1, ^-1)$
10. $(^-3, ^+1)$
11. $(^+1, ^-1)$
12. $(^+2, ^+1)$
13. $(^-4, ^-1)$

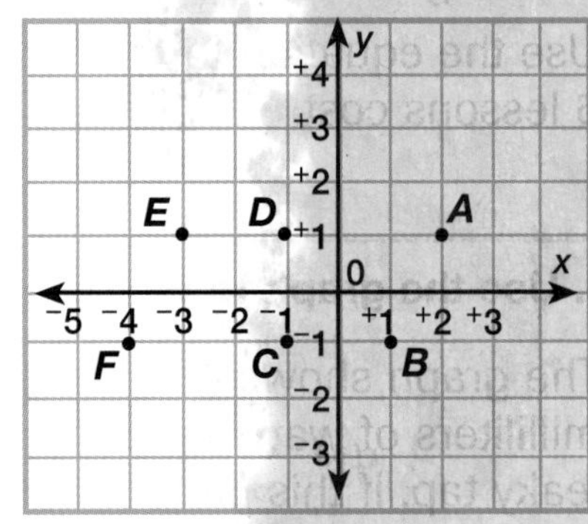

Use the diagram to name the coordinates of figure *LMNO* after each transformation. *(pages 578–579)*

14. Translate right 3 and down 2.
15. Rotate a half turn about point L.
16. Translate left 2 and reflect over the x-axis.

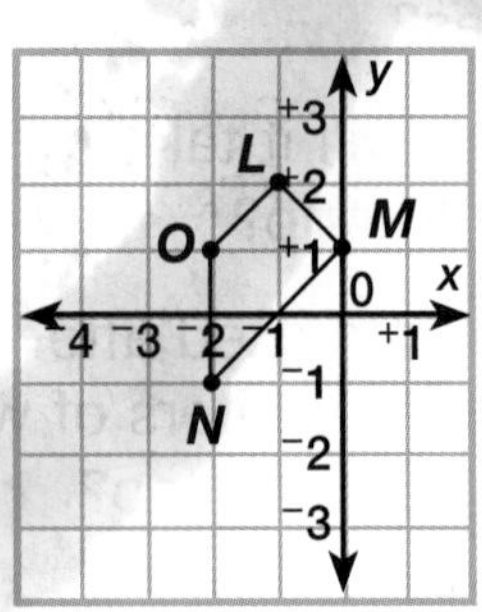

Complete each function table. *(pages 584–585)*

17.

Rule: $y = x + 4$	
x	y
$^-4$	■
$^-2$	■
0	■
$^+2$	■

18.

Rule: $y = x - 1$	
x	y
$^-1$	■
0	■
$^+3$	■
$^+4$	■

19.

Rule: $y = 2x - 3$	
x	y
0	■
$^+1$	■
$^+2$	■
$^+3$	■

Complete each table. Then graph the equation. *(pages 588–589)*

20. $y = x - 5$

x	y
$^-5$	■
$^+1$	■
$^+5$	■
$^-1$	■

21. $y = x + 3$

x	y
$^-3$	■
$^-2$	■
$^-1$	■
0	■

22. $y = 2x + 2$

x	y
$^+3$	■
$^+2$	■
$^+1$	■
0	■

23. $y = 3x - 3$

x	y
0	■
$^+1$	■
$^+2$	■
$^+3$	■

Solve. *(pages 580–581)*

24. Plot the points $A(^+3, ^-3)$, $B(^+3, ^+3)$, and $C(^-1, ^+1)$ and connect them. What figure did you make?

25. Translate figure ABC 2 units to the right and 5 units up. Name the new coordinates of the figure.

Brain Teasers Math Reasoning

Number Reflections

23456789

Which numbers from 2 to 9 resemble uppercase letters when reflected across a vertical line?

Word Reflections

WOW | WOW

HI
HI

Find some other words that can be reflected across horizontal or vertical lines without changing.

Safe Site

Internet Brain Teasers
Visit **www.eduplace.com/kids/mhm** for more *Brain Teasers.*

Chapter Test

Copy the figure on grid paper. Show an example of each transformation.

1. reflection
2. translation
3. rotation

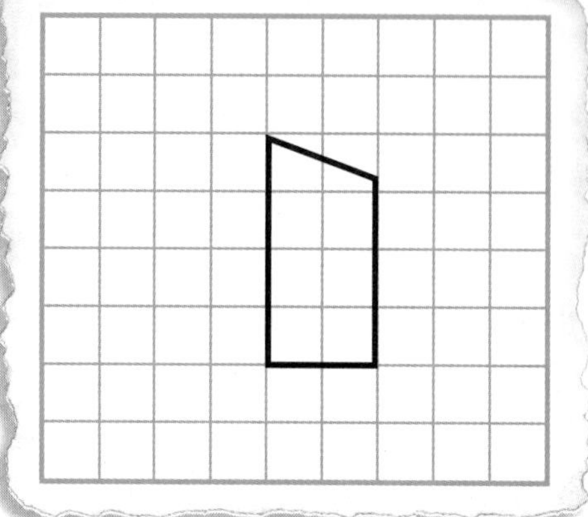

Use the diagram. Name the coordinates of figure *DEFG* after the transformations.

4. Translate right 6, then up 3.
5. Reflect over the *x*-axis.
6. Rotate a half turn about point *F*.
7. Reflect over the *y*-axis, translate down 2.

Find a rule that gives each set of ordered pairs.

8. $(^{+}6, {}^{+}1), (^{+}5, 0), (^{+}4, {}^{-}1), (^{+}3, {}^{-}2)$
9. $(^{+}4, {}^{+}2), (^{+}2, 0), (0, {}^{-}2), (^{-}2, {}^{-}4)$
10. $(0, {}^{+}3), (^{-}3, 0), (^{-}6, {}^{-}3), (^{-}9, {}^{-}6)$
11. $(^{+}2, {}^{-}8), (^{+}4, {}^{-}6), (^{+}8, {}^{-}2), (^{+}10, 0)$

Find three ordered pairs for each equation. Then use them to graph the equation.

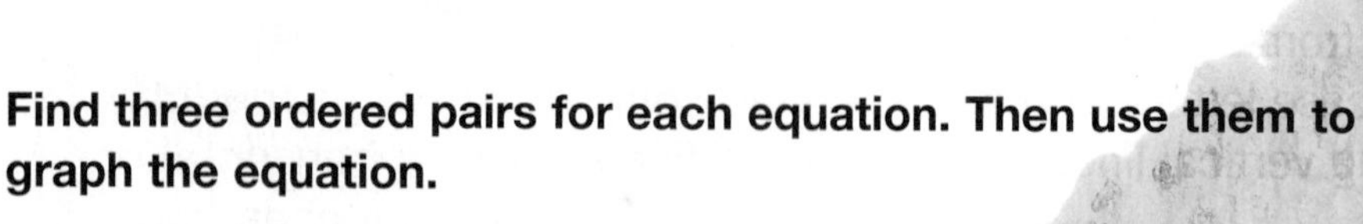

12. $y = x - 1$ **13.** $y = x - 2$ **14.** $y = x + 8$

15. $x - 3 = y$ **16.** $(5x) + 1 = y$ **17.** $y = 3 - (3x)$

Solve.

18. Describe the transformations that moved triangle *ABC*.

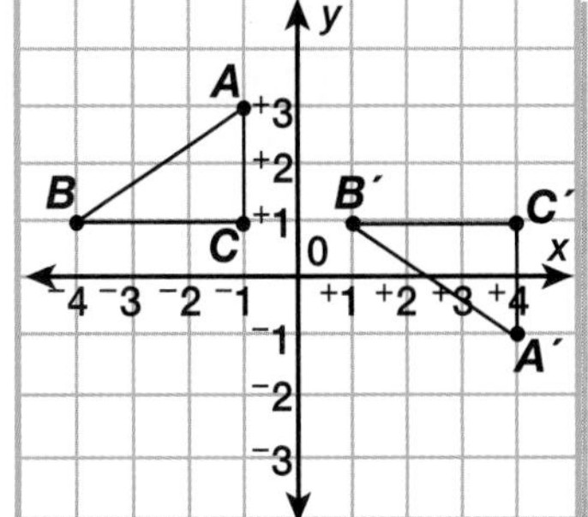

19. A jogger runs along a track at a steady rate.

Time (min)	1	2	3	4	5
Distance (yd)	200	400	600	800	1,000

Which equation describes the relationship between time (t) and distance (d)?

a. $d = 200t$ **b.** $d = 200 + t$

20. Use the equation to find how far the jogger has run after 12 minutes.

Write About It

Solve each problem. Use correct math vocabulary to explain your thinking.

1. Explain.

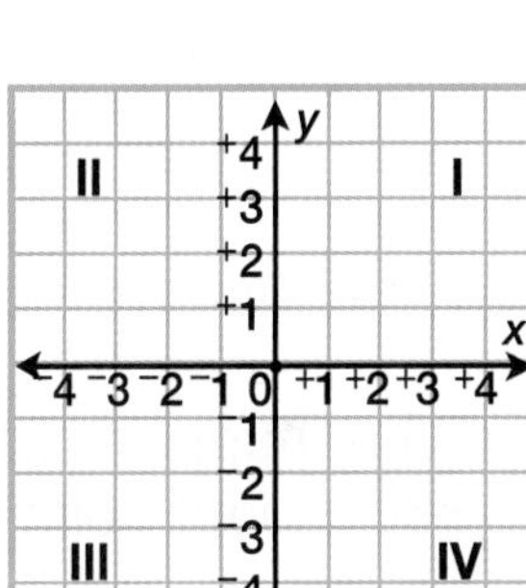

a. Describe the signs of the coordinates (x, y) in each quadrant of a coordinate plane.

b. Why is $(^{+}1, ^{-}2)$ not the same as $(^{-}2, ^{+}1)$?

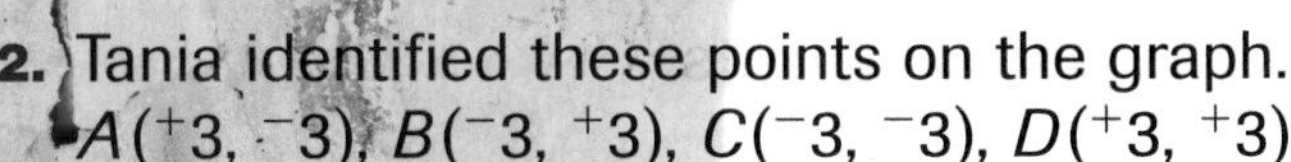

2. Tania identified these points on the graph. $A(^{+}3, ^{-}3)$, $B(^{-}3, ^{+}3)$, $C(^{-}3, ^{-}3)$, $D(^{+}3, ^{+}3)$

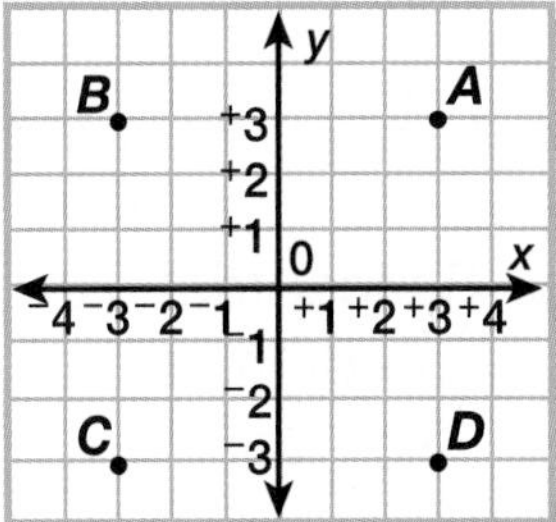

a. Explain what she did wrong.

b. Show how to identify the correct points.

3. Explain the steps you would use to name the coordinates of triangle *ABC* after each transformation if *A* is at $(^{-}3, ^{-}2)$, *B* is at $(^{-}1, ^{-}2)$, and *C* is at $(^{-}3, ^{-}4)$.

a. Translate right 3 and up 5.

b. Reflect across the y-axis.

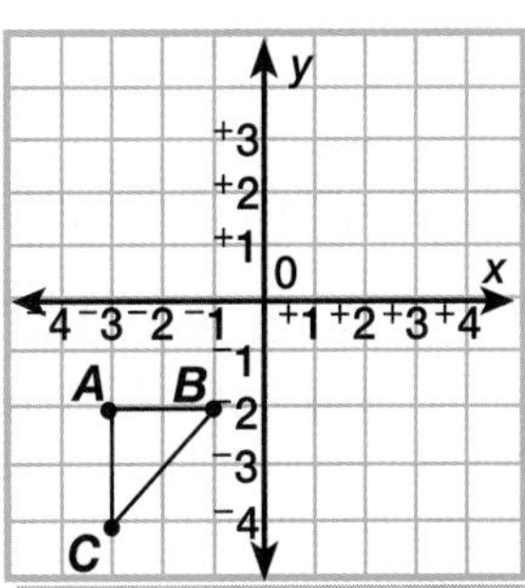

4. Name three points that would appear in a straight line in quadrant II of a graph.

Another Look

Use the graph to solve each problem.

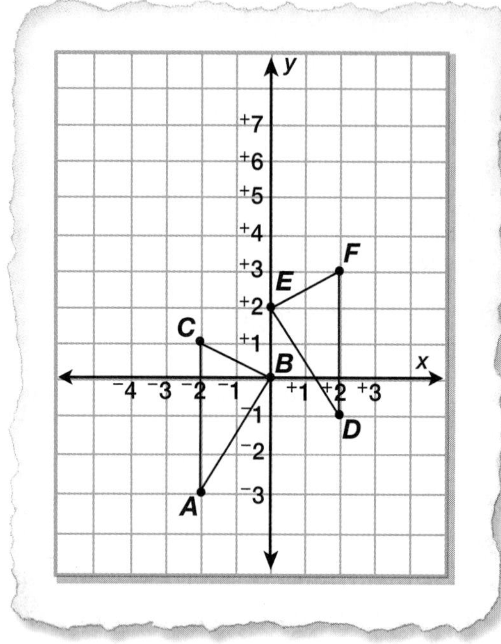

1. Write the ordered pair for point *B*.

2. What happens when you rotate triangle *ABC* 360° about point *B*?

3. Translate triangle *DEF* to the left 3 units and up 4 units. Name the coordinates.

4. Which vertex of triangle *ABC* is in the third quadrant?

5. Reflect triangle *DEF* across the *y*-axis. Name the coordinates.

6. Rotate triangle *ABC* a half turn about point *B*. Name the coordinates.

7. Name a point that is on the line $y = x$.

8. **Analyze** What combination of transformations of triangle *ABC* would place it on top of triangle *DEF*?

Standards AF **1.1, 1.4** SDP **1.5**

Enrichment

Change the Equation

When you graph $y = x$, the graph passes through the origin.

x	y
$^{-}4$	$^{-}4$
$^{-}3$	$^{-}3$
$^{-}2$	$^{-}2$
$^{-}1$	$^{-}1$
0	0
$^{+}1$	$^{+}1$
$^{+}2$	$^{+}2$
$^{+}3$	$^{+}3$
$^{+}4$	$^{+}4$

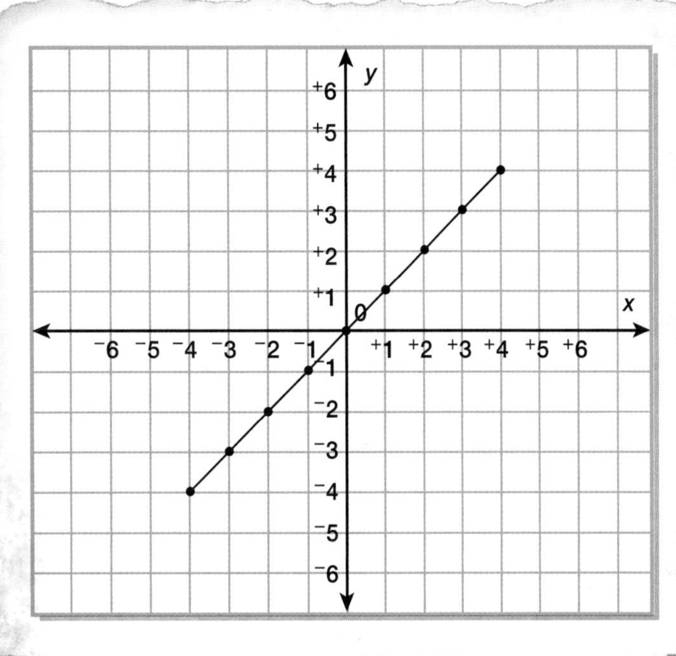

1. Predict what the graph will look like for the equation $y = x + 1$. Check by making a function table and graphing the coordinates.
2. What transformation of the graph of $y = x$ results in the graph of $y = x + 1$?
3. Use what you learned in Problem 2 to graph $y = x + 2$ without using a function table. Test some ordered pairs from your graph to make sure they fit the equation.
4. Predict what the graph will look like for the equation $y = x - 1$. Check by making a function table.

Explain Your Thinking

- How is the graph for $y = x$ transformed each time you increase x by 1? each time you decrease x by 1?
- What do you think would happen to the graph for $y = x$ if you increased y by 1? if you decreased y by 1?

Standards	AF **1.1, 1.4, 1.5** SDP **1.5**

Table of Measures

Customary Units of Measure

Length

1 foot (ft) = 12 inches (in.)
1 yard (yd) = 36 inches
1 yard = 3 feet
1 mile (mi) = 5,280 feet
1 mile (mi) = 1,760 yards

Capacity

1 cup (c) = 8 fluid ounces (fl oz)
1 pint (pt) = 2 cups
1 quart (qt) = 2 pints
1 quart (qt) = 4 cups
1 gallon (gal) = 4 quarts
1 gallon (gal) = 8 pints

Weight

1 pound (lb) = 16 ounces (oz)
1 ton (T) = 2,000 pounds (lb)

Metric Units of Measure

Length

1 meter (m) = 1,000 millimeters (mm)
1 meter (m) = 100 centimeters (cm)
1 meter (m) = 10 decimeters (dm)
1 decimeter (dm) = 10 centimeters
1 kilometer (km) = 1,000 meters
1 centimeter (cm) = 10 millimeters

Capacity

1 liter (L) = 1,000 milliliters (mL)
1 liter (L) = 10 deciliters (dL)

Mass

1 kilogram (kg) = 1,000 grams (g)
1 metric ton (t) = 1,000 kilograms

Units of Time

1 minute (min) = 60 seconds (s)
1 hour (h) = 60 minutes
1 day (d) = 24 hours
1 week (wk) = 7 days
1 year (yr) = 12 months (mo)

1 year = 52 weeks
1 year = 365 days
1 leap year = 366 days
1 decade = 10 years
1 century = 100 years
1 millennium = 1,000 years

Glossary

absolute value The distance of a number from zero on a number line.

acute angle An angle with a measure less than that of a right angle.

acute triangle A triangle in which each of the three angles is acute.

addend A number to be added in an addition expression. In $7 + 4 + 8$, the numbers 7, 4, and 8 are addends.

algebraic expression An expression that consists of one or more variables. It could contain some constants and some operations.

Example: $2x + 3y + 6$

angle An angle is formed by two rays with the same endpoint.

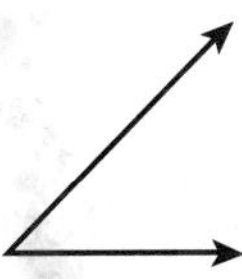

area The number of square units in a region.

array An arrangement of objects, pictures, or numbers in columns and rows.

Associative Property of Addition The property which states that the way in which addends are grouped does not change the sum. It is also called the Grouping Property of Addition.

Associative Property of Multiplication The property which states that the way in which factors are grouped does not change the product. It is also called the Grouping Property of Multiplication.

average The number found by dividing the sum of a group of numbers by the number of addends.

bar graph A graph in which information is shown by means of rectangular bars.

base of a geometric figure A bottom side or face of a geometric figure.

base of a power A factor that is repeated a number of times in a product.

capacity The amount a container can hold.

Celsius The metric temperature scale.

centimeter (cm) A metric unit used to measure length.

100 centimeters = 1 meter

central angle An angle with a vertex at the center of a circle.

chord A segment that connects two points on a circle.

Glossary

circle A closed figure in which every point is the same distance from a given point called the center of the circle.

circle graph A graph used for data that are parts of a whole.

circumference The distance around a circle.

common factor A number that is a factor of two or more numbers.

Commutative Property of Addition The property which states that the order of addends does not change the sum. It is also called the Order Property of Addition.

Commutative Property of Multiplication The property which states that the order of factors does not change the product. It is also called the Order Property of Multiplication.

composite number A whole number that has more than two factors.

cone A solid that has a circular base and a surface from a boundary of the base to the vertex.

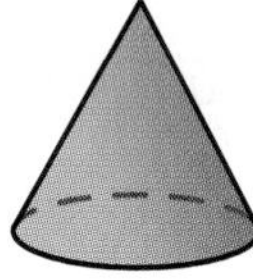

congruent figures Figures that have the same size and the same shape.

coordinate plane A plane formed by two perpendicular number lines in which every point is assigned an ordered pair of numbers.

coordinates An ordered pair of numbers that locates a point in the coordinate plane with reference to the x- and y-axes.

cube A solid figure that has six square faces of equal size.

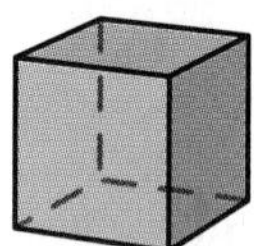

cubic centimeter A metric unit for measuring volume. It is the volume of a cube with each edge 1 centimeter long.

cylinder A solid with two circular faces that are congruent and a cylindrical surface connecting the two faces.

decimal A number with one or more digits to the right of a decimal point.

denominator The number below the bar in a fraction.

diameter of a circle A segment that connects two points on the circle and passes through the center.

difference The result of subtraction.

Distributive Property The property which states that when two addends are multiplied by a factor the product is the same as if each addend was multiplied by the factor and those products were added.

dividend The number that is divided in a division problem.

divisible One number is divisible by another if the quotient is a whole number and the remainder is 0. For example, 10 is divisible by 2, since 10 ÷ 2 = 5 R0.

divisor The number by which a number is being divided. In 6 ÷ 3 = 2, the divisor is 3.

double bar graph A graph in which data are compared by means of pairs of rectangular bars drawn next to each other.

double line graph A graph that is used to show data by means of two broken lines.

edge The segment where two faces of a solid figure meet.

endpoint The point at either end of a line segment. The beginning point of a ray.

equation A mathematical sentence with an equals sign.

Examples: $3 + 1 = 4$ and $2x + 5 = 9$ are equations.

equilateral triangle A triangle that has three congruent sides.

equivalent fractions Fractions that show different numbers with the same value.
Example: $\frac{1}{2}$ and $\frac{4}{8}$ are equivalent fractions.

estimate A number close to an exact amount. An estimate tells *about* how much or *about* how many.

evaluating an expression Substituting the values given for the variables and performing the operations to find the value of the expression.

even number A whole number that is a multiple of 2. The ones digit in an even number is 0, 2, 4, 6, or 8. The numbers 56 and 48 are examples of even numbers.

event In probability, a result of an experiment that can be classified as certain, likely, unlikely, or impossible to occur.

exponent The number in a power that tells how many times a factor is repeated in a product.

F

face A flat surface of a solid figure.

fact family Facts that are related, using the same numbers.

Examples: $1 + 4 = 5$; $4 + 1 = 5$; $6 - 4 = 2$; $6 - 2 = 4$; $3 \times 5 = 15$; $5 \times 3 = 15$; $15 \div 3 = 5$; $15 \div 5 = 3$

factor One of two or more numbers that are multiplied to give a product.

factorization A number written as a product of its factors.

factor of a number A number that divides evenly into a given number.

Fahrenheit The customary temperature scale.

Glossary

fraction A number that names a part of a whole, a part of a collection, or a part of a region.

Examples: $\frac{1}{2}$, $\frac{3}{4}$, and $\frac{2}{3}$ are fractions.

function A rule that gives exactly one value of *y* for every value of *x*.

greatest common divisor The greatest whole number that is a common factor of two or more numbers. It is also called the greatest common factor.

greatest common factor The greatest whole number that is a common factor of two or more numbers. It is also called the greatest common divisor.

histogram A graph in which bars are used to display how frequently data occurs within equal intervals.

horizontal axis The *x*-axis in a coordinate system. It is a number line that locates points to the left or to the right of the origin.

Identity Property For addition the sum of any number and 0 is that number; for multiplication the product of any number and 1 is that number.

improper fraction A fraction that is greater than or equal to 1. The numerator in an improper fraction is greater than or equal to the denominator.

inch (in.) A customary unit used to measure length.
12 inches = 1 foot

inequality A sentence that contains $>$ (is greater than) or $<$ (is less than).

Examples: $8 > 2$, $5 < 6$

integers The set of positive whole numbers and their opposites (negative numbers) and 0.

$\ldots, {}^{-}3, {}^{-}2, {}^{-}1, 0, {}^{+}1, {}^{+}2, {}^{+}3, \ldots$

intersecting lines Lines that meet or cross at a common point.

isosceles triangle A triangle that has two congruent sides.

kilogram (kg) A metric unit used to measure mass.
1 kilogram = 1,000 grams.

kilometer (km) A metric unit used to measure length.
1 kilometer = 1,000 meters.

least common multiple The least number that is a multiple of two or more numbers.

Example: 12 is the least common multiple of 3 and 4.

like denominators Denominators in two or more fractions that are the same.

line A straight, continuous, and unending set of points in a plane.

line graph A graph that uses a broken line to show changes in data.

line of symmetry The line along which a figure can be folded so that the two halves match exactly.

line plot A diagram that organizes data using a number line.

line segment A part of a line that has two endpoints.

line symmetry A figure has line symmetry if it can be folded in half and the two halves are congruent.

liter (L) A metric unit used to measure capacity.
1 liter = 1,000 milliliters

mean Arithmetic mean, also called *average*. The number found by dividing the sum of a group of numbers by the number of addends.

measures of central tendency The mean, median, and mode.

median The middle number when a set of numbers is arranged in order from least to greatest.

Examples: The median of 2, 5, 7, 9 and 10 is 7. For an even number of numbers, it is the average of the two middle numbers. The median of 2, 5, 7, and 12 is $\frac{(5 + 7)}{2}$ or 6.

meter (m) A metric unit used to measure length.
1 meter = 100 centimeters

milliliter (mL) A metric unit used to measure capacity.
1,000 milliliters = 1 liter

mixed number A number that is the sum of a whole number and a fraction.

mode The number or numbers that occur most often in a set of data.

multiple A number that is the product of the given number and a number.

negative integer An integer less than 0.

Examples: $^{-}4$, $^{-}7$, $^{-}100$

Glossary

negative number A number that is less than 0.

Examples: $^-\frac{7}{8}$, $^-5$, and $^-2.8$ are negative numbers.

net A flat pattern that can be folded to make a solid.

number line A line on which numbers are assigned to points.

numerator The number above the bar in a fraction.

obtuse angle An angle with a measure greater than that of a right angle and less than 180°.

obtuse triangle A triangle that has one obtuse angle.

odd number A whole number that is not a multiple of 2. The ones digit in an odd number is 1, 3, 5, 7, or 9. The numbers 67 and 493 are examples of odd numbers.

opposite of a number The same number but of opposite sign. Examples of opposite numbers are $^+2$ and $^-2$, $^-7$ and $^+7$, and $^-12$ and $^+12$. The opposite of a number is also called its additive inverse.

ordered pair A pair of numbers in which one number is considered to be first and the other number second.

origin A point assigned to zero on the number line or the point where the *x*- and *y*-axes intersect in a coordinate system.

outcome A result in a probability experiment.

outlier A number or numbers that are at one or the other end of a set of data, arranged in order, where there is a gap between the end numbers and the rest of the data.

parallel lines Lines that lie in the same plane and do not intersect. They are everywhere the same distance apart.

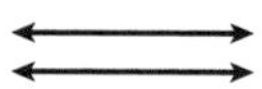

parallelogram A quadrilateral in which both pairs of opposite sides are parallel.

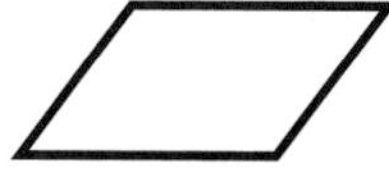

percent Per hundred. Ratio of a number to 100.

Example: 7% means 7 out of 100 or $\frac{7}{100}$.

perimeter The distance around a figure.

perpendicular Two lines or line segments that cross or meet to form right angles.

plane A flat surface made up of a continuous and unending collection of points.

point An exact location in space, represented by a dot.

polygon A simple closed plane figure made up of three or more line segments.

positive numbers Numbers that are greater than zero.

pound (lb) A customary unit used to measure weight.
1 pound = 16 ounces

prime factorization Factoring a number into its prime factors only.

Example: the prime factorization of 30 is $2 \times 3 \times 5$.

prime number A whole number, greater than 1, that has exactly two factors.

prism A solid figure that has two parallel congruent bases and rectangles and parallelograms for faces.

probability The chance of an event occurring. A probability can be any number from 0 through 1.

product The answer in a multiplication problem.

proper fraction A fraction in which the numerator is less than the denominator.

Example: $\frac{4}{7}$

Property of Zero for Multiplication The property which states that if 0 is a factor, the product is 0.

pyramid A solid figure whose base can be any polygon and whose faces are triangles.

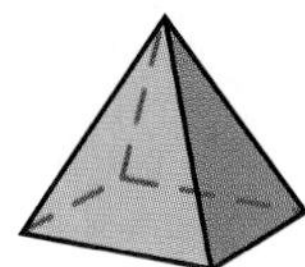

quadrant Each of the four parts into which a plane is separated by the *x*-axis and the *y*-axis. The axes are not parts of the quadrant.

quadrilateral A polygon with four sides.

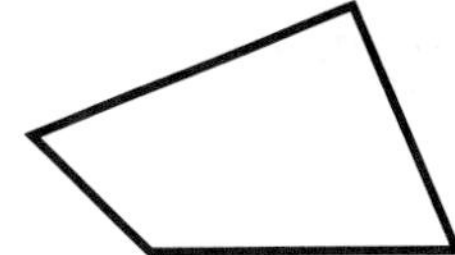

quart (qt) A customary unit to measure capacity.
4 quarts = 1 gallon

quotient The answer in a division problem.

radius A segment that connects the center of a circle to any point on the circle.

range The difference between the greatest and least numbers in a set of data.

rate A comparison by a ratio of two quantities using different kinds of units.

ratio A comparison of two numbers by division.

ray Part of a line that starts at an endpoint and goes on forever in one direction.

Glossary

reciprocal The product of a number and its reciprocal is 1.

Example: $\frac{2}{3} \times \frac{3}{2} = 1$, so $\frac{2}{3}$ and $\frac{3}{2}$ are reciprocals of each other.

rectangle A polygon with opposite sides parallel and four right angles.

rectangular prism A solid figure with six faces that are rectangles.

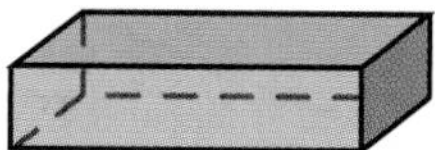

rectangular pyramid A solid figure whose base is a rectangle and whose faces are triangles.

remainder The number that is left after one whole number is divided by another.

rhombus A parallelogram with all four sides the same length.

right angle An angle that measures 90°.

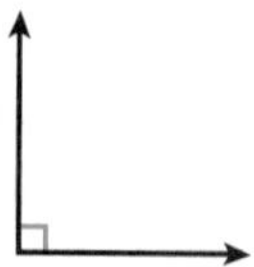

right triangle A triangle that has one right angle.

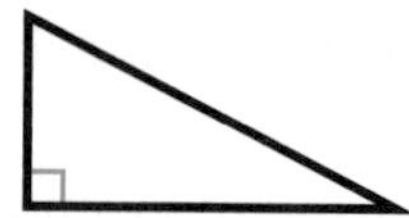

rotational symmetry A figure has rotational symmetry if, after the figure is rotated about a point, the figure is the same as when in its original position.

rounding To find about how many or how much by expressing a number to the nearest ten, hundred, thousand, and so on.

scalene triangle A triangle with all sides of different lengths.

side of a polygon One of the line segments that make up a polygon.

similar figures Figures that have the same shape but not necessarily the same size.

simplest form of a fraction A fraction whose numerator and denominator have the number 1 as the only common factor.

simplest form of an algebraic expression An algebraic expression is in simplest form if no terms can be combined.

solution of an equation A number or numbers that, when substituted for the variable or variables in an equation, give a true statement.

solid figure A three-dimensional figure in space.

sphere A solid figure that is shaped like a round ball.

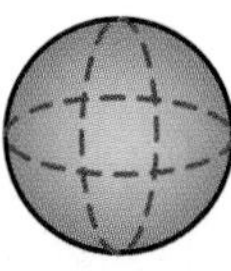

square A polygon with four right angles and four congruent sides.

stem-and-leaf plot A frequency distribution that arranges data in order of place value. The last digits of the number are the leaves. The digits to the left of the leaves are the stems.

surface area The total area of the surface of a solid.

symmetric figure A figure that has symmetry.

symmetry (line symmetry) A figure has line symmetry if it can be folded along a line so that the two parts match exactly.

trapezoid A quadrilateral with exactly one pair of parallel sides.

tree diagram A diagram that shows combinations of outcomes of an event.

triangle A polygon with three sides.

triangular prism A prism whose bases are triangles.

triangular pyramid A pyramid whose base is a triangle.

two-variable equation An equation that has two different variables.

unit fraction A fraction in which the numerator is 1.

Example: $\frac{1}{5}$

variable A letter or a symbol that represents a number in an algebraic expression.

vertex of an angle A point common to the two sides of an angle.

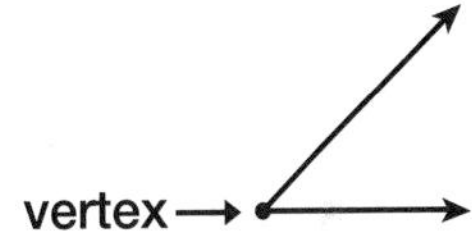

vertex of a polygon A point common to two sides of a polygon.

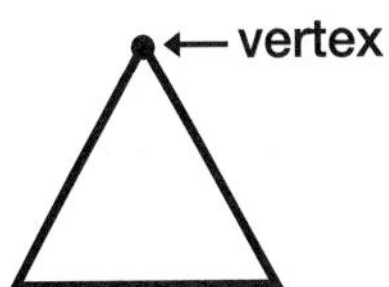

vertex of a prism A point common to three edges of a prism.

vertical axis The *y*-axis in the coordinate system. It is a number line that locates points up or down from the origin.

volume The number of cubic units that make up a solid figure.

weight The measure of how heavy something is.

***x*-axis** The horizontal number line in a coordinate system.

***x*-coordinate** The first number of an ordered pair of numbers that names a point in a coordinate system.

***y*-axis** The vertical number line in a coordinate system.

***y*-coordinate** The second number of an ordered pair of numbers that names a point in a coordinate system.

Zero Property of Addition The property which states that the sum of any number and 0 is that number.

Zero Property of Multiplication The property which states that the product of any number and 0 is 0.

Index

Index

D

Index

Index

Index

Index

Index

Credits

PHOTOGRAPHY

All photographs by Houghton Mifflin Company (HMCo.) unless otherwise noted.

Coin photography by Mike Tesi for HMCo. xi: C.J. Allen/Stock Boston. xvi: F. Hasler/M. Jentoft-Nilsen/H. Pierce/K. Palaniappan/NASA Goddard Lab for Atmospheres/NOAA. xviii: *t.* Benjamin Rondel/The Stock Market; *b.* Bob Gomel/The Stock Market. xix: *l.* Roger Wood/Corbis; *m.* © Dale E. Boyer/Photo Researchers, Inc.; *r.* Yann Arthus-Bertrand/Corbis. xxvi-1: © 1996 Richard T. Nowitz Photography. 5: *b.* Steve Owlett/Bruce Coleman Inc. 10: *t.* Vladimir Pcholkin/FPG International; *b.* Ken Straiton/The Stock Market. 11: *b.* Michael Gaffney for HMCo. 12: Archive Photos. 13: *l.* Archive Photos; *r.* Courtesy, Library of Congress. 15: Massimo Borchi/Bruce Coleman Inc. 18: Llewellyn/Uniphoto Pictor. 21: Mike Tesi for HMCo. 28: © David Sailors. 30–31: Canadian Special Olympics. 32: Stephen Green-Armytage/The Stock Market. 35: *l.* Michael Keller/The Stock Market; *r.* Robert Fried/Stock Boston. 54: Richard T. Nowitz Photography. 56: *t.* PhotoDisc, Inc. 57: *l.* L. Kolvoord/The Image Works Inc.; *r.* David Young-Wolff/PhotoEdit. 58: *l.* C.J. Allen/Stock Boston. 59: Michael Gaffney for HMCo. 60: *l.* Michael Newman/PhotoEdit; *r.* Wolfgang Kaehler/Corbis. 61: Jack Fields/Corbis. 62: Bob Daemmrich Photos/Stock Boston. 70: ICS/Photo Network/Picture Quest Network International/PNI. 74: Michele Burgess/Index Stock Imagery. 78: Richard Hutchings for HMCo. 79: *l.* Sagamore Hill National Historic Site/National Portrait Gallery, Smithsonian Institution; *r.* Underwood and Underwood/Corbis. 92–93: © Alan Detrick/Photo Researchers, Inc. 98: Llewellyn/Uniphoto Pictor. 100: © Gary J. Benson. 106: © Kent Wood/Science Source/Photo Researchers, Inc. 110: Mercedes-Benz USA, Inc. 112: *t.* John Paul Endress for HMCo. 114: Long Photography/Pasadena Tournament of Roses. 116: Steve Simonsen/Marine Scenes. 117: Forestier/Corbis/Sygma. 130–131: Telegraph Colour Library/FPG International. 137: The Kobal Collection. 140: *b.* Michael Newman/PhotoEdit. 141: PhotoDisc, Inc. 142: *t.* Miro Vintoniv/Stock Boston; *b.* Vic Bider/PhotoEdit. 143: Don Eastman/Scenic & Nature Photography, Inc. 146: Paul Ambrose/Picture Quest Network International/PNI. 147: *t.* NASA; *b.* Color-Pic, Inc. 148: *bkgd.* Gary Chowanetz/Corbis. 150: Archive Photos. 151: *t.l.* Anup Shah/Dembinsky Photo Associates; *t.r.* Stan Osolinski/Dembinsky Photo Associates; *b.l.* Color-Pic, Inc. 152: *bkgd.* Andy Sotiroiu/PhotoDisc, Inc. 154: John S. Zeedick/AP/Wide World Photos. 156: *t.* Mitsuhiro Wada/Liaison Agency Inc.; *b.* David Bookstaver/AP/Wide World Photos. 158: Jan Butchofsky-Houser/Corbis. 159: Joseph Sohm/Visions of America, LLC/Picture Quest Network International/PNI. 162: Novastock/Stock Connection/Picture Quest Network International/PNI. 170: Preston Lyon/Index Stock Imagery. 172: *t.* Chip Henderson/Index Stock Imagery. 174: *t.* Bob Daemmrich Photography. 175: Kevin Horan/Stock Boston. 186: Dean Conger/Corbis. 188–189: Jeff Schultz/Alaska Stock Images. 190: *t.* R. Rathe/FPG International; *b.* Peter Johnson/Corbis. 193: Richard Hutchings for HMCo. 194: Michael Gaffney for HMCo. 198: Telegraph Colour Library/FPG International. 200: © Joseph Nettis/Photo Researchers, Inc. 201: Nik Wheeler/Corbis. 203: *t.* © Penny Tweedie/Corbis; *b.* Wally McNamee/Corbis. 204: Richard Hutchings for HMCo. 206: David Fleetham/FPG International. 209: Jeffry W. Myers/Corbis. 210: Richard Hutchings for HMCo. 214: *t.* Kevin Fleming/Corbis; *b.* ICS/Photo Network/Picture Quest Network International/PNI. 218: Richard Hutchings for HMCo. 226: Kevin Fleming/Corbis. 227: *l.* Joe Sohm/Chromosohm/Stock Connection/Picture Quest Network International/PNI. 240–241: Bob Daemmrich/Stock Boston. 244: John Paul Endress for HMCo. 250: *t.* Brian Seed Associates; *b.* Kevin Fleming/Corbis. 253: *t.* David Liebman Photography; *b.* © A. Rider/Photo Researchers, Inc. 254: *t.* AFP/Corbis. 258: Bob Daemmrich Photography. 260: *t.l.* Ted Streshinsky/Corbis; *t.r.* Courtesy, Ronald Reagan Library; *b.l.* Franklin D. Roosevelt Library; *b.r.* National Park Service/Courtesy, The Dwight D. Eisenhower Library. 264: Michael Grecco/Stock Boston. 265: PhotoDisc, Inc. 267: C Squared Studios/PhotoDisc, Inc. 268: *l.* Janis Burger/Bruce Coleman Inc.; *r.* David A. Northcott/Corbis. 269: Dominique Braud/Dembinsky Photo Associates. 280: *l.* FPG International. 281: A. Ramey/Stock Boston/Picture Quest Network International/PNI. 294–295: Index Stock Imagery. 302: *l.* © Photo Researchers, Inc.; *r.* Arthur Tilley/FPG International/Picture Quest Network International/PNI. 305: Richard Hutchings for HMCo. 313: Ralph Corwin. 327: *l.* PhotoDisc, Inc.; *r.* Steve Lee (University of Colorado)/Jim Bell (Cornell University)/Mike Wolff (Space Science Institute)/NASA. 330: John Paul Endress for HMCo. 332: F. Hasler/M. Jentoft-Nilsen/H. Pierce/K. Palaniappan/NASA Goddard Lab for Atmospheres/NOAA. 334: *t.* Stephen Frisch/Stock, Boston Inc. /Picture Quest Network International/PNI. 336: *l.* David Madison/Bruce Coleman Inc.; *r.* William Waterfall/The Stock Market. 338: *l.* Mohamed Amin/Bruce Coleman Inc.; *m.* Stan Osolinski/FPG International; *r.* John Eascott/Yva Momatiuk/DRK Photo. 340: *b.* Michael Gaffney for HMCo. 341: Michael Gaffney for HMCo. 344: Joe Sohm/Chromosohm/Stock Connection/Picture Quest Network International/PNI. 345: Catherine Karnow/Corbis. 347: Larry Lawfer/Black Star. 348: Mike Tesi for HMCo. 349: Michael S. Yamashita/Corbis. 360: *l.* David Perdew/Stock South/Picture Quest Network International/PNI; *r.* Dean Conger/Corbis. 362–363: NASA. 375: Richard Megna/Fundamental Photographs. 378: *bkgd.* Bill Horsman/Stock Boston/Picture Quest Network International/PNI. 382: *t.* Harry Bartlett/FPG International/Picture Quest Network International/PNI; *b.* Mike Blank/Tony Stone Images. 384: Tom Stewart/The Stock Market. 386: Steven E. Sutton/Duomo Photography. 387: Jose Carrillo/Stock Boston. 388: Spencer Grant/Stock Boston. 390: Richard Hutchings for HMCo. 391: *l.* Tony Freeman/PhotoEdit/Picture Quest Network International/PNI; *r.* Arthur Grace/Stock Boston/Picture Quest Network International/PNI. 404–405: Rob & SAS/The Stock Market. 408: *r.* Bob Daemmrich Photography. 409: T. Duffy/Allsport Photography, Inc. 410: Shinichi Kanno/FPG International. 411: *t.* Benjamin Rondel/The Stock Market; *b.* Bob Gomel/The Stock Market. 414: *bkgd.* Bill Horsman/Stock Boston/Picture Quest Network International/PNI. 417: Ross Durant/©FoodPix. 420: *l.* © Oliver Meckes/Ottawa/Photo Researchers, Inc.; *r.* © Peter Skinner/Photo Researchers, Inc. 421: *t.* © Maslowski/Photo Researchers, Inc. 422: Corbis. 424: Michael Gaffney for HMCo. 425: *l.* David Young-Wolff/PhotoEdit; *r.* Jackie Foryst/Bruce Coleman Inc. 426: *t.* Courtesy, R. Landsberg/University of Chicago, the Center for Astrophysical Research in Antarctica (CARA), a NSF Science and Technology Center, & the NSF Advanced Technological Education Program, The Art Institue of Pittsburgh; *b.l.* Tom Van Sant/The

Stock Market; *b.r.* Ann Hawthorne/Black Star. 429: Mark Downey/Lucid Images/Picture Quest Network International/PNI. 430: Jacob Hutchings/Richard Hutchings Photography. 432: Partners for Youth with Disabilities. 436: Michael Krasowitz/FPG International. 437: Lawrence Migdale/Stock Boston. 450–451: Bruce Mcnitt/Panoramic Images. 454: Robert Srenco/FPG International. 462: Michael Gaffney for HMCo. 464: Morton Beebe/Corbis. 471: Henry Diltz/Corbis. 474: Andre Jenny/Focus Group/Picture Quest Network International/PNI. 476: *l.* Yann Arthus-Bertrand/Corbis; *r.* Roger Wood/Corbis. 478: *t.* © Dale E. Boyer/Photo Researchers, Inc. 480: Stockbyte. 483: *l.* Jim Newberry Photography; *r.* Wayne Kusy/All From Just Toothpicks. 486: John Paul Endress for HMCo. 489: Larry Lefever/Grant Heilman Photography, Inc. 492: *b.* Michael Gaffney for HMCo. 494: Michael Graves & Associates. 500: Robert Holmes/Corbis. 501: Karen Su/FPG International. 514–515: David Young-Wolff/PhotoEdit. 522: Tom Craig/FPG International. 527: *l.* Gary N. Crabbe/Enlightened Images Photography; *r.* Lee Foster/Bruce Coleman Inc. 532: Richard Hutchings for HMCo. 533: *t.* Joanna B. Pinneo/AURORA/Aurora & Quanta Productions; *b.* David Madison/Bruce Coleman Inc. 534: Brian Bailey/Tony Stone Images. 537: Terry Eggers/The Stock Market. 538: *r.* Lawrence Migdale/Pix. 544: PhotoEdit. 548: Betty Crowell/Faraway Places. 550: Richard Hutchings for HMCo. 551–552: Michael Gaffney for HMCo. 554: David Young-Wolff/PhotoEdit. 555: © Bettman/Corbis. 568–569: Chris Michaels/FPG International. 572: Billy McDonald Jr./Bruce Coleman Inc. 574: Roger Ressmeyer/Corbis. 586: David Brooks/The Stock Market. 587: © G. Savage/Vandistadt/Photo Researchers, Inc. 590: Tony Freeman/Picture Quest Network International/PNI. 591: *l.* Wolfgang Bayer/Bruce Coleman, Inc./Picture Quest Network International/PNI; *m.* Mitsuaki Iwago/Minden Pictures; *r.* Robert Houser/Index Stock Imagery.

ILLUSTRATIONS

vi–ix: Chuck Primeau. 4: Gary Antonetti. 6: Russel Benfanti. 8: Dale Glasgow. 12–13: Tom Barrett. 14: Gary Antonetti. 15: Chi Chung. 16: Dave Joly: 18: Leah Palmer. 24: Stephen Wagner. 26: Russell Benfanti. 29: Jonathan Simon. 46: Guy Smalley. 52–53: Margo De Paulis. 54: Tom Barrett. 60–61: Art Thompson. 63: Andrew Shiff. 66: Patrick Gnan. 74–75: Margo De Paulis. 89: Joe Taylor. 101: Jim Kopp. 108: Art Thompson. 109: Joe Taylor. 110: Carlyn Iverson. 113: Doug Horne. 116: Scott McDougall. 127–128: Joe Taylor. 136: Christian Musselman. 140: Rob Schuster. 150: Trevor Keen. 154: Tom Barrett. 163: Patrick Gnan. 166: Bob Kayganich. 181: Andrew Shiff. 186: Margo De Paulis. 192: Ken Batelman. 196: *t.* Barbara Cousins; *b.* Patrick Gnan. 200–201: David Meikle. 202: Ken Batelman. 208–209: Doug Horne. 211: Lori Anzalone. 214: Sam Ward. 215: Ortelius Design. 233: Garry Colby. 248: John Kovaleski. 249: Ken Batelman. 252: John Kovaleski. 255: Phil Wilson. 260: Margo De Paulis. 263: Terry Guyer. 271: Kevin Karl. 278–279: Rob Schuster. 299: Tim McGarvey. 302: Garry Colby. 303: Gary Antonetti. 308: Robert Forsbach. 313: Doug Horne. 318: Margo De Paulis. 321: Dave Joly 322: David Christensen. 326: Terri Chickos. 333: Atomic Battery. 336: Keith Locke. 346: Dan Clyne. 360: Rob Schuster. 366: Patrick Gnan. 368: Patrick Gnan. 370: Margo De Paulis. 373: Tom Powers. 383: Doug Horne. 390–391: Rob Schuster. 410: Doug Horne. 412–413: T.L. Ary. 416: Carlyn Iverson. 428: T.L. Ary. 447: Joe Taylor. 458: Ken Batelman. 467: Robert Santora. 475: Ken Batelman. 483: Patrick Gnan. 485: Ken Batelman. 488: Gary Torrisi. 490: Michael Anderson. 492: Ken Batelman. 494–500: Bermar Technical Corporation. 524: Doug Horne. 525: Patrick Gnan. 535: Joe Taylor. 536: Gary Antonetti. 541: Bot Roda. 546: Neil Stewart. 554: Bryan Friel studio. 566: Patrick Gnan. 567: Deborah Drummond. 574: Walter Stuart. 576: Walter Stuart. 578: John Youssi. 581: Dave Joly. 606: Saul Rosenbaum. 611–612: Saul Rosenbaum.